The Growth of American Politics

Volume II

Since the Civil War

The Growth of American Politics

❧ Volume II
Since the Civil War

A Modern Reader

edited by Frank Otto Gatell, Paul Goodman, and Allen Weinstein

New York · OXFORD UNIVERSITY PRESS
London 1972 Toronto

Contents

Contents

Introduction

Toward a New Political History

The student of politics has traditionally divided his attention between the art of gaining power and the craft of retaining it. Any dictionary definition of the term "politics" will recognize these dual functions: on the one hand, "policies or affairs of a government"; on the other, "the conducting of or engaging in political affairs, often professionally." When examined in tandem, they should provide a thorough understanding both of the way political power operates within a society, and some of its uses. Americans have been far from unique in asking questions of their political history that might help explain their contemporary society. In recent years, however, we have experienced a heightened sense of confusion concerning the directions of present-day America, and this lends special urgency to our desire for additional perspective through an understanding of our political past.

A century ago, even as recently as fifty years ago, United States political history seemed to most Americans (and to the country's historians) a refreshing and epic drama of expanding liberty and declining tyranny. This morality tale, pounded home in countless orations and sermons delivered on the Fourth of July and just about every other day, survived with hardly a phrase altered in the lectures of American history teachers from one-room grade schools to the universities. The United States, the story ran, had been founded in crisis by seventeenth-century North Europeans searching for religious and political freedom, created in revolution by eighteenth-century colonials struggling against imperial despotism, and consecrated in civil war by nineteenth-century

Unionists vindicating the national commitment to freedom by fighting against an aggressive slave power. Even in the nineteenth century, of course, there were dissents from this candy-coated version of political history. American Negroes (*after* Reconstruction), Socialists, utopian reformers, non-English-speaking immigrants, and Indians might be forgiven a dash of pardonable skepticism concerning the universality of America's reputed Mission to extend equally the boundaries of freedom. Nonetheless, for a majority of Americans, the prevailing image of libertarian nationalism, an "empire for liberty," seemed a reasonably adequate approximation of the realities of political life.

Growing doubts concerning the merits of this largely mythical and uncritical view of the American past emerged around 1900 as certain new perspectives began to take shape. Late nineteenth-century science had helped transform the way in which American history, along with other non-scientific disciplines, was studied in the universities. History became a profession, and historians became more exacting in their research techniques and increasingly more critical in their interpretations of the American past. When the historians of the first half of the nineteenth century did their work the American Revolution remained a still-vivid experience for many of their countrymen. Similarly, scholars in the latter half of the nineteenth century, both North and South, wrote under the lengthening and inhibiting shadow of a Civil War mythology. Historians who pioneered in critical assessments of their national past early in the twentieth century lived in a country fresh from easy yet disquieting imperial adventures and, moreover, touched everywhere by the ferment of a new reform wave.

The Progressive Era provided additional impetus, if any were needed, for historians to engage in a critical appraisal of the American past, if only to understand why industrialism and urbanization had brought in their wake so much political corruption, economic exploitation, and social misery. The hallmark of "Progressive history," as it came to be called, was a searching and present-minded view of contending forces within society. The American past seemed no longer the simple tale of freedom's triumph over oppression, but, instead, another simple tale—this one recounting a constant moral struggle of democratic against privileged elements. For Frederick Jackson Turner and others who saw the westward movement as the central interpretive clue to American development, conflicts between an expanding egalitarian frontier and stratified, older regions supplied the unifying theme. Shortly after Turner developed the frontier interpretation, another scholar, Charles A. Beard, presented another theory: he described American political history as a struggle among rival economic interest groups, a view that has remained powerful and influential among historians to this day. In Beard's analysis, class interests rather than sectional ties determined the fundamental lines of political cleavage in American history: farmers opposing merchants, workers opposing factory owners, Southern planters opposing Northern industrialists.

Progressivism had reflected the prevailing anxiety among Americans of most classes over "plutocracy," or unrestrained economic power, the threat posed to a democratic society by unsupervised business enterprise. Beard and his followers discovered similar threats at each stage in American political growth, which they interpreted as a constant struggle between competing economic classes for control of the government. Although these conflicts had sometimes produced positive advances in democratic government, such as the abolition of slavery, suffrage extension, and government regulation of business, Progressive historians still worried over what lay ahead. The past had been a struggle; the future would inevitably be shaped by struggle as well. Whether twentieth-century American democracy could survive such violent clashes in an era of giant cities, conglomerate industries, massive concentrations of economic power, and new techniques for manipulating the public will remained questionable. Largely due to the work of scholars such as Turner and Beard, American political history no longer seemed a providential story of liberty's demanding yet unstoppable triumph over tyranny. If anything, the Progressive historians made the outcome of the imminent struggle appear to be a fifty-fifty proposition.

Before Beard died in 1948, the United States had become engulfed in global conflicts, first with German and Japanese fascism in the early 1940's, and then, since 1945, with Russian and Chinese communism—foreign conflicts which forced serious reappraisals of the American past by political historians.

Increased attention to a comparison of American political history with the experiences of European and Asian nations led a number of younger scholars, in the wake of World War II, to challenge the assumption of Progressive historiography that conflict had been *the* dominant aspect of United States history. Both Beard's stress on class antagonisms and Turner's model of sectional hostility evoked growing, sometimes massive skepticism among historians who saw that, when compared with social struggles in other countries, American disputes appeared milder, less internecine, and more capable of compromise through existing institutional channels. Historians during the 1950's also stressed the comparatively high degree of individual freedom and material prosperity enjoyed in the United States, and for the first time since the turn of the century, most of the major innovative studies of American history bypassed the assumptions and visions of angry reformism.

Many factors helped produce this new burst of historical *un*-criticism, or "consensus" history—among them the stress on comparative history, the anxieties over national survival in an atomic age, and the growing body of scholarship which questioned numerous errors or oversimplifications in the work of the early masters such as Beard and Turner. For whatever reasons, the 1950's witnessed the brief heyday of consensus history, a bland yet often eloquent rewriting of American political history that accentuated the positive features while muting the importance of past conflicts.

An abrupt reversal of this "consensus" among American historians accompanied the growing economic, generational, and racial conflicts, in the 1960's. With the increase of social tension during the 1960's came a revival of the reform impulse among younger historians, a neo-Beardianism that owes far more to its originator's historical premises than its practitioners often recognize or care to admit. "New Left" akademicians, stressing class struggles as the determining factor in American political history, have yet to produce their own Beard or even a synthesis

of our past equivalent to his. Yet they have voiced the disenchantment of liberal scholars, as well as radicals, with a political
history based on "consensus" assumptions which, all too often,
either whitewashed or neglected the ample record of political op-
presion and social injustice in America.

Yet changes in American historiography do not result simply
from altered climates of opinion, but often proceed from new
methodology and new research within the historical profession
itself. Thus, a procession of historians had scrutinized the Progressive historians' arguments for several decades, beginning long
before World War II, and rejected many of them not because
of changing values but because of conflicting evidence. Historians
were trained and continue to be trained to examine new data and
to question received explanations in an effort to achieve deeper
understanding of the past. Thus, in analyzing frontier society in
specific areas much more systematically than Turner alone was
able to do, several historians discerned a highly stratified or, at
the very least, contradictory social structure rather than the democratic fluidity which Turner theorized. Similarly, recent scholarship has exploded Beard's portrait of Confederation era politics
as a clear-cut struggle between the mass of anti-Federalist farmers against a coalition of merchants, planters, and bondholders
who favored the new frame of government. Later historians,
studying a myriad of local economic and political groupings, ex-
humed a complex set of responses toward the Constitution absent
from Beard's simple economic demonology. Beard's world portrayed a constant procession of clashing economic interests;
Turner's, a welter of contending sectional interests. While not rejecting entirely either view of the American past, contemporary
historians have shown greater interest than their major predecessors in evaluating other keys to American political history. Such
factors as ethnic and religious ties, ideological commitments, and
irrational drives have been isolated as powerful determinants of
American political behavior by historians using a variety of new
techniques borrowed from the social sciences.

Much of this scholarship—"the new political history" as some
of its votaries dub it—cannot be explained merely through the

recovery of vast bodies of data previously untapped by indolent historians, although new historical evidence has indeed proliferated of late. The primary influence behind recent major reinterpretations of American political history lies in the profound impact of the social sciences upon historians over the past several generations. The discipline of history has traditionally straddled the humanities and social sciences, pivoting toward the former in that it sometimes enjoys status as a literary art, yet eyeing enviously the claims for certitude and predictability made by the latter. Having grown restless with this half-caste intellectual classification, a growing number of scholars have struggled to introduce a more precise technical analysis of available data than has previously characterized historical generalizations. The "new political history" has attempted to apply methods of analysis perfected by the various social sciences—political science, psychology, sociology, economics, and anthropology—to the search for a more accurate rendering of America's political past.

Although influenced just as heavily by today's social climate of opinion as were their scholarly, "non-scientific" predecessors of previous eras, much of the best new work in political history at least makes an attempt to counter inevitable present-mindedness by rigorous, and hopefully fair-minded, application of techniques such as the systematic quantification of political data, the analysis of group ideology, and multivariate analysis of political behavior.

In the selections that follow, students will find samples of the older as well as of the new political history, sometimes blended in the same selection. Traditionally, political historians have formulated hypotheses to account for a historical development and then tested their theories against the available evidence through a wide-ranging yet frequently impressionistic and unsystematic examination of relevant data. The impressionistic method, and the intuition upon which it relies so heavily, will always remain among the historian's principal tools, if only because in most cases the data needed to answer with certainty many of the most significant historical questions are lacking, and will remain so.

But quantification, though no panacea, offers a valuable additional method, a precision tool for writing political history. Techniques of quantitative analysis have allowed for more accurate measurement of voting patterns among important groups in American life, both at the national and local levels. They have also allowed inept practitioners, those with a tendency to quantificate, to publish numerical gibberish; but then no methodology, traditional or super-modern, is any better than the people who apply it. Yet quantification permits historians to speculate more securely on the motivations behind group political attitudes and behavior. We can learn more easily, for example, what kinds of people voted for William Jennings Bryan or supported William McKinley in 1896; we can determine which groups were most likely to support the Democrat Andrew Jackson against his Whig opponents in the 1830's; we can guage the composition of the "ethnic vote" in 1860 (or in 1960); or evaluate similar voting behavior at other critical points in the American past.

Recent quantitative analysis of American political behavior has shown, for example, that United States politics cannot be understood solely in terms of economic class categories, although in their time such Beardian explanations represented a considerable advance in American historical writing. Today's historians must take into account equally powerful influences on political behavior, such as race, religion, ethnic background, cultural milieu, and ideology. Those who assume that people invariably vote their pocketbooks will find that a systematic culling of voting data does not always bear out that assumption. Variables other than economic class shape the complex manner in which people perceive and respond to political events. No discussion of the origins of the Civil War that fails to include the pathological elements in Southerners' fears over slavery, or the similarly irrational components in the anxieties of antebellum Northerners, can hope to explain that war's background adequately.

All of which is yet another way of saying that political history is more than the study of past politics. Recognizing the axiom that political behavior cannot be comprehended in isolation from other patterns of human behavior, political history has broadened its range. Such factors as group psychology, racism, ethnicity, economic development, immigration, nativism, and urban-rural conflicts have all become critically important (indeed, essential), to the study of American political history in recent years.

The analysis of American politics within broader social and cultural contexts has alerted historians to the influence of ideology, which is sometimes decisive for political action. The ideas and values which men believe in and sometimes die for are rarely accidental, and the forms they assume at any given time and place reflect the delicate adjustments made by individuals between their cultural beliefs and group interests. Yet ideas can become so powerful at critical moments in the history of a society as almost to assume a life of their own, exerting influences beyond the intellectual vanguard, often few in number, who transmit them. Thus the proto-revolutionaries of the 1760's and the Republicans of the 1850's both constructed ideologies that helped prepare their fellow countrymen for the impending realities of civil conflict. The natural rights doctrines of colonial dissidents during the Revolutionary era and the Republican party's free labor ideology nearly a century later both produced consequences that far exceeded their narrow class or group origins: American independence in the first instance, and the abolition of slavery in the second.

The newer political methodology, with its social analysis of politics and quantification of political behavior, along with the inconoclastic dismantling of the Progressive synthesis in recent decades, has left American political history in a state of confusion and disarray. Since World War II revisionist historians, using both new and traditional analytical techniques, have relentlessly and persuasively modified traditional views on almost every major question, often causing them to be discarded altogether. No alternative synthesis has yet emerged, however, to provide a coherent and systematic account of the growth of American politics. The story itself, an embarrassment of riches, was slighted by Progressive historians, and we are left with the difficulty of assimilating leads offered by the social sciences. Our bequest is a historical Tower of Babel that thus far defies synthetic reinterpretation.

Scholars also confront the compounding difficulties of the rapidly changing attitudes within the United States during the past decade—a growing loss of faith in progress, a profound skepticism over the worth of intellect, a reluctant recognition of the irrational and uncontrollable aspects of human behavior, and a fundamental loss of confidence in America's national destiny—all of which have denied to political historians a firm ground of current and universally accepted beliefs from which they could base a systematic treatment of the past.

In time, if our society can survive its present crises, a new overview of American political growth will emerge. We hope that at least some of the selections represented in this anthology will contribute to that synthesis. Certainly it is too soon to chart the exact contours of this new political history, but it will most likely rest on a more sophisticated understanding of the complexities of individual and social psychology than its predecessors did. It will also probably devote greater attention than did earlier twentieth-century political syntheses to explaining how geographic and vocational mobility, ethno-cultural and religious diversity, racial hostilities, and regional diversity have kept Americans from dividing along clear-cut economic class lines. It may examine in greater depth the manner in which American voters and their politicians have responded to constantly-changing urban and industrial patterns from the mid-nineteenth century to the present, and it may make more effective use of the quantitative method to sharpen our knowledge of how specific groups organize and act politically. The following selections should serve the student as a reliable and stimulating introduction to some of the work already done and to other larger projects yet in progress.

It is fairly safe to predict that no new synthesis can hope either to be accepted or long-lived unless it grapples with the past in all its puzzling complexity. That complexity, and the existing gaps in our knowledge which historians have recently become sensitized to, stand as formidable obstacles in the path of providing a revised, modern interpretation of the growth of American politics. But without such an interpretation, we shall not know where we came from—and in that blissful state of ignorance, we can hardly expect to know where we are headed.

I

Political Reconstruction, 1865–1877

Reconstruction: A National View

Negro Suffrage and Republican Politics

by La Wanda and John H. Cox

The nation emerged from four years of Civil War only to plunge at once into a decade of political conflict for control of the former slave states. Radical Republicans and Johnson Democrats, freedmen and ex-rebels all shared at least one fundamental perception throughout the "Reconstruction Era," namely a common recognition of its uniqueness. The partisan quarrels of the years 1865–1877 were grounded on a dilemma which all politicians faced: the singular absence of precedents to guide political decision-making.

At war's end, there existed an unwieldly governing coalition in the North, the "Union party" composed of Republicans and some "War Democrats" such as President Andrew Johnson. As Johnson and the congressional Radicals struggled for power, both confronted a revolutionary situation for which neither the Constitution nor the ordinary processes of American government had made provision. What political rights, if any, remain for leaders and followers of a defeated secessionist movement? What place in the Republic's political life should a freed Negro population assume—be given, rather? Which branch of the national government, executive or legislative, should dominate postwar policy

*formation? The confrontation between Andrew Johnson and the
Radicals arose out of these unanswered constitutional and moral
questions. Not even the takeover of national government by Republican congressional leaders in 1867 provided firm answers either
to the legal or political questions involved. In the process, however,
Congress assumed responsibility for imposing its own version of
Reconstruction upon the South.*

*Who were the Radicals and what were their major goals? His-
torians have argued over these problems almost from the moment
Reconstruction ended, often disagreeing vehemently on Republican motives in supporting Negro suffrage through passage of the
Reconstruction Acts and the Fourteenth and Fifteenth Amendments. Some have labeled the Radicals either self-serving political
opportunists or pro-black zealots, bent upon cynically manipulating a Southern Negro electorate in order to ensure their own continued domination of national politics and to punish former
Confederates. Others have seen congressional Radicals as tools of
Northern industrialists determined to block the Democrats'
return to power and preserve the economic benefits of Republican rule. Still others have pointed to the contradictions between
the general opposition of most white Northerners to Negro suffrage in their own states and Radical support for such legislation
in the South. Were Republican politicians "sincerely" in favor
of federal support for the freedman—including his enfranchisement—and, if so, how did their policies triumph temporarily in
spite of their constituents' strong anti-Negro bias? In the following
article La Wanda and John Cox explore these questions by reviewing the historiography of Negro suffrage and interpreting the
complexities of Republican motivation.*

Republican party leadership of the 1860's was responsible for
establishing the legal right of Negro citizens to equal suffrage,
first in the defeated South by act of Congress and then through-

From *The Journal of Southern History*, XXXIII (August 1967), 303–30.
Copyright 1967 by the Southern Historical Association. Reprinted by permission of the Managing Editor; most footnotes omitted.

out the nation by constitutional amendment.[1] Whether historians have condemned or applauded the grant of suffrage to Negroes in the post–Civil War years, they have more often than not viewed the motives behind this party action with considerable cynicism. The purpose of this article is to review their treatment and to raise for re-examination the question of what moved Republicans in Congress to such far-reaching action.

The earliest study of the origins of the Fifteenth Amendment was prepared by a scholarly lawyer from western Virginia, Allen Caperton Braxton, for presentation to the state bar association in 1903. The work is still cited, and a new edition was printed in the 1930's. Braxton held that Negro suffrage was the result of "gratitude, apprehension and politics—these three; but the greatest of these was politics." To Radical leaders of the Republican party, enfranchisement early appeared "a promising means of party aggrandisement"; it soon became "essential to the perpetuation of their power." In the struggle with President Andrew Johnson over Reconstruction, they had alienated "the entire white race of the South" for at least a generation to come. Once the Southern states were restored to the Union and the white vote of the South added to the Democratic vote of the North, the Republican party would face hopeless defeat; the only means of escape lay through the Southern Negro. In the legislation of March 1867 Radicals effected "a *coup d'etat* of the first magnitude," but it was not a stable foundation on which to build future political power. The law might be rescinded by Congress, overturned by judicial decision, or defied by the Southern states after their readmission. Only a constitutional amendment could provide security. It would also mean votes from an increasing Negro pop-

---

1. The First Reconstruction Act, passed over President Andrew Johnson's veto March 2, 1867, and the Fifteenth Amendment, passed by Congress February 26, 1869, and declared ratified March 30, 1870. In 1860 the only states with equal suffrage for Negroes were Maine, New Hampshire, Vermont, Massachusetts, and Rhode Island. New York permitted Negroes with a $250 freehold estate to vote. By 1869 the following Northern states had been added to the above list: Nebraska, Wisconsin, Minnesota, and Iowa.

ulation in the North as a potential balance of power in close elections. A few footnotes and quotations, notably one from Charles Sumner, appear as illustrative, and there is a flat assertion that debates in Congress on the Fifteenth Amendment "leave no room to doubt" its political inspiration. It is clear, however, that the author felt no need either to scrutinize or to document his interpretation; a primary relationship between Negro suffrage and party expediency appeared to him self-evident.

Braxton did examine in detail a thesis and the historic contradiction that it implied. "One may well question," he wrote in conclusion, "whether the popular will was executed or thwarted when negro suffrage was written into the fundamental law of this nation." No reader would doubt that the author's answer was "thwarted." Despite some overstatement and minor distortions of fact, this thesis is sound history. The national guarantee of an equal vote to the Negro did not reflect a popular consensus, even in the North. Braxton's attempt to explain how an unwanted policy became the fundamental law of the land, though less convincing, raised an important historical problem.

Despite his emphasis upon political expediency as the impelling causal element behind equal suffrage, the Virginia attorney might have considered Republican leaders who had imposed this result upon the nation, at least a few of their number, men sincerely concerned with the Negro's right to vote. References to "fanaticism," "bigotry," and "negrophiles" suggest that he did, though obviously without sympathy. This implication, however, is explicitly disavowed and with specific reference to Senator Sumner. Braxton found "shocking" evidence of insincerity in the fact that men who argued for the inalienable right of the Negro to vote agreed to exclude Indians and Chinese from the franchise. He considered leaders of the party to be distinguished from the rank and file of Northerners neither by principle nor by lack of prejudice. Unlike their constituents, congressmen were removed from personal competition with the Negro, and their national perspective made them aware of the dependence of Republican party power upon Negro enfranchisement. Braxton's indictment of Republican motivation showed charity on just one count. He granted that some leaders were moved neither by "malice toward the South" nor by "heartless political ambition." They had come to equate the life of the Republican party with the life of the nation and honestly feared a Democratic victory as a national disaster.

The second study of the fifteenth Amendment, by John M. Mathews, appeared in 1909 and was to remain the standard historical account for more than half a century. Originally prepared as a paper for a seminar in political science at Johns Hopkins University, it is a most unhistorical history in the sense that its author was more concerned to analyze concepts than men or events. He narrowly delimited the chronology and substance of his "legislative history" and showed special interest in the judicial interpretation of the amendment. Neither the historic problem posed by Braxton's study nor the question of men's motives as individuals or as party leaders presented a challenge to Mathews; he did not even consider it important to identify with particular congressmen or with political parties the four elements in his analysis—the humanitarians, the nationalists, the politicians, and the local autonomists. Indeed, he explicitly stated that "These forces were primarily principles, rather than men or groups of men. They were not always separable except in thought, for the same senator or representative was often influenced by more than one of them at the same time."

Yet the Mathews monograph does carry certain implications in respect to motivation. The statement that "There was little real difference of opinion among the leaders in Congress as to the desirability of enlarging the sphere of political liberty for the negro race" might be read as an assumption of genuine concern for the Negro on the part of the lawmakers. On the other hand, a quite different interpretation could be given to statements that "The politician was the initiator and real engineer of the movement," that he labored for a concrete objective "fraught with definite,

practical results," and that he was not altogether satisfied with
the final form of the amendment "because it did not directly and
specifically guarantee the African's right to vote" and hence might
be evaded. In this study so long considered authoritative, there
is nothing to confirm Braxton's identification of equal suffrage
with partisan advantage, but neither is there anything that would
cause its readers to question that assumption.

The writings of William A. Dunning and of James Ford
Rhodes, the two most influential scholars with accounts of Reconstruction published during the first decade of the twentieth
century, did sound a warning. To Southerners it had been "incon-
ceivable," Dunning pointed out, that "rational men of the North
should seriously approve of negro suffrage *per se*"; hence they assumed that the only explanation was "a craving for political
power." Dunning was implying a fallacy in their understanding.
Yet he himself attributed Republican sponsorship of Negro suffrage in the First Reconstruction Act of 1867 to the "pressure of
party necessity and of Sumner's tireless urging." In writing of the
Fifteenth Amendment, Dunning assumed that he had established the motivation behind it. He cited an earlier paragraph as
support for the statement: "We have already seen the partisan
motive which gave the impulse to the passage of the Fifteenth
Amendment." Any reader who took the trouble to turn back the
pages would find a passage which, far from proving the contention, did not necessarily imply it. Dunning had written that after
the presidential election of 1868 in which Democrats gained majorities in Georgia and Louisiana through the use of violence,
moderate Republicans had no uncertainty as to "the policy
of maintaining what had been achieved in enfranchising the
blacks."

Rhodes was more explicit in his warning and more direct in
crediting to humanitarian feelings within Republican party ranks
an influence in "forcing negro suffrage upon the South." He cautioned readers not to lose sight of the high motives involved "for
it would be easy to collect a mass of facts showing that the sole

aim of congressional reconstruction was to strengthen the Republican party." Neither the statement quoted nor his account as a whole would stir to skepticism anyone who had assumed with Braxton the predominance of political expediency. He did not analyze or criticize the Braxton assumption but rather supplemented it. In Rhodes's view, there were men with "intelligence and high character" who were "earnest for the immediate enfranchisement of the freedmen," but they were "numerically small." His writing at times carried an unintended innuendo. For example, he stated that the majority of Republicans in Congress when they reassembled after the Christmas holidays of 1866 did not favor the imposition of Negro suffrage upon the South, a policy which they sustained by a two-thirds vote a few weeks later. The explanation lay in "The rejection of the Fourteenth Amendment by the South, the clever use of the 'outrages' argument, the animosity to the President . . . which was increased to virulence by his wholesale removals of Republicans from office," factors that "enabled the partisan tyranny of Stevens and the pertinacity of Sumner to achieve this result."

The ambivalence in Rhodes's treatment arose primarily from his strong conviction that the grant of suffrage to the Negro during Reconstruction was a major mistake in policy. This judgment was evident in a paper which he delivered before the Massachusetts Historical Society while writing his account of Reconstruction and also in the volumes of his *History of the United States* which appeared two years later. Suffrage had been an abysmal failure which "pandered to the ignorant negroes, the knavish white natives and the vulturous adventurers who flocked from the North" and "neutralized the work of honest Republicans. . . ." Experience in the North, in his opinion, also discredited the grant of equal suffrage to the Negro—he had shown little political leadership, rarely identified himself "with any movement on a high plane," such as civil service, tariff reform, honest money, or pure municipal government, and "arrogantly asserts his right to recognition" because he is "greedy for office and emolument." All this had not been the Negro's fault; he had been "started at the top" despite "all the warnings of science and political experience." Rhodes believed that the findings of science were clear and that they had been available to Sumner and his fellow advocates of Negro enfranchisement through the distinguished Harvard scientist Louis Agassiz, who was Sumner's friend. He did not place all blame on Sumner, however, but indicated that the fault lay in our national character. "I think that England or Prussia would have solved the negro problem better"; they would have "studied the negro scientifically"; in the "age of Darwin and Huxley" Americans had made no attempt to do so.

In discussing the problem with fellow historians, Rhodes revealed more sharply than in his writings his personal assessment of motivation: "From a variety of motives, some praiseworthy and others the reverse, we forced negro suffrage upon the South. . . . Party advantage, the desire of worthless men at the North for offices at the South, co-operated with a misguided humanitarianism." The warning which he sounded, and the less explicit one from Dunning as well, reflected a conscientious desire on the part of these distinguished historians to be fair, restrained, and judicious. The assumption that most Republican members of Congress who voted for equal Negro suffrage did so primarily if not solely, for reasons of political expediency, was an assumption they accepted; it apparently did not occur to either man that there was need for any careful scrutiny to establish the validity of this accusation.

For three decades, until the post–World War II years, few historians handled the question of Republican motivation with as much fairness as had Rhodes and Dunning. Ellis P. Oberholtzer, in his multivolume *History of the United States Since the Civil War*, wrote that "Just as the war had not been waged to free the negro from bondage" so the postwar strife "except to a few minds, had little enough to do with the improvement of the lot of the black man." He continued: "The project to make voters out of black men was not so much for their social elevation as for the further punishment of the Southern white people—for the capture of offices for Radical scamps and the intrenchment of the Radical party in power for a long time to come in the South and in the country at large." The small but influential volume in the Yale *Chronicles of America* series written by Dunning's foremost student, Walter L. Fleming, made the indictment specific. The election of 1868, Fleming wrote showed that Democrats could command more white votes than could Republicans "whose total included nearly 700,000 blacks." This prompted the Radicals to frame the Fifteenth Amendment which, as it appeared to them, would not only "make safe the negro majorities in the South" but also add strength from Negroes previously denied the ballot in the North, thus assuring "900,000 negro voters for the Republican party."

During the late 1920's and the 1930's, a period in Reconstruction historiography which saw the "canonization" of Andrew Johnson, little charity was shown to those who had been Johnson's opponents. Claude G. Bowers developed the "conspiracy" approach to Negro suffrage, seeing it as the culmination of a plot hatched by Sumner and a few Radicals and dating back at least to the early days of 1865. He quoted approvingly the Georgian, Benjamin H. Hill, who charged that Negro suffrage was a matter of knaves using fools " 'to keep the Radical Party in power in the approaching presidential election, . . . to retain by force and fraud the power they are losing in the detection of their treason in the North.' " George Fort Milton recognized that "The Radicals had mixed motives in this insistence on negro suffrage," but his lack of sympathy for the "old Abolitionists" led him to gibe at Sumner. From a letter of the Senator, he quoted, " 'We need the votes of all,' " then observed, "Could it be that practical political necessities moved him as well as lofty idealistic views?" Milton did little more than mention the Fifteenth Amendment but could not resist using the opportunity to belittle its Republican sponsors: ". . . one or two Senators shamefacedly admitted that perhaps an intelligent white woman had as much right as an ignorant

negro plow-hand to determine the destinies of the nation. But
there seemed little political advantage in women suffrage. . . ."
James G. Randall, whose substantial volume on the Civil War
and Reconstruction served as a standard college textbook from
the 1930's to the 1960's, handled the subject of Negro suffrage
with restraint; yet in substance he accepted a mild version of
Bowers' conspiracy thesis. Randall's variant was that "the importance of the Negro vote to the Republican party North and
South caused leading Radicals to keep their eye upon the issue"
although Northern sentiment would not support nationwide Negro suffrage. Gradually, as the power of the Radicals increased,
they moved toward their goal. "Step by step they were able to
enact laws promoting Negro suffrage without an amendment, and
finally to carry the suffrage amendment itself in the first year of
Grant's administration." This account was allowed to stand without modification when the volume was revised in 1961 by David
Donald.

The chronological limits of Howard K. Beale's study of the
election of 1866, perhaps the most influential scholarly product
of the pro-Johnson historiography, precluded an examination of
the Reconstruction Acts of 1867 and the Fifteenth Amendment.
However, there is a chapter devoted to Negro suffrage as a general issue. Beale divided its Radical proponents into four groups
—old abolitionists, who believed in the principle of equal suffrage;
friends of the Negro, who saw the ballot as his only means of
defense; men hostile to racial equality, who would use Negro
suffrage to humiliate the defeated South; and, lastly, "a more
numerous group" to whom "expediency was the motive." Curiously, his classification had the same weakness as Mathews' dis-
embodied analysis; it offered the reader no evidence that any one
of the four "groups" was identifiable in terms of specific individuals. In fact, despite a deep personal commitment to Negro equality and intensive manuscript research, Beale added little new
except to link the suffrage issue with his general thesis that Radical leaders were motivated by economic as well as political ends.

"If the South could be excluded, or admitted only with negro suffrage," he wrote, "the new industrial order which the Northeast was developing, would be safe."

Yet Beale did not dismiss fhe suffrage issue as summarily as had the Republicans in the 1866 campaign. His treatment suggests his interest in the subject, and particularly in the claim made during 1865 and after that the Negro would never be safe unless protected by the ballot. Beale considered it "a powerful [argument]" even though he looked with sympathy upon those who mistrusted a grant of unqualified suffrage to naïve and uneducated freedmen. After struggling with the argument for several pages, he concluded that no one could say with certainty whether without the ballot the status of the newly freed slave among white Southerners would have been shaped by "the fair-minded" or "the vicious." Then he added: "Few cared to know. Extreme Radicals wanted negro suffrage; outrages against the negroes, and an exaggeration of cruel codes would reconcile Northerners to it." In other words, the "powerful argument" was essentially a propaganda device; its prevalence in the 1860's would not lighten the charges against the Republican Radical leadership.

Another election study, Charles H. Coleman's analysis of the Grant–Seymour campaign of 1868, was published in the 1930's and at once took its place as the standard, perhaps definitive, account. Coleman's discussion of the Negro suffrage issue in the elections of 1867 and 1868 is exceptionally fair and informative. Without raising the question of motivation or passing judgment, it yet provides considerable material pertinent to the problem. Also, Coleman, like Walter Fleming, was interested in the importance of the Negro vote. He estimated that it had provided Grant with 450,000 of his total, without which the Republicans would not have gained a popular majority. While Coleman believed that a majority of the white voters of the country favored the Democratic party in 1868 and implied that this remained true until 1896, unlike Fleming, he did not point to any connection between the 1868 election results and the movement immediately thereafter for an equal-suffrage amendment. The omission may have been due to his clear recognition that Grant's victory in the electoral college would have been secure without any Negro votes. The Democrats with better leadership, according to Coleman, might have contended with the Republicans on almost equal terms in 1868, but they did not lose the election "through the operation of the reconstruction acts." Despite a generally careful and balanced presentation, in his opening paragraphs Coleman made reference incidentally and uncritically to "Republican ascendancy" as the motive behind the Fifteenth Amendment. He had not given thought to the relationship between his findings and the time-honored charges of Braxton and Fleming.

By the 1950's a new direction was evident in historical writings dealing with the Negro in nineteenth-century America, one that rejected the assumption of racial inferiority and cherished the quest for racial equality. This trend, which reached major proportions in the 1960's, drew stimulus and support both from the contemporary social and intellectual climate and from interior developments within historical research. During the thirties revisionist articles dealing with so-called "Black" Reconstruction in the South had anticipated postwar attitudes toward race relationships and had upset the negative stereotypes of "scalawags," "carpetbaggers," and "Radical" regimes. In the forties the National Archives provided material for new departures in Reconstruction scholarship by making available the manuscript records of the Freedmen's Bureau with a useful checklist. The extremes to which vindication of Andrew Johnson had been carried in the thirties, together with a program to assemble and publish his papers, led to re-examination of his record and that of his opponents. Military confrontation with Hitler stimulated a challenge to the "needless war" interpretation of the American civil conflict, redirecting attention to slavery as a moral issue. Antislavery agitators became the focus of renewed interest and sympathy, the latter reinforced by a growing sophistication in the historian's borrowings from psychology and sociology. Leadership of Negroes in the contemporary struggle for equality found a counterpart in an increased recognition of the role of Negro leadership during the nineteenth century. Through new biographies and analytical articles, a beginning was made in reassessing the record and motives of leading Radicals. Finally, the coincidence of the Civil War centennial with the great public civil rights issues of the 1960's quickened the pace of historical writings concerned with the status of the Negro.

Out of these recent studies has come a new perspective on the post–Civil War grant of suffrage to the Negro, once widely regarded with dismay. The Fifteenth Amendment is now seen as a "momentous enactment." It included Negroes within "the American dream of equality and opportunity," gave the United States distinction as being the first nation committed to the proposition that in a "bi-racial society . . . human beings must have equal rights," and established an essential legal substructure upon which to build the reality of political equality.

There has also emerged an explanation of political Radicalism during Reconstruction, even of Republicanism generally, in terms of ideas and idealism. The case has been subtly argued and dramatically summarized by Kenneth M. Stampp: ". . . radical reconstruction ought to be viewed in part as the last great crusade of the nineteenth-century romantic reformers." If anything, Radicals were less opportunistic and more candid than the average politician. "To the practical motives that the radicals occasionally revealed must be added the moral idealism that they inherited from the abolitionists." The case for Radicalism has also been persuasively presented by the English historian William Ranulf Brock, who has written that the cement binding together the Radicals as a political group was "not interest but a number of propositions about equality, rights, and national power." In fact, Brock does not limit this generous interpretation of motives to the Radicals, but includes moderate Republicans as well. He was gone even further and identified "the great moving power behind Reconstruction" with "the conviction of the average Republican that the objectives of his party were rational and humane." The study by the present authors led to the conclusion that the moderates in Congress broke with the President in 1866 primarily because of their genuine concern for equal civil rights short of suffrage.

With the ferment and new direction of Reconstruction historiography, the old Braxton–Rhodes–Fleming assumption of party expediency as the controlling motive behind support for Negro suffrage by Republican congressmen might reasonably be expected to meet one of three fates: it might be quietly replaced by the opposite assumption that congressional votes reflected in large measure the strain of idealism in Republicanism; it could be dismissed on the ground that there had been a fusion of principle and expediency so intimate and indivisible as to preclude further inquiry; or it could be subjected to an incisive, detailed, and comprehensive examination. At the present writing neither the first nor third alternative appears at all likely. As for the second, the problem of motivation deserves a better resolution, for it is important both to our understanding of the past and to our expectations of the future.

The "practical" view of Republican motivation is too casually accepted in historical writings and too consonant with prevailing attitudes toward politicians and parties to be in danger of just disappearing. Leslie H. Fishel, Jr., Emma Lou Thornbrough, and Leon F. Litwack in their sympathetic pioneering studies of Negroes in the North all assume that Republican politicians had little interest in the Negro except to obtain his vote. In staking out the well-merited abolitionist claim of credit for having championed the cause of Negro equality during the Civil War and Reconstruction, James M. McPherson perpetuates the traditional attitude toward Republicans: the abolitionists provided moral justification, but party policies "were undertaken primarily for military or political reasons." Indeed, McPherson condemns the whole North for a failure of conscience and belittles the public support given to equal rights as "primarily a conversion of expediency rather than one of conviction." David Donald has attempted to bypass the "difficulty of fathoming . . . motives" by disregarding individuals in favor of "objective behavior patterns" and "quantitatively measurable forces." His procedures and logic, however, start with the assumption that politicians wish either re-election or higher office and that this fact is controlling in presidential policy and congressional voting. It is startling to read that Lincoln's policies could have been arrived at by "A rather simple computer installed in the White House, fed the elementary statistical information about election returns and programed to solve the recurrent problem of winning re-election. . . ."

Even Stampp, who restates the old hostile arguments regarding the political motivation of Radicals in order to challenge them, replies directly only with the observation that conservatives as well were thinking how best to keep the Republican party in power—to them Negro suffrage simply appeared an obstacle rather than an instrument of party unity and control. Stampp also strikes a disparaging note evident elsewhere in recent scholarship. This is the charge of "timidity" and "evasion" leveled against Republican politicians on the question of Negro suffrage. There is irony in the shifting basis of attack upon the reputation of Republican politicians. Once berated from the right for plots and maneuvers to thwart the popular will and establish Negro suffrage, these whipping boys of history are now in danger of assault from the left for having lacked the boldness, energy, and conviction needed for an earlier and more secure victory.

There finally appeared in 1965 to supersede the Mathews monograph an intensive, scholarly work by a young historian, William Gillette, on the passage and ratification of the Fifteenth Amendment. Reflecting the modern temper in its rejection of caste and commitment to equality, the new study nevertheless represents a vigorous survival of the Braxton-Fleming tradition. Gillette's thesis transfers to the North the emphasis formerly placed on the South, but political expediency remains the heart of the matter: "The primary object of the Amendment was *to get the*

Negro vote in the North. . . ." As revealed by the election results of 1868, "prospects for both northern and southern Republicans were not bright" and, according to Gillette, "Republicans
had to do something." They were pessimistic about reliance upon
the Negro vote in the South but alert to its potential in the
North. This prospect motivated the framing of the amendment
and accounted for ratification in the face of widespread opposition since it "made political sense to shrewd politicians. . . ." In
effect, Gillette accepts as his thesis the judgment pronounced in
1870 by the Democratic party-line newspaper, the New York
World, that Republican leaders " 'calculated that the Negro vote
in the doubtful Northern states would be sufficient to maintain
the Republican ascendancy in those states and, through them, in
the politics of the country. It was with this in view that they
judged the Fifteenth Amendment essential to the success of their
party.' "

In challenge to the dominant pattern of interpretation from
Braxton through Gillette, we should like to suggest that Republican party leadership played a crucial role in committing this
nation to equal suffrage for the Negro not because of political expediency but *despite* political risk. An incontestable fact of Reconstruction history suggests this view. Race prejudice was so
strong in the North that the issue of equal Negro suffrage constituted a clear and present danger to Republicans. White backlash may be a recently coined phrase, but it was a virulent political phenomenon in the 1860's. The exploitation of prejudice by
the Democratic opposition was blatant and unashamed.

The power base of the Republican party lay in the North. However much party leaders desired to break through sectional boundaries to create a national image or to gain some measure of security from Southern votes, victory or defeat in the presidential
elections of the nineteenth century lay in the Northern states.
With the exception of the contested election of 1876, electoral
votes from the South were irrelevant—either nonexistent or unnecessary—to Republican victory. It was the loss of Connecticut,

Indiana, and New York in 1876 and 1884, and of those states plus Illinois in 1892, which was critical; had they remained in the Republican column, Democrats would have waited until the twentieth century to claim residence for one of their own in the White House.[2]

What has been charged to timidity might better be credited to prudence. The caution with which Republicans handled the Negro suffrage issue in 1865, 1866, and again in 1868 made political sense. Had the elections of 1866 and 1868 been fought on a platform supporting equal suffrage, who could say with certainty, then or now, that Republicans would have maintained their power?[3] In the state elections of 1867, when Negro suffrage was a major issue, the party took a beating in Connecticut, New York, Pennsylvania, and New Jersey, suffered losses in local elections in Indiana and Illinois, and came within 0.4 per cent of losing the Ohio governorship despite the personal political strength of their candidate Rutherford B. Hayes. In Ohio the issue was clearly drawn, for, in addition to the nationwide commitment to Negro suffrage in the South made by the First Re-

2. For the election of 1868, see Coleman, *Election of 1868*, p. 363. Calculations for the other years are based upon the electoral vote as given in W. Dean Burnham, *Presidential Ballots, 1836–1892* (Baltimore, 1955), 888–89. In 1872 Republicans had 286 electoral votes and would have held a substantial majority without the six Southern states and the two border states which were included in the total. Republicans could have won in 1876 without the 19 contested votes of Florida, Louisiana, and South Carolina had they retained either New York (35 votes), or both Connecticut (6) and Indiana (15). In the elections of 1880, 1884, 1888, and 1892, the Republican candidate gained no electoral votes from any former slave state. In 1884, as in 1876, either the New York vote or a combination of those of Indiana and Connecticut would have won the election for the Republicans. In 1892 the electoral count was 277 Democratic, 145 Republican, and 22 Populist. Republicans needed an additional 78 votes for a majority, which could have come from New York (36), Illinois (24), Indiana (15), and Connecticut (6). The party kept Pennsylvania and Ohio (except for one vote); it had not held New Jersey (10 votes) since 1872.

3. More than a simple majority would have been necessary to retain control of Reconstruction in the face of President Johnson's vetoes and to pass the Fifteenth Amendment. Johnson supporters welcomed Negro suffrage as an issue on which they expected to redress their 1866 defeat.

construction Act of March 1867, the Republican party bore responsibility for a state-wide referendum on behalf of equal suffrage at home. The proposed suffrage amendment to the state constitution went down to defeat with less than 46 per cent of the votes cast. Democrats gained control of both houses of the state legislature, turning a comfortable Republican margin of forty-six into a Democratic majority of eight. Even judged by the gubernatorial vote, Republicans suffered a serious loss of support, for the popular Hayes gained 50.3 per cent of the vote as compared to 54.5 per cent won by the Republican candidate for secretary of state in 1866.

There was nothing exceptional about Ohioans' hostility to Negro suffrage. In Republican Minnesota and Kansas equal-suffrage amendments also went down to defeat in the fall elections of 1867, with a respectable 48.8 per cent of the vote in the former but with less than 35 per cent in the latter despite the fact that Kansas Repubilcans in the 1860's constituted 70 per cent of the electorate. From 1865 through 1869 eleven referendum votes were held in eight Northern states on constitutional changes to provide Negroes with the ballot; only two were successful—those held during the fall of 1868 in Iowa and Minnesota. The Minnesota victory, gained after two previous defeats, has been attributed to trickery in labeling the amendment. The issue was never placed before the white voters of Illinois, Indiana, Pennsylvania, or New Jersey; and this fact probably indicated a higher intensity of race prejudice than in Connecticut, New York, and Ohio, where equal suffrage was defeated.[4] These seven were marginal states of critical importance to the Republicans in national elections. The tenacity of opposition to Negro enfranchisement is well illustrated in New York, where one might have expected to find it minimal since Negroes had always voted in the state although subjected to a discriminatory property qualification since 1821. After a Republican legislature ratified the Fifteenth

4. The other two states where equal suffrage was defeated were Wisconsin and Michigan.

Amendment in April 1869, New Yorkers defeated a similar change in the state constitution, swept the Republicans out of control at Albany and returned a Democratic majority of twenty, which promptly voted to rescind New York's ratification.

In short, Republican sponsorship of Negro suffrage meant flirtation with political disaster in the North, particularly in any one or all of the seven pivotal states where both the prejudice of race and the Democratic opposition were strong. Included among them were the four most populous states in the nation, with corresponding weight in the electoral college: New York, Pennsylvania, Ohio, and Illinois. Negroes were denied equal suffrage in every one of these critically important seven, and only in New York did they enjoy a partial enfranchisement. If Negroes were to be equally enfranchised, as the Fifteenth Amendment directed, it is true that Republicans could count upon support from an overwhelming majority of the new voters. It does not necessarily follow, however, that this prospect was enticing to "shrewd politicians." What simple political computation could add the number of potential Negro voters to be derived from a minority population that reached a high of 3.4 per cent in New Jersey and 2.4 per cent in Ohio, then diminished in the other five states from 1.9 to 1.1 per cent, a population already partially enfranchised in New York and to be partially disenfranchised in Connecticut by the state's nondiscriminatory illiteracy tests; determine and subtract the probable number of white voters who would be alienated among the dominant 96.6 to 98.9 per cent of the population; and predict a balance that would ensure Republican victory?

The impact of the Negro suffrage issue upon the white voter might be softened by moving just after a national election rather than just before one; and this was the strategy pursued in pushing through the Fifteenth Amendment. Yet risk remained, a risk which it is difficult to believe politicians would have willingly assumed had their course been set solely, or primarily, by political arithmetic. Let us, then, consider the nature of the evidence cited

to show that Republican policy sprang from narrow party interests.

Since the days of Braxton, historians have used the public statements of public men, straight from the pages of the *Congressional
Globe*, not only to document the charge of party expediency but
also to prove it by the admission of intent. The frequency with
which either Senator Charles Sumner or Thaddeus Stevens. has
been quoted on the arithmetic of Negro enfranchisement might
well have suggested caution in using such oral evidence for establishing motivation. As craftsmen, historians have been alerted
against a proclivity to seize upon the discovery of an economic
motive as if, to quote Kenneth Stampp, they then were "dealing
with reality—with something that reflects the true nature of man."
Stampp cites Sumner as an example of the fallacy: ". . . when he
argued that Negro suffrage was necessary to prevent a repudiation
of the public debt, he may *then* have had a concealed motive—
that is, he may have believed that this was the way to convert
bondholders to his moral principles." An equal sophistication is
overdue in the handling of political motivation. With reference
to the Reconstruction legislation of 1867, Sumner did state—
frankly, as the cynically inclined would add—that the Negro
vote had been a necessity for the organization of "loyal governments" in the South. He continued with equal forthrightness:
"It was on this ground, rather than principle, that I relied most.
. . ." A man remarkably uncompromising in his own adherence
to principle, Sumner obviously did not believe it wise to rely
upon moral argument alone to move others. Thaddeus Stevens's
belief in the justice of equal suffrage and his desire to see it
realized were as consistent and genuine as Sumner's own, but
Stevens was a much shrewder practitioner of the art of politics. It
is worth noting, then, that Negro suffrage was not the solution
to which he clung most tenaciously in order to guarantee "loyal
governments" in the South; he looked more confidently to the
army and to white disfranchisement. In the last critical stage of
battle over Reconstruction policy, it was the moderate Repub-

licans who championed an immediate mandate for Negro suffrage in the South, while Stevens led the fight to delay its advent in favor of an interlude of military rule.

All this suggests the need for a detailed analysis of who said what, when, in arguing that Negro suffrage, South or North, would bring Republican votes and Republican victories. Did the argument have its origin with the committed antislavery men or with the uncommitted politician? Was it used to whet an appetite for political gain or to counter fear of losses? Such a study might start by throwing out as evidence of motivation all appeals to political expediency made after the Fifteenth Amendment was sent to the states for ratification. By that time Republicans were tied to the policy and could not escape the opprobrium it carried; a leadership that used every possible stratagem and pressure to secure ratification in the face of widespread opposition could be expected to overlook no argument that might move hesitant state legislators, particularly one that appealed to party loyalty and interest.

It has been implied that election results in the 1870's and 1880's were evidence of political motivation behind the Fifteenth Amendment. The logic is faulty. Consequences are not linked causally to intentions. Favorable election returns would not constitute proof that decision-making had been dependent upon calculation, nor would election losses preclude the existence of unrealistic expectations. Yet it would be of interest to know the effect of the enfranchisement of Negroes upon Republican fortunes, particularly in the marginal Northern states. Election returns might serve to test the reasonableness of optimistic projections of gain by adding black voters, as against the undoubted risk of losing white voters. If the end result of Negro enfranchisement in the North was one of considerable advantage to Republicans, we may have overestimated the element of political risk. If enfranchisement brought the Republicans little benefit, the case for a careful re-examination of Republican motivation is strengthened. Inquiry can reasonably be restricted to the results of presidential and congressional contests, since these were of direct concern to the Republicans in Congress responsible for the Fifteenth Amendment.[5]

Negro votes in the critical Northern states were not sufficient to ensure victory in three of the six presidential elections following ratification of the Fifteenth Amendment in 1870. For purposes of comparing the "before" and "after" vote, the election of 1872 is unfortunately of no utility. Horace Greeley proved so weak a Liberal Republican-Democratic candidate that in every one of the critical seven states Grant would have won without a single Negro ballot.[6] In the 1876 contest, which affords the best comparison with 1868, the Republican percentage of the vote dropped in every one of the marginal states, four of which were lost to the Democrats. Comparison of the number of Republican losses in the seven states for the three elections before 1872 with those for the three elections after 1872, shows four losses in the earlier period as against nine losses after Negro enfranchisement.[7] Of course, it could be argued that Republicans would have done even worse without the Negro vote and the politicians in 1869 could not have anticipated the depression of 1873. Politicians would have known, however, that Negroes in the North, outside the border states, were too few to constitute a guarantee of victory

5. Local elections did, of course, have consequences for senators, who were elected by state legislatures; and a shift of political fortune in a critical state was always of national interest. However, the Fifteenth Amendment was not generated from local politics. The argument of political expediency implies political profit in national elections.

6. The percentage of Negroes in the population as compared with the percentage margin of victory in 1872 follows: Connecticut, 1.8 per cent with 2.4; New York, 1.2 per cent with 3.1; Pennsylvania, 1.9 per cent with 12.1; New Jersey, 3.4 per cent with 4.4; Ohio, 2.4 per cent with 3.2; Indiana, 1.5 per cent with 3.2; Illinois, 1.1 per cent with 6.2. The Negro percentage is from Gillette's convenient chart, Right to Vote, 82; the percentage of the Republican vote was calculated from the election figures in Burnham, Presidential Ballots, as was that of 1868 and 1876.

7. Before 1872: New Jersey in 1860 (in part), 1864, and 1868, and New York in 1868. After 1872: Connecticut, New York, and Indiana in 1876 and 1884; New Jersey in 1876, 1880, and 1884.

in the face of any major adversity. In 1880 and 1888, years of success, Republicans might have lost Indiana without the Negro, but they would not have lost the Presidency. The only presidential contest in the nineteenth century in which Negro voters played a critical role was that of 1876, and the voters lived not in the North but in the South. Analysis of ballots in the 1870's and 1880's does not confirm the reasonableness of expectations for a succession of Republicans in the White House as the result of Negro enfranchisement.

As to Congress, Republicans could hope to gain very little more than they already held in 1869. Of thirty-six Democrats seated in the House of Representatives from the seven marginal states, only four came from districts with a potential Negro electorate large enough to turn the Republican margin of defeat in 1868 into a victory.[8] Of the four, Republicans gained just one in 1870, in Cincinnati, Ohio. Their failure to profit from the Negro vote in the Thirteenth District of Illinois, located at the southern tip of the state, is of particular interest. The district had gone Republican in 1866 and had a large concentration of Negro population. In 1868 the Republican share of the vote had been a close 49.1 per cent; in 1870 it actually decreased with the Democratic margin of victory rising from 503 to 1,081. In the two counties with the highest proportion of Negroes to whites, over 20 per cent, a jump in the Republican percentage plus an increase in the actual number of Republican votes cast—unusual in a nonpresidential year—indicate that Negroes exercised their new franchise. How-

8. The four were the Second District in New Jersey, the First in Ohio, the Sixth in Indiana, and the Thirteenth in Illinois. This conclusion is based upon an inspection of election returns as reported in the *Tribune Almanac,* comparing the margin of victory for Democratic winners in 1868 with an approximation of the number of potential Negro voters estimated as one-fifth of the Negro population in the counties comprising each district. Population figures were taken from the *Ninth Census of the United States,* 1870 (Washington, 1872). Districts where Republican candidates were seated as the result of a contest were not counted as Democratic even though a Democratic majority was shown in the *Tribune Almanac* election returns.

ever, this apparently acted as a stimulus for whites to go to the
polls and vote Democratic. In three of the five counties in the
district where Negroes constituted over 5 per cent of the population, more Democratic votes were recorded in 1870 than in 1868.[9]

The Republicans did better in holding seats won by slim margins in 1868 than in winning new ones. Eighteen congressional
districts in the critical seven states had gone to Republicans by a
margin of fewer than five hundred votes. Of these, Republicans
retained fourteen and lost four to the Democrats in 1870.[10] Three
of the four districts lost had a potential Negro electorate large
enough to have doubled the Republican margins of 1868. The
record of voting in congressional elections from 1860 through
1868 in the fourteen districts retained suggests that half might
have remained Republican without any benefit of the Fifteenth
Amendment.[11] It is doubtful whether three of the other seven, all
districts in Ohio, would have been placed in jeopardy had Negro
suffrage not been raised as an issue in 1867 both at home and in
Washington, for the margin of victory dropped sharply from 1866

9. That Negroes were responsible for the increase in the Republican vote cannot, of course, be proved but appears highly probable; similarly, the explanation
for the larger Democratic vote is inference. The Republican vote in Alexander
County with a Negro population of 21.73 per cent rose from 656 to 804
(37.8 to 45.6 per cent); in Pulaski with a Negro population of 27.4 per cent
from 543 to 844 (46 to 55.59 per cent). The three counties showing an increase in the number of Democratic votes were Jackson (Republican votes
increased there also), Massac, and Pulaski.
10. Districts lost were the Sixteenth Pennsylvania, the Third and Fourth Ohio,
and the Seventh Indiana. Districts retained were the Second Connecticut, the
Eleventh and Twelfth New York, the Third, Fifth, Tenth, and Thirteenth
Pennsylvania, and Fourth New Jersey, the Second, Sixth, Seventh, Fourteenth,
and Sixteenth Ohio, and the Fourth Indiana.
11. This tentative conclusion is based upon Republican victories in at least
four of the five congressional elections before 1870. The winner in 1860 had to
be estimated on the basis of the county vote because district boundaries were
changed in 1862. In only one of the seven had the margin of Republican
victory in 1866 been less than five hundred. This district, the Fifth in Philadelphia, may have needed Negro votes for victory in 1870 despite its Republican record. Together with it, the Thirteenth in Pennsylvania and the Fourth
in Indiana had slim majorities in 1870. In the latter two, however, the margin
decreased as compared with 1868, making it unlikely that Negro enfranchisement helped more than it hurt the Republican candidates.

to 1868.[12] One of the remaining four, the Second District in Connecticut, consisted of two counties, Middlesex with a Negro population of 372 and New Haven with 2,734, the largest concentration of Negroes in the state. New Haven had gone Democratic in
1869 (Connecticut elected its congressmen in the spring) by 62
votes, though the Republican won the district; two years later,
with Negroes enfranchised, the Democratic margin in New Haven actually increased to 270! Middlesex saved the day for the incumbent, who barely survived by 23 votes. This suggests that the
district remained Republican not because of Negro enfranchisement, but despite it. Two seats, one in Pennsylvania and the
other in New Jersey, were retained by an increase in the margin of
victory larger than the number of potential Negro voters.[13] The
last of the fourteen districts, the Eleventh of New York, consisting of Orange and Sullivan counties, may have been saved by
Negro voters, although the election results there are particularly
difficult to interpret.[14]

If we consider the total picture of the 1870 congressional races,
we find that the Republican share of the vote decreased in five of
the seven critical states, remained practically constant in Ohio,
and increased in New Jersey. The party did best in the two states
with the highest percentages of Negroes in their population,

12. In every one of the seven close Ohio districts, the majority vote had been
against the state's Negro suffrage amendment in 1867. Their congressmen,
however, supported Negro suffrage, all having voted for the First Reconstruction Act of March 1867, and also for Negro suffrage in the District of
Columbia on January 18, 1866, and again on December 14, 1866. These
men, each of whom served both in the Thirty-ninth and Fortieth Congresses
(1865–1869) were Rutherford B. Hayes, Robert C. Schenck, William Lawrence, Reader W. Clarke, Samuel Shellabarger, Martin Welker, and John A.
Bingham.
13. The Tenth District in Pennsylvania, made up of Lebanon and Schuylkill
counties, had a Negro population of 458, or about 90 potential voters. The
Republican margin increased by 404 votes. The Fourth District in New Jersey
had a larger Negro population, but the incumbent's margin jumped from 79
to 2,753.
14. The Republican incumbent lost in 1868 by 322 votes but contested the
outcome and was seated. In 1870 another Republican won by 500 votes.
There were 2,623 Negroes, somewhat more than 500 possible voters, of whom
some would have qualified under the old freehold requirement.

Ohio and New Jersey, netting one additional seat in each. However, in the seven states as a whole Republicans suffered a net loss of nine representatives. Democrats gained most in New York and Pennsylvania, almost doubling their congressional delegation in the latter from six to eleven out of a total of twenty-four. Republicans retained control in Congress but with a sharply reduced majority. In short, results of the Northern congressional elections of 1870 suggest that Negro voters may have offset to some extent the alienation of white voters by the suffrage issue, that they did little, however, to turn Republican defeats into Republican victories, and that the impact of the Fifteenth Amendment was in general disadvantageous to the Republican party.

Election returns blanket a multitude of issues, interests, and personalities. In an effort to relate them more precisely to the impact of Negro enfranchisement, we have identified all counties in the seven marginal states in which Negroes constituted a higher-than-average percentage of the population. Using 5 per cent, we found thirty-four such counties.[15] An analysis of the number of Republican voters in 1868 as compared with 1870 and of the changing percentage of the total vote won by Republicans in 1866, 1868, 1870, and 1876 would indicate that Negroes did go

15. One in New York (Queens); three in Pennsylvania (Chester, Delaware, Franklin); eight in New Jersey (Cape May, Cumberland, Salem, Camden, Mercer, Monmouth, Somerset, Bergen); ten in Ohio (Meigs, Gallia, Pike, Ross, Brown, Clinton, Fayette, Clark, Greene, Paulding); five in Indiana (Clark, Floyd, Spencer, Vanderburgh, Marion); and seven in Illinois (Alexander, Jackson, Gallatin, Massac, Pulaski, Randolph, Madison). The three urban centers with the largest aggregate number of Negroes in 1870 did not meet the 5 per cent criterion and are not included. Leslie Fishel has compiled a revealing table showing Negro and foreign-born urban population: Table II, Appendix III-B, "The North and the Negro, 1865–1900: A Study in Race Discrimination" (unpublished Ph.D. dissertation, Harvard, 1954). For the three cities with over 5,000 Negroes, the comparative figures in 1870 were:

	Colored	Foreign-born	Total
Philadelphia	22,147	183,624	674,022
New York	13,072	419,094	942,292
Cincinnati	5,900	79,612	216,239

to the polls and vote Republican in numbers which more than offset adverse white reaction, but this appears to have been the case in less than half the counties.[16] The net effect upon Republican fortunes was negligible, if not negative. Thus, in the first congressional election after Negroes were given the ballot, three of the thirty-four counties shifted from Democratic to Republican majorities, but another three went from the Republicans to the Democrats. The record was no happier for Republicans in the 1876 presidential election. Again, only six counties changed political alignment as compared with the 1868 balloting. Two were added to the Republican column, and four were lost!

From whatever angle of vision they are examined, election returns in the seven pivotal states give no support to the assumption that the enfranchisement of Northern Negroes would help Republicans in their struggle to maintain control of Congress and the Presidency. This conclusion holds for all of the North. Any hope that may have been entertained of gaining substantial strength in the loyal border states was lacking in realism. It failed to take into account the most obvious of facts—the intensity of hostility to any form of racial equality in communities recently and reluctantly freed from the institution of Negro slavery. Only Missouri and West Virginia had shown Republican strength in 1868; of the ten congressional seats which Republicans then won, half were lost in the elections of 1870. Kentucky had the largest Negro population in the North, but in seven of its nine congressional districts the Democratic margin of victory

16. Twelve counties showed an increase in both the number and percentage of Republican votes in 1870 as compared with 1868; in nine of these, Republicans also made a better showing than in 1866. In 1876 twelve counties had a higher percentage of Republican votes than in 1868. Of these, eight were identical with counties showing marked gains in 1870. The eight, with an indication of their pre-1870 party record, are: in New Jersey, Camden (R), Mercer (D/R), and Somerset (D); in Ohio, Pike (D) and Ross (D/R); in Indiana, Clark (D); in Illinois, Alexander (D) and Pulaski (D/R). The two clear instances of contested counties turning Republican in 1870 and remaining Republican were Mercer in New Jersey and Pulaski in Illinois, the former with a Negro population of 5.1 per cent and the latter with 27.3 per cent.

was so overwhelming that the state could not possibly be won by
the Republican opposition, and, in fact, all nine seats remained
Democratic in 1870. Although no Republican had won a seat
from Maryland in 1868, there the odds were better. The outcome, however, was only a little more favorable. In 1870 Republicans failed to make any gain; in 1872 they were victors in two
of the six congressional districts; these they promptly lost in 1874.
The pattern of politics in Delaware was similar, consistently
Democratic except in the landslide of 1872.

The lack of political profit from the Negro vote in pivotal
states of the North reinforces the contention that Republican
sponsorship of Negro suffrage in the face of grave political risk
warrants a re-examination of motive. There is additional evidence
which points to this need. Circumstances leading to the imposition of unrestricted Negro suffrage upon the defeated South
are not consistent with an explanation based upon party expediency. Two detailed accounts of the legislative history of the Reconstruction Act of March 2, 1867, have recently been written,
one by Brock and the other by David Donald; in neither is there
any suggestion that the men responsible for the Negro suffrage
provision, moderates led by John A. Bingham, James G. Blaine,
and John Sherman, placed it there as an instrument of party advantage. They were seeking a way to obtain ratification of the
Fourteenth Amendment, which the Southern states had rejected,
and to restore all states to the Union without an indefinite inter-
val of military rule or the imposition of more severe requirements.

The nature of the Fifteenth Amendment also suggests the inadequacy of the view that its purpose was to make permanent
Republican control of the South. The amendment did not constitute a guarantee for the continuance of Radical Republican
regimes, and this fact was recognized at the time. What it did
was to commit the nation, not to universal, but to *impartial* suffrage. Out of the tangle of legislative debate and compromise
there had emerged a basic law affirming the principle of nondis-
crimination. A number of Republican politicians, South and

North, who measured it in terms of political arithmetic, were not happy with the formulation of the amendment. They recognized that under its provisions the Southern Negro vote could be reduced to political impotence by literacy tests and other qualifications, ostensibly equal.

If evidence of Republican concern for the principle of equal suffrage irrespective of race is largely wanting in histories dealing with Negro enfranchisement, it may be absent because historians have seldom considered the possibility that such evidence exists. With the more friendly atmosphere in which recent scholarship has approached the Radicals of Reconstruction, it has become apparent that men formerly dismissed as mere opportunistic politicians—"Pig Iron" Kelley, Ben Wade, Henry Wilson—actually displayed in their public careers a genuine concern for the equal status of the Negro. It is time to take a fresh look at the Republican party record as a whole. For example, let us reconsider the charge that Republicans were hypocrites in forcing equal suffrage upon the South at a time when Northern states outside New England did not grant a like privilege and were refusing to mend their ways. Aside from disregarding the sequence of events which led to the suffrage requirement in the legislation of 1867, this accusation confuses Republicans with Northerners generally. In the postwar referendums on Negro suffrage, race prejudice predominated over the principle of equality but not with the consent of a majority of Republican voters. Thus the 45.9 per cent of the Ohio vote for Negro suffrage in 1867 was equivalent to 84.6 per cent of the Republican electorate of 1866 and to 89 per cent of the Republicans who voted in 1867 for Rutherford B. Hayes as governor.[17] In truth, Republicans had

17. Republican support in Kansas was the weakest, with the 1867 referendum gaining only 54.3 per cent of the vote for the party's candidate for governor the previous year. In the 1867 defeat for Negro suffrage in Minnesota, the proposal had the support equal to 78.7 per cent of those voting for the Republican governor. The 1865 vote on the constitutional proposal in Connecticut amounted to 64 per cent of the vote for the Republican candidate for governor; that in Wisconsin, to 79 per cent of the Republican gubernatorial

fought many lost battles in state legislatures and in state referendums on behalf of Negro suffrage. What is surprising is not
that they had sometimes evaded the issue but that on so many
occasions they had been its champion. Even the most cynical of
observers would find it difficult to account for all such Republican effort in terms of political advantage. What need was there in
Minnesota or Wisconsin or Iowa for a mere handful of potential
Republican voters? In these states, as in others, the movement to
secure the ballot for Negroes antedated the Civil War and cannot be discounted as a mere maneuver preliminary to imposing
Negro suffrage upon a defeated South.

Historians have not asked whether Republicans who voted for
the Fifteenth Amendment were acting in a manner consistent
with their past public records. We do not know how many of
these congressmen had earlier demonstrated, or failed to demonstrate, a concern for the well-being of free Negroes or a willingness publicly to support the unpopular cause of Negro suffrage.
The vote in the House of Representatives in January 1866 on the
question of Negro suffrage in the District of Columbia offers an
example of neglected evidence. The issue was raised before a
break had developed between President Johnson and Congress; it
came, in fact, at a time when an overwhelming majority of Republicans accepted the President's decision not to force Negro
suffrage upon the South, even a suffrage limited to freedmen who
might qualify by military service, education, or property holding. In other words, this vote reflected not the self-interest but
the conscience of Republicans. They divided 116 for the measure, 15 against, and 10 recorded as not voting. In the next Congress, which passed upon the Fifteenth Amendment, support for
that measure came from seventy-two representatives elected from
Northern states which had not extended equal suffrage to Negroes. Were these men acting under the compulsion of politics

vote. New York rejected equal suffrage in 1869 with supporters equaling 60
per cent of the 1868 Republican vote for governor and 80 per cent of the
party's 1869 vote for secretary of state.

or of conscience? More than half, forty-four in all, had served in the House during the previous Congress. Every one of the forty-four had voted in favor of Negro suffrage for the District of Columbia. Why can they not be credited with an honest conviction, to use the words of a New York *Times* editorial, "that a particular color ought not of itself to exclude from the elective franchise . . . ?"

The motives of congressmen doubtless were mixed, but in a period of national crisis when the issue of equality was basic to political contention, it is just possible that party advantage was subordinated to principle. Should further study rehabilitate the reputation of the Republican party in respect to Negro suffrage, it would not follow that the 1860's were a golden age dedicated to the principle that all men are created equal. During the years of Civil War and Reconstruction, race prejudice was institutionalized in the Democratic party. Perhaps this very fact, plus the jibes of inconsistency and hypocrisy with which Democrats derided their opponents, helped to create the party unity that committed Republicans, and through them the nation, to equal suffrage irrespective of race.

Reconstruction: A Local View

The South Carolina Politicos

by Joel Williamson

World events have seriously undermined American mythology in recent decades, and one of the prominent casualties has been the national image of Reconstruction in the South. Having themselves undertaken to occupy and "reconstruct" Germany and Japan following World War II, Americans could no longer view the Southern experience as unique. Nor did growing knowledge of the usual manner in which victors dealt with vanquished in modern civil wars—whether in Russia, Spain, China, Cuba, or elsewhere—support the contention made by previous generations of American historians that Northern treatment of the South had been harsh beyond measure. The images conjured up by such films as "The Birth of a Nation" or "Gone With the Wind," which portrayed an entire region under the oppressive thumb of rapacious Radical carpetbaggers and bestial freedmen, seem from today's perspective more a product of desire than memory. There never was any Black Reconstruction, and the notion that "black excesses" turned Radical rule into a nightmare for the South endures largely as a monument to America's national neurosis—racism.

In light of the Black Revolution of the 1960's which helped produce changing American racial attitudes, changes already well underway in the academic community have undertaken a more thorough and less mythical assessment of the Negro's role during Reconstruction. No longer treating blacks solely as objects of fear and abuse, more sympathetic scholars have begun probing the manner in which Negroes experienced their new freedom. They have found that although blacks clearly did not dominate Reconstruction, they were much more than merely subservient and unwitting tools of ruling, white politicians. Despite the humble post-emancipation status of most Southern Negroes as landless farmers, the Fifteenth Amendment had promised Constitutional protection for their right to vote. In every Southern state under Radical rule, politicians eagerly competed for their ballots. Local Southerners or Northern emigrants, many of them black, often wrestled for power among themselves in the name of principle, economic privilege, or simple plunder—and all needed votes.

One of the period's most undeniably tragic aspects concerned the aborted development of a Negro leadership class, particularly in state and local politics. By the time the South had reverted completely to conservative white domination in 1877, the Negro's political leaders had either fled the South or been silenced. In the following selection, Joel Williamson describes the development of such a group and the problem it faced during the Reconstruction period in South Carolina.

❧ The alliance of Negroes with the Republican party was a logical outgrowth of the pursuit by individuals of their own interests. Yet, some allowance must be made for the leadership that focused and organized the political energy of the Negro masses. The men who supplied this leadership and the manner in which they pursued their objectives are the subjects of this chapter.

The traditional story that Radical Republicans in the North dispatched paid organizers to South Carolina to encourage Ne-

From Joel Williamson, *After Slavery: The Negro in South Carolina During Reconstruction*, 1861–1877 (Chapel Hill: University of North Carolina Press, 1965), pp. 363–83, 387–92, 394, 416–17. Reprinted by permission; footnotes omitted.

groes to claim their political rights and join the Republican party only after they plotted to pass the first Reconstruction Act is a patent exaggeration. Actually, Republican organization in South Carolina began during the war. As if by deliberate selection, the great majority of Northern civilians and the higher officers of the military who came to the Sea Islands before the surrender were of the Republican persuasion. In 1864, Republicans on the islands were well enough organized to send a delegation to the national convention of the party and in the following year to elect the Radical editor of the Beaufort *Free South*, James G. Thompson, to the otherwise all-Democratic state constitutional convention which met at Johnson's call. Many of these Sea Island Republicans were abolitionists who, after emancipation, passed on to Radicalism. Before 1867, however, most of them were much more avid in pursuing their professions than in organizing potential Negro voters as Republicans.

The tradition also asserts that governmental employees, military officials, and, particularly, the agents of the [Freedmen's] Bureau were hand-picked Republican emissaries. Assuming that subsequent political prominence would mark most such people, this, too, is clearly untrue. Indeed, with the exception of the educational department of the Bureau, less than a dozen Republican leaders emerged from the hundreds thus employed. Albert Gallatin Mackey, Daniel T. Corbin, and Charles P. Leslie were the only federal officials who took leading parts in organizing Republicanism in South Carolina. Mackey, a native Charlestonian and a persistent Unionist, received the choicest post in the state— that of collector of the port of Charleston. Mackey became the very able presiding officer of the convention that drafted the Constitution of 1868. Corbin, a Vermonter who had been a captain of Negro troops during the war, became the federal district attorney after the war. Corbin acted as a legal adviser to the Constitutional Convention of 1868, was a perennial senator from Charleston, and remained an active Republican leader in the state long after Redemption. Leslie came to the state as a collector of internal revenue. By the spring of 1867, however, when he emerged an active Republican, he had already left the service of the treasury department and was eminently unsuccessful as a planter in Barnwell District.

The military was even less political. From early 1866 into the summer of 1867, the commanding general was Daniel Sickles, a close personal friend of Orr. Sickles's relief, E. R. S. Canby, evinced a mild Republicanism which even the native whites found inoffensive. Only two officers in the entire command became active Republicans. One of these, a Colonel Moore who commanded the Sixth Infantry, was relieved after appearing at several political meetings in the Columbia area. The other, A. J. Willard, pursued a peculiar political career. A New York lawyer who came South as the lieutenant-colonel of a Negro regiment, he remained to become a legal adviser to the commanding general. In 1867, he was given the duty of registering voters in the two Carolinas. There is no indication that he was an active Republican until after he was seated on the supreme court bench by the first Republican legislature.

Outside of its educational division, the Bureau was hardly more political. Saxton had never been able to make an abolitionist stronghold out of his various commands. His successor in the Bureau, Scott, became the first Republican governor and laid the Bureau open to the obvious charge. Yet, the Bureau under Scott was as often accused of anti-Republicanism as otherwise. Indeed, his staff seemed to tend away from Republicanism and certainly from Radicalism. "They are often more pro-slavery than the rebels themselves," scandalized Laura Towne, "and only care to make the blacks work. . . ." Leaving aside its educators and Scott, only three Bureau agents were active Republican organizers. R. C. De Large and Martin Delany held minor offices in the Bureau, and J. J. Wright was Scott's legal adviser.

It is true that before the passage of the first Reconstruction Act South Carolina Negroes were not organized by and as Republicans in any significant degree. They were, however, organized *for* Republicanism. They were associated in such a way that when they were enfranchised, the establishment of the party amounted to little more than formalizing a pattern which already existed. The elements most responsible for this pre-conditioning of the Negro voter-to-be were the Bureau schools, the Northern churches, and the native Negro leadership. Moreover, these three sources supplied a ready-made core of chiefs to South Carolina Republicanism.

Many early Republican leaders found their first postwar employment in the educational division of the Bureau. Reuben Tomlinson, a Pennsylvania Quaker who had been among the first experimenters to come to the Sea Islands during the war, was for nearly three years the Bureau's superintendent of education in South Carolina. In the summer of 1868, he took a seat in the first Republican legislature. Two of Tomlinson's assistant superintendents, Whittemore and Randolph, were front rank leaders in the organization of the state's Republicans. Whittemore was particularly influential in the northeastern quarter of the state, represented Darlington in the Constitutional Convention of 1868, and became the first Republican congressman elected in that area. Randolph was active in the vicinity of Orangeburg and was that county's first Republican state senator. A number of Northern-born Negro soldiers also became Bureau teachers and passed into the Republican leadership. London S. Langley and Stephen A. Swails were two who belonged to this class.

In addition, the Bureau recruited as teachers a host of Charleston Negroes (many of whom had been free before the war) and sent them into the hinterland. There they did yeoman work, not only as educators, but in imparting a sense of political awareness to the parents of their scholars. Many of them returned to Charleston as delegates to the Constitutional Convention of 1868. Examples of such cases are numerous and worth close attention because they indicate one means by which Republicanism spread among the Negro population before they actually obtained the vote. These examples also reveal much of the character of what might be called the second echelon of Republican leadership in the state. Henry L. Shrewsbury, twenty-one years old in 1868, a mulatto offspring of the free Negro population of Charleston and well educated, was sent to Cheraw as a Bureau teacher soon after the war. In 1868, he returned to Charleston as Chesterfield's Negro delegate to the Constitutional Convention. Henry E. Hayne, who had also been free before the war and became a sergeant in the First South, was sent to Marion as a Bureau teacher and returned to Charleston in 1868 as the leader of the three-man Negro delegation from that district. William J. McKinlay and T. K. Sasportas went to Orangeburg from Charleston as Bureau teachers. Both were scions of free Negro families which were prominent in the trades. Sasportas was the son of a butcher who had himself owned slaves before the war. Sasportas was educated in Philadelphia, remained there during the war, and was said to be intelligent and very well informed. The work of Randolph, Sasportas, and McKinlay goes far toward explaining the large Negro vote cast for the convention in Orangeburg District in the fall of 1867 and the subsequent development of Orangeburg as the stronghold of Republicanism, Northern Methodism, and Negro education. All three of these educators returned to Charleston in 1868 as delegates to the convention. What these men did in Orangeburg was duplicated by James N. and Charles D. Hayne in Barnwell District. Offspring of the free Negro society of Charleston, the brothers probably came to Barnwell as Bureau teachers and, along with Northern Methodist minister Abram Middleton, formed the core of Republican leadership in that district. James Hayne was apparently the leader of the trio which combined with ex-slave Julius Mayer to represent Barnwell in the Convention of 1868. Interestingly, in the convention, Sasportas voted with Randolph on every recorded vote, and the Negro delegates from Barnwell paralleled Randolph's vote six out of seven times. . . .

Technically all these teachers were employed by private parties, the function of the Bureau being simply to supply the physical materials necessary. Actually, however, as superintendent of education, Tomlinson had a large degree of control over recruiting, assigning, and overseeing the performance of teachers in schools supported by the Bureau.

Also prominent in early Republican organization in South Carolina and in the Constitutional Convention of 1868 were two Negroes who came to the state as the direct agents of the American Missionary Association for the purpose of establishing schools and, hence, were closely associated with the Bureau. These were F. L. Cardozo, who was the principal of the largest Negro school in the state, and J. J. Wright who passed into full Bureau service soon after entering the state.

Of the seventy-four Negroes who attended the Constitutional Convention of 1868, certainly eleven and probably thirteen . . . came by way of their involvement in Negro schools. Even though Tomlinson did not himself attend the convention, he followed the same path into the Republican legislature. It could hardly be denied that this phase of the Bureau's program in South Carolina was politically vital.

Probably as significant in conditioning the Negro population for Republicanism were the labors of religious missionaries from the North. The real meaning of their work was that they taught and practiced a religion which did not discriminate against the freedman because of his race. . . . Many leading ministers did manage to avoid direct political participation. Many others, however, devoted themselves wholeheartedly to promoting the interests of the Republican party.

Northern Methodists were especially prominent politically. French, Whittemore, and Randolph might well be considered politicians rather than ministers, but when formal Republican organization began in the spring of 1867 they moved easily and familiarly among the Northern Methodist congregations of the state. It is no coincidence that the very areas in which Northern Methodism was strongest—Camden, Greenville, Kingstree, Orangeburg, Summerville, Florence, Maysville, Sumter, Darlington,

Aiken, Barnwell, and Charleston—were also areas in which Republican organization proceeded comparatively rapidly and successfully. . . .

At least five of the 124 members of the Constitutional Convention of 1868 were Northern Methodist ministers. At least one delegate—Barney Burton, a forty-year-old ex-slave who had moved to Chester after the war—and perhaps several others were among the 102 local preachers in the conference.

Aside from Bishop Payne nearly every leading minister in the African Methodist Church was also a practicing politician. R. H. Cain was the most successful in both careers, but there were others who were hardly less active than he. William E. Johnston of Sumter was a delegate to the Constitutional Convention of 1868 and later the senator from that county. Richard M. Valentine was an early organizer for the African Church in Abbeville and, although not a delegate to the convention, he sat as a representative in the first Republican legislature. It is virtually a fact that the African Methodists moved their 30,000 members into the Republican party as a solid phalanx.

Individual ministries in other churches were also active politicians. Altogether at least thirteen of the seventy-four Negro delegates who sat in the convention of 1868 were professional or lay ministers.

By 1867 in South Carolina, a numerous resident leadership had already evolved among Negro laymen to make the work of Republican organization easy. The coastal Negro population who had won their freedom before the end of the war supplied a disproportionately large number of top-level leaders for their race. Many of these came directly out of the Union Army to assume prominent places in their communities. At least nine members of the Constitutional Convention of 1868 had been soldiers in the Negro regiments. Three of these had been in South Carolina regiments and became active Republican organizers in the interior districts—H. E. Hayne in Marion, Prince R. Rivers in Edgefield, and Richard Humbird in Darlington. Six were Northerners who had joined the Massachusetts regiments and remained in the coastal area after the war. . . .

Negroes in the interior were not without their natural leaders and some of these appeared in the Constitutional Convention of 1868. W. Beverly Nash, a middle-aged, ex-hotel waiter who had once belonged to William C. Preston, gained national attention in 1866 by his criticism of the Bureau's activities in the middle districts. By 1868, Nash was unquestionably the chief spokesman for the Negro electorate of Richland, a position which he maintained over all rivals throughout Reconstruction. Even in the most remote districts, Negro communities pressed forward a home-grown leadership. . . .

Utilizing the ready-made organization and leadership provided by Bureau schools, churches, and the native Negro community, Republicans in South Carolina rapidly marshaled their powers. Almost simultaneously, in mid-March, organizing meetings were held in Columbia and Charleston. Early in May, Republicans from as far away as Greenville met in Charleston for the purpose of establishing the party on a statewide basis. The Charleston meeting was decidedly not representative, but it did call for a Columbia convention in July and formed a committee to accelerate formal organization in areas not represented. . . . When the referendum on the calling of a constitutional convention was held in November, Republicans were able to present a slate of candidates in each district and to muster some 69,000 votes to secure their election.

Obviously, Republican organization in South Carolina was largely homespun rather than imported as tradition maintains. However, Northern emissaries were not entirely lacking. In March, 1867, heretofore strange Negro ministers from Washington appeared in Charleston and Columbia. In May, Senator Wilson (escorted by Parson French), was circulating through the state, and "Pig Iron" Kelley was expected to follow soon. A white woman residing in Abbeville in August saw some of the lesser lights in the field. "With Rev. Nick Williams's & Armstrong's lecturing our semi-chimpangee brethren at our very doors," she wailed, "God only knows what will come, & I have decided to hide my head." A few of the lesser Northern politicos remained to participate in the constitutional convention. William N. Viney, for instance, was an Ohio-born Negro who came to the state as a paid political organizer and went to the convention as a delegate from Colleton District. . . .

In 1867 and 1868, Union or Loyal Leagues were an important part of Republican activity in the state. Possibly, Leagues had existed in South Carolina in 1865 and 1866, but it was only after the passage of the first Reconstruction Act that the organizational device was widely used. Leagues were used to indoctrinate Negroes with Republicanism, but they were also schools to instruct Negroes in their civic responsibilities. It was perhaps no accident that the first president of the League in South Carolina was Gilbert Pillsbury, a long-time abolitionist who had first headed the military's school system in the Charleston area. Negroes must have found the Leagues entertaining. Visiting his low-country plantation near Adams Run in December, 1867, The Reverend Cornish found that "Sam—the then negro boy that waited on me when I lived at the Hermitage on Edisto Island— . . . is now president of the Loyal Leage [sic] & a very influential character among the Negroes—is Sam Small——" Leagues were not always harmless, however. Sometimes they assumed a militant front. Early in January, 1868, the mistress of Social Hall, also near Adams Run, noted that the Negroes in the vicinity were well organized. "The men have weekly meetings for the purposes of drill—fife, fine dinners, uniforms, drum, flags & c. Prince Wright acting Brig. Gen., Ned Ladson (R. knows him) Colonel!" As described above, in the mountain district of Oconee, the threat passed into open violence when members of a League killed a white boy in the course of a riot and proceeded to seize control of the community. Occasionally the whites retaliated. A year after the Oconee riot, Elias Kennedy, a Negro minister living in adjacent Anderson County and well known as a League organizer, was killed while on a League mission in a neighboring Georgia town. Leagues were numerous in South Carolina, but outside of the cities they were not durable. After the heated campaigns of 1867 and 1868, the great mass of Negro voters apparently faded out of the organization. The subsequent character of the League in South Carolina was accurately reflected in the politics of their president, F. L. Cardozo, one of the most conservative Negro politicians in the state.

Far more permanent and effective than the League was the regular party organization, which had developed in the traditional pattern. The grass roots were represented by individual Republicans who met either in township or, frequently, in county conventions to nominate candidates for local offices and to choose delegates to conventions representing larger districts—counties, congressional districts, or the state and nation. Each convention chose its permanent executive committee which, with its chairman, was responsible for carrying on the party's business until relieved by the next convention. At the peak of the pyramid was the state executive committee. After 1870, control of this committee by Negroes gave them important power in the heart and core of Republican politics in South Carolina.

The character of professional Republican politicians in South Carolina during Reconstruction has often been debated. The Redeemers, who wrote most of the history of the period, damned them all. The scalawags were poor whites without character, education, or position. The carpetbaggers—except those with money—were bootless ex-officers of the Union Army and unprincipled adventurers in search of political plunder. And Negro politicians were either Northern-sprung zealots in various stages of mental derangement or ignorant and deluded freedmen who moved directly from the cotton fields into office without so much as a change of clothes. Even a cursory survey of these groups reveals the inaccuracy of such a description.

Actually, scalawags represented—in economic status, education, and, to a large extent, social standing—every phase of Carolina society. The single quality found in the backgrounds of most native white Republican leaders was a spirit of Unionism distinctly deeper than that of their neighbors. Even here, however, scalawags as a group were still in some degree representative of the community, mustering a few first-line fire-eaters in their ranks. Franklin J. Moses, Jr., for instance, had been the secretary of the secession governor and had personally hauled the United States flag down from over Fort Sumter in 1861. Some scalawags were poor. Solomon George Washington Dill of Charleston and Kershaw, by his own report, had always been a poor man and identified himself with the interest of the poor. Others were rich. Thomas Jefferson Robertson, a United States senator throughout the period, was reputedly one of the wealthiest men in the state after the war. Precisely as South Carolina exhibited a high degree of illiteracy in its white population, so too were there ill-educated scalawags. Dill of Kershaw, Allan of Greenville, Owen and Crews of Laurens, and many others apparently possessed only common school educations. On the other hand, many scalawag leaders were at least as erudite as their conservative opponents. Dr. Albert Gallatin Mackey graduated first in his class in Charleston's Medical School, and a Northern correspondent, visiting him in the book-lined study in his Charleston home, found him highly learned. . . . Doubtless some native whites became Republicans out of expediency, but it is also certain that many adopted the party out of principle. John R. Cochran and John Scott Murray of Anderson and Simeon Corley of Lexington, for instance, were Republican leaders whose principles were above reproach even by the opposition. Although none of the self-styled aristocracy became open Republicans, a fair proportion of the scalawag leadership had been accepted in the elite social circle of their own communities before becoming Republicans, and in most cases, apparently they did not immediately lose social prestige by crossing the political divide. . . .

Carpetbaggers exhibited the same degree of variety. . . . The average carpetbagger was rather better educated than his Southern counterpart of the same age and economic background. . . .

Indeed, one seeks in vain among the leading carpetbaggers for one who was ill-educated, and many of those least educated in the formal sense were, like Timothy Hurley, intelligent men of wide experience. Few political carpetbaggers were received socially by the aristocracy, but they obviously remained fully acceptable in their home communities in the North. . . .

The Redeemers' estimate of Northern Negroes in the South was nearly correct—they were zealots. Some, like R. H. Gleaves, came to further their material fortunes by business pursuits. Others, like Whipper and the lawyer class in general, probably saw a chance for personal profit in representing the claims of the newly emancipated. But, most of them came (or, having left the army, remained) primarily as religious, educational, and cultural missionaries, hoping to accomplish an elevation of their racial brothers which was not possible in the restricted and less populous Negro communities in the North. Just as the Massachusetts Negro regiments drew off the cream of young manhood from the Northern Negro population during the war, Reconstruction attracted the cream in peace.

The one thing that most native Negro leaders were not was fresh from the cotton fields. Of the seventy-four Negroes who sat in the Constitutional Convention of 1868, fourteen were Northerners. Of the fifty-nine Negroes who had been born or settled in South Carolina before the war, at least eighteen and probably twenty-one had been free. A dozen of these were Charlestonians. Nearly all had been tradesmen. Roughly two-thirds of this group continued to pursue their trades after the war and at least until the time of the convention. The remainder took service as Bureau teachers. T. K. Sasportas, Henry Shrewsbury, and others had risen to the educational level of the high school graduate in the North. Most possessed the equivalent of a common school education, while several were, apparently, barely literate. F. L. Cardozo, of course, having attended the University of Glasgow and the London School of Theology, was as well educated as any man in the state.

Thirty-eight of the delegates were clearly former slaves. The occupations of twelve of these are not known, but not one was described as an agricultural worker. Twenty-six were trades-, professional, or business men. Eight of the twenty-six were ministers (some being tradesmen as well), four were carpenters, two blacksmiths, two shoemakers, two had been coachmen and the remaining eight included a businessman, a businessman and steamer captain (Smalls), a tanner, a barber, a teacher, a waiter, a servant, and a carriage maker. Most of those who were tradesmen had pursued the same occupation as slaves. For instance, John Chesnut, the barber, was the son of a Camden barber whose father had been freed by the first General James Chesnut. John was born of a slave mother and, hence, was a slave but had been allowed to learn his trade in his father's shop. The degree of education possessed by these freedmen was not high. However, nearly all appeared to be literate in some degree, and a few were amazingly well read. Nash, for example, could quote Shakespeare with apparent ease and obviously read the leading Northern papers. During the war, Robert Smalls had been taught intensively by two professional educators while he was stationed for a year and a half in the Philadelphia Naval Yard. It is true that conservatives had considerable grounds for complaint against the ignorance of their late-slaves become legislators, but their charges of stupidity changed with the political climate. Early in 1866, the Camden press lauded John Chesnut and Harmon Jones as "two intelligent freedmen" for their speeches to the Negroes denying that the government was to give them lands and urging them to return to work. After 1867, when John Chesnut went into Republican politics, became a delegate to the convention which drafted a new constitution, and served thereafter in the Republican legislature, words strong enough to describe Chesnut's lack of talent were not available.

In view of the high degree of natural ability extant among leading Republicans of both races, it is hardly surprising that the higher offices were filled with men who were quite capable of executing their responsibilities.

In the executive area, the abilities of such white office holders as Dr. Ensor as the director of the insane asylum and H. L. Pardee as superintendent of the penitentiary and such Negro office holders as F. L. Cardozo and H. E. Hayne withstood the closest criticism. Although he was frequently overridden by a less careful legislature, Cardozo as treasurer of the state from 1872 until the summer of 1876 (after which his office was virtually nullified by a boycott of white taxpayers) revealed the highest capacities. . . .

Even political opponents generally recognized the capacity of leading Republican legislators. South Carolina's Negro congressmen—Elliott, Rainey, Ransier, De Large, Cain, and Smalls—were usually conceded to be able enough for their posts. Though Democrats in the House scoffed, Elliott's speech to Congress on the Ku Klux was widely celebrated. Capable Negro solons also appeared in the Constitutional Convention of 1868 and in the Republican legislatures which followed. Ransier, Gleaves, and Swails as presiding officers in the Senate and Samuel J. Lee and, again, Elliott as speakers of the house were remarkably effective managers in view of their sudden elevation to their posts. There were others, like Whipper, who were virtually professional legislators and became excellent parliamentarians.

It was inevitable that combinations of intelligence, education, experience, and natural ability were in short supply among Republicans in South Carolina. After all, there were comparatively few Negroes in South Carolina who could claim to possess a high level of education or significant experience in government. In the legislature, and in local offices in many areas, there was obviously a lack of competence among Republican leaders. This absence was usually identified with the presence of the Negro officeholder.

Yet, what one saw in the legislature was obviously determined by what one was conditioned to see. . . . The more astute visitors, however skeptical they may have been of the results, invariably saw something vital in the proceedings of Republican and Negro legislatures in the state. "It is not all sham, nor all burlesque," wrote James Pike after his celebrated visit in the winter of 1873. "They have a genuine interest and a genuine earnestness in the business of the assembly which we are bound to recognize and respect unless we would be accounted shallow critics."

Conservative native whites were distressed by what they saw even before they entered the legislative chambers. . . .

The proceedings of the House particularly offended whites. In August, 1868, an upcountry editor was shocked to find seven "dusky belles" seated on the platform with Speaker Moses. A year later, another observer noted that members frequently defied the chair, conversed with debaters on the floor, and, on one occasion, T. K. Sasportas answered an argument from Representative De Large with his fist. A Northern visitor in 1874 was amazed by the lack of respect accorded to some members by others. As an instance, he noted that Representative Holmes of Colleton called on the speaker for the yeas and nays on a measure, but the speaker refused to recognize him until the vote had been announced. Holmes then rose to a question of privilege and was overruled. He persisted and other members began to cough. Holmes tried to talk over the noise. The coughing grew louder. Finally, E. W. M. Mackey suggested that someone call a doctor and the house roared in amusement, while the exasperated Holmes collapsed in his chair.

Capacity and incompetence frequently traveled side by side in the legislature, but incapacity was often glaringly in evidence among officeholders of the lower echelons. "Our letters are often lost now," wrote a resident of Camden to her son, "Adamson is travelling Agent to distribute the letters and Boswell and Frank Carter, Ned's son, are Postmaster[s] here." The cause, of course, was apparent: "In Columbia and elsewhere, they have negroes in the Post office, and I have no doubt our letters go astray." County and city officers elicited similar complaints. Much distressed, the grand jury of Williamsburg County, in the spring of 1871, charged that the county commissioners permitted the county's prisoners to roam the streets of Kingstree after the jail burned in 1867, kept no records worthy of the name, and had allowed the roads and bridges of the county (some of which had not been worked upon in two years) to become almost impassable. Further, they feared that the county poor farm was "calculated to do more harm to the County than good."

The great problem of the Republican regime in South Carolina, however, was not so much a lack of capacity among its leaders as it was an absence of a sense of responsibility to the whole society, white as well as black. In the idealistic days of the Constitutional Convention of 1868, Republicans often reflected verbally upon the fact that their work was for the benefit of all. Yet, within two months after the close of the convention, election results showed that, willingly or not, the Republican party in South Carolina was the party of the Negro and for the Negro. Within a short time, it also became a party by the Negro. This was a line which the whites themselves had helped to draw. There emerged among Republican leaders a new concept that their first loyalty was due, not to their total constituency, but to that particular Republican and Negro element which had put them into office. This attitude was evident in the inclination of Republicans to drive Democrats and native whites of the conservative persuasion completely out of the government. It was also evident in a certain superciliousness which developed among members of the party in power toward the opposition. In this atmosphere, the protests of the white minority became proper subjects for Republican disdain and, indeed, ridicule. "Please read where I have marked, and judge the class of men which composed the late Taxpayer's convention of South Carolina," Negro Congressman Rainey jeered quietly in a confidential communiqué to President Grant's secretary early in 1874. Three years earlier, while the first taxpayers' convention was in session, A. O.

Jones, the mulatto clerk of the house, suggested to his partner in a corruption-laden ring of public printers that their Republican Printing Company enter a bid for the printing of "Ye Taxpayers." "R. P. C.," he jested, "That's as effective on the State Treasury as the other terrible triad is on Radical office holders—eh?" If the opposition had no political rights, they also had no economic rights. Attacks on the property by heavy taxation and then by the theft of those tax moneys was perhaps within the limits of this new morality.

Among Republican politicos in Reconstruction South Carolina, there is no correlation between intelligence, education, wealth, experience, and competence on the one hand and, on the other, integrity. The thieves included men who claimed all or most of these qualities, as well as men who could claim none. The relationship which did exist was the logical one: among those who did steal, the most successful thieves invariably combined high intelligence and large administrative talents with generous endowments of education, wealth, and experience. Petty frauds were numerous and widespread, but the truly magnificent peculations were conceived and executed by a relatively few men, usually residing in Columbia or Charleston. However, these larger schemes frequently required the purchase of the co-operation of scores of state officers and legislators, and thus corruption was spread.

The first and always the most gigantic steals consisted simply of issuing state bonds in excess of the amounts authorized by the legislature. In the summer of 1868, the legislature sanctioned the issue of one million dollars worth of bonds to pay the interest on the state debt and to re-establish its credit. The financial board, consisting of Governor Scott and the other leading officers in the state government, was authorized to market the bonds through a financial agent, H. H. Kimpton, in New York. The authorized issue was promptly made. Probably under Kimpton's management, another million was clandestinely added. Since Scott had to sign each bond and Treasurer N. G. Parker had to

issue them and honor payments of interest, it is certain that they
were implicated in the plot, but the involvement of other members of the board is not clear. When the legislature directed the
issue of another million dollars in bonds in 1869, the fraud was
repeated. After passing and repealing an act to re-finance the debt
through London sources, the legislature repudiated about half of
the state's twelve-million-dollar debt and converted the remainder
into a single loan guaranteed by about six million dollars' worth
of "Conversion Bonds." But again the actual issue almost doubled
the amount authorized. By flagrantly misrepresenting the state's
finances and by buying and selling his own issues, Kimpton kept
the bond bubble afloat. To its authors, a part of the appeal of the
bond scheme was that it needed the co-operation of the inner
few only and did not require the wide-scale bribery of state officials. Indeed, the fewer to profit the better. Moreover, the ring
only served its own interest when it encouraged efforts at financial
reform and re-establishing the state's credit, because these displays
tended to drive up the market price and to prepare the way for
further illicit issues. . . .

There were a number of other major "jobs" pushed through
the legislature. During the first Scott administration, a group of
native white conservative Charleston businessmen combined with
several carpetbag politicians to gain, over Scott's veto, a fabulously
lucrative monopoly of the mining of phosphates (for fertilizer)
from the river beds of the state. Agent for the job was Timothy
Hurly, a Boston-born Republican who reportedly came to Columbia carrying a carpetbag containing $40,000 which he used, partly
through scalawag Speaker Moses, to win the desired legislation.

The most effective jobber, however, was always Patterson. It
appears that the Pennsylvania financier enjoyed legislative bribery
as a game. In the fall of 1871, he and his henchman, H. C. Worthington, one-time Nevada congressman, Union general, and minister to Brazil, volunteered to defend Governor Scott from a
threatened impeachment. They used $50,000 of the state's money
provided by Scott. On the morning before the vote initiating pro-

ceedings was taken, Patterson arranged the usual caucus through Rivers, who "was always looked to as a leader of certain members, about fifteen or twenty." As host, Rivers served drinks, "viands," and cigars. Patterson and Worthington attended and spoke against the impeachment. Afterward, only Patterson and Rivers were in the room. "So when Patterson saw me in the room," Rivers later testified, "he just said: 'You go and vote against the impeachment and I'll give you $200;' and I said: 'All right.' " By the same methods, and at the cost of $40,000, Patterson bought himself a seat in the United States Senate and promptly had Worthington appointed collector of the port of Charleston where both doubt-less soon earned several times that amount by soliciting bribes from merchants. In the fall of 1873, Senator Patterson again lent his special legislative talents to a friend, Hardy Solomon, and succeeded in getting legislation passed to pay the obligations of the state to that merchant and banker.

There were other patterns of corruption in the legislature. Pre-siding officers in both houses and their clerks conspired to issue fraudulent pay certificates and to honor claims for legislative expenses which were without justification. Between 1870 and 1874, a steady source of bribe money was the Republican Print-ing Company, an organization administered and ostensibly owned by the clerks of the two houses, A. C. Jones, a Negro, and Jo-sephus Woodruff, a Charleston and Columbia journalist become scalawag. Through bribery, the clerks patched together enough support to secure the contract for state printing, but actually they were constantly pressed for funds by some legislators as if the company were co-operatively owned by the members and Wood-ruff and Jones merely the managers. Virtually every election by the legislature elicited a rash of bribery; but there were also other forms of graft. The sumptuous furnishings of Columbia com-mittee rooms somehow seemed to find their way into the homes of members and of attachés in all parts of the state. A com-mittee clerk from Aiken later testified that Speaker Samuel J. Lee, a Negro also from Aiken, during one session furnished rooms for himself and his wife over a Columbia restaurant as a "Committee Room." Later the clerk saw the same "marble-top table, settees, cushioned chairs, sideboards, &c" in the parlor of Lee's Aiken home. John Williams, the sergeant-at-arms for the house, furnished rooms for himself and Prince Rivers in the same way. Williams, too, carried furniture to his Hamburg residence and transferred other pieces so that "a house of ill fame kept by a colored woman named Anna Wells was also furnished."

Corruption at the local level was less spectacular, but it was prevalent enough. In many places, e.g., Beaufort, Negro officers maintained high standards of integrity, but all too often Negroes and whites were knaves together. The grand jury of Williamsburg, looking over the books—such as they were—of the clerk of the county commissioners in the spring of 1874, found that "upon many occasions when money was received, it was forthwith divided out between the members of the board and the clerk." Further, the commissioners had drawn pay for more than the maximum number of days allowed per year; the Negro school commissioner could not account for his funds; and the county treasurer paid only such claims as he chose to honor. By June, 1874, no less than twenty-four county commissioners, three county treasurers, two sheriffs, and one school commissioner had been presented by grand juries, indicted, or convicted. During Moses's gubernatorial term, punishment was neither swift nor certain for the guilty. . . . After 1874, when reform was in the air and public peculation had become precarious, thievery seemed almost entirely halted. . . .

Cities, too, frequently fell victim to the spoilers. Columbia, which underwent an expansion of its boundaries to give the Republicans absolute control and Negro officers from mayor to policeman, suffered an increase in its debt from some $426,000 in 1872 to $620,000 in 1874, and to $677,000 in 1875. Meanwhile, Charleston's debt swelled prodigiously beyond the two-million-dollar mark.

The average Negro officeholder realized very little profit by resorting to rascality. Those who became wealthy by thievery were few, and all the most successful were white—Scott, Parker, Kimpton, Patterson, and, perhaps, Neagle and Woodruff. These were the men who conceived, organized, and directed steals on a statewide basis. Key figures who abetted them in their predatory operations, either as officers of the government or as lobbyists, also received substantial sums—Moses, Hurley, Leslie, Worthington, Whittemore, Elliott, Samuel J. Lee, and Swails—amounting over the entire period from scores of thousands to several hundred thousand dollars each. The average Negro legislator and officeholder, however, found that the wages of sin were pitifully small. There were only four occasions when large sums of money were passed out as bribes; other divisions were made of the printing money, and occasionally some office seeker was willing to buy votes. Senators were usually paid from $500 to $5,000 for their support on such occasions. Members of the House received much less. . . .

The real profits of the corruptionists, large and small, were often much less than quoted. For instance, the bond ring sold its issues to doubtful investors at much less than par value (usually at about sixty cents on the dollar). As more bonds flooded the market and criticism of the government rose, good issues and bad dropped to fractions of their face value. One issue eventually fell to 1 per cent of its nominal value. Blue Ridge Railroad scrip, used to pay the largest bribe bill contracted during the Reconstruction Period, circulated at less than its face value. Legislative pay certificates, whether or not legitimately obtained, were usually sold at a considerable discount by impecunious members of businessmen like Hardy Solomon. Such circumstances existed because the treasury was itself perennially empty and those having claims against it had to await the pleasure or indulgence of the treasurer. While Parker held that position, large sums of tax money were sent North to Kimpton to keep the bond bubble inflated by interest payments on both good and bad issues. Local obligations were very liable to be neglected. After 1872, each claimant had to face the suspicious Cardozo, who soon became the bane of every corruptionist's existence by his miserly management of the treasury. The officers of the Republican Printing Company, to which a generous legislature appropriated $385,000 for the state fiscal year 1873–1874, had the greatest difficulty during the summer of 1874 in squeezing $250 to $300 out of the treasurer every Saturday to meet their minimum operating expenses. Lecturers in history are fond of titillating their classes with the story of how the Negro legislature voted Speaker Moses a gratuity of $1,000 for his services as presiding officer after his having lost that amount to Whipper in a horse race. Yet, Moses probably thought the gesture something less than generous since pay certificates, if the holder were fortunate enough to find any buyer, seldom sold at more than three-fourths of face value. Moreover, Moses probably considered it an ordinary reward for the extra duty demanded by his office, a burden which many legislatures, North and South, customarily eased by voting special compensation.

There *was* plush living in Columbia during Reconstruction. The senators maintained a bar in one of their cloak rooms in the Capitol and fine food, smooth whiskey, and the best Havana cigars were copiously available. The legislative halls, the offices in the Capitol, and the committee rooms located in privately owned buildings (many were in Parker's Hall, often spelled "Haul" by contemporaries) were lavishly furnished. Yet the bar, which was allegedly supported by the senators from their private resources, was closed to other officers except by invitation, and the enjoyment of the accommodations afforded by other rooms were usually limited to those who used them officially.

The average Negro representative came to Columbia on his own money. He roomed and took his meals—usually on credit—in an ordinary boarding house with a dozen or so other legislators, clerks, and legislative attachés. Many could not afford appropriate clothing. Hardy Solomon found one member on the street so ill

clad that he took him to his store and fitted him into a suit without requiring a vote in return. Occasionally some affluent Republican might offer the favorite "oyster supper" at a local dining
room, or a caucus be held in which refreshments were served; but
these were rare events. Such high living as was done by the legislators was done in the barrooms and, typically, on credit. . . .

Far from a jubilee, attending a session of the legislature was for
many Negro members a prolonged torture. Occasionally, political
excitement ran high, as during 'the Ku Klux troubles and recur-
rently during elections. But the typical legislator followed a dull,
drab, daily routine. During the mornings, he attended committee
meetings or caucuses, stood on the streets or about the Capitol
grounds, or remained in his boarding house. Beginning at noon,
he attended a three- or four-hour legislative session, most of
which were uneventful and, indeed, unimportant. In the late
afternoons, he repeated the morning's performances, had his com-
munal dinner at his boarding house, and retired. Throughout the
session, he was plagued by a lack of money and by a worrying
uncertainty whether he would be able to collect his pay at all,
regardless of how much he voted himself, and whether he would
realize from his nominal salary enough cash to meet his debts in
Columbia and his obligations at home, familial and otherwise.
Retrospectively, the life of the Reconstruction Negro legislator
was rather monkish when compared to the annual excursions to
the capital of his antebellum counterpart. . . .

If, as Chamberlain alleged in the summer of 1874, the mass of
Negro voters thought that public peculation was no less wrong
than private thievery, the question arises of how the thieves remained in office year after year. The circumstances suggest a series
of obvious answers. First, the period of blatant corruption was
actually quite short, beginning when the railroad and printing
schemes got out of hand in 1870 and ending as reform pressures
became increasingly strong in the spring and summer of 1874.
Further, the full extent of corruption became known only after

Redemption, if then. Very few Republican officials admitted to
any robbery before 1877, and even the conservative native whites,
in the Taxpayers' Convention of 1871, certified the soundness of
Republican fiscal administration.

Rumors there were of fraud, and probably many Negro voters
realized something of the state of affairs, but Republican politicos
sagaciously chose to accentuate the positive aspects of their activities and to call the roll of the offenses of the whites. With a fair
degree of honesty, Republican campaigners could point with pride
to a legislative program dedicated fully to the Negro's economic,
educational, and political interests, and the paper pattern had at
least some fraction of reality in every county. . . .

During their first dozen years of freedom in South Carolina,
Negroes realized a progressive expansion of the meaning of their
new liberty. From slaves and quasi-slaves they burgeoned into
soldiers, farmers, lawyers, businessmen, and investors; elders and
bishops; college students and teachers; jurors, voters, and politicians; family men, Masons, and, even, criminals. In a large
measure, this growth was made possible by an outside political
power which, early in the period, expanded the basis of that
power to include the Negroes themselves. Yet, an irony of the
post-Reconstruction history of the Negro is that the very political
freedom under which other liberties were early nurtured could not
sustain itself in a period in which those liberties continued to
grow. Negro losses in the political realm were largely the result of
the effectiveness of the Redeemer campaign in vilifying Republicanism in South Carolina. The extravagant charges levied in the
report of the Fraud Committee (attested to by scores of witnesses
who were confessed participants) seemed ample by its very volume and redundancy to cover the whole body of Republicanism
with layers of slime. The numerous indictments against absent
Republicans and the apparent ease with which convictions were
obtained where the state chose to prosecute was proof enough of
the guilt of all. It is hardly surprising that many native white

contemporaries convinced themselves and the following generation that Republicanism meant "corruption," and that Negro
Republicanism meant "corruption compounded." In time, Northerners accepted the Southern argument as it applied to the South
and found in it a certain measure of relief from a sense of guilt
for their apostasy. The results were unique; the men who had lost
the war in South Carolina had won the peace. Not many vanquished can claim such a victory.

2

The Gilded Age, 1877–1892

The Business of Politics

National Party Structure in the Gilded Age

by Robert D. Marcus

After the collapse of Radical rule in the South, national political debate clustered around a group of issues that defined most partisan conflict for the next two decades. No great constitutional crisis such as Andrew Johnson's impeachment trial nor any profound moral question such as Negro suffrage troubled Democratic and Republican politicos as they haggled over the tariff, silver policy, civil service reform, and regulation of trusts. While mass immigration, urban growth, and especially rapid industrialization transformed the contours of American society, most politicians responded to the process of change largely by aligning themselves with the industrial elites who dominated late-nineteenth-century economic life. Both parties contained business-oriented factions, primarily (but not exclusively) among Eastern politicians. No clear-cut ideological divisions separated the major parties after Reconstruction, in fact, until the silver issue split them both into sectional wings in 1896, a circumstance made possible by the growth of the Populist third-party threat and three years of depression.

Some historians have argued that the remarkable cohesion displayed by both parties during the "Gilded Age" (Mark Twain's *catchy but meaningless label for the period) simply pointed up the hollowness of most national political contests. In this view, both major parties had been transformed largely into mouthpieces of the business community, and their quadrennial struggles for the presidency turned into sham battles. Recently, however, some scholars have reassessed the notion of Gilded Age politicians as business-dominated and concluded instead that both major parties showed considerable skill in absorbing business support while retaining a large measure of independence in political decision-making.*

The selection by Robert D. Marcus that follows explores the complicated, revealing, and often surprising interrelationships between national politics and the business community.

American political parties are what Maurice Duverger calls "cadre parties." They have no official roster of supporters. There are no dues to pay or cards to carry and no rigid membership requirements. Before the twentieth century, the parties had no definable legal status, nor was there any official listing of who had a right to participate in their nominating procedures. They were simply, as Lord Bryce observed, "extra-legal groupings of men." The concept of party membership had "no meaning at all" in the American system, Duverger correctly notes. Rather one could only enumerate in the order of their importance the political roles men played: "the militants who are part of the 'machine,' the supporters who reinforce it during election campaigns, the people who take part in 'primaries,' and the citizens who vote for the party's candidates at election." The politician, not the party member, had the central role.

In the Gilded Age, the men we would call professional politicians did not form a distinct interest group, as reformers then and historians since have often supposed. The professional politician

From Robert D. Marcus, *The Grand Old Party: Political Structure in the Gilded Age,* 1880–1896 (New York: Oxford University Press, 1971), pp. 3–21. Copyright © 1971 by Oxford University Press, Inc. Reprinted by permission; footnotes omitted.

did not necessarily earn his living directly from politics (although there were many who did). He was simply the man from whatever walk of life who made a continuous identification between his own political interests and that of an ongoing organization, which in American politics has always meant a state or local organization, a "machine."

These political leaders included a large number of businessmen. The great political boss of Michigan, Zachariah Chandler, was a wealthy lumber merchant; Pennsylvania's Simon Cameron a banker and railroad director; and New Yorker Tom Platt a banker, president of a lumber company, and director of an express company. Theodore Roosevelt conceded that Boss Platt's political lieutenants throughout New York State included "the leading and substantial citizens"—bankers, railroad and traction executives, and manufacturers. Most railroad company presidents engaged actively in politics in this era; and in fields facing public regulation, such as banking and insurance, some executives like John A. McCall, insurance company president and prominent Democrat, or Chauncey Depew, railroad counsel and important Republican, held positions that depended on their political activities.

The parties also included the actors kept alive in the textbooks: the letter carriers and veterans, the customs-house tide waiters and the ward heelers, the "shoulder-hitters" and thugs, as well as the ambitious lawyers, the butchers, the barbers, and the saloon keepers. Politics was a national pastime to a far greater degree than it would be in the twentieth century, and the personnel of the parties—although one could find spectacular local exceptions —constituted a fair cross-section of the population. The same social class would not provide both letter carriers and Senators, but the parties, in sharp contrast to twentieth-century experience, reached all the way across the social spectrum.

When the politician, however wide or narrow his gaze, viewed his electorate, what he counted on most was an overwhelming party regularity. From the seventies until 1889, national elections were close, voters tended to vote straight tickets—supporting the

party generally, not just particular candidates—and voting turnout
was very high. Walter Dean Burnham in a careful statistical study
found that between 1876 and 1896, 78.5 per cent of the eligible
voters turned out for presidential elections and 62.8 per cent for
off-year elections, figures remarkably high by twentieth-century
standards. He also found that about two-thirds of the voters
habitually voted straight tickets, with about an additional 10 per
cent voting with a relatively high frequency for one party's candidates. Moreover, this electorate constituted a genuine national
cross-section: poor people, rural Americans, and (with numerous
and shocking local exceptions) Negroes voted along with their
more affluent and socially favored compeers in a way that is no
longer typical of the American electorate.

The parties of the Gilded Age continued the political system
that had matured before the Civil War. Political fervor remained
high for a forty-year period after the log cabin campaign of 1840:
campaigns were major events offering entertainment, information,
and emotional satisfaction. Then in the 1880's politicians noted a
slackening of enthusiasm as "the brass band, the red light, and
the mass meeting seemed suddenly to have lost their power."
This mood deepened until 1892, when politicians complained that
it was "difficult to tell from the manners of the people that this
[was] a presidential campaign." The decline in political enthusiasm and participation gave way momentarily to a new and
intense interest in the battle of the standards, but in the twentieth
century American voters have failed to show the level of interest
in political contests which they manifested in the past.

The closeness of elections, high turnout, and party regularity of
the period seemed to be mutually reinforcing phenomena. The
voters who identified with a party were—then as now—those who
cared enough about the election to vote, while the expectation that
an election will be close spurred both the voter to make his
franchise count and the political organization to get to the polls
everyone likely to vote its way. Close elections also supported
party regularity by raising the cost of expressing one's dissatis-

faction with the party above what most voters were willing to pay. When Tom Platt during the depression year of 1894 hoped to get New York Democrats to vote for a Republican congressional candidate, he instructed his canvassers to remind voters that they were not threatening the Democratic majority in Congress, but only serving "a warning to the Democrats that they must go slow in the passage for laws that interfere with industry." In short, Platt did not think that voters ordinarily were willing to sacrifice a possible party victory to express their dissident opinions.

These three factors—close party balances, high turnout, and party regularity—gave a particular form to presidential contests of the Gilded Age. In the twentieth century, these elections have been marked by periodic "surges" of voter participation—the result of a charismatic and prominent candidate who could bring out the potential voters not in the habit of exercising their franchise, not bound by party ties, and needed to break the stranglehold of a majority party. The election of Dwight Eisenhower in 1952 and 1956 is, of course, the best example. Gilded Age presidential contests did not and indeed could not show such a trend. Since most eligible people voted, the possibility of a radical surge of otherwise non-participatory citizens was not the usual expectation and statistics clearly indicate that it did not occur. Also, the "independent" voters who might be swayed by an especially attractive candidate were not a huge statistical quantity as at present, but a small number of usually well-to-do and college-educated men whose role as publicists far out-shadowed their size as a voting group. Moreover, neither party felt the need for a presidential candidate with the independent and individual strength of the charismatic leader when they could very well hope to win with some regular party member so long as he was "available."

After 1880, when Republican politicians began to worry about the waning of the old-time enthusiasm of the Civil War era, the party turned for the first time to a "prominent" rather than an "available" leader. James G. Blaine, with a long, colorful, and controversial national record, was a man whom we would call charismatic and whom contemporaries described as "magnetic." He had a personal following, especially among Irish nationalists, in addition to normal Republican support, and he seemed capable of re-arousing the traditional dedication among party workers.

Modern students of voting behavior have discovered that Blaine's 1884 campaign was reasonably successful in retrieving significant losses suffered two years previously in the off-year elections. But his contemporaries saw only the more obvious results: that the new strategy of appealing to voters not normally Republican led to dangerous incidents upsetting the loyalties of both new and old Republicans, and most of all that Blaine had been the first unsuccessful Republican candidate since Frémont in 1856. And as Blaine's magnetism had seemed to fail in 1884, so did Grover Cleveland's issue-oriented tariff campaign four years later. These incidents of the eighties slowed the tendency to put prominence over party, postponing for several years longer the era of the charismatic, issue-oriented national leader that Theodore Roosevelt was to inaugurate.

There is a more sophisticated explanation of Blaine's and Cleveland's failure to inaugurate the era of presidential leadership and charisma. For the nineteenth-century analogue to the "surge" election was what we might call the "decline" election. One could expect the normal party vote for virtually any reasonable candidate. But someone of national prominence was liable to have made a few enemies in his political career. He was unlikely to gain opposition votes in an age of straight-ticket voting, there were few independent surge votes to pick up, and he might keep a few of the otherwise faithful who disliked his past record away from the polls. This in fact was the only kind of swing election the era saw: 1872, when Democrats stayed home rather than vote for Greeley; and probably 1892, when a few hundred thousand Republicans must have neglected to support Benjamin Harrison, who as President had committed enough sins of omission or commission to alienate many party members. Blaine in 1884 probably suffered this "decline" effect among Republicans, but apparently compensated for it by picking up normally Democratic support from Irish-Americans. Throughout the period, Presidents found it hard to win a second term for just this reason: they had become too prominent. The unpopular Lincoln had had to create a new "Union" party and needed the good fortune of major military victories to win re-election; Grant had been equally unpopular and had had to withstand a party split, triumphing only because the opposition party split even more completely. For the remainder of the era no other leader could do it until the fundamental facts of voting behavior had changed.

The leaders of the Gilded Age have long been excoriated for their colorlessness and their failure to confront significant issues. But this accusation—which is wholly just—must be understood in terms of the voting public the politicians represented. Recent students of voting behavior have demonstrated that the questions that voters of the Gilded Age found salient revolved almost exclusively about local cultural conflicts: native versus immigrant, Protestant versus Catholic, evangelical temperance-oriented church groups versus liturgical tradition-oriented Lutherans. National politicians avoided these explosive cultural issues, capitalized on immediate circumstances such as economic downturns, and depended on close party organization. Blaine's perennial problem as a presidential candidate was his facility for reflecting the deep-seated cultural issues, especially the overriding one of anti-Catholic prejudice among the Protestant electorate. His early advocacy of national campaigns based on the tariff was not—as many have interpreted it—an effort to rearrange the politics of the age, but an attempt to move personally to a more neutral national position.

The national political results of the era show clearly that anything which detracted from the overt appeal of partisanship, such as issues or personalities, brought a decline in support. Even the third parties, the era's characteristic expression of political dissatisfaction, bear this out. They not only withheld votes from the major parties, their presence actually was a sign of shrinking political participation. They flourished in off-year elections when

fewer voters turned out; in the two presidential years of the
Gilded Age in which third-party movements were serious forces,
1872 and 1892, voting turnout dipped significantly. The third-
party issues of reform and economic regulation by which twentieth-
century historians have judged the era apparently frightened and
confused the electorate of the Gilded Age, who probably were
either baffled into political impotence or sent scurrying back into
the comfortable and familiar world of the old parties.

The major parties rapidly moved into a modern personality and
issue-oriented style in the twentieth century. But the world in
which McKinley could easily win re-election and in which Teddy
Roosevelt became so outstanding a national leader that he dared
create a party in his own image, was one in which the electorate
had wholly changed: the Republicans were the clear majority
party, voter turnout had mysteriously shrunk, and "insurgency"
became a major political style. It was, in Burnham's image, a
newly shaped political universe, stressing well-defined issues,
much independent voting, active national leadership, and the
confinement of the national political family to those with a stake
in society. This last came about in part by systematic exclusion, as
in the case of the Negro, and in part by the elaboration of electoral
machinery that made the political system more accessible to, and
more controlled by, educated issue-oriented elites, and also better
buffered against the vagaries of a lower class that—under the new
dispensation—became increasingly depoliticized.

II

The late nineteenth century was preoccupied, in Robert Wiebe's
phrase, with a "search for order." Men grasped for elements of
predictability and continuity amid furious social and physical
change. Politics was one area where men sought a link with the
past. This theme was especially prominent in the seventies and
eighties when the events of the Civil War and Reconstruction
continued to provide the main topics of national debate. These

issues, in stabilizing political loyalties by keeping eyes focused on a past full of familiar friends and enemies, fulfilled some of the need for order, even if this psychological advantage came at the cost of any meaningful attempt to control the world of early industrialism.

The men actively engaged in party politics welcomed and encouraged the electorate's disposition to re-live and relieve the traumas of the sixties: it helped them maintain their own order in the world of politics by keeping the behavior of voters generally predictable. Politicians could usually tell how various groups would vote. They talked, as politicians usually do, about the "Germans" or the "wheat farmers" or the "wool-growing counties." They knew roughly where there were Democrats and where Republicans. They could predict with considerable accuracy sure victories, certain defeats, and which contests would be close and require attention. This was not because they possessed insight superior to that of the politicians of other eras, but because of three related factors: the predictable party voting of the electorate, the party structure which provided them with a range and level of information that the modern politician with all his computers and survey data clearly does not have, and the forms of political indoctrination to which their electorate was exposed.

Although the men of the nineteenth century knew about sampling the close counties where minor changes would mirror what a larger voting public was doing, it was not the main prop of their information structure. Instead they relied on virtually total polling. When they wanted information about the "condition" of an electorate, in some cases over as large an area as an entire state, they got it through an attempt at a full poll of the state. The state committee chairman would request the information from his county chairmen, who would enlist all available workers to visit every voter. These workers included the post-masters in the little villages, the editors of the party paper—and rare was the small town outside the South without its Republican and its Democratic newspapers—every federal official wherever he held a post, as well as men engaged in work for the state, county, or town governments, and any of a number of businesses (street cars, railroads, banks, utilities) having extensive dealings with these governments. In short, with politics a hobby to hundreds of thousands and a livelihood or part of one to hundreds of thousands more, there was usually enough labor to conduct a full survey.

The results were impressive. The "inside polls"—those for party use, not for scare tactics—often were amazingly accurate. Politicians complained that 1892 was a particularly hard year to tell in advance how the "silent vote" tended. Yet the Indiana Democratic poll showed a statewide margin of 6000 votes against an actual victory by 6482 votes. Similarly, the chairman of the Republican state committee of Maine figured a 12,000 vote victory against a final margin of 12,531 votes. Not all polls were so accurate, but they suggest the capability of the politicians to get accurate information when they required it.

Politicians calculated their chances by handfuls of votes. They pinpointed the areas where a few votes would make the difference, and sought means to gain them. Their principal method was to stir up "enthusiasm" to bring their potential voters to the polls, or, less frequently, to demoralize the opposition into staying home. They knew what students of voting behavior have since confirmed, that campaigns rarely change voters' minds, that "a candidate's major resources should go into getting out his supporters and latent supporters and only peripherally attempting to convert the opposition." Only in very special circumstances when voter allegiances seemed to be shifting did they actually expect to convert waverers.

Their other mainstay in making up votes which their polls told them were lacking was a set of hoary but not hallowed methods, which included buying up purchasable voters, intimidating fearful ones into staying away from the polls, voting "repeaters," stuffing ballot boxes, falsifying returns, and creating imaginary voters on the rolls and producing them from out of town on election day. Some of these techniques, such as intimidation and repeating, were apparently most common in the cities; others, such as out-right vote-buying, seem to have been practiced most often in the small towns and rural areas.

There is far too much evidence to dismiss these techniques as folklore, and sensible and successful politicians were too frank about their use to discount them as factors in over-all results. Surely many an election on every level was determined by who was in the best position for perpetrating frauds. One source of political stability must have been the built-in advantage a majority party had in any given area in being able to control the election machinery, or often simply the balance of physical force at a polling place. Its importance in the South was too overwhelming to question. But in many northern localities it was crucial as well, and "election-day expenses and operations" were a large item in the party managers' organization and expenditures.

Corruption was a real factor in political calculations. Neverthe-less two major qualifications must be entered to place this force into a proper perspective. As charges and counter-charges during each campaign bear witness, both parties practiced it, so that in national politics over the long run much of the impact must have canceled out. And most important of all, the widespread fraud in this era must be understood as far more a product than a cause of the close elections. No one would pay as much as $15 per vote (as Indiana politicians did in 1888) in a runaway con-test. Only because the parties were so closely balanced did chica-nery have this importance in the calculations of the professionals. Historians today tend to underestimate this factor in response to the fantastic overestimation of it by the Progressives, but an image of clean politics in the Gilded Age would be much like Sophocles's *Philoctetes* without the wound.

The electorate itself helped mightily in the politicians' efforts to keep track of it. Crucial to party regularity in the era's voting pat-terns was the delimited body of political information available to most of the electorate. Charles Sellers has argued that the flow of political information in the antebellum period was probably greater

than at present, even if far less varied. This appears true of the
post–Civil War period as well. Rather than a mass of relatively
independent media in competition for the attention of voters, most
political information came in the direct party form: newspapers
were party newspapers, and political conversations, which were
clearly innumerable, were among committed party members. In
short, the party in each area had a far larger degree of control of
the political information flow than at present, and this in turn reinforced party loyalty.

Survey data has confirmed that voters with a clear party commitment are more easily swayed by propaganda during a campaign
than those who are more party-oriented. In the nineteenth century
few people would be greatly influenced by outside, independent
sources of political information. This naturally discouraged the production of such material. The era sported independent political
journalism of a high order in periodicals such as *Harper's Weekly*
and *The Nation*, but their clientele was extremely restricted and
their indirect political influence through that small but select read-
ership seems also to have been slight. The world of the magazines
was the world of sensibility which, as cultural historians have repeatedly observed, was ruled by women in the late nineteenth
century. Roscoe Conkling scored a direct hit when he stigmatized
George William Curtis, the editor of *Harper's Weekly* and a leading civil service reformer, as a "man-milliner." Men, the politicians
shouted, had party labels. The caustic Kansas Republican Senator,
John J. Ingalls, berated the "new school of political philosophers
who announce that nonpartisanship is the panacea for all the evils
that afflict the Republican party" as "the neuter gender not popular either in nature or society." They were "a third sex."

Politics, the Gilded Age believed, was masculine, and culture
feminine. Men got their information from the stump speech, the
party paper, and the smoke-filled tavern and meeting room, while
women read magazines and novels and attended lectures and sermons. Judging from their rhetoric, practical politicians worked
hard to maintain the artificial separation between these two realms.

They attacked political independence with its attendant interest in civil service, women's rights, prohibition, and general efforts to raise the tone of politics, with a vehemence that suggests they knew their real enemy. Politics was that generation's moral equivalent of war, and politicians did not welcome a middle ground between friend and foe. The party faithful were inured against enemy propaganda, but politicians knew from experience that an independent appeal could be seductive. In 1884, for example, an Iowa Republican reported to a party leader on the "Edmunds feeling . . . at Stanwood," caused, he explained, by *The Nation*, "which has a small circulation there." Politicians rejoiced that the audience for independent political attitudes remained small and its influence limited either by standards of literacy or by the official cultural dichotomy reinforced by the ridicule of politicians. Thus did these small men make their contribution to the great bifurcation between the masculine life of business and politics and the feminine genteel culture of the age.

Everything about this picture: the party regularity, the well-coordinated information structure of both parties, and the general party control of political information started to fade in the late eighties as voting habits began to shift in one of those mysterious cycles which have come once a generation throughout the history of the republic. Politicians worried all during the eighties over slackening enthusiasm and the weakening of old means of campaigning. They experimented unsuccessfully with new forms of political organization designed to appeal to more genteel citizens. They tried one makeshift after another to catch the changing moods of restless workingmen and immigrants. As the decade advanced the old moorings began to slip everywhere. The rise of the Knights of Labor, the Haymarket affair, and Henry George's strong showing in the New York mayoralty race of 1886 sent tremors throughout middle-class America. Agricultural depression shook the countryside. People expressed their fear of the "trusts," unhappiness over the railroads rose to a crescendo, and a new concern over the dangers of unlimited immigration settled upon the land. Even the

Negroes, the most loyal of Republican groups, manifested discontent by forming a short-lived "Afro-American National League" hoping to organize the entire black community independent of the Republican party.

The off-year election of 1889 showed that this discontent had reached the parties, as long-held voting patterns gave way, especially in the Midwest, revealing a significant trend away from the Republican party. In the cycle of fluctuation into which the parties plunged thereafter, the politician found himself no longer certain of his electorate. The degree of predictability had abruptly shrunk. Previously only a limited part of the electorate had eluded the politicians' estimates. Workingmen in times of economic hardship and restive Irish voters in periods of intense agitation of the "Irish question" in the British Isles were the outstanding examples. Other groups, such as the harder-pressed farmers, had gone through various third-party romances, but in most cases this had been a measurable quantity in political calculations and Republican party managers could closely gauge the size of such movements and the probabilities of arranging fusions with them or avoiding fusions with the Democrats. But after 1889 politicians were never sure of their votes. The congressional election of 1890 showed a massive defection from the Republicans, a revitalization of the Democratic party, and the growth of the Populists. On the other hand, four years later, the Republicans scored the greatest congressional victory in their party's history. The changeability of the electorate became as much a byword among politicians as its predictability had been years before. The most astute politicians shared the general feeling of crisis that so clearly marked the nineties.

The parties' control of the flow of political information was seriously diminished as well. Suddenly a spate of utopian and muckraking books appeared and commanded wide audiences. William Allen White recalled years later the "tremendous thrill" of "the books from the late Eighties and early Nineties" that broke down the conservatism of his upbringing. The most influential of these, and the one most indicative of their place in the political changes of the nineties, was Edward Bellamy's *Looking Backward,* *2000–1887,* published in 1888. The first and most successful of some fifty utopias committed to paper in the few years after its publication, this pleasant—if somewhat static—utopian romance not only sold half a million copies, it also gave rise to a network of Nationalist clubs which Bellamy and many of his supporters hoped would become "a party aiming at a national control of industry with its resulting social changes."

That never happened, but many erstwhile Nationalists found their way into the People's party and then into various socialist or progressive movements in the ensuing years. An incipient American socialist movement which, Howard H. Quint has argued, "owed more for its inspiration to Edward Bellamy's *Looking Backward* than it did to Karl Marx's *Das Kapital*" began to show the first signs of what many expected would be a massive political future. Leading Americans voiced hysterical fears of social revolution, and some of the most sober politicians quietly calculated the probabilities.

The gap between culture and politics, which, artificial as it was, men like Henry Adams despaired of bridging, slowly gave way of itself in the nineties. The older magazines suddenly confronted competition from newer, cheaper, and more topical journals such as *Munsey's, McClure's,* and *Cosmopolitan.* These magazines aimed at capturing the middle-class family audiences of the age by appealing to the father of the household, not the mother. Under pressure of this competition, the older magazines became increasingly political as well. Ministers started to become far more vocal in their comments on the political order while reformers in numerous localities challenged the parties and their methods in ways similar to the more successful challenges of the progressive era.

Beneath all of this was the obvious and palpable fact that the voters' long-ingrained habits were changing, that some kind of vast generational shift was occurring whose end no man could see and no man—not even Mark Hanna—could hope to guide. Politicians could only guess at the direction in which the electorate was

moving and wonder if the party system they knew was capable of
containing the new populations, the new pressures, and the new
demands that all parts of an increasingly interconnected society
made on the political system.

National leaders had their first glimmering of this changing
electorate in 1888. The old world of hard, recognizable factions
had become blurred and indefinite, and the landmarks of sure
Republican or Democratic states with but a few marked "doubtful" had eroded to a grey mass of marginally doubtful states
stretching across the country. Yet the older mold was strained
rather than broken, and party leaders, puzzled but still basically
confident, pushed on in the old way, discounting the alarms of
local politicians, and concentrating their resources where they had
in years past. In the end, 1888 proved an Indian Summer for the
Gilded Age, the last moment before the optimism of the eighties
gave way to the insecurities of the next decade.

Four years later there could be no doubt of the changed world
that the politicians faced. The Republican party seemed in a continuing crisis with its traditional support threatened all over the
country, its national structure chaotic, and its personnel demor-
alized. The rise of the Populists, the growth of the Democratic
party, and the unpopularity of the administration suggested an unhappy future for the Grand Old Party. Its national leadership,
confused by change and riddled with discontent, seemed at a loss
to adjust to the equally confused discontent of the electorate.

Yet within two years, the whole political scene had been transformed. Instead of the Republican demise which many had feared,
the Democrats collapsed under the pressure of a grinding depression, exacerbated ethnic tensions, and a national administration
even more unpopular than its predecessor. In 1896, both parties
had to make a major attempt to accommodate the new and mysterious electorate of this period of fluctuation, although neither
effort disrupted the traditional forms of national party politics.

On the surface, the Democrats made the most radical attempt
to reform their party within the old identity. Behind William Jen-

nings Bryan, the silverite, anti-administration Democracy made
the old machinery labor for a new western-based coalition. With
few experienced engineers to move the levers and practically no
money to lubricate the gears, the clanking and grinding reverber-
ated across the plains and the engine never reached the farms of
the Midwest and the cities of the East, where new fuel might be
located. The Republicans, on the other hand, found nothing but
pleasant surprises when they brought out the old engine for its
quadrennial journey. Massive shifts in voter preference offered unprecedented majorities in many areas; a frightened business community turned its financial support almost exclusively to the Republican candidate; local party politicians rushed to aid the national cause that promised campaign funds and electoral success.
It was still the old machine, but fresh fuel and oil had radically
improved its performance, preparing it to lumber on into the
twentieth century.

The 1896 campaign was the first clear test of the ability of an
amorphous national party system to absorb massive changes in
political demands without great structural alterations. For certainly
the Civil War had pointed ambiguous political lessons to the next
generation. Then, new demands had seemed to fracture the parties,
although in retrospect, one is impressed with how the party system continued unchanged despite the replacement of the Whigs
by the Republicans. The men of the nineties could not see that
this would happen again—and this time without a war or a new
party. They did not know whether the parties and the whole national system would metamorphize into some strange new form,
or if its evolution was to be brief but final, like the ganoid fish,
Pteraspis, which (along with the progress in Presidents from
Washington to Grant) had cost Henry Adams his belief in evolution.

The Senate Club and Its Constituency

The Structure of State Politics

by David J. Rothman

In the late nineteenth century, presidential power suffered considerable decline as a procession of half-hearted Chief Executives (with the partial exception of Grover Cleveland) followed one another into the White House. National political authority passed largely into the hands of Congress, where leaders of Democratic and Republican senatorial caucuses controlled policy-making. Their influence stemmed in part from the increasingly disciplined partisan voting behavior observable in Congress, as party caucuses shaped congressional treatment of pending legislation.

The power which leading senators held over legislation was enjoyed by state political leaders in making Presidents. National politics depended in both parties upon shifting alliances, delicately constructed by state bosses and their machines around candidates distinguished mainly by their inoffensiveness. Politically interested businessmen would often attach themselves to candidates angling for the presidency, and national party leaders struggled throughout the late nineteenth century to dominate this feudal bargaining process. At the turn of the century, control of party machinery remained generally in the hands of professional state bosses, although their role as presidential king-makers had been challenged

David J. Rothman 81

by a series of ambitious political managers, most successfully, Mc-
Kinley's 1896 Warwick, an Ohio industrialist named Mark Hanna.
David J. Rothman here describes the career patterns of the
period's leading professional politicos.

❀ Effective leaders rarely dominated the pre–Civil War parties.
Webster, Clay, and Calhoun enjoyed great prominence, leaving
indelible marks on Washington, but they did not systematically
attend to the narrow and detailed concerns of Massachusetts, Kentucky, and South Carolina politics. There were times when several
vigorous Whig county bosses joined together or the head of a Jeffersonian city machine united with two upcountry politicians; but
these alliances were usually designed to secure only local control.
In the post-Reconstruction decades, however, a new pattern transformed state affairs: centralized power became the norm, not the
exception. Party heads and their subordinates exerted consistent
authority that reached into isolated hamlets as well as into the
populous capitals, into rural counties as well as into city wards.
By 1900 the monarch had displaced the feudal princes.

The chamber's sturdy leather chairs were plush thrones for the
new party bosses. During the last years of the nineteenth century,
would-be leaders contested Senate elections, and the victor won
party power as well as the trip to Washington. The coincidence
was not surprising. The senatorship satisfied a politician's grandest
ambition, and state authority was at once a prerequisite for and a
guarantee of a place in the chamber.

Each state party nominated a Senate candidate in caucus, and
the majority then elected its choice in formal session. This system
compelled Senate hopefuls to exert wide influence. The more supporters in the caucus, the better the opportunity for nomination;
the larger the numbers in the assembly, the greater the chance for

From *Politics and Power: The U. S. Senate, 1869–1901* (Cambridge, Mass.:
The Belknap Press of Harvard University Press, 1966), pp. 160–90. Copyright 1966 by the President and Fellows of Harvard College. Reprinted by
permission; footnotes omitted.

election. To make their position secure, aspirants vigorously courted the ward captains, the county chairmen, and the convention presidents. They had ample time to marshal forces and distribute favors for commitments in the Senate race were almost as well known as party labels. Constituents demanded that a candidate for the legislature declare his allegiances well in advance, and state laws often compelled him to respect the pledge. Invariably, the Washington contest entered every election district.

Would-be senators regularly linked private ambitions to the party's welfare. In the first place, it made no sense to win the endorsement of a perennial minority. Moreover, no one could risk antagonizing a substantial portion of the membership; dissidents might ally with the opposition, turning victory into defeat. Under these circumstances, candidates relied upon the organizational machinery to smooth over animosities, confident that it could forestall any bolts. In Maryland, Arthur Gorman always asked the Democrats to convene in caucus to approve his re-election, even when the meetings became empty formalities, and in Rhode Island, Charles Brayton, Nelson Aldrich's clever manager, followed identical tactics. The reasoning was straightforward: any mechanism that consolidated and harmonized party ranks was to be carefully maintained. Thus, from the start of their careers, senators encouraged caucus action to promote unity. They would retain the habit long after coming to Washington.

Political observers could predict the outcome of January Senate elections once the November ballots were counted. Factional squabbles might occasionally confuse matters, but a party chieftain was usually in firm control. In Wisconsin, for example, the 1896 Republican majority prepared, without debate or dissension, to send John Spooner to the Capitol. With equanimity, Spooner noted: "No other name has been mentioned." The state leader also frequently dictated the choice of junior senator. With Aldrich's approval, George Wetmore ended his worldwide traveling to join the Philosophy Club at McMillan's. New York's Chauncey Depew satisfied an old dream because Tom Platt finally consented, and West Virginia's outstanding glass manufacturer, Nathan Scott, came to the chamber when Stephen Elkins approved his candidacy. Such efforts were not always successful. Indiana's Republican senior senator, Charles Fairbanks, owned one place but he could not prevent the extraordinarily eager Albert Beveridge from grabbing the other. In most instances, however, a close friend, obliging partisan, or potential heir accompanied the head of the party to Washington. Order now characterized Senate elections as well as proceedings.

Senators, through their own efforts or by carefully delegating responsibility, exercised unprecedented state authority. As professional politicians dedicated to the needs of the party, they ruled their organizations. Always prepared to meet and satisfy the most burdensome political demand, they would not hesitate to undertake a long and tiring campaign to win votes. When tact would cajole opponents, they exercised it, and when the party chest was low, they energetically set about filling it. As a result, centralized control defined the structure of state politics at the end of the nineteenth century.

This new type of leadership often originated with the Republican organization. In fact, a few of the men who led the young party to its first victories still retained and exercised power forty years later. Justin Morrill, the first Republican congressman to be elected from Vermont, opened his fourth campaign for Senate re-election in 1891 by promising to withdraw from the race should any opposition develop. Having issued a similar pronouncement six years before, he knew full well that no one would challenge his carefully maintained organization, and talented young men like Redfield Proctor understood the necessity of waiting their turn. So long as Morrill held the reins, Vermont's politics remained orderly.

Some party leaders of the 1890's inherited power from their predecessors and systematically managed to increase its scope and intensity. Their organizations were machines but they did not deteriorate in time. Succession was not always as evident as when Simon Cameron, furious with newly elected President Hayes, resigned his place in favor of his son, Donald. Greenville Dodge, in greater privacy, selected William Allison to run for senator. Yet both men consciously and successfully named the party's future chief. The procedure could assume biblical overtones: Mark Hanna took his seat from John Sherman just as the crafty Jacob snatched his blessing from an aging and near blind Isaac. In each instance the political heirs fulfilled their tasks even more skillfully.

Party chiefs often increased their stature by prudently settling disruptive and lingering factional disputes. New York's Roscoe Conkling informed Simon Cameron in 1871 that the "party had never been so united in this state, never in better fighting order," but within a decade the Republicans were divided into two warring camps and Conkling's career terminated because of the split. By 1890, however, Tom Platt securely controlled the organization, bringing a new authority to New York politics.

"There is nothing more singular in political history," Chauncey Depew recounted to a fascinated President Harrison, "than the strange mixture of antagonisms in the reorganization of the party. . . . I write this bit of history because it shows how little is left of the ancient feuds." The old guard that surrounded Conkling in the 1870's, Chester Arthur, Alonzo Cornell, and Tom Platt, had long since disbanded. "After Arthur's election and the defeat of Conkling's efforts to return to the Senate," recounted Depew, "they quarreled, and the feud became so bitter that neither Conkling, Arthur, Cornell, or Platt spoke to each other." Joining the anti-Arthur forces, Platt was soon identified with the anti-Conkling wing. "The two most prominent leaders of the anti-Conkling forces were Hiscock and General Merritt. Now again Hiscock and Platt are together and Merritt has for some years . . . taken no part in party manipulation. Again, while I led the fight in the Senatorial contest which ended in the retirement of Mr. Conkling," Depew concluded, "the most enthusiastic and devoted of my

friends at Chicago [the national convention] were the immediate
friends of Mr. Conkling."

Platt's reward was commensurate with the difficulty of his task:
"Four-fifths of the legislators at Albany would have no wish" except to record his wants. And for many years, he dominated the
most powerful organization in New York's history.

Similarly Philetus Sawyer, the Wisconsin lumber millionaire,
rose to command the state's Republicans. In the early 1870's the
Madison Regency, as the State House ring was known, engaged
in typical court intrigues as feuding leaders switched alliances and
maneuvered for position. Selecting his allies prudently, Sawyer
defeated Elisha Keyes, the one-time undisputed boss, for party
control and for the Senate seat. Naming John Spooner his co-
senator, political lieutenant, and heir apparent, Sawyer ruled the
organization until his voluntary retirement in 1893. Without losing
momentum, Spooner took over the reins.

Most often, however, dogged hard work accounted for political
success. The state's first Republican senator and boss, Zach
Chandler, was not a novice in leadership; and having earned two
million dollars in Detroit mercantile and real estate investments,
he unquestionably possessed the wherewithal to run an organization. In fact Hamilton Fish considered Chandler not a bad fellow
but too much the political manager. Nevertheless, dissident Republicans defeated his re-election bid in 1874 and he could not
recapture power. . . .

The merger of competing business interests at the close of the
nineteenth century sometimes helped to consolidate the state party
leadership. Events in New Hampshire exemplified the process.
The coalition that united the Republican party there during the
Civil War disbanded in the following decade and left various factions competing for supremacy. The state's old and viable tradition of rotation in office plagued many successful incumbents.
But the most important barrier facing any potential leader was
the competition between the Concord Railroad and the Boston &

Maine. When one company endorsed a candidate, the other automatically sponsored a rival, disrupting the majority organization.

Into this turmoil stepped William Chandler. The one-time railroad lobbyist, National Republican Committee Chairman, and Secretary of the Navy was appointed in 1887 to fill an unexpectedly vacant Senate seat. When he ran for re-election two years later Jacob Gallinger, congressman and chairman of the state Republican Committee, challenged him. Gallinger championed the Concord Railroad, regularly urging its claims before the legislature, while Chandler, long absent from the state, was not identified with either line. The Boston & Maine, preferring neutrality to certain enmity, backed Chandler's candidacy and their efforts, together with his experience, brought victory. But in these peculiar circumstances, Chandler could not dominate the party and Gallinger carried on the struggle. In 1891 the Concord man captured the second Senate seat and factionalism continued to split the Republican ranks.

In 1895 the Boston & Maine merged with its competitor, and the political repercussions soon became evident. Gallinger was easily re-elected in 1897, but in 1900 the newly consolidated railroad set out to defeat Chandler. The former lobbyist had recently delivered long harangues on the illegal use of passes, the corruption of the legislature, and the nefarious powers of the corporation; the lines responded by resolving to remove him from the Senate. Convinced that defeat was certain unless the company ended its hostility, the unpredictable Chandler changed tactics. He dispatched letter after letter to anyone who might carry influence with the road's president, Lucius Tuttle. Eugene Hale suggested contacting his co-senator, William Frye, a director of the Maine Central which was part of the Boston & Maine network; but Frye could only state that Tuttle revealed no sign of antagonism. Vermont's new senator, Redfield Proctor, sent his sympathies but little more, explaining that in his state the roads were too competitive to undertake joint action.

Chandler finally persuaded Aldrich to call on Tuttle; the Rhode Island Senator, however, reported that Tuttle had promised to continue in the future as he had in the past and not interfere with the election. Despite these assurances, Chandler recognized that Tuttle's "subordinates all over the state are as busy as the devil in a gale of wind nominating Senators and Representatives whom they believe will be hostile to me and whom they can control. The railroad and the money machine in New Hampshire is against me and it may not be possible to divert its assaults." His fears were valid. The 1901 legislature turned down his bid and Gallinger gained undisputed control. The moral seemed clear: one railroad, one political leader.

The powers of a great corporation also proved to be invaluable assets for other state chieftains. Donald Cameron inherited the Republican organization from his father, but the rights to his patrimony did not go uncontested. When he tried to capture the second Senate seat for a loyal partisan in 1881, a revolt broke out; aggrieved Republicans hoped to ally with the Democratic minority and select a more acceptable candidate. The Democrats, however, under the authority of William Wallace, refused to join the dissidents, rejecting the opportunity to elect one of their own men. Wallace's solicitude for Cameron's welfare seemed unusual only to those who did not understand their mutual allegiance to the Pennsylvania Railroad. When the Democratic leader faced a similar challenge some years before, Cameron had secured Republican neutrality. Wallace was now pleased to repay the kindness.

Events in New Hampshire and Pennsylvania were not typical of the nation; elsewhere, the concentration of business enterprises, by itself, did not smooth the way for leadership. Professional political skills rather than economic connections usually stabilized state power.

The mine owners of Colorado often shared a harmony of interests; nevertheless, politics remained faction-ridden for several decades. In the 1870's and 1880's Henry Teller, a successful

Central City lawyer and investor, competed with Denver's Jerome Chaffee for dominance of the territorial Republican party. As the capital swelled in importance and the gulch towns died, Chaffee gained the advantage. When statehood came, he captured the first Senate seat and authority over the organization. His control, however, was weak and short-lived. He could not prevent his rival from also winning election, and when Chaffee soon lost interest in politics and neglected its duties, Teller's influence immediately rose.

Nevertheless, succession to power was still not easily accomplished for Teller's ambitions were quickly challenged by Nathaniel Hill. The Brown-educated chemist had come West and made his fortune by devising an inexpensive process for extracting precious metals from their ores. Despite common stakes with Teller in mining enterprises, Hill continued to oppose him. The contest was balanced and funds were no problem for either man. Eventually, Teller's superior political skills determined the outcome. Consolidating the younger members behind his candidacy, he defeated Hill for the 1885 Senate vacancy. Conscientiously rewarding his followers, Teller proceeded to rule the state until well into the twentieth century. . . .

Party chieftains, utilizing every prerogative at their disposal, ordered the politics of a majority of states. By the 1890's they dominated organizations in California as well as Rhode Island, in Iowa as well as New York, in Wyoming as well as Wisconsin. Nevertheless, the Democrats could not generally match the authority of their Republican rivals. The differentiation was not the result of two fundamentally distinct political styles but rather reflected the fact that southern parties did not regularly duplicate the national pattern. The Democrats were by no means untouched by the movement. David Hill in New York, Calvin Brice in Ohio, Henry Davis in West Virginia, Arthur Gorman in Maryland, Thomas Martin in Virginia, William Vilas in Wisconsin, and George Hearst in California effectively administered their organizations. But for peculiar reasons, many southern states followed a unique course.

The divergence began with Reconstruction. Although the Republicans temporarily suppressed rival parties, they could not harmonize their own ranks. The paths to political power were diverse, running through the Florida Freedman's Bureau for Thomas Osborn, the Collectorship of the Port of New Orleans for William Kellogg, and the military governorship of Mississippi for Adelbert Ames. In state after state two contending factions divided the organization. Native Republicans, favoring moderate Reconstruction policies, competed with more radical newcomers, prepared to enact punitive measures. Ames, a native of Massachusetts, opposed James Alcorn, a local and conservative planter; Alabama's Willard Warner held much milder views than his recently arrived antagonist, George Spencer. The contests invariably came to a deadlock and each faction's leader took one of the chamber's seats. In Washington, Ames served alongside Alcorn and Warner sat beside Spencer.

Even after the Democrats returned to power, two opposing camps continued to divide the Senate places. In the course of serving the Confederacy and throwing off Republican rule, generals and redeemers gained fame and popularity. Not surprisingly, these advantages were often used to win Senate elections; in typical fashion, Augustus Garland in Arkansas, Wade Hampton in South Carolina, and Richard Coke in Texas directed Democratic efforts, served short terms in the state capital, and then began long careers in Washington. Despite the invaluable advantages of medals and heroics, these leaders could not unite southern parties. A basic cleavage still separated them. Politicians receptive to industrial advancement competed with colleagues more devoted to traditional ways, and no one was able to bridge the gap. In the end a member of each school shared party control and a Senate seat. North Carolina's popular and agrarian-minded Zebulon Vance served with Matt Ransom, a New Departure sympathizer. James Barbour satisfied Virginia's capitalists and John Daniel pleased her old-fashioned citizens, while Mississippi's Edward Walthall and L. Q. C. Lamar maintained an identical balance. In Alabama, John Morgan faithfully corresponded with his mentor, antebellum senator C. C. Clay, and his colleague, James Pugh, kept in close touch with Birmingham's businessmen.

New Departure senators, unable to overcome the appeal of the past and the rural political bias, rarely exerted undisputed authority. But traditionalists, boasting impressive military and government records, were in a better position to capture the organization. The one-party system in the South, however, decreased any potentiality for harmony; elsewhere, the contending factions might have supported different groups. Even more important, the traditionalists, devoted to strict constitutionalism, rarely approached politics with such modern goals as efficiency and organization. Enjoying personal popularity and the assurance of Senate re-elections, they did not direct their talents and ambitions to the orderly exertion of power. They contentedly gave rivals their due and shared the honors.

Friction between the two camps heightened during the last decade of the century. The Populist threat strengthened the rural wing of the Democratic party and agrarian spokesmen in Texas, Kentucky, Georgia, Tennessee, and South Carolina grew more powerful. Nevertheless, clear-cut victories even during the 1890's were unusual; most organizations remained divided and leaderless.

The structure of southern politics complicated Gorman's tasks as chairman of the Senate caucus. The customary distribution of the chamber seats between opposing factions made his efforts to achieve national unity especially trying. Disharmony was built into the process of election, and Gorman was forced to exercise every talent for compromise to offset its effects. On the other hand, Allison and Aldrich faced Republican colleagues with no such obstacles.

The western states admitted to the Union between 1889 and 1897 also failed to emulate the political development of their more mature predecessors even though territorial government encouraged effective party leadership. The office of governor, federally appointed, and Territorial Delegate to Congress, popularly elected, possessed unusual potentiality for power. Governorships were filled in Washington, and party men with excellent connections usually received the posts. National influence, together with a large amount of local patronage, helped chief executives like Wyoming's Francis Warren and Idaho's George Shoup to build up dependable followings. After statehood, both men translated their control into Senate elections. Delegates, for their part, occupied the most significant positions available to the territory's inhabitants. The campaigns brought invaluable prominence and the opportunity to perfect dependable organizations. After this apprenticeship, South Dakota's Richard Pettigrew and Wyoming's Joseph Carey traveled to Washington.

The divisive issues of the 1890's and the concomitant rise of the Populists, however, soon ended the brief authority of western leaders. By accommodating silver sentiment, Francis Warren survived as head of the party, but his good fortune was unique. George Shoup stood out against currency expansion and suffered defeat, while his colleague, Fred Dubois, joined the Silver Republicans only to be dislodged by an alliance of Democrats and Populists. Pettigrew remained in office as a Silver Republican, but the 1900 victory of the regulars destroyed his power. In a less tumultuous era, the new states might have maintained centralized party organizations.

Finally, the Populists were less affected by the tendencies of these decades than either major party. Like the Southern Republicans during Reconstruction, they too divided into two factions. Moderates, with particular grievances and concrete reforms, confronted radicals, determined fundamentally to alter American society. The competition was intense, and without effective leadership, Populist attempts to elect senators often ended in disgust, confusion, or failure.

When the People's party, for example, gained a small majority in the 1891 Kansas legislature, the moderates predominated numerically over a highly vocal band of radicals led by Jerry Simpson and Mary Lease. Republican incumbent John Ingalls, famous for his frequent speeches vilifying the Democrats, made a desperate

attempt to gain Populist support; but despite his Senate proposal to outlaw all speculation in agricultural commodities, the
Simpson–Lease wing vetoed his candidacy. The moderates, more
frightened of the radicals than of the Democrats, settled on William Peffer, an undistinguished conservative editor of the *Kansas
Farmer*; in case the left-wingers bolted, Democratic votes would
probably secure his election. The stopgap proved unnecessary since
all the Populists remained loyal; yet because of party divisions, a
lackluster and untalented senator went to Washington. Similarly,
Populists carried Washington in 1896, but unable to agree on a
candidate of their own, they promoted Silver Republican George
Turner. Richard Pettigrew could not control the South Dakota
organization in 1897, and Mark Hanna persuaded enough Populists
to elect James Kyle; the new Senator, in return, promised to vote
for Republican organization in the chamber. A new party could
anticipate factional difficulties, but the Populists proved extraordinarily untractable.

The southern branch performed just as poorly, frequently passing over fellow members to elect Democratic senators. Despite a
Populist majority in the 1891 Florida legislature, Democrat Wil-
kinson Call captured the seat. Unable to resist Zebulon Vance's
appeals, the North Carolina Populists returned him to the chamber; Vance promised his sympathy but refused to agree to a
major platform proposal, the sub-treasury plan. And the election
by Georgia Populists of John Gordon, a Civil War veteran and
hapless investor in less than reputable schemes, was even more
of a blunder. Vance at least had a reputation for supporting
farmer demands. Election procedures were intricate and the Populists could not usually master the techniques. Not surprisingly,
direct election was prominent in their list of reforms.

In post–Civil War America, Senate contests were so vitally
linked to state leadership that they assumed unprecedented importance. Elections usually proceeded with efficiency and dispatch;
but at times the significance of the outcome was the cause of delay
and obstruction. Between 1893 and 1899 nine legislatures, caught

in a deadlock, were unable to select anyone to go to Washington. The public and the press blamed the silver sentiments of a determined minority; yet even in 1899, after the movement waned, four states were unable to complete the electoral process. Currency agitation, in fact, accounted for only a few of the incidents. Gold and silver factions thus divided the Democrats in Kentucky and the Republicans in Washington and Oregon. Wyoming's Populists, holding the balance of power in the 1893 legislature, refused to ally with either party. In most instances, however, personal ambitions, unrelated to the silver question, blocked action. In Pennsylvania, John Wanamaker, the mercantile king, feuded with Matt Quay, preventing any election in 1899; Delaware Republicans split their support between John Addicks, a newcomer and millionaire, and Anthony Higgins, an old party regular, and no one was chosen. William Clark and Marcus Daly disrupted Montana's Democrats, internal divisions stymied California's Republicans, and both states lost full representation. But factionalism, not rival ideologies, separated Wanamaker and Quay, while individual designs, not political principles, kept Higgins and Addicks apart. When states could not elect a senator, personal designs were usually at fault.

This was not the first time in American political history that factionalism disrupted party harmony, yet theretofore, deadlocks did not characterize Senate elections. For example, when the Liberal Republicans bolted in 1872, they joined with Democrats in the state legislature to elect acceptable candidates; in Minnesota, Samuel McMillan replaced Alexander Ramsey and in Michigan, Isaac Christiancy succeeded Zach Chandler. Even during the silver controversy, partisans formed suitable alliances, circumventing barriers to election. In the 1890's, however, the traditional recourses were no longer appropriate or applicable. The Senate race had become the battleground for party leadership. There were no issues to attract the opposition, no incentives to prompt interference. Unable to distinguish among antagonists, the minority was frequently just as pleased to see the state's seat vacant as to have another vote cast in the chamber against its national party.

Moreover, Senate contestants rarely solicited outside assistance. Support by a rival party settled no questions of power and ostensibly gave credence to charges of disloyalty. Stalemates were overcome when one candidate gained dominance within the organization. Eventually, Warren won out over Carey, Quay defeated Wanamaker, and Wyoming and Pennsylvania were once again represented by two senators. The stakes were high and the parties autonomous. Fierce competition was sometimes bound to end in a draw.

The rule of Senate party leaders affected the political process in scattered capitals as well as in Washington. When state chieftains turned attention to national affairs, they often delegated local control to trusted subordinates; from the perspective of Capitol Hill, management for its own sake seemed a minor accomplishment. Of course, party victories and personal ascendancy had to be assured for the tickets to Washington were not one-way. But there was no sense in over-extending the capacities of the organization. Prudence and caution rather than dreams of a monopoly of state power determined the course of action. Moreover, secure in their position at home, senators carried few debts as they entered the chamber. National party spokesmen, from the President to the chairman of the campaign committees, and vast economic interests, from steel to sugar, would not, or could not, undermine their authority. As ambassadors from sovereign states, senators surveyed the chamber.

State bosses utilized their powers with discrimination, not attempting to dictate every aspect of politics. Attentive to men and offices rather than to the legislative work of assemblies, they still preferred not to intervene unless some important personal interest was at stake. James McMillan, for example, kept clear of the gubernatorial contests of 1890 and 1894. Publicly, he announced that party success rather than individual advancement was his primary concern; privately, the genial host confided to his son

that it was unwise to meddle in contests except against an avowed
enemy: disappointed office-seekers could form dangerous combinations. After his election, McMillan continued to avoid too prominent a role in state gatherings and disliked serving as chairman of
the central committee. Other colleagues also preferred to distribute honors widely and often purposefully abstained from serving as delegates to national or state conventions. The skills of
leadership demanded that the limited ammunition be fired only
on the proper occasions.

Among the various state offices, senators devoted much attention to the selection of the speaker of the state assembly. By controlling the committee assignments, he was an invaluable ally
when canvassing support; with the bait of fine places, friends
could be rewarded and new supporters attracted. . . .

The governor's office posed tactical difficulties. Potential opponents, emulating the careers of many senators themselves, could
build up strength in the state capital; but party chieftains' frequent interference here might bring disagreeable publicity as well
as unwanted factionalism. McMillan suffered no inconveniences
for his restraint, but in Ohio, Governor Joseph Foraker gained
enough influence to alarm Hanna and secure a Senate seat. Decisions demanded the most skillful exercise of power for the line
between negligence and foresight was difficult to discern.

The election of state legislators posed far less complex issues.
The risks in any one race were small, and the rewards, a vote for
the Senate, were considerable. "If I were you," Richard Pettigrew
instructed Idaho's candidate, George Shoup, "I would put a man
in every single legislative district and have them report to you
every day. They can assist the men in their election in the district.
These fellows, so elected, will stay by you in the legislature."
Stephen White, the masterful California politician, told friends:
"I am more than ordinarily interested in the nominations made
for the assembly; first, to see that they are strong men, and second,
that they are not personally inimical." Interference was expected
and not at all dangerous. Even so established a person as John

Sherman prodded his managers to secure him a unanimous caucus nomination; it would "strengthen me in my position in the Senate and enable me to do what I so much desire to do." The successful candidates, knowing whom to thank, customarily gave a party for the legislators, and in January, Sherman promptly complied with the custom. But always the astute politician, he reminded his lieutenants that "in deference to the public sentiments in Ohio," liquor had best be omitted.

Senators invariably helped select their junior colleagues for the difficulties of serving with an active rival in Washington were patent and to be avoided at all cost. They also supervised the legislature's choices for other, more abstruse, reasons. In many states powerful customs dictated a geographical division of the chamber seats, and senators did not wish to see anyone elected by chance from their particular region since that would only complicate their own re-election. Detroit, as McMillan well knew, enjoyed the rights to one senatorship, but not both. Similarly, precedent allowed Omaha, Indianapolis, and St. Paul one place, and the rural sections the other. According to statute, one senator was to be elected from eastern and one from western Maryland, while the mountains that bisected Vermont provided her apportionment. Despite cogent arguments that sectional divisions were irrelevant since senators labored for the entire state's welfare, the divisions were usually maintained. Leaders therefore respected these considerations with typical prudence, directing their efforts, here as elsewhere, to securing re-election, not revolutionizing political practices.

Senators conscientiously supervised state organizations to protect their authority. Consequently, they could act freely in the capital, without fear of reprisals from the national party. Insofar as organizational needs were concerned, tact and caution were most necessary in local affairs. In Washington, a senator's independence, at worst, could cost him influence within the chamber; but his authority at home would not necessarily be diminished. No national figure, from the President to the National Committee

Chairman and the head of the caucus, could seriously threaten him. State leadership brought political immunity.

Presidents in post–Civil War America preferred to avoid the entangling webs of state politics. When John Logan campaigned for Illinois' 1879 Senate place by openly and resolutely attacking the policies of Hayes, W. H. Smith, a good friend of the President, moved to retaliate. "You may be sure," Smith advised the Chief Executive, "that if Logan is elected, he will make life a burden to you if he can do it." Nevertheless, Hayes, unwilling to take a part, refused to sanction his plans. Two years later James Garfield utilized every strategy to force his New York nominations through the Senate over Conkling's opposition; but when the Senator abruptly resigned his seat and attempted to win a vote of confidence from the legislature, the President pulled back. "I have fought the assumption of Mr. C[onkling] against my authority," he scrawled in his diary, "but I do not think it best to carry the fight into New York." Grover Cleveland shared less of this reluctance; still McKinley entered the executive offices and revived the habits of his Republican predecessors.

James Blaine, as Garfield's Secretary of State, revealed the potentialities of presidential power to effect state decisions. Garfield hesitated to attack Conkling in New York but Blaine shared none of his reservations. "Everything possible or impossible must be done to beat those fellows at Albany," he instructed his friend and ally, Stephen Elkins. "Do what you can, but don't go to Albany," he concluded with more than usual circumspection. The limitations of travel proved minor. According to J. P. Jones, partisan but still in a position to know the details, offers of federal posts of every sort were made to the New York legislators if they would vote against Conkling's re-election. And not surprisingly, the New York Senator lost his bid. But such systematic and effective exercise of the federal patronage was rarely duplicated by Garfield's nineteenth-century successors.

Presidential unwillingness to wield the leverage of the patronage paralleled its diminishing importance. In the years immediately following the close of the Civil War, the distribution of federal offices could determine factional disputes. Conkling headed the New York Republicans after Grant gave him, and not Reuben Fenton, patronage control; similarly, Simon Cameron and Henry Anthony profited from the General's favoritism. By the 1890's, however, state leaders were no longer overly concerned with particular executive decisions; only a vendetta would provoke their retaliation. Senators possessed sufficient resources within their own organizations to obviate any simple dependence upon the whims of the White House. Usually entering the chamber after having consolidated state power, they infrequently needed reinforcements to bolster tenuous positions.

The distribution of federal offices now often appeared bothersome and hardly worth the effort; for every ally attracted through some sinecure, ten others went away angry. So keen a politician as Stephen White told Theodore Roosevelt, then chairman of the Civil Service Commission, in all honesty: "I do not believe that you will find me hostile to the reformations which have been inaugurated with reference to the Civil Service." Hoping to extend rather than curtail the system, White observed: "At present, members of Congress and Senators are annoyed from day to day by the persistent demands of persons for place, and it is a question whether we were elected to legislate, or procure employment." To lighten the burden, state senators of the same party split the offices down the middle. Nevertheless, at the start of each session members devoted their correspondence to answering the innumerable applications and complaining that patronage was a deadly plague.

Perhaps the greatest advantage to controlling the offices was the assurance that no rival could benefit from them. State leaders would not permit a contending faction to feed and grow on the patronage and should a hostile President disagree, they were not without protection. Senatorial courtesy could be invoked against an overactive executive, and usually, if not invariably, the chamber supported any beleaguered colleague. David Hill headed the

New York Democrats despite the machinations of Grover Cleveland, and the Senate assisted him by rejecting several appointments. Members were rarely forced to retreat to their defenses
but in any event they were adequately insulated from the power
of the President.

The national committees, organized to help in election contests, exerted minimal influence; their efforts were sporadic and
temporary, and their occasional victories, rarely durable. With
their assistance, a senator might win one trip to Washington but
he would not capture state dominance.

Democrats and Republicans vigorously contested Senate elections in the 1890's, for party strength in the chamber was so
evenly divided that the outcome of any one race could determine
majority and minority status. As margins grew slimmer, the national committees increased their labors. The National Republican Committee Chairman, Mark Hanna, knew the value of
travel. His first circuit through the South pinpointing Republican
delegates had helped secure McKinley's nomination and in the
autumn of 1896, after working for the party victory, he undertook a second journey to capture the Senate for the incoming
President. The confused political conditions of several states invited his skills and where Republicans had not won outright majorities in the legislature, he effectively arranged alliances. The
election of Senator Kyle over the protests of Populist leader Richard Pettigrew was a typical success. Hanna owned no monopoly
of intrigue, even if James K. Jones, his Democratic counterpart,
was usually less adroit. But for all their energy, national interference remained haphazard. They tackled a specific assignment,
be it in Delaware or Idaho, and then turned attention elsewhere.

The Senate could not select its members. The constitutional
right to judge senators' qualifications and the legality of their
elections was rarely abused. During Reconstruction, the authority
was sometimes exercised for partisan purposes, but by the very
next decade judicial evaluations were again the rule. Despite a
Republican majority in 1899, Matt Quay was denied his seat;

paying no attention to party lines, the chamber voted that governors could not appoint a senator when legislatures failed to elect one. The institution gained no political influence through this constitutional prerogative.

To be sure, senatorial associates often aided one another. Colleagues serving in high party positions would tap national committee funds for an extra sum; some money from the congressional campaign fund was available, but it had to be distributed nationally to House and Senate hopefuls. Wealthy senators donated liberally to friends' campaigns. . . .

Senators also enjoyed a great deal of freedom from economic as well as political pressures. During the last decades of the century, business interests frequently meddled in state affairs, but insofar as Senate elections were concerned, their achievements were not often notable. The influences they exerted were balanced by the strength of political organizations, and party leaders were not compelled to defer to their demands.

It is not always easy to uncover the part that corporations played in electing senators, but in most instances their authority was limited. Companies were unusually reticent to discuss their efforts at the polls. Thomas Kimball, an agent for the Union Pacific Railroad, told investigators in 1888 the full details of his lobbying techniques; yet when asked about attempts to influence the choice for senator, he would admit only to individual, not company, activities. Political involvement, alleged Kimball, was "a right I exercised as a citizen and not as a representative of the Union Pacific." Corporation executives ostensibly participated in campaigns simply as ordinary Americans.

Soon, however, business leaders dropped this dubious distinction and acknowledged what everyone already knew: companies were involved in the political process. Henry Havermeyer, head of the largest American sugar refining enterprise, explained his policies to an 1894 congressional board of inquiry. The organization, its president declared, distributed state campaign contributions, although none of the funds went to national races. "As we look upon it," added Theodore Havermeyer, partner and brother, "we are simply large real estate owners." The corporation supported good government because efficient police and fire facilities were essential to its welfare. No special favor were asked and none were expected. "I have long since learned," one business official told his questioners, "the truth of the colored man's version of: 'Blessed are dem what 'spects nuffin, den dey don't get disappointed.'" Donations were not even intended to secure "fair treatment," for that would have been forthcoming in any event. Every economic interest tendered contributions, Havermeyer complaisantly concluded. Sugar only followed the popular example.

Despite its few concessions, such testimony was an inaccurate and incomplete guide to the political roles of the corporation. For one thing, the differentiation between state and national campaigns was not firm; to elect a legislature was to affect the selection of senators. Moreover, a company's interest obviously extended beyond the requirements of good government. Without question it wished to see receptive and well-meaning representatives serving in the Senate. The corporations were not as innocent as their public statements would have it. But that is not to say that they could effectively prejudice the course of politics.

There can be no doubt that in a few states, such as New Hampshire, Pennsylvania, and New Jersey, a company dominated the assembly so completely that promoting friendly members to the Senate was not very difficult. Yet this control was exceptional. In most states a wide range of interests tried to influence the power structure, and no one group could be confident that its demands would be favored. In New York, Ohio, Wisconsin, Michigan, California, and Oregon, all sorts and sizes of manufacturing, transportation, banking, mining, real estate, mercantile, and agrarian enterprises took some active part in politics; and their aims were by no means identical. Manufacturers and suppliers did not always agree on tariff questions, mine owners and railroad operators frequently divided on questions of transportation regulation, and merchants often disputed bankers on fiscal policy. Moreover, particular corporations could not effectively direct politics in more than one or two capitals; no business was so vast that it could command the sympathies of a substantial minority of the Senate by manipulating state politics. Even giant insurance companies, for example, preferred national regulation to state control because the difficulties of dealing with several legislatures were too burdensome. As a result of these limitations, corporations had to resort to more indirect methods to try and insure favorable treatment in Washington. Campaign contributions thus became typical in post–Civil War America.

Several considerations combined to limit the influence that companies could exert through their political gifts. In the first place, corporations hoped to win the regard of the men who actually gained power; accordingly they distributed their monies as broadly as possible and all possible winners received part of their largess. The practices of railroad president C. P. Huntington were common. "Some of us," he instructed his Republican-minded partners, "ought to act with the Democratic party. I think there is little difference between them now; it is only the seven reasons: the five loaves and the two fishes." The logic was clear. The railroad "cannot afford to be too openly for the man that loses."

When one party firmly commanded a state, gifts were not squandered on the minority. "Wherever there is one dominant party," Havermeyer affirmed, "that is where we give the contribution." Otherwise, corporation funds were readily forthcoming to both political organizations. Sometimes the internal corporate structure encouraged this tactic; directors, divided in their political loyalties, would not permit the exclusive support of one organization. In other instances the threat of reprisal neutralized favoritism. The Union Pacific may have preferred to support John Thurston for senator from Nebraska, but his competitor, Charles Manderson, was not without powerful friends. John Gear, chairman of the Senate Railroad Committee, informed Grenville Dodge, a Union Pacific associate, that the road had better refrain from action. There were some vital matters to be adjusted in Congress and Gear threatened that "they will be held up if the U.P. people are going to put anything in the path of Manderson. Of course," he instructed Dodge, "you can put it on the ground that you are intimate with some of the Committee especially so with myself, the Chairman." Undoubtedly Dodge relayed the message.

Then too, companies were not necessarily efficient in their attempts to gain power. Politics was an intricate business, and outsiders were not always familiar with its complexities. Friends informed Senator Henry Dawes that Massachusetts' manufacturers "do not give the attention to the primaries they ought; the management of the caucuses is (therefore) in other hands." The companies might try to influence the legislature on Dawes's behalf in January, but "businessmen," he was warned, "neglect as a rule their political duties in all preliminary matters."

Campaign contributions usually entered politics after the fact, adding their weight when the balance was already tipped. Party leaders did not require the talents of money raising, for corporations spread their gifts widely. Then too, the era of exorbitant election costs was still in the future and funds seem to have been available in more or less of an adequate supply. Complaints on this score were rare, and from all indications, the problem was minor. Moreover, the size of campaign chests did not decide political contests. . . .

Rather, enlarged treasuries facilitated expanded political efforts, helping to extend and entrench the power of party chieftains in all parts of the state. Campaign contributions meant that the election costs of friendly legislators could be more easily paid, trains could be ordered, speakers dispatched, and leaflets distributed. Organizations, buttressed by funds, were more secure in power—and thus, less susceptible to external control. Money was a tool for the political artisan and he used it artfully.

The heightened power of party forced corporations to seek favors as supplicants, not as patrons, proving their good will by giving rather than receiving donations. Appeals for action were couched in terms of party welfare. James Swank, for example, representing the American Iron and Steel Association, asked William Allison to try and treat the group well for they had pledged large sums and were likely to respond again. "Human nature is human nature all the world over," Swank noted. "We would not for one moment think of using any improper means to secure the favorable consideration by your Committee of the steel rail duty. But our friends on the Committee are Republicans striving for the success of our party in the coming election. I beg you, therefore, to make it easy for me . . . to secure . . . additional collections." As Swank realized, senators gave first allegiance to the party, and its organization shaped the vital political decisions. The party's importance made contributions necessary. Yet at the same time, its power restricted a donor's influence to a minimum. More than equal to particular economic interests, Republicans and Democrats could safely ignore any specific demand.

Centralization set the tone of post–Civil War state politics, and local politicians, senators, businessmen, and reformers recognized the change. Contemporaries offered explanations, but their interpretations were usually confused, contradictory, and misleading. Most observers, like Moisei Ostrogorski, related the movement to the other portentous event of these years: the rise of the corporation. Monopoly, Ostrogorski asserted, had its counterpart in political unity. In those states "where capitalistic interests were concentrated," senators ruled the party on their behalf. As company hirelings, bosses dominated every facet of local government and followed its bidding in Washington as well. This sort of analysis was popular for the two frightening innovations were related and, at the same time, a solution was proposed. Break up the trusts and the bosses will disappear; eradicate the party and the corporation would disintegrate. The neatness of the formula, however, did not validate it.

Even those most certain that monopolies prompted political centralization could not consistently define the relationships between these two spheres. Economic interests, first stated Ostrogorski "equipped and kept up political organizations for their own use, and ran them as they pleased, like their trains." This argument conveniently fitted into his scheme and yet he was soon forced to conclude: "It was with them [the politicians] that the corporation now had to deal, whether they liked it or not, by purchasing their support or by submitting to blackmail." The confusion was inevitable, for during these years party unity occurred in states lacking monopolistic business interests and failed to mature elsewhere despite their presence. Political leadership was a political development.

The economic changes that followed the Civil War were not irrelevant to this process, but they did not establish it. Progressive spokesman Herbert Croly rather than Moisei Ostrogorski perceptively grasped this distinction. "Just as business had become specialized and organized," wrote Croly in *The Promise of American Life* (1909), "so politics also became the subject of specialization and organization . . . But to consider the specialized organization of American business is wholly to misunderstand its significance." Political efficiency, Croly maintained, demanded the boss. He is "an independent power who has his own special reasons for existence. He put in an embryonic appearance long before the large corporations had obtained anything like their existing power in American politics; and he will survive in some form their reduction to political insignficance. He has been a genuine and within limits a useful product of the American democracy; and it would be fatal either to undervalue or to misunderstand him." The industrial leader, Croly accurately concluded, did not create the boss, although through his support "he has done much to confirm the latter's influence."

The skills and strategies of Republican and Democratic leaders then, not the appearance of the trusts, altered state parties. Professionals devoted full time to its concerns, investing it with a new authority. When men trained in business, like James McMillan and Mark Hanna, achieved political success, it was testimony to personal genius for administration and meticulous attention to organization, not to the firms of McMillan and Newberry or Mark Hanna and Company. Private wealth may have smoothed the first steps but it was not ultimately responsible for power. J. P. Jones complained but he toured Nevada again and again; McMillan composed individual notes to every Republican legislator. Leadership was never grasped or maintained without the devotion of unrelenting effort.

By 1900 party chiefs were secure against defeat and would not be effectively challenged until the Progressive revolt. Their surest protection was a statewide power. Losses in one district barely affected over-all control; reverses in one ward were matched by victories elsewhere. Only a counter-organization able to strike with uniform strength over an entire state could threaten their dominance. Understanding that organization was essential to politics, that the Platts, Allisons, and Gormans could be beaten only with their own techniques, the Progressives first made the necessary effort. Hiram Johnson in California and Bob La Follette in Wisconsin proved capable of attracting and administering large political followings. The leaders of 1900 were often defeated a decade later, but only after setting the future course of state politics.

Secure in power, chamber members were not dependent upon national party organizations for their future careers. And since senators, unlike the members of Parliament, were free from the danger of reprisal, it is no wonder that discipline in the Senate never equaled the standard set in Commons. But perhaps more remarkable, independence did not make these ambassadors to Washington cantankerous. The chairman of the caucus could not bolster or weaken their authority at home and yet he frequently welded diverse members into an effective chamber party. The very dedication to organizations that rendered state leaders impervious to external threats also made them good party senators. Trained in the virtues of the binding caucus, they understood the necessity for discipline. Devoted to the exercise of power, they were willing to pay obeisance in order to share in it. They were professional in Washington as well as in Albany or Sacramento, and could no sooner play the maverick in one capital than in another. To be sure, Allison and Gorman resorted to flattery more often than intimidation. Nevertheless, they stood before a caucus filled with politicians ready to compromise for the sake of party. The Senator from Iowa and the Senator from Maryland knew how to manage this sort of gathering.

3

Ferment in the 'Nineties,
1892–1900

Populism and the American Spirit

The Populist Heritage and the Intellectual

by C. Vann Woodward

Until the rise of Populism, national party politics in the Gilded Age rarely confronted the major economic and social problems produced by industrialization. Republicans and Democrats alike avoided serious debate over the nature of the Federal government's obligations to farmers and workers until a significant agrarian third-party challenge during the 1890's coincided with a severe industrial depression to force such a debate.

Since the 1870's, farmers had agitated for national regulation as an antidote to agricultural problems. The economic roots of agrarian distress were complex and not always understood by ordinary farmers. Partly because of government land disposal, rural education, and immigration programs, production of staple crops such as wheat, corn, and cotton expanded greatly during the Gilded Age. Farmers contributed to the surplus by using modern equipment and through massive indifference to marketing problems. Agricultural protest groups throughout the Gilded Age directed their grievances against those enemies of the farmer whom they believed politically vulnerable: railroads, bankers, and manufacturers.

Populism inherited and built upon traditional sources of late nineteenth century agrarian protest, especially its complaints concerning excessive railroad rates, the absence of an adequate supply of money and credit in rural areas, and discriminatory high tariff and freight rates. In addition to the familiar litany of demands— railroad regulation, free and unlimited coinage of silver, and tariff reduction—Populists added a simple but significant marketing scheme known as the "subtreasury plan." Besides the economic proposals, Populists also demanded political reforms that acknowledged for the first time that the national government should play a direct part in combatting the degrading realities of daily life for both farmer and worker within industrial America.

The Populists have enjoyed a "good press" among most subsequent American historians, reared in the traditions of liberal reform. In the decade after World War II, however, dissenting voices began to be heard. Yet Richard Hofstadter and other critics never swept the historical field, and more sympathetic students in the past decade have challenged almost every one of their anti-Populist premises. The scholarly assault on Populism during the 1950's and the reaction it provoked have ended in a surprising degree of agreement that the movement was more rational than romantic in its programs, more tolerant than bigoted in its social attitudes, more realistic than paranoid in its view of the world. C. Vann Woodward's essay, which defends Populism as a reform movement, launched the counterattack against its detractors.

✿ Thirty years after Secession and Civil War, the South suffered a second alienation from the dominant national spirit. This received expression in the Populist upheaval of the nineties. The Populist movement won more sympathy in the West than had the Secessionist movement. It did not win the allegiance of as large a proportion of Southerners as had the Lost Cause, nor did it involve those it did win quite so deeply. But the alienation was real enough, and the heritage it left was a lasting one.

During the long era of the New Deal, one had little difficulty

From *The Burden of Southern History* (Baton Rouge: Louisiana State University Press, rev. ed., 1968), pp. 141–66. Reprinted by permission.

living in comparative congeniality with the Populist heritage. The two periods had much in common, and it was easy to exaggerate the similarities and natural to seek antecedents and analogies in the earlier era. Because of the common setting of severe depression and economic dislocation, Populism seemed even closer to the New Deal than did Progressivism, which had a setting of prosperity. Common to both Populists and New Dealers was an antagonism to the values and dominant leaders of the business community. Among both was a sense of urgency and an edge of desperation about the demand for reform. And in both, so far as the South and West were concerned, agricultural problems were the most desperate, and agrarian reforms occupied the center of attention. It seemed entirely fitting that Hugo Black of Alabama and Harry Truman of Missouri—politicians whose political style and heritage were strongly Populistic—should lead New Deal reform battles. From many points of view the New Deal was neo-Populism.

The neo-Populism of the present bred a Populistic view of the past. American historiography of the 1930's and 1940's reflects a strong persuasion of this sort. The most popular college textbook in American history was written by a Midwesterner, John D. Hicks, who was friendly to Populism and the foremost historian of the movement. The leading competitor of this book was one that shared many of the Populist leanings, even though one of its authors was a Harvard patrician and the other a Columbia urbanite. A remarkably heterogeneous assortment of men and ideas struck up congenial ties in the neo-Populist coalition. Small-town Southerners and big-city Northerners, Texas mavericks and Hudson River aristocrats, Chapel Hill liberals and Nashville agrarians were all able to discover some sort of identity in the heritage. The South rediscovered ties with the West, the farmer with labor. The New York–Virginia axis was revived. Jacksonians were found to have urban affiliations and origins. Not to be outdone, the Communists staked out claim to selected Populist heroes.

Many intellectuals made themselves at home in the neo-

Populist coalition and embraced the Populist heritage. They had prepared the way for the affiliation in the twenties when they broke with the genteel tradition, adopted the mucker pose, and decided that conventional politics and the two major parties were the province of the boobocracy and professional politicians were clowns or hypocrites. In the thirties intellectuals made naïve identification with farmers and workers and supported their spokesmen with enthusiasm. The Populist affinity outlasted the New Deal, survived the war, and perhaps found its fullest expression in the spirit of indulgent affection with which intellectuals often supported Harry Truman and his administration.

Even before Truman left the White House, however, the Populist identification fell into disgrace, and intellectuals began to repudiate the heritage. "Populist" suddenly became a term of opprobrium, in some circles a pejorative epithet. This resulted from no transfer of affection to Truman's successor, for there was very little of that among intellectuals. The origins of the altered temper came earlier.

Disenchantment of the intellectual with the masses was well under way in the forties. Mass support for evil causes in Germany and elsewhere helped to undermine the faith. The liberal's feelings of guilt and impotence were reflected in the interest that the writings of Sören Kierkegaard and Reinhold Niebuhr aroused, and the mood of self-flagellation was expressed in the vogue of the novels of Franz Kafka and George Orwell. The shock of the encounter with McCarthyism sustained and intensified the mood. Liberals and intellectuals bore the brunt of the McCarthyite assault on standards of decency. They were rightly alarmed and felt themselves betrayed. They were the victims of a perversion of the democracy they cherished, a seamy and sinister side of democracy to which they now guiltily realized they had too often turned a blind or indulgent eye. Stung by consciousness of their own naïveté, they responded with a healthy impulse to make up for lost time and confront their problem with all the critical resources at their command. The consequence has been a formidable and often valuable corpus of social criticism.

Not one of the critics, not even the most conservative, is prepared to repudiate democracy. There is general agreement that the fault lay in some abuse or perversion of democracy and was not inherent in democracy itself. All the critics are aware that these abuses and perversions had historic antecedents and had appeared in various guises and with disturbing frequency in national history. These unhappy tendencies are variously described as "mobism," "direct democracy," or "plebecitarianism," but there is a surprising and apparently spontaneous consensus of preference for "Populism." Although the word is usually capitalized, the critics do not as a rule limit its reference to the political party that gave currency to the term. While there is general agreement that the essential characteristics designated by the term are best illustrated by an agrarian movement in the last decade of the nineteenth century, some of the critics take the liberty of applying it to movements as early as the Jacksonians, or earlier, and to twentieth-century phenomena as well.

Reasons for this convergence from several angles upon "Populism" as the appropriate designation for an abhorred abuse are not all clear. A few, however, suggest themselves. Populism is popularly thought of as an entirely Western affair, Wisconsin as a seedbed of the movement, and Old Bob La Follette as a foremost exponent. None of these assumptions is historically warranted, but it is true that Senator McCarthy came from Wisconsin, that much of his support came from the Middle West, and that there are some similarities between the two movements. The impression of similarity has been enhanced by the historical echo of their own alarm that modern intellectuals have caught in the rather hysterical fright with which Eastern conservatives reacted to Populism in the nineties.

This essay is not concerned with validity of recent analysis of the "radical right" and its fascistic manifestations in America.

It is concerned only with the tendency to identify Populism with these movements and with the implied rejection of the Populist tradition. It is admittedly very difficult, without risk of misrepresentation and injustice, to generalize about the way in which numerous critics have employed the Populist identification. They differ widely in the meaning they attribute to the term and the importance they attach to the identification. Among the critics are sociologists, political scientists, poets, and journalists, as well as historians, and there is naturally a diversity in the degree of historical awareness and competence they command. Among points of view represented are the New Conservative, the New Liberal, the liberal-progressive, the Jewish, the Anglophile, and the urban, with some overlapping. There are no conscious spokesmen of the West or the South, but some are more or less unconscious representatives of the urban East. Every effort will be made not to attribute to one the views of another.[1]

Certain concessions are due on the outset. Any fair-minded historian will acknowledge the validity of some of the points scored by the new critics against the Populist tradition and its defenses. It is undoubtedly true that liberal intellectuals have in the past constructed a flattering image of Populism. They have permitted their sympathy with oppressed groups to blind them to the delusions, myths, and foibles of the people with whom they sympathized. Sharing certain political and economic doctrines and certain indignations with the Populists, they have attributed to them other values, tastes, principles, and morals which the

1. Daniel Bell (ed.), *The New American Right* (New York, 1955), especially essays by Richard Hofstadter, Peter Viereck, Talcott Parsons, and Seymour Martin Lipset; Edward A. Shils, *The Torment of Secrecy* (Glencoe, Ill., 1956) and "The Intellectuals and the Powers: Some Perspectives for Comparative Analysis" in *Comparative Studies in Society and History*, I (October, 1958), 5–22; Peter Viereck, *The Unadjusted Man* (Boston, 1956); Oscar Handlin, *Race and Nationality in American Life* (Boston, 1957), and "American Views of the Jews at the Opening of the Twentieth Century," *Publication of the American Jewish Historical Society*, No. 40 (June, 1951), 323–44; Richard Hofstadter, *The Age of Reform* (New York, 1955); Victor C. Ferkiss, "Ezra Pound and American Fascism," *Journal of Politics*, XVII (1955), 174–96; Marx Lerner, *America as a Civilization* (New York, 1958).

Populists did not actually share. It was understandably distasteful to dwell upon the irrational or retrograde traits of people who deserved one's sympathy and shared some of one's views. For undertaking this neglected and distasteful task in the spirit of civility and forbearance which, for example, Richard Hofstadter has shown, some of the new critics deserve much credit. All of them concede some measure of value in the Populist heritage, though none so handsomely as Hofstadter, who assumes that Populism and Progressivism are strongly enough established in our tradition to withstand criticism. Others are prone to make their concessions more perfunctory and to hasten on with the job of heaping upon Populism, as upon an historical scapegoat, all the ills to which democracy is heir.

The danger is that under the concentrated impact of the new criticism the risk is incurred, not only of blurring a historical image, but of swapping an old stereotype for a new one. The old one sometimes approached the formulation that Populism is the root of all good in democracy, while the new one sometimes suggests that Populism is the root of all evil. Uncritical repetition and occasional exaggeration of the strictures of some of the critics threaten to result in establishing a new maxim in American political thought: *Radix malorum est Populismus.*

Few of the critics engaged in the reassessment of Populism and the analysis of the New American Right would perhaps go quite so far as Peter Viereck, when he writes that "beneath the sane economic demands of the Populists of 1880–1900 seethed a mania of xenophobia, Jew-baiting, intellectual-baiting, and thought-controlling lynch-spirit." Yet this far from exhausts the list of unhappy or repulsive aberrations of the American spirit that have been attributed to Populism. Other aberrations are not pictured as a "seething mania" by any one critic, but by one or another the Populists are charged with some degree of responsibility for Anglophobia, Negrophobia, isolationism, imperialism, jingoism, paranoidal conspiracy-hunting, anti-Constitutionalism, anti-intellectualism, and the assault upon the right of privacy—these among others.

The Populist virus is seen as no respecter of the barriers of time or nationality. According to Edward A. Shils, "populism has many faces. Nazi dictatorship had markedly populistic features. . . . Bolshevism has a strand of populism in it too." And there was among fellow travelers a "populistic predisposition to Stalinism." On the domestic scene the strand of Populistic tradition "is so powerful that it influences reactionaries like McCarthy and left-wing radicals and great upperclass personalities like Franklin Roosevelt." And according to Viereck, Populistic attitudes once "underlay Robespierre's Committee of Public Safety" and later "our neo-Populist Committee on un-American Activities."

Among certain of the critics there is no hesitancy in finding a direct continuity between the nineteenth-century Populists and twentieth-century American fascism and McCarthyism. Victor C. Ferkiss states flatly that "American fascism has its roots in American populism. It pursued the same ends and even used many of the same slogans. Both despaired of achieving a just society under the joined banners of liberalism and capitalism." His assertion supports Viereck's suggestion that "since the same impulses and resentments inspire the old Populism and the new nationalist right, let us adopt 'neo-Populism' as the proper term for the latter group." Talcott Parsons believes that "the elements of continuity between Western agrarian populism and McCarthyism are not by any means purely fortuitous," and Shils thinks the two are connected by "a straight line." It remains for Viereck to fill in the gap: "The missing link between the Populism of 1880–1900 and the neo-Populism of today—the missing link between Ignatius Donnelly and the McCarthy movement—was Father Charles Coughlin."

There is a strong tendency among the critics not only to identify Populism and the New Radical Right but to identify both with certain regions, the West and South, and particularly the Middle West. "The areas which produced the populism of the end of the nineteenth century and the early twentieth century have continued to produce them," writes Shils. Viereck puts it somewhat more colorfully: "The Bible-belt of Fundamentalism in religion mostly overlapped with the farm-belt of the Populist, Greenback, and other free-silver parties in politics. Both belts were anti-intellectual, anti-aristocratic, anti-capitalist." Parsons and Ferkiss likewise stress the regional identity of Populist–Radical Right ideology, and Viereck supplies an interesting illustration: "Out of the western Populist movement came such apostles of thought-control and racist bigotry as Tom Watson."

If so many undesirable traits are conveniently concentrated along geographical lines, it might serve a useful purpose to straighten out the political geography of Populism a bit. In the first place, as Hofstadter and other historians of the movement have noted, Populism had negligible appeal in the middle western states, and so did the quasi-Populism of William Jennings Bryan. Wisconsin, Minnesota, Iowa, Illiniois, and states east of them went down the line for William McKinley, Mark Hanna, gold, and the Old Conservatism (and so did Old Bob La Follette). Only in the plains states of North and South Dakota, Nebraska, and Kansas were there strong Populist leanings, and only they and the mountain states went for Bryan in 1896. At the crest of the Populist wave in 1894 only Nebraska polled a Populist vote comparable in strength to that run up in Alabama, Georgia, and North Carolina.

For the dubious distinction of being the leading Populist section, the South is in fact a strong contender; if the test used be merely quasi-Populism the pre-eminence of the former Confederacy is unchallengeable. It was easily the most solidly Bryan section of the country, and its dogged loyalty long outlasted that of the Nebraskan's native state. However, a more important test was third-party Populism, the genuine article. The remarkable strength the Populists manifested in the Lower South was gained against far more formidable obstacles than any ever encountered in the West. For there they daily faced the implacable dogmas of racism, white solidarity, white supremacy, and the bloody shirt. There was indeed plenty of "thought control and racist bigotry and lynch-spirit," but the Populists were far more often the victims than the perpetrators. They had to contend regularly with fore-closure of mortgages, discharge from jobs, eviction as tenants, exclusion from church, withholding of credit, boycott, social ostracism, and the endlessly reiterated charge of racial disloyalty and sectional disloyalty. Suspicion of loyalty was in fact *the* major psychological problem of the Southern Populists, as much so perhaps as the problem of loyalty faced by radicals of today. They contended also against cynical use of fraud comparable with any used against Reconstruction, methods that included stuffed ballot boxes, packed courts, stacked registration and election boards, and open bribery. They saw election after election stolen from them and heard their opponents boast of the theft. They were victims of mobs and lynchers. Some fifteen Negroes and several white men were killed in the Georgia Populist campaign of 1892, and it was rare that a major election in the Lower South came off without casualties.

Having waged their revolt at such great cost, the Southern Populists were far less willing to compromise their principles than were their Western brethren. It was the Western Populists who planned and led the movement to sell out the party to the Silverites, and the Southern Populists who fought and resisted the drift to quasi-Populism. The Southerners were consistently more radical, more insistent upon their economic reforms, and more stubbornly unwilling to lose their party identity in the watered-down quasi-Populism of Bryan than were the Westerners.

There is some lack of understanding about *who* the Southern Populists were for and against, as well as *what* they were for and against. Edward Shils writes that the "economic and political feebleness and pretensions to breeding and culture" of the "older aristocratic ruling class" in the South provided "a fertile ground for populistic denunciation of the upper classes." Actually the Southern Populists directed their rebellion against the newer ruling class, the industrialists and businessmen of the New South, instead of the old planters. A few of the quasi-Populists like

Ben Tillman did divert resentment to aristocrats like Wade Hampton. But the South was still a more deferential society than the rest of the country, and the Populists were as ready as the railroads and insurance companies to borrow the prestige and name of a great family. The names of the Populist officials in Virginia sounded like a roll call of colonial assemblies or Revolutionary founding fathers: Page, Cocke, Harrison, Beverley, Ruffin. There were none more aristocratic in the Old Dominion. General Robert E. Lee, after the surrender at Appomattox, retired to the ancestral home of Edmund Randolph Cocke after his labors. His host was later Populist candidate for governor of the state. As the editor of their leading paper, the allegedly anglophobic Populists of Virginia chose Charles H. Pierson, an ordained Anglican priest, English by birth, Cambridge graduate, and theological student of Oxford. To be sure, the Populist leaders of Virginia were not typical of the movement in the South. But neither were Jefferson, Madison, Monroe, and John Taylor typical of *their* movement in the South: there were simply never enough aristocrats to go around. Some states had to make do with cruder customers as leaders in both Jeffersonian and Populist movements, and in the states to the west there was doubtless less habitual dependence on aristocrats, even if they had been more readily available.

In their analysis of the radical right of modern America, the new critics have made use of the concept of "status resentment" as the political motivation of their subjects. They distinguish between "class politics," which has to do with the correction of economic deprivations, and "status politics," which has no definite solutions and no clear-cut legislative program but responds to irrational appeals and vents aggression and resentment for status insecurity upon scapegoats—usually ethnic minorities. Seymour Martin Lipset, who appears at times to include Populism in the category, has outlined the conditions typical of periods when status politics become ascendant. These are, he writes, "periods of prosperity, especially when full employment is accompanied by inflation, and when many individuals are able to improve their economic position." But the conditions under which Populism rose were exactly the opposite: severe depression, critical unemployment, and crippling curency contraction, when few were able to improve their economic position—and certainly not farmers in a cash-crop staple agriculture.

The Populist may have been bitten by status anxieties, but if so, they were certainly not bred of upward social mobility, and probably few by downward mobility either—for the simple reason that there was not much further downward for most Populists to go, and had not been for some time. Populism was hardly "status politics," and I should hesitate to call it "class politics." It was more nearly "interest politics," and more specifically "agricultural interest politics." Whatever concern the farmers might have had for their status was overwhelmed by desperate and immediate economic anxieties. Not only their anxieties but their proposed solutions and remedies were economic. While their legislative program may have often been naïve and inadequate, it was almost obsessively economic and, as political platforms go, little more irrational than the run-of-the-mill.

Yet one of the most serious charges leveled against the Populists in the reassessment of the new critics is an addiction to just the sort of irrational obsession that is typical of status politics. This is the charge of anti-Semitism. It has been documented most fully by Richard Hofstadter and Oscar Handlin and advanced less critically by others. The prejudice is attributed to characteristic Populist traits—rural provinciality, an ominous credulity, and an obsessive fascination with conspiracy. Baffled by the complexities of monetary and banking problems, Populist ideologues simplified them into a rural melodrama with Jewish international bankers as the principal villains. Numerous writings of Western Populists are cited that illustrate the tendency to use Jewish financiers and their race as scapegoats for agrarian resentment. Hofstadter points out that Populist anti-Semitism was entirely verbal and rhetorical and cautions that it can easily be misconstrued and exaggerated. He is nevertheless of the opinion "that the Greenback–Populist tradition activated most of what we have of modern popular anti-Semitism in the United States."

In the voluminous literature of the nineties on currency and monetary problems—problems that were much more stressed by silverites and quasi-Populists than by radical Populists—three symbols were repetitively used for the plutocratic adversary. One was institutional, "Wall Street," and two were ethnic, the British and Jewish bankers. Wall Street was by far the most popular and has remained so ever since among politicians of agrarian and Populistic tradition. Populist agitators used the ethnic symbols more or less indiscriminately, British along with Jewish, though some of them bore down with peculiar viciousness on the Semitic symbol. As the new critics have pointed out, certain Eastern intellectuals of the patrician sort, such as Henry and Brooks Adams and Henry Cabot Lodge, shared the Populist suspicion and disdain of the plutocracy and likewise shared their rhetorical anti-Semitism. John Higham has called attention to a third anti-Semitic group of the nineties, the poorer classes in urban centers. Their prejudice cannot be described as merely verbal and rhetorical. Populists were not responsible for a protest signed by fourteen Jewish societies in 1899 that "no Jew can go on the street without exposing himself to the danger of being pitilessly beaten." That happened in Brooklyn, and the mob of 1902 that injured some two hundred people, mostly Jewish, went into action in Lower East Side New York.

Populist anti-Semitism is not to be excused on the ground that it was verbal, nor dismissed because the prejudice received more violent expression in urban quarters. But all will admit that the charge of anti-Semitism has taken on an infinitely more ominous and hideous significance since the Nazi genocide furnaces than it ever had before, at least in Anglo-American society. The Populists' use of the Shylock symbol was not wholly innocent, but they used it as a folk stereotype, and little had happened in the Anglo-Saxon

community between the time of Shakespeare and that of the
Populists which burdened the latter with additional guilt in repeating the stereotype.

The South, again, was a special instance. Much had happened
there to enhance the guilt of racist propaganda and to exacerbate
racism. But anti-Semitism was not the trouble, and to stress it in
connection with the South of the nineties would be comparable to
stressing anti-Negro feeling in the Arab states of the Middle
East today. Racism there was, in alarming quantity, but it was
directed against another race, and it was not merely rhetorical.
The Negro suffered far more discrimination and violence than the
Jew did in that era or later. Moreover, there was little in the
Southern tradition to restrain the political exploitation of anti-
Negro prejudice and much more to encourage its use than there
was in the American tradition with respect to anti-Semitism.
Racism was exploited in the South with fantastic refinements and
revolting execesses in the Populist period. Modern students of the
dynamics of race prejudice find marked similarities between anti-
Negro feelings and anti-Semitism and in the psychological traits of
those to whom both appeal. First in the list of those traits under
both anti-Negro attitudes and anti-Semitism is "the feeling of
deprivation"; another, lower in the list but common to both, is
"economic apprehensions." The Southern Populists would seem
to have constituted the perfect market for Negrophobia.

But perhaps the most remarkable aspect of the whole Populist
movement was the resistance its leaders in the South put up against
racism and racist propaganda and the determined effort they made
against incredible odds to win back political rights for the Negroes,
defend those rights against brutal aggression, and create among
their normally anti-Negro following, even temporarily, a spirit of
tolerance in which the two races of the South could work together
in one party for the achievement of common ends. These efforts
included not only the defense of the Negro's right to vote but also
his right to hold office, serve on juries, receive justice in the courts
and defense against lynchers. The Populists failed, and some of

them turned bitterly against the Negro as the cause of their failure. But in the efforts they made for racial justice and political rights they went further toward extending the Negro political fellowship, recognition, and equality than any native white political movement has ever gone before or since in the South. This record is of greater historical significance and deserves more emphasis and attention than any anti-Semitic tendencies the movement manifested in that region or any other. If resistance to racism is the test of acceptability for a place in the American political heritage, Populism would seem to deserve more indulgence at the hands of its critics than it has recently enjoyed.

Two other aspects of identification between the old Populism and the New Radical Right require critical modification. Talcott Parsons, Max Lerner, and Victor Ferkiss, among others, find that the old regional strongholds of Populism tended to become the strongholds of isolationism in the period between the two world wars and believe there is more than a fortuitous connection between a regional proneness to Populism and isolationism. These and other critics believe also that they discern a logical connection between a regional addiction to Populism in the old days and to McCarthyism in recent times.

In both of these hypotheses the critics have neglected to take into account the experience of the South and mistakenly assumed a strong Populist heritage in the Middle West. Although one of the strongest centers of Populism, if not the strongest, the South in the foreign policy crisis before the Second World War was the least isolationist and the most internationalist and interventionist part of the country. After the war, according to Nathan Glazer and Seymour Lipset, who base their statement on opinion poll studies, "the South was the most anti-McCarthy section of the country." It is perfectly possible that in rejecting isolationism and McCarthyism the South was "right" for the "wrong" reasons, traditional and historical reasons. V. O. Key has suggested that among the reasons for its position on foreign policy were centuries of dependence on world trade, the absence of any concentration of Irish or Germanic population, and the pre-dominantly British origin of the white population. Any adequate explanation of the South's rejection of McCarthy would be complex, but part of it might be the region's peculiarly rich historical experience with its own assortment of demagogues—Populistic and other varieties—and the consequent acquirement of some degree of sophistication and some minimal standards of decency in the arts of demagoguery. No one has attempted to explain the South's anti-isolationism and anti-McCarthyism by reference to its Populist heritage—and certainly no such explanation is advanced here.

To do justice to the new critique of Populism it should be acknowledged that much of its bill of indictment is justified. It is true that the Populists were a provincial lot and that much of their thinking was provincial. It is true that they took refuge in the agrarian myth, that they denied the commercial character of agricultural enterprise and sometimes dreamed of a Golden Age. In their economic thought they overemphasized the importance of money and oversimplified the nature of their problems by claiming a harmony of interest between farmer and labor, by dividing the world into "producers" and "nonproducers," by reducing all conflict to "just two sides," and by thinking that too many ills and too many remedies of the world were purely legislative. Undoubtedly many of them were fascinated with the notion of conspiracy and advanced conspiratorial theories of history, and some of them were given to apocalyptic premonitions of direful portent.

To place these characteristics in perspective, however, one should enquire how many of them are peculiar to the Populists and how many are shared by the classes, or groups, or regions, or by the period to which the Populists belong. The great majority of Populists were provincial, ill-educated, and rural, but so were the great majority of Americans in the nineties, Republicans and Democrats as well. They were heir to all the superstition, folklore, and prejudice that is the heritage of the ill-informed. The Populists utilized and institutionalized some of this, but so did their opponents. There were a good many conspiratorial theories, economic nostrums, and oversimplifications adrift in the latter part of the nineteenth century, and the Populists had no monopoly of them. They did overemphasize the importance of money, but scarcely more so than did their opponents, the Gold Bugs. The preoccupation with monetary reforms and remedies was a characteristic of the period rather than a peculiarity of the Populists. The genuine Populist, moreover, was more concerned with the "primacy of credit" than with the "primacy of money," and his insistence that the federal government was the only agency powerful enough to provide a solution for the agricultural credit problem proved to be sound. So did his contention that the banking system was stacked against his interest and that reform in this field was overdue.

The Populist doctrine of a harmony of interest between farmer and labor, between workers and small businessmen, and the alignment of these "producers" against the parasitic "nonproducers" is not without precedent in our political history. Any party that aspires to gain power in America must strive for a coalition of conflicting interest groups. The Populist effort was no more irrational in this respect than was the Whig coalition and many others, including the New Deal.

The political crises of the nineties evoked hysterical responses and apocalyptic delusions in more than one quarter. Excesses of the leaders of a protest movement of provincial, unlettered, and angry farmers are actually more excusable and understandable than the rather similar responses of the spokesmen of the educated, successful, and privileged classes of the urban East. There would seem to be less excuse for hysteria and conspiratorial obsessions among the latter. One thinks of the *Nation* describing the Sherman Silver Purchase Act as a "socialistic contrivance of gigantic proportions," of J. Laurence Laughlin writing of "the great silver conspiracy" in the *Atlantic Monthly* of 1896, or of Police Commissioner Theodore Roosevelt declaring in "the greatest soberness"

that the Populists were "plotting a social revolution and the subversion of the American Republic" and proposing to make an
example of twelve of their leaders by "shooting them dead" against
a wall. There was Joseph H. Choate before the Supreme Court
pronouncing the income tax "the beginnings of socialism and
communism" and "the destruction of the Constitution itself."
For violence of rhetoric *Harper's Weekly*, the *Atlantic Monthly*,
the New York *Tribune*, and the Springfield *Republican* could
hold their own with the wool-hat press in the campaign of 1896.
Hysteria was not confined to mugwump intellectuals with status
problems. Mark Hanna told an assembly of his wealthy friends
at the Union League Club they were acting like "a lot of scared
hens."

Anarchism was almost as much a conspiracy symbol for conserva-
tives as Wall Street was for the Populists, and conservatives
responded to any waving of the symbol even more irrationally, for
there was less reality in the menace of anarchism for capitalism.
John Hay had a vituperative address called "The Platform of
Anarchy" that he used in the campaign of 1896. The Springfield
Republican called Bryan "the exaltation of anarchy"; Dr. Lyman
Abbott labeled Bryanites "the anarchists of the Northwest," and
Dr. Charles H. Parkhurst was excited about the menace of
"anarchism" in the Democratic platform. It was the Populist
sympathizer, Governor John Peter Altgeld of Illinois, who par-
doned the three anarchists of Haymarket, victims of conservative
hysteria, and who partly corrected the gross miscarriage of justice
that had resulted in the hanging of four others. The New York
Times promptly denounced Governor Altgeld as a secret anarchist
himself, and Theodore Roosevelt said that Altgeld would conspire
to inaugurate "a red government of lawlessness and dishonesty as
fantastic and vicious as the Paris Commune." There was more
than a touch of conspiratorial ideology in the desperate conservative reaction to the agrarian revolt. An intensive study of the
nineties can hardly fail to leave the impression that this decade
had rather more than its share of zaniness and crankiness and that

these qualities were manifested in the higher and middling as well as the lower orders of American society.

Venturing beyond the 1890's and speaking of populists with a small "p," some of the new critics would suggest that popular protest movements of the populistic style throughout our history have suffered from a peculiar addiction to scares, scapegoats, and conspiratorial notions. It is true that such movements tend to attract the less sophisticated, the people who are likely to succumb to cranks and the appeal of their menaces, and conspiratorial obsessions. But before one accepts this as a populistic or radical peculiarity, one should recall that the Jacobin Scare of the 1790's was a Federalist crusade and that the populistic elements of that era were its victims and not its perpetrators. One should remember also that A. Mitchell Palmer and the superpatriots who staged the Great Red Scare of 1919–1920 were not populistic in their outlook. One of the most successful conspiratorial theories of history in American politics was the "Great Slave Conspiracy" notion advanced by the abolitionists and later incorporated in the Republican party credo for several decades.

Richard Hofstadter has put his finger on a neglected tendency of some Populists and Progressives as well, the tendency he calls "deconversion from reform to reaction," the tendency to turn cranky, illiberal, and sour. This happened with disturbing frequency among leaders as well as followers of Populism. Perhaps the classic example is the Georgia Populist, Tom Watson, twice his party's candidate for President and once for Vice President. When Watson soured he went the whole way. By no means all of the Populist leaders turned sour, and there has been an over-emphasis on a handful of stock examples, but there are several valid instances. Even more disturbing is the same tendency to turn sour among the old Populist rank and file, to take off after race phobias, religious hatreds, and witch hunts. The reasons for this retrograde tendency among reformers to embrace the forces they have spent years in fighting have not been sufficiently investigated. It may be that in some instances the reform movement appeals to personalities with unstable psychological traits. In the case of the Populists, however, it would seem that a very large part of the explanation lies in embittered frustration—repeated and tormenting frustration of both the leaders and the led.

Whatever the explanation, it cannot be denied that some of the offshoots of Populism are less than lovely to contemplate and rather painful to recall. Misshapen and some times hideous, they are caricatures of the Populist ideal, though their kinship with the genuine article is undeniable. No one in his right mind can glory in their memory, and it would at times be a welcome relief to renounce the whole Populist heritage in order to be rid of the repulsive aftermath. Repudiation of the Populist tradition presents the liberal-minded Southerner in particular with a temptation of no inconsiderable appeal, for it would unburden him of a number of embarrassing associations.

In his study of populist traits in American society, Edward Shils has some perceptive observations on the difficult relations between politicians and intellectuals. He adds a rather wistful footnote: "How painful the American situation looked to our intellectuals when they thought of Great Britain. There the cream of the graduates of the two ancient universities entered the civil service by examinations which were delightfully archaic and which had no trace of spoils patronage about them. . . . Politics, radical politics, conducted in a seemly fashion by the learned and reflective was wonderful. It was an ideal condition which was regretfully recognized as impossible to reproduce in the United States." He himself points out many of the reasons why this is possible in Britain, the most dignified member of the parliamentary fraternity: respect for "betters," mutual trust within the ruling classes, deferential attitudes of working class and middle class, the aura of aristocracy and monarchy that still suffuses the institutions of a government no longer aristocratic, the retention of the status and the symbols of hierarchy despite economic leveling. No wonder that from some points of view "the British system seemed an intellectual's paradise."

America has it worse—or at least different. The deferential attitude lingers only in the South, and there mainly as a quaint gesture of habit. Respect for "betters" is un-American. Glaring publicity replaces mutual trust as the *modus vivendi* among the political elite. No aura of aristocratic decorum and hierarchal sanctity surrounds our governmental institutions, even the most august of them. Neither Supreme Court nor State Department nor Army is immune from popular assault and the rude hand of suspicion. The sense of institutional identity is weak, and so are institutional loyalties. Avenues between the seats of learning and the seats of power are often blocked by mistrust and mutal embarrassment.

America has no reason to expect that it could bring off a social revolution without a breach of decorum or the public peace, nor that the revolutionary party would eventually be led by a graduate of exclusive Winchester and Oxford. American politics are not ordinarily "conducted in a seemly fashion by the learned and reflective." Such success as we have enjoyed in this respect—the instances of the Sage of Monticello and the aristocrat of Hyde Park come to mind—have to be accounted for by a large element of luck. Close investigation of popular upheavals of protest and reform in the political history of the United States has increasingly revealed of late that they have all had their seamy side and their share of the irrational, the zany, and the retrograde. A few of the more successful movements have borrowed historical reputability from the memory of the worthies who led them, but others have not been so fortunate either in their leaders or their historians.

One must expect and even hope that there will be future upheavals to shock the seats of power and privilege and furnish the periodic therapy that seems necessary to the health of our democracy. But one cannot expect them to be any more decorous or seemly or rational than their predecessors. One can reasonably hope, however, that they will not all fall under the sway of the Huey Longs and Father Coughlins who will be ready to take charge. Nor need they, if the tradition is maintained which enabled a Henry George to place himself at the vanguard of the antimonopoly movement in his day, which encouraged a Henry Demarest Lloyd to labor valiantly to shape the course of Populism, or which prompted an Upton Sinclair to try to make sense of a rag-tag-and-bob-tail aberration in California.

For the tradition to endure, for the way to remain open, however, the intellectual must not be alienated from the sources of revolt. It was one of the glories of the New Deal that it won the support of the intellectual and one of the tragedies of Populism that it did not. The intellectual must resist the impulse to identify all the irrational and evil forces he detests with such movements because some of them, or the aftermath or epigone of some of them, have proved so utterly repulsive. He will learn all he can from the new criticism about the irrational and illiberal side of Populism and other reform movements, but he cannot afford to repudiate the heritage.

Voters and Their Roots

The Politics of Rejection

by Paul Kleppner

For two Gilded Age decades the Republican and Democratic parties competed vigorously. Neither achieved national majority status, though the Republicans generally proved more successful. Presidential contests often turned on a few thousand votes; only in three Congresses did one party control both houses, and only in two did the party that controlled Congress also capture the presidency. This near-deadlock persisted despite the Republicans' apparent electoral advantage after 1865. Smeared with the brush of treason, Democrats had to overcome the bitter heritage of Civil War. Nevertheless, the party swiftly regained strength, aided by the collapse of Radical Reconstruction and resoration of "home" rule which brought the white South back into American politics as a solidly Democratic bloc.

While the South went Democratic, New England remained just as solidly Republican. In the rest of the country the two major parties fought on roughly equal terms. Voting patterns that had been forged in the heat of mid-nineteenth century sectional division and war persisted late into the century. Each party displayed strength among urban and rural voters, wealthy and poor, working class and middle class.

Striking differences in party preference stemmed from ethnocultural and religious backgrounds, however. Thus, Midwesterners of Southern ancestry tended to vote Democratic, while those of New England origin favored the Republicans. Among first- and second-generation immigrants, who were fast becoming a major element in the electorate, Protestants from Germany and Scandinavia tended to enter the Republican fold while Catholics from Ireland and Germany found their political home in the Democratic party. As a party born out of a crusade against the nation's cardinal sin, slavery, a crusade rooted in evangelical, Protestant efforts to purify public life, the Republicans attracted Northern Calvinists, both native and foreign-born, who were alarmed over the growing influence of immigrants with "strange" life styles and mores.

The Democratic party then, committed to negative government and states' rights, had a long history of collaboration with non-WASP ethnic groups. Since Protestants often attempted to use government to impose their standards on unwilling minorities, the Democracy seemed the safest bet for Catholics. On this basis, many of them joined Southern Protestants to form a powerful Democratic coalition. Thus two very distinct groups united in one national party to defend their distinct "gut" interests.

By the 1890's, therefore, the major parties represented coalitions of mixed, often contradictory elements. Political organization brought them together in a common cause and, in the process, provided much-needed cohesion to an otherwise fragmented, though consolidating, society. Americans traditionally divided along ethnocultural and sectional lines far more than they did along class lines, a fact which produced a sobering lesson for the class-oriented politicians of the Populist crusade and the Bryan campaign of 1896. Though the economic and social crises of the 1890's might well have been expected to topple the existing American political structure, and though many thought that the election of 1896 would end in revolution, once Bryan embraced free silver, and once the Populists endorsed him, the American business community closed ranks behind McKinley's candidacy.

Radical realignment failed to materialize, and the return of prosperity ended most talk of class war. Paul Kleppner analyzes the failure of Bryan's 1896 campaign, and points up the persistence of ethno-cultural voting patterns during the crises of 1890's.

⚜ After three years of depression, political parties in 1896 were forced to offer an explanation of economic events and future prospects to the voters. The repudiation of the Democracy in the state and federal elections of 1893 through 1895 created a leadership vacuum within the Democratic party. The defeat of northern and midwestern Democrats in the 1894 congressional elections shifted the leadership roles to the southern and western representatives of the party. Political leaders from these sections, responding to constituency pressures, hoped to remake the image of the party. They hoped to create a political vehicle expressive of, and responsive to, the economic demands of the semicolonial depressed agricultural regions. Aware of this sectional discontent with the eastern party leadership, William Jennings Bryan assiduously cultivated the prospective delegates to the 1896 national convention from the southern and western states. His efforts were capped with the success he had worked for; he was nominated by the Chicago convention as the party's candidate for the presidency. That nomination and the platform that the convention adopted gave the Democratic party's answer to the depression: commodity price inflation.

The Republicans had less difficulty in formulating their explanation of the depression and selecting a candidate whose image was consonant with it. Republican rhetoric following the 1890 defeats had so closely linked William McKinley with the tariff that, when that question assumed new importance, large numbers of party leaders immediately saw him as the "logical" nominee. McKinley encountered opposition from the party's eastern leaders, who were suspicious of his stand on the silver question. But through skillful utilization of his extensive network of personal contacts, and aided by Mark Hanna's organizational techniques, the "Napoleon of Protection" was able to secure his party's nomination for the presidency.

The ensuing contest was a dramatic one. As Bryan toured the

From *The Cross of Culture: A Social Analysis of Midwestern Politics 1850–1900* (New York: The Free Press, 1970), pp. 279–80, 298–315, 369–75. Reprinted by permission.

country preaching the free silver gospel, McKinley waged an energetic "front porch" campaign for tariff protection and honest money. Both were concerned not just with the audience within earshot, but with the broader one that would be exposed to their rhetoric through the written reports of their comments. The Bryan strategy was both apparent and simple. He aimed at uniting the "toiling masses" against the vested interests who oppressed both farmer and laborer. Since, collectively, farmers and urban workers constituted the bulk of the electorate, the strategic aim was pre-eminently reasonable. The crucial question is how well he succeeded in implementing his strategy. . . .

Two dimensions of the failure of the "toiling masses" to cohere in the support of Bryan's Democracy deserve consideration. First, Bryan was not able to restore even the usual levels of Democratic support. Second, he failed to attract workers and farmers *as economic groups*, i.e., he failed to produce a class polarization of politics.

Once we realize that the political configuration that Bryan envisaged did not involve an extension of the old social bases of political action but the creation of an entirely new one, Bryan's lack of attraction for traditional Democrats becomes understandable. Democratic partisan loyalties were not rooted in economic class distinctions, but in religious value systems. In election contests prior to 1896, Democratic strategists had recognized the basis of these traditional attachments and designed their rhetoric *both* to reactivate latent loyalties and to reinforce the proclivity of such voters to support the Democracy.

Current studies of political behavior demonstrate the importance of these types of appeals in a political campaign. One such study offers this assessment of the over-all effects of the campaign on the vote intention: "This is what the campaign does: reinforcement 53%; activation 14%; reconversion 3%; partial conversion 6%; conversion 8%; no effect 16%." [1] The important point to observe

1. Paul F. Lazarsfeld, Bernard Berelson, and Hazel Gaudet, *The People's Choice: How the Voter Makes Up His Mind in a Presidential Campaign*

is that the first three categories, reinforcement, activation, and reconversion, involve a "return," in one sense or another, of the voter to his traditional partisan attachment. These data also indicate the disproportionately important role these effects play in shaping the final voting intention: they sum to 70.0%.

The most obvious fact about the 1896 rhetoric is the absence of reactivating appeals. The Bryanites did not greatly concern themselves with appeals to the underlying bases of traditional Democratic attachments. On the contrary, they explicitly argued that the old bases of political divisions were no longer relevant and that they welcomed support from "old Democrats" only when that arose from an agreement with the party's new program and ideology. We should not, of course, take seriously the claim by Bryan supporters that they sought only votes motivated by complete ideological concurrence. What is important here is not the validity of the claim, but the image being projected to traditional Democrats by the fact that the claim was being made and the fact that the party's rhetoric was devoid of the customary and expected types of reactivating appeals. In brief, that image was one of a *new* and *different* Democracy. It was *not* the image of the traditional Democratic party, the image of negative government and of maximum "personal liberty." [2]

Nor was it merely Bryan's enemies, Republican or Democratic, who were responsible for projecting such an image. Indeed, Democratic organs that opposed Bryan reiterated the theme that he did not represent the traditional Democracy. Their concern with this type of theme was a reflection of their awareness of the potency of party identifications in mobilizing voters. That anti-Bryan organs

(2nd ed.; New York, 1948), p. 103, and also see Table V, p. 102, for a more detailed breakdown of its effects by categories of "vote intention in May."

2. My description of the public image projected by Bryanites in 1896 is based upon a systematic content analysis of the relevant state and national platforms, Bryan speeches, numerous excerpts of which are in *The First Battle* (Chicago, 1896), and full texts of which are available in contemporary newspapers, and of more than 1,000 pro-Bryan newspaper editorials that appeared in September and October, 1896. . . .

projected such an image to Bryan's Democracy was less important than the fact that this was *by design* the image the Bryanites projected of themselves. Their concern was not with the reactivation of *old* loyalties, but with the creation of a *new* configuration of political forces. That involved *conversion*, not mere reactivation and reinforcement of old loyalties.

Late nineteenth-century midwestern partisan identifications were not rooted in economic class identifications. Voting behavior was not signficantly determined by differences in relative degrees of economic prosperity. Bryan's appeals were directed to class awareness and designed to polarize voters along economic lines. To produce such a configuration required that large numbers of voters not only accept a new set of priorities, ones that placed economic considerations above ethnic and religious ones, but that they structure entirely new political perspectives. Essentially, Bryan was asking Democrats to view their party not as a preserver of their religious value system, not in the way in which they had seen it since the 1850's, but as a vehicle through which they could implement class objectives. In formal terms, such rhetoric was *disruptive* rather than *reactivating*. That is, its objective was to orient traditional Democrats to a pattern of values and a basis of party identifications that was specifically in conflict with their time-honored political perspective and its attendant values and definitions.[3]

Since perception is a selective mechanism, and the nature of the selectivity has partisan overtones, numerous Democrats undoubtedly drew the candidate and his program closer to their own positions. But even this mechanism was relatively *less effective* in 1896 than in earlier elections. Misperception requires a certain degree of ambiguity in the objective situation being perceived. In 1896 the objective situation was less ambiguous than usual in

3. See Talcott Parsons, *Essays in Sociological Theory* (Free Press ed.; New York, 1964), ch. viii, "Propaganda and Social Control," pp. 142–76, and especially the distinctions given on pp. 171–72; also see James O. Whittaker, "Cognitive Dissonance and the Effectiveness of Persuasive Communications," *Public Opinion Quarterly*, XXVIII (Winter, 1964), 547–55.

presidential contests. This, coupled with the disruptive impact of Bryan's rhetoric, resulted in his failure to poll even the normal levels of Democratic support.

Conceivably, however, the free silver rhetoric could have served as a reinforcing type of appeal, i.e., it could have provided partisans with a series of arguments with which both to answer their own questions concerning the current economic situation and to counter the opposing Republican arguments. By design it was intended, of course, to do much more than this. It was intended to mobilize the bulk of the "toiling masses," regardless of previous partisan identifications, behind the Bryan candidacy. As the empirical data demonstrate, it achieved neither effect. We can understand this failure by examining that rhetoric in relationship to the social context in which the voter arrived at his partisan decision.

As an economic group urban workers, even those who had previously supported the Democrats, did not respond in a disproportionately favorable way to Bryan. Historians have often explained this on the grounds that the free silver argument offered little advantage to wage earners. There is a large measure of validity in such arguments, but they usually have been posited within a faulty conceptual framework. The implication is that the voter clearly perceived the relationship between the economic effects of free silver and his own class interests. The assumption, in short, is that free silver constituted a substantive "issue" and was rejected, after considerable ratiocination, by issue-oriented voters.[4] There is no factual basis for such assumptions. This does not mean that the free silver rhetoric played no role in Bryan's rejection by urban workers. It means that we have to analyze that

4. While varying in the particular mode of their treatments, the most recent studies of the 1896 contest share this type of framework; see Paul W. Glad, *McKinley, Bryan, and the People* (Philadelphia, 1964), pp. 203–4; Stanley L. Jones, *The Presidential Election of 1896* (Madison, 1964), pp. 332–50; and J. Rogers Hollingsworth, *The Whirligig of Politics* (Chicago, 1963), pp. 84–107. For a much different type of approach, see the perceptive suggestions offered by Hollingsworth in "The Historian, Presidential Elections, and 1896," *Mid-America*, XLV (July, 1963), 185–92, and in "Populism: The Problem of Rhetoric and Reality," *Agricultural History*, XXXIX (April, 1965), 81–85.

rejection within a more useful and realistic conceptual framework.

It is of little analytical value to consider free silver as a substantive issue. But is very meaningful to consider both the money question and the tariff as ideological instruments of voter mobilization and party combat. Both were intended by party strategists to provide voters with an explanation of the 1893 depression and the subsequent economic crisis. Both were designed to offer voters a structured response to their inquiries concerning future economic prospects. In this analytical context the question of whether the tariff or free silver was the major substantive issue in the 1896 election is an irrelevant one; "The important struggle during that campaign was not over two sides of an issue, but over whether or not one issue or the other should be the primary focus of attention. . . . Each [presidential candidate] tried to mobilize voters around explanatory ideological positions with which those voters could identify." [5]

Through the free silver ideology Bryan and his supporters tried to explain both the advent of "hard times" and the process through which prosperity would be restored. The explanations, however, were not consonant with either the experiences or the perceptions of urban workers. An examination of the three major themes of the ideology illustrates the point.

The Bryan rhetoric spoke of the "crime of 1873" and emphasized that "crime" as the underlying cause of all subsequent discontent. The demonetization of silver, the act of "a corrupt and corrupting set of abominable traitors," had "assassinated labor"; it had reduced the "toiling masses" to subservience to "the interest of avarice and greed." [6] The remonetization of silver would undo this great evil and free the "common people" from the yoke of oppression by restoring the pristine virtues and social relationships

5. Samuel P. Hays, "Political Parties and the Local–Cosmopolitan Continuum, 1865–1929" (unpublished paper delivered at Washington University Conference on Political Development, Spring, 1966), p. 13, and his discussion of the importance of conceiving such "proposals" as ideologies rather than substantive issues, pp. 12–14.
6. The quotations are from the *Milwaukee Advance*, October 31, 1896, and the *Monroe Sun Gazette*, September 4, 1896.

that had characterized the earlier era. This type of explanation hardly accorded with the experience of urban workers. They attributed their difficulties, not to a long-term price decline, but to the immediate and severe impact of unemployment and wage reductions that had begun in 1893. The story of twenty years of cumulating hardship hardly accounted for this experience. Nor did the promise of a return to the relationships of a simpler, less complex social system hold out much hope for the restoration of jobs and wages. Free silver, from this perspective, was not a forward-looking, adjustive ideology, not one attuned to the growing complexity of a modern industrial society, not one addressed to the immediate problems of urban workers.[7]

When Bryan and his supporters spoke in terms of immediate solutions they used a theme equally discordant to urban workers. Commodity price inflation was the solution offered to overcome the problems of "the producers of the nation's wealth." This type of explanation bore little relationship to urban workers' perceptions. The size of the job supply was probably more salient to them than that of the money supply, and wage increases more relevant than price increases. But more important was the fact that the explanation revealed the jarringly anachronistic perception the Bryanites held of the role that the wage earner played in the industrial system. To Bryan and his followers commodity price infla-

7. The concern here is with the public image of the free silver ideology, as that image can be reconstructed through a systematic content analysis of the relevant *public* sources. This is both conceptually and analytically a much different approach from that which Norman Pollack criticizes in *The Populist Response to Industrial America: Midwestern Populist Thought* (Cambridge, Mass., 1962), p. 6. Pollack inveighs against the line of reasoning that contends that "Populism did not adjust to industrialism" and was, therefore, "unrealistic." In my opinion the argument, regardless of which side one takes, is an ahistorical one. "Populism" is an abstraction and incapable of adjustment or nonadjustment. It is only through an illogical resort to reification that historians discuss it in such terms. It is more meaningful to speak of *particular* Populists, occupying *particular* positions in the social structure from which they derived *particular*, and often quite conflicting, perspectives. The homogenization of these differences, which is an integral part of Pollack's own research design and which he has combined with an *eclectic* use of both public and *private* qualitative sources, adds little to our understanding.

tion, a producer-oriented solution, was not inconsistent with the best interests of urban workers precisely because the latter *were* producers. Their vision of what the worker *should be*, a petty entrepreneur, was some forty years out of date. The urban laborer, who had accepted the wage system and sought pragmatic adjustments within its confines, saw the normative dictum of the free silver ideology in conflict with the reality he daily experienced.[8]

The third major theme of the free silver rhetoric also created a problem of cognitive dissonance for urban workers. The Bryanites emphasized the primacy of agriculture over industry. They concentrated on the agricultural producer and his role in the creation of the moral and just society. When they turned themselves to the welfare of the urban worker, they attempted to link that directly with the welfare of the farmer. The type of nexus they emphasized was significant. The economic recovery of the farmer had to precede that of the urban worker. Bryan was doing more than displaying his oratorical prowess when, in his address before the Democratic National Convention, he claimed that "the great cities rest upon *our* broad and fertile prairies. Burn down *your* cities and leave *our* farms, and *your* cities will spring up again as if by magic; but destroy *our* farms and the grass will grow in the streets of every city in the country.[9] He was giving verbal expression to his view of the world about him, and enunciating a central theme of the free silver ideology. The relationship between urban workers and farmers that ideology stressed was more than one of mutual interde-

8. Since the 1860's laboring groups had been skeptical of monetary solutions to their difficulties; see Irwin Unger, *The Greenback Era: A Social and Political History of American Finance, 1865–1879* (Princeton, 1964), pp. 94–114 and 181–90.

9. The quotation is from Bryan, *The First Battle*, p. 205, I have added the emphasis. The divergent perspectives that rural and urban "reformers" held created tensions even at the leadership level; see J. H. Berker, August 27, 1894, James P. Corse, September 3, 1894, and L. B. Howrey, September 7, 1894, all to T. C. Richmond, in Richmond MSS, State Historical Society of Wisconsin; Chester McArthur Destler, "Consummation of a Labor–Populist Alliance in Illinois, 1894," *Mississippi Valley Historical Review*, XXVII (March, 1941), 589–602; and William F. Zornow, "Bellamy Nationalism in Ohio, 1891 to 1896," *Ohio History*, LVIII (April, 1949), 162–70.

pendence, it was one in which the worker's concerns had to be subordinate to those of the farmer.

It is a mistake, of course, to suggest, or imply, that contemporary human actors separated one theme of the free silver ideology from another. Voter reactions were not based upon such analytical distinctions. These themes were not separated, but fused into an explanatory ideology through which Bryan hoped to mobilize supporters. That urban workers were not significantly responsive to these attempts was the result of the fact that the free silver ideology was *relatively less* consonant with their experiences and perceptions than the competing ideology offered by the opposition.

The Republican tariff ideology explained the "hard times" in terms that accorded with the urban worker's experiences. Its focus was not on distant causes, but on the very immediate ones that had converted the prosperity of 1892 into the depression of 1893. It addressed itself directly to the immediate problems of the urban worker: employment and wages. It did not propose to solve these problems by increasing prices, or by expanding the purchasing power of *farmers*, but by protecting the laborer's job and his wage levels. It was an ideology which the urban worker could translate into personally relevant terms.

Republican strategists were cognizant of the role played by the tariff ideology, by the "tariff as wage and job protection." Historians have often called attention to the fact that anti-Bryan sources emphasized the harm that would befall the worker whose wages were paid in fifty-cent dollars. To provide their supporters with arguments with which to answer the claims of free silverites. Republicans did use such rhetoric. What is more significant is that in addition to attacking the free silver solution, in urban areas the Republican party newspapers offered a counter-solution. For example, both the *Chicago Tribune* and the *Milwaukee Sentinel* devoted relatively more of their worker-directed symbolism to extolling the necessity of "restoring prosperity by restoring the tariff," than they did to attacks on "funny money."

Midwestern farmers were relatively more responsive to the

Bryan candidacy than urban workers, but as an economic group they failed to provide disproportionate support to his Democracy. Since the Bryanites were especially convinced of their strength among midwestern farmers, the failure is particularly significant. One analysis of the "farm vote" has attempted to explain Bryan's poor showing on the grounds that he was faced with the task of making inroads into a solidly Republican bloc of voters, "Bryan had to convert traditionally Republican farmers to the Democratic cause and convince them to forsake their regular party allegiance." [10] This hypothesis could serve as the basis for an extremely important explanation of the variations in the degree of rural receptivity to Bryan, were it not for the fact that it is in no way congruent with the empirical voting data. Midwestern farmers were not solidly Republican prior to 1896. As a group they had tended to divide rather evenly between the two major parties since at least 1876. Reacting negatively to the party of "hard times," they were more Republican than usual in 1894, but even then a *substantial* minority was anti-Republican. The hypothesis has two more crucial weaknesses. It cannot begin to explain his failure in Michigan and Wisconsin to capture even the normal *Democratic* rural percentage. Nor can it explain the fact that in all three states some of his most pronounced gains came in units that had been solidly and steadfastly Republican during every election in the preceding twenty years.

Bryan's failure to elicit a favorable response from rural voters involved more than farmers voting their traditional party identification. For present purposes, it is adequate to focus on one aspect of this analytical problem: Why didn't these midwestern rural producers, who had suffered from long-term price declines and the short-term impact of the depression, respond favorably to an ideology explicitly designed to attract rural support? No doubt the prospects of repaying their mortgage indebtedness in inflated cur-

10. Gilbert G. Fite, "Republican Strategy and the Farm Vote in the Presidential Campaign of 1896," *American Historical Review*, LXV (July, 1960), 804–5.

rency, and of rising commodity prices, were attractive to midwestern farmers. But the farmer did not approach the 1896 election without his own explanation of the ills that had befallen him during the previous two decades. He had his own perception of both the nature of his problems and the possible solutions available to him. That he found little congruence between these perceptions and the free silver ideology resulted in Bryan's failure to translate rural dissatisfaction into a favorable partisan voting intention.

Although they all had been squeezed between falling commodity prices and rising costs, farmers in the Midwest, the East, the trans-Missouri West, and the South, did not define their problems in the same way. Those definitions varied because the structure of agriculture and the impact of the "overproduction crisis" differed among regions. While no region was similar to any of the others, and none was internally homogeneous, it is adequate here to focus on the ways in which the midwestern farmer's perception of his problems diverged from those held by rural producers in the South and the West.[11]

Producers in the latter areas saw their difficulties arising from exploitation by the financial interests of the East. Capital and credit shortages required the importation of eastern money, at what western producers saw as ruinous interest rates. The absence of nearby large urban centers required the shipment of their products to eastern markets and made him highly vulnerable to changes in transportation costs. Involvement in an impersonal price and marketing system controlled by easterners merely intensified their sense of powerlessness. While these and other particulars could be endlessly extended, it suffices to observe that southern and western producers explained their problems to themselves in terms of exploitation by avaricious easterners. To them, "Wall Street" became a potent symbolic expression of what was wrong with their world.

11. Lee Benson's analysis of the reaction of New York farmers to Populism is unusually perceptive and served as the basis for the following reexamination of the reaction of midwestern farmers; see "The New York Farmers' Rejection of Populism: The Background" (unpublished M. A. thesis, Columbia University, 1948). The explanation here overtly follows Benson's model.

The solution that they envisaged involved wresting political and financial control from the exploiters. Bryan's free silver ideology was addressed to precisely such perspectives.

Midwestern farmers lived in a region that had a different set of structural relationships with the East. They tended to see their world, to define their problems in entirely different ways; they came, as a result, to propose different genera of solution.

When the midwestern farmer asked himself what was wrong with his world, why his prices were declining and his property depreciating in value, his response gave no consolation to his western counterpart. The principal problem was not exploitation by eastern capitalists, nor excessive railroad freight rates, but the "unfair" competition created by western production. The availability of cheap land frequently provided by the government, relatively lower taxes, and advantageous long-haul freight rates enabled the western producer to send his beef, hogs, corn, and wheat "to enter and compete in markets which by natural contact should belong to others." Midwestern farm leaders attributed the depression of agriculture to an oversupply of production, not to an undersupply of currency. The chief villain was not the eastern financier but the western farmer, who was responsible for the overproduction. The president of the Ohio Agricultural Society translated the causative sequence into directly and personally relevant terms when he claimed that, "It has been overproduction by the opening up of the great West . . . that has placed mortgages upon the farmers' homes of this state." [12]

The antagonism of interests that the midwestern farmer perceived between himself and his western brethren found expression in the frequent resolutions adopted by all types of agricultural organizations against continued government expenditures for western

12. The respective quotations are from *Annual Report of the Ohio Farmers' Institutes, 1891–92*, p. 47, and the *Annual Report of the Ohio State Board of Agriculture, 1891*, p. 58. These, and the other sentiments described here, recurred frequently in the relevant agricultural sources. For more detailed documentation of all these matters, see Paul Kleppner, "The Politics of Change in the Midwest: The 1890's in Historical and Behavioral Perspective" (unpublished Ph.D. dissertation, University of Pittsburgh, 1967), pp. 476–85.

irrigation and reclamation projects. In what they frequently described as "an age of competition," it made little sense to the embattled midwestern farmer for the federal government to appropriate public funds to aid his competitor. Midwestern farmers showed little sympathy for what they viewed as "a scheme to bring in competition with the farmer east of the Mississippi all these vast acres of land at the expense of the general government." [13]

The midwestern farmer was not content with a monistic explanation of his difficulties. He constructed a litany of troubles. But this shared little in common with the southern and western ejaculatory recitation. When the midwesterner railed against the railroads, he more often than not criticized them for the role they played in abetting the "unfair" western competition. His focus of complaint was not so much that his rates were too high, but that rates on western shipments were *too low*. He attributed some portion of his difficulty to the tax structure, and supported legislation to reduce the tax levels on real property and increase those on personal property. He sought to eliminate the "unfair" competition created by "fraudulent" products, oleo and filled-cheese, through legislative proposals at both state and national levels to outlaw or severely restrict the sale of such products. Such attempts involved farmers in conflict and combat with *local* Grocers and Retailers Associations. When the farmer directed his ire against financial manipulators, it was not eastern capitalists, not "Wall Street," that fell under fire, but "the *local* Boards of Trade" that speculated in futures, coerced local dealers, and depressed prices. Finally, he raised his voice against the tariff: not to oppose its principle, but to demand the extension of its protection to the products of the farm. Though midwestern farmers frequently complained that manufacturing interests received relatively too great a measure of tariff protection, and demanded a counterbalancing increase in the level of protection afforded their own products, they did not op-

13. The quotations are from the *Proceedings of the Annual Meeting of the Illinois State Dairymen's Association*, 1890, p. 29, and *Annual Report of the Ohio State Board of Agriculture*, 1890, p. 3–4.

pose the principle of tariff protection for industry. To the contrary, this protection guaranteed full employment in cities and a nearby, lucrative market for farm products. The farmers' objective was to "protect" that market both by continued high employment and by eliminating the "unfair" competition of western producers and "fake goods." [14]

When the midwestern producer sought relief, he turned to measures designed to combat *his* problems. He pressed for I.C.C. rulings to increase the freight rates on shipments from the West. He advocated legislation to eliminate the tax disparity between real and personal property. He favored legislative enactments to reduce the power of his *local* enemies, the Grocers and Retailers Associations and the Boards of Trade. But he did not confine himself to suggestions aimed only at changing the roles played by others. His own role, too, had to change.

Western and southern producers blamed their repressed condition on eastern exploiters, but rural opinion leaders in the Midwest allotted a major portion of the responsibility to the farmer himself. Success required farmers doing more than "going over the same routine of work that their fathers have laid out before them." If the farmer was not receiving a just share of society's profits, it

14. For examples of such sentiments, see *Annual Report of the Indiana State Board of Agriculture*, 1890–91, pp. 419–20, 1891–92, pp. 351–52, 1893–94, p. 349; *Proceedings of the Annual Meeting of the Illinois State Dairymen's Association*, 1890, pp. 497–98, 1891, p. 47, 1895, p. 272; *Prairie Farmer* (Chicago), September 30 and November 13, 1893, and April 21 and August 4, 1894; *Annual Report of the Michigan State Board of Agriculture*, 1890, p. 483; *Transactions of the Michigan Dairymen's Association*, 1895, pp. 29, 34–35, 56–66, and 114, 1896, p. 16–17, 27, 28–32, 96, and 159; *Annual Report of the Ohio State Board of Agriculture*, 1893, p. 223, 1894, pp. 192–94, 1895, pp. 278–81; *Proceedings of the Annual Session of the Ohio Dairymen's Association*, 1895, p. 564; *Ohio Farmer* (Cleveland), January 2 and 23, 1886, September 14, and October 12 and 26, 1889, August 22 and 29, 1891, February 1 and 8, March 1, April 19, June 14 and 28, 1894, January 2 and 23, February 13, March 5, 1896; *Annual Report of the Wisconsin Dairymen's Association*, 1894, pp. 190–91, 1895, pp. 35 and 170–72, 1896, pp. 50–51 and 193–95; *Transactions of the Wisconsin State Agricultural Society*, 1876, p. 164, 1889, pp. 281–82, 1892, pp. 237–42, 1895, pp. 260–76, 1896, pp. 123 and 139–43; and *Hoard's Dairyman* (Fort Atkinson), January 3, 1896.

was not enough for him to "settle down to the role of the chronic grumbler." Nor should he expect solutions to be bestowed upon him by either a kindly providence or a munificent government. The remedy lay in self-help:

How long O! Lord, how long will it take the average American farmer to learn that the Lord helps those who help themselves? . . . Go out of the ruts then ye grumblers. Go to work and do your full share in trying to remedy existing evils, and until you have done that, shut up, and let us hear no more of your unmanly grumbling.[15]

It was not a *general* self-help ideology that distinguished mid-western solutions from southern and western ones, but the *specific* approaches into which that ideology channeled rural energies. If the midwestern producer was squeezed between falling prices and rising costs, the solution was "to economize," to adopt improved production techniques and thus reduce his costs. When his products sell for less than usual, the practical farmer "does not waste his vitality in trying to raise prices by grumbling about the times, but immediately turns his attention to producing an article at less cost." Even at the height of the depression, some farmers were able to make a profit. These, the opinion leaders argued, were the farmers who had adopted and adapted the "new knowledge" to the practical task of farming; the ones who had emulated, rather than castigated, businessmen and their principles and practices. If all farmers would model themselves after these, if they would follow the much-admired methods of the business world, then "every farmer can make a living, no matter how low prices are." [16]

In the Midwest, rural opinion leaders used two themes to elaborate their self-help ideology. First, businessmen were not enemies

15. The quotations are from *Ohio Farmers' Institutes*, 1890–91, p. 117; *Prairie Farmer* (Chicago), February 15, 1890; and *Journal of Proceedings, Annual Session of the Illinois State Grange*, 1889, p. 22. Also see the responses of Wisconsin farmers to a question concerning the causes of agricultural distress, in *Seventh Biennial Report of the Bureau of Labor, Census and Industrial Statistics, State of Wisconsin*, 1895–1896 (Madison, 1896), pp. 112–23.
16. Quotations are from *Wisconsin Farmers' Institutes, Session of 1889*, p. 82, and *Ohio Farmer* (Cleveland), October 1, 1896.

to be fought, but exemplars to be followed. If the captains of industry enriched themselves in "the battle of life," if the number of millionaires in the country was growing, this was not evil: "Let us put ourselves in the places of the successful individuals . . . and methinks we should have done as they have done and thought it no crime, but an honor." The farmers could learn from these men, they could learn how to be successful; they could learn the efficient, business-like principles of management and operation that they, too, had to adopt in order to "get out of the ruts worn deep by the sluggish, slow motion of our fathers." Profitable farming required the producer to adopt such methods.[17]

The necessity of conducting the farm as a business operation dovetailed with the second theme, the need for a higher level of practical education among farmers. Rural opinion leaders of all types preached the doctrine of scientific farming. The farmer who did not take advantage of the "new knowledge" emanating from the experiment stations and agricultural colleges was the *"hayseed, long-haired, backwoods clod-hopper."* If he expected to convert his farm into a practical and profitable business operation, the farmer had to "keep step with the advancing progress of the age, [or] he may as well throw up the sponge." [18]

Of course, not all midwestern farmers would have structured the same rank-ordering of the sources of their economic difficulties. Nor did they all, or even a majority, idolize businessmen and revere the test tube as deeply as the plow. There was undoubtedly considerable animosity toward local merchants and middlemen; and probably the majority of farmers ridiculed "kid-glove" farming. The opinions and attitudes expressed in the rural press, agricultural journals, Grange meetings, the conventions of agricultural societies and dairymen's associations, and the farmers' institutes were those of a much more cosmopolitanly oriented group than the average

17. The quotations are from the *Journal of Proceedings, Annual Session of the Illinois State Grange,* 1893, p. 10, and 1894, p. 18.
18. *Ibid.* 1896, p. 18, and *Transactions of the Wisconsin State Agricultural Society,* 1891, p. 229.

"hayseed." Nor was there a one-to-one relationship between these attitudes and grass-roots sentiments.

But in the midst of a severe depression such attitudes served an important function to farmers who were not of the leadership strata. Reiterated over a twenty-year period, collectively they created a climate of opinion which conditioned the political response of midwestern farmers to the "hard times" of the 1890's. The severity of the depression created a set of conditions beyond the experience of most rural producers; it created a literally unstructured situation. Atempting to impart meaning to that situation, to explain it to himself, the farmer was more likely to turn first to those ideologies which struck familiar chords. "Practical, or scientific, farming," "business-like management," "the tariff"; these were explanations whose terms and implications he could understand; these were ideologies through which his support could be mobilized.[19]

When the depression struck, and more farmers *actively* concerned themselves with seeking solutions to their problems, these ideologies channeled their discontent. It was no coincidence that the worst years of the depression, 1894–96, saw marked increases in the popularity of the farmers' institutes and in the circulation of the bulletins of the agricultural experiment stations. By 1896 experiment stations bulletins were reaching 70.0% more readers in Indiana than they had in 1892, 125.0% more in Michigan, and over 300.0% more in Wisconsin. The average attendance at sessions of the farmers' institute more than doubled in every one of the five midwestern states during each year between 1893 and 1896, and the number of institutes held also increased. While even after 1896 the "farmer constituency anxious to bring science down out

19. For useful insights see David O. Arnold and David Gold, "The Facilitation Effect of Social Environment," *Public Opinion Quarterly*, XXVIII (Fall, 1963), 513–16; James G. March and J. S. Coleman, "Group Influences and Agricultural Innovations," *American Journal of Sociology*, LXI (May, 1956), 588–94; and S. E. Asch, "Effects of Group Pressure Upon the Modification and Distortion of Judgments," in Harold Guetzkow (ed.), *Groups, Leadership and Men* (Pittsburgh, 1951), pp. 177–90.

of the skies and hitch it to the plow" was probably still only a minority, those who *actively* sought solutions to the economic difficulties during the depression were relatively more responsive to familiar ideologies than they were to one that inveighed against unfamiliar enemies and promised its chief benefits to groups that midwestern farmers saw as competitors.[20]

Bryan's free silver ideology did not elicit a cohesive and favorable response from midwestern farmers precisely because they could see in it little that was consonant with their perceptions of either the nature of their problems or what constituted feasible solutions.

Although he preached the free silver gospel with the zeal of a Methodist circuit-rider, Bryan failed to polarize the vote of the "toiling masses" in his favor. But if he was unable to realign the social bases of partisan support along class lines, he did succeed in producing considerable political movement among other categories of social groups. . . .

The voter realignment of the mid-1890's shattered a twenty-year political stalemate. The "politics of equilibrium" gave way to those of Republican dominance. Thereafter, through the first decade of the new century, the "party of McKinley" commanded the allegiance of a majority of the electorate, nationally and in the Midwest. This new Republican majority was quite different socially from that which the party had mobilized in the 1850's. This was not the party of evangelical Protestantism, not the "party of piety," but the "party of prosperity."

The voter realignment of the 1850's had produced a new structural configuration of political allegiances. Old personal and intrastate sectional loyalties were broken down. Sharing a common commitment to pietistic religious values, "reform" elements united in the support of a political party through which they could use the

20. The quotation is from Vernon Carstensen, "The Genesis of an Agricultural Experiment Station," *Agricultural History*, XXIV (January, 1960), 20; the estimates of the increase in circulation of agricultural experiment station bulletins and attendance at farmers' institutes are based on data in the annual reports of the experiment stations for the years 1892–96 and in the reports of the institutes for the same years.

power of government to impose their own canons of behavior upon the broader society. Native and immigrant pietists sublimated ethnic animosities and translated a shared religious perspective into a politically salient identification. Through united action they hoped to purge society of "ungodly" acts of behavior; they hoped to eliminate the "sins" of intemperance and Sabbath desecration and, through the agency of their public schools, to socialize the children of the "sinners" into a "righteous" value system.

But the "sinners" resisted. They condemned the fulsome zeal of the pietists and their tendency to see "sin" where there was none. Viewing their world from a much different religious perspective, the ritualists distinguished spiritual from secular activities and did not view as sinful those social customs against which the pietists inveighed. Clinging to their religious values as ardently as the pietists, they sought, through their own school system, to preserve and perpetuate them. In defense of their religious values, they mobilized for combat against the encroachments of imperialistic pietism in the ranks of the party of "personal liberty."

The conflicts between pietists and ritualists, in the 1850's and thereafter, focused on substantive issues. Not being able to convert the "sinner," the pietist would at least control him. The pietist sought to "reform" the sinner through legislative enactment. He sought government edicts, of various forms, against the "saloon power," to prevent the "desecration" of the Sabbath, and, eventually, to undermine the parochial school system. In the 1870's and 1880's, conflicts at the local and state levels over specific "reform" proposals kept alive the animosities between the two groups and reinforced the commitment of each to its chosen political vehicle of expression.

These conflicts involved much more than "policy positions" taken by groups of voters. It was not merely a specific temperance proposal, nor a particular Sunday closing law, that was at stake. It was a conflict rooted in divergent and conflicting religious perspectives. When the pietist defended temperance, he defended more than a legislative measure. Quite literally, he was defending his religious value system. When the ritualist, the "reformee," resisted, he was doing more than acknowledging his subservience to the "saloon power," he was defending and trying to preserve a sanctified set of values.

The conflict was not "unreal," not some distraction from the human actor's "real," or class, values. The contemporary human actor did not see his world as one in which economic values were somehow the ultimate and transcendent reality. Instead, he concerned himself with those matters which were an integral part of his daily life and experiences. He did not react to protracted and complex debates in "far away" Washington over the intricacies of national tariff policy. It is unlikely that he even perceived the ways in which such policies impinged upon his daily life. But he could perceive, and without the benefit of external instruction, the ways in which his religious values were relevant. He could see, also, the ways in which those values were imperiled by the onslaughts of religious groups whose values were antithetical. It was these perceptions, rooted in familiar grounds, that prompted his action.

Contemporary political leaders were not unaware of the motive impulses which underlay the structure of partisanship. They were not unaware that cultural identifications were stronger than economic ones in mobilizing voter support. Strategically, their problem was to forge a link between the activities of national and state party leaders, on the one hand, and the concerns of grass-roots voters, on the other. While they used the matter of current events as the subjects of their rhetorical appeals, they shaped the "style" component of that rhetoric to reflect their perceptions of their supporters' concern with cultural matters.

The national and regional majorities that the Republicans had mobilized in the 1850's dwindled throughout the 1870's and 1880's. But while the Democracy increased its strength somewhat, it did not emerge as the new majority party. Instead, elections became closely fought contests in which neither party commanded a majority of the electorate. The political stalemate grew from a combination of two factors. First, the Republicans suffered from the fact that those groups that were strongly Democratic were coming to cast an increasing share of the ballots. Second, the Republicans suffered from the rise of third parties, especially the Prohibitionists, who siphoned off support.

The two developments were not unrelated. As strongly Democratic groups grew in relative electoral size, some Republican political leaders saw the need to broaden their party's social base of support. This required appealing to the one Democratic group that could potentially be led to support of the Republican Party, the German Lutherans. It was not that the party sought to convert the old German Lutherans voters, but that particular leaders hoped to win support among the new generation of Lutheran voters and from those immigrants who had not shared the Know-Nothing trauma of the 1850's.

To appeal to German Lutheran voters required the Republican party to reshape its strategy. It required that the party de-emphasize those cultural factors that had alienated Lutherans voters, especially temperance and sabbatarian measures. These, however, were precisely the measures that the pietists espoused. The attempts to integrate German Lutheran voters into the party's coalition produced a sense of sociological alienation among its intensely pietistis supporters. No longer perceiving congruence between their political goals and the Republican party as a means of achieving them, these voters were susceptible to mobilization by other political organizations in which they could perceive that congruence.

The factionalism that characterized both major parties during the "era of stalemate" was largely an outgrowth of differential leadership responses to conflicting subcoalitional demands. In Ohio, the Foraker faction responded favorably to the demands of the pietists. Hayes, McKinley, and Sherman were much more concerned with adjusting the party to changing demographic realities. In Wisconsin, the pietistic faction, led by La Follette, Haugen, and Hoard, inveighed against the pragmatists with the normative epithets of "bossism" and "corruption." In Michigan, the urban-based leadership of the party contended against its pietistic rural wing.

The temporary Democratic resurgence from 1889 through 1892

was the product of another act in the half-century-long struggle
between the adherents of conflicting religious values. Ohio's
pietists saw their champion, Governor Foraker, act to enforce
Sunday-closing in Cincinnati and threaten to extend his concern
for morality to other "sinful" areas of the state. They also saw the
German Lutherans abandon the Republicans and provide the
margin of victory for a Democratic candidate in the 1889 gubernatorial election. In Wisconsin, the pietists staged an assault against
the parochial school system and earned, for their efforts, the election of a Democratic governor. In Michigan, the urban, non-
pietistic wing of the party dominated its 1890 state convention
and nominated a "wet" as its gubernatorial candidate. Capitalizing on the aroused disaffection of rural pietists, the Democrats
offered a rural "dry" and captured the state house.

Even by 1892 the Democrats had lost the major portion of
these gains. In 1894 they lost more than that. The industrial depression, which began to be felt in the late spring of 1893, dominated the elections of that and the following year. Unemployment, underemployment, and reduced wages led voters of all social groups to turn away from the party of "hard times." Though
the rate of movement away from the Democracy varied over space,
and with the degree of the group's commitment to the party, the
central tendency persisted. But this anti-Democratic movement
did not always benefit the Republicans. Frequently, Democratic
voters turned to third parties to express their dissatisfaction. In
those contexts in which the Populists were culturally neutral they
tended to benefit from this type of anti-Democratic movement. At
the same time, in some localities, the Populists garnered voting
support from the Prohibitionists. The movement of new voters
into the Populist party in 1894 did not signify the acceptance by
those voters of the Populist program and its goals. To a large number, especially to the defecting Democrats, it was simply a convenient and reasonably safe means of expressing their dissatisfaction with their own party's inability to come to terms with the
"hard times."

The Bryan–McKinley contest in 1896 did not produce a continuing movement of voter groups along the lines congruent with past partisan loyalties. It did not produce increasing levels of urban–rural tension; nor did it unite the "poor" in political opposition to the "rich." But it did produce a unique movement of voter groups and a new political alignment.

Groups that had been staunchly Democratic and had been the most resistant to the 1894 movement away from the Democracy moved toward the "party of McKinley" in 1896. Bryan's Democracy was not the old Democracy to which they had pledged their fealty for fifty years; it was a new entity, with a new leadership, crusading in the name of evangelical Protestantism for the creation of a moral society. As they had resisted the encroachments of imperialistic pietism for over fifty years, when those came in Republican dress, so they resisted them in their new attire. The Republicans could not mobilize such voters as the party of "personal liberty," but they could, and did, sublimate potentially divisive cultural concerns to a shared concern with "prosperity." The party could, and did, use its tariff ideology to mobilize a new coalition of voting groups.

Conversely, anti-Democratic groups, especially native, Norwegian, and Swedish pietists, tended to give higher levels of support to the Democracy of Bryan than they had to any Democratic candidate since the 1850's. Alienated from McKinley's brand of Republicanism, and not interested in a party that sacrificed morality to the pragmatic concern of building a winning electoral coalition, these voters turned to the new "party of morality," to the party of William Jennings Bryan.

The relative responses of these groups were not born solely of the events of 1896. They occurred against a half-century background of religious–political conflict. The partisan identifications formed as a consequence of that strife were tenaciously held commitments. Men did not take lightly their party identifications, because they did not take lightly their religious values. It was precisely because the Bryan crusade did not reactivate and reinforce that commitment among religious ritualists that these voter groups rejected his candidacy. It was precisely because they had identified with the Democracy as the party of "personal liberty," the party of negative government, that they were unresponsive to his evangelical fervor. Pietistic groups responded favorably because they, for half a century, had sought the type of moral "reformation" Bryan promised.

The realignment of the 1890's meant that the major parties faced the new century as much different social entities than the ones that had done battle since the 1850's. The Republican party was no longer a narrowly based social vehicle in the hands of evangelical crusaders. It was a functioning integrative mechanism with a much-broadened social base of support. The Democracy of Bryan was not the party of "personal liberty," but an instrument in the hands of "reformers" who aimed at the creation of a moral social order. Its leaders did not seek to come to terms with the complexities of a modern social system, but to eliminate these by sublimating them to a centuries-old morality. As the Bible contained all that was sufficient for human knowledge, so the morality it envisioned was the only solution to all social maladies.

4

Reforms and Repressions, 1900–1920

Progressives and the Issues

Social Tensions and the Origins of Progressivism

by David P. Thelen

The Progressives were expert not only at publicizing the needs of reform but at establishing a positive public image of their own activities. American historians who first dealt with the many reform movements of the early twentieth century tended to inherit and embellish the reformers' own self-portraits. Thus the notion of a unified movement of reformers, selflessly dedicated to curbing the abuses of runaway industrialism through stern regulation, while at the same time ministering to the victims of poverty and injustice, passed from reportage and memoirs into history. This favorable collective self-portrait painted the Progressives as humane fighters for the extension of American democracy against corruption and interest group politics, compassionate friends of the underprivileged, unselfish agitators for preservation of America's natural and human resources.

On most scales of historical measurement, the Progressive self-portrait has recently been toned down. Even during the 1920's and 1930's, critics pointed to the Progressives' inability to alter significantly their era's political, social, and economic patterns. Several leading liberal historians joined the attack on the Progressive self-image in the decade after World War II. George Mowry and Richard Hofstadter, in particular, took aim at the reformers' vaunted selflessness, depicting Progressives as socially distraught, psychologically anxious burghers, intent upon capturing government as an instrument with which to reverse the declining status of middle-class Americans in a society ruled by giant corporations and immigrant voting blocs. Class fears, not public interest, dictated the concerns of Progressive politics, according to Hofstadter and Mowry.

Their work heralded even more drastic historical re-evaluations (some might argue under-valuations) of America's turn-of-the-century reformers. Christopher Lasch in The New Radicalism in America, for example, viewed the reform impulse among certain leading Progressives as expressions of deep-seated psychological needs and suggested the utter failure of most twentieth-century American reformers (including that early generation) to translate their cultural grievances into successful political programs. On a different tack, Gabriel Kolko saw Progressivism even more starkly: he considered it a deliberate attempt by business and financial leaders to rationalize their economic practices and privileges through the use of regulatory agencies designed largely to fulfill the needs of giant corporations. Robert H. Wiebe and Kolko demonstrated the degree to which specific pieces of reform legislation enjoyed widespread support from segments of the business community, but Kolko held a more relentless vision of the Progressives as political puppets, manipulated by the directors of American capitalism. Wiebe's synthesis of the period, published as The Search for Order, described the ultimately unsuccessful Progressive effort to impose an orderly bureaucratic structure upon the chaotic social and economic environment in which they functioned.

Most recent studies of early twentieth-century political leadership have disclosed that Progressives and their conservative political opponents shared similar social characteristics. David P. Thelen not only demonstrates this similarity in the case of Wisconsin politicians, whether reformers or regulars, but seriously calls into question the general practice by some historians of dabbling unsystematically in such borrowings from the social sciences as "status loss." Thelen's view of Progressive origins leans heavily *on the traumatic effect of the depression of the 1890's on politicians from every class.*

❧ Recent historians have explained the origins of the Progressive movement in several ways. They have represented progressivism, in turn, as a continuation of the western and southern farmers' revolt, as a desperate attempt by the urban gentry to regain status from the new robber barons, as a thrust from the depths of slum life, and as a campaign by businessmen to prevent workers from securing political power. Behind such seemingly conflicting theories, however, rests a single assumption about the origins of progressivism: the class and status conflicts of the late nineteenth century formed the driving forces that made men become reformers. Whether viewed by the historian as a farmer, worker, urban elitist, or businessman, the progressive was motivated primarily by his social position; and each scholar has painted a compelling picture of the insecurities and tensions felt by the group that he placed in the vanguard of progressivism. Pressures and threats from other social groups drove men to espouse reform. In these class and status conflicts can be found the roots of progressivism.

How adequately does this focus on social tensions and insecurities explain the origins of progressivism? Since some of these scholars have invoked concepts from social science to support their rejection of earlier approaches, the validity and application of some of the sociological and psychological assumptions which make up the conceptual framework for the idea that social tensions impelled the progressive require analysis. Is the focus on social classes relevant to the rise of political movements like progressivism? Is it useful to rely upon a narrow, untestable, and unproved conception of motivation when other approaches are available? How much of a concrete situation does an abstract model explain?

From *The Journal of American History*, LVI (September 1969), 323–41. Reprinted by permission; most footnotes omitted.

First, theories borrowed from one discipline are not designed to encompass the data of another. In questioning the application of models from physiology and physics to psychology, the noted personality theorist George A. Kelly explained: "We are skeptical about the value of copying ready-made theories which were designed for other foci of convenience"; and he urged his fellow psychologists to resist the temptation of "poking about in the neighbors' back yards for methodological windfalls." Just as physiology and physics encompass only part of the psychologist's realm, so psychology, sociology, and political science are concerned with only part of the historian's realm.

Those historians who have borrowed the idea that social stratification explains the rise of political movements like progressivism illustrate the dangers inherent in borrowing theories from other fields. Most sociologists and political scientists now doubt the relevance of social stratification to the emergence of political movements. Reinhard Bendix, for example, maintained that "the study of social stratification, whether or not it is adumbrated by psychological analysis, is not the proper approach to an understanding of the role of cumulative political experience." In their pleas for more pluralistic approaches to political power, such political scientists as Nelson W. Polsby and Robert A. Dahl have found that social stratification is largely irrelevant to the exercise of political power. So severe were these criticisms of the assumption that social class determined political power that one sociologist, reviewing the literature of the field in 1964, concluded that "the problem has simply been dropped."

But an even greater problem with placing emphasis on social tensions is that it is ahistorical. Even sociologists like Seymour M. Lipset and Bendix have complained about the "increasingly ahistorical" drift of the focus of this field. After analyzing the major models of social change, another sociologist concluded that the fundamental error of these models was their failure to incorporate the dimension of time. Few scholars would deny that social tensions exist at all times and in all societies. For at least twenty years before 1900, various business groups had tried to take political power away from workers and bosses. But to focus on the social class motivation of businessmen is to obscure the basic historical problem of why progressivism emerged *when* it did. Conflicts between businessmen and workers were hardly unique to the years around 1900. The emphasis on social tensions obscures chronology. When sociologists are disturbed about this problem, historians should be wary indeed.

The assumption that progressivism derived from social tensions is at least as vulnerable to attack by psychologists. If the kinds of questions historians generally ask about the origins of political and social movements are reduced to the psychological level, then the theories of class and status motivation would seem to be premised on very debatable assumptions about individual motivation. Most historians would want to know the conditions that existed before a change occurred, why the change happened, and what were the results of that change.

The first problem—the conditions before a change occurred—reduces in psychological terms to the way an individual perceives himself, his self-image. Psychologists have approached this question in many ways, but a theory of change which assumes that social tensions were the basic cause implicitly accepts only one of these approaches. It assumes that an individual defines himself primarily in terms of his particular social role, that his behavior is motivated mainly by his class and status role perceptions. Only about one out of every three psychologists, however, would accept this premise to any real extent. Even some sociologists and anthropologists, who have traditionally seen individual behavior as primarily determined by culture, have retreated from that position and now see a more symmetrical interaction in which personality also influences culture. An overwhelming majority of psychologists have rejected role theory as an adequate explanation for the way an individual who enlists in a reform movement forms his self-image.

The second problem—why the change happened—reduces in

psychological terms to the mechanism by which an individual feels impelled to join a political movement like progressivism. Here again those scholars who emphasize social tensions have implicitly chosen only one of several alternatives offered by psychologists. They assume that the threat from some other social group frustrated the would-be progressive who, in turn, reacted aggressively against that threat. Very few psychologists, however, would claim that social tensions are the main source of frustration. Furthermore, individuals are generally capable of reacting to new roles without experiencing any major frustrations. The different ways in which Theodore Roosevelt and Calvin Coolidge, for example, remade the role of the presidency to fit their own personalities suggest how flexible roles can be without deeply frustrating an individual. Furthermore, different members of the same social class will perceive social challenges in different ways; many will experience no frustration at all.

Even if historians concede that social stresses can frustrate an individual, does it follow that he will react aggressively toward the source of that frustration? The frustration-produces-aggression model is one of the most debated propositions in psychology. Extreme critics have called it "nonsensical." Others have shown that frustration more often produces anxiety, submission, dependence, or avoidance than aggression. Even presumably simpleminded creatures like rats and pigeons do not necessarily react aggressively when they are frustrated. If some psychologists have shown that aggression is only one possible result of frustration, others have shown that frustration is only one possible source of aggression. Indeed, prior to 1939 most psychologists accepted Sigmund Freud's *Beyond the Pleasure Principle*, which contended that aggression derived from the Death Wish. Others have found the source of aggression in neither frustration nor the Death Wish. The assumption that social tensions will frustrate an individual and drive him to react aggressively has been riddled by the artillery of a great many psychologists. For historians to continue to assume that men react primarily to social threats is to ignore an impressive body of psychological literature.

The third problem—what were the results of that change—reduces in psychological terms to the way an individual outwardly expresses the internal change. If an individual felt angry following threats from another social group, how would he express that anger? The idea that he will sublimate his aggressive propensities into cries for political reform is one which is endorsed by many Freudians who follow *Civilization and Its Discontents*. But even some psychoanalysts claim that Freud never adequately explained sublimation. Other personality theorists have asserted that "everyone recognizes . . . that at present we have no theory which really explains the dynamics" of sublimation. Many psychologists have seen sublimation as only one possible way of expressing aggressive proclivities. Political reform is only one of hundreds of directions an individual can channel hostile impulses. But most personality theorists are so unimpressed by the concept of sublimation that they simply ignore it in their own theories.

By assuming that social tensions produced progressivism, historians have approached the basic questions about social and political movements from a very narrow psychological viewpoint. Even more important, the psychological underpinnings of this assumption are either disproved, disputed, ignored, or "untestable" by modern psychologists.

Moreover, the whole psychological framework which includes these theories has recently come under attack. Both behaviorists and psychoanalysts had previously assumed that individuals were motivated by "a state of tenseness that leads us to seek equilibrium, rest, adjustment, satisfaction, or homeostasis. From this point of view, personality is nothing more than our habitual modes of reducing tension." Men become reformers to relieve tensions, perhaps impelled by class and status anxieties. Now, however, many psychologists contend that personality theorists too long overemphasized the irrational components in motivation. As

early as 1953 Gordon Allport reported that the trend in motivational theory was away from the tension reduction approach and
toward an emphasis on the rational and healthy side of individuals. By stressing the rationality of free choice, these psychologists have argued that a commitment to reform, for example, may
in fact be the ultimate expression of a mature personality and reflect a man who is capable of getting outside of his self-preoccupa-
tion. Indeed, Erich Fromm has said that the revolutionary leader
might well be the only "sane person in an insane world." The decision to embrace progressivism may simply represent a conscious
choice between alternative programs, not an attempt to reduce
tensions which grew out of a man's efforts to maintain his social
position.

There is another problem in borrowing models: the more in-
clusive the model, the farther it is removed from the reality it is
attempting to explain. The data must be squeezed and distorted
to make them conform to the model. Many social scientists themselves have revolted against the top-heavy and abstract models
which have prevailed in their fields. One student of social stratification, for example, concluded from a review of 333 studies that
his field suffered from "the disease of overconceptualization." Similarly, many psychologists have rejected the abstract personality
constructs used to explain motivation because they are too far removed from the reality of individual people. Arguing for a focus
on the "life style" of each person, Allport has attacked theories
which emphasize "the abstract motivation of an impersonal and
therefore non-existent mind-in-general," preferring "the concrete,
viable motives of each and every mind-in-particular." In a like
vein, Kelly has argued that most psychological constructs ignore
an individual's "private domain, within which his behavior aligns
itself within its own lawful system." These abstract constructs can
only account for the individual as "an inert object wafted about
in a public domain by external forces, or as a solitary datum sitting
on its own continuum." Allport even charged that psychologists
who build universal models to explain human motivation are

seeking a "scientific will of the wisp"; the " 'irreducible unlearned motives' of men" they are seeking cannot be found because they do not exist.

This is not a critique of any particular psychological theory or approach to behavior. Rather it is a plea to be aware of the dangers in building a conceptual approach to such a problem as progressivism upon so many rickety psychological foundations. Historians should recognize that psychologists are not that different; they are at least as divided in their interpretations as we are. For historians to accept the assumptions that underlie the idea that social tensions produced progressivism would be similar to a psychologist borrowing Frederick Jackson Turner's frontier hypothesis for his research. Many of us would complain that there are other explanations for the development of American history; and a great many psychologists, in effect, are shuddering at the weak psychological underpinnings of the assumption that their social backgrounds made men become reformers.

The real test for the soundness of any approach is not theoretical, of course, but empirical. In this case the inadequacy of the sociological and psychological ideas which inform the assumption that social tensions produced progressivism becomes obvious after an examination of the types of men who became progressives and conservatives. If social tensions were relevant to the rise of progressivism, then clearly the class and status experiences of progressives should have differed in some fundamental way from those of the conservatives.

How different, in fact, were the social origins of progressives and conservatives? Following George E. Mowry's publication in 1951 of *The California Progressives*, several scholars examined the external social class attributes of progressive leaders and concluded that the reformers were drawn from the young urban gentry. But because they neglected to sample a comparable group of conservatives, these studies failed to prove their contention that class and status experiences impelled the progressives. Subsequent profiles of both progressive and conservative leaders in the election of

1912 and the legislative sessions of 1911 in Washington and 1905 in Missouri showed that both groups came from nearly the same social background. Objective measures of their social origins failed to predict the programs and ideologies of political leaders.

Scholars may not accept this finding because they question whether the 1912 campaign reflected political ideologies so much as the personalities of leaders and the desire for office. The studies of legislatures in Washington and Missouri might be questioned because in a single session such extraneous pressures as the personality of a powerful governor or the use of bribes might have interfered with a legislator's expression of his natural preferences. Furthermore, neither Washington nor Missouri was ever noted as a banner progressive state. Perhaps the issues in these states were not as hotly contested—and hence did not reveal as sharp social tensions—as in the more radical states.

The following profile of Wisconsin legislators was designed to avoid some of the possible objections to the other studies. Since contemporaries and historians alike have agreed on the pivotal position of Wisconsin, it is an ideal state to test whether social tensions were important in the development of progressivism. This sample begins with the 1897 session because it was then, for the first time, that the Progressive Republicans identified in their speeches, platforms, and votes the issues which divided them from the stalwarts, and concludes with the 1903 session, when many of their programs were enacted. The index for "progressivism" was based on votes growing out of the campaigns for a more equitable distribution of the tax burden, for regulation of quasi-public corporations, and for purification of the electoral and legislative processes. These were the issues which gave the thrust and tone to Wisconsin progressivism and served as the dividing lines between the old guard and the insurgents.

During these four sessions there were 286 roll calls on these issues. A "progressive" legislator was defined as one who voted for more than 75 per cent of the progressive measures; a "moderate" favored between 50 and 75 per cent of the progressive measures;

and a "conservative" opposed more than half of the progressive
measures. Of the 360 Republican legislators included in this profile, 40 per cent were progressives, 38 per cent were moderates, and
22 per cent were conservatives.[1]

If social conflicts were important to the emergence of progressivism, the variable which would be most likely to reveal that fact
would be the occupations of legislators. Convincing generalizations from [Table 1] would need to be based upon large statistical
differences, since the relatively small sample is divided so many
ways. Occupation clearly made little difference in a legislator's
vote on progressive measures.

Table 1

	Farmer	Merchant	Professional	Manufacturer	Financier	Worker
	%	%	%	%	%	%
Progressives	20	27	26	13	9	5
Moderates	22	24	29	6	13	6
Conservatives	12	27	32	16	10	3

The extent of a man's education helps to locate his social position. In Wisconsin neither progressives (22 per cent), moderates
(24 per cent), nor conservatives (27 per cent) were dominated by
college graduates. At a time and place where college degrees were
rare, perhaps a better measure of educational aspirations would be
the proportion of men who sought any kind of formal schooling—
high school, business college, night school—beyond the level of
the common school. Here again, however, the differences in
achievement between progressives (58 per cent), moderates (60
per cent), and conservatives (66 per cent) are insignificant.

1. The handful of Democrats, who seldom comprised over one-tenth of the
legislators, were excluded because they contributed no programs to the development of Wisconsin progressivism and because they used their meagre
numbers primarily to embarrass the conflicting Republican factions. Because
absences could be interpreted in many ways, those legislators who were absent
for more than 20 per cent of the roll calls on these issues were also excluded
from the sample.

The place of a man's birth also indicates his social background. But the nativity of Wisconsin's legislators failed to differentiate progressives from conservatives (see Table 2).

If the Wisconsin sample corresponds roughly to those of other states in the occupations, education, and nativity of political leaders, it differs from them in two other respects. Students of the 1912 election found the progressives to be considerably younger than the conservatives in both age and political experience, a fact which led them to see progressivism as a revolt of the young, would-be politicians. In Wisconsin, however, progressives and conservatives both had an average age of forty-eight, and the moderates averaged forty-six. The median ages of progressives (49),

Table 2

	Midwest	East and New England	Canada	Europe
	%	%	%	%
Progressives	47	29	6	18
Moderates	61	24	2	13
Conservatives	49	30	5	16

moderates (45), and conservatives (47) likewise fail to suggest the existence of any generational conflict between progressives and conservatives.

Nor were Wisconsin's progressives the most politically immature of the rival factions. While service in the legislature is only one measure of political experience, it does reveal the effectiveness of politicians in winning renomination from their local organizations. Although Wisconsin's conservatives had the longest tenure in the legislature, they contrasted not so much with the progressives as with the moderates. Table 3 indicates the number of previous sessions attended by legislators.

The social origins of Wisconsin legislators between 1897 and 1903 clearly suggest that no particular manner of man became a progressive. Such variables as occupation, education, nativity, age, and previous legislative experience fail to differentiate the average progressive from the average conservative. The theories that progressivism was motivated by status or class tensions felt by the urban gentry, the businessmen, the workers, the farmers, or the incipient politicians are challenged in Wisconsin by the fact that members of these groups were as likely to become conservatives as progressives. And the Wisconsin profile parallels other studies. To the extent that social class allegiance can be measured by such attributes as occupation, nativity, education, and age, social tensions were apparently irrelevant to the formation of progressivism since the "typical" progressive and conservative came from the same social background.

Table 3

	None	One	Two or more
	%	%	%
Progressives	52	28	20
Moderates	62	27	11
Conservatives	35	37	28

Collective statistical profiles can, however, obscure more than they reveal. The five more prominent early Wisconsin progressive leaders, the men who forged the issues which Robert M. La Follette subsequently adopted, were most noteworthy for their different social origins. The man contemporaries hailed as the "father of Wisconsin progressivism" was Albert R. Hall, a small dairy farmer in the western part of the state. Nephew of national Grange head Oliver Kelley, Hall was basically an agrarian radical who developed the reputation of a fearless enemy of the railroads and other large corporations. No less important was John A. Butler, the lengthened shadow of the powerful Milwaukee Municipal League. A sharper contrast to Hall could scarcely be found than this independently wealthy and highly educated Brahmin who seemed to spend more time in his villa than he did in his Milwaukee office. Milwaukee also contributed Julius E. Roehr, organized labor's leading champion in the legislature. Born in New York City—the son of German immigrants—this hardworking lawyer and dissident Republican politician would have been extremely uncomfortable with the smells of either Hall's farm or Butler's villa. James H. Stout, the most respected of the early progressives in the legislature, was born and raised in Iowa and educated at the University of Chicago. A fabulously wealthy lumber baron, Stout used his company town of Menomonie to pioneer in vocational education and in welfare benefits for his workers. The orator of these early legislative progressives was James J. McGillivray, a self-made Canadian-born architect and manufacturer who lived in Black River Falls and authored the state's antitrust acts. It would seem almost pointless to hunt for a common social "type" in these early progressives. A Brahmin man of leisure and self-made manufacturer, an agrarian radical who knew no workers and a lawyer who never lived outside a large city and was the workers' champion, young men and old men, Yankees and immigrants, these were the leaders who made common cause in Wisconsin and developed the progressive program.

The widely scattered backgrounds of the most prominent early leaders and the remarkable collective similarity between the average progressive and conservative confirm the weaknesses in the sociological and psychological framework for the assumption that progressivism was rooted in social tensions. The widespread emphasis on social tensions is unsound sociologically because it draws upon only a narrow spectrum of personality theory, and those models upon which it does draw are either unproved or unprovable. The statistical profiles from Wisconsin and elsewhere reveal empirically that the origins of progressivism cannot be found by studying the social backgrounds and tensions of progressive leaders. Remembering Kelly's injunction to avoid "poking about in the neighbors' back yards for methodological windfalls," historians must develop alternative approaches which encompass not only the realm of sociology and psychology but also that of history.

Such an alternative approach should at least restore chronology, a major casualty in the repeated emphasis on men's class and status feelings, to a more prominent position. At this point it is possible to offer a tentative explanation for the origins of progressivism when that movement is placed in the context of the chronological evolution of both industrialism and reform.

When the Progressive era is put against the backdrop of the growth of industrialism in America, the remarkable fact about that period is its relative freedom from social tensions. If conflicts between city and farm, worker and boss, younger and older generations, native-born and immigrant are more or less natural results of industrialization, then the years between the late 1890's and the early 1910's stand as a period of social peace when contrasted with either the Gilded Age or the 1920's, when those conflicts were raw and ragged. Not competition but cooperation between different social groups—ministers, businessmen, workers, farmers, social workers, doctors, and politicians—was what distinguished progressivism from such earlier reform movements as Mugwumpery, Populism, the labor movement, and civil service reform. To the extent that men and groups were motivated by tensions deriving from their class and status perceptions, they would have been unable to cooperate with men from different backgrounds. In focusing on the broadly based progressive thrust, the real question is not what drove groups apart, but what drove them together? To answer this question, progressivism must be located in the development of reform in the late nineteenth century.

The roots of progressivism reach far back into the Gilded Age. Dozens of groups and individuals in the 1880's envisioned some change that would improve society. Reformers came forward to demand civil service reform, the eight hour day, scientific agriculture, woman suffrage, enforcement of vice laws, factory inspection, nonpartisan local elections, trust-busting, wildlife conservation, tax reform, abolition of child labor, businesslike local government, regulation of railway rates, less patronizing local charity, and hundreds of other causes which would subsequently be identified with progressivism. Younger social scientists, particularly economists, were not only beginning to lambast the formalism and conservatism in their fields and to advocate the ideas which would undergird progressivism but they were also seeking to force governments to accept their ideas. Richard T. Ely's work on the Maryland Tax Commission in the mid-1880's, for example, pioneered in the application of the new economics to government and generated many of the programs which future reformers and politicians would soon adopt.

But this fertility of reform in the Gilded Age did not conceal the basic fact that individuals and groups remained fragmented. There was no common program which could rally all groups, and the general prosperity tended to reassure people that industrialism might cure its own ills. As late as 1892 one editor, reflecting this optimistic frame of mind, could state that "the rich are growing richer, some of them, and the poor are growing richer, all of them." Men and groups seeking major changes, whether elitists or Populists, were generally stereotyped as cranks who were blind to the vast blessings and bright future of industrialism. Circumscribed by such problems and attitudes reformers were understandably fragmented in the Gilded Age.

The catastrophic depression of 1893–1897 radically altered this pattern of reform. It vividly dramatized the failures of industrialism. The widening chasm between the rich and the poor, which a few observers had earlier called a natural result of industrialism, could no longer be ignored. As several tattered bands of men known as Coxey's Army tramped from town to town in 1894, they drew attention to the plight of the millions of unemployed and vividly portrayed the striking contrasts between the way of life of the poor and the "conspicuous consumption" of the rich. Furthermore, as Thorstein Veblen observed, they showed that large numbers of Americans no longer cherished the old gospel of self-help, the very basis for mobility in a democratic society. As desperation mounted, businessmen and politicians tried the traditional ways of reversing the business cycle, but by 1895 they realized that the time-honored formulas of the tariff and the currency simply could not dispel the dark pall that hung over the land. Worse still, President Grover Cleveland seemed utterly incapable of comprehending, let alone relieving, the national crisis.

The collapse of prosperity and the failure of national partisan politicians to alleviate the crisis by the traditional methods generated an atmosphere of restless and profound questioning which few could escape. "On every corner stands a man whose fortune in these dull times has made him an ugly critic of everything and everybody," wrote one editor. A state university president warned his graduates in 1894 that "you will see everywhere in the country symptoms of social and political discontent. You will observe that these disquietudes do not result from the questions that arise in the ordinary course of political discussion . . . but that they spring out of questions that are connected with the very foundations of society and have to do with some of the most elemental principles of human liberty and modern civilization." Was the American dream of economic democracy and mobility impossible in an industrial society? Would the poor overthrow an unresponsive political and economic system? Such questions urgently demanded answers, and it was no longer either wise or safe to summarily dismiss as a crank anyone who had an answer. "The time is at hand," cried one editor, "when some of the great problems which the Nineteenth century civilization has encountered are crying for a solution. . . . Never before in the history of the world were people so willing to accept true teaching on any of these subjects and give to them a just and practical trial." A man's social origins were now less important than his proposals, and many men began to cooperate with people from different backgrounds to devise and implement solutions.

This depression-inspired search for answers sprouted hundreds of discussion groups at which men met, regardless of background, to propose remedies. These groups gave men the habit of ignoring previously firm class lines in the face of the national crisis. When Victor Berger urged the Milwaukee Liberal Club to adopt socialism as the answer, for example, his audience included wealthy

bankers, merchants, and lawyers. In the same city, at the Church
and Labor Social Union, banker John Johnston urged a "new
society" where "class privileges will be abolished because all will
belong to the human family," and the discussion was joined by
Populists and Socialists as well as clergymen and conservative editors. In this context, too, all types of people sought the wisdom
of the men who had made a career of studying the social and economic breakdown. No one was surprised when unions, Granges,
women's clubs, and other groups wanted University of Wisconsin
economists like Ely to address them. Maybe they had an answer.
The social unrest accompanying the depression weakened class
and status allegiances.

The direct political effects of the depression also broke down
the previous rigidity and fragmentation of reform. The depression
created a clear sense of priorities among the many causes which
Gilded Age reformers had advocated. It generated broadly based
new issues which all classes could unite behind. One such program
was the urgent necessity for tax reform. When the depression
struck, individuals and corporations were forced to devise ways of
economizing as property values, sales, and revenues declined pre-
cipitously. Caught between higher taxes to cover the rising costs
of local government and their own diminishing revenues, many
wealthy individuals and corporations began to hide their personal
assets from the assessors, to lobby tax relief through local governments, and even to refuse to pay any taxes. The progressive program was forged and received widespread popular support as a
response to these economies. Citizens who lacked the economic or
political resources to dodge their taxes mounted such a crusade
against these tax dodgers that former President Benjamin Harrison
warned the wealthiest leaders that unless they stopped concealing
their true wealth from the tax assessors they could expect a revolution led by enraged taxpayers. The programs for tax reform—
including inheritance, income, and ad valorem corporation taxes—
varied from place to place, but the important fact was that most
citizens had developed specific programs for tax reform and had

now agreed that certain individuals and corporations had evaded a primary responsibility of citizenship.

A second major area which proved capable of uniting men of different backgrounds was "corporate arrogance." Facing declining revenues, many corporations adopted economies which ranged from raising fares and rates to lobbying all manner of relief measures through city and state governments. Even more important, perhaps, they could not afford necessary improvements which elementary considerations of safety and health had led local governments to demand that they adopt. Corporate arrogance was no longer a doctrinaire cry of reformers. Now it was an unprotected railway crossing where children were killed as they came home from school or the refusal of an impoverished water company to make improvements needed to provide the healthful water which could stop the epidemics of typhoid fever. Such incidents made the corporation look like a killer. These specific threats united all classes: anyone's child might be careless at a railroad crossing, and typhoid fever was no respector of social origins.

From such new, direct, and immediate threats progressivism developed its thrust. The more corporations used their political influence to resist making the small improvements, the more communities developed increasingly radical economic programs like municipal ownership or consumer-owned utilities and fought to overthrow the machines that gave immunity to the corporations. Political reforms like the initiative, direct primary, and home rule became increasingly important in the early stages of progressivism because, as William Allen White said, men had first to get the gun before they could hit anything with it. But it was the failure of the political system to respond to the new and immediate threats of the depression that convinced people that more desperate programs were needed.

Perhaps there are, after all, times and places where issues cut across class lines. These are the times and places where men identify less with their occupational roles as producers and more with their roles as consumers—of death-dealing water, unsafe railway

crossings, polluted air, high streetcar rates, corrupt politicians—
which serve to unite them across social barriers. There are also
universal emotions—anger and fear—which possess all men regardless of their backgrounds. The importance of the depression of the
1890's was that it aroused those universal emotions, posed dramatic and desperate enough threats to lead men of all types to
agree that tax dodging and corporate arrogance had to be ended
and thereby served to unite many previously fragmented reformers
and to enlist the support of the majority that had earlier been
either silent or enthusiastic only about partisan issues like the tariff
or symbols like Abraham Lincoln. The conversion of the National
Municipal League showed how issues were becoming more important than backgrounds. Originally composed of elitists who favored such Mugwumpish concerns as civil service reform, the
League by 1898 had become so desperate with the domination
over political machines by utility companies that it devoted its
energies to municipal ownership and to political devices which
promised "more trust in the people, more democracy" than its
earlier elitism had permitted. The attitude of moral indignation,
such an obvious feature of the early stages of progressivism, was
not rooted in social tensions but in the universal emotion of anger.

Whether this emphasis on the results of the depression—unrest,
new threats and new issues, and cooperation among social groups
—has widespread relevance or validity remains to be seen, but it
does help to explain the roots of progressivism in Wisconsin. The
most important factor in producing the intensity of Wisconsin
progressivism was the cooperation between previously discrete and
fragmented social groups both in forging popular issues and getting reforms adopted. And the most important factor in defining
the popular issues was the arrogance of certain corporations. In
Milwaukee the traction and electricity monopoly between 1894
and 1896 alone, for reasons ranging from extreme overcapitaliza-
tion to confidence in its political powers, raised both its lighting
and streetcar fares, refused to arbitrate with its striking employees,

enjoined the city from enforcing ordinances lowering its fares, and used its political power—the company's chief manager was the state's leading Republican boss—to cut its tax bill in half, kill an ordinance which would have prevented it from polluting the air, and thwart generally popular attempts at regulation. Each time the monopoly refused to obey an order, lobbied special favors from the city or state, or prostituted the Republican party to the company, the progressive coalition grew. By the end of the depression, the coalition drew together both ends of the economic spectrum— the Merchants and Manufacturers Association and the Chamber of Commerce as well as several labor unions and the Federated Trades Council. Politically it included the country Republican Club, the Democratic Jefferson Club, and the Socialists and Populists. The Mugwumpish and upper-class Municipal League was joined by German social clubs like the Turnvereine. So defiant was the company—so desperate were the people—that the traction managers became the state's most hated men by 1899; and humorist-politician George Peck observed that Wisconsin's parents "frighten children when they are bad, by telling them that if they don't look out," the traction magnates "will get them." Four hundred miles away, in Superior, the story was remarkably similar. Angered by the repeated refusals of that city's water company to provide the city with healthful enough water to prevent the typhoid fever epidemics that killed dozens of people each year, and blaming the company's political power within both parties for the failure of regulation, labor unions and Populists cooperated with business and professional men and with dissident politicians to try to secure pure water and to overthrow the politicians owned by the company. In Superior, political debate had indeed narrowed, as an editor observed, to a fight of "the people against corporate insolence." The water company, like the traction monopoly at Milwaukee, stood isolated and alone, the enemy of men from all backgrounds. In Wisconsin, at least, the community's groups continued to perform their special functions; and, by the

end of the depression, they were all agreed that corporate arrogance had to be abolished. Their desperation made them willing
to speak, lobby, and work together.

If, as the Wisconsin experience suggests, cooperation was the
underpinning of progressivism, historians should focus on reformers not as victims of social tensions, but as reformers. At any given
time and place, hundreds of men and groups are seeking supporters for their plans to change society and government. The
basic problem for the reformer is to win mass support for his
program. In Wisconsin a reformer's effectiveness depended on
how well he manipulated acts of corporate and individual arrogance that infuriated everyone in order to demonstrate the plausibility of his program. Desperate events had made tax dodging, corporate defiance and control of politics the main political issues
and had allowed this program to swallow the older reformers at
the same time that they created a much broader constituency for
reform. The question then becomes: Why did some succeed while
others failed? North Dakota never developed a full-blown progressive movement because that state's progressives never demonstrated the plausibility of their programs. Wisconsin's early progressives did succeed in drawing together such diverse groups as
unions, businessmen, Populists, and dissident politicians because
they adapted their program and rhetoric to the menacing events
which angered everyone. Reformers operate in their hometowns
and not in some contrived social background which could as easily
apply to New York or Keokuk, and it is in their hometowns that
they should be studied. Historians should determine why they
succeeded or failed to rally the support of their communities to
their programs, for the most significant criterion for any reformer
is, in the end, his effectiveness.

When the progressive characteristically spoke of reform as a
fight of "the people" or the "public interest" against the "selfish
interests," he was speaking quite literally of his political coalition
because the important fact about progressivism, at least in Wisconsin, was the degree of cooperation between previously discrete

social groups now united under the banner of the "public interest." When the progressive politician denounced the arrogance of quasi-public corporations and tax-dodgers, he knew that experiences and events had made his attacks popular with voters from all backgrounds. Both conceptually and empirically it would seem safer and more productive to view reformers first as reformers and only secondarily as men who were trying to relieve class and status anxieties. The basic riddle in progressivism is not what drove groups apart, but what made them seek common cause.

City Fathers and Reform

The Politics of Reform in Municipal Government

by Samuel P. Hays

In a second selection that manages to incorporate many of the recent critical perspectives on Progressive reform, Samuel P. Hays shows how the Mowry-Hofstadter "status loss" interpretation founders badly when applied to municipal reformers. Further, Hays, studying municipal reform in the early twentieth century, questions whether Progressive agitation at the local level can be understood in moral terms (as many contemporaries did), as a conflict between altruistic reformers and corrupt machine bosses.

Hays also challenges the more recent view that Progressives, concerned with a loss in status, tried to gain control of government at every level in order to regulate the corporations which had come to dominate levers of prestige and power in America. He finds little evidence that the municipal reform movement represented an effort to reassert democratic control of the cities against the tyrannical combination of machine bosses and corporations described by muckrakers such as Lincoln Steffens. Rather, Hays discovers the major sources of support for municipal reform among precisely those professional and business groups which composed a city's upper-class elite, men determined to gain control of city politics to further their own class interests. These groups, according to Hays, became attracted to the idea of efficient, nonpartisan municipal government as their best vehicle for winning and retaining power.

✿ In order to achieve a more complete understanding of social change in the Progressive Era, historians must now undertake a deeper analysis of the practices of economic, political, and social groups. Political ideology alone is no longer satisfactory evidence to describe social patterns because generalizations based upon it, which tend to divide political groups into the moral and immoral, the rational and the irrational, the efficient and the inefficient, do not square with political practice. Behind this contemporary rhetoric concerning the nature of reform lay patterns of political behavior which were at variance with it. Since an extensive gap separated ideology and practice, we can no longer take the former as an accurate description of the latter, but must reconstruct social behavior from other types of evidence.

Reform in urban government provides one of the most striking examples of this problem of analysis. The demand for change in municipal affairs, whether in terms of over-all reform, such as the commission and city-manager plans, or of more piecemeal modifications, such as the development of city-wide school boards, deeply involved reform ideology. Reformers loudly proclaimed a new structure of municipal government as more moral, more rational, and more efficient and, because it was so, self-evidently more desirable. But precisely because of this emphasis, there seemed to be no need to analyze the political forces behind change. Because the goals of reform were good, its causes were obvious; rather than being the product of particular people and particular ideas in particular situations, they were deeply imbedded in the universal impulses and truths of "progress." Consequently, historians have rarely tried to determine precisely who the municipal

From *The Pacific Northwest Quarterly*, LV (October 1964), 157–69. Reprinted by permission; footnotes omitted.

reformers were or what they did, but instead have relied on reform ideology as an accurate description of reform practice.

The reform ideology which became the basis of historical analysis is well known. It appears in classic form in Lincoln Steffens' *Shame of the Cities*. The urban political struggle of the Progressive era, so the argument goes, involved a conflict between public impulses for "good government" against a corrupt alliance of "machine politicians" and "special interests."

During the rapid urbanization of the late nineteenth century, the latter had been free to aggrandize themselves, especially through franchise grants, at the expense of the public. Their power lay primarily in their ability to manipulate the political process, by bribery and corruption, for their own ends. Against such arrangements there gradually arose a public protest, a demand by the public for honest government, for officials who would act for the public rather than for themselves. To accomplish their goals, reformers sought basic modifications in the political system, both in the structure of government and in the manner of selecting public officials. These changes, successful in city after city, enabled the "public interest" to triumph.

Recently, George Mowry, Alfred Chandler, Jr., and Richard Hofstadter have modified this analysis by emphasizing the fact that the impulse for reform did not come from the working class. This might have been suspected from the rather strained efforts of National Municipal League writers in the "Era of Reform" to go out of their way to demonstrate working-class support for commission and city-manager governments. We now know that they clutched at straws, and often erroneously, in order to prove to themselves as well as to the public that municipal reform was a mass movement.

The Mowry–Chandler–Hofstadter writings have further modified older views by asserting that reform in general and municipal reform in particular sprang from a distinctively middle-class movement. This has now become the prevailing view. Its popularity is surprising not only because it is based upon faulty logic and extremely limited evidence, but also because it, too, emphasizes the analysis of ideology rather than practice and fails to contribute much to the understanding of who distinctively were involved in reform and why.

Ostensibly, the "middle-class" theory of reform is based upon a new type of behavioral evidence, the collective biography, in studies by Mowry of California Progressive party leaders, by Chandler of a nationwide group of that party's leading figures, and by Hofstadter of four professions—ministers, lawyers, teachers, editors. These studies demonstrate the middle-class nature of reform, but they fail to determine if reformers were distinctively middle class, specifically if they differed from their opponents. One study of 300 political leaders in the state of Iowa, for example, discovered that Progressive party, Old Guard, and Cummins Republicans were all substantially alike, the Progressives differing only in that they were slightly younger than the others and had less political experience. If its opponents were also middle class, then one cannot describe Progressive reform as a phenomenon, the special nature of which can be explained in terms of middle-class characteristics. One cannot explain the distinctive behavior of people in terms of characterisics which are not distinctive to them.

Hofstadter's evidence concerning professional men fails in yet another way to determine the peculiar characteristics of reformers. For he describes ministers, lawyers, teachers, and editors without determining who within these professions became reformers and who did not. Two analytical distinctions might be made. Ministers involved in municipal reform, it appears, came not from all segments of religion, but peculiarly from upper-class churches. They enjoyed the highest prestige and salaries in the religious community and had no reason to feel a loss of "status," as Hofstadter argues. Their role in reform arose from the class character of their religious organizations rather than from the mere fact of their occupation as ministers. Professional men involved in reform (many of them—engineers, architects, and doctors—Hofstadter did not examine at all) seem to have come especially from the more advanced segments of their professions, from those who sought to apply their specialized knowledge to a wider range of public affairs. Their role in reform is related not to their attempt to defend earlier patterns of culture, but to the working out of the inner dynamics of professionalization in modern society.

The weakness of the "middle-class" theory of reform stems from the fact that it rests primarily upon ideological evidence, not on a thoroughgoing description of political practice. Although the studies of Mowry, Chandler, and Hofstadter ostensibly derive from behavioral evidence, they actually derive largely from the extensive expressions of middle-ground ideological position, of the reformers' own descriptions of their contemporary society, and of their expressed fears of both the lower and the upper classes, of the fright of being ground between the millstones of labor and capital.

Such evidence, though it accurately portrays what people thought, does not accurately describe what they did. The great majority of Americans look upon themselves as "middle class" and subscribe to a middle-ground ideology, even though in practice they belong to a great variety of distinct social classes. Such ideologies are not rationalizations or deliberate attempts to deceive. They are natural phenomena of human behavior. But the historian should be especially sensitive to their role so that he will not take evidence of political ideology as an accurate representation of political practice.

In the following account I will summarize evidence in both secondary and primary works concerning the political practices in which municipal reformers were involved. Such an analysis logically can be broken down into three parts, each one corresponding to a step in the traditional argument. First, what was the source of reform? Did it lie in the general public rather than in particular groups? Was it middle class, working class, or perhaps of other composition? Second, what was the reform target of attack? Were reformers primarily interested in ousting the corrupt individual, the political or business leader who made private arrangements at the expense of the public, or were they interested in something else? Third, what political innovations did reformers bring about? Did they seek to expand popular participation in the governmental process?

There is now sufficient evidence to determine the validity of these specific elements of the more general argument. Some of it has been available for several decades; some has appeared more recently; some is presented here for the first time. All of it adds up to the conclusion that reform in municipal government involved a political development far different from what we have assumed in the past.

Available evidence indicates that the source of support for reform in municipal government did not come from the lower or middle classes, but from the upper class. The leading business groups in each city and professional men closely allied with them initiated and dominated municipal movements. Leonard White, in his study of the city manager published in 1927, wrote:

The opposition to bad government usually comes to a head in the local chamber of commerce. Business men finally acquire the conviction that the growth of their city is being seriously impaired by the failures of city officials to perform their duties efficiently. Looking about for a remedy, they are captivated by the resemblance of the city-manager plan to their corporate form of business organization.

In the 1930's White directed a number of studies of the origin of city-manager government. The resulting reports invariably begin with such statements as, "the Chamber of Commerce spearheaded the movement," or commission government in this city was a "businessmen's government." Of thirty-two cases of city-manager government in Oklahoma examined by Jewell C. Phillips, twenty-nine were initiated either by chambers of commerce or by community committees dominated by businessmen. More recently James Weinstein has presented almost irrefutable evidence that the business community, represented largely by chambers of commerce, was the overwhelming force behind both commission and city-manager movements.

Dominant elements of the business community played a prominent role in another crucial aspect of municipal reform: the Municipal Research Bureau movement. Especially in the larger cities, where they had less success in shaping the structure of government, reformers established centers to conduct research in municipal affairs as a springboard for influence.

The first such organization, the Bureau of Municipal Research of New York City, was founded in 1906; it was financed largely through the efforts of Andrew Carnegie and John D. Rockefeller. An investment banker provided the crucial support in Philadelphia, where a Bureau was founded in 1908. A group of wealthy Chicagoans in 1910 established the Bureau of Public Efficiency, a research agency. John H. Patterson of the National Cash Register Company, the leading figure in Dayton municipal reform, financed the Dayton Bureau, founded in 1912. And George Eastman was the driving force behind both the Bureau of Municipal Research and city-manager government in Rochester. In smaller cities data about city government was collected by interested individuals in a more informal way or by chambers of commerce, but in larger cities the task required special support, and prominent businessmen supplied it.

The character of municipal reform is demonstrated more precisely by a brief examination of the movements in Des Moines and Pittsburgh. The Des Moines Commercial Club inaugurated and carefully controlled the drive for the commission form of government. In January, 1906, the Club held a so-called "mass meeting" of business and professional men to secure an enabling act from the state legislature. P. C. Kenyon, president of the Club, selected a Committee of 300, composed principally of business and professional men, to draw up a specific proposal. After the legislature approved their plan, the same committee managed the campaign which persuaded the electorate to accept the commission form of government by a narrow margin in June, 1907.

In this election the lower-income wards of the city opposed the change, the upper-income wards supported it strongly, and the middle-income wards were more evenly divided. In order to control the new government, the Committee of 300, now expanded to 530, sought to determine the nomination and election of the five new commissioners, and to this end they selected an avowedly businessman's slate. Their plans backfired when the voters swept into office a slate of anticommission candidates who now controlled the new commission government.

Proponents of the commission form of government in Des Moines spoke frequently in the name of the "people." But their more explicit statements emphasized their intent that the new plan be a "business system" of government, run by businessmen. The slate of candidates for commissioner endorsed by advocates of the plan was known as the "businessman's ticket." J. W. Hill, president of the committees of 300 and 530, bluntly declared: "The professional politician must be ousted and in his place capable business men chosen to conduct the affairs of the city." I. M. Earle, general counsel of the Bankers Life Association and a prominent figure in the movement, put the point more precisely: "When the plan was adopted it was the intention to get businessmen to run it."

Although reformers used the ideology of popular government, they in no sense meant that all segments of society should be involved equally in municipal decision-making. They meant that their concept of the city's welfare would be best achieved if the business community controlled city government. As one businessman told a labor audience, the businessman's slate represented labor "better than you do yourself."

The composition of the municipal reform movement in Pittsburgh demonstrates its upper-class and professional as well as its business sources. Here the two principal reform organizations were the Civic Club and the Voters' League. The 745 members of these two organizations came primarily from the upper class. Sixty-five per cent appeared in upper-class directories which contained the names of only 2 per cent of the city's families. Furthermore, many who were not listed in these directories lived in upper-class areas. These reformers, it should be stressed, comprised not an old but a new upper class. Few came from earlier industrial and mercantile families. Most of them had risen to social position from wealth created after 1870 in the iron, steel, electrical equipment, and other industries, and they lived in the newer rather than the older fashionable areas.

Almost half (48 per cent) of the reformers were professional men: doctors, lawyers, ministers, directors of libraries and museums, engineers, architects, private and public school teachers, and college professors. Some of these belonged to the upper class as well, especially the lawyers, ministers, and private school teachers. But for the most part their interest in reform stemmed from the inherent dynamics of their professions rather than from their class connections. They came from the more advanced segments of their organizations, from those in the forefront of the acquisition and application of knowledge. They were not the older professional men, seeking to preserve the past against change; they were in the vanguard of professional life, actively seeking to apply expertise more widely to public affairs.

Pittsburgh reformers included a large segment of businessmen; 52 per cent were bankers and corporation officials or their wives. Among them were the presidents of fourteen large banks and officials of Westinghouse, Pittsburgh Plate Glass, U.S. Steel and its component parts (such as Carnegie Steel, American Bridge, and National Tube), Jones and Laughlin, lesser steel companies (such as Crucible, Pittsburgh, Superior, Lockhart, and H. K. Porter), and H. J. Heinz Company, and the Pittsburgh Coal Company, as well as officials of the Pennsylvania Railroad and the Pittsburgh and Lake Erie. These men were not small businessmen; they directed the most powerful

banking and industrial organizations of the city. They represented not the old business community, but industries which
had developed and grown primarily within the past fifty years
and which had come to dominate the city's economic life.

These business, professional, and upper-class groups who dominated municipal reform movements were all involved in the rationalization and systematization of modern life; they wished a
form of government which would be more consistent with the
objectives inherent in those developments. The most important
single feature of their perspective was the rapid expansion of
the geographical scope of affairs which they wished to influence
and manipulate, a scope which was no longer limited and narrow, no longer within the confines of pedestrian communities,
but was now broad and city-wide, covering the whole range of
activities of the metropolitan area.

The migration of the upper class from central to outlying
areas created a geographical distance between its residential communities and its economic institutions. To protect the latter required involvement both in local ward affairs and in the larger
city government as well. Moreover, upper-class cultural institutions, such as museums, libraries, and symphony orchestras, required an active interest in the larger municipal context from
which these institutions drew much of their clientele.

Professional groups, broadening the scope of affairs which they
sought to study, measure, or manipulate, also sought to influence the public health, the educational system, or the physical
arrangements of the entire city. Their concerns were limitless,
not bounded by geography, but as expansive as the professional
imagination. Finally, the new industrial community greatly
broadened its perspective in governmental affairs because of its
new recognition of the way in which factors throughout the city
affected business growth. The increasing size and scope of industry, the greater stake in more varied and geographically dispersed facets of city life, the effect of floods on many business
concerns, the need to promote traffic flows to and from work

for both blue-collar and managerial employees—all contributed
to this larger interest. The geographically larger private perspectives of upper-class, professional, and business groups gave rise
to a geographically larger public perspective.

These reformers were dissatisfied with existing systems of municipal government. They did not oppose corruption per se—
although there was plenty of that. They objected to the structure of government which enabled local and particularistic interests to dominate. Prior to the reforms of the Progressive Era,
city government consisted primarily of confederations of local
wards, each of which was represented on the city's legislative
body. Each ward frequently had its own elementary schools and
ward-elected school boards which administered them.

These particularistic interests were the focus of a decentralized political life. City councilmen were local leaders. They
spoke for their local areas, the economic interests of their inhabitants, their residential concerns, their educational, recrea-
tional, and religious interests—i.e., for those aspects of community life which mattered most to those they represented.
They rolled logs in the city council to provide streets, sewers,
and other public works for their local areas. They defended the
community's cultural practices, its distinctive languages or national customs, its liberal attitude toward liquor, and its saloons
and dance halls which served as centers of community life. One
observer described this process of representation in Seattle:

The residents of the hill-tops and the suburbs may not fully appreciate
the faithfulness of certain downtown ward councilmen to the interests of their constituents. . . . The people of a state would rise in
arms against a senator or representative in Congress who deliberately
misrepresented their wishes and imperilled their interests, though he
might plead a higher regard for national good. Yet people in other
parts of the city seem to forget that under the old system the ward
elected councilmen with the idea of procuring service of special benefit
to that ward.

In short, pre-reform officials spoke for their constituencies, inevitably their own wards which had elected them, rather than for other sections or groups of the city.

The ward system of government especially gave representation in city affairs to lower- and middle-class groups. Most elected ward officials were from these groups, and they, in turn, constituted the major opposition to reforms in municipal government. In Pittsburgh, for example, immediately prior to the changes in both the city council and the school board in 1911 in which city-wide representation replaced ward representation, only 24 per cent of the 387 members of those bodies represented the same managerial, professional, and banker occupations which dominated the membership of the Civic Club and the Voters' League. The great majority (67 per cent) were small businessmen—grocers, saloonkeepers, livery-stable proprietors, owners of small hotels, druggists—white-collar workers such as clerks and bookkeepers, and skilled and unskilled workmen.

This decentralized system of urban growth and the institutions which arose from it reformers now opposed. Social, professional, and economic life had developed not only in the local wards in a small community context, but also on a larger scale had become highly integrated and organized, giving rise to a superstructure of social organization which lay far above that of ward life and which was sharply divorced from it in both personal contacts and perspective.

By the late nineteenth century, those involved in these larger institutions found that the decentralized system of political life limited their larger objectives. The movement for reform in municipal government, therefore, constituted an attempt by upper-class, advanced professional, and large business groups to take formal political power from the previously dominant lower- and middle-class elements so that they might advance their own conceptions of desirable public policy. These two groups came from entirely different urban worlds, and the political system fashioned by one was no longer acceptable to the other.

Lower- and middle-class groups not only dominated the pre-reform governments, but vigorously opposed reform. It is significant that none of the occupational groups among them, for example, small businessmen or white-collar workers, skilled or unskilled artisans, had important representation in reform organizations thus far examined. The case studies of city-manager government undertaken in the 1930's under the direction of Leonard White detailed in city after city the particular opposition of labor. In their analysis of Jackson, Michigan, the authors of these studies wrote:

The *Square Deal*, oldest Labor paper in the state, has been consistently against manager government, perhaps largely because labor has felt that with a decentralized government elected on a ward basis it was more likely to have some voice and to receive its share of privileges.

In Janesville, Wisconsin, the small shopkeepers and working-men on the west and south sides, heavily Catholic and often Irish, opposed the commission plan in 1911 and in 1912 and the city-manager plan when adopted in 1923. "In Dallas there is hardly a trace of class consciousness in the Marxian sense," one investigator declared, "yet in city elections the division has been to a great extent along class lines." The commission and city-manager elections were no exceptions. To these authors it seemed a logical reaction, rather than an embarrassing fact that had to be swept away, that workingmen should have opposed municipal reform.

In Des Moines working-class representatives, who in previous years might have been council members, were conspicuously absent from the "businessman's slate." Workingmen acceptable to reformers could not be found. A workingman's slate of candidates, therefore, appeared to challenge the reform slate. Organized labor, and especially the mineworkers, took the lead; one of their number, Wesley Ash, a deputy sheriff and union member, made "an astonishing run" in the primary, coming in second among a field of more than twenty candidates. In fact, the strength of anticommission candidates in the primary so alarmed reformers that they frantically sought to appease labor.

The day before the final election they modified their platform to pledge both an eight-hour day and an "American standard of wages." They attempted to persuade the voters that their slate consisted of men who represented labor because they had "begun at the bottom of the ladder and made a good climb toward success by their own unaided efforts." But their tactics failed. In the election on March 30, 1908, voters swept into office the entire "opposition" slate. The business and professional community had succeeded in changing the form of government, but not in securing its control. A cartoon in the leading reform newspaper illustrated their disappointment; John Q. Public sat dejectedly and muttered, "Aw, What's the Use?"

The most visible opposition to reform and the most readily available target of reform attack was the so-called "machine," for through the "machine" many different ward communities as well as lower- and middle-income groups joined effectively to influence the central city government. Their private occupational and social life did not naturally involve these groups in larger city-wide activities in the same way as the upper class was involved; hence they lacked access to privately organized economic and social power on which they could construct political power. The "machine" filled this organizational gap.

Yet it should never be forgotten that the social and economic institutions in the wards themselves provided the "machine's" sustaining support and gave it larger significance. When reformers attacked the "machine" as the most visible institutional element of the ward system, they attacked the entire ward form of political organization and the political power of lower- and middle-income groups which lay behind it.

Reformers often gave the impression that they opposed merely the corrupt politician and his "machine." But in a more fundamental way they looked upon the deficiencies of pre-reform political leaders in terms not of their personal shortcomings, but of the limitations inherent in their occupational, institutional, and class positions. In 1911 the Voters' League of Pittsburgh wrote in its pamphlet analyzing the qualifications of candidates that "a man's occupation ought to give a strong indication of his qualifications for membership on a school board." Certain occupations inherently disqualified a man from serving:

Employment as ordinary laborer and in the lowest class of mill work would naturally lead to the conclusion that such men did not have sufficient education or business training to act as school directors. . . . Objection might also be made to small shopkeepers, clerks, workmen at many trades, who by lack of educational advantages and business training, could not, no matter how honest, be expected to administer properly the affairs of an educational system, requiring special knowledge, and where millions are spent each year.

These, of course, were precisely the groups which did dominate Pittsburgh government prior to reform. The League deplored the fact that school boards contained only a small number of "men prominent throughout the city in business life . . . in professional occupations . . . holding positions as managers, secretaries, auditors, superintendents and foremen" and exhorted these classes to participate more actively as candidates for office.

Reformers, therefore, wished not simply to replace bad men with good; they proposed to change the occupational and class origins of decision-makers. Toward this end they sought innovations in the formal machinery of government which would concentrate political power by sharply centralizing the processes of decision-making rather than distribute it through more popular participation in public affairs. According to the liberal view of the Progressive Era, the major political innovations of reform involved the equalization of political power through the primary, the direct election of public officials, and the initiative, referendum, and recall. These measures played a large role in the political ideology of the time and were frequently incorporated into new municipal charters. But they provided at best only an occasional and often incidental process of decision-making. Far more important in continuous, sustained, day-to-day processes of government were those innovations which centralized decision-making in the hands of fewer and fewer people.

The systematization of municipal government took place on both the executive and the legislative levels. The strong-mayor and city-manager types became the most widely used examples of the former. In the first decade of the twentieth century, the commission plan had considerable appeal, but its distribution of administrative responsibility among five people gave rise to a demand for a form with more centralized executive power; consequently, the city-manager or the commission-manager variant often replaced it.

A far more pervasive and significant change, however, lay in the centralization of the system of representation, the shift from ward to city-wide election of councils and school boards. Governing bodies so selected, reformers argued, would give less attention to local and particularistic matters and more to affairs of city-wide scope. This shift, an invariable feature of both commission and city-manager plans, was often adopted by itself. In Pittsburgh, for example, the new charter of 1911 provided as the major innovation that a council of twenty-seven, each member elected from a separate ward, be replaced by a council of nine, each elected by the city as a whole.

Cities displayed wide variations in this innovation. Some regrouped wards into larger units but kept the principle of areas of representation smaller than the entire city. Some combined a majority of councilmen elected by wards with additional ones elected at large. All such innovations, however, constituted steps toward the centralization of the system of representation.

Liberal historians have not appreciated the extent to which municipal reform in the Progressive Era involved a debate over the system of representation. The ward form of representation was universally condemned on the grounds that it gave too much influence to the separate units and not enough attention to the larger problems of the city. Harry A. Toulmin, whose book, *The City Manager*, was published by the National Municipal League, stated the case:

The spirit of sectionalism had dominated the political life of every city. Ward pitted against ward, alderman against alderman, and legislation only effected by "log-rolling" extravagant measures into operation, mulcting the city, but gratifying the greed of constituents, has too long stung the conscience of decent citizenship. This constant treaty-making of factionalism has been no less than a curse. The city manager plan proposes the commendable thing of abolishing wards. The plan is not unique in this for it has been common to many forms of commission government. . . .

Such a system should be supplanted, the argument usually went, with city-wide representation in which elected officials could consider the city "as a unit." "The new officers are elected," wrote Toulmin, "each to represent all the people. Their duties are so defined that they must administer the corporate business in its entirety, not as a hodge-podge of associated localities."

Behind the debate over the method of representation, however, lay a debate over who should be represented, over whose views of public policy should prevail. Many reform leaders often explicitly, if not implicitly, expressed fear that lower- and middle-income groups had too much influence in decision-making. One Galveston leader, for example, complained about the movement for initiative, referendum, and recall:

We have in our city a very large number of negroes employed on the docks; we also have a very large number of unskilled white laborers; this city also has more barrooms, according to its population, than any other city in Texas. Under these circumstances it would be extremely difficult to maintain a satisfactory city government where all ordinances must be submitted back to the voters of the city for their ratification and approval.

At the National Municipal League convention of 1907, Rear
Admiral F. E. Chadwick (USN Ret.), a leader in the Newport,
Rhode Island, movement for municipal reform, spoke to this
question even more directly:

Our present system has excluded in large degree the representation
of those who have the city's well-being most at heart. It has brought,
in municipalities . . . a government established by the least educated,
the least interested class of citizens.

It stands to reason that a man paying $5,000 taxes in a town is more
interested in the well-being and development of his town than the
man who pays no taxes. . . . It equally stands to reason that the man
of the $5,000 tax should be assured a representation in the committee
which lays the tax and spends the money which he contributes. . . .
Shall we be truly democratic and give the property owner a fair
show or shall we develop a tyranny of ignorance which shall crush him.

Municipal reformers thus debated frequently the question of
who should be represented as well as the question of what
method of representation should be employed.

That these two questions were intimately connected was revealed in other reform proposals for representation, proposals
which were rarely taken seriously. One suggestion was that a
class system of representation be substituted for ward representation. For example, in 1908 one of the prominent candidates
for commissioner in Des Moines proposed that the city council
be composed of representatives of five classes: educational and
ministerial organizations, manufacturers and jobbers, public utility corporations, retail merchants including liquor men, and the
Des Moines Trades and Labor Assembly. Such a system would
have greatly reduced the influence in the council of both mid-
dle- and lower-class groups. The proposal revealed the basic
problem confronting business and professional leaders: how to
reduce the influence in government of the majority of voters
among middle- and lower-income groups.

A growing imbalance between population and representation

sharpened the desire of reformers to change from ward to city-wide elections. Despite shifts in population within most cities, neither ward district lines nor the apportionment of city council and school board seats changed frequently. Consequently, older areas of the city, with wards that were small in geographical size and held declining populations (usually lower and middle class in composition), continued to be overrepresented, and newer upper-class areas, where population was growing, became increasingly underrepresented. This intensified the reformers' conviction that the structure of government must be changed to give them the voice they needed to make their views on public policy prevail.

It is not insignificant that in some cities (by no means a majority) municipal reform came about outside of the urban electoral process. The original commission government in Galveston was appointed rather than elected. "The failure of previous attempts to secure an efficient city government through the local electorate made the business men of Galveston willing to put the conduct of the city's affairs in the hands of a commission dominated by state-appointed officials." Only in 1903 did the courts force Galveston to elect the members of the commission, an innovation which one writer described as "an abandonment of the commission idea," and which led to the decline of the influence of the business community in the commission government.

In 1911 Pittsburgh voters were not permitted to approve either the new city charter or the new school board plan, both of which provided for city-wide representation; they were a result of state legislative enactment. The governor appointed the first members of the new city council, but thereafter they were elected. The judges of the court of common pleas, however, and not the voters, selected members of the new school board.

The composition of the new city council and new school board in Pittsburgh, both of which were inaugurated in 1911, revealed the degree to which the shift from ward to city-wide representation produced a change in group representation. Members of the upper class, the advanced professional men, and the large business groups dominated both. Of the fifteen members of the Pittsburgh Board of Education appointed in 1911 and the nine members of the new city council, none were small businessmen or white-collar workers. Each body contained only one person who could remotely be classified as a blue-collar worker; each of these men filled a position specifically but unofficially designed as reserved for a "representative of labor," and each was an official of the Amalgamated Association of Iron, Steel, and Tin Workers. Six of the nine members of the new city council were prominent businessmen, and all six were listed in upper-class directories. Two others were doctors closely associated with the upper class in both profession and social life. The fifteen members of the Board of Education included ten businessmen with city-wide interests, one doctor associated with the upper class, and three women previously active in upper-class public welfare.

Lower- and middle-class elements felt that the new city governments did not represent them. The studies carried out under the direction of Leonard White contain numerous expressions of the way in which the change in the structure of government produced not only a change in the geographical scope of representation, but also in the groups represented. "It is not the policies of the manager or the council they oppose," one researcher declared, "as much as the lack of representation for their economic level and social groups." And another wrote:

There had been nothing unapproachable about the old ward aldermen. Every voter had a neighbor on the common council who was interested in serving him. The new councilmen, however, made an unfavorable impression on the less well-to-do voters. . . . Election at large made a change that, however desirable in other ways, left the voters in the poorer wards with a feeling that they had been deprived of their share of political importance.

The success of the drive for centralization of administration
and representation varied with the size of the city. In the smaller
cities, business, professional, and elite groups could easily exercise a dominant influence. Their close ties readily enabled them
to shape informal political power which they could transform
into formal political power. After the mid-1890's the widespread
organization of chambers of commerce provided a base for political action to reform municipal government, resulting in a
host of small-city commission and city-manager innovations. In
the larger, more heterogeneous cities, whose subcommunities
were more dispersed, such community-wide action was extremely
difficult. Few commission or city-manager proposals materialized
here. Mayors became stronger, and steps were taken toward centralization of representation, but the ward system or some modified version usually persisted. Reformers in large cities often had
to rest content with their Municipal Research Bureaus through
which they could exert political influence from outside the municipal government.

A central element in the analysis of municipal reform in the
Progressive Era is governmental corruption. Should it be understood in moral or political terms? Was it a product of evil men
or of particular socio-political circumstances? Reform historians
have adopted the former view. Selfish and evil men arose to take
advantage of a political arrangement whereby unsystematic government offered many opportunities for personal gain at public
expense. The system thrived until the "better elements," "men
of intelligence and civic responsibility," or "right-thinking people" ousted the culprits and fashioned a political force which
produced decisions in the "public interest." In this scheme of
things, corruption in public affairs grew out of individual personal failings and a deficient governmental structure which could
not hold those predispositions in check, rather than from the
peculiar nature of social forces. The contestants involved were
morally defined: evil men who must be driven from power, and

good men who must be activated politically to secure control of municipal affairs.

Public corruption, however, involves political even more than moral considerations. It arises more out of the particular distribution of political power than of personal morality. For corruption is a device to exercise control and influence outside the legal channels of decision-making when those channels are not readily responsive. Most generally, corruption stems from an inconsistency between control of the instruments of formal governmental power and the exercise of informal influence in the community. If powerful groups are denied access to formal power in legitimate ways, they seek access through procedures which the community considers illegitimate. Corrupt government, therefore, does not reflect the genius of evil men, but rather the lack of acceptable means for those who exercise power in the private community to wield the same influence in governmental affairs. It can be understood in the Progressive Era not simply by the preponderance of evil men over good, but by the peculiar nature of the distribution of political power.

The political corruption of the "Era of Reform" arose from the inaccessibility of municipal government to those who were rising in power and influence. Municipal government in the United States developed in the nineteenth century within a context of universal manhood suffrage which decentralized political control. Because all men, whatever their economic, social, or cultural conditions, could vote, leaders who reflected a wide variety of community interests and who represented the views of people of every circumstance arose to guide and direct municipal affairs. Since the majority of urban voters were workingmen or immigrants, the views of those groups carried great and often decisive weight in governmental affairs. Thus, as Herbert Gutman has shown, during strikes in the 1870's city officials were usually friendly to workingmen and refused to use police power to protect strikebreakers.

Ward representation on city councils was an integral part of grass-roots influence, for it enabled diverse urban communities, invariably identified with particular geographical areas of the city, to express their views more clearly through councilmen peculiarly receptive to their concerns. There was a direct, reciprocal flow of power between wards and the center of city affairs in which voters felt a relatively close connection with public matters and city leaders gave special attention to their needs.

Within this political system the community's business leaders grew in influence and power as industrialism advanced, only to find that their economic position did not readily admit them to the formal machinery of government. Thus, during strikes, they had to rely on either their own private police, Pinkertons, or the state militia to enforce their use of strikebreakers. They frequently found that city officials did not accept their views of what was best for the city and what direction municipal policies should take. They had developed a common outlook, closely related to their economic activities, that the city's economic expansion should become the prime concern of municipal government, and yet they found that this view had to compete with even more influential views of public policy. They found that political tendencies which arose from universal manhood suffrage and ward representation were not always friendly to their political conceptions and goals and had produced a political system over which they had little control, despite the fact that their economic ventures were the core of the city's prosperity and the hope for future urban growth.

Under such circumstances, businessmen sought other methods of influencing municipal affairs. They did not restrict themselves to the channels of popular election and representation, but frequently applied direct influence—if not verbal persuasion, then bribery and corruption. Thereby arose the graft which Lincoln Steffens recounted in his *Shame of the Cities*. Utilities were only the largest of those business groups and individuals who requested special favors, and the franchises they sought were only the most sensational of the prizes which included such items as favorable tax assessments and rates, the vacating of streets wanted for factory expansion, or permission to operate amid antiliquor and other laws regulating personal behavior. The relationships between business and formal government became a maze of accommodations, a set of political arrangements which grew up because effective power had few legitimate means of accomplishing its ends.

Steffens and subsequent liberal historians, however, misread the significance of these arrangements, emphasizing their personal rather than their more fundamental institutional elements. To them corruption involved personal arrangements between powerful business leaders and powerful "machine" politicians. Just as they did not fully appreciate the significance of the search for political influence by the rising business community as a whole, so they did not see fully the role of the "ward politician." They stressed the argument that the political leader manipulated voters to his own personal ends, that he used constituents rather than reflected their views.

A different approach is now taking root, namely, that the urban political organization was an integral part of community life, expressing its needs and its goals. As Oscar Handlin has said, for example, the "machine" not only fulfilled specific wants, but provided one of the few avenues to success and public recognition available to the immigrant. The political leader's arrangements with businessmen, therefore, were not simply personal agreements between conniving individuals; they were far-reaching accommodations between powerful sets of institutions in industrial America.

These accommodations, however, proved to be burdensome and unsatisfactory to the business community and to the upper third of socio-economic groups in general. They were expensive; they were wasteful; they were uncertain. Toward the end of the nineteenth century, therefore, business and professional men sought more direct control over municipal government in order to exercise political influence more effectively. They realized their goals in the early twentieth century in the new commission and city-manager forms of government and in the shift from ward to city-wide representation.

These innovations did not always accomplish the objectives that the business community desired because other forces could and often did adjust to the change in governmental structure and re-establish their influence. But businessmen hoped that reform would enable them to increase their political power, and most frequently it did. In most cases the innovations which were introduced between 1901, when Galveston adopted a commission form of government, and the Great Depression, and especially the city-manager form which reached a height of popularity in the mid-1920's, served as vehicles whereby business and professional leaders moved directly into the inner circles of government, brought into one political system their own power and the formal machinery of government, and dominated municipal affairs for two decades.

Municipal reform in the early twentieth century involves a paradox: the ideology of an extension of political control and the practice of its concentration. While reformers maintained that their movement rested on a wave of popular demands, called their gatherings of business and professional leaders "mass meetings," described their reforms as "part of a world-wide trend toward popular government," and proclaimed an ideology of a popular upheaval against a selfish few, they were in practice shaping the structure of municipal government so that political power would no longer be broadly distributed, but would in fact be more centralized in the hands of a relatively small segment of the population. The paradox became even sharper when new city charters included provisions for the initiative, referendum, and recall. How does the historian cope with this paradox? Does it represent deliberate deception or simply political strategy? Or does it reflect a phenomenon which should be understood rather than explained away?

The expansion of popular involvement in decision-making was

frequently a political tactic, not a political system to be established permanently, but a device to secure immediate political victory. The prohibitionist advocacy of the referendum, one of the most extensive sources of support for such a measure, came from the belief that the referendum would provide the opportunity to outlaw liquor more rapidly. The Anti-Saloon League, therefore, urged local option. But the League was not consistent. Towns which were wet, when faced with a county-wide local-option decision to outlaw liquor, demanded town or township local option to reinstate it. The League objected to this as not the proper application of the referendum idea.

Again, "Progressive" reformers often espoused the direct primary when fighting for nominations for their candidates within the party, but once in control they often became cool to it because it might result in their own defeat. By the same token, many municipal reformers attached the initiative, referendum, and recall to municipal charters often as a device to appease voters who opposed the centralization of representation and executive authority. But, by requiring a high percentage of voters to sign petitions—often 25 to 30 per cent—these innovations could be and were rendered relatively harmless.

More fundamentally, however, the distinction between ideology and practice in municipal reform arose from the different roles which each played. The ideology of democratization of decision-making was negative rather than positive; it served as an instrument of attack against the existing political system rather than as a guide to alternative action. Those who wished to destroy the "machine" and to eliminate party competition in local government widely utilized the theory that these political instruments thwarted public impulses, and thereby shaped the tone of their attack.

But there is little evidence that the ideology represented a faith in a purely democratic system of decision-making or that reformers actually wished, in practice, to substitute direct democracy as a continuing system of sustained decision-making in place of the old. It was used to destroy the political institutions of the lower and middle classes and the political power which those institutions gave rise to, rather than to provide a clear-cut guide for alternative action.

The guide to alternative action lay in the model of the business enterprise. In describing new conditions which they wished to create, reformers drew on the analogy of the "efficient business enterprise," criticizing current practices with the argument that "no business could conduct its affairs that way and remain in business," and calling upon business practices as the guides to improvement. As one student remarked:

The folklore of the business elite came by gradual transition to be the symbols of governmental reformers. Efficiency, system, orderliness, budgets, economy, saving, were all injected into the efforts of reformers who sought to remodel municipal government in terms of the great impersonality of corporate enterprise.

Clinton Rodgers Woodruff of the National Municipal League explained that the commission form was "a simple, direct, business-like way of administering the business affairs of the city . . . an application to city administration of that type of business organization which has been so common and so successful in the field of commerce and industry." The centralization of decision-making which developed in the business corporation was now applied in municipal reform.

The model of the efficient business enterprise, then, rather than the New England town meeting, provided the positive inspiration for the municipal reformer. In giving concrete shape to this model in the strong-mayor, commission, and city-manager plans, reformers engaged in the elaboration of the processes of rationalization and systematization inherent in modern science and technology. For in many areas of society, industrialization brought a gradual shift upward in the location of decision-making and the geographical extension of the scope of the area affected by decisions.

Experts in business, in government, and in the professions measured, studied, analyzed, and manipulated ever wider realms of human life, and devices which they used to control such affairs constituted the most fundamental and far-reaching innovations in

decision-making in modern America, whether in formal government or in the informal exercise of power in private life. Reformers in the Progressive Era played a major role in shaping this new
system. While they expressed an ideology of restoring a previous
order, they in fact helped to bring forth a system drastically new.

The drama of reform lay in the competition for supremacy between two systems of decision-making. One system, based upon
ward representation and growing out of the practices and ideas of
representative government, involved wide latitude for the expression of grass-roots impulses and their involvement in the political
process. The other grew out of the rationalization of life which
came with science and technology, in which decisions arose from
expert analysis and flowed from fewer and smaller centers outward
to the rest of society. Those who espoused the former looked with
fear upon the loss of influence which the latter involved, and those
who espoused the latter looked only with disdain upon the waste-
fulness and inefficiency of the former.

The Progressive Era witnessed rapid strides toward a more centralized system and a relative decline for a more decentralized system. This development constituted an accommodation of forces
outside the business community to the political trends within business and professional life rather than vice versa. It involved a tendency for the decision-making processes inherent in science and
technology to prevail over those inherent in representative government.

Reformers in the Progressive Era and liberal historians since
then misread the nature of the movement to change municipal
government because they concentrated upon dramatic and sensational episodes and ignored the analysis of more fundamental political structure, of the persistent relationships of influence and
power which grew out of the community's social, ideological, economic, and cultural activities. The reconstruction of these patterns
of human relationships and of the changes in them is the historian's most crucial task, for they constitute the central context
of historical development. History consists not of erratic and spas-

modic fluctuations, of a series of random thoughts and actions, but of patterns of activity and change in which people hold thoughts and actions in common and in which there are close connections between sequences of events. These contexts give rise to a structure of human relationships which pervade all areas of life; for the political historian the most important of these is the structure of the distribution of power and influence.

The structure of political relationships, however, cannot be adequately understood if we concentrate on evidence concerning ideology rather than practice. For it is becoming increasingly clear that ideological evidence is no safe guide to the understanding of practice, that what people thought and said about their society is not necessarily an accurate representation of what they did. The current task of the historian of the Progressive Era is to quit taking the reformers' own description of political practice at its face value and to utilize a wide variety of new types of evidence to reconstruct political practice in its own terms. This not to argue that ideology is either important or unimportant. It is merely to state that ideological evidence is not appropriate to the discovery of the nature of political practice.

Only by maintaining this clear distinction can the historian successfully investigate the structure of political life in the Progressive Era. And only then can he begin to cope with the most fundamental problem of all: the relationship between political ideology and political practice. For each of these facets of political life must be understood in its own terms, through its own historical phenomena. The relationship between them for the Progressive Era is not now clear; it has not been investigated. But it cannot be explored until the conceptual distinction is made clear and evidence tapped which is pertinent to each. Because the nature of political practice has so long been distorted by the use of ideological evidence, the most pressing task is for its investigation through new types of evidence appropriate to it. The reconstruction of the movement for municipal reform can constitute a major step forward toward that goal.

A Giant Step Backward

The Negro and Disfranchisement

by Sheldon Hackney

The end of Radical Reconstruction in 1877 had not terminated all Negro voting in the South. Even under the Redeemer governments, blacks continued to vote, although in smaller numbers, depending on the degree of physical coercion or economic pressures brought to bear on them in different localities. Yet in state after state, even during the 1870's and 1880's, black voting declined significantly as white Redeemer politicians stuffed the ballot boxes, complicated voting procedures for Negroes, and, if necessary, sanctioned violence. Throughout the 1880's, however, Southern white politicians continued to play with the dwindling Negro vote in order to bolster their particular factions. It was mainly the minority of prosperous Southern blacks or Negro politicians who allied their supporters with local groups of Redeemer politicians and kept disfranchisement from becoming complete even without legal impediments.

But even this controlled and harmless exercise in voting by blacks soon became anathema to the mass of white voters, and demands for total disfranchisement began to grow, reaching their peak during the Progressive Era. Beginning in the 1890's the restraints on black voting in the South became imbedded in con-

stitutional law. The movement for complete disfranchisement arose during the height of the agrarian Populist crusade and continued during the following decade, largely under the leadership of Southern demagogues who were Progressives in other matters but also bitter-end racists, "anti-trust and anti-Negro." Almost every Southern state during the 1890's and 1900's revised its constitution, state laws, or local ordinances to require some combination of poll taxes, literacy tests, and property qualifications that could generally be applied at the discretion of local voting registrars. Seven states even introduced into their constitutions the so-called "grandfather clause," waiving all other requirements for lineal descendants of persons who could vote in 1867, a provision designed to permit those poor whites to vote who were unable to meet the other new qualifications.

In addition, Southern states also passed legislation during this period allowing the Democratic party, which completely dominated the region's politics, to set its own rules for membership and primary voting, in other words, permitting "whites only" voting in the primary elections. Starting with Mississippi in 1890 and ending with Georgia in 1908, the South effectively excluded the Negro from voting through patently unconstitutional but "legal" devices. In the following selection Sheldon Hackney describes this dismal process in Alabama.

Emancipation Day was celebrated on January 1, 1901, in Negro communities throughout Alabama just as it had been for many years. Numerous Negro speakers enumerated and detailed the progress of Negroes since the Civil War: progress made in literacy, land ownership, business, the professions, and the aggregate of personal achievements that reflected material progress. Measured against the lowly status of Negroes 35 years before, these advances seemed spectacular. But measured against the promise of American life, they were not great enough to dissuade whites from their belief in the doctrine of Negro inferiority. Some people felt Ne-

From *Populism to Progressivism in Alabama* (Princeton: Princeton University Press, 1969), pp. 180–208. Reprinted by permission; footnotes omitted.

groes had failed their test as Americans and deserved to be proscribed. Others, such as those for whom Tom Heflin spoke, feared
that Negroes were succeeding too well. For whatever reason, most
white men in Alabama agreed on the necessity of disfranchisement. It was the biggest and most important downward readjustment in the long and bitter process of redefining the Negro's
place in Southern life.

The trend in race relations had been evident in the South ever
since Florida enacted the first Jim Crow law in 1887. The tendency was to replace informal, fluctuating, and nonuniform patterns with legal, static, and uniform methods of treating Negroes.
For example, Negroes could vote and participate in politics in
various ways in some places during the 1890's. In other places
countless stratagems of dubious morality were employed to neu-
tralize or utilize their votes. The constitutional convention, said
James Weatherly, was called to replace "this revolutionary method
by legal machinery. . . ."

The revolutionary methods had grown out of the vague feeling
among many whites that there was something impermanent and
not right about existing relations between the races. As a friend
wrote to John W. DuBose, probably in 1902, "The Civil War
. . . did not settle the problem. It is still unsettled and must remain so until settled right." But with no model of "right," there
was no agreement on the spheres of life from which even the
deferential Negro should be excluded.

Consequently the pattern of race relations was highly fluid in
Alabama in the period 1890 to 1910. Inconsistency was the primary characteristic. The law in its various guises brought increasing order to the situation, and in doing so abolished both the
freedom and the insecurity that went with inconsistency. The
workings of the law could be seen in various fields. The city council of Montgomery passed an ordinance segregating the seating on
streetcars in 1900. A Negro boycott that year failed to reverse the
decision. Jim Crow did not come to the railroad stations until
January 6, 1902, when the Alabama Railroad Commission issued

an order to the railroads operating in the state to maintain comfortable waiting rooms for their passengers. The order also required railroads to furnish separate waiting rooms for the two races. The last company of Negro state militia, the Capitol City Guards, was not disbanded until 1905. Meanwhile Birmingham's mayor announced that the new Birmingham jail, famed in folk song and pamphlets of protest, would be segregated at last.

While recognizing the law's creative role in the structure of segregation, the growing separation of the races did exist independent of the law. This separation was even extended to the domain of death. A Negro newspaper noticed in 1900 that the Mississippi legislature had ordered the removal of the remains of the Honorable James Lynch from the white cemetery where they rested since his death. Two years later a Birmingham paper reported that "Will Mathis has requested Judge Lowry to have his hanging at a different hour from the time that the negro, Orlando Lester, will be hanged, and also that he be hanged from a different set of gallows."

Labor was a particularly sensitive area of race relations. The vice president of the Alabama Federation of Labor in 1902 was J. H. Beanes, a Negro, who was host for the organization's annual convention in Selma in that year. Community pressure was strong for the meeting to be segregated, but there was resistance. A delegate from Typographical Union Local 104 in Birmingham stated that "rather than see one accredited delegate, black or white, thrown out of this convention I would go to the woods and hold this meeting." Union locals were thoroughly segregated, but conventions and governing bodies admitted Negroes in order to protect unionism from an increasingly hostile Negro labor force.

Perhaps nothing better captures the flux of patterns of segregation in the South at the turn of the century than the case of a Southerner with an impeccable pedigree, Mary Custis Lee, the daughter of Robert E. Lee. In 1902 she was arrested on the Washington, Alexandria & Mt. Vernon Railroad for refusing to move from the Negro section of the car where she had taken her seat. She was not a freedom rider; she simply was not aware that there was a law segregating the races on that railroad, and evidently was not used to such a practice being dictated by custom.

Pathological evidence of the disturbed state of race relations was available in the statistics on lynching. The ten-year period 1889 to 1899 witnessed the most dramatic rise and decline of lynch law. The peak years were 1891 and 1892; in each year 24 people were dispatched by mobs in Alabama. The low point of a mere four lynchings was reached in 1900. But in 1901, a year of prosperity and rising cotton prices, contrary to the notion that the frequency of lynchings fluctuated in response to deviations from the long-term trend in cotton prices, there were 16 mob murders. It was no accident that disfranchisement was the single most important public issue that year. This raises the question of the cause of the ebb and flow in this form of physical aggression. It is certainly true that "respectable" groups in society carried on campaigns to discourage people from resorting to rope and faggot. Thomas G. Jones went so far as to argue that the Thirteenth and Fourteenth Amendments gave federal courts jurisdiction in lynching cases against mob members who deprived Negro victims of equal protection and due process of law. Governor William Dorsey Jelks (1901–1906) was sincerely devoted to the prevention of lynching, for which he suffered some criticism. He was deeply disturbed by the fact that "human life is about as cheap in Alabama as it is anywhere. . . ." Yet he was unable to get lynchers convicted even when the evidence appeared overwhelming. In view of the continued immunity of lynchers it would seem that some factor other than social disapproval was responsible for the decline of lynching.

It is likely that the high rate of extralegal sanctions against Negroes in the 1890's was related to the fluidity and uncertainty in patterns of race relations. The potential for conflict was greater as long as patterns of permissible conduct were poorly defined and changing. At the end of the decade and after, as legal devices were used increasingly to define and make uniform the prescribed boundaries of the permissible in race relations, anxious whites felt less need to assert their superiority. The Negro leader and president of Alabama A. and M. College at Normal, W. H. Councill, sensed this when he told an Emancipation Day audience in 1901 "that the salvation of the negro in this country depends upon drawing the social lines tighter, tighter all the while, North and South. The moment they become slack the white man becomes brutal—the negro goes down forever."

Councill's statement also reflected the deepening disillusionment of Negroes in the face of their increasing proscription. This despair was expressed in the half-dozen extant Negro newspapers in Alabama. As the 1890's wore on, Negroes postponed their quest for full citizenship through political self-assertion and turned to the more traditional paths favored by Booker T. Washington and W. H. Councill. Accommodation, material self-improvement, and dependence on upper-class whites seemed to be the only choice short of emigration for Negroes. H. C. Binford, schoolteacher, city alderman, and newspaper editor, in 1899 told his readers: "there is nothing in politics for us, it makes no difference which side wins none of them want the Negro." A year later he glumly admitted that "we have gotten use to being slighted and have ceased to kick. What's the use?" Negro newspapers of all shades of opinion put increased emphasis on the need to acquire education and property.

Prospects were so gloomy that Washington thought that "before we [Negroes] can make much progress we must decide whether or not the Negro is to be a permanent part of the South." Not only was there a Negro emigration movement of unknown strength, and white propagandists of colonization like John Temple Graves, Thomas Pearce Bailey, and John Tyler Morgan, but newspapers were full of plans to replace the Negro labor force and population of the South with white immigrants. The atmosphere was so tense that W. H. Councill surrendered to pessimism. In a controversial article in *The Forum* in 1899 he arrived at the conclusion that everything the Negro had was at the sufferance of the whites and that there was no future for the Negro in America.

Councill's despair led to two patterns of thought. On the one hand there was the policy of accommodation—and Councill was an expert accommodator. In 1901, as always, he needed funds from the state government, and applied to Governor Samford hat-in-hand. His letter argued that the state was getting a good deal because "all of this vast property is deeded to the State of Alabama. The State has donated money only for a normal school which is putting into rural districts as well as the towns teachers who are not only competent to teach, but who are in harmony with the institutions and customs of the South." To complete this example of the policy of accommodation, Councill's request was endorsed by General William C. Oates who played the role of upper-class paternalist. Oates wrote that he thought "Councill a good man and fine manager of this school and politically all right."

The other fork of Councill's two-pronged pessimism was the assertion of a perennial American Negro myth, "repatriation." The redemption of Africa from barbarism by American Negroes was a satisfying dream for Negroes who were alienated from American life and suffering from a poor self-image.

The progressive alienation of Negroes sprang from several sources. One prime cause was the dwindling sphere of economic opportunity. Negro newspapers in Alabama were aware, as was Councill, of the Negro's weakening position in the job market. But while the Negro is anxious to work," commented the *Southern Watchman*, "there are those who are using every effort to deprive him of the wherewithal to earn his daily bread."

But it was the total impact of adverse change that Negroes experienced. One Negro newspaper reacted with bitterness, indignation, despair, bewilderment, and resignation:

The "Jim Crow" car law, which forces the respectable and the disrespectable Negro to travel in the same car is infamous enough, an insult is being added to injury continually. Have those in power forgotten that there is a God, and do they not know that every seed of unjust discrimination sown will in some due time come up. . . . The Negro is as docile as he can be . . . and day after day he is reminded through the daily papers . . . that some additional project is on foot, or is about to be promulgated to stand as a menace to his development, or a curb to his ambitious manhood . . . and we wonder what the harvest will be.

Leaders of the white community were as aware as Negroes were of the deterioration in race relations, for the future of the Negro was a popular topic of public discussion. One evidence of this concern and interest was The Southern Society for the Promotion of the Study of Race Conditions and Problems in the South. Edgar Gardner Murphy conceived the idea and quickly enlisted Hilary Herbert and a blue-ribbon membership. The result was a widely publicized meeting in May 1900 in Montgomery. The conference aired a broad range of opinion, from John Temple Graves's call for colonization of Negroes in Africa to William A. MacCorkle's insistence that Negroes be treated as citizens. A Negro observer reported that there was no support for Graves's proposal nor for the argument of a North Carolina man that Southern states ought not to educate Negroes. Other speakers evidently met significant opposition when they expressed their belief in the inherent inferiority of Negroes, when they maintained that Negro criminality was getting worse, and when they thought that Negro religious life should be guided and controlled by whites. Everyone was opposed to lynch law. According to Murphy, even the Northerners agreed that enfranchising Negroes was a mistake.

This is an important indication of the state of informed opinion at the time of the Alabama Constitutional Convention. Booker T. Washington himself was yielding before it. In November 1899 he had tried unsuccessfully to rally Negro opposition to a disfranchising measure pending before the Georgia Assembly. At the same time, however, he was talking of backing an educational qualification for suffrage as a means of ensuring that Negroes would be judged on the same basis as whites. G. W. Atkinson of West Virginia questioned the wisdom of such a deal with white leaders. Atkinson advised Washington that he thought the Democratic leaders of the South were using Washington and that any voting law would be administered so as to discriminate against Negroes.

As later events proved, it was naïve of Washington to think registrars would apply suffrage tests fairly to both races. Atkinson grasped the essential evil of the Southern system when he understood this. But Washington understood that he had very little choice; he was simply trying to use his contacts among white leaders to make the best deal possible under the circumstances.

The problem was, those bent on disfranchisement were no longer restrained by the federal government or by opposition from within the state. The small force of 14 Populists and Republicans in the 155-member convention could do little, though they stood fast against limiting suffrage. The sizable opposition to disfranchisement registered in the referendum, more interested in white votes than black, was not nearly sufficient to block the powerful coalition whose divergent interests happened to focus on disfranchisement. There was so little resistance of any kind that there was little need to camouflage the purpose and intent of the convention.

"And what is it that we want to do?" asked John B. Knox in his presidential address to the Constitutional Convention of Alabama as it opened its deliberations on May 22, 1901. "Why it is within the limits imposed by the Federal Constitution, to establish white supremacy in this State." The subordinate position of the Negro race was about to be written into the fundamental law. "Our purpose is plain," delegate Thomas Watts asserted some days later. "It is not denied by any man upon the floor of this Convention or in this State."

There was such a consensus on disfranchising Negroes that the main question facing the convention was not whether to do it but how to do it without violating the Federal Constitution on the one hand and the pledge not to disfranchise any white men on the other hand.

The committee of the convention in charge of the delicate task of drafting the suffrage article was the Committee on Suffrage and Elections, composed of 21 lawyers and including 9 members from the Black Belt. The chairman of the committee was Thomas W. Coleman from Eutaw in Greene County. Coleman was a graduate of Princeton and the University of Alabama Law School, a former Associate Justice of the Alabama Supreme Court, an officer in the Confederate army, a member of the Constitutional Convention of 1875, and the president of the Merchants and Farmers Bank of Eutaw. Of such stuff was the convention made.

While the rest of the convention settled down for an uncomfortably hot and contentious summer of parliamentary maneuvering . . . the Suffrage Committee met for the first time on May 29 and began its long and arduous task of shaping a suffrage article. It drew on the suffrage provisions of other Southern states, as well as many ordinances submitted by delegates, sent by constituents, and published by newspapers. Through the month of June the committee debated in private the sundry suggestions of how best to disfranchise the Negro. Even without diabolical registrars, the constitution could eliminate Negroes by applying tests that took advantage of differing social conditons. Property tests, literacy tests, residence requirements, the poll tax, and disqualification for conviction of certain crimes all fell into this category.

The central problem was how, or whether, to provide for the whites who would be disfranchised by the anti-Negro provisions unless some special loophole were created for them. There is no doubt that many people in the state envisaged the disfranchisement of poor whites as well as poor Negroes.

In his opening address President Knox provided a rationale for those wishing to disfranchise whites while not violating the pledge of the party. On the one hand there were 236,476 white males of voting age of whom 31,681 were illiterate but who were not to be disfranchised. On the other hand there were 181,345 Negro males of voting age of whom 107,946 were literate and who were to be disfranchised. "We are pledged," said Knox, " 'not to deprive any white man of the right to vote,' but this does not extend unless this Convention chooses to extend it beyond the right of voters now living."

The Committee on Suffrage and Elections accepted Knox's rationalization. When it finally made its recommendations on June 30, the majority report was a grotesquely complicated document that eventually became Article VIII of the new constitution with very few alterations.

Article VIII, as finally passed, contained two distinct "plans." The permanent plan contained the disfranchising provisions, the qualifications that were to be a permanent part of the organic law. The temporary plan consisted of the devices designed to permit those of the favored race (or party) who would not be able to qualify under the permanent rules to register under special provisions. The temporary plan expired on January 1, 1903.

The permanent plan set up a most elaborate maze through which one had to grope to claim the privilege of becoming an elector. The basic conditions for registration were that a person must be a male citizen, or alien who had declared his intention of becoming a citizen, twenty-one years of age who had resided in the state for two years, the county for one year, and the precinct for three months. The second requirement was the ability to read and write any article of the United States Constitution, unless physical disability caused the deficiency. Except for the physically disabled, the prospective elector also must have been engaged in some lawful employment for the greater part of the preceding twelve months. If this requirement could not be met there was the alternative property qualification of 40 acres of land on which the prospective elector lived, or the ownership of real or personal property assessed for taxes at a value of $300 and on which the taxes had been paid. There was, in addition, a long list of disqualifying crimes, including vagrancy. Having become an elector, the last cul-de-sac in the labyrinth was the cumulative poll tax of $1.50 per year that had to be paid on or before the first day of February preceding the election in which the elector offered to vote.

Those who could meet all but the literacy and property qualifications were provided with loopholes that were to be open for only a few months. For this purpose Louisiana's famous "grand-father clause" was adapted by Alabama, indeed the only novelty of the suffrage article, so that it became the "Fighting Grandfather Clause." This device allowed those to register who had served honorably in the land or naval forces of the United States or Confederate States in any war from 1812 on, or who were descendants of such veterans. If this were not enough, there was the further provision to register "all persons who are of good character and who understand the duties and obligations of citizenship under a republican form of government."

From July 23 to August 3 the convention gave itself over to a remarkably frank debate on the suffrage article. The most significant attack on the article came from an important group of men who questioned the "Fighting Grandfather" clause. In their minority report, they pointed out that the clause set up an arbitrary standard which discriminated against citizens of the United States on the basis of race and was therefore a violation of the Federal Constitution. They also asserted that it was undemocratic, that it insulted white men by requiring less of them than of Negroes, that it was open to manipulation, fraud, and perjury. These men wanted suffrage requirements that applied to all alike.

William C. Oates, the chief spokesman of the minority of the Committee on Suffrage and Elections, received support on the floor from Thomas G. Jones who spoke in the tradition of patrician paternalism. George P. Harrison and Stanley H. Dent, prominent men who had been colleagues of Jones in the gold Democratic Party in 1896, also signed the minority report. Senators Morgan and Edmund W. Pettus made their opposition known in letters to the convention. The instructive thing about this opposition to the granfather clause was that it was not all of one coloration.

The fourth signer of the minority report was Frank S. White of Birmingham who doubled at the convention as the leader of Comer's crew of railroad regulators. J. L. M. Curry was also opposed to providing loopholes for ignorant white men, and Robert J. Lowe of Birmingham, Chairman of the State Democratic Executive Committee and a man with some Progressive leanings, thought the grandfather clause was "the very repudiation of fairness."

Evidently, the Big Mules and the Progressives shared a pessimism about human nature as well as a passion for social order. Much of the discussion of the grandfather clause and white suffrage was based on a belief in the existence of a large, powerful, and dangerous portion of the population that was "ignorant and vicious." The convention was dedicated to limiting the suffrage to the "intelligent and virtuous." Samuel Blackwell, a Progressive from Morgan County, expressed his desire to put the suffrage only in the hands of competent men so as to ensure good government. He affirmed his belief that "nature has marked the weak and incompetent to be protected by Government, rather than to be the directors of the Government."

This outlook received support from Alabama's most famous reformer, Edgar Gardner Murphy. The crusading rector of St. John's Episcopal church in Montgomery wrote an "open letter" to the constitutional convention, in which he voiced his opposition to the grandfather clause. Then in the midst of a campaign to free the state of the evil of child labor, Murphy expressed doubts about the natural goodness of man. His social reforms were essentially aimed at putting institutional limits on human capacity for evil. But he also believed in secular progress, in industrialization, and in improving the material and moral condition of man. He wanted to release the creative energies of men who were cramped and rendered inefficient by human institutions. An aristocracy of the educated would achieve that progress, so limiting suffrage to the "intelligent and virtuous" was a step in the right direction.

It is quite likely that some of the opposition to the grandfather clause was influenced by personal obligations to Booker T. Washington who was actively soliciting the aid of white businessmen for a letter-writing campaign. Murphy and Oates, in particular, were on easy terms with him, and Thomas G. Jones was appointed to a federal district judgeship in October 1901 by his grace. Washington's most open move was a petition to the convention signed by fifteen prominent Negroes which humbly asked that Negroes be allowed to share in the choice of their rulers.

This "humble and unnecessary" petition was not well received in some quarters of the Negro community. The *Southern Watchman* stigmatized Washington as "the white man's ideal Negro" and entered an eloquent plea for racial justice. "Do not show us how to be men and then blame us for being men," wrote the *Watchman*, which claimed to be speaking for "every intelligent Negro in America" when it asserted "that they are not satisfied with the present condition of things in the South."

Neither protesting Negroes, with whatever tone of voice, nor sympathetic whites could budge the majority. Defending the suffrage article from attacks on the left as well as the right, the convention tabled the minority report by a vote of 109 to 23. The "no" votes were cast by the opponents of the grandfather clause, joined by Populists and Republicans who were against the whole idea of suffrage restriction in spite of the inducements offered by the temporary plan.

To Knox and Coleman and other prominent champions of the clause, the most beautiful thing about the temporary plan was that it was temporary. Delegates who represented poor-white voters, whose support for the new constituion the compromise was designed to secure, made several attempts to widen and lengthen the loophole. A minor irony is the fact that the principal doctrinal support for belief in the common (white) man, or in the "democratic myth," was white supremacy—the doctrine that "the white man was always qualified to vote. He inherits his qualities. . . . The meanest white man in the State is within the saving clause. . . ." The adherents of such a philosophy failed in their attempt to make the grandfather clause permanent, and the convention also

•

defeated other attempts to postpone the terminal date of the temporary plan.

In order to move the convention in the other direction representatives from the Black Belt tried to raise the age at which a man became exempt from the poll tax from forty-five to sixty. This was in reality a fight over white disfranchisement. After a series of close votes that indicated the restrictionists had a slight majority, the issue was compromised by setting the age of exemption at forty-five, but providing that the legislature could raise it to sixty. Similarly, for fear of creating opposition to the new constitution in the ratifying referendum, the convention gave north Alabama its way by defeating the Black Belt's attempt to raise the property requirements for suffrage.

The only victory won by those who wanted to expand the electorate beyond the limits set by the majority of the Committee on Suffrage and Elections came in regard to aliens. The majority report had reversed existing practice by not providing for the registration of aliens who had declared their intention of becoming citizens. On the motion and initiative of C. P. Beddow, a spokesman for Birmingham labor, the convention changed the majority report so that "first paper" aliens could register and vote. Beddow won another victory by getting the wording of the article changed so that strikers would not be proscribed by the ban against persons who were not regularly employed.

The meager results of attempts to change the suffrage article might give the impression that the debates were dull. Nothing could be further from the truth.

Among other things, the debates disclosed the gnawing sense of guilt that permeated the convention. They bore witness to the recent suggestion of Professor C. Vann Woodward that the peculiarities of the Southern identity owe much to the un-American experiences of defeat, poverty, and guilt. Every time electoral fraud was mentioned, every time a delegate argued that the suffrage article did not violate the Fifteenth Amendment, every time the pledge not to disfranchise any white man was explained away, the uneasy conscience was briefly exposed. Dr. Russell M. Cunningham remarked in a revealing jest that he had often in his life wanted to be a lawyer. "This is one time," he said, "I am glad that I am not. If I were a lawyer I would not only be expected to have a conscience, but I would also be expected to have an opinion, and leave the conscience to rest. (Laughter)."

Mike Sollie could not ignore his conscience. A rather traditional thinker who nevertheless supported Comer's drive for railroad regulation, Sollie was oppressed by the thought that the South's "history records a grievous error. . . . It was contrary to the principles of freedom and liberty embedded deep in the American heart that slavery should exist in our midst." And Sollie feared that the South's present and future woes were growing out of this sin of the fathers. "Our prostrated and devastated South," he said, "our unequal opportunities in the race of progress and the graves of our dead heroes are all parts of the painful accounting we have thus far given for the sin committed."

The uncomfortable themes of sin and retribution were suffocated under the patchwork quilt of the orthodox view of the past. This popular view gained authority from repetition, and dissent became perilous. The best of the speeches evoked all of the proper and approved historical symbols: the pernicious Yankee Slave Trader, the hallowed Founding Fathers, the Happy Slave, the glorious Lost Cause, the Faithful Retainer, Black Reconstruction, the Depraved Negro, the Blessed Redemption, the Required Corruption to maintain White Supremacy, and the Necessary Purification of the Ballot. The past was marshaled to justify the present.

The present that needed justifying was a time of racial proscription. In the melange of opinion four varieties of racial attitudes can be isolated. They might be called: (a) Orthodox White Supremacy, (b) Paternalism, (c) Radicalism, and (d) race-bating Demagoguery. The orthodox white supremacy was based on what was taken to be the simple and demonstrable fact of the superiority of the white race and its inherited capacity to rule. This fact was supported by an evolutionary conception of history, but Providential rather than Darwinian evolution. In this view, "the records of history are largely narratives of man's advancement from barbarism to civilization. The great, dominant, white races of the earth have been thousands of years in reaching their present state of development." Meanwhile the Negro race had been completely stationary. The turn-of-the-century euphoria about western civilization, which did so much to abet the forces of uplift, in this case contributed to the contrast between the races which justified the conclusion that "the white race must dominate because it is the superior race. . . ."

The key concept in the orthodox outlook was that there should be little or no differentiation among Negroes. Every Negro should carry the value that was assigned to the race as a whole by the white community's stereotype.

By looking at Negroness in much the same way that they looked at membership in the lower class, paternalists were able to recognize differences among Negroes. They normally wanted to hold out hope to the Negro that in the future he might individually improve his status and attain some of the rights of citizenship of which he was being denuded. Where orthodox racism was based on a vague and erroneous genetics, paternalism was based on a more plastic social judgment. Some paternalists hoped that in the distant future, equal education and employment opportunities would enable the Negro to stand on his own as a full citizen.

But in 1901 the Negro was not a full citizen. In fact, it seemed as if he was being pushed entirely out of society. In this atmosphere the distinctive note of paternalism was its insistence that society was an organic whole of which the Negro was an integral, although subservient, part and that the white man was chaged with moral responsibility for his welfare. "The negro race is under us," argued ex-Governor Thomas G. Jones, ". . . we have shorn him of all political power. . . . In return for that, we should extend to him . . . all the civil rights that will fit him to be a decent and self-respecting, law-abiding and intelligent citizen of this state."

Even more feeble in 1901 was the idealistic hope of racial cooperation. This radical point of view, extraordinary for the time, found its spokesmen among the Republicans and Populists. There was, for instance, John H. Porter from Coosa County who had in turn been a Whig, a Populist, and a Republican. Porter was not afraid to dispute the orthodox view of the past or of the present. He stated that all the Negro asked for as a citizen of the state was "to choose between two or more the one he prefers to rule over him. This right," said Porter, "in my judgment, he should have."

The Republicans had been the original experimenters with biracial politics and still had obligations to their constituents. But it would be too much to say that the Populists had taken up where the Republicans left off. I. L. Brock chided O. D. Street, who was in the process of becoming a Republican, for his opposition to disfranchisement. "You know the populists always were willing and ready for the negro to be disfranchised if it could be done without disfranchising the white man, . . ." he wrote. But the fact is that the foremost champion of Negro suffrage at the convention was a Populist who was also in transit to the Republican party.

Newton B. Spears was a Tennesseean and the son of a Union general. These facts do not explain his radical views on race, but perhaps they help account for his antipathy toward the Democratic Party and his freedom from its mythology. Men who were still Populists in 1901 were likely to be more unorthodox in their views on race relations than was the mass of Populists when the party was at full strength in 1894–96. Only congenital "outsiders" would cling to such an obviously dead party. In addition to this, those Populist politicians who wanted to make the shift to Republicanism had to prove they were good Republicans at heart, and standing up for Negro suffrage was one way to do this in 1901, for the lily whites had not yet taken over the party.

Spears declared that Negroes could no longer be treated as slaves. They were citizens. He challenged any delegate to stand up and "contend that the ordinance we are now considering does not abridge the privilege of voting . . ." of both black and white men. He praised the Thirteenth, Fourteenth, and Fifteenth Amendments, characterized the proposed voter registration system as tyranny, lauded William Lloyd Garrison and Lincoln, swore by Old Hickory Jackson, called the equalitarian Jefferson the greatest Populist, and thoroughly antagonized the convention.

Spears's defiance of the convention extended to thinking that Negroes should have the right to vote. He thought, in fact, that they should have justice. As the convention recovered from that idea, he asked it most prophetically if it wanted "to pursue a course and a policy that will make the negro look to Washington and not to Montgomery for protection?"

Another theme, and one not at all muted, was that of strident and aggressive racism cast in terms of race conflict. This jarring chord was struck by the budding demagogue, J. Thomas Heflin. On the verge of a political career that would take him to the United States Senate, Tom Heflin was a new type in Alabama. He became famous as a storyteller and spokesman for the common white man. But if his performance in the convention of 1901 is a true indication, while he was talking for the poor whites he was voting for the rich ones.

The tone of Heflin's depiction of race relations, even where he was not diverging from the orthodox view, was aggressive and antagonistic. The Negro was not merely subordinate to the white race, but he was ordained by God to be the white man's servant. And Heflin did not stop at this sort of revival of the old pro-slavery argument. When, in order to rationalize its action on suffrage, the convention resorted to the theory that the ballot was not a right but a privilege, Heflin went one step further and maintained that it was a natural right for the white man but a privilege for the Negro. He insisted that Negroes and whites should never be required to compete on the same level. "If you want to make a foot race," said Heflin, "let us make it with the descendants of our own tribe." Tribalism and race conflict were basic to Heflin's philosophy.

Heflin thought the impending conflict rendered it mere folly to educate or otherwise equip the Negro. Consequently he supported the move (which ended in a compromise) to provide for separate Negro and white school systems, each supported by the taxes paid directly by that race. In the first place, thought Heflin, "he doesn't need encouragement. . . . Why as soon as you elevate him you ruin him." But more importantly, it was dangerous. Heflin gave new clothes to the old antebellum fear of educating the slaves. "The negroes are being educated very rapidly," he told his fellow delegates who professed to think Negroes incapable of education, "and I say in the light of all the history of the past, some day when the two separate and distinct races are thrown together, some day the clash will come and the survival of the fittest, and I do not believe it is incumbent upon us to lift him up and educate him on an equal footing that he may be armed and equipped when the combat comes." Heflin spoke with the voice of twentieth-century frustrations.

The shrewdness of the authors of the suffrage article, in reconciling the aims of the various racial theories, was revealed when the debates and motions to amend had run their ineffective course. The vote to approve the entire article showed an overwhelming victory, 95–19. The minority consisted of those on the right who opposed the grandfather clause and those on the left who adhered to the principle of universal manhood suffrage. Eleven of the "no" votes came from the Republicans and Populists. All of the "yes" votes were Democratic. Disfranchisement was a reality after ten years of talk and agitation.

The differential in voting between the races was immediate and marked. In 1906 there were 205,278 whites registered in Alabama, 83 per cent of the male whites of voting age. Only 3,654 Negroes, 2 per cent of the adult men, were registered. That has been much the ratio until the campaign to increase Negro registration in the South in the 1960's.

The effect of the new constitution on white voting is more debatable. Governor Jelks was anxious to prove that the constitution worked properly. One of the big fears of white-county delegates was that the registrars would not register white men whom they suspected of improper political leanings. Could Christ and his Disciples register under the good character clause? "That would depend entirely on which way he was going to vote," said John W. A. Sanford. After the constitution was in effect, Senator Morgan became quite worried about reports that registrars in the Black Belt were registering "politically reliable" Negroes.

> I think you are perhaps unnecessarily alarmed [responded Jelks]. The Board of Appointment spent thirty days selecting these Registrars and in every instance we were assured positively that the appointees would carry out the spirit of the Constitution, which looks to the registration of all men not convicted of crime, and only a few negroes. . . .
> What is distressing me now is the general apathy on the subject of the Payment of polls.

Whether or not it resulted from apathy or poverty, Governor Jelks had cause for concern about the nonpayment of the poll tax. However, the figures for registration and for poll tax receipts might shed some light on a murky point of interpretation. Scholars are in dispute about the reasons for the rapid decline in white voting. Undoubtedly both apathy and disfranchisement played a part. The question is, which should get the greater emphasis? The crux of the problem is that there is no way to measure the number of adult men who would have voted had they not been prohibited by some legal barrier.

Perhaps some rough indication can be devised to measure the effect of at least the poll tax requirement in Alabama. The separate acts of registering *and* paying poll tax *both* had to be accomplished to enable one to vote. Men over forty-five years of age were exempt from the poll tax but still had to register. By assuming that everyone forty-five or older actually did register, it is possible to calculate that there were at least 132,117 men registered in 1904 who were required also to pay the poll tax. Only 79,151 polls were actually paid. If we assume that registration was a declaration of interest in voting, then failure to pay poll tax was caused by something other than apathy. On such a basis, a minimum of 5 per cent of the native white males between the ages of twenty-one and forty-four years, or 23.6 per cent of the total white, male, voting-age population was disfranchised by the poll tax alone. The convention had done its job well: white voters declined, Negro voters practically ceased to exist.

5

The Abnormal 'Twenties, 1920-1932

Harding the Politician

The Myth and the Reality

by Robert K. Murray

Almost before the corpse had time to grow cold, most writers on the presidency began treating Warren G. Harding with contempt. His term in office, shortened by his death in August 1923, came between the longer administrations of Woodrow Wilson and Calvin Coolidge, two men righteously upstanding in private life and public utterance. Harding, by contrast, appeared sordid and unseemly, both in his personal and official capacities. Recently, however, the bulk of Harding's private papers became available to researchers, and their examination has already produced a softening of earlier, negative appraisals.

Students of American history know at least a few details of the Harding legend, some factual but even more tidbits lacking foundation. The story, spread first by a few of Harding's cronies and embellished subsequently by journalists and historians, runs something like this: Harding was a weak-willed, "unbelievably ill-informed" (William Allen White's words) Ohio senatorial nonentity whom a smoke-filled room of unscrupulous G.O.P. politicos fingered for the presidency in 1920. Once in the White House, he paid little attention to the affairs of state, domestic or foreign, leaving such matters in the hands of subordinates, some of whom

betrayed the President's trust. Harding supposedly preferred hard
drinking, poker playing, and illicit love-making to affairs of state.
In a series of revelations that shook the administration shortly before the President's death, the country learned that corruption and
thievery, reminiscent of scandals around Grant (the President with
whom Harding is most often compared), had occurred at the highest levels.

This view of Harding achieved its acerbic apogee in a judgment made by Theodore Roosevelt's daughter, Alice Roosevelt
Longworth, that "the brevity of his tenure of office was a mercy
to him and to the country. Harding was not a bad man. He was
just a slob."

Harding's most recent biographer, Robert K. Murray, finds him
neither a slob nor a boob. Murray, the first historian to use Harding's official and personal papers extensively, believes that previous writers badly underestimated the Harding administration's
important achievements. Murray considers that it established a
successful national "breathing period" following Wilson's tumultuous second term, a period in which the country had entered
World War I, had rejected the Treaty of Versailles, and had undergone a savage post-war flurry of political repression—the "Red
Scare" of 1919–1920. Harding eased the transition of a tense and
energized nation into a quieter decade of domestic prosperity.
Murray also believes that the Coolidge administration, generally
credited with creating the close alliance of business and government interests that characterized the 1920's, followed policies set
down first under Harding. Murray concentrates on refurbishing
Harding's presidential reputation, especially his leadership role,
and however questionable some of the judgments, Murray's study
skillfully charts the onset of conservative national politics during
the "Tory 'Twenties."

❧ "President Harding is dead and I have a telegram for the Vice-
President." So shouted a delivery man to Colonel John Coolidge
whose head popped out of a bedroom window in the small white
cottage where his son was vacationing in Plymouth, Vermont. It

From Robert K. Murray, *The Harding Era* (Minneapolis: University of
Minnesota Press, 1969). Copyright © 1969 by the University of Minnesota.
Reprinted by permission; footnotes omitted.

was after midnight on the morning of August 3, 1923. Calvin Coolidge was quickly awakened by his father and with mingled feelings read the brief message from Attorney General Daugherty which urged him immediately to "Take the oath of office as successor to the Presidency." In a dramatic and homey scene, Colonel Coolidge administered the presidential oath to his son on the spot. It mattered little that the legality was dubious and the ceremony had to be repeated later in Washington, D.C.

Technically the Harding era was over and the Coolidge years had begun. But not really. Until his election in his own right in 1924, Coolidge actually served as caretaker for the Harding program, and for the time being he belonged more to the Harding period than to his own. No more unlikely person could have been saddled with such custodial responsibility. Often described as "a small, hatchet-faced, colorless man, with a tight-shut, thin-lipped mouth," Coolidge had not been impressive during the Harding era. William Allen White had referred to him in the *Emporia Gazette* as a "runty, aloof, little man, who quacks through his nose when he speaks," while Mark Sullivan had found Harding to be much "the bigger man, the larger personality."

Aside from presiding over the Senate, Coolidge's contributions to the Harding administration had been minimal. He had not participated in policy-making or in administration decisions. He stuck close to the Capitol end of Washington and consorted neither with Harding's cronies nor with the aristocracy of the cabinet. There is no record of his suggesting anything significant and the Harding Papers do not disclose any attempt on the President's part to consult regularly or purposefully with him. To Harding, Coolidge was simply "that little fellow from Massachusetts." Indeed, Harding apparently did not even consider him a permanent member of the administration. As early as 1922 there was some discussion of retiring Coolidge in 1924 and sending him back to Massachusetts to run against David Walsh for the Senate. Certainly there was no thought that Coolidge would ever succeed to the presidency.

Ironically, considering his lack of loquaciousness and his general

parsimonious attitudes, Coolidge's primary importance to the
Harding administration was social. He may have been "weaned
on a dill pickle" (which Alice Roosevelt Longworth later denied
ever having said about him), but he faithfully showed up at the
many functions which Harding could not attend. He became "the
official diner-out of the administration." Once, asked why he
accepted so many dinner invitations, he allegedly replied: "Got to
eat somewhere." Only his wife, Grace, whose charm and gracious-
ness made him more bearable, knew how miserably restless he was
in this role and how useless he felt. Coolidge's personal letters during this time were filled with uncertainty, pessimism, and irritation,
and he frequently spoke of his "barren life." Yet in his later *Autobiography* he called this "a period of most important preparation"
and revealed that presiding over the Senate was fascinating to him.
In any event, despite his restlessness, he apparently was proud to
be included as a member of the Harding cabinet and had no
thought of giving up the vice-presidency.

Coolidge's sudden succession to the presidency was a shock.
"Imagine—Calvin Coolidge, President! My God!" was the first
reaction of veteran newspaper reporters. Somehow Harding, with
all his shortcomings, seemed suited to the job—but Coolidge?
Then began an amazing metamorphosis. Newspapers created a
Coolidge image and a Coolidge myth. According to newspaper-
man Thomas L. Stokes, "It was one of the greatest feats of newspaper propaganda that the modern world has seen. It was really
a miracle. He said nothing. Newspapers must have copy. So we
grasped little incidents to build up human interest stories and we
created a character." Frank R. Kent, *Baltimore Sun* correspondent,
later commented on the phenomenon: "Not in the memory of
anyone now living has there been a President who leaned so
heavily on this newspaper tendency to praise and protect, who
profited by it so much, who would shrivel so quickly if he lost it,
as Calvin Coolidge."

Coolidge was neither as silent nor as wise as the artificially
created popular belief thereafter suggested. But because of the

scandals, the presidential office needed bolstering and this was hardly the time for the press to undermine the incumbent, whoever he was. Fortunately certain facets of the Coolidge personality fitted neatly into the desired image. Being less gregarious and affable than Harding, Coolidge naturally tempered the open and easy atmosphere surrounding the White House. This "change" was quickly heralded as a conscious effort on his part to get rid of the poker players and the "carousing" that went on during the Harding years. But this shift would have occurred anyway, regardless of the scandals. Immediately upon assuming office Coolidge told the chief usher, Ike Hoover, "I want things as they used to be —before!" Notice was served that the occupants of the White House were no longer "just folks" nor could people causually "drop in." The habitual tolerance of Harding gave way to Coolidge's inscrutable aloofness. Unlike Harding, Coolidge "slapped no man on the back, he pawed no man's shoulder, he squeezed no man's hand." A kind of puritanism descended which was certainly worthy of respect, but was not exciting. And just as they had earlier made Harding's affability a virtue, now newspapers praised Coolidge's restraint.

This Coolidge "change," however, only extended to superficialities and did not affect the Harding administration's program, or its top personnel. The claim by some that the death of Harding ushered in "a new period in American politics" was simply not true. The Harding cabinet was kept intact until public and congressional pressure forced out Daugherty and Denby. Coolidge retained all Harding appointees on regulatory boards and commissions until 1925. In the diplomatic corps the only significant change was the appointment of Frank Kellogg to replace George Harvey as ambassador to Great Britain and this was occasioned by Harvey's resignation, not Coolidge's initiative. Coolidge retained Wood in the Philippines and Crowder in Cuba. He even reappointed Dr. Sawyer as White House physician. Besides Harvey, the only major resignation following Harding's death was that of George Christian as private secretary, who left to handle Mrs.

Harding's personal affairs and who was replaced by former Representative C. Bascom Slemp of Virginia.

As for Harding's policies, Coolidge's support was immediate. In officially announcing Harding's death he stated: "It will be my purpose to carry out his polices which he has begun for the service of the American people." After his first cabinet meeting on August 14, 1923, Coolidge stated that all the policies of the Harding administration, not just some of them, would be continued. Hence, despite the cries for change from insurgent Republicans, Coolidge early staked his political future on the Harding program. Among those policies which he listed as receiving his wholehearted support were (1) the collection of all war debts, (2) participation in the World Court, (3) prevention of Soviet recognition, (4) the improvement of relations with Latin and South America, (5) further restriction of immigration, (6) continuation of economy in government, (7) maintenance of the protective tariff system, and (8) additional remedial legislation for the farmer. Two weeks later in a press conference, the new president also announced that, like his predecessor, he would oppose a soldier's bonus and enforce the Volstead Act.

In his first message to Congress in December 1923, Coolidge reaffirmed these policies and added a few more: the return of all shipping to private ownership, railroad consolidation along the lines suggested by Harding, and the maintenance of naval strength up to Washington Treaty limits. Instead of Coolidge's high-pitched voice, it could have been Harding's mellifluous tones for the hour and four minutes it required to stake out these positions. Except for his unequivocal endorsement of the Mellon tax plan of 1923, not one straying step did Coolidge take from Harding's orthodoxy, not one new idea did he advance. Strangely, the press did not remark on this fact; indeed, newspapers avoided mentioning it. They talked instead of Coolidge's "constructive policy" and his "emergent wise leadership." But it had all been advocated before and represented well-known Harding views. The Ohioan had cleared the path; now a new President walked down it with the approval of the nation.

Until 1925 Coolidge followed the Harding pattern remarkably well. He declared the League a dead issue, but retained the tenuous ties with that organization that had been established during the Harding years. He resisted all pressure for debt cancellation and, although he was willing to be malleable on interest terms and time schedules, he insisted that the debts be paid. He restated Harding's proposal for joining the World Court and supported it in the face of a recalcitrant Senate. He encouraged the rapid completion of recognition negotiations with Mexico and endorsed the removal of troops from the Dominican Republic. He reinforced the Harding decision against immediate Philippine independence and supported General Wood against the demands of Filipino politicians. Toward Russia, Coolidge at first appeared to adopt the same concilatory tone which Harding had shown in the last months before his death, but not long thereafter, mainly under the guidance of Hughes, embraced the same intransigent postion which had characterized the Harding years.

On the domestic front Coolidge's actions were also distinctly Hardingesque. In the brief anthracite coal strike in the late fall of 1923, he insisted on remaining neutral and relied on outside mediators to bring the disputants together. His hope rested primarily on local action and ultimately Governor Pinchot of Pennsylvania provided the tact and the drive which produced a favorable settlement. Like Harding, Coolidge encouraged Secretary of Labor Davis to overhaul the immigration system and endorsed the Johnson bill which was designed to curb the incoming flow even further. He strongly upheld Mellon's hand in continuing to reduce the national debt and supported the Budget Bureau. He exhorted the states to tighten their prohibition enforcement procedures, but evidenced little more interest than Harding in expending large sums of federal money on enforcement. On the bonus question, Coolidge proved to be as adamant as Harding.

When in mid-May 1924 the Congress presented him with a new bonus law, he immediately vetoed it. Unlike Harding, however, Coolidge was not able to hold Congress in line as it hurriedly passed the bill over his veto.

The bonus struggle highlighted yet another striking similarity between Harding and Coolidge. Coolidge, no less than his predecessor, continued to experience difficulty with Congress. Coolidge tried various tacks in dealing with the Republican insurgents who were either elected or re-elected in the fall of 1922. His most elaborate and naïve attempt to placate them was his announcement in September 1923 that La Follette was welcome at the White House and that the President hoped he could rely on the Wisconsin senator to support this program. La Follette, whose presidential ambitions were predetermining his actions, was not impressed. At the same time, other insurgents indicated that they intended to monitor the administration carefully and pointedly warned that on certain issues they held the balance of power.

During the first session of the 68th Congress (December–June 1924), Coolidge was treated shabbily. In the first four months after his December message not one executive proposal was acted on. Not only did Congress run roughshod over his opposition to the bonus, it ignored his plea for adherence to the World Court. It manhandled the Mellon tax plan. It even squabbled over his appointment of Harlan F. Stone to succeed Daugherty as attorney general. In the end the public felt rather sorry for Coolidge and, just before the nominating conventions in June, newspapers caught the general mood by declaring that the "public rejoices at Congress passing its resolution to adjourn." As one editor summed up its work: "a Republican Congress has devoted itself to bloodying the President's nose, boxing his ears, and otherwise maltreating him." The Harding pattern was repeating itself.

In one respect, however, the situation was markedly different—the scandals. Here Coolidge operated under a severe handicap. He had to remain pure himself while leading a party which was obviously tainted by corruption. As already noted, throughout

February, March, and early April, newspapers wallowed delightedly in the muck churned up by the various investigations. The reading public was fascinated and devoured rumors with even greater relish than the facts. In mid-March the *New York Times*, not noted for sensational reporting, was devoting three and four full pages daily to investigation matters.

Fortunately for Coolidge and the Republicans there was a limit to public credulity. By late March there were those who began to complain about excesses and especially about Wheeler's "grandstanding." Editorials began to warn readers that much of the testimony was dubious and cautioned against anything but tentative conclusions. Even the *New Republic* admitted that most of the Stinson–Means charges in the Daugherty investigation were "intrinsically improbable." More important, there were increasing complaints by businessmen and local chambers of commerce that the constant round of investigations was hurting the economy. Coolidge, recovering from his earlier fright regarding the disclosures, by mid-April began to show impatience at the Wheeler–Walsh drive to uncover more dirt. Surprisingly, the public, while still intrigued by the scandals, apparently agreed with him. As April moved into May and there were no new disclosures, the scandals disappeared into the inner recesses of the newspapers. By May 8 not a single spectator attended the dying hearings of the Teapot Dome investigation.

In the case of the Justice Department investigation, as Wheeler ultimately failed to deliver on his constant promises of other revelations of an "almost unbelievable nature," public interest not only waned but turned against him. By May both Walsh and Wheeler were receiving angry letters condemning them for their actions, and some Democrats found it necessary to explain to irate constituents why their two Montana colleagues were so zealous. It became increasingly obvious, in view of the upcoming presidential nominating conventions, that the Walshes, La Follettes, and Wheelers were less avenging angels than ambitious politicians with personal axes of their own to grind. In June, when the final Walsh report admitted that only Fall, Sinclair, and Doheny were culpable in the Teapot Dome affair, it was greeted with derision. One editor remarked: "After the thunder and the earthquake, the still small voice . . . the report of Senator Walsh." Said another, "If this is all that Senator Walsh had to recommend, we might as well not have undertaken the investigation at all." Concluded the *American Federationist:* "The single, solemn truth is that the Walsh report is a flat fizzle."

Thus the investigation mania ran its course and Coolidge, by doing nothing more than appointing a two-man special counsel and waiting for public reaction to set in, emerged virtually unscathed. He did not tamp down the fires of public discontent or party insurrection by shrewd and calculated maneuvering. He simply did what was natural for him—kept quiet and waited. The fires of discontent had never burned brightly enough to demand careful attention anyway and ultimately flickered out of their own accord. Coolidge was further aided by the fact that the electorate was still generally distrustful of Congress and observed all its actions with a jaundiced eye. Moreover the public's sense of morality had been blunted by the war and, as Will Rogers said, it was difficult to convince a jury of serious wrongdoing when most of the jurors secretly admired those who committed the crimes. Then, too, it was impossible to sustain interest in a few government scandals when several times each year the nation was witnessing other events which the headline-hungry press blew up into gigantic proportions. In the late spring of 1924 the Bobby Franks kidnapping and murder quickly supplanted the more mundane crime of Albert Fall, and not many months later the public was infinitely more concerned with the lonely plight of Floyd Collins in a cave in Kentucky than in the honesty of its government officials. The Hall–Mills murder, with its "pig woman" and various other revelations, had far more emotional impact than malfeasance in the Veterans' Bureau or the alien property custodian's office. The precise topography of De Russey's Lane in New Jersey where the murdered rector and his choir-singer mistress were found dom-

inated the news while a Forbes and a Miller were quickly forgotten.

But of all the factors in the rapid decline of public interest in
the scandals perhaps none was so important as the return of business prosperity. Throughout the spring of 1924, the scandal disclosures had to compete on the front pages of the newspapers with
bold evidence of increasing dividends, profits, and spiraling sales.
On the very day, March 24, that the oil investigating committee
voted to charge Harry Sinclair with contempt, one of the front-
page headlines in the *New York Times* read: "U.S. Steel Gained
Half Billion in 1923; Profit $108,707,064." Such indications of an
expanding economy not only turned the public mind away from
the scandals but encouraged the continuing defection of the
middle and upper-middle classes from the tenets of progressivism.
These groups rapidly embraced the new buoyant philosophy of
welfare capitalism whose chief exponent was the large efficient
business corporation and whose goals were full employment,
relatively high wages, widespread consumption, mass production,
increased leisure time, and mounting profits. In the midst of burgeoning optimism and ample evidence of affluence, these middle-
and upper-middle-income groups (the professional classes, the
small manufacturer, the tradesman, the businessman, and even
the white-collar worker) had money in their pockets, and the
feeling that soon they would have more. This rising expectation,
coupled with the outward signs of prosperity, robbed progressivism
of much of its relevancy. Die-hard liberals might long to combat
existing pockets of poverty or right society's social wrongs, but
these middle-group Americans were generally satisfied with their
lot. From their point of view, the scandals notwithstanding, there
was no need to be disturbed about the state of the nation.

Hence, it was not only public apathy, moral insensibility, emotional satiety, Democratic ineptitude, or Coolidge's purity which
rendered the impact of the Harding scandals less significant. It
was also the amazing postwar economic success of the Harding
program. Ironically, if Harding bequeathed to his successor the

awesome liability of the scandals, he also left him an asset in the form of returning industrial prosperity which politically more than made up the deficit.

The election campaign of 1924 actually began in 1922. The opening battle was the fall congressional campaign of that year and the outcome caused insurgents, Democrats, and anti-Harding opponents of all types to conclude that the Harding program was unacceptable to the public and that their own hazy plans could be substituted.

From the beginning the Republican insurgent group, in particular, miscalculated both the nature of the public discontent in mid-1922 and the actual support for its own ideas. Resting primarily on western farm dissatisfaction, this insurgency did not have the broad national appeal necessary for permanence. Instead of possessing a truly enlightened political philosophy, most of the insurgents embraced a hodgepodge of relatively unsophisticated and outmoded beliefs. Too much myth and lore of a bygone day encrusted their attitudes; they inadequately understood modern economic development; and they insisted on repeating the clichés and slogans of the late nineteenth century. By 1923 this group, in spite of La Follette, possessed poor leadership and could not rely on any substantial help from either of the major parties. Indeed, as the economic picture brightened slightly on the farm in early 1924, this element even began to lose some of its rural support.

While La Follette insurgents and remnants of the earlier farm bloc continued to blow their anti-Harding horns, especially during the scandal investigations, other anti-administration elements quietly sought new polical alignments. As early as 1919, a group of die-hard liberals met in New York City to examine the possibility of forming a national progressive political organization. This group included labor men, Socialists, old Populists, single-taxers, Bull Moosers, intellectuals, and a few La Follette insurgents. The meeting dissolved after passing a few resolutions and calling for a second gathering in St. Louis later in the year. This latter conference then created a "Committee of Forty-Eight," which was not a new political party but was intended to be a step toward one. Among the forty-eight were such divergent personalities as J. A. H. Hopkins (a former Bull Mooser), McAlister Coleman (a Debsian Socialist), Gilbert E. Roe (a La Follette lieutenant), Arthur Garfield Hays (a prominent liberal intellectual), and Frederic C. Howe (a former Tom Johnson supporter).

There matters stood until February 1922 when, in a separate move, fifteen railroad brotherhoods convened a Conference for Progressive Political Action in Chicago to "bring about political unity" and promote "a better understanding" among prolabor liberals. Representatives of the Committee of Forty-Eight attended as did members of various socialist and farmer-labor parties. It was agreed to meet again after the 1922 fall elections to establish a third-party organization if that seemed feasible. All these various elements united in their efforts to oppose the Harding administration at the polls in 1922, denouncing "the invisible government of plutocracy and privilege." Especially effective was the work of the Committee of Forty-Eight in several western states.

The fall election returns provided the impetus for further action. As planned, a second meeting of the Conference for Progressive Political Action was held in Cleveland in December, two weeks after the Washington gathering of the newly elected progressive senators and representatives under the aegis of La Follette and Norris. There was no official connection between these two groups, although some who attended the Washington meeting also turned up in Cleveland. The Cleveland affair was certainly no love feast. First, the Communists under William Z. Foster created dissension by attempting unsuccessfully to gain representation. Then a cleavage appeared between the farmer elements and the labor groups. The intellectuals were disowned by both. Finally, there was a squabble over the advisability of creating a third party. The farm groups wanted to move very slowly and perfect state organizations first. The unions also dragged their feet. Only the Socialists and more militant elements argued for immediate third-party action. A final decision was postponed until 1923.

Again in 1923 no consensus was reached and not until 1924 was it finally decided to create a third party. There was a constant struggle, meanwhile, to prevent infiltration by the Communists and to hold the various diverse elements together. Important in the final decision to create a third party were the emergence of the Harding scandals, the political demise of McAdoo as a Democratic nominee (before the Doheny disclosures he was the favorite of the railway unions), and La Follette's willingness to be a third-party candidate. Six hundred delegates flocked to the nominating convention of the Progressive party in 1924 and agreed unanimously on the Wisconsin senator as their presidential nominee. For vice-president they selected the *bête noire* of the Justice Department—Senator Wheeler. Their platform condemned the Mellon tax program, denounced protective tariffs, favored a soldier's bonus, called for the abolition of injunctions in labor disputes, and rejected the current "mercenary system of degraded foreign policy." In short, the Progressives' position represented a direct challenge to the Harding program and an indictment of almost everything for which it stood, Significantly, in the eyes of these dissident elements it was Harding who was on trial in the election of 1924, not Coolidge. Coolidge was still merely the custodian of the Harding program.

Coolidge was certainly not ashamed of that program nor was he reluctant to run on it. No sooner had Harding died than Republican politicians speculated on who would be the party's nominee in 1924. Hughes told Taft as they rode back from the station after Harding's funeral that under no circumstances would he make the race. Taft declared the same thing. There were others not so self-effacing. La Follette would eagerly have taken the nomination if the party had asked him. Hiram Johnson was waiting in the wings, as were other hopefuls. But it was clear that they could wrest the nomination from Coolidge only with great difficulty. Coolidge wanted it and intended to have it.

As early as December 8, 1923, Coolidge formally announced his candidacy. From that time forward the issue was never in doubt. One by one Harding's cabinet members endorsed him. By the spring of 1924 Hiram Johnson dropped his presidential aspirations. By mid-April Coolidge had 530 of the 555 delegates necessary for the nomination already pledged to him. It was freely predicted that by convention time he would have over 1000.

Coolidge possessed certain obvious advantages which became the favorites of historians thereafter—his incumbency, his integrity, his honesty, his silence, and so forth. Often overlooked, however, was the fact that Coolidge decided to stand on the Harding program and the 1920 platform. By so doing he automatically garnered the support of all former Harding supporters. The Harding organization now became a factor in keeping Coolidge in the White House. It was a marriage of mutual interest. As Taft wrote to Root in June 1924, "The only hope of the party is in Coolidge." Conversely, the only hope of Coolidge was in the Harding record, scandals notwithstanding.

The Republican convention was anticlimactic. Rigidly organized by Coolidge's hand-picked manager, William M. Butler, and his ubiquitous secretary, C. Bascom Slemp, the convention quickly nominated him and endorsed a reiteration of the 1920 platform. The only suspense came in the selection of a vice-presidential nominee. Various names were proposed, even Borah's. When the latter's name came up, Butler turned to Mellon and said, "Mr. Secretary, what do you think of Borah?" Looking off in the distance and taking his little black cigar from his mouth, Mellon replied: "I never think of him unless somebody mentions his name." Significantly, the convention settled on Charles Dawes as Coolidge's running mate, a man whom Harding had once mentioned as his own presidential successor and who, even during the height of the scandals, did not hide his admiration for the dead Ohioan.

Rarely before had the Democrats been so hopelessly divided as they were in 1924. That party was experiencing the first ground

swell of cataclysmic change which confronted it with an entirely
new set of circumstances. The bitter cleavage between the emerg-
ing northern urban wing and the conservative southern element
marked the beginning of a fierce internal struggle over such matters as immigration restriction, religion, and prohibition, and symbolized the cultural and ideological schism between the older and
the newer America. In the midst of such turmoil, the party's
ability to combat the Republicans was limited. The Democrats
attempted to paper over their disunity and displayed righteous
indignation at the Harding scandals by making Senator Walsh
permanent chairman of their 1924 convention. On opening day
12,000 of them jammed into Madison Square Garden to hear Senator Pat Harrison scream about the saturnalia of corruption in
Washington. Then followed the shattering experience of twenty-
nine sessions and 102 ballots to arrive at the selection of John W.
Davis, a conservative lawyer and former ambassador to Great
Britain, as presidential nominee. This folly was compounded by
naming western radical Charles W. Bryan, brother of William
Jennings Bryan, as Davis's running mate. By this action, as one
wag said, the Democratic party had succeeded in "snatching defeat from the jaws of victory."

Victory was never in sight. Neither the Democrats nor the
Progressives were able to mount a sustained offensive against the
incumbent Republican party. The alternative represented by La
Follette was obviously not acceptable to the public, while the
Democrats, with the conservative Davis at the helm, were unable
to offer any alternative at all. In some matters, such as prohibition
and Negro rights, neither of the opposing parties presented anything novel or genuinely liberal. And while Davis lapsed into a
pattern of dull campaigning, La Follette succumbed to the same
regional and class orientation which in the past had proved the
undoing of other third-party movements. Mouthing old Populist
shibboleths, La Follette tried to energize the country with warnings about "Wall Street," "bloated plutocrats," and "money
piracy." What he got for his pains was largely apathy. La Follette's

political philosophy was almost as archaic as that of bona fide reactionaries. Moreover, he found himself the leader of competing groups which possessed little basis for harmony. La Follette had to be different things to too many different men. For example, caught between labor on the one hand and the farmer on the other he often had no alternative but to utter absolute economic nonsense. He had to preach "high beef on the hoof and low beef on the table."

Surprisingly neither the Progressives nor the Democrats concentrated their fire on the one area where the Republicans were the most vulnerable—the scandals. The Republicans expected this attack and at the time of the nominating conventions many believed the scandals would cost the party the election. But events showed differently. Embarrassed by their own indirect involvement through Lane, McAdoo, and others, and fearful of a public backlash, the Democrats generally steered clear of the scandals. Here Coolidge's own purity was important. As between Davis and Coolidge there was no issue of corruption.

The Progressives were more aggressive on the subject, but even they fell short of expectations. While La Follette attacked both major parties by claiming that "fraud, graft and corruption under the last Democratic administration [Wilson's] equaled in magnitude, if not in venality, that of the administration now in power," he was too busy raking Wall Street for its "gigantic robberies" to be particularly bothered with such peripheral thievery as that committed by Fall. Of all the candidates, only La Follette's running mate, Senator Wheeler, made corruption the hallmark of his campaign. His favorite tactic was to debate an empty chair, representing Calvin Coolidge, at which he would fire demands such as "tell the people of New York City why you kept Harry M. Daugherty as Attorney General." Of course there would be no response, after which he would quip, "There, my friends, is the usual silence that emanates from the White House."

The Republican strategy was inevitable—perhaps masterful as some claimed—considering the personality of their candidate.

The scandal issue was met with silence. Coolidge stuck to the theory that no candidate was ever injured by not talking too much. Coolidge knew that public-opinion polls showed him ahead and that all he had to do was avoid mistakes. In July the *Wall Street Journal* was already proclaiming a Coolidge victory. Charles Michelson, a veteran Washington reporter, later stated he could not "recall anybody who thought John W. Davis had a chance." There was even talk that La Follette might lose Wisconsin and the Northwest. By late October the *Literary Digest* poll showed Coolidge outstripping his closest rival by more than two to one and receiving a minimum of 327 electoral votes. Even such a Democratic stalwart as Senator Walsh despaired of his party's winning and began to hold a post-mortem long before the votes were counted.

Of the 28,647,000 votes cast, Coolidge received 15,275,000, or 54 per cent, in a three-way race, a phenomenal showing. Davis collected a little over 8,385,000 and La Follette 4,826,000. Coolidge carried thirty-five states with 382 electoral votes; Davis twelve with 136; and La Follette one (Wisconsin) with 13. Later it was fashionable for historians, striving to show the continuance of the progressive spirit, to emphasize La Follette's vote. But, by any test, his showing was poor. Of his 4,826,000 votes, 3,798,000 were cast as Progressive; 858,000 as Socialist; and 170,00 as Farm-Labor. Roughly 2,500,000 of his votes came from agrarians and a little over 1,000,000 from labor. In other words, even in the Midwest fewer than one-third of all the votes cast went to La Follette. The election results in Kansas, Iowa, and Nebraska represented a complete La Follette collapse. Here neither farmers nor laborers voted for him in the numbers expected. In the nonindustrialized, sparsely populated regions of the country, where his vote was greatest, he never ran higher than second, and only in Wisconsin was he first. Thus in no area, except in the senator's own home state, was the only real alternative to the Harding program endorsed by the electorate.

In analyzing their own defeat, Democrats, and some later historians, claimed the major factor was the suicidal Madison Square Garden convention fight and sighed, "if only McAdoo had been nominated." This was wishful thinking. As Josephus Daniels wrote to Franklin Roosevelt in 1927: "I believe that [if McAdoo] had been nominated in 1924 before the bitter feeling of Madison Square [Garden], that he would have pulled the labor vote and . . . have won the party many of the dissatisfied farmers in the West, but I do not think he could have been elected." Few persons really believed that Smith could have beaten Coolidge either, but most agreed that Davis was certainly the wrong candidate. Even this, however, can be debated. In view of returning prosperity and the general conservatism of the public at that moment, Davis may have made a better, not a worse, showing than the other available Democratic candidates.

As for La Follette, the reasons for his defeat were obvious. Labor support was not wholehearted, the public was suspicious of many of the groups that championed him, his agrarian support was not unified, he had little monetary backing, he possessed no effective party organization, he harped on worn-out issues, and, most important, his program had no popular appeal. The rapid demise of the Progressive party after the election attested to the impermanency of his support and the quixotic political behavior of the elements that made up his following. Immediately after the defeat, the Socialists, agrarians, and labor groups came to a parting of the ways. Progressive congressmen who had supported La Follette quickly scurried back into the Republican or Democratic fold. In February 1925, amid considerable wrangling, the Conference for Progressive Action was formally liquidated. Four months later, in June 1925, La Follette followed it into the grave.

Coolidge's victory was ascribed to various factors—his political shrewdness, his honesty, his silence, and so on. Some observers went so far as to claim that his victory was purely a personal one and did not represent a public endorsement of his party. This conclusion belied the facts. Republicans gained in both houses and increased their control in state and local communities. The election of 1924 was actually a repetition of 1920—it demonstrated a continued public desire for "normalcy," but with this significant difference. In 1920 the voting public had no point of reference to what constituted "normalcy"; in 1924 it had such a reference— the Harding policies, which Coolidge had promised to continue. Therefore, voter endorsement was not made in the dark in 1924, nor was it the result of the campaign magic of one silent, honest man. Harding and his administration had constructed a program which by 1924 was so basically acceptable that even the shock effect of scandal could not affect it.

Business prosperity was probably the major campaign factor. Prosperity represented the consummation of the Harding policies and gave them validity. Without such prosperity the election prospects for Coolidge would have been far different. Prosperity did several things. It justified conservatives in their beliefs and it convinced many others, even some liberals, that whatever caused such outstanding economic advance had to possess some "progressive" qualities. Old doctrinaire labels became blurred in the glow of economic progress, and even some former Progressives after 1924 embraced the new economic order as a logical extension of Wilsonian liberalism.

In any case, Coolidge's election marked the true end of the Harding era. Henceforth American politics carried Coolidge's special stamp and he no longer lived so directly under the shadow of his predecessor. Beginning in 1925 several changes were made in the cabinet, especially in State and Agriculture, which permitted Coolidge to influence more personally both foreign affairs and domestic economic matters. After 1925 Coolidge rapidly packed regulatory boards and agencies with his type of men. Thereafter he openly showed a big-business bias in contrast to Harding who had struggled to maintain some kind of balance between business and agriculture. As Coolidge's most recent biographer said, he stood in awe of the Dodsworths and respected his fellow Babbitts. Just after Harding's death, William Gibbs McAdoo prophesied that Coolidge would prove to be "a more useful servitor of the interests than Harding was." Indeed, from the beginning, the *Wall Street Journal* enthusiastically hailed Coolidge's elevation to the presidency and proclaimed that he was "sound from every angle." Clarence W. Barron, who accurately reflected the feelings of big business, greeted the opening of Coolidge's administration with "He has never made a mistake in action or in his public utterances on economic questions." Coolidge's lackluster message to Congress in December 1924, which was not even delivered in person but was read in a monotone by disinterested clerks, was highly praised in business circles precisely because it recommended nothing more than the status quo. Chief Justice Taft uttered a widely held business opinion when he wrote to Elihu Root: "It isn't essential that we should have a great amount of legislation. . . . What we need is stability and not movement at the present time."

Business could well afford to be satisfied. In contrast to the Harding era, Secretary Mellon emerged after 1925 as the single most important presidential adviser. Coolidge thereafter rested his political life on Mellon's economics and consulted closely with him before making any moves. Hoover continued as secretary of commerce and also played a part in enhancing the business image, but he was never in as much presidential favor as he had been under Harding. Coolidge often referred to Hoover as the "Wonder Boy" and in a fit of pique in 1928 remarked: "that man has offered me unsolicited advice for six years, all of it bad!" Along with others, Hoover was oftentimes in sharp disagreement with Mellon's theories. For example, after 1925 Mellon reversed his earlier stand and increasingly supported easy money policies while Hoover constantly warned of their dangers. In cases involving such opposing opinions, Coolidge would customarily admonish: ". . . if I were in your position, I think I would yield my views to that of the Treasurer [Mellon]."

"Business seems to be in the saddle," said *Harper's* in early 1925. "Let us see what it can make of the job." If there was any real change after Harding, this was it. A business civilization emerged triumphant and the Harding era of conciliation, consensus, and accommodation gave way to the business-dominated "wonderful nonsense" of the subsequent period with its growing stock speculation, bull market, ticker-tape parades, Mayor Jimmy Walker, Peaches Browning, flagpole sitting, and bunion derbies. But still it must be remembered that in this mad race for pleasure, quick riches, and affluence the Harding era had supplied the starting gun, loaded the cartridge, and pulled the trigger.

Through it all the taciturn little man in the White House could "sit tight." He could do so because, despite the momentary danger and aggravation of the scandals, his predecessor had provided him with an economic and political philosophy which was well suited to the times, and had bequeathed him mainly settled problems rather than unsettled ones. This was a much different legacy from the one left Harding by his predecessor.

"The accurate historian will rank Warren G. Harding as one of the really great Presidents of the United States of America. No other historical verdict will be possible." So wrote George Christian in an article for *Current History* in September 1923, just a month after Harding's death. Almost forty years later, Arthur M. Schlesinger published the results of a poll of seventy-five American historians who were asked to rate the Presidents, and with "little dissent" they agreed that Warren G. Harding was a flat failure. Scandals, suspected personal immorality, and ineffective leadership were mentioned as the chief factors which prompted such an adverse verdict. Thus, despite Christian's high hopes of 1923, historians, in whom he had placed such supreme confidence, by mid-century had relegated Warren Harding to the bottom of the pile as the worst President ever to hold that high office. How this came about represents a final irony in the Harding story.

In August 1923 the *Outlook* in its obituary of Harding wrote this epitaph: "Among American Presidents Harding will be one of the least misunderstood. No myth will obscure his personality."

Except for Washington and Lincoln, no American President has
been surrounded by as many myths, as much misunderstanding,
and as many inaccuracies as Harding. Immediately after his death,
well-meaning but highly emotional eulogies crowded the pages
of magazines and newspapers, bestowing on him attributes which
he did not possess and which he would have been the first to deny.
The years 1923–24 saw the appearance of no fewer than four
full-length biographies deifying him. All were hopelessly sentimental and generally useless except for demonstrating one fact:
Harding was briefly remembered as one of the nation's most
loved Presidents.

The corrosive effect of the scandals, Nan Britton's disclosures in
The President's Daughter, and Gaston Means's compendium of
lies, *The Strange Death of President Harding*, prompted a devastating reaction. This set the pattern for much subsequent
mythmaking and muckraking. Throughout the thirties and forties,
pulp magazine such as *True Detective Stories* continued to titillate
readers with wholly fictional exposés of Harding's private life,
while tabloids like the *New York Daily News* discovered that
sensational tales about the former President still sold newspapers.
Even as late as 1963, such publications as *Inside Story* and *Fact*
carried reports which "proved" that Harding was "America's First
Negro President," while Clare Booth Luce loaned her prestige
to an article in *McCall's*, entitled "All for the Love of a Lady," in
which she gave millions of modern housewives a warmed-over
version of the Britton episode direct from the pages of Nan's own
book.

Never at any time after the onset of the thirties did the works
of Harding's apologists, such as Daugherty's *The Inside Story of
the Harding Tragedy*, offset the cumulative effect of this muckraking activity and, as Oswald Villard had prophesied, the muckrakers continued to capture public attention. To Harding's friends
this appeared as rank injustice. But in terms of historical accuracy,
justice would not have been served if only apologists like Daugherty had emerged victorious. Inaccuracies, gross errors, and faulty

conclusions were shared by apologists and muckrakers and both groups contributed to a clouded picture of the twenty-ninth President.

Ultimately, neither of these groups proved to be the most significant element in creating a mythical Harding for posterity. From the outset the main bulk of lasting impressions concerning the Ohioan and his administration came from the journalistic world—especially from the so-called liberal journalists. Representing only a small minority of the working press, these men were extremely articulate and were mainly political mavericks or Roosevelt–Wilson followers. In their treatment of Harding, they made him the last major victim of their own wartime and postwar disillusionment. In him they discovered a convenient outlet for all their own frustrations arising from a feeling of ideological betrayal and defeat. Harding became their scapegoat for the wartime and postwar degeneration of Wilsonian liberalism. . . .

Although such sensational matters as sexual escapades and mixed-blood stories continue to appeal to popular writers and the prurient-minded public, they remain of peripheral value in any over-all historical assessment of the Harding era. While Carrie Phillips hinted darkly several times at "exposing" Harding if he did not do her bidding and Nan Britton claimed that she received some "spending money" from him, there is absolutely no evidence of any aberrant political activity on Harding's part which can be traced to his extramarital dalliances. His relationship with Nan, whatever the facts, in no way altered the pattern of his political beliefs or the character of his political life. Even Carrie's angry and violent pleas in 1917 that he vote against the war with Germany, a situation on which she expended most of her threats, did not prevent him from speaking out in favor of it on the Senate floor. These amorous detours apparently had no impact on his senatorial career, his nomination or election, or his presidency. With or without their existence, the Harding administration's agricultural, labor, business, conservation, marine, immigration, tariff, fiscal, and overseas policies would have remained the same. This latter is also true in relation to Harding's other personal habits or traits—his drinking, smoking, swearing, card playing, and golfing had little to do with his administration's success or failure. Too long have Harding's detractors obscured his contributions by stirring up emotional dust over these personal activities; conversely, too long have Harding's relatives and friends struggled to whitewash his personal immorality. Ultimately, his historical significance, if any, lies in the nature and effectiveness of his presidency.

Over the years that presidency has almost become a cliché. The "Harding administration" has been used in virtually every presidential election since 1924 as an example of evil and the epitome of a bankrupt "do-nothing" political philosophy. On the basis of the record, this picture is grossly unfair. Coolidge exaggerated when he claimed, "It would be difficult to find two years of peacetime history in all the record of our republic that were marked with more important and far-reaching accomplishments." But he was closer to the truth than William Allen White, who once claimed: "President Harding's administration from 1921 to 1923 was an episode, a sort of intermezzo between President Wilson with his illusion of world peace unfairly negotiated and President Coolidge with his speculative boom."

Taken separately, the Harding administration's achievements were rather impressive—the peace treaties, the Budget Bureau, the Washington Conference, agricultural legislation, economy in government, debt reduction, and business recovery—but the total was more important than any of the parts. The Harding administration acted as a cushion against the friction and the acrimony of the Wilson days and eased the transition of the nation to a prosperous peacetime existence. The period 1921–23 was one of crisis and readjustment—these were years of tremendous economic and social change. Harding was able to secure a general consensus during this period which facilitated national progress rather than blocked it. By all standards of political compromise, the Harding administration was a success. Harding's personal contribution as an emollient and mediator was immense.

If the net effect was restorative for the nation, contrary to contemporary appearances, it was also constructive for the Republican party. Out of office for eight years, that party had no policy and no program. The Harding administration provided it with both. Partly the result of conscious endeavor and party accidental, this program proved so adaptable that it was retained with only minor variations throughout the rest of the twenties and elicited the support of two succeeding Presidents. Endorsed wholeheartedly by the public in 1924 and again, indirectly, in 1928, this "normalcy" program in longevity alone has to be classified as highly significant. In a very real sense the entire decade was the "Harding era."

In terms of honesty and frankness of purpose, the Harding administration was relatively unique. This seems like a ridiculous statement in view of the scandals. However, rarely has an administration been so open about its goals and proceeded so rapidly to achieve them. In 1920 Harding was no unknown quantity and represented no political surprise. Everything for which he stood he had articulated in his campaign speeches and few Presidents have so conscientiously attempted to translate campaign promises into reality. That many of these were "conservative" and at variance with the thinking of numerous "liberals" is beside the point. If a criterion for political success is that the electorate receive almost exactly what it has been told to expect, then in Harding's case the criterion was fully met.

The Harding administration also deserves considerable credit in view of the recalcitrant role of Congress. Not since the Reconstruction period had Congress been so obstreperous as during the immediate post–World War I years. In opposing Wilson this Republican-controlled body had gotten so used to trampling on the prerogatives of the chief executive that it could not stop even after a Republican was elected to that office. Harding, of course, was no strong executive, but in view of congressional attitudes it was perhaps just as well. More often than not he handled Congress masterfully and, since that body was not prepared for domination by the executive anyway, it probably gave him as much as, if not more than, it would have given to a more aggressive President. Yet Harding sometimes displayed unusual political courage, especially when congressional intransigency threatened his ability to maintain economy in government or undergird a sound America First.

Perhaps more important, the Harding administration represented a momentary salutary balance between the various competing forces in the American economic system. In this respect Harding was able to accomplish what neither Coolidge nor Hoover could do after him. Under Harding, business had not yet succeeded in infiltrating government to the exclusion of other interests. Harding, more than his two successors, was actually "President of all the people" and a champion of no specific interest. Too, Harding remained remarkably open-minded and malleable on most questions. During his administration, although they did not then realize it, liberals and progressives alike had a greater opportunity to influence decision making at the top level of government than at any other time during the rest of the decade. Despite the scandals, Harding's administration was less controlled by vested interests or by pressure groups than the administrations of either of his successors. Furthermore, the economy was in better balance under Harding by 1923 than it was thereafter under either Coolidge or Hoover.

Obviously, the Harding administration possessed serious defects. No amount of new manuscript materials or reevaluations can alter this fact. Its solutions to pressing domestic problems were oftentimes shallow and makeshift. Its economic philosophy, particularly in relation to the tariff and war debts, was outmoded and no longer fit realities. Its lack of sensitivity to the needs of the working man was patently clear. Its economic conservatism precluded any real experimentation in dealing with the grave problems of agriculture. While it showed some interest in the social and welfare sectors, it moved only gingerly and without the required enthusiasm. Its various attempts at international cooperation were less than aggressive and its approach to the problems of war and peace was relatively unsophisticated.

But of all the administration's defects perhaps none was so crippling as the qualities of Harding himself. Certain of his virtues —his gentleness, his humaneness, his affability, and his gregariousness—so highly prized in Marion, became faults in Washington, D.C. Undoubtedly a more discriminating mind than Harding's would have detected the unworthy men among his associates and blocked them from securing high office. Harding's particular friends and acquaintances represented a heavy burden for any President to bear. The President himself obviously had a number of skeletons in his own closet—skeletons which, if not affecting his administration while he was alive, plagued it after his death.

In the American political system there is no such thing as an innocent bystander in the White House. If Harding can rightly claim the achievements of a Hughes in State or of a Hoover in Commerce, he must also shoulder responsibility for a Daugherty in Justice and a Fall in Interior. Especially must he bear the onus for his lack of punitive action against such men as Forbes and Smith. By his inaction he forfeited whatever chance he had to maintain the integrity of his position and salvage a favorable image for himself and his administration. As it was, the subsequent popular and scholarly negative verdict was inevitable, if not wholly deserved.

It is perhaps to Harding's credit that he had few illusions about himself. He was "small town" and unsophisticated and he knew it. He was a conservative whose political values came from a bygone day when men looked more to themselves for their salvation than to Washington. This he freely admitted. Not long before his death, in words highly reminiscent of a later, younger, and more liberal President, he exhorted one audience, "think more of what you can do for your government than what your government can do for you." Moreover, his intellectual talents were not outstanding and his mental capacity was not enriched either by a first-class education or by rigorous self-discipline. This he also admitted. He once said: "I know my limitations; I know how far removed from greatness I am." Such laudable frankness cannot be accepted as a substitute for ability nor can it compensate for the many errors made or the opportunities lost. Yet Harding was not, as one New York editor once called him, "an indistinguished and undistinguishable unit in the ruck of Republican Senators." And, as Harry New later put it, "he was a much abler man than he thought himself."

Still, as many observers later claimed, Harding probably should never have been President. Possibly that was the key mistake which, in view of his personal shortcomings and his past, Harding's own native intelligence should have prevented. But he *was* President and as such he was certainly the equal of a Franklin Pierce, an Andrew Johnson, a Benjamin Harrison, or even a Calvin Coolidge. In concrete accomplishments, his administration was superior to a sizable portion of those in the nation's history. Indeed, in establishing the political philosophy and program for an entire decade, his 882 days in office were more significant than all but a few similar short periods in the nation's experience. Yet the Harding era is still mainly remembered for its smoke-filled room, its Nan Britton, and its Teapot Dome. The record notwithstanding, its myths still command more attention than its realities.

The Urban Thrust

American Political Parties and the Rise of the City

by Carl N. Degler

The overwhelming majority of urban political machines today are Democratic, not Republican, and in nearly all presidential elections since 1928, most Northern industrial cities have gone Democratic. These facts, along with large doses of Democratic rhetoric, have reinforced the popular notion that one party, the Democratic, has throughout our history been identified with urban voters. "Artisans for Jefferson" somehow blended into "Mechanics for Jackson," and these, in turn, blended into "Immigrant Workers for Cleveland" and all his Democratic successors, on up to the present. Historians have known for some time that actually urban voting patterns have shifted more erratically from party to party, depending on such factors as the specific issues in a campaign (rational or emotional), the candidates' ethnic and religious backgrounds, regional variations among cities in different sections; and voting distinctions between cities with predominantly native-born or immigrant populations.

From time to time major shifts in the over-all party allegiance of urban voters have taken place, but never in any simplistic or total fashion, of course. During the Gilded Age both major parties competed for the nation's cities, and each party possessed its par-

ticular urban strongholds. Yet during the congressional elections
of 1894 a dramatic surge toward the Republican party occurred
in most major metropolitan areas. This surge ushered in a period
of Republican domination of national, urban politics which lasted
until the equally significant election of 1928, when the loser, Al
Smith, began the process of regaining for his party Democratic
strength among urban voters, especially among immigrants and
their children. During the next decade, the 1930's, Democratic
control of the cities would become one of the most important
realities of American politics, and Franklin Roosevelt would cash
in the chips bought by Al Smith. Carl Degler highlights these
shifts, and explains urban voting patterns over the previous cen-
tury, in the following article.

The ending of Reconstruction in 1877 deprived both Republican and Democratic parties of the issues that had sustained their
rivalry for half a century. As a result, in the presidential elections
from 1876 to 1892, neither party won decisively; never before nor
since has popular political inertia been so noticeable. More important, this indecision of the voters obscured the significant fact
that the Republican party was popularly weak. For despite the
preponderance of Republican Presidents during these years, only
James A. Garfield secured a popular plurality and his was the
smallest in history. The party's weak popular base was even more
evident in the congressional elections between 1874 and 1892
when the Democrats captured sizable majorities in the House of
Representatives in eight out of ten Congresses. So serious was this
popular weakness of the party that Republican Presidents from
Rutherford B. Hayes to Benjamin Harrison, as both Vincent P.
De Santis and Stanley P. Hirshson has shown, worked in a variety
of ways to build up a stronger Republican party in the South, but
with very limited success.

Thus in the opening years of the 1890's the Republicans as a

From *The Journal of American History*, Vol. LI (June 1964), pp. 41–59.
Reprinted by permission; most footnotes omitted.

national party were in obvious trouble. The elections of 1890 and 1892 were disastrous for them as the Democrats swept into firm control of the House of Representatives and into the White House as well. Despite the party's proud association with the winning of the War for the Union, the Republicans were no more popularly based than at their founding forty years earlier; the majority of the nation's voters remained stubbornly Democratic. Moreover, with each passing election the political value of that vaunted association depreciated further as memories grew dimmer. The party seemed destined to recapitulate the history of the Whigs by serving only as a convenient alternative to the Democrats.

At that point, though, a complete reversal in party prospects took place. In the congressional election of 1894 the Republicans clearly emerged as the majority party, leaving the Democrats to wander in the political wilderness for a generation. The transfer of seats in the election of 1894 from the Democratic to the Republican side of the House was the largest in history. The Republicans gained a majority of 132, whereas in twenty-four states not a single Democrat was elected and in six others only one Democrat was returned in each. Moreover, prominent Democrats like William L. Wilson of West Virginia, William McK. Springer of Illinois, and Richard L. Bland of Missouri—men associated with important Democratic doctrines like low tariffs and free silver—lost their places. This overwhelming Republican congressional victory in 1894 was confirmed two years later by what for the Republicans was to be their first decisive presidential victory without benefit of federal protection of Negro voting in the South. Measured against the margins of defeat in previous elections, William Jennings Bryan's defeat was crushing; he ran farther behind the winner than any candidate of a major party since Ulysses S. Grant trounced Horace Greeley.

Dramatic as the Republican victories for 1894 and 1896 undoubtedly were, their enduring significance lies in the continuance of the trend they began. For the next sixteen years the Republicans, without interruption, commanded the majorities in the House and elected the Presidents. Thus in the middle of the 1890's the Republicans, for the first time, emerged as the majority party of the nation.

The question which arises is: why? At the outset one can reject the hypothesis of challenging new leadership, since the party enjoyed none in the 1890's. Furthermore, since the shift in votes took place when Grover Cleveland, an acknowledged conservative, was President, and continued when a radical Democrat, Bryan, was the party's candidate, the policies of the opposition party do not offer much help in explaining the change. The only place left to look is among the voters themselves. It is their attitudes that changed as the United States passed from an agricultural to an industrial economy.

In spite of all that has been written to emphasize that the 1890's was the period during which this agrarian to industrial transition occurred, there are valid reasons for placing this momentous shift in the preceding decade. It was, for example, during the 1880's that the production of manufactured goods surpassed farm goods in dollar value, and it was in this same decade that a majority of the nation's work force became engaged in non-agricultural rather than agricultural pursuits. Also during the 1880's railroad construction reached unprecedented heights, with more miles of track laid than in any other decade in American history. These were years of peak membership of the Knights of Labor, something over 700,000; the American Federation of Labor was formed, and the number of industrial strikes sharply increased. It was the decade of the frightening Haymarket riot in Chicago, which, in its nationwide notoriety, epitomized the arrival of the new world of the factory, the city, and the immigrant. In fact the number of immigrants who flooded into the country in that decade exceeded that of any other similar period in the century. Furthermore, those ten years were the seedtime of the city. According to a contemporary analysis of the census, the number of cities with 8,000 or more population jumped from 286 in 1880 to 443 in 1890.

Many cities doubled in size in the ten years, and some, like Chicago, had been already large at the beginning of the decade. A few made spectacular records of rapid growth. Minneapolis jumped from 47,000 to 165,000; Omaha reached 140,000 in 1890, though ten years before its population had been no more than 31,000; Denver nearly tripled its population.

During that decade of transition neither the political parties nor the people were prepared by previous experience for the problems and nature of the new industrial, urban age. Hence the politics of the 1880's were sterile, uninteresting, and often trivial, as the parties and the voters rehashed stale issues and only reluctantly faced the new. Then, in the early 1890's, it would seem, the decision was made; the commitment of the voters hardened. The question then remains: why did the Republican party, which thus far had been sectionally based and numerically weak, rather than the popular Democratic party, emerge from this period of indecision as the dominant party of the nation?

A part of the answer seems to lie in the public image of the two parties. The Republican party was more suited to the needs and character of the new urban, industrial world that was beginning to dominate America. In those years the Republicans were the party of energy and change. They inherited from their antebellum beginnings as well as from the experience of Reconstruction a tradition which looked to the national authority first and to the states second. The party and its leaders had not hesitated to use the national power in behalf of economic growth by sponsoring such measures as the Homestead Act, land grants and loans to railroad construction companies, and protective tariffs. During the Civil War the Republicans demonstrated their willingness to use income and inheritance taxes, and fiat money when the nation's survival had seemed to require such novel measures. In the 1880's, it was Republican Senator Henry W. Blair who sought to employ the federal revenues and power in behalf of aid to the public schools. In each of the four times that the Blair education bill came before the Congress, Republican support always exceeded Democratic support.

This nationalistic tradition and these specific measures, of course, also added up to a national image of the party that would appeal to urban voters and immigrants. As the self-proclaimed party of prosperity and economic growth, the Republicans could expect to win support from those who managed the expanding factories and crowded into the tenements of the burgeoning cities. Certainly party spokesmen made appeals to the urban working class. In 1892, for example, President Harrison told the Congress: "I believe that the protective system, which has now for something more than thirty years continuously prevailed in our legislation, has been a mighty instrument for the development of our national wealth and a most powerful agency in protecting the homes of our workingmen from the invasion of want. I have felt a most solicitous interest to preserve to our working people rates of wages that would not only give daily bread, but supply a comfortable margin for those home attractions and family comforts and enjoyments without which life is neither hopeful nor sweet." Nor should such appeals be hastily brushed aside as empty rhetoric. Republican claims received substance, if not proof, from the steady rise in real wages during the last three decades of the century. Moreover, foreign observers, like Friedrich Engels, who certainly could not be accused of being partial to Republican propaganda, cited the tariff as one of the principal reasons why American workingmen were better off than European. In 1893 Engels wrote to his friend Friedrich A. Sorge that "through the protective tariff system and the steadily growing domestic market the workers must have been exposed to a prosperity no trace of which has been seen here in Europe for years now. . . ."

The Democratic party, to a greater extent than the Republican party, was more a congeries of state organizations than a national party. Certainly in the South and in a northern state like Illinois, there were many Democrats in the 1890's who were far from agreement with the national leadership. But even with these cautionary observations, of the two parties between 1880 and 1896, the Democrats undoubtedly presented the more conservative face to the electorate. The hallmark of the party under the dominance of Cleveland was economy, which in practice meant the paring down of government assistance to business, opposing veterans' pensions, hoarding the national resources, lowering the tariff, and, in general, stemming the Republican efforts to spur economic growth and to enhance the national power. Besides, the Democrats were ideologically unsuited to any ventures in the expansion of governmental activities. Still steeped in the Jeffersonian conception of the limited role of the federal government, the national Democrats were less likely than the Republicans to use federal powers in new ways to meet new problems. It was Cleveland, after all, who had vetoed a meager $10,000 relief appropriation for drought-stricken Texas farmers with the stern warning: "though the people support the Government the Government should not support the people."

The election results of the 1880's suggest that the Republicans were even then receiving returns from their bid for working-class support. Today it is axiomatic that the big cities of the country will vote Democratic, but in that period most of the large urban centers outside the South were more likely to be Republican than Democratic. It is true that cities like New York, Boston, and San Francisco were usually safely Democratic, but in the three presidential elections of the 1880's a majority of the nation's cities over 50,000 outside the South went Republican. In these three elections—even though in two of them Cleveland polled a larger vote than his Republican opponents—eastern and midwestern cities like Philadelphia, Chicago, Cleveland, Cincinnati, Buffalo, Providence, Milwaukee, Newark, Syracuse, Paterson, and Minneapolis invariably appeared in the Republican column. In the election of 1884, which was won by Democrats, the Republicans captured twenty of the thirty-three non-southern cities over 50,000.

In 1888 the Republicans took twenty-six of the forty-four largest non-southern cities listed in the census of 1890.[1]

Furthermore, many of these Republican cities contained substantial proportions of immigrants. The 1890 census showed thirty per cent or more of the population of Chicago, Milwaukee, Paterson, Cleveland, Buffalo, Pittsburgh, Providence, and Rochester to be foreign-born.[2] All of these cities voted consistently Republican in the three presidential elections of the 1880's.

But the tendency for Republicans to do better than Democrats in northern cities must not be exaggerated. The election of 1892, with its upsurge of Democratic strength in the cities, demonstrated that Republican popularity in the urban centers was neither so overwhelming nor so fixed that the popular Democracy might not reduce it. Clearly some other force, some other ingredient in the mixture, was operative. That additional factor appears to be the depression of 1893.

The depression of the 1890's was an earth-shaker. Not only did it last five years or more, but it was the first economic decline since the United States had made the transition to full-scale industrialism. As a consequence its effects were felt especially in the growing cities and among the working class. A recent historian of this depression has estimated that real earnings for the population

1. According to the *Tribune Almanac of 1881* there were thirty-six cities in 1880 with a population of 50,000 or more. The two southern cities of Richmond and New Orleans, and Washington, D.C., which did not possess a national vote, have been excluded from my count. In the tabulation for 1888, Memphis, Nashville, and Atlanta, as southern cities, have also been excluded in addition to the three excluded for 1880 and 1884. It might be noted for the benefit of those unfamiliar with the form of the statistics in Burnham's and Robinson's compilations of the presidential vote that the county is the smallest unit reported. Thus, my figures for the cities are actually the returns for the counties in which the cities are located and not strictly the cities themselves.

2. See table in *Eleventh Census: 1890, Population* (Washington, 1895), pt. 1, xcii. Strictly speaking, these figures are not comparable with those on voting since the immigration statistics are for the city only while the voting figures are for the county. Nevertheless, the city figures certainly suggest the importance of the immigrant in these Republican districts and that is all that is intended.

dropped 18 per cent between 1892 and 1894. The single year of 1894 witnessed Coxey's army as well as other less well-known armies of unemployed workers on the march, widespread labor unrest, and the violence of the Pullman and Chicago railroad strikes. More workers went out on strike in that year than in any other in the century. The number was not equalled again until 1902.

Since it is true that the Republicans for all their belief in the national power would not have taken any stronger anti-depression measures than the incumbent Democrats, the election upset of 1894 might be considered as nothing more than a case of blind, rather than calculated, reprisal against the incumbents. Furthermore, it might be said that the Republicans had been chastised in much the same fashion in 1874 when they chanced to be in power at the beginning of the depression of 1873. The objection is not as telling as it appears. In the election of 1894 there was a third party, and if simple dissent were operating, the Populists should have benefited as much from it as the Republicans. But this they did not do. Although the total Populist vote in 1894 was higher than in 1892, not a single state that year, John D. Hicks has observed, could any longer be called predominantly Populist. Four western states, Kansas, Colorado, North Dakota, and Idaho, all of which had voted Populist in 1892, went Republican in 1894. In a real sense, then, the election was a victory for the Republican party and not simply a defeat for the Democrats.

If the terrible impact of the depression polarized the voting in a new way, thereby helping to explain the massive shift to the Republicans, the activities of the Democrats in 1896 could only confirm the urban voters in their belief that the Republican party was the more responsive political instrument. In their convention of 1896 the Democrats hardly noticed the cities; they had ears only for the cries of the farmers demanding currency reform. Many Populists, it is true, stood for something more than free silver, but the money issue was certainly accepted by Bryan and the vast majority of Democrats as the principal issue of the cam-

paign. Free silver was at best uninteresting to the urban population and, at worst, anathema to them. The adoption of such a
monetary policy would be inflationary and therefore contrary to
the interests of all urban consumers, whether bankers, petty
clerks, or factory workers. Mark Hanna, McKinley's campaign
manager, sensed this defect in Bryan's appeal from the outset.
Early in the campaign he said about Bryan: "He's talking silver
all the time, and that's where we've got him."

And they did have him. The cities, where the industrial workers were concentrated, voted overwhelmingly Republican. Only
twelve of the eighty-two cities with a population of 45,000 or
more went for Bryan—and seven of the twelve were in the Democratic South while two others were located in silver-producing
states. Seven of the seventeen cities in the states that Bryan carried gave a majority to McKinley; on the other hand, only three
of the sixty-five cities in states going to McKinley provided a
majority for Bryan. Bryan was hopeless in the industrial East; he
did not carry a single county in all of New England, and only one
in New York, and eleven rural counties in Pennsylvania. He even
lost normally Democratic New York City.

Taken together, the elections of 1894 and 1896 mark the emergence of the Republican party as the party of the rising cities.
Even a cataclysmic event like the Civil War, in which the Democrats were on the losing side, had not been able to dislodge the
Democracy from its favored place in the voters' hearts. But the
impact of an industrial-urban society with its new outlook and
new electorate had done the trick. It is significant that several
cities like San Francisco, Detroit, Indianapolis, Columbus, and St.
Paul, which had been Democratic in the 1880's and early 1890's,
voted Republican in 1896 and remained Republican well into the
twentieth century. None of the large cities which had been Republican in the 1880's and early 1890's, on the other hand, changed
party affiliation in 1896 or for decades thereafter. Another indication of the continuity between the elections of 1894 and 1896 is
that the states which showed the greatest Republican congres-

sional gains in 1894 also showed increased Republican strength in
the presidential election two years later. There were twelve states,
each of which gave the Republicans four or more new seats in
1894; of these, eight were among the states which in 1896 showed
the greatest number of new counties going to the Republicans.
Significantly, they were mainly industrial-urban states like Illinois,
New Jersey, New York, Ohio, and Pennsylvania.

It is commonplace for textbooks to depict the Republican party
of the late nineteenth century as the political arm of the Standard
Oil Trust, but if the election returns are to be given any weight
at all, that is not the way the voters saw the party in the 1890's.
Not only was it the party of respectability, wealth, and the Union;
it was also the party of progress, prosperity, and national authority. As such it could and did enlist the support of industrial workers and immigrants as well as merchants and millionaires. As one
analyst of the 1896 New England vote saw it, the Democrats may
have obtained their most consistent support among the poor and
the immigrants of the cities, but the Republicans gained strength
there, too, "just as they did in the silk-stocking wards. . . . They
were able to place the blame for unemployment upon the Democrats and to propagate successfully a doctrine that the Republican
party was the party of prosperity and the 'full dinner pail.' "

Ideologically, it is true, the Republican party in the 1890's had a
long way to travel before it would translate its conception of the
national power into an instrument for social amelioration. But it
is suggestive that Robert M. La Follette in Wisconsin and Theodore Roosevelt in Washington, who are the best known of the
early Progressives, were also Republicans. It is these men, and
others like them in the party, who carried on the political revolution of 1894, which had first announced the Republican party as
the majority party in the new America of cities and factories.

The significance of that political revolution is that the pattern
of party allegiance then established continued for many years to
come. To be sure, in 1912, because of a split in the Republican
party, Woodrow Wilson was able to break the succession of Re-

publican Presidents. But it is also evident that the success of the Democrats in 1912 and 1916 should not be taken as a sign of a fundamental change in voter preferences. One reason for thinking so is that in 1916 Wilson was re-elected by the very close margin of 600,000 popular and twenty-three electoral votes and in 1920 the Republicans swept back into the White House on a landslide. Another reason is provided by the Democratic losses in the House of Representatives after 1912. That year the Democrats achieved a margin of 160 seats over the Republicans, one of the largest in congressional history, but by the mid-term elections the difference between the parties was down to 35; by 1916 it was less than 10. In 1918 the Democrats lost control of the House.

The most persuasive evidence for believing that the Republicans continued to be the majority party of the nation, despite the interruption of the Wilson administrations, is the history of elections during the 1920's. In 1920 Warren G. Harding received over 61 per cent of the votes cast, a proportion of the total not achieved since the advent of universal manhood suffrage and only equalled once thereafter. Although other Republican presidential victories in the 1920's did not reach the proportions of the Harding landslide, they were all substantial. Furthermore, at no time between 1920 and 1928 was the Republican margin of strength in the House of Representatives endangered; it never went below twenty seats. In fact, near the end of the decade, Republican strength in the House was reaching out for a new high; in 1928 it was one hundred seats greater than the Democratic proportion. In the presidential election that year Herbert Hoover's majority over Alfred E. Smith was more than six million votes. In short, by the end of the 1920's the Republicans were as much the majority party of the nation as they had been in 1894 when the tide of history first turned in their favor.

Within four years, though, another political revolution had been consummated, this time returning the Democrats to the position of the majority party of the nation. In 1932 the Democrats elected their second president in forty-two years and cap-

tured the House of Representatives with a majority of unprecedented size, something like 190 seats. The true measure of the
reversal of political patterns, though, did not come until 1934 and
1936. For with their overwhelming victories in those two elections,
the Democrats showed that 1932 was not simply another 1912,
when a large Democratic victory had been quickly eroded away in
subsequent elections. Instead, in 1934 the Democrats reversed the
patterns of the preceding fifty years; rather than losing seats in the
House, as was customary in off-year elections, they actually added
ten more to their swollen total. And then in 1936 they succeeded
in re-electing Franklin D. Roosevelt by an overwhelming majority, with a proportion of votes that came very near topping Harding's landslide of 1920.

Because the Roosevelt revolution in politics coincided with the
onset of the Great Depression, it is tempting to argue that it was
economic adversity in 1932, much as it had been in 1894, which
accounts for the shift in the voters' preferences. Certainly the impact of the depression had much to do with the long-range change;
it undoubtedly accounts for the overwhelming character of the
shift. But there is also much evidence to suggest that the shift
which first became evident in 1932 was already in progress four
years before. Beneath the surface of Hoover's victory the forces
which would consummate the Roosevelt revolution were already
in motion in 1928 in behalf of Alfred E. Smith.

The most obvious comment to be made about Smith's vote
was its large size. Smith's 15 million votes were 6.5 million more
than John W. Davis had polled in 1924, when La Follette's Progressive candidacy had drawn away some Democratic votes, and
5 million more than James M. Cox and Roosevelt had been able
to capture in 1920. With this enormous gain, if by nothing else,
Smith showed himself to be the most popular Democratic candidate since Bryan in 1896.

But important as Smith's ability to attract votes may have been,
his contribution to the turn to the Democrats lay in something
more than mere numbers. After all, Hoover increased the Re-

publican vote by some five million over Coolidge's total in 1924 and Harding's in 1920. What was significant was that Smith's unique combination of politically effective personal attributes was attracting a new class of voters to the Democratic party. Many years after the election, Hoover pointed out that in 1928 the candidates of both major parties had risen from small beginnings to become figures of national prominence. But if this was true of the origins of Smith and Hoover, by 1928 the two men were poles apart. Unlike Hoover, or any previous presidential candidate of either party, Smith was both of lower class social background and a native of a big city. As is well known, his life and his career in politics were closely associated with New York City and the Tammany political machine. It is true that his four terms as governor of New York showed him to be progressive in thought and action as well as honest and courageous, but his loyalty to Tammany was both well known and unshakeable. Furthermore, Smith was a Roman Catholic and, though he had no intention of making his religion a political issue, many Protestants did. In fact, in 1927, an article that gained national prominence challenged him to show that his religion would not interfere with his proper execution of the duties of president. Although Smith's parents were native New Yorkers, his religion, his mother's Irish background, and his close association with Irish-dominated Tammany Hall stamped him as a spokesman for the urban immigrants. In short, he was the first presidential candidate to exhibit the traits of a part of the population that had never before been represented by a candidate of a major party.

Smith's religion, which hurt him in the South and helped to explain why Hoover was able to capture four southern states, undoubtedly assisted him in the North. Massachusetts and Rhode Island, both heavily Catholic in population, went Democratic in 1928 for the first time since the Civil War. In fact, while Hoover was taking 200 southern counties from the Democrats, Smith took 122 northern counties that had been consistently Republican. Moreover, of these 122 counties, 77 were predominantly Roman

Catholic; most of these 77 counties remained in the Democratic column, it is worth emphasizing, in subsequent elections.

Since Roman Catholicism in America is an immigrant religion and its communicants are largely concentrated in the big cities, most of the new counties Smith gained were urban. Indeed, the striking thing about Smith's candidacy was that it attracted the big city vote away from the Republicans for the first time since the 1890's. In 1920 Harding had taken all of the twelve cities with a population over 500,000, but in 1928, among these twelve, New York, Cleveland, St. Louis, Milwaukee, and San Francisco went for Smith though their states did not. Moreover, Pittsburgh and Baltimore failed to give Smith a majority by fewer than 10,000 votes each. Of the twelve cities only Los Angeles was strongly for Hoover. If the votes of all twelve cities are added together, Smith secured 38,000 more votes than Hoover; in 1920 the Republicans had carried the same cities by 1,638,000 votes. In a broader sample, a recent student of the election has shown that in 1920 Harding carried all twenty-seven of the principal cities outside the South; in 1928, Smith captured eight, and made appreciable gains in the others. He ran behind Cox and Roosevelt in only three of the twenty-seven. Such a reversal was one sign that a socio-political revolution was under way.

Despite all that has been written about Smith's appeal to the voters of the big cities, the significant point, often overlooked, is that his appeal was not of equal force in all cities. For example, he ran badly in southern cities, the residents of which exhibited, when compared with other southerners, the weakest commitment to the historic party principles that had made the South a stronghold of the Democrats. In fact, Dallas and Houston in Texas, and Birmingham in Alabama went Republican in 1928. More important was Smith's strikingly uneven attraction for the cities of the North. His attractive power was considerably stronger in those cities in which immigrant stock predominated than in those in which it was in the minority. (Immigrant stock is defined here as foreign-born whites and native whites born of one or more foreign-born parents.) According to the census of 1930, the closest to the election of 1928, there were thirty-six cities with populations in excess of a quarter of a million. In nineteen of these cities, immigrants and children of immigrants constituted 50 per cent or more of the population. In the presidential election of 1920, all of these nineteen cities voted Republican; in the election of 1924 all but one voted Republican. In the election of 1928, though, seven of them turned Democratic.

On the other hand, in the seventeen cities out of the thirty-six in which the native-born whites of native-born white parents constituted a majority of the population in 1930, only four went Democratic in 1928, and three of them were located in the traditionally Democratic South (Atlanta, New Orleans, and Memphis). The fourth was St. Louis. In fact, Democratic strength in these "native-white" cities actually declined in 1928, for in the 1920 and 1924 elections six of the seventeen had gone Democratic. All six of them, it should be noted, were in the Democratic South. Thus in the election of 1928 among the cities in which native whites consituted a majority, there was actually a loss in Democratic strength. In short, Smith's appeal to urban voters was not simply that he was of urban origin but that his Catholicism and Irish background stamped him as a champion of immigrants and children of immigrants. At the same time, those cities in which the immigrant stock was in the minority retained their allegiance to the Republican party—an allegiance which had been first clearly established in the 1890's for the big cities as a whole.

Yet it might be said that Smith failed, after all, to carry even a majority of the cities with a preponderance of immigrant stock. He won only seven of the nineteen cities of immigrant stock. Does not this fact call into serious question the assertion that there was a relationship between the social character of these cities and Democratic voting?

Closer analysis suggests not. As inspection of Table 1 makes evident, in every one of the cities with 50 per cent or more immigrant stock, whether they were carried by Smith or not, the Demo-

cratic vote increased enormously in 1928 over 1920, when the
Republican majorities had been very large. In fact, in none of the
cities in which immigrant stock predominated was the Democratic
increase less than 100 per cent, and in many it was considerably
higher. In these same cities, on the other hand, the Republican
vote increased as much as 100 per cent in only one of the nineteen
cities and in only three did it go above 50 per cent (Oakland,
Pittsburgh, and Seattle). In several of the cities that Smith carried, the Republican vote actually fell from that of 1920.

Table 1

Cities with 50 Per Cent or More Immigrant Stock *

City	Democratic vote in nearest thousand		% Change	Republican vote in nearest thousand		% Change
	1920	1928		1920	1928	
Boston	68	205	202	108	99	−7.7
Buffalo	40	126	215	100	145	45.0
Chicago	197	716	266	635	812	27.8
Cleveland	71	166	132	149	195	30.7
Detroit	52	157	201	221	265	19.9
Jersey City	63	153	143	102	100	−1.9
Los Angeles	56	210	275	178	514	189.0
Milwaukee	25	111	344	73	82	12.2
Minneapolis	143	396	178	519	561	8.1
Newark	41	118	188	116	169	45.6
New York	345	1,168	239	786	715	−9.1
Oakland	21	61	190	73	119	63.2
Philadelphia	90	276	209	308	420	36.5
Pittsburgh	40	161	301	139	216	55.5
Providence	46	97	112	80	86	7.5
Rochester	29	74	156	74	100	35.2
St. Paul	21	57	171	40	53	32.5
San Francisco	33	97	195	96	96	0.0
Seattle	17	47	176	59	96	62.9

* Two cities in this list, Oakland and Seattle, counted 47.8 and 48.2 per cent,
respectively, of immigrant stock, but they have been included here rather than
in Table 2, because they also have less than 50 per cent of native white population. Their proportions of native white population are 46.4 and 47.7 per cent,
respectively. The missing proportions are accounted for by colored persons.

If one examines the Democratic performance in those cities in which the native-white population predominated, the conclusion that there was a close association between the increase in Democratic votes and immigrant stock is further strengthened. In none of these cities was there much of an increase in either the total vote or in the vote for the Democratic candidate. (See Table 2.)

Table 2

Cities with Less than 50 Per Cent of Immigrant Stock

Cities	Democratic vote in nearest thousand		% Change	Republican vote in nearest thousand		% Change
	1920	1928		1920	1928	
Akron	28	32	14.3	44	79	79.5
Atlanta	9	7	−22.5	3	6	100.0
Baltimore	87	126	44.8	126	135	7.3
Birmingham	25	17	−32.0	7	18	157.0
Cincinnati	78	110	41.0	113	148	31.0
Columbus	48	47	−2.3	60	92	53.2
Dallas	14	17	21.4	5	27	440.0
Denver	23	41	78.5	44	74	68.1
Houston	15	22	47.7	8	27	237.0
Indianapolis	61	73	19.7	80	110	37.4
Kansas City, Mo.	77	97	26.0	80	127	58.6
Louisville	56	64	14.3	68	98	44.3
Memphis	16	18	12.5	9	12	33.3
New Orleans	33	56	70.0	18	14	−22.2
Portland, Ore.	28	45	60.5	45	76	68.8
St. Louis	106	176	66.0	163	162	−0.68
Toledo	30	45	50.0	52	78	50.0

Only in Denver did the Democratic vote increase as much as 75 per cent; in no city did it reach as high as 100 per cent as it did in every one of the cities in Table 1. In five the increase was less than 25 per cent and in three there was actually a loss of Democratic votes. The median value is 26.0 per cent.

The Republican vote in Table 2 provides a revealing contrast with the Democratic vote in Table 1, for now it can be seen that the "native-white" cities produced no upsurge in voting for Republans comparable to that in the cities of immigrant stock. Except for a marked—and what turned out to be temporary—upturn in Republican strength in the southern cities of Atlanta, Birmingham, Dallas, and Houston, the increase between 1920 and 1928 in none of these cities was as much as 100 per cent. The median value is 53.2 per cent.

From this examination of the variability in the response of the cities to Smith's candidacy it seems clear that Smith brought out the immigrant vote in unprecedented numbers. Some of these voters of immigrant stock had probably been voting Republican all along and now switched to the Democrats. But many more, it would seem, voted for the first time, for otherwise one cannot explain the enormous increase in Democratic votes in the short span of eight years without a commensurate decline in Republican votes. These same people, backed by even greater numbers, would come out in 1932 to vote for Franklin Roosevelt and consummate the Roosevelt Revolution in politics. But it was Smith, the Catholic and the recognized champion of the urban-based immigrant, who first made the Democratic party the party of the cities and the immigrant. This upsurge in immigrant voting in 1928 helps to explain, at least negatively, the apparent paradox of urban support for a Republican party in the 1920's that defended Prohibition and pushed for restrictions on immigration. Prior to the galvanizing appearance of Smith on the political landscape, most urban imigrants just did not vote at all and many probably did not even think of themselves as part of the body politic. And to those who did vote, the Democratic party offered no candidates, other than Wilson, to lure them away from the party of national power, Theodore Roosevelt, and prosperity. Samuel Lubell has suggested, further, that the broadening educational opportunities of the 1920's also help to explain the upsurge in immigrant political participation in 1928.

Despite familiarity with the connection between the cities and the Democratic party today, that connection was not forged, as far as the nation was concerned, until 1928–1932. Indeed it is the conclusion of this paper that it was the political activity of urban voters which raised the Republican party to a position of dominance in American politics for a third of a century, just as it has been the cities which have been largely responsible for the Democratic party's leading place in the nation's political life for the most recent third of this century. For Franklin Roosevelt after the landslide of 1936 continued to receive the support of the vast majority of the 37 principal cities of over 250,000 population, carrying 32 of them in 1940 and 30 in 1944.[3] Harry Truman in 1948 did about as well, even though the Dixiecrat candidate took three of the traditionally Democratic southern cities. Truman's score was 30 of the big cities against 4 for Thomas E. Dewey.

The real test of the Democratic power in the cities came in 1952 with the first campaign of Dwight D. Eisenhower, certainly the most popular Republican of the twentieth century. In that election and the next, Eisenhower made substantial inroads into the urban territory of the Democrats. In his first election, for example, he carried 21 of the 39 cities over 250,000 and in 1956 he did even better by taking 28 of them—almost as many as Franklin Roosevelt did in 1944.[4]

But there are two good reasons for seeing this resurgence of Republican strength in the cities as temporary and nothing more than a reflection of the special appeal of Eisenhower rather than as a basic shift in popular party allegiance. The first reason is that Eisenhower was able to carry a majority of the House of Representatives for his party in only the first of his four congressional

3. The cities are those listed in Tables 1 and 2 above, but with San Antonio added since it passed 250,000 population by 1940. Conclusions about urban strength of the parties have been derived from the county voting statistics compiled in Edgar Eugene Robinson, *They Voted for Roosevelt: The Presidential Vote, 1932–1944* (Stanford, 1947) and from those in *The Political Almanac, 1952* (New York, 1952).
4. The thirty-nine cities are those listed in Tables 1 and 2 but with Fort Worth, Omaha, San Antonio, and San Diego added because they reached the 250,000 population mark by 1950 and with Providence eliminated because it fell below that level. The conclusions on the urban strength of the parties and the results of the congressional elections have been derived from Richard M. Scammon, ed., *America Votes* (4 vols., New York, 1956–1962).

elections. Indeed, his own popular vote in 1956 was greater than that of 1952, but he proved unable, nonetheless, to do what every popular president since Zachary Taylor had been able to do: carry a majority of his party into the House of Representatives.

In this failure the cities played a part since many of them that voted for Eisenhower did not grant the same degree of support to the Republican congressional candidates. This tendency was most obvious in the southern cities, where he showed great strength. In 1952 he carried six of the eight southern cities and in 1956 he captured all but Atlanta. Yet in the congressional races in all of these cities, Democratic congressmen, because of the South's one-party system, were almost invariably returned. More important, the same tendency could be observed in cities outside the South. For example, in the Ninth Ohio District (Toledo) a Democratic congressman was returned in all four of Eisenhower's congressional elections, though the General personally carried the city in 1952 and 1956. Although Eisenhower won Cook County, Illinois in 1956, eight of the twelve congressional districts of the city of Chicago went Democratic. Newark and Denver, both of which supported Eisenhower in 1952 and 1956, sent only Democratic congressmen to Washington throughout the Eisenhower years. Eisenhower won Milwaukee in 1956, but the two congressmen elected from the city that year were Democrats.

The second reason for seeing Eisenhower's substantial victory as more personal than partisan is that in the election of 1960 John F. Kennedy, despite his close victory in the national popular vote, regained the cities for the Democrats. He carried 27 of the 39 cities, even though he did less well than Stevenson in 1952 among southern cities, capturing only New Orleans, San Antonio, and ever-faithful Atlanta. A large part of the explanation for Kennedy's failure to regain southern big city support commensurate with his general increase in urban backing is to be found, of course, in southern dislike of the Democratic party's stand on civil rights which began with Truman and which Kennedy went out of his way to support and advance. Nevertheless, the defection also calls attention to the quite different social character of southern, as compared with northern, big cities. There are very few Catholics or children of immigrants in southern cities, so that an Al Smith and a John F. Kennedy have no religious or social appeal there as they do in the North. That this difference was influential is suggested by the return to the Democratic fold in 1960 of San Antonio and New Orleans, the only two southern cities containing substantial numbers of Catholics and children of immigrants.

In short, as the congressional strength of the Democrats throughout the Eisenhower years had suggested, the election of 1960 showed that the Democrats still retained the long-term allegiance of the big city voters, whose support had first been evident thirty-two years before in another campaign by a Roman Catholic grandson of an Irish immigrant.

WASP America's Pyrrhic Victory

Folklore of the Campaign of 1928

by Paul A. Carter

Calvin Coolidge may have sensed the dangers that lay ahead before he announced that he would not run for re-election in 1928. Republicans then turned to Herbert Hoover, "the Great Engineer," a Coolidge cabinet officer who was not the professional politicians' choice but who seemed the best available Republican. Hoover rose meteorically before World War I as a mining engineer and self-made millionaire. He won international fame and admiration during the war itself, directing American relief efforts in Europe.

To millions of Americans, Hoover came to symbolize the Progressive businessman at his best, a man who had harnessed administrative and organizing talents to humane purposes. As Secretary of Commerce from 1921 to 1928 he had brought advanced business ideas to Washington. Hoover wanted to replace conflict between capital and labor with welfare capitalism; cutthroat competition with trade associations and business cooperation; and negative government with active encouragement to all economic sectors, promoting prosperity and social stability. One of the most effective exponents of a more responsible "American individualism," his countrymen regarded him as an impartial public servant *rather than a professional, and presumably self-serving, politician. Hoover seemed blessed with the vision and the technical expertise required to lead a modern, industrial society.*

In this sense, Hoover represented a shift in Republican leadership from figures like Harding and Coolidge, men whose appeal stemmed largely from their ability to evoke nostalgia for a simpler, bygone America. In contrast, Hoover thoroughly identified with the view that America had entered a new era created by the genius of American business and capable of producing unprecedented affluence. Four more years of Republican rule, Hoover and his party promised, would bring the country closer to the day when it would achieve final victory over poverty.

Hoover's Democratic opponent, Governor Alfred E. Smith of New York, ran despite several political handicaps. He was the first representative of the Newer Americans, the first Catholic, and the first poor boy from a big city to run for President. In 1924 Southern and Western rural Democrats had blocked Smith's nomination, apparently willing to lose an election rather than accept someone with Smith's cultural background. When Smith did win the nomination four years later, many rural Democrats crossed party lines. Political feelings ran so high in 1928 that Republicans cracked the Solid South for the first time since Reconstruction. Many of the bolters voted for Hoover to save America, they thought, from a Catholic orgy of rum and Romanism. Conflicts between the two cultures, urban and rural, dominated the 1928 campaign and had been nationally divisive throughout the decade. Yet it is doubtful that any Democrat, even a Methodist bishop, could have beaten Hoover in that prosperity year.

Hoover won impressively, yet the extent of his victory obscured for a time an awareness of important shifts in voting behavior which would have long-term consequences. Smith ran unusually well in the Republican farm belt (though he did not, of course, carry it), and this was a clear sign of rural discontent with the GOP. His strength lay in the cities with their large ethnic populations. Although his New York (Noo Yawk) accent and manners evoked laughter and derision among the native-born Protestants, the urban immigrants accepted Smith as one of their own. Newer Americans who had previously voted Republican or had not both-

*ered to vote trooped to the polls in 1928 to support Smith and
help swing most big cities into the Democratic column.*

*"The cities exist," catechized Walter Lippmann in 1927, "but
they are felt [by old-stock Americans] to be alien, and in this uncertainty as to what the cities might yield up, men turn to the
old scenes from which the leaders they always trusted have come.
. . . Here are the new people, clamoring to be admitted to America, and there are the older people defending their household
gods." Hoover, though a technocrat and a business enthusiast,
reflected this village sense of virtue far more strongly than his opponent did in 1928. Paul A. Carter comments below on the meaning of the election for both American politics and society.*

❦ At an early stage in the presidential campaign of 1960, Denis
Brogan, interpreting that campaign from a foreign perspective,
wrote: "American politicians live to an extraordinary degree by
historical shorthand, by the memory of past . . . episodes that
'prove' that this *must* happen or that this *cannot* happen. And
high on the list of such political rules of thumb is the belief that
'Al' Smith was defeated in 1928 because he was a Catholic."

Up until election night of 1960, and indeed in some worried
minds up until the meeting of the electoral college in December,
the conclusion commonly drawn from this rule of thumb was that
any Catholic American who sought the Presidency could expect
the same fate as Smith. But even before the nomination and election of John F. Kennedy as the first Catholic President of the
United States, the rule of thumb had begun to be challenged.
Richard Hofstadter, for example, said in an article published early
in 1960: "There was not a Democrat alive, Protestant or Catholic,
who could have beaten Hoover in 1928." John D. Hicks in a review in 1958 declared: "Had Smith been nominated in 1932, he
would almost certainly have won." And in 1952 Samuel Lubell,
in an arresting sentence which is already reshaping the historiog-

From *Wisconsin Magazine of History*, XLVI (Summer 1963), 263–72.
Reprinted by permission; footnotes omitted.

raphy of the 1920's, maintained that the 1928 election demonstrated, not the fatal weakness of a Catholic candidate for the Presidency, but precisely the reverse: "Before the Roosevelt Revolution there was an Al Smith revolution."

Yet political folklore dies hard. As recently as 1956 . . . Edmund A. Moore examined the 1928 presidential campaign and warned that the supposed "unwritten law" against Catholic Presidents might still be in effect; therefore, politicians who were Catholics would be better advised to aim at the relatively modest office of the Vice-Presidency as a more realistic personal and political goal. Two years later, in the *dénouement* of his lucid and moving biography of Al Smith, Oscar Handlin wrote that at the time Smith's death "no Catholic . . . could aspire to be President, whatever other avenues of advance might be open."

"Can a Catholic be President?" As early as 1924, at least one American Catholic, Martin Conboy, put the question in such a way as to imply the answer "yes." In that era, when Alfred E. Smith was Governor of the nation's most populous state, there had already been a number of Catholic Governors and Senators, and two Chief Justices of the United States: "Short of the Presidency, Catholics have held every position of importance within the gift of their fellow citizens"—therefore, Conboy reasoned, why not the Presidency? The closing of the question in the affirmative as of 1960 invites at least a re-examination of the question as of 1924 and especially as of 1928.

One of the discoveries of the 1960 election has been that when Americans ask themselves the question "Can a Catholic be President of the United States?" it is necessary to specify what kind of Catholic. During 1959 and 1960, the thought of John F. Kennedy as a prospective President prompted all kinds of misgivings, among both liberals and conservatives, which had nothing whatever to do with religion. *Mutatis mutandis*, the same may be presumed of Al Smith in his day—although the misgivings roused by the man from Fulton Street would have been of a different sort from those roused by the man from Hyannis Port. One of President Kennedy's pre-election critics, for example, summed up his impression of the candidate in the title of an article: "The Cool Eye of John F. Kennedy." It is difficult to imagine anyone making precisely this assessment of Smith. Stock campaign jokes of 1960 about the Democratic candidate's Harvard accent and his father's millions —related no doubt to the "country squire" stereotype of Franklin Roosevelt still popular among aging Republicans—are a far cry indeed from the Al Smith portrayed in some of the more savage political cartoons of 1928: a bibulous, ungrammatical roughneck.

Professor Moore in his study of the 1928 campaign has shown that the anti-Smith feeling contained a considerable element of sheer social snobbery, connected perhaps with the traditional middle-class Republican image of the Opposition as shiftless good-for-nothings—the image classically set forth in 1896 in the editorial "What's the Matter with Kansas?" "Can you imagine Al Smith in the White House?" the Republican National Committeewoman for Texas asked a W.C.T.U. meeting in Houston, visualizing for them a President Smith committing *gaucheries* of grammar and etiquette; and, more to the point for that audience, "Can you imagine *Mrs.* Smith in the White House?" Those last words would have rather a different ring had they been said about the former Jacqueline Bouvier!

While Moore's point on the effect of snobbery in the 1928 election is well taken, mere snobbism can not fully account for the detestation of Smith on the part of many who, like Al, could claim a heritage from the wrong side of the tracks. The most militant of all the anti-Smith forces, the Klansmen, liked to think of themselves as plain and even poor people (which some of them were), "open to the charge of being 'hicks' and 'rubes' and 'drivers of second hand Fords.'" For such voters to concur with W. C. T. U. ladies from Houston, there had to be something more than simple social condescension to unite them. The common bond most frequently assumed has been anti-Catholicism. But the Woman's Christian Temperance Union had quite another primary concern, and the members of the Ku Klux Klan spent a part of their energies in destroying whisky stills. An inescapable political issue throughout the 1920's for any candidate, regardless of his church or his manners, was Prohibition.

Common causes which unite rather widely disparate kinds of Americans—anti-Masonry, Free Soil, free silver, world peace, and most recently anti-subversion—are of course an old chapter in the republic's history. When they have been comparatively short-lived, or when they have not seemed clearly related to issues which are alive for a later generation, the emotions which such movements can arouse have often seemed inexplicably intense. Robert Moats Miller has wisely noted: "Nothing is more difficult than for an individual indifferent to a certain issue to appreciate that to others it might be of transcendent importance." It can only be said again that Prohibition *was* deemed to be of transcendent importance by millions of Americans both "wet" and "dry"; the sheer bulk of serious public discussion of the issue during the 1920's is enough to document the point. Since the anti-liquor crusade of the twentieth century emerged from nineteenth-century conflicts which pitted Protestant against Protestant, it would be begging the question to insist that the prohibitionist case against Smith was nothing but a cover for anti-Catholicism. Hoover was "sound" on liquor; Smith was not. For many a voter the issue was as simple as that.

Edmund A. Moore, in the able study of the 1928 election previously referred to, up to a certain point makes this same judgment: "There can be no doubt that the enforcement, by statute, of the ban on alcoholic beverages was an issue of great importance in its own right." But he warns us that "Prohibition . . . was often made to play hide-and-seek with the religious issue," and suggests that the extensive debate on Prohibition may have been a sublimated version of a debate on Catholicism, frank discussion of which was "limited by a widespread sense of delicacy and shame."

But to speculate on what discussants *may* have meant—on the "latent" as opposed to the "manifest" content of their discussion,

so to speak—is to play a very dangerous historiographic game indeed. Having in mind some of the imputations of religious prejudice in the 1960 campaign, as for example the journalistic treatment of the West Virginia presidential primary, the historian of
the 1928 campaign ought perhaps to be less concerned with
searching out anti-Catholicism assumed to be masquerading as
something else than with avoiding the error of assuming what
might be called "anti-Catholicism by association." This effort,
which would now be superfluous in the case of John Kennedy, is
still necessary when discussing Al Smith.

And yet a further pitfall awaits the historian of Prohibition,
after he has disentangled it from anti-Catholicism: the temptation to construe such a question in terms of equivalent *political*
ideas, so that the Wets become "liberal" and the Drys become
"conservative." This reading of the question then becomes as-
similable to a liberal-versus-conservative reading of the Smith-
Hoover campaign more generally, especially when one notices that
four of the conservative "solid-South" states carried by Herbert
Hoover were subsequently to be twice carried by Dwight Eisenhower, and three of them again by Richard Nixon. But in the case
of Prohibition, as least, these "left"–"right" categories of political
ideology break down; the present writer has shown elsewhere that
a progressive, social-welfare, and even radical outlook pervaded
the anti-liquor movement at least in its incipient stages and to
some extent throughout its existence. So unquestionably liberal
a journal as the *Christian Century* justified supporting Hoover in
1928 on prohibitionist grounds; and one social radical in 1932,
finding the Democrats, the Republicans, and the Socialists either
insufficiently liberal, insufficiently "dry," or both, by process of
elimination voted Communist!

Conversely, there were "wet" conservatives. Senator Oscar Underwood, for example, in his later years condemned the Eighteenth
Amendment because it "challenged the integrity of the compact
between the States" and compelled men "to live their lives in the
mold prescribed by the power of government." The Alabama Sen-

ator argued, furthermore, that the Drys could no more force their interpretation of the Eighteenth Amendment on the Wets than the North could force its interpretation of the Fourteenth Amendment on the South. When one reflects that this same conservative Southern Senator had courageously denounced the Ku Klux Klan at the Democratic Convention of 1924 and thereby ruined his own chances of being a presidential nominee, the campaign of 1928 which followed becomes even harder to see in "liberal" versus "conservative" terms.

Yet Smith himself is persistently seen by his latter-day admirers as a "liberal" who became "conservative" only upon the failure of his "liberal" expectations. He was not always seen in this light, however, by his contemporaries; Walter Lippmann wrote in 1925: "[Smith] is really a perfectly conservative man about property. . . . He believes in the soundness of the established order. . . . He is what a conservative ought to be always if he knew his business." When one finds a *New York Times* story on June 27th, the second day of the 1928 Democratic National Convention, headlined "Stocks up in 'Smith Market' as Raskob tells business it need not fear, the governor," one begins to understand what Lippmann was talking about: "Market leaders such as General Motors, United States Steel, Anaconda Copper, Allied Chemical and New York Central, had a sharp run-up. . . . Buying orders poured in so rapidly . . . that Wall Street began talking of a 'Smith market.' Friends of the Governor were said to be actively in the market, prepared to demonstrate that the financial and business interests are not hostile to his candidacy."

One of these friends of the Governor was John J. Raskob, whose remarks, the *Times* noted apparently without irony, "frequently have stimulated buying enthusiasm in the stock market." Franklin Roosevelt, among others, had serious misgivings about Smith's choice of Raskob as Democratic national chairman, largely on account of this Wall Street taint—yet some of Smith's putative liberalism has rubbed off on the General Motors financier, who is described in Oscar Handlin's biography of Al Smith as "another

poor boy who had come up in the world." Raskob grew up, Handlin writes, in "the free-and-easy atmosphere of Detroit where
religious prejudice seemed altogether out of place." Remembering the notorious anti-Semitism of the then president of the leading competitor of General Motors, one is a little surprised at
hearing Detroit described as being a city altogether free of religious prejudice; here is another indication that a straight liberal/
conservative interpretation of the campaign of 1928 must be burdened with more ideological freight than it can carry.

Moore, in contrast to Handlin, sees Raskob's role in the campaign in terms not of liberalism but of expediency: the Democrats
had to win some of the business community away from its prosperous love affair with Hoover Republicanism, and Raskob was
their instrument for this purpose. But had not the candidacies of
stanch "gold standard" advocate Alton B. Parker in 1904 and corporation counsel John W. Davis in 1924 demonstrated that
Democratic attempts to beat Republican conservatism at its own
game usually failed? Moore does note that Raskob's appointment
as national chairman "seemed like an insult to the dry, Protestant,
rural South"; was it not equally an insult to the Democratic Party's anti-corporate, anti-speculative Progressives and liberals?

If, then, the campaign of 1928 will not reduce to a campaign
between liberals and conservatives, snobs and plain people, or
Wets and Drys, are we then left with Protestant against Catholic
by process of elimination? Not necessarily. Let us return again to
the contemporary assessment of Smith by Walter Lippmann:
"The Governor's more hasty friends show an intolerance when
they believe that Al Smith is the victim of purely religious prejudice. . . . There is an opposition to Smith which is as authentic
and, it seems to me, as poignant as his support. It is inspired by
the feeling that the clamorous life of the city should not be acknowledged as the American ideal."

Closely allied to the image of the corner saloon in American
folklore has been the image of the Eastern city slicker. It is a

venerable one; dissipated urban vice in contrast to abstemious rural virtue are themes as old in history as are cities themselves. In America, as witness Jefferson's *Notes on Virginia* and Royall Tyler's play *The Contrast*, they antedate the Constitution. There is also a long-standing tradition of the South and the West perennially arrayed politically against the urban East, almost regardless of the specific political issues confronting America at any given moment. The anti-Smith country in the election of 1928 was, by and large, the old Bryan country—which suggests that the Prohibition issue, and the Klan issue, and possibly even the Catholic issue, were surface stirrings of animosities of another kind. It may be noted in passing that this same trans-Mississippi Bryan country of 1896, which had become Hoover country by 1928, was to become Nixon country in 1960 and Goldwater country in the maneuverings which followed; so perhaps President Kennedy and Governor Smith had more in common as actors of an American political role than simply their religion, or their status as (by definition) liberal Democrats.

"The principal obstacle in Smith's way," wrote a contemporary observer of the pre-convention maneuverings of 1928, "never becomes palpable. . . . It lies in the fact that to millions of Americans he . . . embodies something alien. Not something alien in race or religion, but something alien to themselves . . . something they do not understand and which they feel does not understand them. . . . Some of the perturbed Methodist clergymen in the South opposed to Smith's nomination unconsciously revealed what really moves them most profoundly . . . when they said he was 'New York minded.' "

Had these words been written by one of those same perturbed Methodist clergymen, or indeed by any other Protestant, or even by a secularist liberal such as Lippmann, they could be cited as merely an unusually tortuous rationalization for anti-Catholicism. But they were written *by a Catholic*, and were printed in the Catholic liberal weekly *Commonweal*. And, conscious that bogey-

men are not slain by one magazine article, the writer, Charles
Willis Thompson, returned to the fray some months later in the
Catholic World, with a piece entitled "The Tammany Monster."
This second article was a ringing defense of the "monster" against
attacks by the kind of outlander (Thompson mentioned Iowa,
Nebraska, Oklahoma, and Little Rock, Arkansas) who viewed the
mysterious East and all its works as evil, saying: "Tammany and
Wall Street are the same thing, aren't they?"

Smith's own managers and friends were aware of this widespread
fear of the urban East in the American hinterland. Norman Hapgood and Henry Moskowitz, in their campaign biography of Smith
in 1927 (significantly titled *Up From the City Streets*), faced the
problem squarely. The story of Al Smith, they wrote, "suggests that
in the future our vast cities may do better by humanity than we
have feared." Specifically, the politics characteristic of great cities,
abhorred by some as "machine" or "Tammany" politics, might
have creative possibilities undreamed of in the Mississippi Valley.
Smith, in particular, "has been a product of the machine and . . .
has remained a member of it, and at the same time has become a
leader of the most progressive thought of the United States." Corner saloon politics, these authors argued, were not in essence very
different from country store politics. Far from regarding "the machine" as oppressive and corrupt, the urban poor among whom Al
Smith had grown up "were convinced that Tammany Hall was
kind to them." Pressing this interpretation perhaps a shade too
far in their enthusiasm, Hapgood and Moskowitz defined machine
politics as "neighborliness—which on election day is translated
into votes."

For the rural voter, who on successive days during the spring of
1928 might have seen headlines such as "Chicago's Election Starts
with Kidnapping" and "Deneen Ticket Leads; His Candidate
Slain," such a concept of big-city neighborliness was rather hard
to take. New York was, of course, not Chicago, especially in 1928
when the Capone organization was near its peak; but to the rural

mind one big city was much like another. With this problem in mind, local leaders in some rural areas—not all of them Democrats—strove to bridge the chasm between their constituents' world and Al Smith's.

One of the most interesting of these attempts, particularly in the light of what happened later in the campaign, was made by the Republican editor of the Emporia *Gazette*, William Allen White. Writing to Franklin D. Roosevelt on February 11, 1928, on behalf of the Kansas State Editorial Association, White invited Al Smith to come out to Kansas, "the center of the world which Smith does not know and which does not know Smith." "Smith is supposed to have horns and a tail out west," he wrote, and a confrontation between the New York Governor and a bipartisan group of Western newspaper editors "would do more for him politically than any other one thing he might possibly do." Frank Freidel has noted that Roosevelt tried to persuade Smith to accept this invitation, but failed; in that failure may lie a subtle indication of one reason for the failure of Smith's entire campaign.

The aftermath of this friendly gesture was saddening and distasteful. Throughout his life, William Allen White was the kind of partisan who can be a man of good will toward the Opposition "three and a half years out of every four," as Franklin Roosevelt himself later put it. As the campaign grew hotter than it ever could have been in February, even in 1928, an organization man "regular" enough to have supported Harding and Coolidge when the time came could have been expected to be drawn into the fray against Smith, even though White credited Al with "one of the important brains now functioning in American politics." But, as Professor Moore has shown at length in his study of the campaign, White's attacks on Smith went far beyond the generally acceptable limits of campaign behavior. White wrote that Smith's record as governor showed the New Yorker to be "soft" not only on Prohibition but also on gambling and prostitution. Worse, when he realized the enormity of such a charge when unproven, his retraction was grudging and ambiguous. It was, Moore concludes, a shocking lapse in a theretofore conspicuously honorable political career.

Professor Moore conjoins William Allen White's charges against the Governor with those of the Fundamentalist Baptist leader in New York City, the Rev. John Roach Straton—a conjunction which strongly implies that White's and Straton's warfare with Smith comes down essentially to the same thing, namely, anti-Catholicism. White in this period of the campaign saw Al Smith as a threat to "the whole Puritan civilization which has built a sturdy, orderly nation"; and Moore comments: "Of course one important facet of the 'whole Puritan civilization' was its stanchly Protestant character." Moore finds this attitude of the Kansas editor particularly "confused and distressing" because White, in a book which was already in press while these attacks were going on, "was about to present Smith in an essentially favorable light."

A re-reading of *Masks in a Pageant*, the work referred to, leads the present writer to a conclusion somewhat different from Professor Moore's. References to "Puritanism" and "a Puritan civilization" occur throughout White's writings in contexts having little or nothing to do with Smith or Catholicism. His apt characterization of Calvin Coolidge as "a Puritan in Babylon," for example, loses all its bite if the most cautious of all of America's Presidents is made merely a *Protestant* in Babylon. And parenthetically it may be observed that President Kennedy has had some notoriously kind words to say about Puritanism. What worried White far more than Al Smith's religious affiliation, or even his "wet" sympathies, was the old Jeffersonian bugbear of the great city as an enemy of liberty. In *Masks in a Pageant*, White was trying not only to reassure his readers about Smith but also to reassure himself about Smith's background.

William Allen White was aware that great cities had brought forth American Presidents before, and he cited Theodore Roosevelt—whose faithful vassal he himself had been—and Chester A. Arthur. But neither of these two men "was purely urbanite" (re-

call Mark Hanna's "damn cowboy" epithet hurled at T.R., for
example), whereas Al Smith was "urbanite with an urbanity un-
strained . . . city born, city bred, 'city broke,' city minded, and
city hearted." And, White's urban reader might well have asked,
why not? The Kansas editor did his best to agree: "There is no
reason why the back alley cannot produce as good moral, spiritual,
mental, and physical timber for politics as the backwoods. . . .
The streets educated [Smith] as the woods and fields educated
Lincoln." And yet, backwoods and back alley were inevitably
headed for conflict in the twentieth century; "industrial democracy" was destined to "struggle for supremacy with . . . rural
democracy—the America of our past."

As a determined political progressive, White was intellectually
on the side of the new order; as a product of the Kansas frontier
he was emotionally drawn to the old. The most revealing fact
about the Al Smith sketch in White's *Masks in a Pageant* is that
the author grouped it at the end of the book in a section titled
"The Young Princes of Democracy"—and his other young prince
was Mayor William Hale "Big Bill" Thompson of Chicago. The
Al Smith essay *was*, in the main, favorable to Smith; but Al and
Big Bill were of the same species in White's mind. In the epigraph
to that part of the book, White wrote: "When we have sloughed
off our rural philosophy—our fundamental Puritanism—we shall
crown the young princes. In the meantime the warning is plain:
'Put not your trust in princes!' "

With mistrust of White's sort rampant throughout the Bryan
country, it is understandable that practicing Democrats in the
spring of 1928 might have cast about for a candidate who could
hold Al Smith's constituents without alienating Willam Allen
White's; ideally, a Catholic who was not one of the young princes.
Predictably, some of them found him, in a state even more rural
than Kansas. On March 4, Senator Thomas J. Walsh of Montana
tossed his hat into the ring. On May 1, he was knocked out of
the running in the California presidential primary; but in the
meantime he had posed a major obstacle for the hypothesis of an

"unwritten law" governing Catholic candidates. What is one to make of the fact that, in Professor Moore's words, "The two leading candidates for the Democratic nomination in 1928 were Catholic [and] one of them was nominated"? If the Walsh candidacy was a stalking-horse to divide the Catholic vote, as has been suggested, clearly the effort was unsuccessful; and if it was a serious bid for the presidency, then the "unwritten law" was already well on the way to being a dead letter. In either case, conclusions about toleration in American life more optimistic than those which have been customarily drawn for the 1920's would seem to be in order.

6

The New Deal, 1932–1945

The Roosevelt Coalition

Revolt of the City

by Samuel Lubell

The New Deal's urban-ethnic power base originated, as political analyst Samuel Lubell points out, during the realignment of voting patterns in the 1928 presidential election, a phenomenon previously discussed in the selection by Paul A. Carter. "In many ways," Lubell argues, "Smith's defeat in 1928, rather than Roosevelt's 1932 victory, marked off the arena in which today's politics are being fought," since Smith "first hacked out the rural-city cleavage which generates so much of the force behind the present struggle between Congress and the President." The 1928 returns disclosed not only that Herbert Hoover had split the previously Democratic "Solid South," but that Smith had won 122 previously Republican Northern counties, most of them urban, and 77 of them in heavily Catholic areas. Whatever its previous history, clearly a new "Democracy" was then forming, and it has remained the dominant political force in urban America ever since.

The foreign-born urban masses, already in political revolt by 1928, consummated their transformation into a cohesive segment of the Democratic coalition under the New Deal of the 1930's. "By 1936," in William E. Leuchtenburg's words, "Franklin Roosevelt had forged a new political coalition firmly based on the masses in the great Northern cities, and led in Congress by a new political type: the Northern, urban, liberal Democrat typified by [a United States Senator from] New York, Robert F. Wagner." This fundamental political realignment gained added impetus from the popularity of New Deal relief programs among the urban poor, hard-hit by the Depression. For them, federal welfare payments or public works jobs often meant the difference between marginal poverty and desperate privation.

Beyond these tangible economic benefits, however, the New Deal distributed certain equally important political and psychological rewards to the urban immigrant electorate. For the first time in the history of American patronage, large numbers of "new immigrants" from Ireland and southern and eastern Europe, or their children, began to receive employment as federal bureaucrats and executives. For example, of the 214 federal judges appointed by three Republican Presidents from 1920 to 1932, only 8 had been Catholics, whereas Franklin Roosevelt named 51 Catholics among his 196 federal judicial appointments. Not only did Roosevelt work closely with Catholic and Jewish political leaders in the Northern cities, but many of his advisers came from these previously neglected ethnic groups. FDR even made some second or third line appointments of blacks, though only a thimbleful at this point. The urban immigrant, opening his morning paper (perhaps still a foreign-language periodical), could follow the latest actions and statements of men such as James A. Farley, Felix Frankfurter, or Joseph P. Kennedy, among many other Catholics and Jews at the administration's highest levels; and men such as New York's Fiorello H. La Guardia, or Chicago's Anton J. Cermak, had become mayors of some of the nation's largest cities.

All of these factors—increased political influence, economic assistance, and the important intangible known as "recognition" —helped create the all-important urban base for the New Deal coalition.

A *Little Matter of Birth Rates*

In the winter of 1910 Congress received the longest report ever submitted by a government investigating body up to that time. From early 1907 a special commission had been studying almost every imaginable aspect of immigration, filling forty-two fat volumes with its findings. Buried in that statistical mountain was at least one table of figures which was to prove peculiarly prophetic for our own times.

This table showed that a majority of the children in the schools of thirty-seven of the nation's leading cities had foreign-born fathers. In cities like Chelsea, Fall River, New Bedford, Duluth, New York and Chicago more than *two out of every three* school children were the sons and daughters of immigrants.

Viewed in today's perspective, it is clear that those figures forecast a major political upheaval some time between 1930 and 1940. By then all of these children, plus baby brothers and sisters not enrolled in school, would have grown to voting age. Massed as they were in the states commanding the largest electoral vote, their sheer numbers would topple any prevailing political balance.

No matter what else had happened, the growing up of these children of the 13,000,000 immigrants who poured into the country between 1900 and 1914 was bound to exert a leveling pull on American society. As it was, the Great Depression—striking when most of them had barely entered the adult world—sharpened all their memories of childhood handicaps. When Roosevelt first took office, no segment of the population was more ready for "a new deal" than the submerged, inarticulate urban masses. They became the chief carriers of the Roosevelt Revolution.

The real revolutionary surge behind the New Deal lay in this coupling of the depression with the rise of a new generation,

From *The Future of American Politics*, 3rd rev. ed. (New York: Harper & Row Colophon Books, 1965), pp. 43–48, 55–68. Copyright © 1951, 1952, 1956, 1965 by Samuel Lubell. Reprinted by permission of Harper & Row, Publishers, Inc., footnotes omitted.

which had been malnourished on the congestion of our cities and
the abuses of industrialism. Roosevelt did not start this revolt of
the city. What he did do was to awaken the climbing urban
masses to a consciousness of the power in their numbers. He
extended to them the warming hand of recognition, through
patronage and protective legislation. In the New Deal he supplied
the leveling philosophy required by their sheer numbers and by
the hungers stimulated by advertising. In turn, the big-city masses
furnished the votes which re-elected Roosevelt again and again—
and, in the process, ended the traditional Republican majority
in this country.

In the elections that followed this same big-city generation
would stand like a human wall between the Republicans and
their past dominance. It was this generation—now grown to par-
enthood and in many cases to home-owning, but still bound by
common underdog attitudes—which the Republicans had to crack
to win and hold the presidency.

Twice before in American history a majority party has been
transformed into a minority party. Each time the change was
prefaced by a dramatic reshuffling of population. Jacksonian democracy tramped in to the echoes of the oxcarts which had rolled
westward in the twenty years before. In 1800 only one of twenty
Americans lived west of the Appalachians; when Jackson was
inaugurated the transmountain country claimed one of every three
Americans.

Similarly, the formation of the Republican party was preceded
by a tremendous westward expansion into the Great Lakes and
Midwest regions. Between 1840 and 1860 the nation's population
almost doubled, swelling another 60 per cent by 1880. If it is true
that the pre–Civil War parties were overwhelmed by their inability
to dam back the passions stirred by the slavery controversy, it is
also true that they were unable to channel the flood of new voters.

There were two population currents which cleared the way for
the New Deal:

Between 1910 and 1930 for the first time a majority of the American people came to live in cities. The second population shift might be described as the triumph of the birth rates of the poor and underprivileged over those of the rich and well-born.

Searching for families of five or more, the U.S. Immigration Commission's investigators found two-and-a-half times as many among unskilled laborers as among businessmen. In Minneapolis, for example, the second generation of English stock—the backbone of Republican strength—celebrated a blessed event on the average of one every five years. Among the foreign born a new baby arrived every three years.

As late as 1925 wives of miners and laborers were still having twice as many children as the wives of bankers.

Nor was it the birth rates of the immigrants alone which were threatening the Republican majority. The other prolific baby patches were in the farming areas, particularly in the Appalachian hills and in the South. When World War One shut off the flow of European immigrants, it was into these areas of high human fertility and low living standards that industry sent its recruiting agents searching for cheap labor. Whites and Negroes were sucked north into the cities, especially after 1920 when immigration was curtailed sharply.

Between 1920 and 1930 more than 6,500,000 persons were drawn off the farms and hills; 4,500,000 came into New York, Chicago, Detroit and Los Angeles alone. They hit the cities at roughly the same time that the children of the immigrants were growing up and bestirring themselves. The human potential for a revolutionary political change had thus been brought together in our larger cities when the economic skies caved in.

Through the entire Roosevelt era the Republicans labored on the wrong side of the birth rate. Nor was there anything they could do about it, since the birth rates frustrating them were those of 1910 to 1920. During the last years of Republican victory, from 1920 through 1928, roughly 17,000,000 potential new voters passed the age of twenty-one. From 1936 through 1944, the number ran over 21,000,000, most of them coming from poorer, Democratically inclined families.

Whatever inroads into Roosevelt's popularity the Republicans made was offset largely by these new voters. In 1936, for example, nearly 6,000,000 more ballots were cast than in 1932. While the Republicans gained just under 1,000,000, Roosevelt's vote swelled by almost 5,000,000.

Except for the Polish-Americans and Italo-Americans, the wave of new voters among the immigrant groups passed its crest by 1945. Not until the late 1960's will the record number of births of recent years register politically. Until then the nation's basal political metabolism is likely to remain more sluggish than during the Roosevelt years. The issues of realignment will have to be fought out primarily among existing population elements, whose instinctive voting attitudes are already largely formed.

This prospect, of no abrupt change in the make-up of the electorate, re-emphasizes the decisive importance of the big-city generation, which came of age through the Roosevelt years. Without their overwhelming urban pluralities the Democrats would not have won in either 1940, 1944, or 1948. The 1948 election was so close because Truman's vote in the twelve largest cities fell nearly 750,000 below Roosevelt's 1944 plurality.

Not only does this generation hold the balance of political power in the nation. It also constitutes a radically new political force in American history. The old Republican dominance was rooted in the Civil War and the transcontinental expansion which followed. Most of the immigrants who peopled our larger cities came to these shores long after the Civil War, even after the exhaustion of free lands in the West. To their children and grandchildren the loyalties of Appomattox and the Homestead Act were details in history books rather than a family experience passed down from grandfather to grandson.

Never having known anything but city life, this new generation was bound to develop a different attitude toward the role of government from that of Americans born on farms or in small towns. To Herbert Hoover the phrase "rugged individualism" evoked nostalgic memories of a rural self-sufficiency in which a thrifty, toiling farmer had to look to the marketplace for only the last fifth of his needs. The Iowa homestead on which Hoover grew up produced all of its own vegetables, its own soap, its own bread. Fuel was cut and hauled from the woods ten miles away, where one could also gather walnuts free. "Sweetness" was obtained from sorghums. Every fall the cellar was filled with jars and barrels which, as Hoover observes in his memoirs, "was social security in itself."

To men and women who regulated their labors by the sun and rain, there was recognizable logic in talking of natural economic laws—although even among farmers the murmur for government intervention grew louder, as their operations became more commercialized and less self-sufficient.

In the city, though, the issue has always been man against man. What bowed the backs of the factory worker prematurely were not hardships inflicted by Mother Nature but by human nature. He was completely dependent on a money wage. Without a job, there were no vegetables for his family, no bread, no rent, no fuel, no soap, no "sweetnesss." Crop failures, plagues of grasshoppers, or searing drought could be put down as acts of God. Getting fired or having one's wages cut were only too plainly acts of the Boss.

A philosophy that called for "leaving things alone" to work themselves out seemed either unreal or hypocritical in the cities, where nearly every condition of living groaned for reform. The wage earner had to look to the government to make sure that the milk bought for his baby was not watered or tubercular; he had to look to government to regulate the construction of tenements so all sunlight was not blocked out. If only God could make a tree, only the government could make a park.

Neither the Republicans nor the New Dealers seem to have appreciated how sharp a wrench from the continuity of the past was involved in the rise of this big-city generation. G.O.P. leaders persisted in regarding Roosevelt's popularity as a form of hero worship, abetted by the radio. Only Roosevelt's personal magnetism and political skill were holding together the varied Democratic elements, reasoned the Republicans. With "that voice" quieted, the coalition would fall apart. The nation would then return to safe and sane Republicanism. What this reasoning overlooked was that the Roosevelt generation had no tradition of Republicanism to go back to. For them the weight of tradition was such that if they were undecided about rival Presidential candidates, they instinctively would give the Democrats preference.

The basic weakness of the Republican party stems from this fact, that it has remained rooted in an earlier historical era in which it was dominant. The resilient Democratic strength springs from being so alive—clumsily perhaps, but definitely alive—to the problems with which the newer generation has grown up.

Between the Republican and Democratic appeals, as we shall see, the issue has been less one of conservatism versus liberalism than one of timeliness. . . .

The Year of Decision

Bowls of red roses graced the speakers' table while American flags and tricolored bunting draped the walls of the banquet hall. The occasion was the first annual dinner of the Muncie, Indiana, Chamber of Commerce since the depression. Its immediate inspiration had been the news that General Motors, which had stripped its local plant three years before, was moving back. Mindful that the company was returning to escape a strike in Toledo, the Mayor assured the banqueters that "the citizens of Muncie are in no mood for outsiders to come in and agitate."

Returning to the city that June week in 1935 to begin their study of "Middletown in Transition," Robert and Helen Lynd were struck by the eagerness with which Muncie's community leaders were hailing the return of the "good old days."

But if Muncie's businessmen were ready to forget the depression as "just a bad bump in the road," that was not the feeling across the railroad tracks "in the other world of wage earners." Predominantly native born, drawn mainly from near-by farms, Muncie's "corn-feds," as the local workers were called, had seen no point in labor unions before the depression. Out of a working force of 13,000, hardly 700 had carried union cards, fewer than joined the Klan. Al Smith won a lone precinct in the city, losing one of the two precincts which went Democratic in 1924. With every fourth Muncie worker jobless in 1932, Roosevelt carried thirteen precincts, but still lost the city.

As in so many other communities, the N.R.A. brought a rush among Muncie's workers to join labor unions. At the Ball glass factory and the automotive plants—Muncie's two strongest anti-union citadels—the American Federation of Labor was petitioned to send in organizers. But the A. F. of L. was fumbling and inept, while the business community was militantly efficient. The local police force was secretly increased. Persons distributing handbills advertising a union meeting were picked up. One local newspaper front-paged a photograph of a picket in Oregon being dragged through the streets under the caption, THIS PICKET HAD REAL "DRAG" WITH THE COPS.

By the time the 1936 presidential campaign opened, the drive to unionize Muncie had been broken. But the workers still had the ballot. To the Lynds the 1936 campaign "witnessed perhaps the strongest effort in the city's history by the local big businessmen (industrialists and bankers) to stampede local opinion in behalf of a single presidential candidate." When the ballots were in, Muncie had gone for a Democratic President for the first time since the Civil War. Exulted one worker to the Lynds. "We certainly licked the big bosses."

Muncie was not the only Republican citadel which resisted

Roosevelt in 1932 but fell in 1936. Twenty-three other counties, which the Republicans held in 1932, swung four years later and —like Muncie—stayed Democratic. Among these was "Bloody" Harlan in southeast Kentucky, where efforts to organize the miners in the 1930's exploded in assassinations and pitched battles; also the cities of Philadelphia and Wilmington, the home of the Du Ponts. To defeat Roosevelt, various members of the Du Pont clan contributed more than $500,000 to the Republicans, in addition to their donations to the American Liberty League. The net effect seems only to have advertised more sharply who was on whose side.

So overwhelming was Roosevelt's 1936 victory, that its political decisiveness is often overlooked. With only Maine and Vermont remaining Republican, Roosevelt's re-election seemed primarily a vote of gratitude for lifting the country out of a desperate economic crisis. Certainly many people favored him for that reason. But 1936 was also the year of realignment in which the Democrats became the nation's normal majority party. The traditional dominance which the Republicans had enjoyed since the Civil War was washed away and a new era in American politics began.

The depression vote of 1932 still mirrored the orbit of conflict of the old Republican order. The G.O.P. cleavage had been mainly a struggle between the "progressives" of the Midwest and Far West against the industrial East. Roosevelt's first campaign was directed primarily toward splitting off this "progressive" vote. His best showing came in the Western and Mountain states. All six states he lost—Pennsylvania, Delaware, Connecticut, Vermont, New Hampshire and Maine—were in the East.

The shift in the basis of Roosevelt's appeal "from acreage to population," to use Raymond Moley's phrase, occurred in 1935. Moley credits the change to Huey Long's "Share Our Wealth" agitation and to Roosevelt's ire over the Supreme Court's declaring the N.R.A. unconstitutional. To steal Long's thunder, Roosevelt proposed a "soak the rich" tax bill, which, Moley feels, marked the beginning of the conservative-liberal split inside the Democratic party. Whatever the exact turning point, 1935 saw more social legislation enacted than in any other year in the nation's history—the "wealth tax," the Wagner Labor Relations Act, the Social Security Law, the creation of WPA, the Public Utilities Holding Law, the start of the Rural Electrification Administration.

Not only in Washington but throughout the country 1935 was the year of decision. To go back to the old order or to move forward to something different? That was the question posed for decision in 1935, in countless different ways, in every phase of life.

In the early New Deal days how things were done had been less important than getting the stalled economy going again. By 1935 recovery had progressed to the point where there no longer was any question that the country would be saved. The new issue was: Would the "good old days" of unchallenged business dominance be restored? Or was America to be reshaped?

The more articulate business groups had one answer. As in Muncie, they were ready to resume their annual Chamber of Commerce dinners as if there never had been a depression. But the same processes of recovery which restored the courage of businessmen also enabled the leaders of organized labor to recover their nerve. Early in 1933 John L. Lewis, Phil Murray, and Tom Kennedy lamented to Roosevelt that the United Mine Workers had barely enough members to pay the union's expenses. "Go home and have a good night's sleep," Roosevelt consoled them. "If I don't do anything else in my administration I am going to give the miners an opportunity to organize in the United Mine Workers of America."

Taking Roosevelt at his word, Lewis nearly emptied the UMW treasury to hire organizers, sending them out to tell the miners, "The President wants you to join a union." By 1934 Lewis could stand before the A. F. of L. convention and boast that the UMW was again a fighting force of 400,000 miners. By 1935 he was ready to demand that the A. F. of L. embrace the principle of industrial unionism or let a new labor movement organize the mass production industries.

The hard right to the jaw which Lewis swung at Bill Hutcheson in Atlantic City that October was symbolic of the fact that at least one group of labor leaders were determined not to go back to the old order.

When the first sit-down strike broke in November 1935, it came—significantly—not among workers of immigrant origin, but among the rubber workers of Akron. That city had drawn so many hillbillies from near-by states that it was often jokingly called "the capital of West Virginia." Before taking their place in the picket line, some rubber workers knelt in prayer. After the last "Amen," they picked up their baseball bats and lead pipes and moved into formation around the factories.

This fervor for unions which swept the native American workers —some observers likened it to a religious revival—was of crucial political importance. Al Smith . . . stirred a new sense of political consciousness among workers of immigrant and Catholic origin. But the native workers of the farms and hills had always held suspiciously aloof from those of immigrant stock.

The hillbillies had their own sense of group solidarity. Flint, Michigan, had its "Little Missouri" and "Little Arkansas" residential settlements. In Akron, the West Virginia State Society had 25,000 members and put on an annual West Virginia day picnic. Marked off from the older inhabitants by their accents, manners and dress, the "snake-eaters" were the butt of ridicule and jokes, which were fiercely resented. A judge in Akron suspended sentence on one man on condition that he return to West Virginia. A newspaper reporter wrote up the incident, "Judge Sentences Man to West Virginia for Life." At the next election the hapless judge was badly beaten by the votes of outraged mountaineers.

The formation of the CIO marked the fusing of the interests of the immigrant and native-stock workers, both Negro and white.

That, I believe, is perhaps the most telling accomplishment of the CIO. Its political importance can hardly be exaggerated. The mass production industries had been the ones in which racial and religious antagonisms among the workers were most divisive. Carnegie, Illinois, had sprinkled clusters of different nationalities in each of its mines, reasoning correctly that a Balkanized working force would be more difficult to unionize. In some industries immigrants and Negroes had first been introduced as strikebreakers or because they would work for lower wages than native-born workers. The failure of the Knights of Labor in the 1880's was largely a failure to unite the immigrant working groups. Much of the A. F. of L.'s reluctance to embark on a real organizing drive in the mass production industries reflected the dislike of the "aristocrats of labor" in the skilled crafts for the immigrant "rubbish."

By 1935, of course, the immigrants had made considerable progress toward Americanization. But the key to the change was the rise of a common class consciousness among all workers. The depression, in making all workers more aware of their economic interests, suppressed their racial and religious antagonisms. Put crudely, the hatred of bankers among the native American workers had become greater than their hatred of the Pope or even of the Negro.

This struggle between the old nativist prejudices and the newer class consciousness still remains one of the crucial behind-the-scenes battles in the mass production unions. Class feeling or racial-religious feeling? The future of American labor rests largely on which holds the ascendancy.

This rise in class consciousness among native-American workers was a nation-wide development. In Muncie the Lynds reported the first evidences of class-feeling among the workers, stirred by the sense that the government could do something for them. In "Yankee City" (Newburyport, Mass.) W. Lloyd Warner tells of a similar change among the so-called "Riverbrookers," the proud, clannish, Yankee-stock workers who had always refused to join unions with immigrant workers. When the new shoe union staged the first successful strike in Yankee City's history, the River-brookers supplied the leadership.

Negroes were another voting element which was determined to go forward rather than back. In some cities as many as four out of five Negro families were on relief. "Don't Buy Where You Can't Work" campaigns were being pressed to force white store-owners to hire Negroes. In Harlem the accumulated tensions of the depression years were exploded suddenly by a trivial incident.

On March 19, 1935, a sixteen-year-old boy snatched a ten-cent bread knife from a five-and-ten-cent counter—"just for fun" he later told the police. Two white clerks and the white manager chased the boy to the rear of the store. When they grabbed him, he bit their hands and broke away.

The boy was a Puerto Rican, yet the rumor spread that a Negro had been lynched in the store. Pickets appeared. A soapbox orator on one street corner attracted a growing crowd. When a funeral hearse happened to drive by a woman shrieked, "They've come to take the boy's body!" The Negro mob went on a ram-page. When the riot was over, one man was dead—three others died later of injuries—and a hundred or more whites and Negroes had been shot, stabbed or stoned.

The grisly tragedy was lightened only by the action of a Chinese laundryman. When he saw the mob surging through the streets, heaving stones into store windows, he hastily thrust a sign into his window, "Me colored too."

New York City had four previous race riots, without anything much happening afterward. The 1935 riot, however, set off a series of far-reaching changes. Harlem's shopowners hastily put on Negro employees. Before the year was out Tammany Hall had named its first Negro district leader. Mayor Fiorello La Guardia had appointed the first Negro magistrate. In 1932 most Negro voters in the country were still Republican. In 1936, in many cities two of every three Negro voters were for Roosevelt.

And so it went all through the country. It would be impossible to trace in full all the different ways in which the question—whether to go back or forward—was being asked of the American people. Sometimes the query was put bluntly in so many words. More often it was implicit in the logic of events or in reminders of the depression. At the end of 1935, more than $780,000,000 was still tied up in closed banks, 3,000,000 persons were still on relief; one survey of a group of garment workers showed that half of them had not bought a new coat for four years.

Lifelong Socialists had to ask themselves—did they return to the ivory tower of a futile third party or did they defend their immediate interests by rallying behind Roosevelt? Sidney Hillman and David Dubinsky, whose unions had been saved by the N.R.A., formed a new American Labor party to enable New Yorkers to vote for Roosevelt and still remain independent of the Democrats. Norman Thomas polled 884,000 Socialist votes nationally in 1932 but only 187,000 votes four years later.

On the other side of the political barricades the realignment was equally sharp. In 1932 one-fourth of the Democratic campaign funds was contributed by bankers. In 1936 bankers accounted for a mere 3 per cent of the Democratic party's war chest. (Their total contributions to the Democrats were only about a third of the $750,000 spent by organized labor.)

Particularly in rural areas, the 1936 vote showed that sizable numbers of voters were ready to return to the Republicanism of their ancestors. Winston County, which had seceded from Alabama during the Civil War to remain loyal to the union, swung back to the Republican party in 1936; so did thirty-two counties in Missouri, all but eight bone-dry by tradition. Less than a dozen wheat counties in the whole country had stayed Republican in 1932. Four years later, most of the wheat counties were on their way back to the Republican party.

In the industrial centers, however, the political allegiances that had grown out of the Civil War were uprooted for good. In New York, New Jersey and Pennsylvania, alone, the Democratic vote leaped by roughly 1,800,000. Despite the depression, in 1932,

Roosevelt failed to carry a dozen cities with 100,000 or more population—Philadelphia, Scranton, and Reading in Pennsylvania; Canton, Youngstown, and Columbus in Ohio; Gary, Duluth, Des Moines, Grand Rapids, and Springfield, Massachusetts. Every one swung for Roosevelt in 1936 and except for Grand Rapids have remained Democratic since.

A dramatic glimpse into the nature of this hidden political revolution will be found by comparing the 1928 and 1936 vote in

Cities High Smith			Cities Low Smith		
City	Dem. % 1928	Dem. % 1936	City	Dem. % 1928	Dem. % 1936
Lawrence	71	73	Flint	19	72
Boston	67	63	Wichita, Kan.	24	64
Lowell	64	61	Los Angeles	28	67
Fall River	64	67	Akron	31	71
New York	60	75	Des Moines	31	55
New Haven	57	65	San Diego	32	65
Milwaukee	53	76	Seattle	32	64
New Bedford	52	65	Duluth	32	71
Cleveland	52	76	Canton	34	66
St. Louis	51	66	Spokane	35	71
San Francisco	49	72	Detroit	37	65
Chicago	48	65	Indianapolis	39	57
Pittsburgh	47	67	Philadelphia	39	60
Baltimore	47	67	Youngstown	39	74

our major cities. While Smith won six of every ten voters in some cities, in others he drew only three out of ten. This disparity had narrowed by 1932, but wide divergences in voting still prevailed in different parts of the country. With the 1936 election, as the table above shows, the voting of nearly all our major cities hit a common level.

Whether the cities are heavily foreign-born or native-American in make-up, Catholic or Protestant, with large numbers of Negroes or of whites up from the South, did not make too much difference in their 1936 vote. Nor whether the city had a strong labor tradition like San Francisco or an open shop tradition like Los Angeles, nor whether it was located on the East or West coast or in the Midwest.

A new nationalizing force had clearly been injected into American politics. In the past American political realignments have always followed sectional lines. The Revolt of the City, however, had drawn the same class-conscious line of economic interest across the entire country, overriding not only regional distinctions but equally strong cultural differences.

This development was not without its irony. In drawing the line of cleavage between worker and "economic royalists," Roosevelt unquestionably sharpened the sense of class division in American society. Yet, in doing so, he subordinated the old nativistic prejudices of race and religion, which had divided the lower half of American society for so long, bringing to these lower income elements a greater degree of social unity than they had ever shared before. Was Roosevelt dividing or unifying the country?

By Fire and Water

If the 1936 vote marked the emergence of the new Roosevelt coalition, the third term election brought the crucial trial by fire and water which demonstrated the coalition's durability.

In both 1932 and 1936 Roosevelt would still have been elected without his heavy urban pluralities. In 1940, however, with the war and the third-term issue cutting heavily into his rural strength, the margin of victory that accounted for at least 212 electoral votes was supplied by the dozen largest cities in the country.

In every city I visited while doing a postelection survey I found that the Roosevelt vote broke at virtually the same economic level, between $45 and $60 a month rent. Below that line his pluralities were overwhelming. Above it, they faded away. In Pittsburgh, for example, Roosevelt got three-fourths of the vote in wards whose rentals averaged under $40 a month and only four tenths of the vote where rentals were above $65 a month. Minneapolis, whose social make-up contrasts sharply with Pittsburgh, showed much the same results—about 40 per cent of the vote for Roosevelt in the highest income ward, but seven of every ten voters in the lower rental areas.

The sharpness with which the balloting stratified in city after city—Chicago, Boston, St. Louis, Seattle, Cleveland—left little room for any appreciable shift of votes because of the campaign put on by Wendell Willkie. When I asked one auto unionist in Detroit why the third-term issue had made so little difference he replied, "I'll say it even though it doesn't sound nice. We've grown class conscious." With other unions there may have been less bitterness but the division between worker and "economic royalist" was as sharply drawn. In a Minneapolis ward, inhabited largely by teamsters, the pastor of one church had been outspoken in condemning the third term. He admitted bitterly, "I don't suppose I changed a single vote." John Lewis, who had endorsed Willkie, could have echoed him.

This class consciousness, it should be noted, was not confined to workers. The balloting revealed as much class feeling among the higher income Republicans. If Roosevelt solidified the lower classes, he also welded the upper class.

The one sharp break from "economic voting" came on the basis of ethnic background, reflecting the varying impact upon different groups of Hitler's War. Roosevelt's heaviest losses came in German-American and Italo-American wards, where resentment was strong against his "stab in the back" reference to Mussolini's attack on France. The highest income areas voting for Roosevelt were Jewish. In Brooklyn he carried streets with $15,000 homes— a comfortable valuation in 1940—and apartment houses with doormen. Where low income status coincided with the nationality background of a country invaded by Germany, the vote for Roosevelt was prodigious. Polish-American wards in Buffalo went Democratic nine to one, with individual precincts running as high as twenty to one, his heaviest pluralities in the whole country.

Curiously, the ethnic elements most bitterly antagonized by Hitler were largely those contributing the heaviest numbers of new voters. In Buffalo, in 1940, the Polish-Americans mustered enough votes to elect a Polish-American judge for the first time. One Democratic ward leader, John Kryzinski, a tavern keeper, was foaming with enthusiasm at the significance of this victory.

"Out in ritzy Humboldt Park they get two voters to a family," he snorted contemptuously. "I get six out of my house. I got neighbors who give me eight. We elected a judge this year. The way things are going in eight years we'll elect a mayor."

Nine years later Buffalo did elect Joseph Mruc its first Polish-American mayor.

In every city one could see the same inexorable spread of numbers and the same leveling pressures. Almost it seemed, in fact, that the Republicans had decided to abandon the cities to the Democratic masses, taking refuge in the suburbs. In St. Louis the Twenty-eighth Ward had stayed Republican in 1932. By 1940 this G.O.P. stronghold had been reduced to three precincts. Along Lindell Boulevard and Skinker Road, "For Sale" signs were propped in front of mansionlike homes with graveled driveways, flagstone walks and antique-fabricated lampposts. Some of the more imposing residences were being razed to make way for apartment houses. In the old days at the Pageant, the neighborhood movie house, seats were reserved. When I saw it, the lobby was placarded with handbills advertising double features on Wednesdays and Thursdays, with three features for a quarter on Fridays and Saturdays.

In Harlem, as well, the spirit of 1936 had quickened. Along 125th Street Negroes were working in hundreds of establishments which as late as 1935 had been manned completely by whites. Garment workers, janitors, bartenders, waiters and waitresses, Pullman porters, laundry workers, newspaper men, retail clerks and redcaps were flocking into labor unions with a sense of deliverance. To the Negro, unionism promised more than a wage boost. It also seemed the trumpet which would eventually tumble the Jericho walls of discrimination. Some Harlem unions were holding daily classes to teach Negroes selling, typing and stenography, to be able to rebuff employers who protested, "I can't hire Negroes, they're not experienced."

Probably 50 per cent of Harlem's Negroes were still getting relief of some kind. Older Negroes, clinging to the Republican party, might shake their graying heads and mutter, "Our people are selling their birthrights for a mess of pottage." Younger Negroes had a different slant on WPA. "The really important thing about WPA is that it is a guarantee of a living wage," explained Carl Lawrence, a reporter on the *Amsterdam News*. "It means Negroes don't have to work for anything people want to give them. This helps lift the standards of all Negroes, even those not on WPA."

The fall of France in 1940 had spurted the armament program, and the defense boom had been building up steadily in the months before the election. With the boom in employment, a highly significant thing was happening. Older people, who had been thrown out of work during the depression, were not being re-employed. The jobs were going to their children, while the older folk stayed on relief or lived on their savings, plus some help from their children. It hardly had been planned that way, but the New Deal was cushioning a wholesale shift in the working population, by easing the older generation of depression casualties out of the way to make room for a new generation.

In the Charlestown area of Boston one-half of the voters were under forty. The ward leader himself, William Galvin, was thirty-six. Two younger brothers had got out of high school during the depression and had gone into the CCC camps. When employment in the Boston Navy Yard expanded, they got jobs as electrician's and pipe fitter's helpers. From the CCC to the Navy Yard—to these two youths, the government had brought advancement as real as any they could have achieved under a private employer.

As a reporter in Washington I had shared the general belief that the New Deal was hastily improvised and animated by no coherent philosophy. When one translated its benefits down to what they meant to the families I was interviewing in 1940, the whole Roosevelt program took on a new consistency.

The depression had thrown grave strains upon lower income families. Many family heads had last their jobs, never to be employed regularly again. In some instances, the children were old enough to take over the bread-winning, which often robbed the deposed patriarch of his self-respect. In other families the parents had to struggle along until the children grew of age and took over.

In varied ways the New Deal eased these family strains. Through the HOLC a million homes were saved. Many homeowners were too old to have been able to buy a new home, if they had lost their old ones. With their children grown older, I found, many were renting out part of the house, often to a married son or daughter.

Into the CCC camps went 2,750,000 sons of the cities. No longer a drain on the family larder, they even sent some money back home. Children in high school might get NYA aid. Those who went to work usually did so in low-wage industries where the effects of the wage-hour law were most noticeable.

These and other New Deal benefits did not solve all the family problems by any means. They did ease the adjustments that had to be mode as the unfortunates of one generation grew unemployable and another generation finally found its opportunity in defense employment.

The recovery from the depression low helped Roosevelt politically with all groups. It was particularly important in the cities because that recovery coincided with the hatching out of the birth rates of 1910 to 1920 and the rise of a new generation. The very size of the Democratically inclined families helped knit them to the New Deal. Even persons who had done rather well for themselves were likely to have a less fortunate family member lower down the economic ladder being benefited by the New Deal. Old-age pensions and other aid eased the burden of having to care for parents too old to work. Instead of being dragged by family burdens, the rising generation was able to solidify its gains.

How much of all this was "planned that way" and how much of it just happened can be speculated upon endlessly. One can also speculate about what might have happened if Roosevelt had not run for a third term and if the war in Europe had not broken out when it did.

Both Garner and Farley have written that they opposed a third term to keep the Democratic party from degenerating into a personal vehicle for Roosevelt and Roosevelt alone. If Roosevelt runs again, Garner told Bascom Timmons, his biographer, "after he is off the ticket the Democratic party will fall to pieces." Despite Garner's deserved reputation for political shrewdness, he seems to have misjudged the forces at work. But for the third term, it is questionable whether many of the elements who had thrown their strength to the Democrats for the first time in 1936 would have solidified in the party. Early in 1940, for example, Ralph Bunche was still writing of the Negro vote as being "essentially Republican."

Paradoxically, the New Deal also appears to have grown stronger politically after it was abandoned. The outbreak of the war put an end to social reform. But the war boom made unnecessary any additional New Deal measures. In fact, the war succeeded in doing what the New Deal never could accomplish; it brought the country out of the depression.

Unemployment never fell below eight million in 1939 and growing numbers of people wondered whether there ever would be full employment. In the "little steel" strike of 1937 organized labor suffered a serious setback. If the recession of 1938 had dragged on, labor might have had to retreat, instead of entrenching itself as a permanent force in the mass production industries. All through the 1930's surplus sons and daughters had been held back on the farms because of a lack of opportunity in the cities.

The defense boom sparked anew the migration from farm to city. It also sparked new vigor into the marriage rate. In the middle

1930's one of four youths in their late teens and early twenties had never had regular work. By 1939 the marriage rate had risen from the depression low of eight to nearly eleven per thousand population. In 1941 it leaped to almost thirteen per thousand.

Economically speaking, then, the defense boom was the happy ending which saved the New Deal and made it a success story. The years of full employment which followed the outbreak of Hitler's War solved the economic problem of the Roosevelt generation, solidifying them in the Democratic party. But in the process this generation changed markedly. Not only had it aged and taken on responsibilties, but much of this generation had climbed from poverty into the middle class. The rise of this new middle class—whose significance was only dimly sensed even by professional politicians—is worth examining.

FDR in the Saddle

The Roosevelt Reconstruction

by William E. Leuchtenburg

*The Harding-Coolidge decade of relatively prosperous "normalcy"
ended abruptly with the stock market crash of 1929, but few
Americans sensed even then the length and severity of the economic and social crisis that lay ahead. The Great Depression of
the 1930's, the worst such downturn in American history, ushered
into power the nation's longest and most influential modern
presidential administration. Franklin Delano Roosevelt's "New
Deal" turned government energies toward a broad-gauged assault
on the problems of relief, recovery, and reform, and committed
the government in Washington to a degree of involvement in
American economic and social processes which all subsequent
Presidents, Republican and Democratic, have merely extended,
reluctantly or willingly.*

*The situation FDR confronted upon taking office in 1933 left
him little choice: the economy required extensive federal intervention, and an enormous bureaucracy had to be created to manage it. Gross national product (GNP) had fallen from $104 bil-
lion in 1929 to $74 billion by early 1933. During the same period,
American exports had plummeted from over $4.5 billion to less
than $1.5 billion, while national income declined by more than*

half. Most ominous, the legions of unemployed Americans had swollen during the Hoover administration (1929–33) from 3 million to near 15 million, with both public and private relief agencies hopelessly overwhelmed by the dimensions of the distress.

Governmental deference to the business community, the central theme of the earlier decade's "Republican era," would no longer determine American politics. In Roosevelt's inaugural he pledged his administration to an unprecedented peacetime mobilization of economic resources to cope with the national emergency. By the time the New Deal's first hundred days had ended, the country recognized that FDR's initial pledge "to wage a war against the emergency, as great . . . as if we were in fact invaded by a foreign foe" had been more than platform rhetoric. Fifteen major executive programs and a raft of subsidiary bills whizzed through a receptive Congress in little more than three months— an improbable record for speedy passage of controversial legislation that helped alter the economic patterns and social ground rules of American life.

The New Deal struggled for the remainder of the decade to stimulate economic recovery and sidetrack social unrest. In the end, despite its substantial failure to restore the economy to full prosperity, the presidential administration had achieved profound changes upon the attitudes, values, and structure of American society as no other had before. William Leuchtenburg here analyzes the complex and multifarious impact of the New Deal on American life in a synthesis of his larger study of the New Deal years.

🌼 In eight years, Roosevelt and the New Dealers had almost revolutionized the agenda of American politics. "Mr. Roosevelt may have given the wrong answers to many of his problems," concluded the editors of *The Economist.* "But he is at least the first President of modern America who has asked the right questions."

From *Franklin D. Roosevelt and the New Deal, 1932–1940,* by William E. Leuchtenburg. Copyright © 1963 by William E. Leuchtenburg. Reprinted by permission of Harper & Row, Publishers, Inc., footnotes omitted.

In 1932, men of acumen were absorbed to an astonishing degree with such questions as prohibition, war debts, and law enforcement. By 1936, they were debating social security, the Wagner Act, valley authorities, and public housing. The thirties witnessed a rebirth of issues politics, and parties split more sharply on ideological lines than they had in many years past. "I incline to think that for years up to the present juncture thinking Democrats and thinking Republicans had been divided by an imaginary line," reflected a Massachusetts congressman in 1934. "Now for the first time since the period before the Civil War we find vital principles at stake." Much of this change resulted simply from the depression trauma, but much too came from the force of Roosevelt's personality and his use of his office as both pulpit and lectern. "Of course you have fallen into some errors—that is human," former Supreme Court Justice John Clarke wrote the President, "but you have put a new face upon the social and political life of our country."

Franklin Roosevelt re-created the modern presidency. He took an office which had lost much of its prestige and power in the previous twelve years and gave it an importance which went well beyond what even Theodore Roosevelt and Woodrow Wilson had done. Clinton Rossiter has observed: "Only Washington, who made the office, and Jackson, who remade it, did more than [Roosevelt] to raise it to its present condition of strength, dignity, and independence." Under Roosevelt, the White House became the focus of all government—the fountainhead of ideas, the initiator of action, the representative of the national interest.

Roosevelt greatly expanded the President's legislative functions. In the nineteenth century, Congress had been jealous of its prerogatives as the lawmaking body, and resented any encroachment on its domain by the Chief Executive. Woodrow Wilson and Theodore Roosevelt had broken new ground in sending actual drafts of bills to Congress and in using devices like the caucus to win enactment of measures they favored. Franklin Roosevelt made such constant use of these tools that he came to assume a legisla-

tive role not unlike that of a prime minister. He sent special messages to Congress, accompanied them with drafts of legislation
prepared by his assistants, wrote letters to committee chairmen or
members of Congress to urge passage of the proposals, and authorized men like Corcoran to lobby as presidential spokesmen on
the Hill. By the end of Roosevelt's tenure in the White House,
Congress looked automatically to the Executive for guidance; it
expected the administration to have a "program" to present for
consideration.

Roosevelt's most important formal contribution was his creation
of the Executive Office of the President on September 8, 1939.
Executive Order 8248, a "nearly unnoticed but none the less
epoch-making event in the history of American institutions," set
up an Executive Office staffed with six administrative assistants
with a "passion for anonymity." In 1939, the President not only
placed obvious agencies like the White House Office in the Executive Office but made the crucial decision to shift the Bureau
of the Budget from the Treasury and put it under his wing. In
later years, such pivotal agencies as the Council of Economic Advisers, the National Security Council, and the Central Intelligence
Agency would be moved into the Executive Office of the President. Roosevelt's decision, Rossiter has concluded, "converts the
presidency into an instrument of twentieth-century government;
it gives the incumbent a sporting chance to stand the strain and
fulfill his constitutional mandate as a one-man branch of our
three-part government; it deflates even the most forceful arguments, which are still raised occasionally, for a plural executive; it
assures us that the Presidency will survive the advent of the positive state. Executive Order 8248 may yet be judged to have saved
the Presidency from paralysis and the Constitution from radical
amendment."

Roosevelt's friends have been too quick to concede that he was
a poor administrator. To be sure, he found it difficult to discharge
incompetent aides, he procrastinated about decisions, and he
ignored all the canons of sound administration by giving men

overlapping assignments and creating a myriad of agencies which had no clear relation to the regular departments of government. But if the test of good administration is not an impeccable organizational chart but creativity, then Roosevelt must be set down not merely as a good administrator but as a resourceful innovator. The new agencies he set up gave a spirit of excitement to Washington that the routinized old-line departments could never have achieved. The President's refusal to proceed through channels, however vexing at times to his subordinates, resulted in a competition not only among men but among ideas, and encouraged men to feel that their own beliefs might win the day. "You would be surprised, Colonel, the remarkable ideas that have been turned loose just because men have felt that they can get a hearing," one senator confided. The President's "procrastination" was his own way both of arriving at a sense of national consensus and of reaching a decision by observing a trial by combat among rival theories. Periods of indecision—as in the spring of 1935 or the beginning of 1938—were inevitably followed by a fresh outburst of new proposals.

Most of all, Roosevelt was a successful administrator because he attracted to Washington thousands of devoted and highly skilled men. Men who had been fighting for years for lost causes were given a chance: John Collier, whom the President courageously named Indian Commissioner; Arthur Powell Davis, who had been ousted as chief engineer of the Department of the Interior at the demand of power interests; old conservationists like Harry Slattery, who had fought the naval oil interests in the Harding era. When Harold Ickes took office as Secretary of the Interior, he looked up Louis Glavis—he did not even know whether the "martyr" of the Ballinger-Pinchot affair was still alive—and appointed him to his staff.

The New Dealers displayed striking ingenuity in meeting problems of governing. They coaxed salmon to climb ladders at Bonneville; they sponsored a Young Choreographers Laboratory in the WPA's Dance Theatre; they gave the pioneer documentary film maker Pare Lorentz the opportunity to create his classic films *The*

Plow That Broke the Plains and *The River*. At the Composers Forum-Laboratory of the Federal Music Project, William Schuman received his first serious hearing. In Arizona, Father Berard Haile of St. Michael's Mission taught written Navajo to the Indians. Roosevelt, in the face of derision from professional foresters and prairie states' governors, persisted in a bold scheme to plant a mammoth "shelterbelt" of parallel rows of trees from the Dakotas to the Panhandle. In all, more than two hundred million trees were planted—cottonwood and willow, hackberry and cedar, Russian olive and Osage orange; within six years, the President's visionary windbreak had won over his former critics. The spirit behind such innovations generated a new excitement about the potentialities of government. "Once again," Roosevelt told a group of young Democrats in April, 1936, "the very air of America is exhilarating."

Roosevelt dominated the front pages of the newspapers as no other President before or since has done. "Frank Roosevelt and the NRA have taken the place of love nests," commented Joe Patterson, publisher of the tabloid New York *Daily News*. At his very first press conference, Roosevelt abolished the written question and told reporters they could interrogate him without warning. Skeptics predicted the free and easy exchange would soon be abandoned, but twice a week, year in and year out, he threw open the White House doors to as many as two hundred reporters, most of them representing hostile publishers, who would crowd right up to the President's desk to fire their questions. The President joshed them, traded wisecracks with them, called them by their first names; he charmed them by his good-humored ease and impressed them with his knowledge of detail. To a degree, Roosevelt's press conference introduced, as some observers claimed, a new institution like Britain's parliamentary questioning; more to the point, it was a device the President manipulated, disarmingly and adroitly, to win support for his program. It served too as a classroom to instruct the country in the new economics and the new politics.

Roosevelt was the first President to master the technique of reaching people directly over the radio. In his fireside chats, he talked like a father discussing public affairs with his family in the living room. As he spoke, he seemed unconscious of the fact that he was addressing millions. "His head would nod and his hands would move in simple, natural, comfortable gestures," Frances Perkins recalled. "His face would smile and light up as though he were actually sitting on the front porch or in the parlor with them." Eleanor Roosevelt later observed that after the President's death people would stop her on the street to say "they missed the way the President used to talk to them. They'd say 'He used to talk to me about my government.' There was a real dialogue between Franklin and the people," she reflected. "That dialogue seems to have disappeared from the government since he died."

For the first time for many Americans, the federal government became an institution that was directly experienced. More than state and local governments, it came to be *the* government, an agency directly concerned with their welfare. It was the source of their relief payments; it taxed them directly for old age pensions; it even gave their children hot lunches in school. As the role of the state changed from that of neutral arbiter to a "powerful promoter of society's welfare," people felt an interest in affairs in Washington they had never had before.

Franklin Roosevelt personified the state as protector. It became commonplace to say that people felt toward the President the kind of trust they would normally express for a warm and understanding father who comforted them in their grief or safeguarded them from harm. An insurance man reported: "My mother looks upon the President as someone so immediately concerned with her problems and difficulties that she would not be greatly surprised were he to come to her house some evening and stay to dinner." From his first hours in office, Roosevelt gave people the feeling that they could confide in him directly. As late as the presidency of Herbert Hoover, one man, Ira Smith, had sufficed to take care of all the mail the White House received. Under Roosevelt, Smith had to acquire a staff of fifty people to handle the thousands of letters written to the President each week. Roosevelt gave people a sense of membership in the national community. Justice Douglas has written: "He was in a very special sense the people's President, because he made them feel that with him in the White House they shared the Presidency. The sense of sharing the Presidency gave even the most humble citizen a lively sense of belonging."

When Roosevelt took office, the country, to a very large degree, responded to the will of a single element: the white, Anglo-Saxon, Protestant property-holding class. Under the New Deal, new groups took their place in the sun. It was not merely that they received benefits they had not had before but that they were "recognized" as having a place in the commonwealth. At the beginning of the Roosevelt era, charity organizations ignored labor when seeking "community" representation; at the end of the period, no fund-raising committee was complete without a union representative. While Theodore Roosevelt had founded a lily-white Progressive party in the South and Woodrow Wilson had introduced segregation into the federal government, Franklin Roosevelt had quietly brought the Negro into the New Deal coalition. When the distinguished Negro contralto Marian Anderson was denied a concert hall in Washington, Secretary Ickes arranged for her to perform from the steps of Lincoln Memorial. Equal representation for religious groups became so well accepted that, as one priest wryly complained, one never saw a picture of a priest in a newspaper unless he was flanked on either side by a minister and a rabbi.

The devotion Roosevelt aroused owed much to the fact that the New Deal assumed the responsibility for guaranteeing every American a minimum standard of subsistence. Its relief programs represented an advance over the barbaric predepression practices that constituted a difference not in degree but in kind. One analyst wrote: "During the ten years between 1929 and 1939 more progress was made in public welfare and relief than in the three hundred years after this country was first settled." The Roosevelt administration gave such assistance not as a matter of charity but of right. This system of social rights was written into the Social Security Act. Other New Deal legislation abolished child labor in interstate commerce and, by putting a floor under wages and a ceiling on hours, all but wiped out the sweatshop.

Roosevelt and his aides fashioned a government which consciously sought to make the industrial system more humane and to protect workers and their families from exploitation. In his acceptance speech in June, 1936, the President stated: "Governments can err, Presidents do make mistakes, but the immortal Dante tells us that divine justice weighs the sins of the cold-blooded and the sins of the warm-hearted in different scales.

"Better the occasional faults of a Government that lives in a spirit of charity than the constant omission of a Government frozen in the ice of its own indifference." Nearly everyone in the Roosevelt government was caught up to some degree by a sense of participation in something larger than themselves. A few days after he took office, one of the more conservative New Deal administrators wrote in his diary: "This should be a Gov't of humanity."

The federal government expanded enormously in the Roosevelt years. The crisis of the depression dissipated the distrust of the state inherited from the eighteenth century and reinforced in diverse ways by the Jeffersonians and the Spencerians. Roosevelt himself believed that liberty in America was imperiled more by the agglomerations of private business than by the state. The New Dealers were convinced that the depression was the result not simply of an economic breakdown but of a political collapse; hence, they sought new political instrumentalities. The reformers of the 1930's accepted almost unquestioningly the use of coercion by the state to achieve reforms. Even Republicans who protested that Roosevelt's policies were snuffing out liberty voted overwhelmingly in favor of coercive measures.

This elephantine growth of the federal government owed much to the fact that local and state governments had been tried in the crisis and found wanting. When one magazine wired state governors to ask their views, only one of the thirty-seven who replied announced that he was willing to have the states resume responsibility for relief. Every time there was a rumored cutback of federal spending for relief, Washington was besiged by delegations of mayors protesting that city governments did not have the resources to meet the needs of the unemployed.

Even more dramatic was the impotence of local governments in dealing with crime, a subject that captured the national imagination in a decade of kidnapings and bank holdups. In September, 1933, the notorious bank robber John Dillinger was arrested in Ohio. Three weeks later, his confederates released him from jail and killed the Lima, Ohio, sheriff. In January, 1934, after bank holdups at Racine, Wisconsin, and East Chicago, Indiana, Dillinger was apprehended in Tucson, Arizona, and returned to the "escape-proof" jail of Crown Point, Indiana, reputedly the strongest county prison in the country. A month later he broke out and drove off in the sheriff's car. While five thousand law officers pursued him, he stopped for a haircut in a barber shop, bought cars, and had a home-cooked Sunday dinner with his family in his home town. When he needed more arms, he raided the police station at Warsaw, Indiana.

Dillinger's exploits touched off a national outcry for federal action. State and local authorities could not cope with gangs which crossed and recrossed jurisdictional lines, which were equipped with Thompson submachine guns and high-powered cars, and which had a regional network of informers and fences in the Mississippi Valley. Detection and punishment of crime had always been a local function; now there seemed no choice but to call in the federal operatives. In July, 1934, federal agents shot down Dillinger outside a Chicago theater. In October, FBI men killed Pretty Boy Floyd near East Liverpool, Ohio; in November, they shot Baby Face Nelson, Public Enemy No. 1, near Niles Center, Illinois. By the end of 1934, the nation had a new kind of hero: the G-man Melvin Purvis and the chief of the Division of Investigation of the Department of Justice, J. Edgar Hoover. By the end of that year, too, Congress had stipulated that a long list of crimes would henceforth be regarded as federal offenses, including holding up a bank insured by the Federal Deposit Insurance Corporation. The family of a kidnaped victim could call in the federal police simply by phoning National 7117 in Washington.

Under the New Deal, the federal government greatly extended its power over the economy. By the end of the Roosevelt years, few questioned the right of the government to pay the farmer millions in subsidies not to grow crops, to enter plants to conduct union elections, to regulate business enterprises from utility companies to air lines, or even to compete directly with business by generating and distributing hydroelectric power. All of these powers had been ratified by the Supreme Court, which had even held that a man growing grain solely for his own use was affecting interstate commerce and hence subject to federal penalties. The President, too, was well on his way to becoming "the chief economic engineer," although this was not finally established until the Full Employment Act of 1946. In 1931, Hoover had hooted that some people thought "that by some legerdemain we can legislate ourselves out of a world-wide depression." In the Roosevelt era, the conviction that government both should and could act to forestall future breakdowns gained general acceptance. The New Deal left a large legacy of antidepression controls—securities regulation, banking reforms, unemployment compensation—even if it could not guarantee that a subsequent administration would use them.

In the 1930's, the financial center of the nation shifted from Wall Street to Washington. In May, 1934, a writer reported: "Financial news no longer originates in Wall Street." That same month, *Fortune* commented on a revolution in the credit system which was "one of the major historical events of the generation." "Mr. Roosevelt," it noted, "seized the Federal Reserve without firing a shot." The federal government had not only broken down the old separation of bank and state in the Reserve system but had

gone into the credit business itself in a wholesale fashion under
the aegis of the RFC, the Farm Credit Administration, and the
housing agencies. Legislation in 1933 and 1934 had established
federal regulation of Wall Street for the first time. No longer
could the New York Stock Exchange operate as a private club
free of national supervision. In 1935, Congress leveled the mammoth holding-company pyramids and centralized yet more authority over the banking system in the federal government. After a
tour of the United States in 1935, Sir Josiah Stamp wrote: "Just
as in 1929 the whole country was 'Wall Street-conscious' now it
is 'Washington-conscious.' "

Despite this encroachment of government on traditional business prerogatives, the New Deal could advance impressive claims
to being regarded as a "savior of capitalism." Roosevelt's sense of
the land, of family, and of the community marked him as a man
with deeply ingrained conservative traits. In the New Deal years,
the government sought deliberately, in Roosevelt's words, "to
energize private enterprise." The RFC financed business, housing
agencies underwrote home financing, and public works spending
aimed to revive the construction industry. Moreover, some of the
New Deal reforms were Janus-faced. The NYA, in aiding jobless
youth, also served as a safety valve to keep young people out of
the labor market. A New Deal congressman, in pushing for public
power projects, argued that the country should take advantage
of the sea of "cheap labor" on the relief rolls. Even the Wagner
Act and the movement for industrial unionism were motivated in
part by the desire to contain "unbalanced and radical" labor
groups. Yet such considerations should not obscure the more important point: that the New Deal, however conservative it was
in some respects and however much it owed to the past, marked
a radically new departure. As Carl Degler writes: "The conclusion
seems inescapable that, traditional as the words may have been in
which the New Deal expressed itself, in actuality it was a revolutionary response to a revolutionary situation."

Not all of the changes that were wrought were the result of

Roosevelt's own actions or of those of his government. Much of the force for change came from progressives in Congress, or from nongovernmental groups like the C.I.O., or simply from the impersonal agency of the depression itself. Yet, however much significance one assigns the "objective situation," it is difficult to gainsay the importance of Roosevelt. If, in Miami in February, 1933, an assassin's bullet had been true to its mark and John Garner rather than Roosevelt had entered the White House the next month, or if the Roosevelt lines had cracked at the Democratic convention in 1932 and Newton Baker had been the compromise choice, the history of America in the thirties would have been markedly different.

At a time when democracy was under attack elsewhere in the world, the achievements of the New Deal were especially significant. At the end of 1933, in an open letter to President Roosevelt, John Maynard Keynes had written: "You have made yourself the trustee for those in every country who seek to mend the evils of our condition by reasoned experiment within the framework of the existing social system. If you fail, rational change will be gravely prejudiced throughout the world, leaving orthodoxy and revolution to fight it out." In the next few years, teams of foreigners toured the TVA, Russians and Arabs came to study the shelter-belt, French writers taxed Léon Blum with importing "Rooseveltism" to France, and analysts characterized Paul Van Zeeland's program in Belgium as a "New Deal." Under Roosevelt, observed a Montevideo newspaper, the United States had become "as it was in the eighteenth century, the victorious emblem around which may rally the multitudes thirsting for social justice and human fraternity."

In their approach to reform, the New Dealers reflected the tough-minded, hard-boiled attitude that permeated much of America in the thirties. In 1931, the gangster film *Public Enemy* had given the country a new kind of hero in James Cagney: the aggressive, unsentimental tough guy who deliberately assaulted the romantic tradition. It was a type whose role in society could easily be manipulated; gangster hero Cagney of the early thirties was transformed into G-man hero Cagney of the later thirties. Even more representative was Humphrey Bogart, creator of the "private eye" hero, the man of action who masks his feelings in a calculated emotional neutrality. Bogart, who began as the cold desperado Duke Mantee of *Petrified Forest* and the frightening Black Legionnaire, soon turned up on the right side of anti-Fascist causes, although he never surrendered the pose of noninvolvement. This fear of open emotional commitment and this admiration of toughness ran through the vogue of the "Dead End Kids," films like *Nothing Sacred*, the popularity of the St. Louis Cardinals' spike-flying Gas House Gang, and the "hardboiled" fiction of writers like James Cain and Dashiell Hammett.

Unlike the earlier Progressive, the New Dealer shied away from being thought of as sentimental. Instead of justifying relief as a humanitarian measure, the New Dealers often insisted it was necessary to stimulate purchasing power or to stabilize the economy or to "conserve manpower." The justification for a better distribution of income was neither "social justice" nor a "healthier national life," wrote Adolf Berle. "It remained for the hard-boiled student to work out the simple equation that unless the national income was pretty widely diffused there were not enough customers to keep the plants going." The reformers of the thirties abandoned—or claimed they had abandoned—the old Emersonian hope of reforming man and sought only to change institutions. This meant that they did not seek to "uplift" the people they were helping but only to improve their economic position. "In other words," Tugwell stated bluntly, "the New Deal is attempting to do nothing to *people*, and does not seek at all to alter their way of life, their wants and desires."

Reform in the 1930's meant *economic* reform; it departed from the Methodist-parsonage morality of many of the earlier Progressives, in part because much of the New Deal support, and many of its leaders, derived from urban immigrant groups hostile to the old Sabbatarianism. While the progressive grieved over the fate of the prostitute, the New Dealer would have placed Mrs. Warren's profession under a code authority. If the archetypical progressive was Jane Addams singing "Onward, Christian Soldiers," the representative New Dealer was Harry Hopkins betting on the horses at Laurel Race Track. When directing FERA in late 1933, Hopkins announced: "I would like to provide orchestras for beer gardens to encourage people to sit around drinking their beer and enjoying themselves. It would be a great unemployment relief measure." "I feel no call to remedy evils," Raymond Moley declared. "I have not the slightest urge to be a reformer. Social workers make me very weary. They have no sense of humor."

Despite Moley's disclaimer, many of the early New Dealers like himself and Adolf Berle did, in fact, hope to achieve reform through regeneration: the regeneration of the businessman. By the end of 1935, the New Dealers were pursuing a quite different course. Instead of attempting to evangelize the Right, they mobilized massive political power against the power of the corporation. They relied not on converting industrial sinners but in using sufficient coercion. New Dealers like Thurman Arnold sought to ignore "moral" considerations altogether; Arnold wished not to punish wrongdoers but to achieve price flexibility. His "faith" lay in the expectation that "fanatical alignments between opposing political principles may disappear and a competent, practical, opportunisitic governing class may rise to power." With such expectations, the New Dealers frequently had little patience with legal restraints that impeded action. "I want to assure you," Hopkins told the NYA Advisory Committee, "that we are not afraid of exploring anything within the law, and we have a lawyer who will declare anything you want to do legal."

In the thirties, nineteenth-century individualism gave ground to a new emphasis on social security and collective action. In the twenties, America hailed Lindbergh as the Lone Eagle; in the thirties, when word arrived that Amelia Earhart was lost at sea, the *New Republic* asked the government to prohibit citizens from engaging in such "useless" exploits. The NRA sought to drive newsboys off the streets and took a Blue Eagle away from a company in Huck Finn's old town of Hannibal, Missouri, because a fifteen-year-old was found driving a truck for his father's business. Josef Hofmann urged that fewer musicians become soloists, Hollywood stars like Joan Crawford joined the Screen Actors Guild, and Leopold Stokowski canceled a performance in Pittsburgh because theater proprietors were violating a union contract. In New York in 1933, after a series of meetings in Heywood Broun's penthouse apartment, newspapermen organized the American Newspaper Guild in rebellion against the disspiriting romanticism of Richard Harding Davis. "We no longer care to develop the individual as a unique contributor to a democratic form," wrote the mordant Edgar Kemler. "In this movement each individual sub-man is important, not for his uniqueness, but for his ability to lose himself in the mass, through his fidelity to the trade union, or cooperative organization, or political party."

The liberals of the thirties admired intellectual activity which had a direct relation to concrete reality. Stuart Chase wrote of one government report: "This book is live stuff—wheelbarrow, cement mixer, steam dredge, generator, combine, power-line stuff; library dust does not gather here." If the poet did not wish to risk the suspicion that his loyalties were not to the historic necessities of his generation, wrote Archibald MacLeish, he must "soak himself not in books" but in the physical reality of "by what organization of men and railroads and trucks and belts and book-entries the materials of a single automobile are assembled." The New Dealers were fascinated by "the total man days per year for timber stand improvement," and Tugwell rejoiced in the "practical success" of the Resettlement Administration demonstrated by "these healthy collection figures." Under the Special Skills Division of the RA, Greenbelt was presented with inspirational paintings like *Constructing Sewers*, *Concrete Mixer*, and *Shovel at Work*. On one occasion, in attempting to mediate a literary controversy, the critic Edmund Wilson wrote: "It should be possible to convince Marxist critics of the importance of a work like 'Ulysses' by telling them that it is a great piece of engineering—as it is." In this activist world of the New Dealers, the aesthete and the man who pursued a life of contemplation, especially the man whose interests centered in the past, were viewed with scorn. In Robert Sherwood's *The Petrified Forest*, Alan Squier, the ineffectual aesthete, meets his death in the desert and is buried in the petrified forest where the living turn to stone. He is an archaic type for whom the world has no place.

The new activism explicitly recognized its debt to Dewey's dictum of "learning by doing" and, like other of Dewey's ideas, was subject to exaggeration and perversion. The New Deal, which gave unprecedented authority to intellectuals in government, was, in certain important respects, anti-intellectual. Without the activist faith, perhaps not nearly so much would have been achieved. It was Lilienthal's conviction that "there is almost nothing, however fantastic, that (given competent organization) a team of engineers, scientists, and administrators cannot do today" that helped make possible the successes of TVA. Yet the liberal activists grasped only a part of the truth; they retreated from conceptions like "tragedy," "sin," "God," often had small patience with the force of tradition, and showed little understanding of what moved men to seek meanings outside of political experience. As sensitive a critic as the poet Horace Gregory could write, in a review of the works of D. H. Lawrence: "The world is moving away from Lawrence's need for personal salvation; his 'dark religion' is not a substitute for economic planning." This was not the mood of all men in the thirties—not of a William Faulkner, an Ellen Glasgow—and many of the New Dealers recognized that life was more complex than some of their statements would suggest. Yet the liberals, in their desire to free themselves from the tyranny of precedent and in their ardor for social achievement, sometimes walked the precipice of superficiality and philistinism.

The concentration of the New Dealers on public concerns made a deep mark on the sensibility of the 1930's. Private experience seemed self-indulgent compared to the demands of public life.

"Indeed the public world with us has *become* the private world, and the private world has become the public," wrote Archibald MacLeish. "We live, that is to say, in a revolutionary time in which the public life has washed in over the dikes of private existence as sea water breaks over into the fresh pools in the spring tides till everything is salt." In the thirties, the Edna St. Vincent Millay whose candle had burned at both ends wrote the polemical *Conversation at Midnight* and the bitter "Epitaph for the Race of Man" in *Wine From These Grapes*.

The emphasis on the public world implied a specific rejection of the values of the 1920's. Roosevelt dismissed the twenties as "a decade of debauch," Tugwell scored those years as "a decade of empty progress, devoid of contribution to a genuinely better future," Morris Cooke deplored the "gilded-chariot days" of 1929, and Alben Barkley saw the twenties as a "carnival" marred by "the putrid pestilence of financial debauchery." The depression was experienced as the punishment of a wrathful God visited on a nation that had strayed from the paths of righteousness. The fire that followed the Park Avenue party in Thomas Wolfe's *You Can't Go Home Again*, like the suicide of Eveline at the end of John Dos Passos's *The Big Money*, symbolized the holocaust that brought to an end a decade of hedonism. In an era of reconstruction, the attitudes of the twenties seemed alien, frivolous, or—the most cutting word the thirties could visit upon a man or institution—"escapist." When Morrie Ryskind and George Kaufman, authors of the popular *Of Thee I Sing*, lampooned the government again in *Let 'em Eat Cake* in the fall of 1933, the country was not amused. The New York *Post* applauded the decision of George Jean Nathan and his associates to discontinue the *American Spectator*: "Nihilism, dadaism, smartsetism—they are all gone, and this, too, is progress." One of H. L. Mencken's biographers has noted: "Many were at pains to write him at his new home, telling him he was a sophomore, and those writing in magazines attacked him with a fury that was suspect because of its very violence."

Commentators on the New Deal have frequently characterized it by that much-abused term "pragmatic." If one means by this that the New Dealers carefully tested the consequences of ideas, the term is clearly a misnomer. If one means that Roosevelt was exceptionally anti-ideological in his approach to politics, one may question whether he was, in fact, any more "pragmatic" in this sense than Van Buren or Polk or even "reform" Presidents like Jackson and Theodore Roosevelt. The "pragmatism" of the New Deal seemed remarkable only in a decade tortured by ideology, only in contrast to the rigidity of Hoover and of the Left.

The New Deal was pragmatic mainly in its skepticism about utopias and final solutions, its openness to experimentation, and its suspicion of the dogmas of the Establishment. Since the advice of economists had so often been wrong, the New Dealers distrusted the claims of orthodox theory—"All this is perfectly terrible because it is all pure theory, when you come down to it," the President said on one occasion—and they felt free to try new approaches. Roosevelt refused to be awed by the warnings of economists and financial experts that government interference with the "laws" of the economy was blasphemous. "We must lay hold of the fact that economic laws are not made by nature," the President stated. "They are made by human beings." The New Dealers denied that depressions were inevitable events that had to be borne stoically, most of the stoicism to be displayed by the most impoverished, and they were willing to explore novel ways to make the social order more stable and more humane. "I am for experimenting . . . in various parts of the country, trying out schemes which are supported by reasonable people and see if they work," Hopkins told a conference of social workers. "If they do not work, the world will not come to an end."

Hardheaded, "anti-utopian," the New Dealers nonetheless had their Heavenly City: the greenbelt town, clean, green, and white, with children playing in light, airy, spacious schools; the government project at Longview, Washington, with small houses, each of different design, colored roofs, and gardens of flowers and vegetables; the Mormon villages of Utah that M. L. Wilson kept in his mind's eye—immaculate farmsteads on broad, rectangular streets; most of all, the Tennessee Valley, with its model town of Norris, the tall transmission towers, the white dams, the glistening wire strands, the valley where "a vision of villages and clean small factories has been growing into the minds of thoughtful men." Scandinavia was their model abroad, not only because it summoned up images of the countryside of Denmark, the beauties of Stockholm, not only for its experience with labor relations and social insurance and currency reform, but because it represented the "middle way" of happy accommodation of public and private institutions the New Deal sought to achieve. "Why," inquired Brandeis, "should anyone want to go to Russia when one can go to Denmark?"

Yet the New Deal added up to more than all of this—more than an experimental approach, more than the sum of its legislative achievements, more than an antiseptic utopia. It is true that there was a certain erosion of values in the thirties, as well as a narrowing of horizons, but the New Dealers inwardly recognized that what they were doing had a deeply moral significance however much they eschewed ethical pretensions. Heirs of the Enlightenment, they felt themselves part of a broadly humanistic movement to make man's life on earth more tolerable, a movement that might someday even achieve a co-operative commonwealth. Social insurance, Frances Perkins declared, was "a fundamental part of another great forward step in that liberation of humanity which began with the Renaissance."

Franklin Roosevelt did not always have this sense as keenly as some of the men around him, but his greatness as a President lies in the remarkable degree to which he shared the vision. "The new deal business to me is very much bigger than anyone yet has expressed it," observed Senator Elbert Thomas. Roosevelt "seems to really have caught the spirit of what one of the Hebrew prophets called the desire of the nations. If he were in India today they would probably decide that he had become Mahatma—that is,

one in tune with the infinite." Both foes and friends made much
of Roosevelt's skill as a political manipulator, and there is no
doubt that up to a point he delighted in schemes and stratagems.
As Donald Richberg later observed: "There would be times when
he seemed to be a Chevalier Bayard, *sans peur et sans reproche*,
and times in which he would seem to be the apotheosis of a
prince who had absorbed and practiced all the teachings of Machiavelli." Yet essentially he was a moralist who wanted to achieve
certain humane reforms and instruct the nation in the principles
of government. On one occasion, he remarked: "I want to be a
preaching President—like my cousin." His courtiers gleefully recounted his adroitness in trading and dealing for votes, his effectiveness on the stump, his wicked skill in cutting corners to win
a point. But Roosevelt's importance lay not in his talents as a
campaigner or a manipulator. It lay rather in his ability to arouse
the country and, more specifically, the men who served under
him, by his breezy encouragement of experimentation, by his
hopefulness, and—a word that would have embarrassed some of
his lieutenants—by his idealism.

The New Deal left many problems unsolved and even created
some perplexing new ones. It never demonstrated that it could
achieve prosperity in peacetime. As late as 1941, the unemployed
still numbered six million, and not until the war year of 1943 did
the army of the jobless finally disappear. It enhanced the power
of interest groups who claimed to speak for millions, but sometimes represented only a small minority. It did not evolve a way
to protect people who had no such spokesmen, nor an acceptable
method for disciplining the interest groups. In 1946, President
Truman would resort to a threat to draft railway workers into the
Army to avert a strike. The New Deal achieved a more just society
by recognizing groups which had been largely unrepresented—
staple farmers, industrial workers, particular ethnic groups, and
the new intellectual-administrative class. Yet this was still a half-
way revolution; it swelled the ranks of the bourgeoisie but left
many Americans—sharecroppers, slum dwellers, most Negroes—
outside of the new equilibrium.

Some of these omissions were to be promptly remedied. Subsequent Congresses extended social security, authorized slum clearance projects, and raised minimum-wage standards to keep step with the rising price level. Other shortcomings are understandable. The havoc that had been done before Roosevelt took office was so great that even the unprecedented measures of the New Deal did not suffice to repair the damage. Moreover, much was still to be learned, and it was in the Roosevelt years that the country was schooled in how to avert another major depression. Although it was war which freed the government from the taboos of a balanced budget and revealed the potentialities of spending, it is conceivable that New Deal measures would have led the country into a new cycle of prosperity even if there had been no war. Marked gains had been made before the war spending had any appreciable effect. When recovery did come, it was much more soundly based because of the adoption of the New Deal program.

Roosevelt and the New Dealers understood, perhaps better than their critics, that they had come only part of the way. Henry Wallace remarked: "We are children of the transition—we have left Egypt but we have not yet arrived at the Promised Land." Only five years separated Roosevelt's inauguration in 1933 and the adoption of the last of the New Deal measures, the Fair Labor Standards Act, in 1938. The New Dealers perceived that they had done more in those years than had been done in any comparable period in American history, but they also saw that there was much still to be done, much, too, that continued to baffle them. "I believe in the things that have been done," Mrs. Roosevelt told the American Youth Congress in February, 1939. "They helped but they did not solve the fundamental problems. . . . I never believed the Federal government could solve the whole problem. It bought us time to think." She closed not with a solution but with a challenge: "Is it going to be worth while?"

"This generation of Americans is living in a tremendous moment of history," President Roosevelt stated in his final national address of the 1940 campaign.

"The surge of events abroad has made some few doubters among us ask: Is this the end of a story that has been told? Is the book of democracy now to be closed and placed away upon the dusty shelves of time?

"My answer is this: All we have known of the glories of democracy—its freedom, its efficiency as a mode of living, its ability to meet the aspirations of the common man—all these are merely an introduction to the greater story of a more glorious future.

"We Americans of today—all of us—we are characters in the living book of democracy.

"But we are also its author. It falls upon us now to say whether the chapters that are to come will tell a story of retreat or a story of continued advance."

Response to FDR's Challenge

A Conservative Coalition Forms in Congress

by James T. Patterson

Although the New Deal dominated mainstream American politics during the 1930's, considerable opposition to it, both more conservative and more radical, continued throughout the period. A myriad of left-wing organizations demanded more basic changes in the American economic and social structure than those sought or even envisioned by Franklin Roosevelt's government. These changes ranged from traditional demands of the urban-oriented Socialist and Communist parties, whose membership rolls swelled by the hundreds of thousands during the Depression, to newer and even more broadly based programs of neo-Populist agricultural protest movements.

In addition, such demagogue-led assemblages as Father Charles E. Coughlin's National Union for Social Justice, Dr. Francis Townshend's old age pension clubs, and Louisiana Senator Huey P. Long's "Share the Wealth" Movement attracted an aggregate following in the millions. In 1936 some of these elements combined to run a "Union party" candidate·for the presidency. The new group polled less than a million votes and quickly disintegrated, but conservative critics proved more persistent and more long-lived politically.

From the very start of the New Deal, Republicans led by ex-President Hoover had labeled almost all of the New Deal programs as unwarranted and unconstitutional intrusions by the federal government into economic and social policy-making. Beginning in 1934 G.O.P. critics got help from a new organization dominated by Roosevelt's Big Business opponents, which was known as the Liberty League. The League provided a forum for anti-New Dealers of both parties, including none other than "Mr. Urban Democrat" of the 1920's, the Democratic party's candidate in 1928, Al Smith.

Although neither the Liberty League nor the straight Republican opposition alone proved effective in stalling New Deal legislation during Roosevelt's first term, after his re-election in 1936, congressional conservatives from both parties began to cooperate openly against many bills which Roosevelt considered critical to his administration's success. On such issues as Supreme Court "packing," FDR's executive re-organization bill, and increased government aid to depressed urban areas, Democratic and Republican conservatives made common cause to stymie New Deal moves, a common cause described below by James T. Patterson. Thus, in the waning years of the New Deal, the conservative coalition that has controlled Congress through most of the past three decades, and has produced today's "politics of stalemate," took firm and increasingly effective shape.

✿ Few political developments in recent American history have been more significant than the creation of a conservative coalition in Congress. Formed by Republicans and conservative Democrats to combat the New Deal, this "unholy alliance" operated effectively as early as 1937, and by 1939 it was strong enough to block extensions of the administration's program. It has functioned with varying degrees of success since that time, harassing and alarming Presidents of both parties.

Certain aspects of the coalition are well known and open to

From *Journal of American History*, LII (March 1966), 757–72. Reprinted by permission; footnotes omitted.

little question. Undoubtedly, both houses of Congress were more cantankerous in President Franklin D. Roosevelt's second term than they had been in his first, and most of the uncooperative congressmen were conservative on key issues. They tended to favor balanced budgets, to oppose welfare programs, to be suspicious of organized labor, and to speak favorably of states' rights and limited government.

But historians have seldom ventured beyond these generalizations. They have not identified the members of the coalition. They have not tried to generalize about them as a group. They have not probed into the questions of why or when the coalition began. Finally, they have not shown whether the coalition was consciously organized, well disciplined, or coherent on crucial roll calls. These matters deserve attention.

Actually, the conservative leaders were well known. In the House the focus of conservative strength was the Rules Committee, dominated after 1938 by Edward E. Cox, a fiery Georgian who was a ranking Democratic member, and by Howard W. Smith, a Jeffersonian Democrat from Virginia. These two men, with three other southern Democrats and four Republicans, composed a majority of the fourteen-man committee after 1936. Cox was friendly with Joseph W. Martin, Jr. of Massachusetts, the leading Republican member of the committee in 1937–1938 who became House minority leader in 1939. When controversial issues arose, Cox and Martin usually conferred. If they agreed—which was often—Martin instructed his Republican colleagues on the committee to vote with Cox and the southern Democrats. Martin said later that he and Cox were the "principal points of contact between the northern Republicans and the southern Democratic conservatives."

Conservative leadership in the Senate was more diverse. The official Republican leader was Charles L. McNary of Oregon. The popular McNary was neither an orator nor a conservative by nature; indeed, he had voted for most New Deal measures before 1937. Though McNary participated in GOP strategy conferences, the most aggressive Republican senator after 1936 was the moderately conservative Arthur H. Vandenberg of Michigan. Other well-known Republicans who usually voted against major administration proposals included Henry Cabot Lodge, Jr. of Massachusetts, Warren R. Austin of Vermont, and Hiram W. Johnson of California, who became one of the most vitriolic foes of the New Deal after 1936.

Democratic conservatives in the Senate were a varied group. On the extreme right was a cluster of irreconcilables who had voted against most New Deal programs since 1933. These included Carter Glass and Harry F. Byrd of Virginia and Josiah W. Bailey of North Carolina. Bailey was particularly pungent in his criticism of Roosevelt. The President, he wrote,

figures on hard times and does not wish for recovery. He would perish like a rattlesnake in the sun under conditions of prosperity. Pardon the illustration. Mr. Roosevelt is not a rattlesnake. He rattles a great deal, but that is all I am willing to say. Perhaps you know the rattlesnake must stay in the swamp for the reason that he does not have any means of sweating or panting. His heat accumulates. Mr. Roosevelt belongs to that type of man who lives on hard times and discontent.

Other Democrats, equally irreconcilable, joined Bailey in 1935–1936. These included Edward R. Burke of Nebraska, Peter G. Gerry of Rhode Island, Walter F. George of Georgia, and Ellison D. ("Cotton Ed") Smith of South Carolina. Such powerful veterans as Byron ("Pat") Harrison of Mississippi and James F. Byrnes of South Carolina, early supporters of the New Deal, also voted consistently against New Deal spending, tax, and labor programs after 1937. Vice-President John N. Garner of Texas, an influential figure in both houses, was another Democrat who by 1937 was counselling Roosevelt to move in a conservative direction.

While these men were unquestionably the most prominent congressional conservatives, it is not easy to generalize about them as a group. In the main they were not simply old men who had outlived their times. True, some like "Cotton Ed" Smith and Glass undoubtedly had. "Perhaps I am a relic of constitutional government," Glass admitted in 1938. "I entertain what may be the misguided notion that the Constitution of the United States, as it existed in the time of Grover Cleveland, is the same Constitution that exists today. . . ." But others, such as Byrd, Martin, and Howard Smith, were relatively young men. The average age of the most conservative Democratic senators in 1937 was precisely that of the Senate as a whole, while the most conservative Democratic representatives in 1937 averaged fifty years of age, two years less than the entire House.

Furthermore, the conservatives were by no means all veterans whose congressional service preceded the New Deal. Glass, George, and some others fitted this category, but many more first served in 1933 or thereafter, and the percentage of veteran and "coat-tail" Democrats who opposed the New Deal on most crucial roll calls was very much the same. Moreover, the most senior Republicans after 1935 included the moderately progressive McNary, William E. Borah of Idaho, and Arthur Capper of Kansas, while newcomers Austin of Vermont and H. Styles Bridges of New Hampshire tended to be among the most consistent opponents of the New Deal. Democratic veterans included not only conservatives of the Glass variety but New Deal regulars Alben W. Barkley of Kentucky, Hugo L. Black of Alabama, and Robert F. Wagner of New York. As Arthur S. Link has pointed out, the Congresses of the 1920's contained many relics of the progressive era; some of these veteran congressmen became reliable supporters of the New Deal in the 1930's.

Similarly, it is not entirely accurate to say that conservative strength in Congress derived from chairmanships of key committees. In the House, committee chairmen John J. O'Connor of New York and Hattan W. Sumners of Texas occasionally blocked administration proposals. So did "Cotton Ed" Smith, Glass, and Harrison in the Senate. But these men were counterbalanced by such liberal chairmen as Senators Black, Wagner, and Elbert D. Thomas of Utah and Representatives Sam Rayburn of Texas, Adolph J. Sabath of Illinois, and Sol Bloom of New York. More often than not, committee chairmen cooperated with the administration.

Roosevelt's congressional troubles after 1936 stemmed not so much from uncooperative committee chairmen as from more widespread opposition to his programs. In the House, for example, his three most painful defeats on domestic legislation from 1937 through 1939 were the recommittal of the fair labor standards bill in 1937, the recommittal of executive reorganization in 1938, and the defeat of his lending program in 1939. All three came at the hands of the entire House. In the Senate he lost three successive battles for increased relief expenditures in 1939, and each time the reason was the adverse vote of the entire Senate. It is too easy—and too misleading—to blame the seniority rule for Roosevelt's congressional problems.

At first glance it would appear that the conservative bloc was composed of Republicans and southern Democrats, but such was not always the case. It is undeniable that Republicans, especially in the House, opposed the administration with remarkable solidarity after 1936, but the stance of southerners was less easy to determine. Occasionally, it seemed that Cox and Bailey were representative southern spokesmen. For instance, when the House recommitted the fair labor standards bill by a vote of 216–198 in December 1937, 81 of the 99 southern Democrats voted for recommittal, as opposed to but 51 of the remaining 230 Democrats in the House. And when the Senate in August 1937 adopted, 44–39, the so-called Byrd amendment aimed at damaging the Wagner housing bill, 10 of the 22 southern Democrats supported the amendment, while only 19 of the remaining 54 Senate Democrats were with the majority.

Two factors dispel much of this seeming clarity. First, voting alignments depended upon the issue. The labor bill, by proposing to destroy southern competitive wage advantages, upset southerners of all persuasions. Walter Lippmann, in fact, called the bill "sectional legislation disguised as humanitarian reform." On other crucial votes in the House, however, such as those which recommitted reorganization in 1938 and defeated the death sentence provision of the utility holding company bill in 1935, representatives from the South divided as did Democrats from other sections. Secondly, southerners were seldom united. As V. O. Key put it, "while individual southern Senators may frequently vote with the Republicans, a majority rarely does; and when it does, the group as a whole is badly split more than half the time." The New Deal Congresses had their Glasses and Baileys, but they also had their Blacks and Rayburns. Except on race legislation, southern congressmen were never "solid."

Three things, nonetheless, were generally true of the congressional conservatives as a group. First of all, most of the vocal conservatives came from safe states or districts. The Glass–Byrd machine in Virginia, for instance, was able not only to keep veterans like Glass in the Senate but to send new conservatives to the House throughout the period. With all his power and prestige Roosevelt was too often unable to influence congressional nominations; the result was the nomination and election of many conservative Democrats during the New Deal years. In 1935 alone, new Senate Democrats included Rush D. Holt of West Virginia, Gerry of Rhode Island, and Burke of Nebraska, all of whom were soon to become staunch foes of the New Deal. That such men could be nominated in a year of unusually restive and liberal politics indicates both the limitations of presidential political power and the continuing strength of local political organizations.

Second, most of the effective Democratic conservatives, though not committee chairmen, were ranking or near-ranking members of important committees. Cox was the most strategically placed of these men, but there were several others. In the House they included Martin Dies, Jr. of Texas on the Rules Committee and Clifton A. Woodrum of Virginia on appropriations. In the Senate Bailey, George, William H. King of Utah, and many others comprised this group. Those conservative Democrats without responsibility, it seemed, often felt free to act as they pleased.

Thirdly, most conservative congressmen after 1936 were from rural districts or states. Too much should not be made of this fact: so, too, were many liberals. There were also many conservative Democrats from urbanized states, such as Senators Gerry of Rhode Island and Millard E. Tydings of Maryland. The nature of opposition to administration programs depended greatly upon the type of issue: New Deal farm bills, for example, often aroused considerable hostility among urban congressmen. Generally, however, rural congressmen voted against New Deal programs more consistently than did urban congressmen. The coalition was composed not so much of Republicans and southern Democrats as of Republicans and rural Democrats; urban southerners were often more favorably disposed to administration programs than their rural counterparts.

The existence of this urban-rural split upon many economic issues after 1936 was indisputable. Democratic votes in the House against administration measures in the 1937–1939 period were: investigation of sit-downs, 82 per cent rural; recommit fair labor standards, 74 per cent rural; investigate National Labor Relations Board, 77 per cent rural; lending bill, 69 per cent rural; and housing bill, 83 per cent rural. Since the percentage of Democrats who represented rural districts was 54 in 1937 and 57 in 1939, it is clear that the Democratic opposition on these bills was heavily rural in character.

It is difficult to say that any given issue or year "created" the conservative group. Rather, different groups of inherently conservative men switched at different times from unhappy allegiance to the New Deal to open hostility. In most cases these men changed their positions because they discovered that they could oppose the administration without fear of electoral extinction. The state of the President's prestige, as much as the nature of his program, determined the kind of reception he received on Capitol Hill.

Roosevelt's great popularity before 1937 was undeniable. Even

Republicans bowed before it. "There can be no doubt," wrote one Republican senator in 1933, "that at the moment the President has an extraordinary support throughout the country and is able to do with the Congress as he wills. I suppose prudence dictates that one should not attempt to swim against the tide." Thus, Republicans through 1936 split sharply on final votes on major pieces of legislation. Cautious men like Vandenberg supported part of the administration program; others, not so astute, lost in 1934 or 1936. Many congressmen of both parties were unhappy with the New Deal well before 1937, but few dared to publicize their discontent with adverse votes.

Nevertheless, Democratic disaffection in Congress grew ominously as early as 1935. In that year the House three times defeated the death sentence clause of the utility holding company bill, and in the Senate the "wealth tax" bill antagonized not only the Democratic irreconcilables but also moderates like Harrison and Byrnes. Roosevelt's success with his 1935 Congress was indeed remarkable, but it cost him some political capital. Even if he had not thrown Congress into turmoil in 1937 with his court reform plan, he probably would have had great difficulty with the many congressmen who had already chafed at his relentless leadership and who considered the reform era at an end.

The court reform plan, presented in February 1937, provided these fractious congressmen with the ideal occasion for open rebellion. While Harrison and some other leaders remained outwardly loyal, the plan caused many formerly dependable Democrats to oppose the President openly. In addition, it united progressive and conservative Republicans, created intense personal rancor, and left all but the "100 per cent New Dealers" suspicious of the President's motives. Above all, it emboldened congressmen who had not dared speak out before.

Other events after 1936 increased congressional courage. The wave of sit-down strikes in 1937 caused many to blame the New Deal for the growth of labor "radicalism." The recession of 1937–1938 convinced others that the New Deal had failed. The President's plan to reorganize the executive branch, a divisive issue in 1938, provided another occasion for successful coalition effort. And Roosevelt's unsuccessful attempt to purge his conservative opponents in 1938 encouraged disenchanted congressmen to become still more outspoken.

The election of 1938 solidified this trend. Republicans gained 80 seats in the House and 8 in the Senate, increasing their numbers to 169 and 23 respectively. Since unreliable Democrats already numbered some 40 in the House and 20 in the Senate, the administration faced a divided Congress before the session began. The President's achievements in 1939 were negligible; the domestic New Deal, for all intents and purposes, made no more striking gains.

These external events, however, were not the only causes of Roosevelt's difficulties, nor should the President receive all the blame for the change. Two other developments—the changing nature of the liberal coalition and improved economic conditions —also contributed materially to the growth of congressional conservatism after 1936.

Roosevelt's liberal coalition had changed dramatically from the largely southern–western alliance of 1932 to a congeries of politically conscious pressure groups. Composed of labor unions, underprivileged ethnic groups, Negroes, and relief recipients, this aggregation was essentially northern–urban in character. Enormously encouraged by the 1936 election, these groups pressed relentlessly for their objectives in ensuing sessions, often without Roosevelt's approval. The sit-downs, for instance, were not Roosevelt's idea, and he refused to take sides in the matter. Similarly, relief workers and Democratic mayors badgered the President for higher relief expenditures than he was willing to seek. The fair labor standards bill, criticized by conservative southerners, faced even more serious opposition from AFL spokesmen fearful of government interference with collective bargaining. The President did not press either for housing or antilynching legislation, but liberal congressmen insisted upon introducing them, and bitter struggles ensued. Except for the court plan, unquestionably a major presidential blunder, Roosevelt made few tactically serious errors after 1936. But the well-organized elements of his predominantly northern–urban coalition were demanding more aid at the same time that many other congressmen, not so dependent upon these elements for political survival, were convinced of the need for retrenchment. And many rural congressmen, while friendly to much of the New Deal, believed these urban elements were preempting funds or favors which might otherwise have benefited rural areas. The result was a largely urban–rural split within the unwieldy coalition which was the Democratic party. No amount of presidential flattery could have prevented it.

It is also worth noting that the changed emphasis of the New Deal in 1935—such as it was—was not nearly so disturbing to many congressmen as the pressure generated by urban elements in 1937. Southerners, Harrison and Byrnes for instance, had in 1935 approved social security, banking reform, and moderate tax reform. And men like Cox, hostile to abuses by private utilities, had even found it possible to vote for the death sentence clause of the utility bill. But none of these men favored the more urban liberalism espoused by liberal congressmen in 1937–1939. Prior to 1936 the economic emergency, together with the administration's emphasis upon measures benefiting all areas of the nation, had temporarily obscured the urban–rural fissures so apparent in the Democratic party in the 1920's. But when the urban wing of the party, awakened and dominant, sought to gain beneficial legislation in 1937–1939, the split reappeared to plague the New Deal and subsequent liberal administrations.

Improved economic conditions were of great significance to this split, for if one examines executive–congressional relations in the twentieth century, he finds that congressmen were never so tractable as in the desperate years from 1933 through 1935. Without detracting from Roosevelt's able congressional leadership in these years, it is certain that the emergency provided ideal conditions for the success of his program in Congress. Practically every congressman, besieged for relief by his constituents, responded with alacrity to the President's activist leadership. By 1937 this sense of crisis had diminished. Thus many of the same moderate congressmen who had so gratefully supported the administration through 1935 became unreliable two and three years later. And the recession of 1937–1938, far from reviving this sense of crisis, served instead to suggest that Roosevelt was not the magician he had previously seemed to be. Indeed, to many hostile congressmen the period was the "Roosevelt recession." In a sense, the economic state of the nation was the President's greatest ally before 1936, his greatest adversary thereafter.

The sit-down strikes, the defeat of the court plan and the purge, and the recession gave considerable confidence to many inherently conservative congressmen who had already been uneasy or restive with the New Deal in 1935–1936. The beginning of effective conservative opposition in Congress, acccordingly, can be set in 1937. But the roots stemmed at least to 1935, and in retrospect it seems that the court plan merely hastened the development of an inevitable division among the disparate elements of the dominant Democratic party.

One major problem remains: how did the conservative bloc function as a group? Was it a well organized conspiracy, or was it simply a loose combination of the moment?

At a glance, the coalition appears to have been well organized. In the Senate fight against the court plan, Burton K. Wheeler of Montana led a bipartisan team against the President. Senators from both parties not only cooperated but met from time to time in private homes to plan joint strategy. And Republicans agreed to keep quiet lest their partisan charges antagonize moderate Democrats. As Vandenberg admitted later, there was a "bipartisan high command. . . . Only a coalition could succeed—a preponderantly Democratic coalition. This was frankly recognized. There was no secret about it. . . . Republicans voluntarily subordinated themselves and withdrew to the reserve lines. . . ."

Many of the senators who opposed the court plan remained at

odds with the administration in the 1938 and 1939 sessions, and Wheeler led quite similar blocs against executive reorganization. And in the House, 1937 was the year when the conservative bloc in the Rules Committee first began to operate against the administration, refusing three times between August 1937 and May 1938 to report out the fair labor standards bill. Unquestionably, conservatives in both houses developed networks of personal communications across party lines in 1937 and 1938. On crucial roll call votes it was safe to predict that an all but unanimous group of Republicans in both houses would be joined by at least 20 Democrats in the Senate and from 40 to 110 in the House.

Such evidence, however, does not prove the existence of a coordinated group functioning as a team on all—or even most—issues. Wheeler, for example, was not so reactionary as liberals insisted, and he continued after 1937 to back many administration relief, labor, and farm bills. Conversely, Harrison and Byrnes remained loyal to the administration during both the court and reorganization battles, while stridently opposing the fair labor standards bill, increased spending for relief, and the undistributed profits tax. And foreign policy questions created completely different alignments.

That the type of issue determined the composition of the conservative bloc was especially clear in the 1939 session. In the Senate, conservative alliances defeated the administration in struggles over relief spending in January and temporarily over reorganization in March. The crucial votes were 47–46 and 45–44 respectively. On both occasions Republicans voted solidly against the administration; of the 23 in the Senate, 20 voted against relief and 22 against reorganization. Of the 69 Democrats, 26 opposed relief and 21 reorganization. But the bloc was not monolithic. Eleven of the 26 Democrats against the relief bill supported the President on reorganization; 7 Democrats who had backed the President on relief deserted him on reorganization. A conservative nucleus of 20 Republicans and 15 Democrats opposed the administration on both bills. The others shifted in and out at will. For partisan reasons Republicans were remarkably united, but conservative Democrats were seldom able to work together in either house.

Furthermore, even the predictable core of very conservative Democrats ordinarily voted with Republicans because there was a meeting of the minds, not because they had conferred secretly with them in advance of crucial votes. The fate which befell the one serious effort in the direction of long-range conservative planning revealed the insuperable problems involved in developing such bipartisan agreement. This effort occurred in the fall of 1937.

After the Supreme Court's "switch in time that saved nine" in the spring of 1937, Bailey realized that the Senate must replace the court as the bulwark of conservative strength in the country, and he became anxious to form a more cohesive bloc against the New Deal. "What we have to do," he wrote Byrd in September, "is to preserve, if we can, the Democratic Party against his [Roosevelt's] efforts to make it the Roosevelt Party. But above this we must place the preservation of Constitutional Representative Government. We must frame a policy and maintain it—and this must be done in the next Congress. We must ascertain on whom we may rely—get them together and make our battle, win or lose."

When Bailey and his fellow conservatives returned for a special session in November they determined to put their coalition into effect. On December 2 ten conservative Democrats and two Republicans feasted on quail in a Senate dining room and laid plans for the future. As Vandenberg, one of the participants, put it privately, the group "informally resolved upon attempting a coalition statement to the country." For the next ten days this group, led by Vandenberg, Bailey, and Gerry, worked diligently at consulting conservative colleagues and trying to draft a statement of principles. They sought to present Roosevelt with a show of bipartisan strength and to persuade him to adopt a program more conciliatory to business. But their plan was also "replete with the possibility of open coalition upon the floor of the Senate." Senators who subscribed to the principles enunciated in the statement —broad phrases covering tax, spending, and labor policy—were expected to vote accordingly when these issues arose in subsequent congressional sessions.

Bailey's effort failed dismally. To begin with, moderately conservative Democrats like Harrison and Byrnes refused to participate. As southerners they did not relish formal associations with Republicans, nor did they wish to antagonize the President for no good purpose. Others naturally preferred to maintain their freedom of action in the future. And still others feared that such a challenge would drive Roosevelt, then pursuing an uncertain course in dealing with the recession, into the hands of the spenders. Before Bailey and his cohorts had time to circulate the finished document, McNary secured a copy and gave it to the press, which published it without delay on December 16. The surprised conservatives fumed silently. "Premature publicity— *thanks to treachery*—ended the episode,"' Vandenberg noted in his scrapbook. "The next time we want to plan a patriotically dramatic contribution to the welfare of the country, we shall let no one in who is not *tried and true*." Bailey added that the "premature publicity was brought about wholly because this man [McNary] and some of his associates took a partisan view that the declaration of principles would help the Democratic cause and hurt the Republican cause." As both men realized, McNary's action ended the frail hopes for a resounding, well-timed demonstration of conservative strength.

McNary's thinking was indeed partly partisan. At that time he was conferring with Alfred M. Landon, Frank Knox, and other Republican leaders in the Capitol. Encouraged by Roosevelt's declining prestige, these men believed that Republicans could survive without seeking coalitions with conservative Democrats. The idea of a bipartisan statement of conservatism seemed to them considerably less attractive than it did to Vandenberg. Yet McNary's chief motivation was ideological; like other progressive Republicans, he frankly disagreed with the views of the conservatives involved. If Republicans associated with men like Bailey, he believed, they would give the GOP an even more reactionary coloring than it already wore. McNary's "treachery" was evidence both of the power of partisanship and of the divisions within his party.

Neither Bailey nor his fellow conservatives again pressed seriously for the plan. Republicans became increasingly partisan, driving Democrats of all persuasions into uneasy unity for the coming campaign. Despite the attempted purges which followed, both Republicans and Democrats in the ensuing primaries acted along partisan rather than conservative–liberal lines, and the flimsy chances for bipartisan conservative cooperation in the Senate faded quickly. Conservatives continued to vote together in 1938 and 1939 if there was a meeting of the minds; otherwise, as Bailey had feared, they voted apart. As a newsman close to the scene explained at the close of the 1939 session,

in both houses, when a pro- and anti-New Deal issue is squarely presented, a shifting population of conservative Democrats can be counted upon to join the Republicans to vote against the President. The arrangement is not formal. There is nothing calculated about it, except the Republican strategy originated . . . by McNary of refraining from arousing the Democrats' partisan feelings by inflammatory oratory.

A conservative bipartisan bloc was often able by 1939 to block major legislative extensions of the New Deal. But it was not united, and it followed no blueprint. Conservative congressmen, representing widely differing states and districts, faced widely differing political exigencies. They refused to be chained to a "conspiracy." More important, most congressmen were first of all partisans. For all but a few the party organizations of their constituencies were the chief facts of their political careers, and few of these organizations, in 1937 or at any time, wished bipartisanship to operate for long.

7

The Search for Equilibrium, 1945–1960

From FDR to Truman

Congress and the Fair Deal

by Richard E. Neustadt

The French historian André Maurois once described Franklin Roosevelt as a presidential "Moses, [who] led his people through the desert of the depression and the trials of the war toward an awareness of their social and international responsibilities." Maurois shrewdly categorized Roosevelt's less polished successor, Harry S Truman, differently. "Truman's ambition," he observed, "was rather to be a Joshua, the faithful lieutenant who, after the prophet's meeting with his God and the proclamation of the Tables of the Law, undertook the application of them."

Essentially Maurois described Truman's desire, once he became President in 1945, to consolidate and complete "the Roosevelt revolution" in American domestic life. Truman's Fair Deal programs built generally on uncompleted aspects (some barely begun) of the New Deal agenda. Plagued from almost the beginning of his presidency by an uncooperative congressional coalition of Republicans and conservative Southern Democrats, Truman never enjoyed the initial period of harmony between executive and legislative branches that made Roosevelt's first term so spectacularly successful. Thus many of Truman's most cherished domestic programs, including a federally sponsored medical care plan and major civil rights legislation, failed to become law; and Truman's limited talents for congressional arm-twisting (despite some achievements on Capitol Hill), never matched Roosevelt's illustrious record.

Practically from the night he took office upon hearing word of Roosevelt's sudden death, a "night the moon, the stars and all the planets fell on me," Truman recalled, the new President found himself involved in controversy with Soviet Russia, one of America's World War II allies, over the nature of the postwar settlement. During the Truman presidency a Cold War between the world's two superpowers led the United States into forming a series of global alliances with the avowed aim of "containing" Russia. Much of the historiographic debate over the quality of Truman's presidency has pitted a generation of liberal anti-Communist historians who consider Truman's view of Soviet intentions reasonably accurate against a more recent wave of "New Left" revisionists who have placed equal or primary responsibility on Truman for provoking Russian hostility. It is doubtful that the latter group would sustain a 1964 poll among historians that judged Truman as a "near-great" President, but even today, many scholars admire Truman's adroit handling of American foreign policy, particularly considering the Missourian's lack of preparation for the massive presidential responsibilities he inherited.

The verdict on Truman's direction of domestic affairs remains mixed. Despite his passionate opposition to the rise of McCarthyism, recent scholars have demonstrated convincingly the role which the Truman administration's own sweeping investigations of the loyalty of government workers had in preparing the ground for professional Red-baiters such as Joe McCarthy. Truman's presidency, which had begun bright with hope for a peaceful postwar era, ended in cheap scandal, political mudslinging, a grinding and costly Cold War, and with an American army stalemated after a three years of inconclusive fighting in Korea. Yet even his severest critics are frank to acknowledge Truman's honest, candid, and feisty presidential leadership. Richard Neustadt evaluates the President's relationship with Congress in the article that follows, accentuating some of the advantages and drawbacks that affected Truman as FDR's successor.

On September 6, 1945, three weeks after V–J Day, Harry S Truman sent to Congress a twenty-one point program of domestic legislation—his first comprehensive venture in home affairs since Franklin Roosevelt's death five months before. This marked the beginning of a long series of presidential proposals for congressional action in the fields of economic development and social welfare; proposals which streamed out of the White House for nearly seven years, from the first session of the 79th Congress through the second session of the 82nd; a legislative program which became each year more comprehensive, more organized, more definite, receiving after 1948, the distinction of a label: The Fair Deal.

Looking back upon this enterprise, this Fair Deal program and its fortunes in those years, no less an observer than Elmer Davis has ventured the following verdict:

All in all, in domestic affairs, Mr. Truman was an unsuccessful President. [He] presented . . . a liberal program which was coherent and logical as the New Deal had never been. Congress, not being liberal, refused to take it; yet every year he persisted in offering it all to them again and they still wouldn't take it. . . . Truman kept asking for all of it and getting none of it.

This retrospective vision of the President who never changed his pace and of the Congress never altering in opposition is no doubt widely shared these days. No doubt, there is an element of reality behind it. Certainly, President Truman held out for more than he could reasonably hope to gain; certainly his four Congresses persisted in frustrating many of his aims.

Yet in its bold relief and simple black and white, this vision of the Truman record misses much light and shadow in a very complex situation. And by virtue of its very sharpness and simplicity, it becomes a stumbling block to understanding and appraisal. Students of postwar politics and of the presidency, and Congress,

From *Public Policy*, V (1954), 351–81. Reprinted by permission; footnotes omitted.

have need to start their march through Truman's years with a more elaborate guide to the terrain than this quick characterization can supply.

It is much too soon, of course, for the definitive appraisal of the Fair Deal legislative program, its fundamental emphasis and purposes, its ultimate success or failure. But it is not too soon to go behind neat generalizations and draw a balance on the record as it stood when Truman left the White House. What was attempted, what accomplished, what lost? And more important still, what seem now, at this reading, to have been the underlying motivations, the determinative circumstances? These are the questions to which this essay is addressed.

A *General Note on Congress:* 1945 *to* 1952

Before turning to the Fair Deal, as such, something need be said by way of background about the work load and the composition of the four Congresses which Truman faced as President.

These were the Congresses of post-war reconstruction and cold war and Korea. For seven successive years their sessions tackled and put through an extraordinary series of Administration measures in the fields of international cooperation, collective security and national defense; a series which for scope and scale and continuity has no precedent in our history.

On no previous occasion has American foreign policy required —much less received—comparable congressional participation for such a span of time. Rarely before, save at the onset of our greatest wars, has the Congress broken so much new and unfamiliar ground; rarely, if ever, has momentum been so long sustained.

One thinks of Franklin Roosevelt's first four years, and the legislative break-through into broad new areas of Federal action here at home. We look back on that as a revolution—a stunning departure from the traditional limitations of pre-depression years. So, too, were these postwar programs revolutionary—shattering all manner of shibboleths and precedents, in the international sphere untouchable right up to World War II. And what stands out historically is a record of immense accomplishment, in legislative terms, both for the Administration that framed the measures and for the Congresses that put them through.

The record becomes still more impressive when one recalls that President Truman never did command a "safe" working majority of the rank and file in either House of Congress. His "honeymoon" did not outlast the war. There was no bloc of "Truman men," sufficient for his purposes, on which he could rely to follow through, without cavail, whatever leads he gave. Rather, the thing was done through that extraordinary phenomenon, postwar "bipartisanship," a carefully conceived and executed coalition launched by Roosevelt, husbanded by Truman, actively furthered by effective leadership in the congressional power centers of both parties.

This enterprise was in its way as distinctive an achievement, for both President and Congress, as the roster of enactments which it helped to frame and legislate. Of course, the idyl of bipartisanship did not last forever. But even in 1952, the "internationalist" alignment, though reduced in strength by mass Republican defections—and some Democratic backsliding as well—remained a strong bi-factional, if not bipartisan reality, producing —in support of foreign policy—majorities, however bare, which could not have been mustered for a moment behind most Fair Deal domestic programs.

This raises a crucial point: the internationalist coalition, which supported Truman's foreign policy, existed, cheek by jowl, with a "conservative" coalition, which opposed Administration policies at home. What's more, the two most vital elements in the conservative alignment, were also chief participants in the internationalist bloc—the "moderates" of both parties; the Vandenberg Midwest Republicans and the Russell Southern Democrats.

These were the swing groups, joining the "Fair Dealers" to beat off the "extremists" of both parties in their raids on foreign programs; joining the extremists in opposition to most of the

Fair Dealers' pet proposals at home. Internationalism combined with conservatism was the formula which kept two coalitions going, side by side, through issue after issue, Congress after Congress.

A great deal happened after 1949, to sap the strength of the internationalist coalition. On the personality side, of course, came Vandenberg's illness and death, Connally's advancing age, Acheson's unpopularity. Deeper down were the accumulating frustrations of twenty Democratic years, capped with "Communism, Corruption, Korea"—and China; mercilessly exploited by congressional Republicans made desperate after 1948 and cured, thereby, of any faith in "high level" politics, or the "me-too" approach. In addition, after 1950, after Korea, came a development which threatened the whole basis of compatibility between internationalism and conservatism: the full cost of our commitments in the world—in dollars and in human terms as well—took on a new and frightening dimension. Conservatism and internationalism began to come unstuck, to war with one another. And if the Democratic "moderates"—taken as a whole—did not react as sharply or as soon as the Republicans who buried Vandenberg, this may be taken, partly, as a tribute to party loyalties and hopes for 1952.

Taking Truman's four Congresses together, in all these terms of workload and alignment, three further observations are in order. First, had no more been attempted or accomplished, by way of major, controversial, forward measures, than the great landmarks in the international and mobilization fields alone, we would still have to grant, in retrospect, that these were busy and productive years of legislation for the Congress—outstanding years, by prewar standards.

Moreover, whatever else might have been tried, on the domestic front, there was no time, from 1945 to 1952, when Truman's Administration—given its foreign policy and the international situation from year to year—could afford to trade a major objective in the foreign field for some advantage in the domestic. Consistently, it was, and had to be, the other way around.

Finally, considering the integral relationships between the

"internationalist" coalition which supported Truman and the conservative coalition which opposed him, every major venture in home affairs was bound to complicate the progress, endanger the timetable of those all-important measures in his foreign policy. From his first days in office, when he reaffirmed Roosevelt's arrangements for Republican participation in the San Francisco Conference, Truman acknowledged his dependence, in the foreign field, on elements of the anti-New Deal coalition—an enterprise which, always potent after 1937, had spent the wartime "truce" maturing its relations, building its lines and thwarting FDR on secondary issues.

Why, then, did Truman press a host of "hot" Fair Deal domestic issues, sure to arouse the wrath of this entrenched conservative alignment? To this question there is no single, easy answer, but rather a whole series, arising out of motivations and responses which varied with circumstance, over the years. To get at these we need now turn to straight, historical review, beginning with the first Truman "inventory" of legislative needs in home affairs —the twenty-one point program of 1945.

To Reaffirm the Roosevelt Purpose: 1945–46

The original "twenty-one point" program went to Congress by special message on September 6, 1945. Then, within a ten-week span, the President sent Congress six more special messages, each adding a major new proposal to the September list. In January 1946, Truman again presented a "twenty-one point" program, in a radio appeal to the country, reiterated three weeks later in his annual message to the Congress. This second listing was somewhat different from the first. Most of September's minor points had been removed from the enumeration to make room, among the twenty-one, for measures recommended in October and November. And in the annual message there was discussion of additional proposals—over and above the list of twenty-one—which had not previously been mentioned at all.

In summarizing the domestic program which Truman set forth

after V–J Day, it makes no sense at all to attach significance to order or to timing of particular proposals in this confusing sequence. Obviously some things were ready, came to mind, or got approval earlier than others. Obviously, also, these were the days of scatter-shot approach, when everything was put on record fast, in a sort of laundry-listing of postwar requirements with little indication of priority or emphasis.

What counts, here, is that between September 1945 and January 1946, Truman staked out for himself and his Administration a sweeping legislative program in the fields of social welfare and economic development, embracing, in essential outline if not in all details, the whole range of measures we now identify with the Fair Deal.

Nearly everything was there, though later formulations were to alter some specifics. Among September's numbered "points" were full employment legislation, expanded unemployment compensation, the permanent FEPC, an increased minimum wage, comprehensive housing legislation, a National Science Foundation, grants for hospital construction, permanent farm price supports, and—less specifically—protection and assistance for small business and expanded public works for resource conservation and development.

To these, the "points" of January's message added a comprehensive health program—including health insurance—nationalization of atomic energy and development of the St. Lawrence project. In addition, the message stressed, though it did not number, a "thorough-going reconsideration of our social security laws"; financial aid "to assist the states in assuring more nearly equal opportunities for . . . education"; an emergency veterans housing program "now under preparation"; and various kind words for statehood or self-government in the territories and insular possessions and the District of Columbia. Finally, of course, there were appropriate exhortations about extending price and rent controls.

This was the program Truman threw at Congress, the moment the war was won. Roosevelt had supplanted "Dr. New Deal" with

"Dr. Win-the-War." Why then did Truman hurry so to call the old physician in again?

Look back two years, to January 1944, and part of the answer becomes plain. Remember Roosevelt's "Economic Bill of Rights," with which he opened that election year, the year of hoped-for victory in Europe and feared postwar depression here at home:

The right to a useful and remunerative job. . . .

The right to earn enough. . . .

The right of every farmer to . . . a decent living.

The right of every businessman . . . to trade in . . . freedom from unfair competition. . . .

The right of every family to a decent home.

The right to adequate medical care. . . .

The right to adequate protection from . . . fears of old age, sickness, accident and unemployment.

The right to a good education.

All these rights spell security. And after the war is won, we must be prepared to move forward in the implementation of these rights. . . .

Truman was thus reasserting Roosevelt's stated purpose; not in so many words, not necessarily in Roosevelt's way, or with his means, or his specifics—or his men—but consciously and definitely this was for Truman an affirmation of fidelity to the cause and the direction of liberal Democracy; rekindling the social outlook of the New Deal, if not, precisely, of the New Dealers.

The legislative program of 1945 was a reminder to the Democratic party, to the Congress, to the country, that there was continuity between the new national leadership and the old—and not merely in war policy, but in peace policy as well; not only overseas, but here at home.

Beyond this, the new President had a very personal stake in his September message: reaffirmation of his own philosophy, his own commitments, his own social outlook; denial of the complacent understandings, the comfortable assertions that now, with "That Man" gone, the White House would be "reasonable," "sound" and "safe." Harry Truman wanted, as he used to say, to separate the "men" from the "boys" among his summertime supporters. V–J Day brought him his first real chance to think or act in terms of home affairs, and he lost no time in straightening out the record on who he was and what he stood for.

Some of the New Dealers may not have been convinced; conservatives, however, were quick to understand that here, at least on paper, was a mortal challenge. Editors glowered; so did Congressmen. And one of the President's "soundest" advisors, who ornamented the Administration in that capacity from first to last, fought to the point of threatened resignation against sending that "socialistic" message to the Congress.

Here, then, is explanation for the character and over-all direction of Truman's program. But what of its specific scope and range? Granting all this, why was so much territory covered all at once; why so many points; why, in fields like health and housing, go "all out" in a single bite?

Most commentators have seen these things simply as errors in tactics and judgment, charging them off to personal idiosyncrasy, or inexperience. Other Presidents, it is said, would never have concocted so diverse a program, or asked, indiscriminately, for everything at once. But something more was operating here than just the human factor, however significant that may have been. We have no means of knowing what Roosevelt would have done, after the war. But we do know that he had made the "Economic Bill of Rights" an issue in the 1944 campaign—with Truman as his running mate. And in one of his last major campaign addresses, Roosevelt came out strongly, if in general terms, for most of the controversial measures Truman, a year later, urged on Congress.

We also know that in the postwar period, a Democratic President was bound to face a fundamentally different situation, a different set of popular alignments and demands than Roosevelt dealt with in the thirties. Then, the New Deal pioneered, releasing a flood of ideas and impulses for reform that had been dammed up since Wilson's time. And every effort in those years, each new program, every experiment, set into motion, a widening circle of needs and expectations for governmental action—and of organized interest groups to defend the gains and voice the new requirements.

The first Roosevelt Administration broke into virgin territory; the Truman Administration had to deal with the demand for its consolidation and development. Clearly, Roosevelt was aware of this in 1944. Clearly, Truman's sweeping program in 1945 was conceived as a response. And not alone in 1945; from first to last, the Fair Deal legislative program sought to express the vastly heightened expectations of those groups of Americans on which the liberal cause depended for support.

For all these reasons, then, the 79th Congress found itself encumbered with a great, diverse collection of proposals from the President. And what did Congress do? Not very much. This was the Congress elected with the Roosevelt–Truman ticket in 1944. But even before Roosevelt's death, it had shown little disposition to follow the White House lead in home affairs. At the very start of the first session, the conservative coalition got the bit between its teeth and almost overturned Henry Wallace's appointment as Secretary of Commerce. From then on, the coalition remained a power to be reckoned with, its temper not improved by Truman's exhortations, its influence culminating, finally, in emasculation of the price control extender, during the summer of 1946.

From the confusions, irritations and forebodings of defeat, which marked the whole course of its second session, the 79th Congress did produce a number of the major measures Truman had proposed—most notably the Employment Act, the Atomic Energy Act, the Hospital Construction Act and the Veterans Emergency Housing Act. The Congress was not ungenerous in authorizing and appropriating funds for reclamation, flood control, power and soil conservation; these also raised some landmarks on the Fair Deal road. But for the rest, at least in terms of final action, Congress stood still, or even "backslid" here and there—as with the Russell Amendment eliminating the wartime FEPC.

Perhaps, if experience over the months had not dispelled the spectre of postwar unemployment, much more might have been done with Truman's program of September, 1945. But as it was, this turned out to be the least of worries for most Congressmen and their constituents back home. Not job shortages, but strikes, not pay envelopes but price regulations bothered both. The country, like the Congress, far from rallying to presidential visions of a better future, reacted negatively against the irritations of the present, and punished Truman's party with its worst congressional defeat in eighteen years.

To Pillory the Opposition: 1947–48

To gauge the impact of the 1946 election on the attitude and outlook of the Truman Administration, one merely has to contrast the President's address to the incoming 80th Congress, with his wide-ranging message and radio appeal of the preceding year.

The change in tone was very marked. In the annual messages of 1947 domestic affairs were relatively played down; domestic recommendations limited to a few specifics and some gently-phrased, general remarks. In his State of the Union Message, Truman gave more emphasis to budget balancing (e.g., no tax relief) than to any "welfare" measure, save the comprehensive housing program—which had Senator Taft among its sponsors. He also did "urge" action on the balance of his 1945 health program, but not under the heading of "major policies requiring the attention of the Congress." And while brief mention was made of social security, minimum wages and resource development, it is clear from the context that these, too, were relegated to some secondary category.

This was the comparatively mild and qualified domestic program which the President presented to a supremely confident opposition Congress, where he was generally regarded—on both sides of the aisle—as an historical curiosity, a holdover, a mere chair warmer by accident of constitution, for two more years. The view was widely shared. Inside the Administration, many, perhaps most, of Truman's advisers were persuaded, if not that all was over, at least that the postwar reaffirmation of the liberal cause had been a crashing failure at the polls—out of fashion with the public, out of date for officeholders.

The counsels of caution and conservatism within the President's own entourage, muffled somewhat since the fall of 1945, were now heard everywhere, voiced by almost everybody. Whatever Truman's own views may have been, the course of his Administration through much of 1947 seemed to display real hesitancy, real indecisiveness about further assertion of the cause he had so vigorously espoused a year before.

It is true that as the spring wore on, the White House sent up certain special messages along reminiscent lines. In May, another health message repeated the proposals of 1945—but the tone was mild and the issue, then, by no means so inflammable as it was to become in later years. In June, the President vigorously protested inadequacies in the rent control extender and called again for a comprehensive housing program—but this included specific indorsement for Senator Taft's own bill.

Lump these reminders in with the rest, and Truman's domestic program in the spring of 1947 still remains a very conciliatory version of what had gone before. Under the initial impact of defeat, the Administration, clearly, had fallen way back to regroup. And with the Truman Doctrine to be implemented that same spring, by that same opposition Congress, it is no wonder there was hesitation and divided counsel about where to take a stand and when, if ever, to resume the forward march.

Yet, scarcely a year later, Harry Truman was back at the old stand, once again, raising old banners, rubbing salt in old wounds, firing broadsides at Congress more aggressively than ever. What happened here? Wherefore the change from the conciliatory tone of 1947 to the uncompromising challenge of 1948? Obviously, somewhere along the line, the President became convinced that his initial impulse had been correct, that he was right in 1945— that the New Deal tradition, brought up to date, remained good

policy—and good politics—despite the set back of 1946. In this
decision, Truman's temperament, his social outlook, all sorts of
subjective factors, no doubt played a part. But also, in the course
of 1947 there appeared some perfectly objective indications that
a renewed offensive would be not merely "natural" but rational.

Twice, in the early summer of 1947, Truman vetoed tax reductions voted by the Congress. Both times he charged that the reductions were inequitable and ill-timed; that they relieved only
upper income groups, and would add new burdens of inflation
for the rest to bear. Both times there was some stirring of approval
and response around the country—both times his veto was sustained.

In point of fact, these vetoes were no new departure. They had
been foreshadowed from the first by warnings in the annual messages. But the actuality of veto, and the words in which expressed,
did convey a fresh impression: the vision of a sturdy President—
courageous even in the face of lower taxes—defending the "national" interest and the "poor," against a heartless (Republican)
Congress mindful only of the "rich." This was a new note—and
it did not go badly.

Four days after his first tax veto, Truman vetoed the Taft-
Hartley Act. To the general public, the measure was chiefly notable, then and since, because it did something about work stop-
pages in "national emergency" disputes—an issue the President
himself had recognized in prior messages to Congress. But to the
spokesmen for organized labor the act was shot full of unwarrant-
able interferences with basic union rights which had been guaranteed, by law, for half a generation.

And when Truman struck out against these interferences—in
the strongest language he had yet addressed to the 80th Congress
—he evoked a warm response from a part of the public whose
apathy, in 1946, had prominently helped defeat his party and his
postwar cause. The quick congressional override of Truman's
veto merely heightened this response from those who felt themselves despoiled—and further dramatized, for them, the vision of

the presidential "tribune" standing up against the onslaughts of a rapacious (Republican) Congress.

Here, in the summer of 1947, were some straws in the wind. Their meaning was confirmed for the Administration, even enlarged upon, at the special session in the fall.

When Truman called the Congress back to Washington, the principal emergency was international—with the economies of Western Europe verging on collapse. But in his address to the special session, Truman asked not only for interim aid abroad—pending completion of the European Recovery Program—but also for a ten-point program against inflation, billed as an equal emergency at home. And the tenth point of this domestic plan was nothing less than selective restoration of price and wage controls.

This was the first occasion when Truman made an all-out public effort to revive and dramatize an issue which had failed him in 1946, capitalizing on a measure which—as everybody knew—was still anathema to the majority in Congress. This was the first occasion, too, since the election of 1946, when the President presumed to give so controversial a domestic issue equal billing with an essential aspect of his foreign policy.

The program for the 1947 special session was, no doubt, a trial run, in a sense. Had the result been very bad, the President might perhaps have stayed his hand in 1948. In the event, however, the majority in Congress found it expedient to enact something called an "anti-inflation" bill, a most limited measure but indicating that times—and prices—had changed since 1946. Moreover, despite the patent irritations which the price issue aroused, interim aid for Europe went through Congress without a hitch, and just before adjournment, the European Recovery Program was sent up and well received.

By January, 1948, the President had obviously read the signs and portents of the half-year before, and put out of mind the memory of defeat in 1946, with all the cautious counsels it provoked. Truman's address to the new session was confident and sharp, evoking all the liberal issues half suppressed a year before. His presentation was much more coherent than it had been in 1945 or 1946, the language tighter, the focus sharper, the follow-up firmer. But nothing was omitted from the original postwar program and in a number of respects Truman went beyond any earlier commitments.

This was the message which set forth goals for the decade ahead. This was the message which proposed a new, "anti-inflationary" tax program: credits for low income groups to offset the cost of living, with revenues to be recouped by increased levies on corporate profits.

The "tribune" of six months before, who had risen to protect the people against the acts of Congress, now sought their protection in demands on Congress for actions it could not, or would not, take. If the record of Congress could be turned against the opposition, then the President would make that record, not on performance, but on non-performance, not on the opposition's issues but on his issues—those liberal measures which, perhaps, had not gone out of fashion after all.

And as Truman began, so he continued through the spring, with "a message a week," to keep Congress off balance and the spotlight on. In this series there was but one great new formulation—the civil rights message of February, 1948. The legislative program it set forth incorporated most of the proposals of the President's Committee on Civil Rights, which had reported in December 1947. The resulting explosion is still echoing in Congress and the Democratic Party.

Of all Truman's proposals through eight years in office, these were, perhaps, the most controversial. That they loosed a lasting political storm, everyone knows; that they had special political significance in early 1948—appearing just as Henry Wallace made his break to the Progressive Party—is certainly no secret. But there was much more than politics in this. The Civil Rights Committee had originally been established out of genuine concern lest there be repeated in the postwar years, the rioting and retrogression which followed World War I. Congressional indifference had been made manifest in 1946—hence the turn to prominent outsiders. Once having set these people to their task, on problems so potentially explosive, it is hardly credible that Truman could have ignored their report, no matter what the politics of his own situation.

Nothing else, half so dramatic, was unveiled by the President in 1948. But all the older measures were furbished up and trotted out anew. And as the months wore on, Truman's tone to Congress grew steadily more vigorous. He began by lambasting in January, and ended by lampooning in July.

His last address to the 80th Congress was the nearest thing to an outright campaign speech that he—or probably any other President—ever made before the assembled Houses. Opening the post-convention special session, he first demanded action to stop inflation and start more houses—the ostensible purposes for which Congress had been recalled. He then proceeded to list nine other measures which he thought the Congress might be able to enact without delaying the two primary items. Finally he listed every other major proposal advanced since 1945, commenting: ". . . If this Congress finds time to act on any of them now, the country will greatly benefit. Certainly, the next Congress should take them up immediately."

Of course, that hapless session accomplished precisely nothing, in any of these categories. And Truman proceeded to pillory the 80th Congress at every whistle stop across the country, working his way to victory in the presidential election of 1948.

Toward a Liberal Majority: 1949–50

The legislative program Harry Truman presented in 1949, to the new Congress which had shared his victory, reflected all the Fair Deal commitments of the 1948 campaign. "Certainly, the next Congress should take them up immediately," he had proclaimed to the Republicans in July. And he could do no less in January than spread them out—all of them—before his brand-new Democratic majorities.

All interest groups and sponsoring politicians understood the "law of honeymoon"; none was prepared to stand aside, leaving a pet proposal for some later, less naturally advantageous date. All civil rights groups, and most politicians North and South, knew very well that only the extra leverage of an early log jam would suffice, in time, to shut off debate. All trade union spokesmen were agreed that there could be no compromise on Taft-Hartley "repeal" and no delay on any part if it. And so it went, group after group, issue after issue.

Both President and Congress were thus prisoners, in a sense, of the election and the way it had been won. It was one thing to throw a host of highly controversial measures at an opposition Congress which could—and did—reject most of them out of hand. It was quite another thing to throw the same load on a relatively receptive Congress, prepared to make a try at action on them all. Action is much harder than inaction; action on this scale, of this variety, an almost intolerable burden on the complex machinery of the legislative process—and on a President's capacity to focus attention, to rally support.

Despite this handicap, the 81st Congress, be it said, turned out more New Deal–Fair Deal measures than any of its predecessors after 1938, or its successors either; becoming, on its record, the most liberal Congress in the last fifteen years.

This was the Congress that enacted the comprehensive housing program, providing generously for slum clearance, urban redevelopment and public housing; the Congress that put through the major revision of social security, doubling insurance and assistance benefits and greatly—though not universally—extending coverage. This was the Congress that reformed the Displaced Persons Act, increased the minimum wage, doubled the hospital construction program, authorized the National Science Foundation and the rural telephone program, suspended the "sliding scale" on price supports, extended the soil conservation program, provided new grants for planning state and local public works and plugged the long-standing merger loophole in the Clayton Act. And it was principally this Congress that financed Truman's last expansions of flood control, rural electrification, reclamation, public power and transmission lines.

But this record of domestic accomplishment was obscured for commentators, public, and Administration by a series of failures on the most dramatic and most dramatized of 1948's great expectations. In the first session of the 81st Congress—the last full session before Korea—aid to education, health insurance, FEPC and Taft-Hartley repeal were taken up, debated, fought over and either stalled or killed outright somewhere along the line.

General aid to education—that is, maintenance and operation funds for state school systems—had won Senate approval in 1948, in a form that represented careful compromise among religious interests and between the richer and the poorer states. Reintroduced in 1949, the same measure speedily received Senate approval once again. But as the year wore on, these compromises started to unravel; various groups and individuals took second looks, had second thoughts. The whole basis of agreement fell apart before the Senate bill had cleared the House Committee. There the bill remained, unreported at the session's end, eight months after Senate passage. There the second session found it—and left it.

The story on health is similar in some respects. The interest groups supporting Truman's health program and its congressional sponsors did not seriously hope for early victory on compulsory health insurance. But they—and the Administration—saw this issue as a stick with which to beat the Congress into passing other major aspects of the program—increased hospital construction and research, aid to medical education and grants to local public health units; all obvious and necessary preliminaries to effective operation of any general insurance scheme. In the Senate, all four of these secondary measures were approved by early fall of 1949. Hospital construction and research grants—both expansions of existing programs—also fared well in the House. But the medical education and local health bills never got to the House floor. They were smothered to death in committee by a resurgent opposition—medical and other—which seized the stick of health insurance and used it to inflict increasing punishment, not only on these bills, their sponsors and supporters, but on the whole Administration and the Democratic party.

In the case of civil rights, Truman's program was not merely stalled but buried during 1949. At the session's start, the interest groups—supported by the leadership in Congress and Administration—would stand for nothing but a test on the most controversial measure of them all: compulsory FEPC. The measure's proponents were perfectly aware they could not gain compulsion from the House, nor cloture from the Senate, without a major showing of Republican support. This was not forthcoming; the test proved that at any rate. It also helped Democrats, Southern as well as Northern, discharge some pressing obligations toward constituents. But the long filibuster of 1949 was all the Senate could endure. None of its leaders was prepared to face another bloodletting in 1950.

The Congressional failure on Taft-Hartley repeal was just as conclusive as that on civil rights and much more surprising to Administration, press and public. In 1949, the struggle in both Houses was intense, but save for the injunction in emergency disputes—the one feature opponents of repeal could press home to the general public—the advocates of a new law probably would have had their way. The interest groups could not, or would not give on this; the Administration could not, or would not impel them—so everything was lost; lost in 1949 and left, then, to await a new test in a new Congress. A decisive beating in the first session might be compromised in the second, but hardly reversed. And trade union leadership was in no mood for compromise.

Nor was the President. His response to each of these defeats in 1949—and other, lesser scars sustained that year—was a renewed recommendation in 1950. His January messages to the second session of the 81st Congress included virtually all proposals still outstanding, that he had listed to the first session in his moment of honeymoon a year before.

Clearly, there was little hope, in 1950, for much of what he asked. Yet the 81st Congress, as Truman was to say that spring, had "already reversed" its predecessor's backward "trend." And if the "trend" now ran the Fair Deal's way, perhaps what this Congress withheld, would be forthcoming from the next—the 82nd Congress to be elected in November.

Not since 1934, had the Democratic party increased its majorities in a mid-term election; breaking into new terrain in North and West. Yet that, and nothing less, was surely Truman's goal for 1950. "I hope," remarked the President, "that by next January, some of the obstructionists will be removed." And not content with pressing, once again, all the remaining issues of 1948, he urged on Congress three further measures each of which, if it appealed at all, would tap new sources of support, beyond the groups and areas where Democratic power was presumably entrenched.

One of these measures involved a new departure for the President on farm legislation. His 1950 State of the Union Message was the occasion for Truman's first formal use of the magic words connoting the "Brannan Plan." There he first attached the adjective "mandatory" to price supports, first urged "a system of production payments," first declared, "as a matter of national policy," that "safeguards must be maintained against slumps in farm prices," in order to support "farm income at fair levels."

To the uninitiated these words may look very little different from their counterparts in prior presidential messages. But in the language of farm bureaucrats and organizations, these were magic words indeed, fighting words, emphasizing finally and officially, a sharp turn in Truman's agriculture policy—a turn which had begun in 1948, progressively distinguishing Democratic from Republican farm programs, and bringing the Administration now to ground where the Republicans in Congress—not to speak of many Democrats—could not or would not follow.

By the time Truman spoke in January 1950, the more far-reaching measures his words implied had already been rebuffed at the preceding session of the Congress—and the "Brannan Plan" had already become a scare word, rivalling "socialized medicine" in the campaign arsenal the Republicans were readying. Yet by his endorsement Truman seemed to say that scare word or no, here was an issue to cement for Democrats the farm support which he had gained so providentially in 1948.

The second new measure to be proposed in the State of the Union message for 1950, concerned the housing shortage "for middle-income groups, especially in large metropolitan areas." The Housing Act of 1949 had granted more aids for private home financing which swelled the flood of relatively high priced houses. The Act also had promised more public housing, with subsidized rentals for people in the lowest income brackets. Between these two types of housing was a gap, affecting mainly urban and sub-urban "middle" groups of white collar and blue collar families; swing groups politically, as time would show. For them, in 1950, the President proposed "new legislation authorizing a vigorous program to help cooperatives and other non-profit groups build housing which these families could afford."

The third of 1950's new proposals was billed as a mere promissory note in the State of the Union message. "I hope," said Truman, "to transmit to the Congress a series of proposals to . . . assist small business and to encourage the growth of new enterprises." As such, this was no more concrete than the benign expressions in many earlier messages and party platforms. But in the spring of 1950, the President kept his promise and put meat on these old bones with a comprehensive small business program far more elaborate than anything advanced since the emergency legislation of the early thirties. The immediate reaction, in Congress and out, was very favorable. A leading spokesman for "big" business called the Truman message "tempered, reasoned, nonpolitical." Small business groups expressed great interest; even some bankers had kind words to say.

The President's small business program went to Congress as he entrained for the Far West, on his "non-political" tour of May, 1950. The Fair Deal's prospects were then enticing numbers of Administration stalwarts to leave their safe House seats and campaign for the Senate. Many signs encouraged them. The country was prosperous, recession ending; the presidential program popular, to all appearances, attracting interest in useful quarters and stirring overt opposition only where most expected and least feared. Foreign policy was costly but not noticeably burdensome, defense pared down, the budget coming into balance.

Yet on the other side were signs of change, foretastes of things to come, making 1950 a very special year, a year of sharp transition, in retrospect a great divide. The preceding winter saw the last of Chinese Nationalist resistance on the Asian mainland. In January Alger Hiss was convicted in his second trial—and Secretary Acheson quoted from the Scriptures. In February, Senator McCarthy first shared with the public his discovery of Communism's menace here at home. In May, Senator Kefauver's committee began televised crime hearings, exposing criminal connections of political machines in some of the nation's largest cities —where, as it happened, the Democratic party had been long in control.

And on the twenty-fifth of June, the North Korean Communists invaded the Republic of Korea.

Korea: The Great Divide

In legislative terms, the initial impact of Korea on the Fair Deal is symbolized by the collapse of Truman's small business program. Senate hearings had just got under way when the fighting began. They terminated quickly in the first days of July. The Senate committee which had started down this track enthusiastically, turned off to tackle the Defense Production Act—controls for the new, part-way war economy.

All along the line, Fair Deal proposals were permanently shelved or set aside, as Congress worked on measures for defense. And on one of these measures, price controls, which had long been identified with the Fair Deal, not the President but Congress forced the issue—never again was Truman able to resurrect it as his own.

This calls for a short digression. In July, 1950, the President did not raise the price control issue, because he feared it might delay congressional response on other needed measures of control; fearing, moreover, lest opinion overseas might take his call for direct controls as indicating all-out preparation for the general war Korean intervention was intended to avert, not foster.

But Congress proceeded, on its initiative, to include discretionary price and wage controls among the economic powers in the Defense Production Act. The measure became law September 8, 1950. For a variety of reasons, no general application of direct controls was attempted until nearly five months later. Meanwhile the Chinese attack of November 27 set off new buying waves, with consequent sharp price increases. And by the time a general freeze was instituted, January 26, 1951, this sequence of events had thoroughly shaken confidence in the Administration's leadership on the inflation issue.

The fact that Truman subsequently fought for strengthened control legislation, while his congressional opponents shot holes in it at every opportunity, seems not to have restored the President's position in the public mind, nor recreated for the Democrats that popular response the issue had accorded them in 1948. The Republicans, if anyone, drew strength from popular discomfort with high prices, in subsequent elections.

Apart from price controls, the conflict in Korea drew congressional—and national—attention away from the traditional Fair Deal issues. As election time approached, in 1950, there was no back drop of recent, relevant congressional debate to liven up these issues, stressing their affirmative appeal. Instead, the opposition had a field day with the negative refrain of "socialism"— or worse—invoking spectres of the "Brannan Plan," "socialized medicine," and Alger Hiss, to unnerve a public preoccupied with sacrifices in a far-off peninsula, nervous over rumors about "Chinese volunteers."

In the first week of November, the electorate—far from increasing Democratic power—reduced to a bare minimum the Democratic party's lead in both Houses of Congress, abruptly closing the careers of some very senior Senators and some very staunch Administration Congressmen. And in the last week of November the full-scale Chinese intervention in Korea turned virtual victory into disastrous retreat, confronting the Administration and the country with a "new" war, a most uncertain future, and endless possibilities of worse to come.

Mobilization and Reluctant Retreat: 1951–52

On December 15, 1950, the President proclaimed a National Emergency. Three weeks later, in January, 1951, the 82nd Congress assembled to hear, in virtual silence, what Truman had to say.

His State of the Union Message was somewhat reminiscent, in its tight organization and sharp phrasing, of the fighting address of 1948. But in tone and content it was, by far, the most conciliatory annual message since 1947.

The entire address was devoted to events abroad and mobilization at home. Its ten-point legislative program was couched in emergency terms. Among the ten points only one Fair Deal item remained in its entirety—aid for medical education, now billed as a means of "increasing the supply of doctors . . . critically needed for defense. . . ." Two other pillars of the Fair Deal program were included in qualified form. General aid to education was requested, "to meet . . . most urgent needs . . . ," with the proviso that "some of our plans will have to be deferred. . . ." And while there was no specific mention of Taft-Hartley, or its repeal, the President did ask "improvement of our labor laws to help provide stable . . . relations and . . . steady production in this emergency."

Aside from a bland and wholly unspecific reference to "improvements in our agriculture laws," an opening for subsequent proposals never made, these were the only references to Fair Deal measures in the presidential list of "subjects on which legislation will be needed. . . ." They were almost the only references in the entire message; but not quite. After his ten-point numeration, Truman remarked "the government must give priority to activities that are urgent," and offered "power development" as an example. Then he added, "Many of the things we would normally do . . . must be curtailed or postponed . . ."; the door was finally closing, but—the Congress should give continuing attention ". . . to measures . . . for the long pull." There followed four brief and unelaborated but unmistakable references to increased unemployment and old age insurance, disability and health insurance and civil rights.

As in 1947, so in 1951, the President was shifting emphasis, relegating most welfare measures to some secondary order of priority, without quite ceasing to be their advocate. It was too subtle a performance for the press; the distinctions much too fine for headlines or wide public notice—though not, perhaps, for Congressmen to grasp. Yet in its way, this message represented Truman's recognition of the fundamental change in his circumstances and the Nation's; his nearest approach to Roosevelt's sharp, dramatic switch, a decade earlier, from "Dr. New Deal" to "Dr. Win-the-War."

And unlike 1947, this mild beginning, in January 1951, heralded a more conciliatory tone, an increased interest in negotiation, on some of the Fair Deal's most striking programs. As the year wore on, Truman gradually changed tactics on at least three fronts, seeking different ground from that staked out in pre-Korean years.

The first of these shifts came in the field of health. There the Administration was hopelessly on the defensive by 1951. The vocal presence of an aroused and potent medical opposition, victorious in trials of strength at 1950's elections, sufficed to make most Congressmen suspect and fear a taint of "socialized medicine" in any

Truman health measure, however limited its purpose or narrow its scope. The President had barely raised the health insurance issue in January, 1951, but its mere invocation was now enough to halt all legislation in the field. So far had the opposition come, from its days on the defensive, back in 1949.

Finally, Truman voiced his recognition of the situation: "I am not clinging to any particular plan," he told an audience in June. This was followed, six months later, by appointment of the President's Commission on the Health Needs of the Nation, charged with surveying, from the ground up, all problems and proposals in the field. In January 1952, addressing the second session of the 82nd Congress, the President remarked of health insurance, "So far I know it is still the best way. If there are . . . better answers I hope this Commission will find them."

A second change in tactics during 1951 came on the issue of Taft-Hartley. Senator Taft's triumphant re-election, the preceding autumn, had symbolized how futile were the hopes of 1949 for a renewal, in a "better" Congress, of that year's stalled attack. In Truman's January messages of 1951 there was no mention of "repeal." The following October, his first address at a trade-union affair, that year, was notable for subdued treatment of the issue. "We want a law . . . that will be fair . . . ," he said, "and . . . we will have that kind of law, in the long run . . ." and that was all. Two months later, the President enlarged upon this theme, telling the Congress, "we need . . . to improve our labor law . . . even the sponsors . . . admit it needs to be changed. . . ." The issue of "repeal" was dormant, so Truman seemed to say. Amendment, even perhaps piecemeal amendment—anathema in 1949—now measured the ambitions of his Administration.

The President's third shift in emphasis came on his agriculture program. Since the Korean outbreak, farm prices had soared, along with the demand for food and fibre. There was little in the current situation to promote wide interest in Brannan's innovations, or counteract the socialistic spectres that his "plan" invoked. In January 1951, the President had no specific comment on the ideas he had endorsed a year before. By January 1952, Truman was prepared with some specifics, but on much narrower ground. That year, his State of the Union message asked—and Congress shortly granted— renewed suspension of the "sliding scale" on price supports, which otherwise would have become effective at the end of 1952. For the rest, he simply remarked that there was "need to find . . . a less costly method for supporting perishable commodities than the law now provides"—a plug for "production payments," surely, but in a fashion that softpedalled the far-reaching overtones of 1950.

The year of 1951 turned out to be a hard and unrewarding time for the Administration; a year marked by MacArthur's firing, by strenuous debates on foreign policy and on controls, by blighted hopes for quick truce in Korea, by snowballing complaints of government corruption—and by prolonged Congressional indifference to the welfare measures on the trimmed-down Truman list.

The State of the Union message in January, 1952, was less incisive than its predecessor—so was the emergency—but hardly less moderate in its approach on home affairs. Besides the new departures on health insurance, labor laws and farm legislation, the President appealed again for aid to education and the supplementary health bills of a year before. Again he mentioned power needs. Again he raised, briefly and generally, the issues of civil rights. Otherwise, in only two respects did he go beyond specifics urged in 1951—asking cost-of-living increases for social security recipients and readjustment benefits for Korean veterans.

These two requests were granted rather promptly, giving Truman his last minor successes. But in the spring of 1952, the second session of the 82nd Congress was interested less in legislating than investigating; less concerned with pending measures than with Administration struggles over corruption—and the steel dispute; preoccupied above all else with the coming presidential nominations and the campaign to follow in the fall. The session's main contribution to the Fair Deal program was not positive, but negative, rousing one last Truman proposal in opposition to the McCarran Act; creating one more Fair Deal issue; liberalization of the immigration laws.

In this fashion, Truman's last Congress slowed to a close. And in Chicago, that July, appeared a final summary of Fair Deal business left undone—the Democratic platform of 1952.

What Truman had played down, in his last annual messages, the platform now set forth in some detail. It called for action on the civil rights program, avoiding retrogression by a hair; pledged still more improvement in the social insurance laws; promised more resource conservation and development, including public power; urged Federal help for schools, this time stressing construction along with "general" aid; called for a firm stand on public housing and revived the "middle income" issue of two years before; spoke feelingly of protection and assistance for small business, hinting at specifics unmentioned since Korea; adopted Truman's formula on health, with kind words for the President's Commission; followed him also on farm price supports, on immigration and on a host of lesser issues, long the stock-in-trade of Democratic documents.

At one point only did the platform diverge sharply from the President's more recent formulations. On Taft-Hartley it abandoned his new stand, reverting to the cliche of "repeal." The Democratic candidate was put to some trouble by this change, but it cannot be said to have much mattered to the voters.

It had been seven years since Harry Truman, reaffirming Roosevelt's purpose, first charted the Fair Deal in his twenty-one point program of 1945. Now it received its last expression in his party's platform for 1952. This remains the final statement. In January 1953, Truman and his party yielded office to the first Republican Administration in twenty years.

A *Fair Deal Balance Sheet*

Set the platform of 1952 alongside the program of 1945, allow for changing circumstances and particulars, then run a quick calculation on the Fair Deal legislative program. What did Truman gain in seven years from his four Congresses? What came of all the trials and tribulations recorded in this essay?

In the first place, it is clear that Truman managed to obtain from Congress means for modernizing, bringing up to date, a number of outstanding New Deal landmarks in social welfare and economic development among them: social security, minimum wages, public health and housing; farm price supports, rural electrification, soil conservation, reclamation, flood control and public power. Not all of these were strictly New Deal innovations, but all gained either life or impetus from Roosevelt in the thirties. And in the new circumstances of the postwar forties they were renewed, elaborated, enlarged upon, by legislative action urged in Truman's Fair Deal program; even their underlying rationale nailed down in law by the Employment Act of 1946.

This is significant, and not alone by virtue of particulars attained. A generation earlier, the very spirit of Wilsonian New Freedom had been buried deep in the debris of reaction following world war. Not so with the New Deal.

As a consolidator, as a builder on foundations, Truman left an impressive legislative record; the greater part achieved, of course, in less than two years' time, and by a single Congress. Moreover as protector, as defender, wielder of the veto against encroachments on the liberal preserve, Truman left a record of considerable success—an aspect of the Fair Deal not to be discounted. He could not always hold his ground, sustained some major losses, but in the process managed to inflict much punishment on his opponents.

The greater Truman vetoes pretty well define what might be called the legislative program of the conservative coalition in his time. On many of these measures he made his veto stick, as with the offshore oil bills in 1946 and 1952, or natural gas and basing points in 1950. On certain others—like the Gearhardt Resolution in 1948—what one Congress enacted over his veto, the next retracted at his demand. And on a few—especially the two already noted—Congress overrode him, and the ground once lost was not made up in Truman's time: the Taft-Hartley Act in 1947 and the McCarran Act in 1952.

Besides these, Truman asked of Congress four main things which were denied him: aid to education, health insurance, civil rights and—for want of better shorthand—"Brannan Plan." On the outstanding features of these four, he got no satisfaction: no general grants for all school systems; no national prepayment plan for medical care; no FEPC, or anti-poll tax or anti-lynching laws; no wholesale renovation of price supports to insure good returns from general farm production. Here, if anywhere, does Elmer Davis' refrain approach reality: "Truman kept asking for all of it and getting none of it."

Why did he keep asking? From 1945 to 1950, one may concede that year by year there always seemed to be good reason to press on: reason to hope and plan for action, if not in one session then the next, reason to believe the very chance for future action might depend on present advocacy. But after 1950, after Korea, faced with a dozen hard new issues, on the defensive all the way from "Communism to corruption," what then explains the Truman course? He must have known, his actions show awareness, that there had come a real sea change in his affairs and in the country's. Why move so slowly towards a bare minimum of reappraisal, readjustment?

Perhaps the answers lie, in part, in Truman's temperament; partly in his concept of the presidency. Unquestionably he thought these measures right for the country; hence proper for the President to advocate, regardless of their chances in the Congress. He had assumed responsibility as keeper of the country's conscience on these issues; as its awakener, as well, by virtue of stands taken far ahead of the procession. For civil rights, especially, Truman could claim—like Roosevelt after the court fight of 1937—that while he may have lost a legislative battle, the forcing of the issue helped to win a larger war. "There has been a great awakening of the American conscience on the issue of civil rights," he was to say in his farewell report to Congress, "all across the nation . . . the barriers are coming down." This was happening; by his demands for legislation he conceived that he helped make it happen. On that promise, he was bound not to abandon his position, no matter what the legislative outcome, present or prospective.

Even in strictly legislative terms there was, perhaps, much to be

gained by standing firm. Were not some of the fights that failed
a vital stimulus to others that succeeded? Were not some votes
against a measure such as health insurance, repaid by other votes
in favor of reciprocal trade renewal, say? Was not a total presidential program basically advantaged if it overshot the limits of assured congressional response? There are no ready measurements
providing certain answers to these questions. But Presidents must
seek them all the same. And on his record there is little doubt
what answers Truman found.

For Truman then, each of his great outstanding issues had value
as a legislative stalking horse, if nothing more. But that is not to
say he saw no more in them. On the contrary, had he not thought
many things attainable, still actionable in the not too distant future—still meaningful, therefore, in rallying political support—he
scarcely would have bothered, during 1951, to cleanse his farm
and health programs—much less Taft-Hartley—of the worst
taints absorbed in the campaign of 1950, thus rendering them
useable for 1952.

Those changes in approach were hardly aimed at Congress—
not, anyway, the current Congress. Rather, the President was preparing new positions for his party, shifting to ground on which it
could afford to stand with him and to uphold, if in adjusted guise,
the Fair Deal label and the Truman cause.

Right to the last, then, Truman was persuaded that those Fair
Deal issues touched felt needs, roused real response among Americans; no longer viable objectives for his time in office, but crucial
undertakings in his party's future.

Alienated Grownups

McCarthyism as Mass Politics

by Michael Paul Rogin

Concern over subversion has been a major thread in the life of the American republic since its earliest days. In the late nineteenth century, the fear of the anarchism allegedly transplanted to the United States by the new South and East European immigrants became a bogeyman for several decades, to be replaced after the Russian Revolution by anxieties over the spread of communism ("Bolshevism") on American soil. A brief but savagely repressive "Red Scare" in 1919–20 followed World War I, but after 1945 came a much longer and much more systematic hunt for subversives within the American Cold War society.

Red-hunting received sanction at the highest level of government when in 1947 Truman inaugurated a loyalty-security program to examine the patriotism of federal employees. By 1952, almost five million civil servants had been subjected to security checks, and despite the vague yet rigid standards of "loyalty" adopted by government inquisitors, only 1/100th of 1 per cent of all federal employees failed to meet the standards and lost their jobs. This ominous and omnipresent gumshoeing undermined the morale of the federal civil service severely. Similar loyalty checks became standard procedure in many states, universities, school systems, and industries.

Congressional investigating committees, particularly the House Un-American Activities Committee, played an escalating role in stimulating public fears of communist subversion. Spearheaded by a young California congressman, Richard M. Nixon, HUAC helped focus attention on a high former New Deal official, Alger Hiss, a man subsequently convicted for perjury for denying an extended association during the late 1930's with a confessed communist agent named Whittaker Chambers.

Hiss's conviction and the arrest of Julius and Ethel Rosenberg for giving atomic bomb secrets to Russia both occurred in 1950. In February of that year, the junior Wisconsin senator, Joseph R. McCarthy, claimed to have the names of 205 known communists still active in the State Department. McCarthy later pared the figure to 57, but never proved the existence of a single Foggy Bottom Red. In that tense domestic and international climate, however, his charges rang true for many fearful Americans. By the closing years of the Truman administration, Communist armies had won the Chinese civil war, the Soviet Union had exploded its first atomic bomb, and South Korea had been invaded from the Communist North, causing the dispatch of American troops into an undeclared Asian "police action." With public confidence in Truman ebbing, and with Republicans eagerly awaiting the 1952 election, McCarthy's wild charges of top-level subversion in the Roosevelt and Truman administrations received considerable support within the GOP.

McCarthy's meteoric career as a demagogue spanned five years. Then his senatorial colleagues brought him to heel. His censure by the United States Senate in 1954 climaxed a rowdy period dating from Dwight Eisenhower's inauguration during which McCarthy sniped constantly at the executive and snarled at bureaucrats. Although content to allow McCarthy free rein during the 1950–52 period, when he concentrated on attacking Democrats, most Republicans bridled at the Wisconsin maverick's attempts to impugn the patriotism of army generals, Republican cabinet members, and Eisenhower's appointees. The man, clearly, had gone too far.

Seeking an explanation for the rise of "McCarthyism," a num-

ber of historians and political scientists of the 1950's began to view it as a mass movement with significant roots in centers previously noted for agrarian discontent. Although acknowledging McCarthy's evident appeal to the urban Catholic working class, some historians suggested also that McCarthyism represented a mass movement whipped up and given its special urgency by status anxieties and a search for identity among his followers. These might include native-born, old stock Americans anxious over lost power and status, or newer immigrant groups rising too quickly for ideological comfort. Status tensions within both groups were absorbed, according to this argument, by the irrational but convenient "scapegoating" of all sorts of Reds, Ivy Leaguers, Eastern "establishment" figures, radical intellectuals and liberal "dupes."

Several political scientists have challenged this interpretation of McCarthyism as a "mass movement" with roots in the illiberal aspects of the American liberal reform tradition. Most critics of the "status anxiety" thesis assume that McCarthyism can best be understood as a political rather than a sociological phenomenon, that the major core of McCarthy's support came not from Midwestern reform areas, whether once Populist or once Progressive, but from that region's traditional centers of Republican, anti-reform conservatism. Thus McCarthy himself emerges as a stalking horse for old-line Republicanism bent on regaining national power in 1952 after twenty lean years, a view supported by Michael Paul Rogin in an analysis of the sources of McCarthyite strength in three Midwestern states.

From 1950 through 1954, Joseph McCarthy disrupted the normal routine of American politics. But McCarthyism can best be understood as a product of that normal routine. McCarthy capitalized on popular concern over foreign policy, communism, and the Korean War, but the animus of McCarthyism had little to do

From Michael Paul Rogin, *The Intellectuals and McCarthy*, by permission of the M.I.T. Press, Cambridge, Massachusetts, pp. 216–43. Copyright © 1969 by the M.I.T. Press; footnotes omitted.

with any less political or more developed *popular* anxieties. Instead it reflected the specific traumas of conservative Republican activists —internal Communist subversion, the New Deal, centralized government, left-wing intellectuals, and the corrupting influences of a cosmopolitan society. The resentments of these Republicans and the Senator's own talents were the driving forces behind the McCarthy movement.

Equally important, McCarthy gained the protection of politicians and other authorities uninvolved in or opposed to the politics motivating his ardent supporters. Leaders of the GOP saw in McCarthy a way back to national power after twenty years in the political wilderness. Aside from desiring political power, moderate Republicans feared that an attack on McCarthy would split their party. Eisenhower sought for long months to compromise with the Senator, as one would with any other politician. Senators, jealous of their prerogative, were loath to interfere with a fellow senator. Newspapers, looking for good copy, publicized McCarthy's activities. When the political institutions that had fostered McCarthy turned against him, and when, with the end of the Korean War his political issue became less salient, McCarthy was reduced to insignificance.

Politics alone does not explain McCarthyism; but the relevant sociopsychology is that which underpins normal American politics, not that of radicals and outsiders. Psychological insights are not relevant alone to the peculiar politics of the American Right. Equally important, the ease with which McCarthy harnessed himself to the everyday workings of mainstream politics illuminates the weaknesses of America's respectable politicians.

Attention to sociology and psychology must be concentrated within the political stratum, not among the populace as a whole. It is tempting to explain the hysteria with which McCarthy infected the country by the hysterical preoccupation of masses of people. But the masses did not levy an attack on their political leaders; the attack was made by a section of the political elite against another and was nurtured by the very elites under attack.

The populace contributed to McCarthy's power primarily because it was worried about communism, Korea, and the cold war.

The analysis of McCarthyism presented here focuses on political issues, political activists, and the political structure. As an alternative to this interpretation of McCarthyism, the pluralists have suggested an analysis that goes further beneath the surface of American politics. To be sure, unlike La Follette and Hitler, McCarthy mobilized no cohesive, organized popular following. Nevertheless, for the pluralists the concept of mass politics captures both the flavor of McCarthy's appeals and the essence of his threat to American institutions.

In the first place, they argue, McCarthyism drew sustenance from the American "populist" tradition. "Populists," suspicious of leadership, seek to register the unadulterated popular will at every level of government. Giving McCarthyism as his example, Lipset writes,

American and Australian egalitarianism is perhaps most clearly reflected in the relative strength of "populist" movements through which popular passions wreak their aggression against the structure of the polity. . . . Conversely, in Canada as in Britain such problems have been handled in a much more discrete fashion, reflecting in some part the ability of a more unified and powerful political elite to control the system. . . .
The values of elitism and ascription may protect an operating democracy from the excesses of populism . . . whereas emphasis on self-orientation and anti-elitism may be conducive to right-wing populism.

In this view, McCarthy had to go outside the "political stratum" to obtain support; his power came from his ability to exploit mass resentments.

The alleged mass character of McCarthyism flows, in the second place, from the character of the popular resentments he exploited. He is said to have mobilized feelings of uneasiness over a sophisticated, cosmopolitan, urban, industrial society. He focused these vague discontents, the argument continues, on such specific symbols as intellectuals, striped-pants diplomats, homosexuals, and effete eastern aristocrats. McCarthyite status politics was thus radical in its rejection of industrial society as well as in its suspicion of responsible political leadership.

The third perceived mass characteristic of McCarthyism flows from the first two. McCarthyite appeals, it is argued, were not rooted in the traditional cleavages between the major political parties and groups in America. Like other mass phenomena, McCarthyism split apart existing political coalitions. Talcott Parsons sees it as

. . . not simply a cloak for the "vested interests" but rather a movement that profoundly splits apart the previously dominant groups. This is evident in the split, particularly conspicuous since about 1952, within the Republican Party. . . .

But at the same time the McCarthy following is by no means confined to the vested-interest groups. There has been an important popular following of very miscellaneous composition. . . . The elements of continuity between western agrarian populism and McCarthyism are by no means purely fortuitous. At the levels of both leadership and popular following, the division of American political opinion over this issue *cuts clean across the traditional lines of distinction between conservatives and progressives.* . . .

For the pluralists, then, McCarthy disrupted the traditional group basis of politics by exploiting popular resentments over changes in America society. In the view adopted here, McCarthy exploited popular concern over foreign policy, structured by existing political institutions and political cleavages. Four subjects provide evidence relevant to these alternative contentions. The first is the political and social background from which McCarthy rose to power. Did the Wisconsin Senator disrupt political alliances? Did he transform traditional conservative politics? If McCarthy was merely a traditional conservative, why did he achieve so much more notoriety than other conservatives?

Second, we will look at McCarthy's ideology. Was this ideology new for a conservative Republican? Did it exploit populistic resentments and moral indignation? Whom was it likely to attract?

Third, we will investigate the evidence bearing on McCarthy's popular support. What social groups supported the Wisconsin Senator? What psychological characteristics and political attitudes led to sympathy for him? What was the relationship between approving of McCarthy in a public opinion poll and voting for him in the election booth? Was McCarthy's popular support sufficient to explain his influence?

The final inquiry will be directed at the response to McCarthy by political institutions and elites. Did the "political stratum" defend the "rules of the game" against this outsider? Did the education and political sophistication of elites insulate them from suspectibility to McCarthy? Were there important differences among elites in this respect? Do the varying fortunes in the war between elite pluralism and mass populism successfully account for the rise and fall of Joe McCarthy?

The Context

The entry of the Senator from Wisconsin onto the political stage did not split apart a previously united Republican Party. The split in the GOP between the East and the western Middle West goes back decades before McCarthyism. In Populist and progressive days, the West North Central states were the center of liberal opposition to an eastern-dominated Republican Party. During the New Deal and World War II, the two wings of the Republican Party switched places. On "traditional economic issues" as well as on foreign policy, midwest Republicans had been more conservative than their eastern counterparts for a decade before McCarthyism. The midwest wing of the party had been more isolationist for perhaps half a century.

It was this wing that mobilized itself behind McCarthy. It supported him on the censure resolution in the Senate, and Republican businessmen in the Middle West were more sympathetic to McCarthyism than those in the East. McCarthy did not split apart an elite, the parts of which had been equally conservative before him. He rather capitalized on an existing liberal-conservative split within the existing Republican elite.

Former centers of agrarian radicalism, like the plains states, sent right-wing Republicans who supported McCarthy to the Senate. But McCarthy was not the agent who disrupted the traditional agrarian radical base. Before these states supported Mc-Carthy, they had already undergone an evolution from agrarian radicalism to extreme conservatism. (Of the states analyzed here, South Dakota was typical of the trans-Mississippi West and North Dakota the exception.)

The decline of agrarian radicalism increased conservative power in the trans-Mississippi West, but there have been important continuities in the conservative outlook. An ambiguity about the state of the country continues to plague these conservatives; in some ways they are satisfied and in others they are not. The right wing of the Republican Party reveals an uneasiness about cosmopolitan values and styles of life, about large cities and big bureaucracies. In this sense it seeks to change American institutions, not to conserve them. At the same time, it profoundly wishes to preserve the status quo in its own areas—not simply in terms of rural virtues but in terms of the local prestige and economic power of the elites that have since the decline of agrarian radicalism controlled the Republican Parties of the rural and small-town Middle West. This ambiguity—complacency at home and fear of the outside world—is nothing new for midwest conservatism. Half a century ago, it motivated midwestern conservative opposition to agrarian radical movements, which were perceived as alien imports from the bureaucratized and hostile outside world. McCarthy sprang from this conservative background.

For Leslie Fiedler, McCarthy's support among local newspapers indicated his populist roots. Anyone could get the support of a millionaire or two, Fiedler explained, but the

resolutely anti-intellectual small-town weeklies and . . . the professionally reactionary press . . . continue to say in [McCarthy's] name

precisely what they have been saying now for thirty-five years. To
realize this is to understand that McCarthyism, generally speaking, is
the extension of the ambiguous American impulse toward "direct
democracy," with its distrust of authority, institutions, and expert
knowledge; and that more precisely it is the form which populist
theory takes when forced to define itself against such a competing
"European" radicalism as Communism.

The "resolutely anti-intellectual" small-town newspapers, however, led the opposition to every agrarian radical movement from
Populism to La Follette to the contemporary Farmers Union.
The Populists and the Non-Partisan League, for example, had to
start their own newspapers because the existing local press would
not give them a fair hearing in their news columns, much less
support them on the editorial page. The small-town press may be
suspicious of certain authorities and institutions, but it is supported by others—particularly local business interests. The role of
this press provides evidence for McCarthy's conservative inheritance, not his "populist" roots.

There are important continuities between nineteenth century
conservatism and the contemporary variety, but several new developments have had their impact. There has, first, been a change
in the character of eastern conservatism. As the industrial giants
of the East become more established and bureaucratized, they
become less militantly conservative. Taft blamed Eisenhower's victory over him in 1952 on eastern financial interests. This Populist-
sounding charge hardly reflects Taft's Populist roots; the Taft family has always opposed agrarian radicalism. It reflects rather a
change in the politics of "Wall Street."

The New Deal created a balance of forces more opposed to midwest conservatism than this country had seen since the Civil War.
Social legislation and trade unions became prominent, and the
power of the national government increased. It is quite true, as
Parsons argues, that McCarthy directed little fire against trade
unions and the New Deal. Indeed, much of McCarthy's genius
lay in his ability to concentrate on the single issue of communism
—so pressing and popular an issue in the early 1950's—and not

raise other, more divisive appeals. But the activists around the Senator supported him so enthusiastically just because they knew he was attacking their enemies. McCarthy's attacks on foreign polily were often framed as attacks on Roosevelt and the New Deal, and his attacks on Britain were generally tied to its Socialist leadership. A writer for *Fortune* who conducted a survey of business opinion about McCarthy wrote, "Among businessmen who approve of McCarthy's war on subversion there is a satisfaction, subconscious perhaps but very strong, over his incidental licks at all longhairs, eggheads, professors and bright young men of the 1930's and 1940's."

This support, so important to McCarthy, explains why he did not develop an overtly statist appeal. The activists around McCarthy were traditional conservatives, rejoicing in McCarthy's attack on the party of Roosevelt. Like the businessmen in the *Fortune* study, they would have deserted the Senator had he developed a demagogic "liberal" economic program.

Democratic control of national politics added to Republican discontent. By 1952, the GOP had been out of power for twenty consecutive years. And Republicans were not accustomed to opposition; between 1856 and 1932 they failed to control the presidency for a total of only twenty years.

The international situation brought the frustrations of midwest conservatism to a head and at the same time seemed to offer a political issue and a way out. The new long-term importance of foreign policy reinforced an already powerfully moralistic political approach. Much as some progressives at the turn of the century had reacted with defensive moralism to the waves of immigrants, so conservatives now reacted to the Communist threat. There had not yet been time to become accustomed to the new situation.

Traditionally, the Middle West has been isolationist for both ethnic and geographic reasons. Many of the region's political leaders thought Roosevelt had forced the country into a war against Germany; now Truman seemed afraid to fight a much worse enemy. Communism represented to them the epitome of an alien world—atheism, immorality, destruction of the family, and social-ism. But far from defeating this enemy or withdrawing from the outside world that it contaminated, the Democratic Party dealt in an ambiguous atmosphere of international involvement, limited war, and compromise with evil.

Communism in the abstract was threatening enough. The dan-ger became concretized and symbolized by two traumatic events. The first of these was the "loss of China." The right wing insisted with a stridency born of inner doubt that only a failure to apply traditional American values and tactics could have caused this defeat. The loss of China was a loss of American potency; it could only cease to be frightening if those responsible were identified.

Following hard upon the loss of China came the Korean War. Wars in America often produce superpatriotism, and this in turn claims victims. Those suspected of opposing wars have often been the victims of 100 per cent Americanism. But during the Korean War the superpatriots perceived the very prosecutors of the war as the ambivalent ones. This again was something new and rein-forced right-wing Republicans fears that the centers of power in the society were working against them. If Woodrow Wilson had not approved of all the excesses of the superpatriots during and following World War I, he at least approved of the war. In the Korean War, the powers that be seemed unenthusiastic; one had to seek support for superpatriotism elsewhere: This was fertile ground for McCarthy.

If China preoccupied conservative elites, the Korean War at-tracted the attention of the population as a whole. Here real fight-ing brought to a head amorphous cold war anxieties and intensified concern over communism. McCarthy's prominence coincides with the years of the Korean War. He made his famous Wheeling speech in February 1950, and as its impact appeared to be ending the Korean War began in June. Three years later a truce was signed, and a year after that the Senate censured McCarthy.

Less than 1 per cent of a national sample interviewed in the early 1950's voluntereed communism as something they worried about. Many more, however—34 per cent—checked it off a check-list of things they had recently talked about. In addition, almost all families knew someone fighting in Korea. The poll data did not suggest a mass political uprising over the question of communism, but no more did it suggest the issue's political irrelevance.

Of the authors of *The New American Right*, only Parsons placed foreign policy at the center of his analysis, and even he did not mention the Korean War. But Parsons, although he saw the importance of foreign policy, seriously underestimated the role of elites in shaping McCarthyism. Parsons knew that at the popular level "liberal" attitudes about domestic and foreign policy did not go together. He therefore concluded that since the focus of Mc-Carthyism was foreign policy, it cut across the Left–Right cleavage on domestic politics. This analysis failed to comprehend that Mc-Carthyism was the product less of attitude syndromes at the mass level than of the character of political leaders whom the people supported. Parsons failed to see that fear of communism was generally most salient among those who already voted conservative. He overlooked the fact that McCarthy and anticommunism were far more salient to the conservative elite—from precinct workers to national politicians—than to the mass of voters. If the attitude structure at the popular level was not coherent, those whom the people supported did have a coherent set of attitudes. McCarthyism fed into an existing conservative tradition at the elite level, very conservative on both domestic and foreign questions. (Similarly, Parsons found evidence for the "mass" character of Mc-Carthyism in its strength in former agrarian radical territory because he missed the intervention of conservative elites in the political evolution of those states.) This underestimation of the role of political elites in structuring McCarthyism recurs in pluralist analysis, and we will return to it.

Those who did not stress foreign policy in explaining McCarthyism had additional difficulties. They rightly saw that their analysis had to explain why some people supported McCarthy and others did not; presumably everyone was anti-Communist. Therefore they examined the American social structure to find groups particularly prone to status political appeals of the type McCarthy employed. In this view, McCarthy's concern with communism and foreign policy was only the immediate condition which enabled status seeking and populist groups to act out their frustrations. For example, Lipset wrote, "On the national scene, McCarthy's attacks are probably more important in terms of their appeal to status frustrations than to resentful isolationism."

Those who took this approach still had to explain why McCarthyism should be so powerful in the early 1950's and not at some other time. They had to explain why those with personal and status concerns were seeking a political outlet. Bell wrote, "A peculiar change, in fact, seems to be coming over American life. While we are becoming more relaxed in the area of traditional morals . . . we are becoming moralistic and extreme in politics." Bell explained the growing ideological character of American politics by such factors as the prominence of large, symbolic groups like labor, business, and government.

Whatever the plausibility of this interpretation, Bell himself implicitly rejected it a few years later. Entitling a collection of his essays "The End of Ideology," he argued that ideological politics was on the way out in America. He now viewed McCarthyism as an exception to this general trend. In thus contradicting his earlier effort to explain why McCarthyism flourished in the early 1950's, Bell had nothing else to offer. But the aim here is more basic than simply to catch Bell in a contradiction. Pluralist analyses failed to explain the appearance and meaning of McCarthyism because they overlooked the political context in which McCarthy appeared. They underestimated his roots in an already-existing conservative faction inside the GOP—a faction even more concerned about communism, the cold war, and Korea than was the country as a whole. McCarthy came out of an old American Right. What was in part new was the intensity and hysteria he provoked. This in turn is largely explained by changes in American society and politics that agitated the conservatives and by the new importance of foreign policy. Analysis of McCarthy's ideology and of his popular following reveals the role foreign policy and conservative Republicanism played in his power.

The Ideology

When they first became prominent in the middle 1950's, pluralist interpretations of McCarthyism relied very little on empirical evidence. They focused instead on McCarthy's ideological appeals, where the evidence for McCarthy's anticosmopolitan "populism" was strongest. But even McCarthy's ideology was rooted in traditional conservative rhetoric.

In their analyis of McCarthy's rhetoric, the pluralists have accepted the evaluation of McCarthyism presented by its proponents. Both the pluralists and the supporters of McCarthy agreed that McCarthyism was a democratic movement against the elite, that it was opposed to social pretension, that it represented a movement of morality in politics. If liberals have taken Populist rhetoric at face value and analyzed the movement in its own terms, the authors of *The New American Right* have done the same with McCarthyism. But I have argued that moralism was found as much on the Right as on the Left in pre-New Deal American politics and that appeals to the people have been a conservative weapon as well as a liberal one.

A further point is relevant here. In examining the ideology of a movement, one must look beyond the attitudes of the masses. The syndrome of attitudes said to characterize the radical Right does not exist together at the mass level. Trow found in Bennington that authoritarianism, isolationism, political intolerance, ethnocentrism, and a "get-tough" foreign policy were not found in the same people. In the poll data Polsby analyzed, various pro-McCarthy atitudes were not highly associated in the public mind. Similar evidence about liberal ideology also exists. This does not mean that liberalism and the radical Right ideology are unimportant. Rather it points to the importance of elites and activists in structuring disorganized attitudes into a relatively cohesive ideology. An ideology usually reveals more about the preoccupations of elites than of masses.

To his most devoted followers McCarthy was fighting more than the Communists; in this the pluralists are certainly right. Speaking in eulogy of the Senator from Wisconsin, Congressman Smith of Kansas said, "In a world which has lost its understanding of the concepts of right and wrong, truth and error, good and evil, and seeks only to adjust itself to what is expedient, a man like Senator McCarthy is a living contradiction of such Machiavellianism." This sentiment was reiterated in newspaper obituaries. A study of McCarthyism in a Wisconsin county found the same emotion among McCarthy supporters at the grass roots.

That McCarthy should be so widely viewed as a moral figure is no paradox to the pluralists. It is just in his cultivation of a political concern with good and evil that they find his relation to agrarian radicalism. But McCarthy attacked the traditional devils of the conservatives. Just as traditional conservatives had feared the intrusion of alien bureaucrats, alien social legislation, and alien agrarian radicals into their stable world, so McCarthy attacked communism. Godless radicals, intellectuals, and bureaucrats were targets of American conservatism many decades before McCarthyism. If he was more extreme than many conservatives, he was extreme within that tradition.

Moreover, one cannot counterpose McCarthy's moralism to a healthier American pragmatism. For one thing, by McCarthy's use of the document-filled briefcase and the elaborated and detailed untruth, he was able to play upon the devotion of Americans to concrete detail. He promised always to "name names"; he always knew of a specific number of Communists; he had lists, affidavits, reports, right in his hand. McCarthy's "fact-fetishism" played upon our attention to the "real world." Had McCarthy not capitalized on the American weakness in the face of the practical and concrete, he would have been far less effective.

Nor was McCarthy's appeal an alternative to the corrupt but

safer image of the ordinary politician. In many ways, such as his insistent friendliness with men he had just pilloried, McCarthy was a caricature of the ordinary politician. He was deliberately crude and liked to be thought of as a "gut fighter," a tough guy. There was something quite prurient in his atmosphere. As a punishing figure, he could immerse himself in the evil around him— loving both the immersion and the punishing in good sadistic fashion. Perhaps his supporters, turning their guilt at their own illicit desires into anger at the corruption of the outside world, could permit themselves to experience McCarthy's lasciviousness vicariously, since he was wreaking vengeance against their external enemies. In any case, dichotomies between a politics of purity and one tolerant of human corruption hardly do justice to the seaminess of McCarthy's appeal.

McCarthy's rhetoric was hardly principled; what principles there were had traditional conservative antecedents. Yet did not McCarthy attack traditional conservative institutions and defend the virtues of the plain people? How is this part of a traditional conservative approach?

In his Wheeling speech McCarthy attacked

the traitorous actions of those men who have been treated so well by this Nation . . . who have had all the benefits that the wealthiest nation on earth has to offer—the finest homes, the finest college educations, and the finest jobs in Government we can give. . . . The bright young men [in the State Department] who are born with silver spoons in their mouths are the ones who have been most traitorous. . . . [Acheson is a] pompous diplomat in striped pants with a phony British accent.

Demonstrating his disdain for established institutions, McCarthy appealed for classified information from State Department employees. When Senator McClellan charged, "Then you are advocating government by individual conscience as against government by law," McCarthy replied, "The issue is whether the people are entitled to the facts."

A gigantic rally called in honor of McCarthy sang "Nobody Loves Joe But the People," suggesting that if political leaders and institutions could not be relied on, the people could. Other alleged examples of McCarthy's "populism," such as his calling for telegrams against Eisenhower, are examples less of "populism" than of traditional American political practice. Nevertheless, the antielitist flavor of McCarthy's rhetoric is clear.

This fact alone, however, does not remove McCarthy from the conservative tradition. Since the decline of the Federalists, American conservatives have used "populist" rhetoric; in American politics this rhetoric is essential. "Populist" rhetoric does not necessarily reflect a reality of popular enthusiasm and power; often it disguises the power resting in the hands of local and national elites. "Populism" is often an ideological formula used to gain legitimacy, not a factual description of reality.

Moreover, nothing in McCarthy's rhetoric would have frightened several conservative elite groups away. In so far as McCarthy's appeal transcended anticommunism, its roots were in groups disturbed about cosmopolitanism and about the prestige given to the educated and the established families and businesses of the East. Success in their own bailiwick did not insulate the political and economic elites of the Midde West from these concerns any more than prosperity per se insulated the population at large. The nouveaux riches, however wealthy, could still be upset about those born with silver spoons in their mouths. The midwest political elite, however long established, was still upset about striped-pants diplomacy, intellectuals in the State Department, Harvard intellectuals, and British "pinkos." These were McCarthy's targets, and in the Middle West attacks on such targets did not frighten the elite. Furthermore, McCarthy and other midwestern conservatives never went beyond rhetorical attacks on eastern corporate patricians. They never proposed to injure the vital interests of eastern businessmen, who were, like their midwestern business counterparts, members of the moneyed classes.

Nevertheless, there was in McCarthy's rhetoric a heightened

sense of betrayal by the rich and well-born. In part this reflected the growing anxiety of midwestern conservatism in the face of the New Deal and the "liberalism" of Wall Street. Equally important, McCarthy himself was personally very different from other midwestern conservatives. Far from being a man of dangerous principles, McCarthy was a thoroughgoing nihilist. Other conservatives—Goldwater is the prime example—believe in something; he believed in nothing. Whatever the psychological roots of McCarthy's political approach, its sociological roots lay in his one-man struggle for power and prestige, handicapped by a background of relative poverty most unusual in a successful American politician.

McCarthy's personal and social makeup fitted him for the role of destroyer. Perhaps his destructiveness found a sympathy denied his more righteous conservative colleagues. Certainly his outrageous gall catapulted him to a position of power he could exploit.

But McCarthyism is alleged to be more than the exploits of a single man; it is said to reveal the stresses and strains of the American social structure. Analysis of the Senator and of the ideology he employed tells us little about his reception. Did McCarthy's rhetoric in fact embolden the masses to an attack on modern industrial society? Did his "populist" rhetoric in fact attract ex-radicals, or even ex-Democrats? Did the danger from McCarthyism in fact flow from popular passions?

The Popular Following

In January 1954, a majority of the American population approved of Senator McCarthy. For the next eleven months, one third of the total population consistently supported him; eliminate those with no opinion, and the figure rises to 40 per cent (See table 1). This man, terribly dangerous in the eyes of sophisticated observers of American politics, had obtained the backing of millions of American people.

McCarthy's popularity in the polls reenforced a growing belief among intellectuals that the mass of people could not be relied on to defend civil liberties and democratic rights. The Stouffer study of popular attitudes toward communism and civil liberties, published the year following the censure of McCarthy, seemed to demonstrate the willingness of the mass of people to deny civil liberties to socialists and atheists, much less Communists. Community leaders, on the other hand, were much more tolerant of divergent and unpopular points of view. Leaving issues of demo-

Table 1
McCarthy's Popularity in the Gallup Polls *

Date	Favorable	Unfavorable	No opinion
8/51	15%	22%	63%
4/53	19	22	59
6/53	35	30	35
8/53	34	42	24
1/54	50	29	21
3/54	46	36	18
4/54	38	46	16
5/54	35	49	16
6/54	34	45	21
8/54	36	51	13
11/54	35	46	19

* Data reported in Nelson W. Polsby, "Towards an Explanation of McCarthyism, "Political Studies, Vol. 8 (October 1962), p. 252, and Frank J. Kendrick, "McCarthy and the Senate," unpublished Ph.D. dissertation, Department of Political Science (University of Chicago, 1962), p. 331.

cratic rights up to the people was apparently a dangerous business; better if they could be decided among political leaders without resort to popular passions. McCarthy had apparently achieved his successes by taking questions of communism and civil liberties out of the hands of the political elite.

In a simplified form, this theory of McCarthy's power ran into trouble. There is evidence to suggest that mass attitudes are not so different in other countries, such as Britain, without producing anything like McCarthyism. Therefore Lipset has suggested that one must look beyond popular attitudes to the political structure that mobilizes and channels those attitudes. This is an important argument, which could have led the pluralists to question the association between popular attitudes and McCarthy's power. But the pluralists contented themselves with pointing to two elements in the American political structure that *fostered* the translation of popular attitudes into political programs. First, it is alleged that McCarthy supporters lacked group ties to the institutions of modern industrial society. Second, Americans are said to lack deference for political leaders; they are not willing to permit a sufficient amount of elite autonomy. With this "populist" outlook, they will be more willing to trust their own (anti-civil libertarian) views than the views of their elected representatives.

Pluralist explanations focused on the "mass" character of McCarthy's appeal, challenging political leaders and cutting across party lines. But perhaps the single most important characteristic of supporters of McCarthy in the national opinion polls was their party affiliation; Democrats opposed McCarthy, and Republicans supported him. In April 1954, Democrats outnumbered Republicans more than two to one among those having an unfavorable opinion of McCarthy; 16 per cent more Republicans than Democrats had a favorable opinion of the Senator. Totaling support for McCarthy in a series of Gallup Polls in the early 1950's reveals that 36 per cent of the Democrats favored McCarthy while 44 per cent opposed him. The comparable Republican figures were 61 per cent for and 25 per cent against. Democrats were 8 percentage points more against McCarthy than for him, Republicans 36 points more for him than against him. The total percentage point spread by party was 44 points. In these polls, as in the data reported by Polsby, no other single division of the population (by religion, class, education, and so forth) even approached the party split.

Similarly, in October 1954 respondents were asked whether they would be more or less likely to vote for a candidate endorsed by McCarthy. The strong Republicans split evenly, the strong Democrats were five to one against the senator, and the weak and independent Democrats divided four to one against McCarthy. By that date, only hard-core Republicans were actively sympathetic to the Wisconsin senator; even the weak and independent Republicans strongly opposed him.

As Lipset suggests, there is evidence that pro-McCarthy sentiment influenced party preference as well as vice versa. Nevertheless, the great disproportion in support for McCarthy along the lines of previous party commitment was not predicted by the pluralist approach. Pluralism stressed McCarthy's roots in the social structure but not his roots in the existing political structure.

Support for McCarthy was also reasonably close to attitudes on political and economic questions of the day. On a whole range of foreign policy issues, McCarthy adherents had right-wing preferences (see Table 2).

Perhaps more surprising, "McCarthy also drew disproportionately from economic conservatives. Measures of such attitudes as position on liberalism in general, laws to prevent strikes, a federal health program, and support of private development of national resources all indicate that the conservative position on these issues was associated with greater support for McCarthy."

On the other hand, Trow found in Bennington that those with a hostile attitude toward big business as well as big labor were most likely to support McCarthy. This suggested McCarthy's roots in a small business, nineteenth-century mentality. But in a national sample such a relationship did not hold. The antibusiness prolabor group was more anti-McCarthy than any other group, and the "nineteenth-century liberals" were no more pro-McCarthy than those who were antilabor and pro big business or those favoring both big business and big labor. This evidence further locates McCarthy's roots in existing political cleavages.

Clearly McCarthy drew support from the traditional constituency and traditional attitudes of the Republican right wing. However, he also received considerable backing in the polls from traditional Democratic ethnic and social groups. The relevant survey data comes from a variety of different sources, and although

Table 2

Opinions on Foreign Policy Issues and Attitude Toward McCarthy *

Issues		Attitudes Toward McCarthy		
		Pro	Con	N
Break off diplomatic relations with Russia	Yes	21%	32%	(3641)
	No	14	43	(2550)
Withdraw from the United Nations	Yes	28	26	(870)
	No	14	38	(6291)
Peaceful coexistence policy	Favor	32	55	(694)
	Oppose	46	46	(399)
United States should support the United Nations	Favor	33	55	(1042)
	Oppose	47	34	(231)
How to handle the Russians	Offensive war	37	28	(274)
	Keep strong	32	34	(1923)
	Peaceful settlement	26	42	(343)
Korean War policy for United States (asked 1952)	Do as we did	23	40	(577)
	Keep trying for peace	21	43	(665)
	Go further militarily	37	34	(1284)
	Be tough	45	32	(1585)
	Pull out of Korea	31	26	(378)
Give economic aid to underdeveloped countries	Yes	16	37	(5343)
	No	20	32	(1620)
Blocking the coast of Communist China	Favor	43	43	(495)
	Oppose	31	60	(550)
Withdraw foreign aid from nations which refuse to cooperate with the United States	Favor	37	46	(1059)
	Oppose	29	58	(258)

* Data reprinted, with permission, from S. M. Lipset, "Three Decades of the Radical Right: Coughlinites, McCarthyites, and Birchers," in Daniel Bell (ed.), The Radical Right (Garden City, N.Y.: Doubleday Anchor, 1964), p. 409.

the pattern of support for the Senator is consistent, the degree of cleavage varies. Without holding the influence of party constant, religion and occupation best distinguish opponents of McCarthy from supporters. (For the most striking occupational data, see Table 3.) Professional people were more anti-McCarthy than any other occupational group. On five of six reported polls they were the most anti-McCarthy group, and on four of these polls they were far more anti-McCarthy than any other group. Wealthy businessmen were also apparently anti-McCarthy, although there is less evidence about them. Unskilled workers and small business-men were the most consistently pro-McCarthy groups. However, union membership significantly increased the opposition to McCarthy among laborers. Apparently the liberal impact of the union leadership reached significant numbers of workers who would otherwise have been neutral or ignorant about McCarthy.

Farmers also tended to be pro-McCarthy, but their degree of support varied sharply from poll to poll. Perhaps this provides further evidence of farmer political volatility. In one combined group of polls, farmers were clearly the most pro-McCarthy group; in other polls they were no more for McCarthy than were unskilled workers and small businessmen.

The occupational impact on support for McCarthy is clear. In several polls, occupational differences at the extremes equaled or exceeded the party differences. The size of both party and occupa-tional differences is particularly striking since these usually worked against each other. Professionals tended to belong to the pro-Mc-Carthy party, workers to the anti-McCarthy party.

Like occupation, the impact of religion also cut across party loyalties, with the exception of the heavily anti-McCarthy, pro-Democratic Jews. Lipset does not report religious data except within the political parties. Other studies demonstrate that in spite of Catholic and Protestant party affiliations, Catholics were significantly more pro-McCarthy than Protestants (see Table 4). In these polls, the religious differences were greater than the occupational differences, but they were not greater than the occupational differences reported by Lipset, whose occupational measures were more discriminating.

Within the parties the influence of religion was even more apparent. The percentage point spread in attitudes toward

Table 3

Occupation and Attitude Toward McCarthy,* Per Cent Differences Between Approvers and Disapprovers [a]

I.N.R.A. 1954 [b]			*Roper 1952* [c]		
Professional	−35	(731)	Professional and	−17	(219)
Executive and	−24	(511)	Executive		
Manager			Small Business	0	(123)
White Collar	−19	(1144)	Clerical and	−11	(387)
Independent	−14	(583)	Sales		
Business			Factory Labor	−3	(317)
Supervisor and	−16	(405)	Nonfactory	−6	(235)
Foreman			Labor		
Skilled	−14	(2323)	Services	−4	(178)
Unskilled	−14	(1019)	Farm Owner	−6	(184)
Personal Service	−10	(677)	Manager		
Farmers	−21	(824)	*Gallup Dec. 1954* [d]		
Retired	−3	(709)	Professional	−44	(163)
Students	−34	(59)	Executive	−24	(154)
Michigan 1954 [d]			Clerical and	−23	(188)
Professional and	−40	(246)	Sales		
Business			Skilled	−10	(237)
Clerical and Sales	−44	(102)	Unskilled	8	(286)
Skilled	−30	(337)	Labor	7	(68)
Unskilled	−16	(144)	Service	−10	(103)
Farmers	−17	(104)	Farm Owner	−9	(165)

* Table reprinted, with permission, from S. M. Lipset, "Three Decades of the Radical Right: Coughlinites, McCarthyites, and Birchers," in Daniel Bell (ed.), The Radical Right (Garden City, N.Y.: Doubleday Anchor, 1964), p. 400.

[a] Cell entries represent percentage difference between approval and disapproval of McCarthy. The more negative the entry, the greater the predominance of anti-McCarthy sentiment.

[b] Occupation of respondent recorded, or of chief wage earner if respondent is a housewife.

[c] Occupation of respondent recorded; housewives omitted from table.

[d] Occupation of head of household recorded.

McCarthy between strong Democratic Protestants and Catholics was 33. The difference between strong Republican Catholics and Protestants was 21. On the other hand, for strong party identifiers party seems to have been even more important than religion. Strong Democratic Protestants differed in their attitudes from strong Republican Protestants even more than they did from strong Democratic Catholics. And Republican Catholics were closer to Republican Protestants than to Democratic Catholics. Since

Table 4
Religion and Attitude Toward McCarthy *

Religion	Gallup, August 1951–March 1954 attitude toward McCarthy			SRC, October 1954 attitude toward McCarthy-supported candidate			
	Pro	Con	No Opinion	Pro	Con	Neutral	Other
	%	%	%	%	%	%	%
Protestant	45	36	19	9	39	43	9
Catholic	56	29	15	21	24	48	7
Jew	12	83	3	6	53	29	12

* Data reported in Frank J. Kendrick, "McCarthy and the Senate," unpublished Ph.D. dissertation, Department of Political Science, University of Chicago, 1962), p. 330, and Angus Campbell and Homer C. Cooper, Group Differences in Attitudes and Votes (Survey Research Center, University of Michigan, 1956), p. 146.

workers tend to be Catholics, religion and class reinforced each other. Either factor might have declined in importance if the other had been held constant.

Ethnic data also cut across party lines to some extent. Irish and Italian Catholics, traditionally Democratic, were highly pro-McCarthy. However, the influence of party may explain the greater support McCarthy received from German than Polish Catholics, as the latter are strongly Democratic. Among Protestants, differences by ethnic background were small and inconsistent, although Germans were clearly more pro-McCarthy than British.

Finally, level of education was of great significance in explaining support for McCarthy. Without holding party constant, differences are apparent, but they are less significant than occupational influences. However, when party is held constant the effect of education upon support for McCarthy is truly pronounced. The percentage point spread between graduate-school Democrats and grade-school Republicans was 65, the largest spread in all the poll data. However, college-educated Republicans were no more anti-McCarthy than grammar-school Democrats.

The polls provide us with considerable evidence about support for McCarthy, and reveal a broadly consistent pattern. When the influence of party is eliminated and often even when it is not, the lower socioeconomic groups, the more poorly educated, and the Catholics tended to support McCarthy, the big business and professional classes, the better educated, and the Protestants to oppose him. These differences cannot be dismissed as small or insignificant.

There is also clear evidence linking support for McCarthy to the "authoritarian personality." The evidence does not suggest a very strong relationship, however, particularly compared to the impact of party, political issues, and demographic variables. In Bennington, holding education constant, the relationship held only among those who had graduated from high school and not among the grade-school or college educated. In a national sample, there was a slight relationship at all three levels, but it reached substantial proportions only among the college educated. As Lipset writes, "Among the less educated, a high authoritarian score reflects in some part attitudes common to the group, which are also subject to modification by more education. If someone is well educated and still gives authoritarian responses, then the chances are that he really has a basic tendency to react in an authoritarian fashion." Where authoritarianism is simply an artifact of low education, it may reflect broad cultural values that lack psychological or political relevance.

An Alabama study sheds additional light on the relationship between psychological authoritarianism and support for McCarthy. High scorers on authoritarianism not only supported McCarthy;

they also supported agrarian radical Jim Folsom for governor. But Folsom's support among authoritarians was in part an artifact of his strong support in the lower class. If Folsom's relation to authoritarianism had an economic explanation, McCarthy's had a political meaning. McCarthy supporters were less likely to express faith in the viability of the political system. This political factor was more important to McCarthy's support than psychological authoritarianism; when it was held constant, authoritarianism ceased to be significant.

Hofstadter attempts to relate psychological characteristics to pro-McCarthy attitudes by introducing the factor of social mobility. He writes,

Social studies have shown that there is a close relation between social mobility and ethnic prejudice. Persons moving downward, and even upward under many circumstances, in the social scale tend to show greater prejudice against ethnic minorities . . . I believe that the typical prejudiced person and the typical pseudo-conservative are usually the same persons, that the mechanisms at work in both complexes are quite the same, and that it is merely the expediencies and the strategy of the situation today that cause groups that once stressed racial discrimination to find other scapegoats.

Martin Trow, examining the limited evidence cited by Hofstadter, concludes that it does not support a connection between mobility, prejudice, and allegiance to pseudoconservative movements. In Bennington, with education held constant, Trow found no relationship between either political intolerance or ethnocentrism and support for McCarthy. At the national level, there was also no relationship between ethnocentrism and pro-McCarthy sentiments. Nor has it been possible to establish any relationship between social mobility and support for McCarthy. However, one community study has demonstrated that those with felt status incongruities (that is, those who felt they got less money than their education entitled them to) did support the Senator. This is perhaps the best evidence that McCarthy's appeals tapped generalized discontent.

The data, in sum, do not suggest intense, active, mass involvement in a McCarthyite movement. Efforts to relate status frustrations and psychological malformations to McCarthyism have not proved very successful. Party and political issue cleavages structured McCarthy's support far more than pluralist hypotheses predicted. But the ignorant, the deprived, and the lower classes did support McCarthy disproportionately. Were they expressing their animus against respectable groups and institutions?

To answer this question, we must ask two others: Why did McCarthyism attract a large popular following of this character, and what impact did support for the Senator have on political behavior?

Most people supported McCarthy because he was identified in the public mind with the fight against communism. In June 1952, a national sample was asked whether, taking all things into consideration, they thought committees of Congress investigating communism, like Senator McCarthy's, were doing more good than harm. In a period when less than 20 per cent of the population had a favorable personal opinion of the Senator, 60 per cent were for the committees and only 19 per cent against them. The more McCarthy's name was identified with anticommunism, the more support he got from the population. Perhaps because they themselves feared the Communist menace, the pluralists underplayed the anti-Communist component of McCarthy's appeal.

In the Stouffer study, respondents were asked to name someone whose opinions about how to handle communism they especially trusted. Most votes went to J. Edgar Hoover and Eisenhower—27 per cent and 24 per cent respectively. McCarthy was third with 8 per cent. Respondents were then asked whether they trusted this person because they knew his opinions pretty well or because of the kind of person he was. The results were

	Opinions	Person
Hoover	33%	55%
Eisenhower	19	65
McCarthy	58	31

McCarthy's appeal was the functionally specific appeal of a single-issue promoter, not the diffuse appeal which mobilizes the "mass man." McCarthy's stress on communism may have suggested "the weakness of a single issue" for building a right-wing mass movement, but by the same token it explained the strength of McCarthyism.

Popular concern over communism could have symbolized a basic uneasiness about the health of American institutions. So it did for McCarthy and his most vociferous supporters, who saw a government overrun with dupes and traitors. For them, the Communist issue was the issue of Communists in government; internal subversion was the danger. For the American people, however, communism was essentially a foreign policy issue. In the 1952 election, less than 3 per cent expressed concern over Communists in government—fewer than referred to the Point Four program. Foreign policy, on the other hand, was an extremely salient issue, and those concerned over foreign policy were more likely to vote Republican. The external Communist threat and the fear of war benefited the GOP at the polls in the 1950's: the internal Communist danger, salient to committed Republicans alone, did not. Moreover, mass concern about foreign policy did not appear over the loss of China, which the right-wing invested with such peculiar moral signficance. It was only when American soldiers went to Korea that foreign policy became salient at the mass level. And the desire there—as expressed in the election of Eisenhower—was for peace, not for war.

Why then, if McCarthy's appeal had specifically to do with foreign policy and the Korean War, did he receive greater support among the poorer and less-educated groups? Had the working class been actively concerned about McCarthy, we might expect this support to overcome the relative lack of political knowledge among those of low socioeconomic status. But asked to name the man who had done the best job of fighting communism, the less-educated and poorer strata volunteered McCarthy's name no more than did the better-educated and rich. Highly conscious pro-McCarthy sentiments were as prevalent among the upper as the lower classes. (Those of higher socioeconomic status, with more political information and sophistication, were more likely to name McCarthy as someone who had done a particularly bad job.) Disproportionate working-class support for McCarthy thus only manifested itself when his name was actually mentioned in the polls; it was not powerful enough to emerge when workers had to volunteer his name on their own.

The evidence does not suggest that the Communist issue preoccupied the lower classes, or that they were using that issue to vent general grievances about their position in society. More likely, they simply had less information about McCarthy's methods, a less sophisticated understanding of their nature and less concern in the abstract about possible victims of the Senator's techniques. Therefore, when the pollsters specifically mentioned McCarthy's name, it tapped among the middle-class revulsion over McCarthy's crudities and opposition to his infringements of individual rights. Among the working class, it tapped an anticommunism relatively less restrained by these concerns.

Still, lack of sophistication on matters of civil liberties can have as dangerous consequences as the political mobilization of status anxieties and anti-industrial hostilities. It can, that is, if it becomes politically mobilized. But sympathy for McCarthy among the less politically sophisticated was not translated into action. To many Americans, especially those in the lower classes who were not actively in touch with events in the political world, McCarthy was simply fighting communism. Support for McCarthy meant opposition to Communists. This was a long way from being willing to break traditional voting patterns, or vote against other interests, in order to support the Wisconsin Senator. In fact, the issue of McCarthyism was more salient to its opponents than to its sympathizers—precisely because McCarthy's opponents were more concerned with political events. In January 1954, when a majority of the total American population favored McCarthy, only 21 per cent said they would be more likely to vote for a candidate he sponsored, while 26 per cent said they would be less likely to. Three months later 46 per cent of the population had an unfavorable opinion of the Senator and 43 per cent claimed they would be less likely to vote for a candidate he supported. Thirty-eight per cent of the population favored McCarthy; only 17 per cent would let this influence their vote intention. The results in October were similar.

With this relation between opinion and behavior, apparent paradoxes such as occurred in the Maine senatorial primary are easily understandable. Half of a Maine newspaper sample favored McCarthy, but virtually no one supported the candidate he had put up to oppose Margaret Chase Smith. There was no relation in the election between the areas which had supported McCarthy in the poll and those which voted against Mrs. Smith. It was one thing to be against communism, quite another to accept McCarthy's insinuations that Margaret Chase Smith supported communism—or even to have heard of that charge.

Analysis of electoral data confirms both the minimal impact McCarthy had on actual political behavior and his greater salience to opponents than supporters. In Connecticut in 1952, McCarthy made a particular effort to unseat William Benton, but Benton's support was virtually identical to that given the rest of the Democratic ticket. The Eisenhower landslide defeated Benton; McCarthy did not. In Wisconsin and particularly in the Dakotas, McCarthy's impact on the regular party vote was also minimal. There is some evidence that he hurt Republican senators in states where he campaigned for them.

Of the groups that supported McCarthy in the public opinion polls, farmers in Wisconsin voted for him but workers voted against him. Impressionistic evidence from eastern working-class centers like Boston and Brooklyn does suggest strongly felt working-class support for the Senator. Like other impressionistic evidence of McCarthy's popularity, this strength was probably real but exaggerated. Perhaps it would have affected voting behavior more if union leaders and urban liberals had taken a more outspoken anti-McCarthy line (so that workers would have felt forced to choose between pro-McCarthy and pro-Democratic or pro-union sentiments). In any case, whatever intense feelings existed here were probably caused more by religion than by class; these were predominantly Catholic workers, living in cities where church newspapers and the hierarchy were outspokenly pro-McCarthy.

Catholics did vote for McCarthy in South Dakota, Wisconsin, and other states. This may have been little different from the favorite son effect which caused Catholics to vote for Kennedy in 1960. In particular, this would explain McCarthy's strong Irish Catholic following in the polls. Also important is the fact that Catholics generally voted more Republican from 1950 to 1956. In 1956 a majority of the Catholic population voted for Eisenhower. This may have been because of the preaching of the church against communism or simply because increased prosperity weakened traditional Catholic ties to the Democratic Party. In fact, all the "status politics" reasons advanced to explain Catholic support for McCarthy also explain Catholic support for Eisenhower. Eisenhower, no less than McCarthy, permitted Catholics to stop voting Democratic without becoming committed to the Republican Party. Upward social mobility could produce support for Eisenhower no less than for McCarthy. Support for Eisenhower no less than for McCarthy could express conformity to "Americanism." There is, however, one crucial difference between the two figures: Eisenhower was a political moderate.

One need not assume the worst about the motivations for conformity, or about its consequences, or about the aspects of the American tradition that inspire conformity. Compulsive Americanism may have produced Catholic support for Eisenhower. That hardly makes it look like a dangerous source of political extremism. In our society, those with severe personal problems are likely to turn their back on politics. Status anxieties may find an outlet in political moderation. One must not too readily identify personal anxieties or status politics with political extremism. No particular political consequences follow from nonpolitical attitudes such as status anxieties. The intervening political and organizational structures and attitudes are crucial.

The McCarthy years were also the Eisenhower years. Far from demonstrating their discontent with respectable political leadership, the mass of Americans responded to the political anxieties of the cold and Korean wars and whatever social and personal anxieties may also have been relevant by electing Eisenhower. Eisenhower's personal and political appeal depended on the belief that he could be trusted to take care of things without disrupting the society. Eisenhower politics was the politics of deference to responsible leadership, of apolitical moderation. Support for Eisenhower indicates more about the mood of the populace in the America of the 1950's than does support for McCarthy. And McCarthy became prominent in the vacuum of popular apathy and moderation, not on a wave of radical mass mobilization.

What are we to conclude, then, about McCarthy's "mass" appeal? McCarthy's popular following apparently came from two distinct sources. There was first the traditional right wing of the midwestern Republican Party. Here was a group to whom McCarthy was a hero. He seemed to embody all their hopes and frustrations. These were the militants in the McCarthy movement. They worked hardest for him and were preoccupied with his general targets. To them, communism was not the whole story; their enemies were also the symbols of welfare capitalism and cosmopolitanism. These militants were mobilized by McCarthy's "mass" appeal. Yet this appeal had its greatest impact upon activists and elites, not upon the rank-and-file voters. And while McCarthy mobilized the Republican right wing, he did not change its traditional alliances. This was not a "new" American Right, but rather an old one with new enthusiasm and new power.

McCarthy's second source of popular support were those citizens mobilized because of communism and the Korean war. Concern over these issues throughout the society increased Republican strength, although this increase in popular support accrued not so much to McCarthy as to Eisenhower. McCarthy's strength here was not so much due to "mass," "populist," or "status" concerns as it was to the issues of communism, Korea, and the cold war. At the electoral level, there was little evidence that those allegedly more vunerable to "mass" appeals were mobilized by McCarthy to change their traditional voting patterns.

McCarthy had real support at the grass roots, but his was hardly a "movement in which popular passions wreaked their aggression against the structure of the polity." In a period in which the populace gave overwhelming support to Eisenhower, it can hardly be accused of failing to show deference to responsible political leadership. In so arguing, I by no means wish to minimize the danger of McCarthyism. But the pluralists, writing in a context of fear of the masses, have misunderstood both the source and the nature of that danger. They see a rebellious populace threatening the fabric of society. In fact, McCarthy did immense damage to the lives and careers of countless individuals. He exercised an inordinate influence over policy-making. But popular enthusiasm for his assault on political institutions simply cannot explain the power he wielded. In so far as McCarthy challenged political decisions, political individuals, and the political fabric, he was sustained not by a revolt of the masses so much as by the actions and inactions of various elites.

The Politics of Stasis

A Word on Eisenhower

by Emmet John Hughes

*During the 1960's, for almost the same reasons that Harry Tru-
man's presidential leadership declined in reputation among some
historians, Dwight Eisenhower's has grown. Liberal historians,
writing during or immediately after Ike's presidency, had often
criticized Eisenhower for a failure to provide adequate leadership,
especially in domestic affairs, where they quipped "the bland were
leading the bland." Pressing national problems such as widespread
denials of civil rights and civil liberties, the "invisible" poverty of
one out of every five Americans, and the growing dangers of en-
vironmental pollution received almost no sustained attention from
the federal government. "Never has a popular leader who dominated so completely the national political scene," lamented historian Norman Graebner in a widely-shared 1960 appraisal, "affected so negligibly the essential historic processes of his time."*

*More recently, however, historians have begun detecting a sig-
nificant set of accomplishments beneath the bland surface of
Eisenhower's presidency. The single most influential element in
triggering recent reappraisals of American leadership has been
the Vietnamese nightmare. After continuous escalations toward
disaster in Vietnam by two activist Democratic presidents, John*

Kennedy and Lyndon Johnson, many war-weary scholars and students have begun looking back nostaligically at the comparative "normalcy" of Eisenhower's foreign policy. Such historians now claim to find, underlying the apocalyptic world-saving rhetoric of cold-warrior John Foster Dulles and other like-minded administration officials, a basic pattern of restraint in the actual use of American power by Eisenhower himself. American interventions during his presidency tended to be covert, as in the CIA-sponsored Guatemalan coup of 1954, or small-scale, as in the role of U.S. military advisers in selected "trouble spots," or limited, as in the case of a short-lived 1958 Marine landing in Lebanon. Nuclear Armageddon was avoided during the Hungarian and Suez crises of 1956 in large measure due to American restraint, and Truman's prolonged Korean "police action" ended swiftly by truce agreement early in Eisenhower's presidency.

If historical attitudes have changed somewhat on the quality of Ike's statesmanship, however, there are few historians even today who will grant him high marks as a domestic political leader. American professional soldiers who go on to the White House have not proved to be strong Presidents, and Dwight Eisenhower was no exception. His eight years in office provided an extended breathing spell following the super-contentious Roosevelt–Truman years, and most Americans welcomed this caretaker regime which put the presidency into a state of suspended animation. Ike declared that he wanted "to take that straight road down the middle."

Eisenhower was a genuinely modest man, perhaps too much so, since awareness of his intellectual limitations tended to immobilize him. He found details bothersome, and preferred to be briefed in military staff fashion, with analyses of complex issues boiled down to a single page. And he had a limited conception of the role of government. He rejected the examples of a strong presidency set by his two predecessors, regarding himself as a "presiding" officer and little more. In the following selection, a disillusioned former member of Ike's White House staff, Emmet John Hughes, ruminates over the sparse achievements and the many failures of the Eisenhower presidency.

"The human story does not always unfold like a mathematical calculation on the principle that two and two make four. Sometimes in life they make five or minus three; and sometimes the blackboard topples down in the middle of the sum and leaves the class in disorder and the pedagogue with a black eye."

Winston Churchill

A free and prosperous people in the second half of the twentieth century, amply attended by all the time-saving marvels of modern technology and automation, enjoys far greater leisure than any generation of its ancestors. This historic dispensation extends to nearly all phases of a free nation's life. But there is one stunning exception. And this is the enterprise upon which the nation's survival may depend—the attainment of a wise and fair understanding of its own immediate past.

Here the very rhythm of revolutionary change, so generously favoring all other endeavors, harshly exacts its price. For it leaves to a free people—contemplating the sudden crisis or the instant challenge—less time, less chance for perception and reflection, than any other epoch of man. An age not long dead when the sound of musketry on Boston's Bunker Hill would take a fortnight to echo in London's House of Commons—and an age when the firing of an intercontinental missile from the far side of the globe might leave citizens of Detroit a quarter of an hour to prepare themselves for the blast—are two ages distant and distinct from each other by measure more profound than clock or calendar. For the newer of these ages does not challenge merely the speed of sound: it defies the speed of thought. It requires the processes of democratic decision to revolve and to react as fast as all the world in historic upheaval. And it prescribes a rate of obsolescence that dispenses as harshly with yesterday's ideas as with yesterday's weapons.

Thus all witnesses to such an age are denied the chance to wait for those comforting prerogatives of the historian—dispassion and detachment. The witnesses must speak, instead, from the swiftest of glances and the briefest of visits. For the long-deliberated and delicately balanced judgment, finally pronounced after exhaustive examination of amassed archives, can emerge to the light only to peer around for the once-living, once-urgent dilemma—and squint in vain. The dilemma will be dead, beneath the rubble of accomplished facts.

And so, falteringly and presumptuously, one can only try to catch some glimpses of the fleet shapes of the men or the events . . . to touch with the senses some part of their meaning, before they vanish over the rim of remembrance and understanding . . . someday to be recovered for the learning, but too late for the living.

This much one must try to do, as the Eisenhower Years slip fast into the past. . . .

II

What happened to all those fine young people with stars in their eyes who sailed balloons and rang doorbells for us in 1952?
                *Dwight D. Eisenhower (to Sherman Adams), July 1960 **

Dwight David Eisenhower, the man of many paradoxes, left the office of the presidency as the most widely popular—and the most sharply criticized—citizen of his nation. By almost unanimous consensus of all political leaders of both parties, only the constitutional bar to a third term kept him from inflicting upon John Fitzgerald Kennedy an electoral rout as severe and complete as those twice suffered by Adlai Stevenson. By almost equally unanimous consensus of the national community of intellectuals and critics—journalists and academicians, pundits and prophets

* First-hand Report, p. 453.

—his conduct of the presidency was unskillful and his definition of it inaccurate. And these fiercely contradictory judgments inspired two images: the profile acidly etched by his detractors, the portrait warmly painted by his idolators.

The caricature was—as always—easier to draw.

Here, in this vignette, was a weak and irresolute man, surrounded by vastly stronger men, their vision small but their will powerful. To them, this man delegated the powers of the presidency slackly and carelessly. To the role of national leader, he came unequipped by experience, by knowledge, by temperament, or even by taste for politics. To the role of military responsibility, he brought the prejudices of a professional life that had effectively ended before the advent of nuclear weapons. To the role of world statesman, he brought a genial and gregarious disposition, undisciplined and unsophisticated, never holding promise of a diplomacy more profound than a rather maudlin kind of global sociability. On the world scene, he sought to check the power of Soviet Communism by complacent citation of the "spiritual" superiority of American life; and he thereby showed a blindness to national danger reminiscent of a Stanley Baldwin of the 1930's, assuring the people of Great Britain of their serene immunity to the menace of Nazi power. On the national scene, he persisted, too, in facile exhortations on "spiritual" and "moral" values—even while he practiced an aloof neutralism toward the struggle for civil rights that seemed, to many of his citizens, the most pure and urgent moral issue to confront his presidency. As a politician, he set forth to remake the blurred image of the Republican party, but he merely ended by suffering himself to be remade in *its* image. As an intellectual, he bestowed upon the games of golf and bridge all the enthusiasm and perseverance that he withheld from books and ideas. As a President, he sought to affirm the dignity of his high office by the simple device of reducing its complex functions to the circumspect discharge of its ceremonial obligations. As the leader of the world's greatest democracy—charting its flight through all the clouds and storms of the mid-twentieth century, on toward the

mysteries and perils of the Age of Space—he elected to leave his
nation to fly on automatic pilot.

The appreciative portrait was—as almost always—not so easy to
draw.

Here, by this portrait, was a man of selfless and serious patriotism. Physically, he gave of himself unstintingly, in bearing the
burden of the presidency, despite three illnesses that would have
crippled weaker men. Morally, he gave uncompromising scorn to
all temptations of expediency, despite knowing full well the easy
accolades to be won at almost any instant—by publicly chastising a
McCarthy, by blaming congressional leadership for failures, by
wrathfully denouncing a Faubus, by combating recession with tax
reduction or government deficit, by appeasing critics with the replacement of a Dulles or a Benson, or, most dramatically, by proclaiming himself the soldier-champion of gigantic military programs to assure American supremacy in the Age of Space. Whatever the crisis or the clamor, he stayed defiantly faithful to the
policy—or to the man—as honest conviction decreed. As a national
leader, he avoided, through the greater part of a perilous decade,
his and his people's two greatest fears—war in the world and
depression at home. As a partisan leader, he steered Republicanism
toward new historic ground, far from its isolationist traditions; and,
for all the conservatism of his economics, he left the policies of the
New Deal and the Fair Deal intact and secure after eight years of
a Republican Administration. Personally, he led his party to two
successive and smashing national triumphs, after it had endured
twenty years of failure and rebuff. He brought to the White House
itself a personal sense of dignity and honor that could only elevate
the office of the presidency in the eyes of his people. When he
entered this office, the political air of the nation was sulphurous
with bitterness, recrimination, and frustration. And when he left
office, this air was clean of all such rancor, fresh with good will
and good feeling.*

* Nine months after leaving the presidency, Eisenhower cited this as the
first item, when asked to enumerate "your greatest achievements." In his

The two portraits of the man deny and taunt each other. It is easy and obvious to note—as I believe—that each contains some pieces and fractions of the whole truth. It is less easy—but more important—to discern that both suffer from the same flaws and tricks. Both confuse the plausible with the actual, the logical with the reality. Both ignore the capricious and the imponderable and the elusive in history. And so, by the neat fancy of fitting every event to some intent, they contrive the most seductive distortions: the happy occurrence confers credit, where none may be due, and the mourned occasion decrees guilt, where blame may be impossible.

A few instances may give warning. Thus, for example . . .

The hugeness of a President's popularity may be consoling or alarming, according to the viewer's prejudice, but it is of little relevance to a historian's judgment. Through the years, the upward graph of Eisenhower's popularity seemed a fact of formidable meaning. Yet almost immediately upon his departure from office, the significance of this fact seemed dramatically to depreciate, for his successor in the presidency—a man with a wholly different concept of the office and with a record of only mingled successes and reverses—scaled even higher peaks in the favor of opinion polls. The generosity of such popular tributes to both men suggests that these accolades may reveal not much about either of the men, but more about the temper of the nation. For the awareness of national peril seems inevitably to inspire an anxious sense of dependence upon the presidency, unbridled by the strict appraisal of logic or fact. And this sense—of both danger and dependence—may be greatly quickened, in fact, by a manifest lapse in presidential leadership. Thus the humiliation suffered by Eisenhower on his Far Eastern journey, in the summer of 1960, only brought

---

words: "When I came to the presidency the country was rather in an unhappy state. There was bitterness and there was quarreling . . . in Washington and around the country. I tried to create an atmosphere of greater serenity and mutual confidence, and I think that it . . . was noticeable over those eight years that that was brought about." ("Eisenhower on the Presidency," CBS telecast with Walter Cronkite, October 12, 1961.)

forth new signs of popular acclaim. At such moments of national stress, partisans cannot rejoice and critics cannot gloat—and a Chief Executive's political error or diplomatic defeat can acquire a weirdly self-nullifying quality. In a democracy—whose very life may depend upon the clarity and courage of its faculties for self-criticism—this could be an alarming sign of intellectual slackness. It cannot be confused, in any event, with a true estimate of the merit or the vigor of a President's leadership.

And the national political scene, quite as much as the world scene, carries its own warnings against the too simple and sweeping judgment. An indictment of Eisenhower, for example, for allowing himself to be a meek creature of traditional Republican conservatism, rather than a bold creator of a new Republican liberalism, must start from the premise that Eisenhower was not, in fact, a conservative. The passage of years proved this premise largely false. Initially, the reality was obscured by Eisenhower's *foreign* policies, for his stands on mutual security or reciprocal trade invited the label of "liberal," even as they invited the hostility of most Republican traditionalists. But Eisenhower, after leaving the presidency, candidly compared himself and Robert Taft: "I found him to be more liberal in his support of some policies even than I was. . . . I laughed at him one day, and I said, 'How did you ever happen to be known as a conservative and me as a liberal?' " The progress of his presidency brought a more and more heavily conservative accent to Eisenhower's policies and pronouncements. But this was not a matter of slow acquiescence to new political pressures: it meant a gradual reaffirmation of old political persuasions. And to appreciate this, one need only imagine the personal politics of a Dwight David Eisenhower from Abilene, Kansas, who never served in World War II; who passed no memorable years in Europe, there to become the comrade of a Churchill or a De Gaulle; and who became known to the political annals of the 1950's as the quite predictable congressman from the Fourth District of his native Kansas.

For like reasons, there is some unrealism in any tribute to

Eisenhower for ratifying or consolidating the social gains of New Deal and Fair Deal. Eight years of a Republican Administraton did leave intact all such laws and measures. Yet it is hardly accurate to ascribe this to presidential statesmanship, liberalism, or even choice. The Administration was not required to defend these measures against challenge, but merely to accept their immutability, as a matter of political necessity. And even with this tacit act of acceptance, the President himself held an antipathy toward TVA—and at least a tolerance toward right-to-work-laws—scarcely reminiscent of the basic social attitudes of the New Deal. There was exceedingly little here, then, to suggest the labor of a President who was *trying* to be a far-sighted consolidator of past social legislation. And it is not easy to assign historic credit to a man for achievements he never attempted.

All these cautions and qualifications bring some light to the question of the final fate of one of the supreme objectives of the Eisenhower presidency.

This purpose was the invigoration and the rejuvenation of the Republican party.

This purpose ended in defeat.

The size of the defeat was easy to measure. The loss of Executive power in the 1960 elections, despite all advantages enjoyed by the incumbent Administration, could not be ascribed, harshly or entirely, to popular distaste for the personality of Richard Nixon. For the signs of Republican weakness and ineptitude were visible almost everywhere across the political landscape. The Republican party that in 1930 claimed governorships in thirty states could boast of merely sixteen in 1960. Of the nation's forty-one major urban centers, the Democrats in 1960 swept a total of twenty-seven. Through all the Eisenhower Years, in fact, the total polling strength of the GOP had steadily declined despite the President's personal electoral triumphs—from 49 per cent in 1950, to 47 per cent in 1954, finally to 43 per cent in 1958. In the Congress convening as Eisenhower left the presidency, the GOP was outnumbered three to two in the House of Representatives and two to one in the Senate. Such a stark reckoning more than sufficed, in short, to justify Eisenhower's own unhappy query to Sherman Adams: "What happened . . . ?"

The answer clearly lay, in great part, with the man who asked the question. The very definition he imposed upon his roles as President and party leader approached a political philosophy of self-denial. Months after leaving office, for example, he was asked if he had "ever sort of turned the screw on Congress to get something done . . . saying you'll withhold an appointment or something like that." And with disarming accuracy, Eisenhower answered: "No, never. I took very seriously the matter of appointments and [their] qualifications. . . . Possibly I was not as shrewd and as clever in this matter as some of the others, but I never thought that any of these appointments should be used for bringing pressure upon the Congress." The President proudly forswearing the use of "pressure," of course, comes close to brusquely renouncing power itself. And such smothering of his own voice must have two inescapable consequences: the floundering of his legislative program in the halls of the Congress, and the blurring of his party's image in the eyes of the electorate.

As he treated the political present, so, too, Eisenhower faced the future: he served as a passive witness, rather than an aggressive judge, in the choice of leadership to follow him. It is reasonable to accept the sincerity of his belief—by 1960—that "experience" significantly qualified Richard Nixon for the presidency. It is no less certain, however, that—before 1960—Eisenhower constantly reviewed and privately discussed many alternatives to a successor whom he regarded as less than ideal. Along with such personal favorites as Robert Anderson or Alfred Gruenther, he faced—after the 1958 elections—the far more serious political possibility of a Nelson Rockefeller. Even if all calculations of simple political success were disregarded—including John Fitzgerald Kennedy's own calm judgment that his defeat could have been easy—the striking fact is that Eisenhower did nothing to encourage his party to weigh such alternatives, even while he pondered them within himself.

The conclusion must be that—for the Republican party under the leadership of Eisenhower—the 1950's essentially were a lost decade. Let the measure be the growth of the party in popular vote or popular confidence. Let it be the record of specific legislative achievements. Let it be the less specific but more meaningful matter of clear commitment to abiding principles or exhilarating purposes, relevant to an age of revolution. By all criteria, the judgment must be the same. And it darkly suggests no political truth more modern, perhaps, than the venerable warning of Edmund Burke: "The only thing necessary for the triumph of evil is for good men to do nothing."

And yet, there can be no just criticism of a political leader, obviously, without full reference to the political circumstances. And of the Republican party itself, the serious question must be asked: would some other kind of presidential leadership, more vigorous and more creative, have cleanly prevailed over this party's capacity to resist change? The chance of revitalizing a major political organization depends critically upon the nature of the material with which the work must begin. And, in this instance, the circumstances confronting Eisenhower might at least be called mitigating.

For the full half-century since the historic struggle of 1912 between Theodore Roosevelt and William Howard Taft, the Republican party has been known to the nation, of course, as the citadel of conservative orthodoxy. In this span of time, it summoned from its own ranks no President who could lay serious historic claim to greatness. It collectively offered no leadership that could be hailed, by a grateful nation, as imaginative, bold, or memorable. For thirty of those years, the party could not win a presidential election except under the leadership of a war hero. Over this same thirty-year period, it held control of the Congress for a meager total of four years. All this added up to a distinction of the most unwanted kind.

Yet, behind this near-barren half-century, there lies a Republican tradition of a vastly different fiber. This was, almost instantly upon birth, the party that abolished slavery. Throughout the decades of frenetically expanding capitalism—and the lawless acquisitiveness of "the robber barons"—this was the party that conceived and wrote the national laws most vital to the public good and welfare. These included: the first laws of civil service, the anti-trust legislation, the control of the railways, the first federal regulation of food and drugs, the first acts to conserve the nation's natural resources. And throughout this full and rich earlier life, the Republican party logically was both the home and the hope—rather than the enemy and the despair—of the American intellectual.

The third half-century of the story of the Republican party has now just begun. The party, quite obviously, still does not know which of its two selves to *be* in the years immediately ahead. And Dwight David Eisenhower—by his own austere and negative prescription for the role of party leader—could not help it to make up its deeply divided mind.

I have witnessed closely some of this party's recent inner travail. I confess to frequent and sharp dismay at the pettiness of its calculations and the narrowness of its vision. And yet, I presume to believe that the choice before it, as it faces its *third* half-century of life, is as clear as it is historic.

It must, if it is to be a live and generous force in American politics, stir with the energy of enduring convictions, rather than appeal for saving moments to the popularity of a new hero or the plausibility of an ancient shibboleth. It must comprehend and assimilate, in its own mind and spirit, some of the political and intellectual qualities that have enabled British Conservatism to hold power for a full decade and that have animated Christian Democratic parties on the European continent ever since World War II. It must honor, too, its own very origin as a party—by conscientious leadership in the struggle for civil rights. It must learn to use political power in some exercise other than the reflexes of opposition and denunciation. It must forswear the charades of hysterical duels with the imagined menaces of "socialism" and "totalitarianism." It must learn to assess its own political worth by some arithmetic more elevated than the facile addition of its own congressional votes to those of southern Democrats, to contrive the frustration of a fairly impressive number of Executive actions in any congressional session. It must attain a self-respecting sense of identity—and sense of purpose—that can turn cold and confident scorn upon the tawdry political temptations proffered by a Senator Joseph McCarthy or a John Birch Society. And—with these and a host of kindred acts—it might begin to celebrate each political year, each session of the Congress in Washington, by offering the nation a modest minimum of one proud sign of imaginative political action, dedicated unabashedly to the common weal.

To inspire and to lead—indeed, to *re-create*—such a Republican party can only be, still, a patient and painful labor.

To this labor, there was, perhaps, not a great deal that such a President as Eisenhower could bring. This was not only because of the nature of the Republican party long before he encountered it. It was also because of the nature of the man long before the party encountered him. For he appeared upon the national scene as the political father of a phenomenon called "modern Republicanism." Yet his economic and social views could not convincingly be described as "modern." And his political behavior could not, with rare exception, be described as militantly and passionately "Republican." The fact is that the President who was supposed to lead the Republican party toward new, high ground—both "liberal" and "modern"—could not seriously be distinguished from a conservative Democrat.

If this suggests some kind of political paradox about the man, it suggests a more profound paradox about the system of political parties by which America governs itself in the middle of the twentieth century.

And it suggests the final reason why Dwight Eisenhower left the Republican party—politically and intellectually—where first he found it.

> Things are in the saddle,
> And ride mankind.
> *Ralph Waldo Emerson*

The second and the grander of the two high purposes pursued by the Eisenhower presidency was the quest of "peace with justice."

This, too, ended in frustration.

The President's own appraisal of himself as a peacemaker, as fully and finally spoken, sounds rather like a judgment at odds with itself. Thus—on the one side—he publicly recited, within a year of leaving the presidency, what he called "my greatest disappointments," and concluded: "I suppose the most important . . . is a lack of definite proof that we had made real progress toward achieving peace with justice." Yet—on the other side—he had proudly voiced, only a week before surrendering office, a quite different and less disparaging opinion in his final State of the Union Message to the Congress. According to this review of the eight years of his presidency, he professed to see "Communist imperialism held in check." And he invited the Congress to share the Chief Executive's pleasure in his conclusion: "We have carried America to unprecedented heights."

The two contrary appraisals were not as hard to reconcile as they might appear, even apart from the fact that one could not reasonably have expected Eisenhower's final address to the Congress to catalogue his personal disappointments. For the State of the Union message did not, in truth, presume even to suggest "definite proof" of "real progress." Instead, all the alleged achievements merely attested to the practice of a diplomacy of "containment," although its rewards were hailed—now—as "unprecedented heights."

The satisfying summits cited by the departing President were quite specific. They numbered seven in all. And they are worth quick scanning to appreciate the nature of the diplomatic terrain upon which he looked back. . . .

1. Whereas "when I took office, the United States was at war," the nation had "lived in peace" since the Korean Armistice of 1953. *But* . . . there seemed some irony in the fact that this list of eight years of diplomatic accomplishments should be headed by

the prudent acceptance, seven years earlier, of a military status quo whose toleration, even at the time, had elicited only frowns and doubts from the Secretary of State.

2. The United States had "strongly supported" the United Nations in the 1956 Suez Crisis, thus achieving "the ending of the hostilities in Egypt." *But* . . . the prologue to this crisis had entailed the chronic deterioration of Anglo-American relations— and the epilogue had consisted of the alarming expansion of Soviet influence throughout the Middle East.

3. "Again in 1958, peace was preserved in the Middle East"—by prompt American military action in Lebanon. *But* . . . while this action had been vitally required and efficiently executed, its very necessity implied rather critical comment on the political heritage from American Middle Eastern diplomacy two years earlier.

4. "Our support of the Republic of China . . . restrained the Communist Chinese from attempting to invade the offshore islands." *But* . . . the honoring of this defensive action as the major triumph of eight years of diplomacy in the Far East seemed oddly to mock the "initiative" of 1953—supposedly freeing Nationalist China to assume a more menacing military posture toward the Communist mainland.

5. As for Latin America, there was not much that could be said beyond this: "Although, unhappily, Communist penetration of Cuba is real and poses a serious threat, Communist-dominated regimes have been deposed in Guatemala and Iran." The fragile apologia could not even find sufficient supporting evidence in all the Western Hemisphere.

6. As for Europe—while the peripheral issues of an Austrian peace treaty and a Trieste settlement could be remembered from the first term with some justified satisfaction—there was no echo of the 1953 cries of "rollback" or "liberation," but the most modest of observations: "Despite constant threats to its integrity, West Berlin remained free."

7. Finally, there were alleged to be "important advances . . . in building mutual security arrangements." Thus: SEATO was

established in Southeast Asia and the CENTO Pact in the Middle East, NATO was "militarily strengthened," and the Organization of American States was "further developed." *But* . . . a number of dispassionate critics would have felt compelled to note the following: (a) the political or military value of SEATO was highly questionable; (b) the birth of CENTO merely followed the death of the Baghdad Pact when Baghdad itself severed this tie to the West; (c) the political structure of NATO betrayed signs of growing division rather than greater unity; and (d) the OAS probably faced a graver crisis over Cuban Communism than it had ever known in all its political life.

The President's own chosen list of historic events thus strikingly revealed the limits and the lacks of eight years of American diplomacy, and the nation might well ask—as the President himself occasionally must have wondered—why his pursuit of peace, so ample in both motion and emotion, had yielded such meager reward. A part of the answer, it is true, might cite sheer bad luck. Only a glibly assured student of contemporary history could profess to know the course of East-West diplomacy in 1960, at least in its appearances and its amenities, if there had been no disaster with the U-2 flight. But one such mischance could not suffice to explain the sum of nearly a decade of national policy.

The climactic global effort of Eisenhower's peace-making suggested a peacetime variation on a familiar wartime lament. This was the case of—too much, too late. Through all the years ruled by the taut doctrines of John Foster Dulles, the national policy had decreed an almost religious kind of commitment to a moralistic definition of the relations between nations. By the terms of this orthodoxy, the promise of salvation lay in a kind of political excommunication of Soviet power. The means of grace, moreover, were assured: the political weakness of Soviet power was ultimately guaranteed by its moral wickedness. And the contaminating stigma of sin therefore attached to all acts or gestures of diplomacy that, by directly touching the unclean enemy, might give countenance to the damning offenses of his tyranny at home and his conquests abroad. It was as bad and unthinkable as selling indulgences.

Time and history, however, played a cruel trick. For the years when these strictures had been respected were precisely the years when the advantages of politics and power had rested with the United States. Militarily, American nuclear power then had stood beyond challenge. Politically, the Soviet Union had to suffer through all the complex conflicts wracking the Communist state after Stalin's death. But such factors were drastically changed by the time the clenched fist of Dulles came to be replaced, in the world of diplomacy, by the outstreched hand of Eisenhower. The Soviet power that Eisenhower now confronted was the new and ingenious pioneer of the Age of Space. The Soviet leadership that he faced, now no longer strife-torn, was personified by a Khrushchev politically more agile and skillful than a Stalin. Conversely, the American power that Eisenhower now commanded had passed under a cloud of world doubt. The American diplomacy that he directed was caught in a cross fire between colonialism and anti-colonialism, all through the very areas of Asia and Africa marked for political agression by new Soviet leadership. And the American leadership that Eisenhower himself personified now could boast—by the constitutional law of his nation—only a few more months to live.

There was a moral as well as political edge, moreover, to the sad incongruity of all this. The Soviet leadership so righteously shunned by the diplomacy of Dulles stood indicted—a little belatedly—for political crimes essentially rooted in World War II. The Soviet leadership so hopefully encountered by the diplomacy of Eisenhower came—quite freshly—from the savage suppression of Hungarian freedom. And so American policy of the 1950's fashioned its supreme irony: a host of decent intents, generous gestures, and dramatic acts of peace were scrupulously hoarded—through years proclaiming the need for them—to be lavishly spent only when the moral occasion was least appropriate and their political value was least impressive.

The confused timing of such major diplomatic acts had to betray, too, some lack of substance, since the fully reasoned acts would have borne the much earlier dates. And this fact gave to the President's personal diplomacy its disconcerting overtones of impetuosity and improvisation. The reach of the leader was undeniably long, but his grasp did not seem firm; his manner was kind, but uncertain; his words were benign, but unclear. And all this explained why so many national capitals, warm as they felt in the presence of the man, also sensed a little shiver of unreality as they watched and listened. Even as he disarmed his critics, he disquieted his friends. For they could not suppress a fear that perhaps he had never understood the lesson recorded by one historian who had personally witnessed the travail of peace-making, as long ago as 1919: "It would be interesting to analyze how many false decisions, how many fatal misunderstandings, have arisen from such pleasant qualities as shyness, consideration, affability, or ordinary good manners."

The strivings of Eisenhower to conciliate the world of nations thus markedly resembled his equally earnest attempts to conciliate the Congress of the United States. Over the years, the tortuous struggle to evolve Republican legislative programs with the help of political leaders as unreconciled as William Knowland was no more remarkable than the effort to evolve a foreign policy by mingling, in equal measures, Eisenhower's views of the world and those of John Foster Dulles. The truth was that all the public allusions to a "Dulles-Eisenhower" foreign policy were no more sensibly descriptive than some fantastic diplomacy proclaiming itself "radical-reactionary" or "bellicose-pacific." And in the councils closest to Eisenhower, the deep conflict of premises found a kind of analogy in a conflict of persons, also unadmitted by the President. For in Eisenhower's Cabinet, through all the years, no two men stood closer to him than Dulles and Humphrey. In the same Cabinet, no two men clashed more fundamentally on national policy. And the President warmly respected them both—equally.

A foreign policy beset by such inner contradictions inevitably could attain results of only one kind: the negative or the passive. Such results were not wholly to be scorned: they could include acts as important as countering the threatened chaos in Lebanon or the presidential veto upon military intervention in Indochina. But a national policy so nearly schizophrenic was powerless to create a positive political design.

In the deepest sense, it could neither conceive nor execute a truly *historic act.*

This was not because it lacked the courage to act.

This was because it could not decide upon a definition of history.

And so the years inscribed a record, not stained with the blots of many foolish or reckless acts, but all too immaculate. All the acts of omission signified a waste of something more than a briefly enjoyed military superiority. The great waste could be measured only by the vastness of the unused political resources at the command of the most powerful and popular leader of any free nation in the world. For Eisenhower had constantly enjoyed the freedom, so fantastically rare in a modern democracy, of the full and affectionate confidence of a people who would have followed him toward almost any conceivable military enterprise or diplomatic encounter.

The final reckoning upon such a period of singular opportunity truly revealed, in short, a "lack of definite proof" of the achievement of "real progress." At the end of his presidency and confronting his harshest critics, Eisenhower never had to suffer hearing criticism as biting as the accusation that Macaulay once hurled in the House of Commons at Sir Robert Peel: "There you sit, doing penance for the disingenuousness of years." But the chargeable offense might have been the exact opposite: the ingenuousness of years.

A last, small irony was reserved for his last months in office: The President then was fighting an increasingly bitter battle against critics who insistently warned of a faltering of American purpose and American power. While some of these critics focused their concern upon domestic issues—from the health of the aged to the education of the young—the majority saw the world scene as the sharpest cause for anxiety. Essentially, the sources of this anxiety were the multiplying signs of Soviet achievement, from progress of their missile power to education of *their* youth. The President found himself harassed by questions and laments upon a single theme: could not, should not, would not the federal government do more to spur comparable American achievement? Emphatically, then stubbornly, at last almost petulantly, Eisenhower insisted that such demands threatened an enlargement of federal authority that would "take our country and make it an armed camp and regiment it." And he went further—to contend angrily that such acknowledgment of Soviet power implied an almost unpatriotic disparagement of American life, as he gruffly admonished one press conference: "Our people ought to have greater faith in their own system." Thus—strangely—did an intensely patriotic President come finally to argue that the nature of American freedom, and the resourcefulness of the American people, were so limited that they could give retort to the challenge of Soviet Communism only by fractional sacrifice and rationed effort.

The distance in time and in spirit, from the First Inaugural, seemed—in these last days of the Eisenhower presidency—more than the meager sum of seven or eight years. . . . "We must be ready to dare all for our country. . . . The peace we seek . . . is nothing less than the practice and fulfillment of our whole faith. . . . It signifies much more than the stilling of guns, easing the sorrow, of war. More than an escape from death, it is a way of life. More than a haven for the weary, it is a hope for the brave."

The presidency that had followed upon these words had appeared only occasionally to be inspired by any such preachment about peace.

It had settled, instead, for the half-solace of a series of truces.

> O! it is excellent
> To have a giant's strength, but it is tyrannous
> To use it like a giant.
> *Measure for Measure*

The man who, for these several years, entered his office each morning to nod approvingly at the legend on his desk—"Gentle in manner, strong in deed"—would have commended Shakespeare's admonition on "a giant's strength" as an admirable definition of the proper use of power in the presidency of the United States. Because he so believed, he would be charged—quite justly —with refusal to give vigorous leadership even to cherished purposes. And he would also be condemned—not at all justly—for wholly lacking any concept of presidential leadership.

The Eisenhower who rose to fame in the 1940's, under the wartime presidency of Franklin Roosevelt, brought to the White House of the 1950's a view of the presidency so definite and so durable as to seem almost a studied retort and rebuke to a Roosevelt. Where Roosevelt had sought and coveted power, Eisenhower distrusted and discounted it: one man's appetite was the other man's distaste. Where Roosevelt had avidly grasped and adroitly manipulated the abundant authorities of the office, Eisenhower fingered them almost hesitantly and always respectfully—or generously dispersed them. Where Roosevelt had challenged Congress, Eisenhower courted it. Where Roosevelt had been an extravagant partisan, Eisenhower was a tepid partisan. Where Roosevelt had trusted no one and nothing so confidently as his own judgment and his own instinct, Eisenhower trusted and required a consensus of Cabinet or staff to shape the supreme judgments and determinations. Where Roosevelt had sought to goad and taunt and prod the processes of government toward the new and the untried, Eisenhower sought to be both guardian of old values and healer of old wounds.

The contrast was quite as blunt in the case of an earlier—and a Republican—Roosevelt. For the Eisenhower who so deeply disliked all struttings of power, all histrionics of politics, would have found the person and the presidency of Theodore Roosevelt almost intolerable. He would have applied to this Roosevelt, too, the homely phrase of derision that he reserved for politicians of such verve and vehemence: they were "the desk-pounders." Echoing

back across the decades would have come the lusty answer of
T.R.—exulting in the presidency as the "bully pulpit." And it is
hard to imagine a concept of the presidency more alien to Eisenhower: to preach and to yell.

A yet more exact and intimate insight into the Eisenhower
presidency was revealed by his particular tribute to the Abraham
Lincoln of his admiration. He was asked, on one occasion, to
describe this Lincoln. And he chose these adjectives: "dedicated,
selfless, so modest and humble." He made no mention or suggestion of such possible attributes as: imagination, tenacity, single-
mindedness, vision. Pressed gently by his interrogator as to whether
Lincoln were not something of a "desk-pounder," Eisenhower
denied such a notion and spontaneously related the one episode of
Lincoln's life that surged to the surface of memory . . .

> Oh no. Lincoln was noted both for his modesty and his humility.
> For example, one night he wanted to see General McClellan. He
> walked over to General McClellan's house . . . but General McClel-
> lan was out. He . . . waited way late in the evening. But when the
> general came in, he told an aide . . . he was tired and he was going
> to bed, and he would see the President the next day. And when criti-
> cized later . . . someone told Mr. Lincoln he ought to have been
> more arbitrary about this. He said: "I would hold General McClellan's
> horse if he would just win the Union a victory."

The Eisenhower appreciation of Lincoln, in short, reflected one
sovereign attitude: all esteemed qualities of the founder of Republicanism were personal and individual, and not one was political
or historical. And if the logic of such an estimate were carried
coldly to its extreme, it would end in the unspoken implication
that the highest national office should be sought and occupied less
as an exercise of political power than as a test of personal virtue.
To excel in this test, the man would live not *with* the office but
within it—intact and independent, proudly uncontaminated by
power, essentially uninvolved with it. Rather than a political life,
this would be a life in politics. Its supreme symbol would be not
the sword of authority but the shield of rectitude.

While this self-conscious kind of idealism sprang from deep within the man who was Eisenhower, it found reinforcement—and rationalization—in his explicit theory of political leadership. This theory was profoundly felt and emphatically argued. It claimed even to bespeak a sense of responsibility more serious than the conventional shows of leadership. And no words of Eisenhower stated this theory more succinctly than these:

> I am not a . . . leader. I don't want you to follow me or anything else. If you are looking for a Moses to lead you out of the . . . wilderness, you will stay right where you are. I would not lead you into this promised land if I could, because if I could lead you in, someone else could lead you out.

These words might have been spoken by Dwight David Eisenhower—at almost any moment in the years from 1952 to 1960—to the Republican party or, indeed, to the American people at large. They were actually spoken, however, by one of the great leaders of American labor, Eugene V. Debs, more than a half a century earlier. And they are worthy of note here as simple evidence that, quite apart from all impulses of personal character, the political posture assumed by Eisenhower toward the challenge of national leadership could not, in fact, be curtly described as negligent, eccentric, or even entirely original.

This posture *was* Eisenhower—remarkably and unshakably—because it was prescribed for him by *both* the temper of the man and the tenets of his politics. In any President, or in any political leader, these two need not necessarily coincide: they may fiercely clash. A man of vigorous and aggressive spirit, restless with the urge for action and accomplishment, may fight frantically against the limits of a political role calling for calm, composure, and self-effacement. Or a man of easy and acquiescent temper, content to perform the minimal duties of his office, may strain pathetically and vainly to fill the vastness of a political role demanding force, boldness, and self-assurance. Eisenhower suffered neither kind of conflict. The definition of the office perfectly suited and matched the nature of the man. And neither critical argument nor anxious appeal could persuade him to question, much less to shed, an attire of leadership so appropriate, so form-fitting, so comfortable.

The want and the weakness in all this was not a mere matter of indecision. The man—and the President—was never more decisive than when he held to a steely resolve *not* to do something that he sincerely believed wrong in itself or alien to his office. The essential flaw, rather, was one that had been suggested a full half-century ago—when the outrageously assertive Theodore Roosevelt had occupied the White House—and Woodrow Wilson had then prophesied that "more and more" the presidency would demand *"the sort of action that makes for enlightenment."* The requisite for such action, however, is not merely a stout sense of responsibility, but an acute sense of history—a discerning, even intuitive, appreciation of the elusive and cumulative force of every presidential word and act, shaped and aimed to reach final goals, unglimpsed by all but a few. And as no such vision ever deeply inspired the Eisenhower presidency, there could be no true "enlightenment" to shine forth from its somber acts of prudence or of pride.

This is not to say that the record of the Administration wholly lacked zeal—of a kind. It is doubtful if the leadership of any great nation can endure for nearly a decade without at least the flickering of some flame of commitment. The man who came closest to a display of such fervor in these years, however, was not the President but his Secretary of State. This man possessed at least his own understanding of what Theodore Roosevelt meant when he spoke of a "pulpit." And yet, this particular ardor of John Foster Dulles could not be enough. For this kind of zeal was neither creative nor impassioned. It was austere, constrained, and cerebral. And in lieu of fire, it offered ice.

Ultimately, all that Eisenhower did, and refused to do, as a democratic leader was rigorously faithful to his understanding of democracy itself. When the record of his presidency was written and done, he could look back upon it and soberly reflect: "One definition of democracy that I like is merely the opportunity for self-discipline." He lived by this definition. And by all acts of eight years of his presidency, he urged its acceptance by the people of his nation.

The implications of this simple political credo could not instantly be dismissed as shallow. Forbearance and constraint, patience and discipline—those are not virtues for a democracy to deride. They can be fatefully relevant to the ways of free men.

And yet, by the year 1960, they did not seem to serve or to suffice, as full statement of either the nation's purpose or a President's policy.

What was so wrong or wanting in them?

Perhaps one might have caught some hint of the answer, if one were listening attentively, on Inauguration Day in 1961. The provocative moment came shortly before John Fitzgerald Kennedy took his oath of office. At this moment, there stood at the lectern of the Inaugural platform on Capitol Hill not a politician but a poet. His white hair was whipped by the chill January wind. His fingers fumbled clumsily with his text. He was eighty-six years of age—old enough to forget some of his own written lines. But the voice of Robert Frost was strong, and his meaning was clear . . .

> Something we were withholding left us weak
> Until we found it was ourselves
> We were withholding from our land of living
> And forthwith found salvation in surrender.

8

The Modern Distemper, 1960–

Reaffirming the Stalemate

Stability and Change in 1960

by Philip E. Converse, Angus Campbell,
Warren E. Miller, and Donald E. Stokes

*It became certain in 1960 that the presidential father-figure of
Dwight Eisenhower would be replaced by a much younger politician. Vice President Richard M. Nixon, then forty-six, easily
obtained the Republican nomination, while on the Democratic
side, John F. Kennedy, a forty-three-year-old senator from Massachusetts, had run a skillful and successful pre-election campaign.
His principal rival at the Democratic convention, Senator
Lyndon B. Johnson, a Texas conservative and one of the country's
most powerful politicians during the final years of the Eisenhower
administration, surprised the country by agreeing to run with
Kennedy.*

*Although Kennedy criticized the drift and lethargy of the Eisen-
hower years, his election strategy dictated the creation of a positive
image rather than merely assailing the record of a Republican
incumbent who remained personally popular. Kennedy promised
to accelerate the low rate of economic growth and to reduce the
comparatively high existing rate of unemployment; he also promised new and massive federal programs for support of public education and government-financed medical care for those over sixty-
five. "Vigor" became the key word in his appeal: Kennedy con-*

tended that the nation had to "move ahead," and that it could do so only with young, fresh, White House leadership. He also touched bases with the scattered elements of the Democratic coalition, some of which had drifted away from the party during the 'fifties, matching familiar promises to organized labor and farmers with appeals to ethnic minorities and declarations of support for civil rights and racial desegregation.

In contrast, Nixon, though of the same generation as Kennedy, a generation which came to maturity during the Depression and World War II, seemed old-fashioned. As Eisenhower's political heir he dutifully defended the Republican administration's record, stressing the nation's general prosperity and adding a few vague feints in the direction of reform and welfare legislation. Essentially, however, Nixon appealed to those segments of the electorate which were content with the accomplishments of the 1950's, especially those with an economic or psychological stake in the status quo. He opposed, among other Democratic suggestions, federal aid to education and Medicare, charging that they would lead to bureaucratic tyranny and socialized medicine.

Kennedy won in one of America's closest presidential contests, but the result mainly confirmed the previous shift to the center, the stalemate in domestic politics which Dwight Eisenhower's victories had first symbolized and later consolidated. The Democrats kept their stranglehold on Congress, although the "conservative coalition" of Republicans and Southern Democrats remained powerful. The Democrats' majority party status did not extend automatically to the presidency, however. Kennedy won by a hair's breadth: of nearly seventy million votes cast, he obtained only 113,000 more than Nixon, a margin of but 0.2 per cent. Kennedy easily captured the personality contest between the two contenders, but this advantage was nearly offset in November by Protestant defections to Nixon in the South's Bible Belt, where both Kennedy's Catholicism and his support for Negro civil rights cost him votes. Yet 1960 was not like 1928: most of the South stayed Democratic, demonstrating Kennedy's short-term political foresight in placing Johnson on the ticket.

The following article by Philip E. Converse and his associates shows how the 1960 election reaffirmed the "normal" Democratic electoral majority while it failed to provide a new and effective governing majority. As the country was soon to learn, the Eisenhower Era's politics of stalemate left in its wake a legacy of congressional inaction that Kennedy and his New Frontiersmen had not bargained for. It would take the unifying symbolism of Kennedy's assassination and the additional shock of Lyndon Johnson's landslide victory in 1964 to break the legislative logjam, at least temporarily.

❧ John F. Kennedy's narrow popular vote margin in 1960 has already insured this presidential election a classic position in the roll call of close American elections. Whatever more substantial judgments historical perspective may bring, we can be sure that the 1960 election will do heavy duty in demonstrations to a reluctant public that after all is said and done, every vote does count. And the margin translated into "votes per precinct" will become standard fare in exhortations to party workers that no stone be left unturned.

The 1960 election is a classic as well in the license it allows for "explanations" of the final outcome. Any event or campaign stratagem that might plausibly have changed the thinnest sprinkling of votes across the nation may, more persuasively than is usual, be called "critical." Viewed in this manner, the 1960 presidential election hung on such a manifold of factors that reasonable men might despair of cataloguing them.

Nevertheless, it is possible to put together an account of the election in terms of the broadest currents influencing the American electorate in 1960. We speak of the gross lines of motivation which gave the election its unique shape, motivations involving millions rather than thousand of votes. Analysis of these broad currents is not intended to explain the hairline differences in popular vote, state by state, which edged the balance in favor of Kennedy rather than Nixon. But it can indicate quite clearly the

From *The American Political Science Review*, LV (June 1961), 269–80. Reprinted by permission; footnotes omitted.

broad forces which reduced the popular vote to a virtual stalemate, rather than any of the other reasonable outcomes between a 60–40 or a 40–60 vote division. And it can thereby help us to understand in parsimonious terms why a last feather thrown on the scales in November, 1960, could have spelled victory or defeat for either candidate.

1. *Surface Characteristics of the Election*

Any account of the election should not only be consistent with its obvious characteristics as they filtered clear from raw vote tallies in the days after the election, but should organize them into a coherent pattern of meaning as well. These characteristics are, of course, the ones that have nourished post-election speculation. In addition to the close partisan division of the popular vote, the following items deserve mention:

1 *The remarkably high level of turnout.* About 62.7 per cent of estimated adults over 21 voted in the 1952 election, a figure which had stood as the high-water mark of vote turnout in recent presidential elections. The comparable turnout proportion for the 1960 presidential election appears to have been 64.3 per cent.

2 *Upswing in turnout in the South.* The South appears to have contributed disproportionately to the high level in turnout. Outside the South, the increase in total presidential votes cast in 1960 relative to the 1956 election was about 7 per cent, a figure scarcely exceeding estimated population growth in this period. In the South, however, presidential ballots in 1960 increased by more than 25 per cent relative to 1956, an increase far outstripping population growth in this region.

3 *Stronger Republican voting at the presidential level.* On balance across the nation Nixon led Republican tickets, while Kennedy trailed behind many other Democratic candidates, especially outside of the Northeast. These discrepancies in the partisanship of presidential voting and ballots at other levels were not, of course, as striking as those in 1956. Nevertheless, their political significance

has an obvious bearing on the future expectations of the two youthful candidates, and therefore occasions special interest.

4 *The stamp of the religious factor in 1960 voting patterns.* While the Kennedy victory was initially taken as proof that religion had not been important in the election, all serious students of election statistics have since been impressed by the religious axis visible in the returns. Fenton, Scammon, Bean, Harris and others have commented upon the substantial correlation between aggregate voting patterns and the relative concentration of Catholics and Protestants from district to district.

Of these surface characteristics, probably the last has drawn most attention. Once it became clear that religion had not only played some part but, as these things go, a rather impressive part in presidential voting across the nation, discussions came to hinge on the nature of its role. It could safely be assumed that Kennedy as a Catholic had attracted some unusual Catholic votes, and had lost some normally Democratic Protestant votes. A clear question remained, however, as to the *net* effect. The *New York Times*, summarizing the discussion late in November, spoke of a "narrow consensus" among the experts that Kennedy had won more than he lost as a result of his Catholicism. These are questions, however, which aggregate vote statistics can but dimly illuminate, as the disputed history of Al Smith's 1928 defeat makes clear. Fortunately in 1960 the election was studied extensively by sample surveys, permitting more exact inferences to be drawn.

The national sample survey conducted by the Survey Research Center of The University of Michigan in the fall of 1960 had features which give an unparalleled opportunity to comment on the recent evolution of the American electorate. The fall surveys were part of a long-term "panel" study, in which respondents first interviewed at the time of the 1956 presidential election were reinterviewed. In the fall of 1956 a sample of 1763 adults, chosen by strict probability methods from all the adults living in private households in the United States, had been questioned just before and just after the presidential election. This initial sample was constituted as a panel of respondents and was interviewed again in 1958 and twice in connection with the 1960 presidential election. These materials permit the linking of 1960 and 1956 voting behavior with unusual reliability.

2. *The Evolution of the Electorate, 1956–1960*

The difference in presidential election outcome between 1956 and 1960 might depend upon either or both of two broad types of change in the electorate. The first includes shifts in the physical composition of the electorate over time due to non-political factors, *i.e.*, vital processes. Some adult citizens who voted in 1956 were no longer part of the eligible electorate in 1960, primarily because of death or institutionalization. On the other hand, a new cohort of voters who had been too young to vote in 1956 were eligible to participate in the 1960 election. Even in a four-year period, vital processes alone could acount for shifts in the vote. In addition, changes in the electoral vote, though not in the nationwide popular vote margin, might result from voters changing their residences without changing their minds.

Secondly, there are obviously genuine changes in the political choice of individuals eligible to vote in both elections. Such citizens may enter or leave the active electorate by choice, or may decide to change the partisanship of their presidential vote.

The contribution of these two types of change to the shift in votes from a 1956 Eisenhower landslide to a narrow 1960 Kennedy margin—a net shift toward the Democrats of almost 8 per cent—may be analyzed. Somewhat less than 10 per cent of the eligible 1956 electorate had become effectively ineligible by 1960, with death as the principal cause. Older people naturally bulk large in this category. The felt party affiliation or "party identification" expressed in 1956 by these "departing" respondents was somewhat Republican relative to the remainder of the sample. Nonetheless, these people cast a vote for president which was about 48 per cent Democratic, or 6 per cent *more Democratic* than the vote of the 1956 electorate as a whole. Although this appears to be a contradiction, it is actually nothing more than a logical consequence of existing theory. The high Republican vote in 1956 depended on a massive defection to Eisenhower by many people identified with the Democratic party. Since the strength of party attachments increases as a function of age, and since defections are inversely related to strength of party identification, it follows that 1956 defection rates were much higher among younger citizens than among older. The data make it clear that the group of older people voting for the last time in 1956 had cast a much straighter "party vote" than their juniors. Only about 5 per cent of these older Democrats had defected to Eisenhower, as opposed to about a quarter of all Democrats in the electorate as a whole. So both things are true: this departing cohort was more Republican than average in party identification but had voted more Democratic than average in 1956. If we remove them from the 1956 electorate, then, we arrive at a presidential vote of about 60 per cent for Eisenhower among those voters who were to have the option of voting again in 1960. Hence the elimination of this older group from consideration increases the amount of partisan change to be accounted for between 1956 and 1960, rather than decreasing it.

Comparable isolation of the new cohort of young voters in 1960 does very little to change the picture. Little more than one half of this new group of voters normally votes in the first election of eligibility; furthermore, in 1960 its two-party vote division differed only negligibly from that of the nation as a whole. As a result, its analytic removal leaves the vote among the remainder of the electorate nearly unchanged. By way of summary, then, differences in the 1956 and 1960 electorates arising from vital processes do not explain the 1956–1960 vote change; if anything, they extend the amount of change to be otherwise explained.

We may further narrow our focus by considering those people eligible in both 1956 and 1960, who failed to join the active electorate in 1960. A very large majority of these 1960 non-voters had not voted in 1956, and represent Negroes in the South as well as persistent non-voters of other types. Among those who *had* voted in 1956, however, the vote had been rather evenly divided between Eisenhower and Stevenson. As with the older voters, removal of this group leaves an active 1956–1960 electorate whose vote for Eisenhower now surpasses 60 per cent, broadening again the discrepancy between the two-party divisions in the 1956 and 1960 votes. The final fringe group which we may set aside analytically is constituted of those citizens eligible to have voted in 1956 who did not then participate, yet who joined the electorate in 1960. The fact that young voters often "sit out" their first presidential election or two indicates part of the composition of such a group. Once again, however, these newly active citizens divided their ballots in 1960 almost equally between the two major candidates, and the residual portion of the 1960 electorate changes little with their removal.

By this point we have eliminated all the fringe groupings whose entry or departure from the active electorate might have contributed to change in the national vote division between 1956 and 1960. We come to focus directly, then, on the individuals who cast a vote for Kennedy or Nixon in 1960 *and had voted for president in 1956* (Table 1). As we see, paring away the fringe groupings has had the total effect of increasing the net shift in the vote division between the two years from 8 per cent to 11 per cent. If we can explain this shift it will be clear that we have dealt with those broad currents in the electorate which brought the 1960 election to a virtual stalemate.

Naturally, the most interesting features of Table 1 are the cells involving vote changers. In a sequence of elections such as the 1956–1960 series it is a temptation to assume that about 8 per cent of the Eisenhower voters of 1956 shifted to Kennedy in 1960, since this was the net observable change between the two years. Much analysis of aggregate election statistics is forced to proceed on this assumption within any given voting unit. However, we see that the net shift of 11 per cent in the vote of the active 1956–1960 electorate in fact derived from a gross shift of 23 per cent, over half of which was rendered invisible in the national totals because counter-movements cancelled themselves out.

A traditional analysis of these vote changers would specify their membership in various population groupings such as age and occupation category, union membership, race and the like. However, results of this sort in 1960 are so uniform across most of these population groupings that they seem to reflect little more than national trends, and change seems at best loosely connected with location in various of these specific categories. If we took the fact

Table 1
1956–1960 Vote Change Within the Active
Core of the Electorate

1960 Vote for ↓	1956 Vote for		Total %
	Stevenson %	Eisenhower %	
Kennedy	33	17	50
Nixon	6	44	50
	39	61	100

Note: Since we usually think of vote shifts in terms of proportions of the total electorate, percentages in this table use the total vote as a base, rather than row or column totals.

in isolation, for example, we might be struck to note that union members voted almost 8 per cent more Democratic in 1960 than in 1956. However, such a figure loses much of its interest when we remind ourselves that people who are not labor union members also shifted their votes in the same direction and in about the same degree between 1956 and 1960. Such uniform changes characterize most of the standard sociological categories.

There is, of course, one dramatic exception. Vote change between 1956 and 1960 follows religious lines very closely. Within the 6 per cent of the active 1956–1960 electorate who followed a Stevenson-Nixon path (Table 1), 90 per cent are Protestant and only 8 per cent are Catholic. Among the larger group of Eisenhower-Kennedy changers, however, only 40 per cent, are Protestant and close to 60 per cent are Catholic. In the total vote in 1956 and 1960, Protestants show almost no net partisan change. Eisenhower had won 64 per cent of the "Protestant vote" in 1956; Nixon won 63 per cent. Meanwhile, the Democratic proportion of the two-party vote among Catholics across the nation skyrocketed from a rough 50 per cent in the two Eisenhower elections to a vote of 80 per cent for Kennedy. These gross totals appear to substantiate the early claims of Kennedy backers that a Catholic candidate would draw back to the Democratic party sufficient Catholics to carry the 1960 election. Furthermore, it appears that Kennedy must have gained more votes than he lost by virtue of his religious affiliation, for relative to Stevenson in 1956, he lost no Protestant votes and attracted a very substantial bloc of Catholic votes.

The question of net gains or losses as a result of the Catholic issue is not, however, so simply laid to rest. The data cited above make a very strong case, as have the aggregate national statistics, that religion played a powerful role in the 1960 outcome. The vote polarized along religious lines in a degree which we have not seen in the course of previous sample survey studies. Moreover, the few interesting deviations in the 1960 vote of other population groupings, to the degree that they are visible at all, seem with minor exceptions to reflect the central religious polarization. That is, where a group exceeded or fell below the magnitude of the national shift to the Democrats, it is usually true that the group is incidentally a more or less Catholic group. The central phenomenon therefore was religious; the question as to its net effect favoring or disfavoring Kennedy remains open.

In a strict sense, of course, the answers to this question can only be estimated. We know how the election came out, with Kennedy a Catholic. We cannot, without major additional assumptions, know what the election returns might have been if Kennedy were a Protestant and all other conditions remained unchanged. We can make an estimate, however, if we can assume some baseline, some vote that would have occurred under "normal" circumstances. A number of such baselines suggest themselves. We might work from the 1956 presidential vote, as we have done above (42 per cent Democratic); or from the more recent Congressional vote in 1958 (56 per cent Democratic); or from some general average of recent nation-wide votes. But it is obvious that the simple choice of baseline will go a long way toward determining the answer we propose to the question of net religious effect. If we choose the 1958 vote as a baseline, it is hard to argue that Kennedy could have made any net gains from his religion; if we choose the 1956 presidential vote, it is equally hard to argue that he lost ground on balance.

Indeed, the most cogent arguments documenting a net gain for Kennedy—those accounts which appear to express the majority opinion of election observers—use the 1956 presidential vote quite explicitly as a baseline. Yet the second Eisenhower vote seems the most bizarre choice for a baseline of any which might be suggested. The vote Eisenhower achieved in 1956 stands out as the most disproportionately Republican vote in the total series of nation-wide presidential and congressional elections stretching back to 1928. In what sense, then, is this extreme Republican swing plausible as a "normal vote?" Its sole claim seems to lie in the fact that it is the most recent presidential election. Yet other recent elections attest dramatically to the extreme abnormality of the 1956 Eisenhower vote. In the 1954 congressional elections the nation's Democrats, although they turned out less well than Republicans in minor elections, still fashioned a solid majority of votes cast. The fall of 1958 witnessed a Democratic landslide. Even in 1956, "underneath" Eisenhower's towering personal margin, a Democratic popular vote majority exceeding that which Kennedy won in 1960 appeared at other levels of the ticket. Finally, if 1956 is taken as a normal baseline and if it is true that Kennedy did score some relative personal success in 1960, how can we possibly explain the fact that other diverse Democrats on state tickets around the nation tended to win a greater proportion of popular votes than he attracted?

It seems more reasonable to suggest that Kennedy did not in any sense *exceed* the "normal" vote expectations of the generalized and anonymous Democratic candidate; rather, he fell visibly below these expectations, although nowhere nearly as far below them as Adlai Stevenson had fallen. This proposition is congruent not only with the general contours of election returns in the recent period, but with the great mass of sample survey data collected in the past decade as well. With this proposition we can draw into a coherent pattern the several surface characteristics which seemed intriguing from the simple 1960 vote totals. With it, we can locate the 1960 election more generally in the stream of American political history.

3. *The Basic Voting Strength of the Two Parties*

We have found it of great explanatory value to think of election results as reflecting the interplay of two sets of forces: stable, long-term partisan dispositions and short-term forces specific to the immediate election situation. The long-term partisan dispositions are very adequately represented by our measures of party identification. The stability of these dispositions over time is a matter of empirical record. Their partisan division over any period, as it may favor one party or the other, provides the point from which one must start to understand any specific election. This underlying division of loyalties lends itself admirably to the goal of indicating what a "normal" vote would be, aside from specific forces associated with the immediate election.

In these terms, the basic Democratic majority in the nation is scarcely subject to dispute. Year in and year out since 1952, national samples of the American electorate have indicated a preference for the Democratic party by a margin approaching 60–40. However, since no election in recent years has shown a Democratic margin of this magnitude, it would be as absurd to take a 60–40 Democratic majority for a baseline as it would be to work from the 1956 presidential vote. Actually there is little temptation to do so. Over the years large amounts of information have been accumulated on the behavior of people identifying with the two major parties, and it is clear that the realistic voting strength of the Democrats—and this is the sort of baseline which interests us—falls well short of a 60–40 majority. The fact that heavy Democratic majorities in the South are concealed by low voting turnout is but one factor which reduces realistic Democratic strength. Outside the South, as well, Democrats under the same conditions of short-term stimulation are less likely to vote than Republicans.

It is possible to manipulate the data in such a fashion as to take into account all of the significant discrepancies between nominal party identification and realistic voting strength. We thereby arrive at a picture of the vote division which could be expected in the normal presidential election, if short-term forces associated with the election favored neither party in particular, but stood at an equilibrium. In such circumstances, we would expect a Democratic proportion of the two-party popular vote to fall in the vicinity of 53–54 per cent. Outside of the South, such a vote would fall short of a 50–50 split with the Republicans; within the South there would be a strong Democratic majority exceeding a 2-to-1 division.

Short-term forces associated with a specific election may, according to their net partisan strength, send the actual vote in that election deviating to one side or the other of the equilibrium point. In 1952 and 1956 the popularity of Eisenhower constituted one such force, and this force was strongly pro-Republican. The distortions produced in the behaviors of party identifiers of different types have now become familiar. If the net partisan force is strong, as in 1956, identifiers of the favored party vote almost *en bloc*, without defection. The small group of "independents" who do not commit themselves to either party divide very disproportionately in favor of the advantaged party, instead of dividing their vote equally as in the equilibrium case. And members of the disfavored party defect in relatively large numbers, as Democrats did in 1956. A useful description of any specific election, then, is an account of the short-term forces which have introduced these strains across the distribution of party identification.

In such a description, the existing division of deeper party loyalties is taken for granted. Its current character is not to be explained by the immediate political situation. The point is made most clearly by the 1960 election. The fact that the Democrats enjoyed a standing majority was in no way a consequence of the personal duel between Kennedy and Nixon, for it was a majority created long before either candidate became salient as a national political figure, and long before most of the campaign "issues" of 1960 had taken shape. In this perspective, then, we can consider some of the forces which drew the 1960 vote away from its equilibrium state.

4. *Short-term Forces in the 1960 Election*

Popular vote tallies show that Kennedy received 49.8 per cent of the two-party vote outside of the South, and 51.2 per cent of the popular vote cast in the South. The vote outside the South is almost 1 per cent more Democratic than our equilibrium estimates for this part of the nation. In the South, however, the Democratic deficit relative to the same baseline approaches 17 per cent. Naturally, some short-term forces may balance out so that no net advantage accrues to either party. But the comparisons between our baselines and the 1960 vote suggest that we should find some short-term forces which gave a very slight net advantage to Kennedy outside of the South, and yet which penalized him heavily within the South.

As in all elections that attract a wide degree of public attention, a number of short-term forces were certainly at work in 1960. A comprehensive assessment of these must await further analysis. However, there can be little doubt that the religious issue was the strongest single factor overlaid on basic partisan loyalties in the 1960 election, and we have focused most of our initial analyses in this area. Fortunately we know a great deal about the "normal" voting behavior within different religious categories, and can use this knowledge to provide baselines which aid in estimating the net effect of Kennedy's Catholicism upon his candidacy.

The Catholic Vote. As we have observed, the vote division among Catholics soared from a 50–50 split in the two Eisenhower contests to an 80–20 majority in the 1960 presidential vote. However, it is hard to attribute all of this increment simply to the Kennedy candidacy. In the 1958 election, when there were mild short-term economic forces favoring the Democratic party, the vote among Catholics went well over 70 per cent in that direction. Even since our measurements of party identification began in 1952, only a small minority—less than 20 per cent—of Catholics in the nation have considered themselves as Republicans, although a fair portion have typically styled themselves as "Independents." Most of what attracted attention as a Republican trend among Catholics during the 1950's finds little support in our data, at least as a trend peculiar to Catholics. To be sure, many Democratic Catholics defected to vote for Eisenhower in 1952 and 1956. So did many Democratic Protestants. As a matter of fact, the defection rate among Democratic Catholics in 1952 was very slightly less than among Democratic Protestants, and in 1956 was very slightly more. In neither case do the differences exceed sampling error. There is some long-term evidence of a faint and slow erosion in the Catholic Democratic vote; but this has been proceeding at such a glacial pace that the 1956–1960 vote trends which we are treating here dwarf it completely. There is no reason to believe that the short-term personal "pull" exerted on Democrats generally by Eisenhower had a different strength for Catholics than for Protestants. The myths that have arisen to this effect seem to be primarily illusions stemming from the large proportion of Democrats who are Catholics. Their loss was painful in the two Eisenhower votes. But they were at the outset, and remained up to the first glimmer of the Kennedy candidacy, a strongly Democratic group.

We may specify this "normal" Democratic strength among Catholics by applying the same operations for Catholics alone that we have employed for the electorate as a whole. In the equilibrium case, it turns out that one would expect at least a 63 per cent Democratic margin among Catholics. The difference between 63 per cent and the 80 per cent which Kennedy achieved can provisionally be taken as an estimate of the increment in Democratic votes among Catholics above that which the normal, Protestant Democratic presidential candidate could have expected.

We can readily translate this 17 per cent vote gain into proportions of the total 1960 vote, taking into account levels of Catholic turnout and the like. On such grounds, it appears that Kennedy won a vote bonus from Catholics amounting to about 4 per cent of the national two-party popular vote. This increment is, of course, very unequally divided between the South and the rest of the nation, owing simply to the sparse Catholic population in the South. Within the 1960 non-Southern electorate, Kennedy's net gain from the Catholic increment amounts to better than 5 per cent of the two-party vote. The same rate of gain represents less than 1 per cent of the Southern popular vote.

The Anti-Catholic Vote. Respondents talked to our interviewers with remarkable freedom about the Catholic factor during the fall of 1960. This is not to say that all respondents referred to it as a problem. There were even signs that some Protestant respondents were struggling to avoid mention of it although it was a matter of concern. Nonetheless, nearly 40 per cent of the sample voluntarily introduced the subject before any direct probing on our part in the early stages of the pre-election questionnaire. Since this figure certainly understates the proportion of the population for whom religion was a salient concern in 1960, it testifies rather eloquently to the importance of the factor in conscious political motivations during the fall campaign.

These discussions of the Catholic question, volunteered by our respondents, will, in time, provide more incisive descriptions of the short-term anti-Catholic forces important in the election. Our interest here, however, is to estimate the magnitude of anti-Catholic voting in terms of otherwise Democratic votes which Kennedy lost. In such an enterprise, our material on the political backgrounds of our respondents is most useful.

We focus, therefore, upon the simple rates of defection to Nixon among Protestants who were identified in 1960 with the Democratic party. As Figure 1 shows, this defection rate is strongly correlated with regularity of attendance at a Protestant church. Protestant Democrats who, by self-description, never attend church, and hence are not likely to have much identification with it, defected to Nixon only at a rate of 6 per cent. This rate, incidentally, is just about the "normal" defection rate which we would predict for both parties in the equilibrium case: it represents the scattered defections which occur for entirely idiosyncratic reasons in any election. Therefore, for Democrats who were nominal Protestants but outside the psychological orbit of their church, the short-term religious force set up by a Catholic candidacy had no visible impact. However, as soon as there is some evidence of identification with a Protestant church, the defection rate rises rapidly.

Although Protestant Independents are not included in Figure 1, they show the same gradient at a different level of the two-party vote division. The few Protestant Independents not attending church split close to the theoretically-expected 50–50 point. Then the Nixon vote rises to 61 per cent in the "seldom" category; to 72 per cent for the "often" category; and to 83 per cent for the Protestant Independents attending church regularly. This increment of Republican votes above the "normal" 50–50 division for Independents matches remarkably the increment of Republican votes above the "normal" figure of 6 per cent in the case of the Democrats.

We customarily find in our data certain substantial correlations between church attendance and political behavior. The correlation between church attendance and vote among Protestant Democrats and Independents is not, however, one of these. The strong

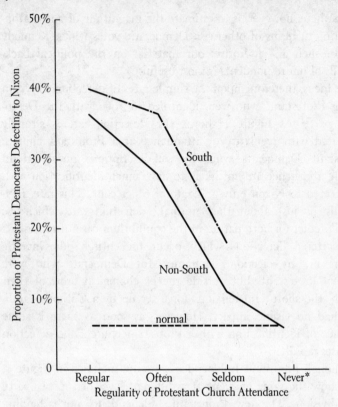

The number of Protestant Democrats who "never" attend church in the South is too small for inclusion.

Figure 1.
Defections to Nixon among Protestant
Democrats as a Function of Church Attendance.

associations seem linked in an obvious way to the 1960 election. We need not assume, of course, that each defection pictured here represents a sermon from the pulpit and an obedient member of the congregation. Social science theory assures us that whether through sermons, informal communication or a private sense of reserve toward Catholicism, the faithful Protestant would react more negatively to the presidential candidacy of a Catholic than would more indifferent Protestants. It remains notable, however, that Democrats who were at the same time regular Protestants defected to Nixon at rates far exceeding those which Eisenhower had attracted in 1952 or 1956.

We may use Figure 1, then, as a tool to estimate the magnitude of the anti-Catholic vote. It is easily argued that the area below the dotted line in Figure 1 represents "normal" defections within each category of church attendance, and that the votes represented by the triangle above the dotted line are votes which Kennedy lost on religious grounds. It is then a simple mechanical matter to convert this triangle into proportions of the popular vote for South and non-South.

On the surface, Figure 1 seems to say that the impact of the religious factor was very nearly the same, North and South, for the Southern gradient of defections is only slightly higher than the non-Southern gradient. If we think of the impact of short-term forces *on individuals* as a function of their party and religious loyalties, this conclusion is proper. Indeed, as we consider in later analyses the impact by different types of Protestantism, it may well be that the character of the impact will show no remaining regional difference whatever. However, to construe Figure 1 as suggesting that the *magnitude* of the anti-Catholic effect was about the same in votes cast in North and South is quite improper. The differences between the regions turn out to be substantial.

We must consider first that less than two-thirds of the active non-Southern electorate is Protestant, whereas within the South the electorate is almost completely (95 per cent) Protestant. Secondly, Protestants are more faithful church-goers in the South than outside it. Quite specifically, we find that over half of the Southern presidential vote is cast by Protestants who go to church regularly, whereas less than 20 per cent of the vote outside the South comes from regular, church-going Protestants. Finally, of the minority outside the South who are Protestant and attend church regularly, only a small proportion are Democratic identifiers: Republicans clearly predominate in this category. In the South, the situation is reversed, with regular Protestants being far more often than not Democratic identifiers.

This conjunction of regional differences means that the defecting votes represented in Figure 1 are of vastly different sizes, South and non-South. It turns out that outside the South regular, church-going Protestants who are Democrats cast only about 5 per cent of the total non-Southern vote. Within the South, however, regular church-going Protestants who are Democrats contributed over 35 per cent of the total Southern vote. Thus it is that the anti-Catholic impact in the South turns out to involve a much larger share of the votes than elsewhere. The anti-Catholic vote in the South fulfills our search for a short-term force of strong net Republican strength in that region.

Summing up these apparent anti-Catholic votes as proportions of the total vote in the South, the non-South, and the nation as a whole, we can compare them with our estimations of the bonuses received by Kennedy from Catholics. Table 2 shows the balance sheet.

There is every reason to believe that these preliminary estimates under-estimate the importance of religion in the 1960 vote and, in particular, under-estimate the magnitude of the anti-Catholic vote. We have at no point taken account, for example, of the possibility that certain Republican identifiers, exposed to short-term forces which would normally have produced defections to the Democrats, may have been inhibited from such defection by Kennedy's Catholicism. In the midwest there were signs of a "farm revolt" favoring the Democrats which failed to materialize in the presidential balloting. At lower levels on farm belt tickets one finds that major Democratic candidates consistently surpassed "normal" Democratic expectations. Yet Kennedy seems to have been peculiarly insulated from any of this profit-taking: in these areas he lagged behind other major Democrats by a rather consistent 5 per cent. It is difficult not to believe that at lower levels of office net short-term forces were favoring the Democrats, and

Republican identifiers were defecting at unusual rates. Analyses may show that religion was a primary force inhibiting such defections at the presidential level.

Other early glimpses of our data also suggest the estimates of anti-Catholicism in Table 2 are conservative. It is likely that a number of non-religious short-term forces generated by the campaign itself were favorable to Kennedy on balance. As a number of other surveys reported, Nixon held a substantial lead over Kennedy in the early stages. At the outset, Kennedy was little known to the public: he stood primarily as the Democratic candidate and a Catholic. As the campaign went on, other and non-religious aspects of the Kennedy image filled in, and the public

Table 2
Offsetting Effects of the Catholic Issue,
1960 Democratic Presidential Vote

Area	% of 2-party vote in area
Outside the South, Kennedy's "unexpected" . . .	
Gains from Catholics	5.2%
Losses from Protestant Democrats and Independents	−3.6
Net	+1.6%
Inside the South, Kennedy's "unexpected" . . .	
Gains from Catholics	0.7%
Losses from Protestant Democrats and Independents	−17.2
Net	−16.5%
For the nation as a whole, Kennedy's "unexpected" . . .	
Gains from Catholics	4.3%
Losses from Protestant Democrats and Independents	−6.5
Net	−2.2%

impression was usually positive. In this crucial shift in sentiment during the campaign, the television debates probably played an important role. Although there were Democrats who reacted warmly to Nixon's performance, our materials show quite strikingly that the net response to the debates favored Kennedy, as has been commonly supposed. In case studies, a reading of interviews has already turned up numerous Protestants of varying partisanship who were much more impressed by Kennedy as a candidate than by Nixon, yet who could not bring themselves to vote for a Catholic. In the measure that Kennedy's attractiveness as a candidate exceeded Nixon's and other short-term forces apart from religion were favoring the Democrats, the total popular vote should have been drawn to the Democratic side of the equilibrium point. The fact that it stayed instead on the Republican side may represent further damaging effects of religion for Kennedy.

Refined analyses at a later date will permit us to estimate more adequately the role which all the major motivational factors, including religion, played in the 1960 outcome. For the moment, however, it is impressive the degree to which the surface characteristics of the 1960 election become intelligible even when viewed simply as the result of an "ancient" and enduring division of partisan loyalties overlaid by a short-term cross-current of religious motivation.

Normally we would expect a national vote falling as close to its equilibrium point as the 1960 case to be a relatively low-turnout election. That is, a vote near the equilibrium point suggests either weak short-term forces or else a balance of stronger forces creating conflict in individuals and thereby lowering their motivation to vote. It is rare that forces strong enough to compel indifferent citizens to come out and vote do not also favor one party over the other quite categorically.

In 1960, however, the motivational picture underlying the vote was somewhat different, and can best be understood by separating the Protestant South from the rest of the nation. In the South, of course, a strong and unidirectional short-term force was reflected in a sharp departure from equilibrium and a surge in turnout, as fits normal expectations. What is abnormal is that this strong Republican short-term force raised motivation in a Democratic preserve, rather than diluting it through conflict. It is likely that conflict *was* created, especially where Democratic partisanship was strong. "Strong" Democrats in our sample made virtually no contribution to the 1960 rise in Southern turnout. The increase came from weaker Democrats, whose participation increased so radically over 1952 and 1956 that their turnout even surpassed that of strong Democrats in very exceptional fashion. For these voters, it seems likely that such forces as anti-Catholic feelings rapidly overcame relatively weak party loyalties and left strong motivation to turn out.

While turnout elsewhere did not show the same remarkable surge which appeared in the South, it remained at the fairly high level characteristic of the 1952 and 1956 elections, despite a partisan division of the vote near the regional equilibrium point. Strong balancing forces appear to have been in operation which did not create much conflict within individuals. The reason is clear: to the degree that religious motivations were engaged, forces were conflicting between groups rather than within individuals. Non-Southern Catholics, predominantly Democratic, were exposed to strong unidirectional short-term forces motivating them to get out and vote for Kennedy. Non-Southern Protestants, predominantly Republican, were exposed to contrary forces, at least where Protestant religious fidelity was strong. Thus the vote fell near the equilibrium point, but there was rather high turnout as well.

The other surface characteristics of the election are equally intelligible in these terms. Despite his position as majority candidate, Kennedy very nearly lost and tended to run behind his ticket. In the northeast, where concentrations of Catholics are greatest, his relation to the rest of the ticket was not generally unfavorable. The penalty he suffered becomes visible and consistent in the Midwest, where Catholics are fewer and Protestant church attendance is more regular. In the South, and for the same reasons, the differences between the Kennedy vote and that of other Democrats become large indeed. Everywhere, if one compares 1956 vote statistics with 1960 statistics, the course of political change is closely associated with the religious composition of voting units.

There was some relief even outside the more committed Democratic circles when the Kennedy victory, slight though it was, demonstrated that a Catholic was not in practice barred from the White House. Yet it would be naive to suppose that a Catholic candidate no longer suffers any initial disadvantage before the American electorate as a result of his creed. Not only did Kennedy possess a type of personal appeal which the television debates permitted him to exploit in unusual measure, but he was also the candidate of a party enjoying a fundamental majority in the land. Even the combination of these circumstances was barely sufficient to give him a popular vote victory. Lacking such a strong underlying majority, which Al Smith most certainly lacked in 1928, it is doubtful that the most attractive of Catholic presidential candidates in 1960 would have had much chance of success. It remains to be seen how far the experience of a Catholic president may diminish the disadvantage another time.

5. *The 1960 Election in Historical Perspective*

In a publication which appeared a few months prior to the 1960 elections we posed the question of "how long a party can hope to hold the White House if it does not have a majority of the party-identified electorate." We had identified the two Eisenhower victories as "deviating elections," in which short-term forces had brought about the defeat of the majority party. We had not found any evidence in our 1952 or 1956 studies that these short-term forces were producing any significant realignment in the basic partisan commitments of the electorate. We felt that unless such a realignment did occur, "the minority party [could] not hope to continue its tenure in office over a very extended period."

We now know that the eight-year Eisenhower period ended

with no basic change in the proportions of the public who identify themselves as Republican, Democrat, or Independent. If there had been an opportunity in 1952 for the Republican party to re-win the majority status it had held prior to 1932, it failed to capitalize on it. The Democratic party remained the majority party and the 1960 election returned it to the presidency. It was, to extend the nomenclature of our earlier publication, a "rein-stating" election, one in which the party enjoying a majority of party identifiers returns to power. The 1960 election was remark-able not in the fact that the majority party was reinstated but that its return to power was accomplished by such a narrow margin. We had recognized the possibility that "the unfolding of national and international events and the appearance of new political figures" might swing the vote away from its natural equilibrium. We now see that such a deflection did occur and that it very nearly cost the majority party the election.

It may be argued that the deficit the Democratic presidential candidate suffered from his normal expectation did not derive from damaging circumstances which were specific to the 1960 election but from a progressive weakening in the willingness of some Democratic partisans to support their ticket at the presiden-tial level. It has been suggested that some voters who consider themselves to be Democrats and customarily favor Democratic candidates at the lower levels of office may have come during the Eisenhower period to have a perverse interest in favoring Republi-can candidates for president, either because of notions of party balance in government, because of local considerations in their states, or simply out of admiration for Eisenhower.

Important differences no doubt exist between voting at the presidential level and voting for a congressman. Our studies have shown, for example, that the popular vote for lesser offices is a more party-determined vote than the vote for president and varies around the normal equilibrium vote figure within a much narrower range than does the presidential vote. However, the supposition that Kennedy failed to win a normal Democratic majority because of a cadre of Democrats who are covertly Republican in their presidential voting is not supported by our data.

Table 1 has already demonstrated that the over-all shift in partisanship of the vote between 1956 and 1960 cannot be explained as a simple unilateral movement of erstwhile Eisenhower Democrats. The election did not depend, as was often supposed, upon the number of Eisenhower Democrats whom Nixon could retain as "covert Republicans." Our panel materials show that if Nixon had been forced to depend only upon the Eisenhower Democrats whom he retained, he would have suffered a convincing 54-46 defeat, assuming that other Democrats had continued to vote for Kennedy. He did not suffer such a defeat because he drew a new stream of Democratic defections nearly sufficient to put him in the White House.

The patterns of short-term forces in the 1960 election were independent of those shaping the 1956 election, then, in the sense that they affected a new set of people, on new grounds. There were Democrats susceptible to Eisenhower in 1956; there were Democrats sensitive to religion in 1960: the two sets of people do not intersect much more than one would expect by chance. In short, there is little evidence that the two Eisenhower elections had created a set of Democrats peculiarly disposed to vote for a Republican presidential candidate.

Analysis of our 1960 data is not sufficiently complete to enable us to describe the entire pattern of forces to which the electorate was reacting on Election Day. We do not know, for example, what the partisan impact of international affairs, which had favored the Republican candidate so strongly in the preceding two elections, was in the 1960 election. We do not know the effect of the Negro discrimination issues. We do not know in detail as yet how the personal attributes of the major candidates, other than their religious affiliations, were evaluated by the public. We feel confident, however, that we will not find any short-term force which moved as large a fraction of the 1960 electorate as did the issue of a Catholic president. This was the major cause of the net departure of the vote totals from the division which the comparative underlying strength of the two parties in 1960 would have led us to expect. After two consecutive "deviating" elections won at a presidential level by the minority party, the 1960 election reinstated the Democratic party. But short-term forces generated by the immediate 1960 situation once again favored the Republicans on balance, and the difference in votes which separated this "reinstating election" from a third "deviating election" was slight indeed.

Lonesome Lyndon

The Wrong Man from the Wrong Place at the Wrong Time

by Eric F. Goldman

The White House years of Lyndon B. Johnson (1963–1969) began in national tragedy, shifted quickly to national euphoria, and ended in national crisis. On the domestic front, Johnson's presidency produced more significant federally sponsored change in American society than any administration since Franklin Roosevelt's.

Johnson had earned his political spurs as a young New Dealer in the National Youth Administration, then as a pro-Roosevelt Texas congressman. He entered the Senate during the Truman administration, became its Democratic leader early in the Eisenhower years, and played a dominant and generally conservative role in Senate policy-making throughout the 1950's. An unsuccessful candidate for the 1960 Democratic nomination, he startled the nation by agreeing to become John Kennedy's running-mate. After the election Johnson chafed noticeably in the reduced role of Vice President for nearly three years. Then Kennedy's assassination in November 1963 gave him the top job.

Johnson's first months as President were occupied necessarily with the business of replacing Kennedy men with his own, and in formulating presidential goals in foreign and domestic policy. The

Kennedy-Johnson transition, on balance, took place less rancorously and with more effective continuity that the shift to a Truman administration after FDR's death.

But mid-1964 a Kennedy faction, "Camelot"-in-exile, had resurfaced in Washington, rallying around the indeterminate yet high-level ambitions of Attorney-General Robert F. Kennedy. Johnson rejected Kennedy, however, and made Hubert H. Humphrey, a long-time Senate colleague, but a liberal, the vice-presidential candidate in 1964. LBJ criss-crossed the country denouncing Republican Barry Goldwater as a trigger-happy rightwinger who might stumble into an unrestricted land war in Vietnam and perhaps beyond that, into nuclear catastrophe. Bolstered by defections among prominent Republican liberals who recoiled from Goldwater, Johnson proposed major advances in health care for the aged, federal aid to education, civil rights legislation, and assistance to the nation's hard-pressed cities—a virtual "war on poverty" that he claimed would produce a "Great Society."

Johnson won the greatest electoral sweep in American history, defeating Goldwater by sixteen million votes, 43 million to 27 million. Goldwater, on his program of uncompromising, doctrinaire conservatism and opposition to civil rights legislation, carried only his home state of Arizona and five others, all in the Deep South. Even more significant than Johnson's 61.1 per cent of the major party vote was the extraordinary length of his presidential coattails; Democrats won two-to-one majorities in both houses of Congress.

Within two years, these congressional majorities passed substantial portions of the "Great Society" program. Before the 1966 congressional elections, Democrats, aided by liberal Republican votes, had passed a major health program for the aged (Medicare); a billion-dollar aid-to-education measure; an even larger anti-poverty program; major public housing and public works legislation; a strong Civil Rights Act that finally provided federal registrars to protect Negro voters in the South; legislation prohibiting racial discrimination in public housing; rent supplements for low-income families; a "model cities" program appropriating federal funds for the nation's under-financed urban areas; and other significant pieces of reform legislation.

In 1966, however, a conservative mood set in, as voters sent 47 more Republicans to the House and 4 more to the Senate, making even the President's strongest congressional supporters leery of further social experiments. By that time riots in the black ghettoes of Northern and Western cities had carved inroads into public support for additional federal civil rights action, and American escalation in Vietnam had produced further bloodshed but no victory. Assailed with increasing ferocity by both conservatives and left-liberals, especially the latter, Johnson's dream of a liberal-moderate coalition supporting a "politics of consensus" evaporated. His once-unassailable popularity had plummeted by 1968. The President announced his decision not to run again in a dramatic March 1968 television speech. The bitter anti-administration primary fights between Eugene McCarthy and Robert Kennedy and Kennedy's June assassination were accompanied by George Wallace's third-party defection, and climaxed by massive demonstrations and police violence at the 1968 Chicago Democratic Convention.

The remnants of Johnson's "Great Society" coalition fought the ensuing campaign in a state of apathetic shock against Richard Nixon's well-organized, well-financed Republican drive. Nixon's victory with a plurality of popular votes over Hubert Humphrey and George Wallace's "American Independents" (a flag-waving label thinly disguising his anti-black party) sealed the demise of Lyndon Johnson's bitter tenure as a national leader. Never had a ruling political party's fortunes been brought so low so quickly and by so few. Eric Goldman, a historian of American reform, who spent several unhappy years as a Johnson adviser, analyzes below "the tragedy of Lyndon Johnson."

❧ Lyndon Johnson is about to leave the White House with every appearance of a thoroughly repudiated President. Since Herbert Hoover rode down Pennsylvania Avenue on a cold day

From the *New York Times Magazine*, January 5, 1969. Copyright © 1969 by Eric F. Goldman, adapted from the book *The Tragedy of Lyndon Johnson* published by Afred A. Knopf.

in 1933, no President has ended his tenure with so few hosannas and so widespread a sense of good riddance.

The story, it seems, is simple: the accident of Dallas made Lyndon Johnson President, and he failed to measure up. So it appears—but in the field of evaluating Presidents, appearances can be sharply deceiving. The cardinal rule for any historian venturing into it is to remember that he is a historian, not History, and that no powers of divination have been bestowed upon him by his profession or even by his abounding faith in his own judgment. Yet I think it should be suggested, and with emphasis, that after the furies of the sixties are laid to rest, Lyndon Johnson may well rank a good deal above where the national mood would now place him.

Certainly in past instances the public esteem of a President during his period in office has borne no particular relationship to future judgment. In 1962, the late historian Arthur M. Schlesinger, Sr., asked 75 well-known scholars of American history to rate the Chief Executives up to John Kennedy. The preponderant opinion called five Presidents "great" in this order: Abraham Lincoln, George Washington, Franklin Roosevelt, Woodrow Wilson and Thomas Jefferson. Again in order, it placed in the "near-great" category Andrew Jackson, Theodore Roosevelt, James Polk, Harry Truman, John Adams and Grover Cleveland. The historians categorized as failures Ulysses Grant and Warren Harding. Popular sentiment in 1962 probably would have gone along with most of these judgments. But of the 11 men called "great" or "near-great," five—Jefferson, Lincoln, T.R., F.D.R. and Truman—were subject to widespread and sustained abuse during their incumbencies. Woodrow Wilson was also roundly repudiated, first by the Senate and then by the voters, on the issue of his most cherished program, the League of Nations. Harry Truman, a man reviled during much of his Presidency, went through an almost identical withdrawal ceremony just 16 years before Lyndon Johnson. Then, while still living, he emerged a favorite of the historians and something of a folk hero. The two Chief Executives deemed failures by a later generation, Ulysses Grant and Warren Harding, were enormously popular during their Presidencies. It is rarely remembered that when the Harding funeral train crossed the United States, it called forth a grief, respect and affection fully equal to, if not exceeding, the public reaction to the death of Abraham Lincoln.

The question of a President's just place in history is complicated not only by shifts in opinion as time passes but by the inherent difficulties of the assessment process. Schlesinger included among the men to whom he sent his 1962 questionnaire a sometime historian, President John Kennedy. J.F.K. was interested, started to fill out the ballot then stopped. "How the hell can you tell?" he remarked. "Only the President himself can know what his real pressures and his real alternatives are. If you don't know that, how can you judge performance?" Historian-President John Kennedy's ultimate test seemed to be concrete achievements. This was an intriguing commentary on the problem of judging Presidents from a Chief Executive who, at least in domestic affairs during his short tenure, was far more notable as an opinion builder than as an achiever of specific legislation.

Of course, central to any long-range judgment of the Johnson Administration is the President's decision to commit American combat forces in the Vietnam war. I happen to be among those who became convinced that the action was a grave mistake; and if this assessment—which seems to be that of so many Americans in 1969—holds, the Vietnam war will certainly prove a heavy drag on the L.B.J. reputation. Just how heavy is quite a different matter. Other Presidents who are today called great or near-great made moves in foreign policy which are now considered serious errors. But with the pasage of the years, the specific was submerged in the general memory of the man. If President Johnson or his successor can bring the Vietnam war to an end without much further damage, in time a kindly haze may obscure the pointless clomp of American soldiers across a defenseless civilization, what amounts to an American defeat, even napalm.

This is the more possible because the future might emphasize that, in a sense, L.B.J. inherited the Vietnam commitment. Three previous Chief Executives had ordered American noncombat involvement in the area. At least two of these Presidents, Eisenhower and Kennedy, believed that preventing South Vietnam from coming under Communist rule was important to American national security. None faced a situation in which the region appeared about to fall, and consequently none had to decide whether preventing a Communist takeover was important enough to justify United States entrance into the fighting war. Lyndon Johnson was forced to make that judgment, and another generation may decide that he committed an error prepared for by his predecessors and one which either President Eisenhower or President Kennedy might have made.

And always there is the possibility which many anti-L.B.J. commentators of the nineteen-sixties simply refuse to entertain: the Vietnam intervention might not have been a mistake at all. President Johnson could be right when he says, let the future decide. A Communist victory in South Vietnam, he was convinced, would be followed by a gradual fall of much of Asia to Communism, the domination of the huge region by a hostile and potentially powerful China and—because China had not been warned by a strong American stand—by ultimate war between China and the United States. If a successor to President Johnson should accept a compromise peace that was followed by such a chain of developments, Lyndon Johnson would be more than forgiven; he would emerge a figure of Churchillian stature, a wise, courageous voice crying out in a crowd of myopic and timid men.

L.B.J.'s place in the long sweep of American domestic affairs can be assessed with much more assurance. Three times in the twentieth century the United States has faced up to the harsh facts of an industrializing, urbanizing civilization—at the beginning of the century, under Theodore Roosevelt and Woodrow Wilson; after the crash of 1929, under Franklin Roosevelt; and then, slowly, in the period following World War II.

The thirties were *sui generis*. The urgency was unique; so too was the public mood. The situations in the early nineteen-hundreds and after World War II were much more alike. In both instances, there was little sense that the country was falling apart. National opinion, jabbed by a zealous left and troubled by the arguments of a dogged right, was gradually forming around the proposition that the general population was being given too little access to economic and social opportunity. More laws were needed; the President ought to lead Congress in getting them.

At the start of the century Theodore Roosevelt bounded into the White House, caught up the strands of dissidence, wove them into an attractive pattern. "Teddy," the journalist William Allen White observed, "was reform in a derby, the gayest, cockiest, most fashionable derby you ever saw." T.R. moved few bills through Congress, but he prepared the way for Woodrow Wilson, who, without derby or gaiety, had the roused public sentiment, the votes in Congress and the Covenanter certitudes to grind the bills through the House and the Senate.

After World War II, the process began all over again. The opinion kept building, the opposition kept fighting and another generation of leaders prepared the way for another wave of action. Harry Truman, his expletives and vetoes poised, fought off a Congress that yearned to turn back. Dwight Eisenhower, before he drifted into his second somnolent term, led the Republican party into some accommodation with the day. John Kennedy appeared, a second Theodore Roosevelt, associating social change with vigor and glamour and the mischievous cocked eye, legislating little but educating many. Then Lyndon Johnson, the cloakroom operator, reenacted the presbyter-professor Woodrow Wilson. He, too, seized the moment to execute the decade's needs—seized it so firmly and wrung it so hard that he built a monument to himself as big as all Texas in that 1965 Congress, which wrote into law just about everything that the public had decided was long past due.

And all the while, breaking out now and again, however explained or explained away, came the voice which spoke of something far removed from cloakroom chicanery, which caught the age-old American insistence that somehow, by some effort of hardheadedness and decency, ordinary men and women can be enabled to live in greater comfort and joy and to walk in the tonic air of self-respect. The voice was there. . . .

. . . when L.B.J., told by a visitor that he was rushing Congress, replied, "An old man on the Hill said to me a long time ago that there are some Administrations that do and some that don't. This one is gonna do";

. . . when he signed an education bill, a mist across his cratered face, and muttered: "Not enough, not nearly enough. But I'm proud, damned proud, to have got this much. Education—that's what's needed, and that's what every kid ought to get, as much of it as he can take, right up to his neck";

. . . when he told a group of corporation executives: "I have thought a great deal the last few days—I missed being an elevator boy by just about that much, when my mother reached up and made me go back to school after laying out for two years. When you're dealing with these [Negro] people, in your company, or in your firm, or in your business, just remember it's some daughter's father, or some boy's mother, or someone's sister, or somebody's brother that you are dealing with. And except for the grace of God, it might be you. And think how you would like it if you lived in a land where you could not go to school with your fellow Americans, where you could not work alongside of them, where you could travel from Texas to Washington, across many states, and not be able to go to the bathroom without hiding in a thicket or dodging behind a culvert. Ask yourself how you would feel";

. . . and when, addressing a White House Conference on Natural Beauty, he shoved aside his prepared text and spoke his memories of boyhood walks: ". . . those hills, and those fields, and the river were the only world that I really had in those years. . . . We were not a wealthy family, but this was my rich inheritance. All my life I have drawn strength, and something more, from those Texas hills. Sometimes, in the highest councils of the nation, in this house, I sit back and I can almost feel that rough, unyielding, sticky clay soil between my toes, and it stirs memories that often give me comfort and sometimes give me a pretty firm purpose.

"But not all the boys in America had the privilege to grow up in a wide and open country. We can give them something, and we are going to. We can let each of them feel a little of what the first settlers must have felt, as they stood there before the majesty of our great land."

History has been generous, and should be, to Presidents who have talked like that and taken action to turn the talk into laws. Probably history will be generous—and it should be—to Lyndon Johnson.

Probably—but all this is in the murky realm of speculation. There remains a hard, clear fact. Lyndon Johnson has served his whole five years in the White House with little genuine hold on the thinking or on the emotions of the American people.

What went so wrong? Obviously, he has been an able, hard-working Chief Executive, eager to serve the interests of the mass of the population, more than eager to win their camaraderie. He tried desperately hard, and he delivered in important respects. Lyndon Johnson not only put through a powerhouse program of legislation. He had taken over the Presidency at a moment of national emotional disarray and conducted a transition that is considered by many experts the most skillful the United States has ever known. He went on to preside over a country marked by that condition which so often has been the prime test of the public's attitude toward an Administration—an America that was generally prosperous, in fact more prosperous than any society in all of man's 5,000 years of recorded history.

White House aides kept telling President Johnson that the whole source of the public's disaffection was what the aides called his "courageous" stand on Vietnam. Well before I resigned from the White House staff, I became accustomed to the litany. Any war creates frustration and resentment, he was told, and discontent is always directed at the leader. Abraham Lincoln himself was assailed with unbridled vehemence. Modern limited wars, with their especially frustrating quality, exacerbate these public feelings.

Yet L.B.J.'s unpopularity cannot be so totally attributed to the Vietnam war. Actually, American wars have generally made of the Commander in Chief a rallying point for support and enthusiasm. Moreover, as early as 1965—before his foreign policy became a major divisive issue and when L.B.J. was at the height of his successes—a widespread distaste for him was plain. Many Americans have been snappish about Lyndon Johnson not so much because they were positive he was wrong on Vietnam but because they believed he was the kind of man who was quite capable of making a bad mistake and, having made it, of not admitting it or moving to correct it.

During the campaign of 1964, when the evidence indicated both that President Johnson would win easily and that the trend was as much anti-Goldwater as pro-Johnson, Lyndon Johnson would remark querulously to visitors, "Why don't people like me?" One guest, too old to be concerned about preferment by the White House and enough of a Washington character to get away with irreverence, answered the question. He said, "Because, Mr. President, you are not a very likable man." Bald as it was, this statement expressed a major part of L.B.J.'s problem with the American people. The fact that he was not a very likable man could not be concealed from the public despite all the arduous efforts of his friends and aides, myself included, who wanted so much to believe otherwise and who did their damnedest to present him in a way that would convince themselves and the country.

Lyndon Johnson may have risen from Johnson City to being the head of a family he cherished, a multimillionaire and the leader of the free world, but he had not risen above something nagging inside him. All the way to the top, and especially at the top, he was cumulatively, combatively insecure. Having started out as the apple of his mother's eye, overloved, overprotected and over-praised, he was thoroughly unprepared for a world that did not view him in such a glow. In his youth he was keenly sensitive to the fact that the Johnsons were not among the leading families of the area. He himself was gawky and no great charmer.

Maturing in an action-worshiping environment, it took him a long time to realize the high value of one resource he had in abundance: brains. By then, the asset was denigrated even in his own eyes by the low status of his schooling (a social abyss existed between his alma mater, Southwest Texas State Teachers College, and the University of Texas). And almost as soon as his career was really started, he had to function in large measure not amid the congenial ways of Texas but in the sharply different atmosphere of Washington.

Of course, the L.B.J. genes dictated that he would have had many of his personal characteristics if he had been born a graceful son of a Brahmin family. But a sense of insecurity was so thoroughly woven into the man by external circumstances that it brought to a high state of development his innate tendencies. Facing a world that he thought looked down on him, he sought constantly to prove, to himself and to it, that he could beat it. Dubious whether people liked him, he pleaded, clawed and maneuvered to have them love him. Desperately seeking proof of loyalty—from friends, aides and the public—he pushed his demand for loyalty close to the point where it meant obeisance. He was ready to give anything—his own driving efforts, sentiment, preferment for their wishes—to hold this loyalty, anything except what people wanted and what his lurking suspicion of them held back, the gift of his genuine self.

Toward the longtime members of his entourage, L.B.J. could be considerate and more than considerate. One aide who found himself overwhelmed by family medical expenses received a substantial financial gift from "a friend"; a person working with the President before a meal—be he a high official or a secretary who had been taking dictation—might be invited to eat with the family. But all the while Lyndon Johnson not only felt it necessary to keep testing the devotion of his most veteran assistants but to assert his mastery in scenes of demeaning tongue-lashing and by manipulating them with extremes of the carrot-and-stick technique. An aide would go along for some time, receiving extravagant praise. Then, for no particular reason, he was excommunicated, his work rejected almost *in toto* and the man himself scarcely spoken to. Just as suddenly, he would be reinstated, and someone else given the treatment.

The insecurity mounted in proportion as President Johnson was removed from familiar situations and types of people. In the spring of 1964, he approved a suggestion that he lunch with a group of writers who had distinguished themselves by their books on Presidents or the Presidency. L.B.J. was at a high point in his administration; his polls were soaring, his bills were rolling through Congress, he had just settled a labor-management deadlock in the railroad industry which two presidents, Congress, three Secretaries of Labor and endless committees and boards had failed to resolve. Yet this group, markedly different from his usual associates, roused all kinds of defenses. He treated the guests warily, almost like a hostile force, and he ended up smothering their efforts at conversation by a near-compulsive monologue. In between, he got onto a protective, complaining theme that he was not given a "fair shake as President because I am a Southerner." It was an intimation of a later Lyndon Johnson who would growl about criticism of the Vietnam war: "I'll never be given credit for anything I do in foreign policy because I didn't go to Harvard."

Always fighting off the devils of insecurity, Lyndon Johnson was vain, not proud; boomerish, not confident; to a considerable extent he was grandiose, not grand, in conceiving his programs and grandiloquent, not eloquent, in expressing them. Gnawed by his inner needs, he turned a Congressional career shot through with instincts for the national good into a feral pursuit of personal domination, and a Presidency marked by a broad streak of idealism into what so often appeared an exercise in self-interest.

Self-interest—here is the only-too-well-recognized part of the

L.B.J. story. As a student of history, I have read a great deal about men who are said to have been motivated merely by self-aggrandizement. I have never really believed the analyses. I think over the array of people I have known well, many of whom are not particularly noble, and they have never seemed totally dominated by self-interest. Neither was Lyndon Johnson—and perhaps Lyndon Johnson especially was not.

But President Johnson, lashed by his insecurity, fought his better angels harder than any man I have ever known. It was a hostile world out there, far removed from mother and Texas and his trusted buddies; you had to keep handling it. Most of the time he appeared afraid to rely on anything except the doctrine that life and politics and government are simply a conflict and confluence between the self-interest of various people and groups. He seemed driven to function as Machiavelli in a Stetson, part of which posture was to keep assuring everyone that rugged he-men in Stetsons would never be Machiavellis.

So lacking in confidence, so defensive and wary, those hard eyes always searching the room or across the country for enemies, he was determined that nobody and no circumstance would get the better of him by playing to his strong personal ideals and emotions. This attitude led to increasing justification for, and ever more extended practice of, his natural bent toward exorbitant secretiveness, labyrinthine maneuverings, a sanctimonious glossing over of reality, the plain withholding of truth which had no need of being withheld and the plain distortion of truth which, at least in part, was much better stated and done with.

The American public delights in ferreting out the shortcomings of its Chief Executives. A nation of President-watchers knew that Franklin Roosevelt was an incorrigible political gamesman, that Harry Truman could sound like the village calliope, that Dwight Eisenhower often tried to grin away massive problems, that John Kennedy had some of the frailties as well as the assets of the charmer. But endlessly critical, it has also shown itself remarkably indulgent, provided that the virtues of the President appear to outweigh his defects. In this balance, the critical weight is the judgment that at bottom the President is a "good man," fundamentally decent, putting the welfare of the nation first in all his really important considerations. Most Americans have believed this to be true of every president from the thirties through 1963. It was a fundamental difficulty of Lyndon Johnson that he did not leave such an impression.

His background of the Texas wheeler-dealers, his long years as a Congressional manipulator and the association with Bobby Baker, his family's accumulation of considerable wealth based on a Government-regulated television station, his very appearance and mannerisms which easily suggested the riverboat gambler—all had prepared the public for skepticism of his basic motives as soon as he entered the White House. Nothing happened to change that attitude. Even the two achievements that President Johnson considered irreproachable brought him no surcease from suspicion.

He felt that he had incontestably established his right to the national leadership by his landslide victory in the election of 1964. But millions came to feel that he had incontestably established that he was ready to double-talk about anything, including taking the country into a grisly war, in order to win votes. He believed that the great success of his legislative program after the election earned him the confidence and admiration of the nation. The great success of that drive was, among other things, his great undoing; it made more people more sure that he did everything only by political legerdemain and only for political advantage.

It was within this context that the charge of credibility gap cut so deeply. Other modern Chief Executives—widely popular ones like Theodore and Franklin Roosevelt, Dwight Eisenhower and John Kennedy—had been known to play fast and loose with the facts. President Johnson not only played faster and looser; he did it amid a widespread conviction that self-serving deceit was part of his essential make-up.

This distrust militated powerfully against his whole Presidential leadership. It went beyond stripping him of much of the credit for his domestic legislative achievements; with the credit blunted, it dulled public interest in helping him make the laws work. "Why don't people, especially young people," President Johnson once complained, "really jump into the poverty program, roll up their sleeves and get it roaring, like we did back in the New Deal?" None of the men in the room with the President had the heart to tell him.

In foreign policy, the pervasive suspicion meant that L.B.J. was given little benefit of the doubt. Worried citizens, facing World War I, World War II or the Korean War, had been inclined to hesitate before opposing the President. He was a good man doing his best, with greater knowledge of the situation than themselves; the odds were that he was right. Few worried citizens hesitated to oppose Lyndon Johnson's Vietnam policy, and once in opposition, their attacks came with special virulence.

There was President Lyndon Johnson, the human being, and then there was President Lyndon Johnson, the maker of and symbol of certain national policies.

Those policies were coming from a man of exceedingly high intelligence. Many times when I have remarked this, during and after my White House days, people have looked at me as if I were a sycophant of the President or as if, during my association with him, I had taken leave of my good sense. Of course, they were thinking of intelligence in terms of a well-educated mind or, I'm afraid, being stuffy and parochial and finding it impossible to associate brains with a man who looked like a polished cowboy and who drawled out so much buncombe and bawdiness. They were decidedly wrong. After years of meeting first-rate minds in and out of universities, I am sure I have never met a more intelligent person than Lyndon Johnson—intelligent in terms of sheer I.Q.— a clear, swift, penetrating mind, with an abundance of its own type of imagination and subtlety.

The point is that little had happened to fill or to stretch this mind. The high school Lyndon Johnson attended, Johnson City High School, was so bad it lacked accreditation even by the lax standards of its region. Southwest Texas State Teachers College taught a watery pedagogese. Almost nothing in such schooling suggested to Lyndon Johnson that, once out of college, he ought to read books, travel, seek out interesting people, try to keep up with new trends, shake himself out of Johnson City and into the later twentieth century. Uncomfortable in the bigger world, obsessed with his political career, he had no personal urge to do these things. The powerful mind was feeding on small fare. The grown man came to the White House with a grab-bag of facts and non-facts, conceptions and misconceptions, ways of thinking and ways to avoid thought which had been gathered largely from his early crabbed environment.

It was this mental matrix which explains why, in his basic policy attitudes, L.B.J. was a passé President all the while he crowded the daily television screens. A man out of a kind of boondocks liberalism that had marked one element in Texas politics, he was easily able to move into New Dealism and to take over much of the tone of the thirties, but for the most part he stopped there. The United States did not stop at all. Nations change not at a steady pace but in slow swings or in rampant rushes, and America had been rampaging between the thirties and the sixties. The alterations were so swift and so deep that the country was changing right out from under President Lyndon Johnson.

Like a good nineteen-thirties man, he expressed his authentic thinking during the campaign of 1964 when he would shout, "Remember Molly and the children," or "We Americans don't want much. We want decent food, housing and clothing." In the nineteen-sixties there were still plenty of Mollies with plenty of troubles. But the essential mass problem had shifted; it was less food, housing and clothing than how to live with a weirdly uneasy affluence, marked by maldistributions that a significant part of the population was no longer ready to accept and a mounting race problem that was only in part economic. Like F.D.R., President Johnson might think of domestic policy in terms of satisfying the economic and social urges of the grand political coalition which dominated the period before World War II—labor, the farmers, the cities, the minorities and the youthful voters. But now much of labor sounded like threatened burghers, and the farm vote was disappearing into technology. The uplifted white minorities had been lifted to a condition where their concern was less social legislation than assuaging their own status trauma. The cities meant more and more the Negroes; the Negroes were wondering how much they wanted to do with any white leadership. The youthful, whether moving left, right or careering down the middle, were inclined to think of bread-and-butter liberalism as quaint, if not downright camp.

Among all age groups, the idealism which had helped sweep along the F.D.R. program, and which L.B.J. kept trying to touch, now sought not simply better pay for teachers and more school buildings but a drastically altered educational atmosphere and curriculum; not simply Medicare but aid for the aged fitted into a whole social welfare structure that found a way of asserting human dignity; not simply civil rights laws but a society in which civil rights laws would not be necessary. A new era, a new pattern of social and political forces, a new agenda—President Johnson, acting upon the kind of consensus domestic policy that would merely codify and expand the programs of the thirties, was about as contemporary as padded shoulders, a night at the radio and Clark Gable.

Again in the mood of the thirties, President Johnson assumed that foreign policy was something you had, like measles, and got over with as quickly as possible. Suddenly forced to confront the world, he reached into the past and laid hold of an attic doctrine which included even apostrophes to the flag and international deeds of derring-do. At the farthest stretch of his modernity, he reached thinking that was substantially of cold war vintage.

In the nineteen-sixties, a considerable and influential part of the public simply would not go along with such a foreign policy. They assumed that international affairs were a constant high-priority subject. Contemptuous of talk of the flag and derring-do, they were alarmed by what they were sure were outmoded cold war attitudes of crusading against Communism and of joining with foreign regimes that sought to use military power to stop social change. Out of a sense of guilt over America's past role in world affairs, a sympathy with the aspirations of underdeveloped nations and fear of nuclear holocaust, they favored accommodation, compromise, political and economic rather than military moves.

Many of these critics were Metro-Americans, part of a group in the cities and even more in the suburbs which was steadily growing in numbers and in its influence in determining national opinion. Relative to the rest of the country, the Metro-American was youthful, well-educated, affluent, more likely to have some minority blood in his veins. His mind had been shaped by an environment which had been good to him. It was no less formed by an American scene of irritating big organizations, brassy media and grinding social dislocations, and by a world situation of wars and threats of still worse wars. His thinking and his attitudes were a tangle of ambivalence. The Metro-American was avidly on the make, economically and socially, but he shied away from the appearance of sheer money-making or sheer caste and preferred the manner of public-spiritedness and cultivation. He had ideals but was skeptical of other people's—and even, a bit, of his own. He was liberal but without ideology; tolerant but intolerant of dogoodism; flexible, pragmatic and a devotee of the ironic edge.

Metro-America was increasingly the focal point of the abrasion between President Johnson and his public. There the uneasiness with him as a human being was greatest; the dissatisfaction with his domestic and foreign policies, the strongest. There, too, was the chief gathering place for a disaffection that joined the criticisms of the man and of his programs and added a third—that one concerning "style"—which really had little to do with the other two but increased the virulence of both.

The Metro-American—whether living in New York, Chicago, San Francisco or Houston—tended to take his style of life from the successful classes of the Northeast; to him, everything else was darkest boorishness. Over the years Texas and Texas mores had become a cherished subject for the gibes of Metro-American cocktail parties. Mention almost any of the personal habits of Lyndon Johnson—whether the sentimentalists or the big white Continental on a roar down a Texas highway—and you brought up something that made Metro-America snicker.

And always there were the Kennedys. After his sweeping victory in 1964, President Johnson may have eliminated virtually all references to President Kennedy in his public remarks. He could not eliminate the fact that his predecessor was legend and that the legend was a restive, bitter, yearning element in the whole life of the generation, especially in Metro-America. Not only did the urge to be different from J.F.K. affect what L.B.J. did and did not do day after day; every difficulty of President Johnson with public opinion was magnified by the Kennedy legend, which made John Kennedy precisely the opposite of all the things that Americans, and especially Metro-Americans, thought were wrong with Lyndon Johnson.

Eight times American Vice Presidents become Presidents have had to cope with the memory of the men they succeeded. Only once has the new Chief Executive been faced not only with a memory but with its living embodiment in a large, talented, energetic, abundantly endowed family, most of whom considered Lyndon Johnson a temporary and unfortunate interruption of the Kennedy years and one of whom thought so from a powerful political base.

Senator Robert F. Kennedy was the looks, the voice, the long stabbing finger of the martyred President. He was youthfulness, celebritese, the Northeast, the new-mode family, canoeing into high rapids and then sitting quoting Aeschylus; the Metro-American's unabashed ambition and the Metro-American's delight in the throw-away manner. He was post-nineteen-thirties politics, talking the quality of American civilization, moving increasingly toward outright opposition to the Vietnam war, centering his domestic legislative program on the cities, probing for a voting coalition based not on the old economic lines but on the new sense of dislocation bringing together Negroes, young people, intellectuals and the suburbanites who had acquired money at the price of malaise.

Nine weeks after President Johnson's speech of withdrawal, more crazed bullets were fired in Los Angeles. An R.F.K. legend immediately started forming, an idealization of the younger brother that joined perfectly with the J.F.K. legend.

The Johnson years were clamped in grim parentheses of happenstance. Lyndon Johnson came into the White House to the caissons for John Kennedy and he was leaving it to the dirges for Robert Kennedy. He entered and he was departing with a Kennedy more central than he in the national thinking and emotions.

In the final months, President Johnson tried hard to appear, what did not come easily to him, philosophical and serene. Strange, complex man in strange, complex circumstances—the towering figure still stalking, endlessly stalking the Oval Office, too astute not to know how seriously things had gone wrong, too limited by background and by self to grasp what had really happened.

No one who worked in Lyndon Johnson's White House can fail to have been moved by the dedication, the abilities and the force he brought to the Presidency of the United States. It is equally difficult not to recall the lines from one of the copybook poems of his school days in Johnson City, John Greenleaf Whittier's "Maud Muller": "For of all sad words of tongue or pen,/The saddest are these: 'It might have been.'" The story of Lyndon Johnson's Presidency is a story of tragedy in the ancient haunting sense of the word, the strong man overwhelmed by forces from within and without.

Hurtled into the leadership of the United States and of the free world in the fiercely demanding nineteen-sixties, he was not ready for them. Seriously flawed in personal characteristics, his virtues could not transform him into an engaging public figure. Functioning in the shadow of a relentless legend, he was beset by a host of attitudes which that legend continuously fed.

Lyndon Johnson could win votes, enact laws, maneuver mountains. He could not acquire that something beyond, which cannot be won, enacted or maneuvered but must be freely given. He could not command that respect, affection and rapport which alone permit an American President genuinely to lead. In his periods of triumph and of downsweep, in peace as in war, he stood the tragic figure of an extraordinarily gifted President who was the wrong man from the wrong place at the wrong time in the wrong circumstances.

Intimations of Mortality

The End of American Party Politics

by Walter Dean Burnham

Upon entering the White House, Richard Nixon inherited a nation more divided, fearful, and embittered by class and generational hostilities than at any time since the Great Depression. Even the inflation-ridden affluence of the Kennedy-Johnson 1960's had failed to restrain the growing alienation of working-class and middle-income voters—traditional Republicans, white ethnics and suburbanites, "Middle Americans" all—repelled by a youthful drug culture, campus political protest and violence, black ghetto riots, and understandably frightened by a growing crime rate which has made life in American cities dangerous, sometimes hellish. Yet this widespread malaise cut two ways, and Nixon's critics began arguing immediately that "the young, the poor and the black" had little place in the new President's political calculations.

Nixon moved cautiously, both in domestic and foreign affairs, apparently choosing to accept most "Great Society" programs at reduced spending levels, rather than attempt a dismantling campaign, especially since Democrats still controlled Congress. Nixon presented only one major new piece of social legislation to his first Congress, a welfare reform bill designed to federalize the largely unsuccessful and financially bankrupting state and local welfare programs. Liberal critics of the idea pointed out that the welfare benefits it proposed were considerably lower than those already paid in most Northern, industrial states, while Nixon's supporters insisted that once the principle of presidential responsibility for handling the welfare mess had been established, payments could be increased in time. Congressional bickering prevented passage of the measure before the 1970 congressional elections, and whatever its ultimate legislative future, the plan's actual impact on the "poverty cycle" among the millions living on welfare remains in doubt.

Nixon also began a highly publicized and cautious policy of American troop withdrawal from Vietnam soon after taking office, reacting to public opinion polls showing that most Americans were sick of the war. American invasions of Cambodia and Laos— Washington preferred to call the comparatively limited moves "incursions"—provoked antiwar demonstrations in the United States even greater than those seen during the Johnson years. Most analysts agree, however, that Nixon appears intent on winding down the role of American ground troops in Vietnam before the 1972 elections to the lowest level compatible with the survival of South Vietnam's government. Whether this is possible will probably determine the administration's future.

Elsewhere, Nixon has pursued a conciliatory policy toward Communist China without abandoning his commitment to protect the Chinese Nationalists on Formosa, a series of moves pointing toward expanded trade and diplomatic contacts in 1970 and 1971 which culminated in China's invitation to Nixon to visit Peking for summit-level discussions. Thus a President who began politicking by accusing Roosevelt and Truman of having "sold out" China to the Communists has come full circle and now appears intent primarily on "buying in." Earlier, Nixon attempted to capitalize on Middle America's hurts in the 1970 congressional elections, but the Nixon–Agnew–Mitchell "law and order" campaign failed to dent liberal Democratic strength in Congress significantly.

America's political future in the early 1970's seems to resist prophecy, so confused and numerous are the complex cross-currents of national problems and prospects. "The nation seems to slouch

*onward into its uncertain future like some huge inarticulate beast,"
historian Richard Hofstadter wrote shortly before his death in
1970, "too much attainted by wounds and ailments to be robust,
but too strong and resourceful to succumb." William Dean Burnham ventures a provocative analysis of the American political future in this concluding yet necessarily inconclusive article.*

American politics has clearly been falling apart in the past
decade. We don't have to look hard for the evidence. Mr. Nixon
is having as much difficulty controlling his fellow party members
in Congress as any of his Democratic predecessors had in controlling theirs. John V. Lindsay, a year after he helped make Spiro
Agnew a household word, had to run for mayor as a Liberal and
an Independent with the aid of nationally prominent Democrats.
Chicago in July of 1968 showed that for large numbers of its
activists a major political party can become not just a disappointment, but positively repellant. Ticket-splitting has become widespread as never before, especially among the young; and George
C. Wallace, whose third-party movement is the largest in recent
American history, continues to demonstrate an unusually stable
measure of support.

Vietnam and racial polarization have played large roles in this
breakdown, to be sure; but the ultimate causes are rooted much
deeper in our history. For some time we have been saying that we
live in a "pluralist democracy." And no text on American politics
would be complete without a few key code words such as "consensus," "incrementalism," "bargaining" and "process." Behind it
all is a rather benign view of our politics, one that assumes that
the complex diversity of the American social structure is filtered
through the two major parties and buttressed by a consensus of
middle-class values which produces an electoral politics of low intensity and gradual change. The interplay of interest groups and

From *Trans-Action*, VII (December 1969), 12–23. Copyright © December
1969 by TRANS-Action, Inc., New Brunswick, New Jersey. Reprinted by
permission.

public officials determines policy in detail. The voter has some leverage on policy, but only in a most diffuse way; and, anyway, he tends to be a pretty apolitical animal, dominated either by familial or local tradition, on one hand, or by the charisma of attractive candidates on the other. All of this is a good thing, of course, since in an affluent time the politics of consensus rules out violence and polarization. It pulls together and supports the existing order of things.

There is no doubt that this description fits "politics as usual," in the United States, but to assume that it fits the whole of American electoral politics is a radical oversimplification. Yet even after these past years of turmoil, few efforts have been made to appraise the peculiar rhythms of American politics in a more realistic way. This article is an attempt to do so by focusing upon two very important and little celebrated aspects of the dynamics of our politics: the phenomena of critical realignments of the electorate and of decomposition of the party in our electoral politics.

As a whole and across time, the reality of American politics appears quite different from a simple vision of pluralist democracy. It is shot through with escalating tensions, periodic electoral convulsions and repeated redefinitions of the rules and general outcomes of the political game. It has also been marked repeatedly by redefinitions—by no means always broadening ones—of those who are permitted to play. And one other very basic characteristic of American party politics that emerges from an historical overview is the profound incapacity of established political leadership to adapt itself to the political demands produced by the losers in America's stormy socioeconomic life. As is well known, American political parties are not instruments of collective purpose, but of electoral success. One major implication of this is that, as organizations, parties are interested in control of offices but not of government in any larger sense. It follows that once successful routines are established or reestablished for office-winning, very little motivation exists among party leaders to disturb the routines of the game. These routines are periodically upset, to be sure, but not by adaptive change within the party system. They are upset by overwhelming external force.

It has been recognized, at least since the publication of V. O. Key's "A Theory of Critical Elections" in 1955, that some elections in our history have been far more important than most in their long-range consequences for the political system. Such elections seem to "decide" clusters of substantive issues in a more clear-cut way than do most of the ordinary varieties. There is even a consensus among historians as to when these turning points in electoral politics took place. The first came in 1800 when Thomas Jefferson overthrew the Federalist hegemony established by Washington, Adams and Hamilton. The second came in 1828 and in the years afterward, with the election of Andrew Jackson and the democratization of the presidency. The third, of course, was the election of Abraham Lincoln in 1860, an election that culminated a catastrophic polarization of the society as a whole and resulted in civil war. The fourth critical election was that of William McKinley in 1896; this brought to a close the "Civil War" party system and inaugurated a political alignment congenial to the dominance of industrial capitalism over the American political economy. Created in the crucible of one massive depression, this "System of 1896" endured until the collapse of the economy in a second. The election of Franklin D. Roosevelt in 1932 came last in this series, and brought a major realignment of electoral politics and policy-making structures into the now familiar "welfare-pluralist" mode.

Now that the country appears to have entered another period of political upheaval, it seems particularly important not only to identify the phenomena of periodic critical realignments in our electoral politics, but to integrate them into a larger—if still very modest—theory of stasis and movement in American politics. For the realignments focus attention on the dark side of our politics, those moments of tremendous stress and abrupt transformation that remind us that "politics as usual" in the United States is not politics as always, and that American political institutions and leadership, once defined or redefined in a "normal phase" seem *themselves* to contribute to the building of conditions that threaten their overthrow.

To underscore the relevance of critical elections to our own day, one has only to recall that in the past, fundamental realignments in voting behavior have always been signalled by the rise of significant third parties: the Anti-Masons in the 1820's, the Free Soilers in the 1840's and 1850's, the Populists in the 1890's and the La Follette Progressives in the 1920's. We cannot know whether George Wallace's American Independent Party of 1968 fits into this series, but it is certain—as we shall see below—that the very foundations of American electoral politics have become quite suddenly fluid in the past few years, and that the mass base of our politics has become volatile to a degree unknown in the experience of all but the very oldest living Americans. The Wallace uprising is a major sign of this recent fluidity; but it hardly stands alone.

Third-party protests, perhaps by contrast with major-party bolts, point up the interplay in American politics between the inertia of "normal" established political routines and the pressures arising from the rapidity, unevenness and uncontrolled character of change in the country's dynamic socioeconomic system. All of the third parties prior to and including the 1968 Wallace movement constituted attacks by outsiders, who felt they were outsiders, against an elite frequently viewed in conspiratorial terms. The attacks were made under the banner of high moralistic universals against an established political structure seen as corrupt, undemocratic and manipulated by insiders for their own benefit and that of their supporters. All these parties were perceived by their activists as "movements" that would not only purify the corruption of the current political regime, but replace some of its most important parts. Moreover, they all telegraphed the basic clusters of issues that would dominate politics in the next electoral era: the completion of political democratization in the 1830's, slavery and sectionalism in the late 1840's and 1850's, the struggle between the industrialized and the colonial regions in the 1890's, and welfare liberalism vs. laissez-faire in the 1920's and 1930's. One may well view the American Independent Party in such a context.

The periodic recurrence of third-party forerunners of realignment—and realignments themselves, for that matter—are significantly related to dominant peculiarities of polity and society in the United States. They point to an electorate especially vulnerable to breaking apart, and to a political system in which the sense of common nationhood may be much more nearly skin-deep than is usually appreciated. If there is any evolutionary scale of political modernization at all, the persistence of deep fault lines in our electoral politics suggests pretty strongly that the United States remains a "new nation" to this day in some important political respects. The periodic recurrence of these tensions may also imply that—as dynamically developed as our economic system is—no convincing evidence of *political* development in the United States can be found after the 1860's.

Nationwide critical realignments can only take place around clusters of issues of the most fundamental importance. The most profound of these issues have been cast up in the course of the transition of our Lockeian-liberal commonwealth from an agrarian to an industrial state. The last two major realignments—those of 1893–96 and 1928–36—involved the two great transitional crises of American industrial capitalism, the economic collapses of 1893 and 1929. The second of these modern realignments produced, of course, the broad coalition on which the New Deal's welfarist-pluralist policy was ultimately based. But the first is of immediate concern to us here. For the 1896 adaptation of electoral politics to the imperatives of industrial-capitalism involved a set of developments that stand in the sharpest possible contrast to those occurring elsewhere in the Western world at about the same time. Moreover, they set in motion new patterns of behavior in electoral politics that were never entirely overcome even during the New Deal period, and which, as we shall see, have resumed their forward march during the past decade.

As a case in point, let me briefly sketch the political evolution of Pennsylvania—one of the most industrially developed areas on earth—during the 1890–1932 period. There was in this state a preexisting, indeed, preindustrial, pattern of two-party competition, one that had been forged in the Jacksonian era and decisively amended, though not abolished, during the Civil War. Then came the realignment of the 1890's, which, like those of earlier times, was an abrupt process. In the five annual elections from 1888 through November 1892, the Democrats' mean percentage of the total two-party vote was 46.7 per cent, while for the five elections beginning in February 1894 it dropped to a mean of 37.8 per cent. Moreover, the greatest and most permanent Republican gains during this depression decade occurred where they counted most, numerically: in the metropolitan areas of Philadelphia and Pittsburgh.

The cumulative effect of this realignment and its aftermath was to convert Pennsylvania into a thoroughly one-party state, in which conflict over the basic political issues were duly transferred to the Republican primary after it was established in 1908. By the 1920's this peculiar process had been completed and the Democratic party had become so weakened that, as often as not, the party's nominees for major office were selected by the Republican leadership. But whether so selected or not, their general-election prospects were dismal: of the 80 statewide contests held from 1894 through 1931, a candidate running with Democratic party endorsement won just one. Moreover, with the highly ephemeral exception of Theodore Roosevelt's bolt from the Republican party in 1912, no third parties emerged as general-election substitutes for the ruined Democrats.

The political simplicity which had thus emerged in this industrial heartland of the Northeast by the 1920's was the more extraordinary in that it occurred in an area whose socioeconomic division of labor was as complex and its level of development as high as any in the world. In most other regions of advanced industrialization the emergence of corporate capitalism was associated with the development of mass political parties with high structural cohesion and explicit collective purposes with respect to the control of policy and government. These parties expressed deep conflicts over the direction of public policy, but they also brought about the democratic revolution of Europe, for electoral participation tended to rise along with them. Precisely the opposite occurred in Pennsylvania and, with marginal and short-lived exceptions, the nation. It is no exaggeration to say that the political response to the collectivizing thrust of industrialism in this American state was the elimination of organized partisan combat, an extremely severe decline in electoral participation, the emergence of a Republican "coalition of the whole" and—by no means coincidentally—a highly efficient insulation of the controlling industrial-financial elite from effective or sustained countervailing pressures.

Irrelevant Radicalism

The reasons for the increasing solidity of this "system of 1896" in Pennsylvania are no doubt complex. Clearly, for example, the introduction of the direct primary as an alternative to the general election, which was thereby emptied of any but ritualistic significance, helped to undermine the minority Democrats more and more decisively by destroying their monopoly of opposition. But nationally as well the Democratic party in and after the 1890's was virtually invisible to Pennsylvania voters as a usable opposition. For with the ascendency of the agrarian Populist William Jennings Bryan, the Democratic party was transformed into a vehicle for colonial, periphery-oriented dissent against the industrial-metropolitan center, leaving the Republicans as sole spokesmen for the latter.

This is a paradox that pervades American political history, but it was sharpest in the years around the turn of this century. The United States was so vast that it had little need of economic colonies abroad; in fact it had two major colonial regions within its own borders, the postbellum South and the West. The only kinds of attacks that could be made effective on a *nationwide* basis against the emergent industrialist hegemony—the only attacks that, given the ethnic heterogeneity and extremely rudimentary political socialization of much of the country's industrial working class, could come within striking distance of achieving a popular majority—came out of these colonial areas. Thus "radical" protest in major-party terms came to be associated with the neo-Jacksonian demands of agrarian smallholders and small-town society already confronted by obsolescence. The Democratic party from 1896 to 1932, and in many respects much later, was the national vehicle for these struggles.

The net effect of this was to produce a condition in which—especially, but not entirely on the presidential level—the more economically advanced a state was, the more heavy were its normal Republican majorities likely to be. The nostalgic agrarian-individualist appeals of the national Democratic leadership tended to present the voters of this industrial state with a choice that was not a choice: between an essentially backward-looking provincial party articulating interests in opposition to those of the industrial North and East as a whole, and a "modernizing" party whose doctrines included enthusiastic acceptance of and cooperation with the dominant economic interests of region and nation. Not only did this partitioning of the political universe entail normal and often huge Republican majorities in an economically advanced state like Pennsylvania; the survival of national two-party competition on such a basis helped to ensure that no local reorganization of electoral politics along class lines could effectively occur even within such a state. Such a voting universe had a tendency toward both enormous inbuilt stability and increasing entrenchment in the decades after its creation. Probably no force less overwhelming than the post-1929 collapse of the national economic system would have sufficed to dislodge it. Without such a shock, who can say how, or indeed whether, the "System of 1896" would have come to an end in Pennsylvania and the nation? To ask such a question is to raise yet another. For there is no doubt that in Pennsylvania, as elsewhere, the combination of trauma in 1929–33 and Roosevelt's creative leadership provided the means for overthrowing the old order and for reversing dramatically the depoliticization of electoral politics which had come close to perfection under it. Yet might it not be the case that the dominant pattern of political adaptation to industrialism in the United States has worked to eliminate, by one means or another, the links provided by political parties between voters and rulers? In other words, was the post-1929 reversal permanent or only a transitory phrase in our political evolution? And if transitory, what bearing would this fact have on the possible recurrence of critical realignments in the future?

Withering Away of the Parties

The question requires us to turn our attention to the second major dynamic of American electoral politics during this century: the phenomenon of electoral disaggregation, of the breakdown of party loyalty, which in many respects must be seen as the permanent legacy of the fourth party system of 1896–1932. One of the most conspicuous developments of this era, most notably during the 1900–1920 period, was a whole network of changes in the rules of the political game. This is not the place for a thorough treatment and documentation of these peculiarities. One can only mention here some major changes in the rules of the game, and note that one would have no difficulty in arguing that their primary latent function was to ease the transition from a preindustrial universe of competitive, highly organized mass politics to a depoliticized world marked by drastic shrinkage in participation or political leverage by the lower orders of the population. The major changes surely include the following:

The introduction of the Australian ballot, which was designed to purify elections but also eliminated a significant function of the older political machines, the printing and distribution of ballots, and eased a transition from party voting to candidate voting.

The introduction of the direct primary, which at once stripped the minority party of its monopoly of opposition and weakened the control of party leaders over nominating processes, and again hastened preoccupation of the electorate with candidates rather than parties.

The movement toward nonpartisan local elections, often accompanied by a drive to eliminate local bases of representation such as wards in favor of at-large elections, which produced—as Samuel Hays points out—a shift of political power from the grass roots to citywide cosmopolitan elites.

The expulsion of almost all blacks, and a very large part of the poor-white population as well, from the southern electorate by a series of legal and extralegal measures such as the poll tax.

The introduction of personal registration requirements the burden of which, in faithful compliance with dominant middle-class values, was placed on the individual rather than on public authority, but which effectively disenfranchised large numbers of the poor.

Breakdown of Party Loyalty

Associated with these and other changes in the rules of the game was a profound transformation in voting behavior. There was an impressive growth in the numbers of political independents and ticket-splitters, a growth accompanied by a sea-change among party elites from what Richard Jensen has termed the "militarist" (or ward boss) campaign style to the "mercantilist" (or advertising-packaging) style. Aside from noting that the transition was largely completed as early as 1916, and hence that the practice of "the selling of the president" goes back far earlier than we usually think, these changes too must be left for fuller exposition elsewhere.

Critical realignments, as we have argued, are an indispensable part of a stability-disruption dialectic which has the deepest roots in American political history. Realigning sequences are associated with all sorts of aberrations from the normal workings of American party politics, both in the events leading up to nominations, the nature and style of election campaigning and the final outcome at the polls. This is not surprising, since they arise out of the collision of profound transitional crisis in the socioeconomic system with the immobility of a nondeveloped political system.

At the same time, it seems clear that for realignment to fulfill some of its most essential tension-management functions, for it to be a forum by which the electorate can participate in durable "constitution making," it is essential that political parties not fall below a certain level of coherence and appeal in the electorate. It is obvious that the greater the electoral disaggregation the less effective will be "normal" party politics as an instrument of countervailing influence in an industrial order. Thus, a number of indices of disaggregation significantly declined during the 1930's as the Democratic Party remobilized parts of American society under the stimulus of the New Deal. In view of the fact that political parties during the 1930's and 1940's were once again called upon to assist in a redrawing of the map of American politics and policymaking, this regeneration of partisan voting in the 1932–52 era is hardly surprising. More than that, regeneration was necessary if even the limited collective purposes of the new majority coalition were to be realized.

Even so, the New Deal realignment was far more diffuse, protracted and incomplete than any of its predecessors, a fact of which the more advanced New Dealers were only too keenly aware. It is hard to avoid the impression that one contributing element in this peculiarity of our last realignment was the much higher level of electoral disaggregation in the 1930's and 1940's than had existed at any time prior to the realignment of the 1890's. If one assumes that the end result of a long-term trend toward electoral disaggregation is the complete elimination of political parties as foci that shape voting behavior, then the possibility of critical realignment would, by definition, be eliminated as well. Every election would be dominated by TV packaging, candidate charisma, real or manu-factured, and short-term, ad hoc influences. Every election, there-fore, would have become deviating or realigning by definition, and American national politics would come to resemble the formless gubernatorial primaries that V. O. Key described in his classic *Southern Politics*.

The New Deal clearly arrested and reversed, to a degree, the march toward electoral disaggregation. But it did so only for the period in which the issues generated by economic scarcity re-mained central, and the generation traumatized by the collapse of 1929 remained numerically preponderant in the electorate. Since 1952, electoral disaggregation has resumed, in many measurable dimensions, and with redoubled force. The data on this point are overwhelming. Let us examine a few of them.

A primary aspect of electoral disaggregation, of course, is the "pulling apart" over time of the percentages for the same party but at different levels of election: this is the phenomenon of split-ticket voting. Recombining and reorganizing the data found in two tables of Milton Cummings' excellent study *Congressmen and the Electorate*, and extending the series back and forward in time, we may examine the relationship between presidential and con-gressional elections during this century.

Such an array captures both the initial upward thrust of disag-gregation in the second decade of this century, the peaking in the middle to late 1920's, the recession beginning in 1932, and espe-cially the post-1952 resumption of the upward trend.

Other evidence points precisely in the same direction. It has generally been accepted in survey-research work that generalized partisan identification shows far more stability over time than does actual voting behavior, since the latter is subject to short-term factors associated with each election. What is not so widely understood is that this glacial measure of party identification has suddenly become quite volatile during the 1960's, and particularly during the last half of the decade. In the first place, as both Gallup and Survey Research Center data confirm, the proportion of independents underwent a sudden shift upwards around 1966: while from 1940 to 1965 independents constituted about 20 per cent to 22 per cent of the electorate, they increased to 29 per cent in 1966. At the present time, they outnumber Republicans by 30 per cent to 28 per cent.

Second, there is a clear unbroken progression in the share that independents have of the total vote along age lines. The younger the age group, the larger the number of independents in it, so that among the 21–29 year olds, according to the most recent Gallup findings this year, 42 per cent are independent—an increase of about 10 per cent over the first half of the decade, and representing greater numbers of people than identify with either major party. When one reviews the June 1969 Gallup survey of college students, the share is larger still—44 per cent. Associated with this quantitative increase in independents seems to be a major qualitative change as well. Examining the data for the 1950's, the authors of *The American Voter* could well argue that independents tended to have lower political awareness and political involvement in general than did identifiers (particularly strong identifiers) of either major party. But the current concentration of independents in the population suggests that this may no longer be the case. They are clearly and disproportionately found not only among the young, and especially among the college young, but also among men, those adults with a college background, people in the professional-managerial strata and, of course, among those with higher incomes. Such groups tend to include those people whose sense of political involvement and efficacy is far higher than that of the population as a whole. Even in the case of the two most conspicuous exceptions to this—the pile-up of independent identifiers in the youngest age group and in the South—it can be persuasively argued that this distribution does not reflect low political awareness and involvement but the reverse: a sudden, in some instances almost violent, increase in both awareness and involvement among southerners and young adults, with the former being associated both with the heavy increase in southern turn-out in 1968 and the large Wallace vote polled there.

Third, one can turn to two sets of evidence found in the Survey Research Center's election studies. If the proportion of *strong* party identifiers over time is examined, the same pattern of long-term inertial stability and recent abrupt change can be seen. From 1952 through 1964, the proportion of strong Democratic and Republican party identifiers fluctuated in a narrow range between 36 per cent and 40 per cent, with a steep downward trend in strong Republican identifiers between 1960 and 1964 being matched by a moderate increase in strong Democratic identifiers. Then in 1966 the proportion of strong identifiers abruptly declines to 28 per cent, with the defectors overwhelmingly concentrated among former Democrats. This is almost certainly connected, as is the increase of independent identifiers, with the Vietnam fiasco. While we do not as yet have the 1968 SRC data, the distribution of identifications reported by Gallup suggests the strong probability that this abrupt decline in party loyalty has not been reversed very much since. It is enough here to observe that while the ratio between strong identifiers and independents prior to 1966 was pretty stably fixed at between 1.6 to 1 and 2 to 1 in favor of the former, it is now evidently less than 1 to 1. Both Chicago and Wallace last year were the acting out of these changes in the arena of "popular theater."

Finally, both survey and election data reveal a decline in two other major indices of the relevance of party to voting behavior: split-ticket voting and the choice of the same party's candidates for President across time.

It is evident that the 1960's have been an era of increasingly rapid liquidation of pre-existing party commitments by individual voters. There is no evidence anywhere to support Kevin Phillips' hypothesis regarding an emergent Republican majority—assuming that such a majority would involve increases in voter identification with the party. More than that, one might well ask whether, if this process of liquidation is indeed a preliminary to realignment, the latter may not take the form of a third-party movement of truly massive and durable proportions.

The evidence lends some credence to the view that American electoral politics is undergoing a long-term transition into routines designed only to fill offices and symbolically affirm "the American way." There also seem to be tendencies for our political parties gradually to evaporate as broad and active intermediaries between the people and their rulers, even as they may well continue to maintain enough organizational strength to screen out the unacceptable or the radical at the nominating stage. It is certain that the significance of party as link between government and the governed has now come once again into serious question. Bathed in the warm glow of diffused affluence, vexed in spirit but enriched economically by our imperial military and space commitments, confronted by the gradually unfolding consequences of social change as vast as it is unplanned, what need have Americans of political parties? More precisely, why do they need parties whose structures, processes and leadership cadres seem to grow more remote and irrelevant to each new crisis?

Future Politics

It seems evident enough that if this long-term trend toward a politics without parties continues, the policy consequences must be profound. One can put the matter with the utmost simplicity: political parties, with all their well-known human and structural shortcomings, are the only devices thus far invented by the wit of Western man that can, with some effectiveness, generate countervailing collective power on behalf of the many individually powerless against the relatively few who are individually or organizationally powerful. Their disappearance as active intermediaries, if not as preliminary screening devices, would only entail the unchallenged ascendancy of the already powerful, unless new structures of collective power were somehow developed to replace them, and unless conditions in America's social structure and political culture came to be such that they could be effectively used. Yet *neither* of these contingencies, despite recent publicity for the term "participatory democracy," is likely to occur under immediately conceivable circumstances in the United States. It is much more probable that the next chapter of our political history will resemble the metapolitical world of the 1920's.

But, it may be asked, may not a future realignment serve to recrystallize and revitalize political parties in the American system?

The present condition of America contains a number of what Marxists call "internal contradictions," some of which might provide the leverage for a future critical realignment if sufficiently sharp dislocations in everyday life should occur. One of the most important of these, surely, is the conversion—largely through technological change—of the American social stratification system from the older capitalist mixture of upper or "owning" classes, dependent white-collar middle classes and proletarians into a mixture described recently by David Apter: the technologically competent, the technologically obsolescent and the technologically superfluous. It is arguable, in fact, that the history of the Kennedy-Johnson Administrations on the domestic front could be written in terms of a coalition of the top and bottom of this Apter-ite mix against the middle, and the 1968 election as the first stage of a "counterrevolution" of these middle strata against the pressures from both of the other two. Yet the inchoate results of 1968 raise some doubts, to say the least, that it can yet be described as part of a realigning sequence: there was great volatility in this election, but also a remarkable and unexpectedly large element of continuity and voter stability.

It is not hard to find evidence of cumulative social disaster in our metropolitan areas. We went to war with Japan in 1941 over a destruction inflicted on us far less devastating in scope and intensity than that endured by any large America city today. But the destruction came suddenly, as a sharp blow, from a foreign power; while the urban destruction of today has matured as a result of our own internal social and political processes, and it has been unfolding gradually for decades. We have consequently learned somehow to adapt to it piecemeal, as best we can, without changing our lives or our values very greatly. Critical realignments, however, also seem to require sharp, sudden blows as a precondition for their emergence. If we think of realignment as arising from the spreading internal disarray in this country, we should also probably attempt to imagine what kinds of events could produce a sudden, sharp and general escalation in social tensions and threatened deprivations of property, status or values.

Conceivably, ghetto and student upheavals could prove enough in an age of mass communications to create a true critical realignment, but one may doubt it. Student and ghetto rebellions appear to be too narrowly defined socially to have a *direct* impact on the daily lives of the "vast middle," and thus produce transformations in voting behavior that would be both sweeping and permanent. For what happens in times of critical realignment is nothing less than an intense, if temporary, quasi revolutionizing of the vast middle class, a class normally content to be traditionalists or passive-participants in electoral politics.

Yet, even if students and ghetto blacks could do the trick, if they could even begin, with the aid of elements of the technological elite, a process of electoral realignment leftward, what would be the likely consequences? What would the quasi revolutionizing of an insecure, largely urban middle class caught in a brutal squeeze from the top and the bottom of the social system look like? There are already premonitory evidences: the Wallace vote in both southern and nonsouthern areas, as well as an unexpected durability in his *postelection* appeal; the mayoral elections in Los Angeles and Minneapolis this year, and not least, Lindsay's narrow squeak into a second term as mayor of New York City. To the extent that the "great middle" becomes politically mobilized and self-conscious, it moves toward what has been called "urban populism," a stance of organized hostility to blacks, student radicals and cosmopolitan liberal elites. The "great middle" remains, after all, the chief defender of the old-time Lockeian faith; both its material and cultural interests are bound up in this defense. If it should become at all mobilized as a major and cohesive political force in today's conditions, it would do so in the name of a restoration of the ancient truths by force if necessary. A realignment that directly involved this kind of mobilization —as it surely would, should it occur—would very likely have sinister overtones unprecedented in our political history.

Are we left, then, with a choice between the stagnation implicit in the disaggregative trends we have outlined here and convulsive disruption? Is there something basic to the American political system, and extending to its electoral politics, which rules out a middle ground between drift and mastery?

The fact that these questions were raised by Walter Lippmann more than half a century ago—and have indeed been raised in one form or other in every era of major transitional crisis over the past century—is alone enough to suggest an affirmative answer. The phenomena we have described here provide evidence of a partly quantitative sort which seems to point in the same direction. For electoral disaggregation is the negation of party. Further, it is—or rather, reffects—the negation of structural and behavioral conditions in politics under which linkages between the bottom, the middle and the top can exist and produce the effective carrying out of collective power. Critical realignments are evidence not of the presence of such linkages or conditions in the normal state of American electoral politics, but precisely of their absence. Correspondingly, they are not manifestations of democratic accountability, but infrequent and hazardous substitutes for it.

Taken together, both of these phenomena generate support for the inference that American politics in its normal state is the negation of the public order itself, as that term is understood in politically developed nations. We do not have government in our domestic affairs so much as "non-rule." We do not have political parties in the contemporary sense of that term as understood elsewhere in the Western world; we have antiparties instead.

Power centrifuges rather than power concentrators, they have been immensely important not as vehicles of social transformation but for its prevention through political means.

The entire setting of the critical realignment phenomenon bears witness to a deep-seated dialectic within the American political system. From the beginning, the American socioeconomic system has developed and transformed itself with an energy and thrust that has no parallel in modern history. The political system, from parties to policy structures, has seen no such development. Indeed it has shown astonishingly little substantive transformation over time in its methods of operation. In essence, the political system of this "fragment society" remains based today on the same Lockeian formulation that, as Louis Hartz points out, has dominated its entire history. It is predicated upon the maintenance of a high wall of separation between politics and government on one side and the socioeconomic system on the other. It depends for its effective working on the failure of anything approximating internal sovereignty in the European sense to emerge here.

The Lockeian cultural monolith, however, is based upon a social assumption that has come repeatedly into collision with reality. The assumption, of course, is not only that the autonomy of socioeconomic life from political direction is the prescribed fundamental law for the United States, but that this autonomous development will proceed with enough smoothness, uniformity and generally distributed benefits that it will be entirely compatible with the usual functioning of our antique political structures. Yet the high (though far from impermeable) wall of separation between politics and society is periodically threatened with inundations. As the socioeconomic system develops in the context of unchanging institutions of electoral politics and policy formation, dysfunctions become more and more visible. Whole classes, regions or other major sectors of the population are injured or faced with an imminent threat of injury. Finally the triggering event occurs, critical realignments follow, the universe of policy and of electoral coalitions is broadly redefined, and the tensions generated by the crisis receive some resolution. Thus it can be argued that critical realignment as a periodically recurring phenomenon is as centrally related to the workings of such a system as is the archaic and increasingly rudimentary structure of the major parties themselves.

Party vs. Survival

One is finally left with the sense that the twentieth-century decomposition of partisan links in our electoral system also corresponds closely with the contemporary survival needs of what Samuel P. Huntington has called the American "Tudor polity." Electoral disaggregation and the concentration of certain forms of power in the hands of economic, technological and administrative elites are functional for the short-term survival of nonrule in the United States. They may even somehow be related to the gradual emergence of internal sovereignty in this country—though to be sure under not very promising auspices for participatory democracy of any kind. Were such a development to occur, it would not necessarily entail the disappearance or complete suppression of sub-group tensions or violence in American social life, or of group bargaining and pluralism in the policy process. It might even be associated with increases in both. But it would, after all, reflect the ultimate sociopolitical consequences of the persistence of Lockeian individualism into an era of Big Organization: oligarchy at the top, inertia and spasms of self-defense in the middle, and fragmentation at the base. One may well doubt whether political parties or critical realignments need have much place in such a political universe.

A Selected Modern Bibliography

General Works

Richard Hofstadter, *The American Political Tradition* . . . (New York, 1954)

Ralph H. Gabriel, *The Course of American Democratic Thought* . . . (New York, 1940)

Arthur A. Ekirch, Jr., *The American Democratic Tradition* . . . (New York, 1963)

Louis Hartz, *The Liberal Tradition in America* . . . (New York, 1955)

Arthur A. Ekirch, Jr., *The Decline of American Liberalism* (New York, 1955)

Clinton Rossiter, *Conservatism in America* . . . (2nd edition, New York, 1962)

Daniel J. Boorstin, *The Genius of American Politics* (Chicago, 1953)

Wilfred E. Binkley, *American Political Parties: Their Natural History* (4th edition, New York, 1962)

Herbert Agar, *The Price of Union* (Boston, 1950)

William Nisbet Chambers and Walter Dean Burnham (eds.), *The American Party Systems, Stages of Political Development* (New York, 1967)

Kirk H. Porter and Donald B. Johnson (eds.), *National Party Platforms, 1840–1956* (Urbana, 1956)

Pendleton Herring, *The Politics of Democracy: American Parties in Action* (New York, 1940)

Clinton Rossiter, *Parties and Politics in America* (Ithaca, N.Y., 1960)

Joseph LaPalombara and Myron Wiener (eds.), *Political Parties and Political Development* (Princeton, 1966)

V. O. Key, Jr., *Politics, Parties, and Pressure Groups* (5th edition, New York, 1964)

Hugh A. Bone, *Party Committees and National Politics* (Seattle, 1958)

Cornelius P. Cotter and Bernard C. Hennessy, *Politics Without Power: The National Party Committees* (New York, 1964)

Frank R. Kent, *The Democratic Party, a History* (New York, 1928)

Henry A. Minor, *The Story of the Democratic Party* (New York, 1928)

Ralph M. Goldman, *The Democratic Party in American Politics* (New York, 1966)

Ronald F. Stinnett, *Democrats, Dinners and Dollars* (Ames, Iowa, 1967)

William T. Cash, *History of the Democratic Party in Florida* (Tallahassee, 1936)

George L. Willis, *Kentucky Democracy* (3 vols., Louisville, 1935)

Thomas E. Powell, *The Democratic Party of . . . Ohio* (Columbus, 1913)

Malcolm C. Moos, *The Republicans: a History* . . . (New York, 1956)

George H. Mayer, *The Republican Party, 1854–1966* (2d edition, New York, 1967)

Francis Curtis, *The Republican Party . . . 1854–1904* (2 vols., New York, 1904)

Charles O. Jones, *The Republican Party* . . . (New York, 1965)

Milton Viorst, *Fall From Grace: The Republican Party and the Puritan Ethic* (New York, 1968)

Paul D. Casdorph, *A History of the Republican Party in Texas . . .* (Austin, 1965)

Eugene H. Roseboom, *A History of Presidential Elections* (New York, 1957)

James W. Davis, *Springboard to the White House: Presidential Primaries* . . . (New York, 1967)

William B. Brown, *The People's Choice: The Presidential* . . . *Campaign Biography* (Baton Rouge, 1960)

W. Dean Burnham (comp.), *Presidential Ballots, 1836–1892* (Baltimore, 1955)

V. O. Key, *The Responsible Electorate: Rationality in Presidential Voting, 1936–1960* (Cambridge, 1966)

Lucius Wilmerding, Jr., *The Electoral College* (New Brunswick, 1958)

Wallace S. Sayre and Judith H. Parris, *Voting for President: The Electoral College* . . . (Washington, 1971)

George F. Milton, *The Use of Presidential Power, 1789–1943* (Boston, 1944)

Edward S. Corwin, *The President: Office and Powers, 1787–1948* . . . (3rd edition, New York, 1948)

Morton Borden (ed.), *America's Ten Greatest Presidents* (Chicago, 1961)

Harold J. Laski, *The American Presidency* . . . (New York, 1940)

Sidney Hyman, *The American President* (New York, 1954)

Sidney Hyman (ed.), "The Office of the American Presidency," *Annals of the American Academy of Political and Social Science*, Vol. 307 (September, 1956)

Clinton Rossiter, *The American Presidency* (2d edition, New York, 1960)

Herman Finer, *The Presidency* . . . (Chicago, 1960)

Richard E. Neustadt, *Presidential Power* (New York, 1960)

Wilfred E. Binkley, *The Man in the White House: His Powers and Duties* (revised edition, New York, 1964)

Carleton Jackson, *Presidential Vetoes, 1792–1945* (Athens, Ga., 1967)

James Hart, *The Ordinance Making Powers of the President* . . . (Baltimore, 1925)

Richard P. Longaker, *The Presidency and Individual Liberties* (Ithaca, 1961)

James E. Pollard, *The Presidents and the Press* (New York, 1947)

Rexford G. Tugwell, *The Enlargement of the Presidency* (New York, 1970)

Mary L. Hinsdale, *A History of the President's Cabinet* (Ann Arbor, Mich., 1911)

Richard F. Fenno, Jr., *The President's Cabinet: . . . from Wilson to Eisenhower* (Cambridge, 1959)

Dorothy G. Fowler, *The Cabinet Politician: The Postmasters General 1829–1909* (New York, 1943)

Carl Russell Fish, *The Civil Service and the Patronage* (New York, 1905)

Paul P. Van Riper, *History of the United States Civil Service* (Evanston, Ill., 1958)

W. Lloyd Warner, et al., *The American Federal Executive . . .* (New Haven, 1963)

Harold Seidman, *Politics, Position and Power: The Dynamics of Federal Organization* (New York, 1971)

Wilfred E. Binkley, *President and Congress* (3rd edition, New York, 1962)

Clinton Rossiter, *The Supreme Court and the Commander in Chief* (Ithaca, 1951)

Glendon A. Schubert, Jr., *The Presidency in the Courts* (Minneapolis, 1957)

Ernest S. Griffith, *Congress: Its Contemporary Role* (3rd edition, New York, 1961)

Randall B. Ripley, *Majority Party Leadership in Congress* (Boston, 1969)

Charles O. Jones, *The Minority Party in Congress* (Boston, 1970)

Barbara Hinckley, *The Seniority System in Congress* (Bloomington, Indiana, 1971)

Marshall E. Dimock, *Congressional Investigating Committees* (Baltimore, 1929)

Emmy E. Werner, "Women in Congress, 1917–1964," *Review of Politics*, XIX (March, 1966)

George H. Haynes, *The Senate of the United States: Its History and Practice* (2 vols., Boston, 1938)

Joseph P. Harris, *The Advice and Consent of the Senate: . . . Confirmation of Appointments . . .* (Berkeley, 1953)

Donald R. Matthews, *U.S. Senators and Their World* (Chapel Hill, 1960)

George B. Galloway, *History of the House of Representatives* (New York, 1961)

H. B. Fuller, *The Speakers of the House* (Boston, 1909)

Robert G. McCloskey, *The American Supreme Court* (Chicago, 1960)

Leo Pfeffer, *This Honorable Court* . . . (Boston, 1965)

John R. Schmidhauser, *The Supreme Court, Its Politics, Personalities, and Procedures* (New York, 1960)

Carl B. Swisher, *The Supreme Court in Modern Role* (revised edition, New York, 1965)

Conyers Read (ed.), *The Constitution Reconsidered* (New York, 1938)

Robert K. Carr, *The Supreme Court and Judicial Review* (New York, 1942)

Charles G. Haines, *The American Doctrine of Judicial Supremacy* (revised edition, Berkeley, 1932)

William W. Crosskey, *Politics and the Constitution* . . . (2 vols., Chicago, 1953)

Martin Shapiro, *Law and Politics in the Supreme Court* . . . (Glencoe, Ill., 1964)

Richard Claude, *The Supreme Court and the Electoral Process* (Baltimore, 1970)

Horace B. Davis, "The Occupations of Massachusetts Legislators, 1790–1950," *New England Quarterly*, XXIV (March, 1951)

DeAlva S. Alexander, *A Political History of the State of New York* (4 vols., New York, 1906–1923)

V. O. Key, *Southern Politics in State and Nation* (New York, 1949)

Perry H. Howard, *Political Tendencies in Louisiana, 1812–1952* (Baton Rouge, 1957)

Jasper B. Shannon, *Presidential Politics in Kentucky, 1824–1948* (Lexington, 1950)

J. Stephen Turett, "The Vulnerability of American Governors, 1900–1969," *Midwest Journal of Political Science*, XV (February, 1971)

Allan G. Bogue, "United States: The 'New' Political History," *Journal of Contemporary History*, III (January, 1968)

George M. Belnap, "A Method for Analyzing Legislative Behavior," *Midwest Journal of Political Science*, II (November 1958)

Lee F. Anderson, et al., *Legislative Roll-Call Analysis* (Evanston, Ill., 1966)

Robert P. Swierenga, "Ethnocultural Political Analysis: A New Approach to American Ethnic Studies," *Journal of American Studies*, V (April, 1971)

Charles A. McCoy and John Playford, *Apolitical Politics: A Critique Of Behavioralism* (New York, 1967)

I *Political Reconstruction, 1865–1877*

Herman Belz, *Reconstructing the Union: Theory and Policy during the Civil War* (Ithaca, 1969)

William B. Hesseltine, *Lincoln's Plan for Reconstruction* (Chicago, 1967)

Wilbert H. Ahern, "The Cox Plan of Reconstruction: . . . Ideology and Race Relations," *Civil War History*, XVI (December, 1970)

John G. Sproat, "Blueprint for Radical Reconstruction," *Journal of Southern History*, XLV (December, 1958)

W. E. B. DuBois, *Black Reconstruction* . . . (New York, 1935)

John Hope Franklin, *Reconstruction* . . . (Chicago, 1961)

Kenneth M. Stampp, *The Era of Reconstruction* . . . (New York, 1965)

Rembert W. Patrick, *The Reconstruction of the Nation* (New York, 1967)

David Donald, *The Politics of Reconstruction* . . . (Baton Rouge, 1965)

Albert Castel, "Andrew Johnson: His Historiographical Rise and Fall," *Mid-America*, XLV (July, 1963)

Eric L. McKitrick, *Andrew Johnson and Reconstruction* (Chicago, 1960)

Lawanda and John Cox, *Politics, Principle and Prejudice:* . . . *1865–1866* (Glencoe, Ill., 1963)

W. R. Brock, *An American Crisis: Congress and Reconstruction, 1865–1867* (New York, 1963)

Michael Perman, "The South and Congress's Reconstruction Policy, 1866–1867," *Journal of American Studies*, IV (February, 1971)

Theodore B. Wilson, *The Black Codes of the South* (University, Ala., 1965)

Joe M. Richardson, "The Florida Black Codes," *Florida Historical Quarterly*, XLVII (April, 1969)

Martha M. Bigelow, "Public Opinion and . . . the Mississippi Black Codes," *Negro History Bulletin*, XXXIII (January, 1970)

Larry Kincaid, "Victims of Circumstance: . . . Changing Attitudes Toward Republican Policy Makers and Reconstruction," *Journal of American History*, LVII (June, 1970)

John G. Clark, "Historians and the Joint Committee on Reconstruction," *Historian*, XXIII (May, 1961)

Richard N. Current, *Old Thad Stevens* . . . (Madison, Wisc., 1942)

Fawn M. Brodie, *Thaddeus Stevens* . . . (New York, 1959)

David Donald, *Charles Sumner and the Rights of Men* (New York, 1970)

Hans L. Trefousse, *The Radical Republicans* . . . (New York, 1968)

George R. Bentley, *A History of the Freedmen's Bureau* (Philadelphia, 1955)

William S. McFeeley, *Yankee Stepfather: General O. O. Howard and the Freedmen* (New Haven, 1968)

Jacobus TenBroek, *The Antislavery Origins of the Fourteenth Amendment* (Berkeley, 1951)

Joseph B. James, *The Framing of the Fourteenth Amendment* (Urbana, Ill., 1956)

George P. Smith, "Republican Reconstruction and Section Two of the Fourteenth Amendment," *Western Political Quarterly*, XXIII (December, 1970)

Alfred H. Kelly, "The Congressional Controversy Over School Segregation, 1867–1875," *American Historical Review*, LXIV (April, 1959)

James E. Sefton, "The Impeachment of Johnson: A Century of Writing," *Civil War History*, XIV (June, 1968)

Bertram Wyatt-Brown, "The Civil Rights Act of 1875," *Western Political Quarterly*, XVIII (December, 1965)

Ronald B. Jager, "Charles Sumner . . . and the Civil Rights Act of 1875," *New England Quarterly*, XLII (September, 1969)

J. David Hoeveler, Jr., "Reconstruction and the Federal Courts: The Civil Rights Act of 1875," *Historian*, XXXI (August, 1969)

Charles O. Lerche, Jr., "Congressional Interpretations of the Guarantee of a Republican Form of Government . . . ," *Journal of Southern History*, XV (May, 1949)

Stanley I. Kutler, *Judicial Power and Reconstruction Politics* (Chicago, 1968)

Harold M. Hyman, *Era of the Oath: Northern Loyalty Tests* . . . (Philadelphia, 1954)

David Montgomery, *Beyond Equality: Labor and the Radical Republicans* . . . (New York, 1967)

LaWanda and John H. Cox, "Negro Suffrage and Republican Politics: The Problem of Motivation in Reconstruction Historiography," *Journal of Southern History*, XXXIII (August, 1967)

Charles H. Coleman, *The Election of 1868* (New York, 1933)

Leslie H. Fishel, Jr., "Northern Prejudice and Negro Suffrage, 1865–1870," *Journal of Negro History*, XXXIX (January, 1954)

Glenn M. Linden, ". . . Negro Suffrage and Republican Politics," *Journal of Southern History*, XXXVI (August, 1970)

Edgar A. Toppin, ". . . The Negro Suffrage Issue in Post-Bellum Ohio Politics," *Journal of Human Relations*, XI (Winter, 1963)

G. Galin Berrier, "The Negro Suffrage Issue in Iowa . . . ," *Annals of Iowa*, XXXIX (Spring, 1968)

Robert R. Dykstra and Harlan Hahn, "Northern Voters and Negro Suffrage: The Case of Iowa, 1868," *Public Opinion Quarterly*, XXXII (Summer, 1968)

William Gilette, *The Right to Vote: Politics and the Passage of the Fifteenth Amendment* (Baltimore, 1965)

Everette Swinney, "Enforcing the Fifteenth Amendment . . . ," *Journal of Southern History*, XXVIII (May, 1962)

George R. Woolfolk, *The Cotton Regency: The Northern Merchants and Reconstruction* . . . (New York, 1958)

Frank B. Evans, *Pennsylvania Politics, 1872–1877* . . . (Harrisburg, 1966)

Felice A. Bonadio, *North of Reconstruction: Ohio Politics, 1865–1870* (New York, 1970)

Richard O. Curry (ed.), *Radicalism, Racism, and Party Realignment: The Border States During Reconstruction* (Baltimore, 1969)

Allen W. Trelease, "Who Were the Scalawags?" *Journal of Southern History*, XXIX (November, 1963)

Jack P. Maddex, Jr., *The Virginia Conservatives, 1867–1879: A Study in Reconstruction Politics* (Chapel Hill, 1970)

W. McKee Evans, *Ballots and Fence Rails: Reconstruction on the Lower Cape Fear* (Chapel Hill, 1967)

Francis B. Simkins and Robert H. Woody, *South Carolina During Reconstruction* (Chapel Hill, 1947)

Olive H. Shadgett, *The Republican Party in Georgia, from Reconstruction through 1900* (Athens, Ga., 1964)

Elizabeth S. Nathans, *Losing the Peace: Georgia Republicans and Reconstruction* . . . (Baton Rouge, 1968)

David Donald, "The Scalawag in Mississippi Reconstruction," *Journal of Southern History*, X (November, 1944)

William C. Harris, "A Reconsideration of the Mississippi Scalawag," *Journal of Mississippi History*, XXXII (February, 1970)

Howard A White, *The Freedman's Bureau in Louisiana* (Baton Rouge, 1970)

W. C. Nunn, *Texas Under the Carpetbaggers* (Austin, 1962)

Thomas B. Alexander, *Political Reconstruction in Tennessee* (Nashville, 1950)

Robert Cruden, *The Negro in Reconstruction* (Englewood Cliffs, N.J., 1969)

Samuel D. Smith, *The Negro in Congress, 1870–1901* (Chapel Hill, 1940)

Alrutheus A. Taylor, *The Negro in the Reconstruction of Virginia* (Washington, 1926)

Joel Williamson, *After Slavery: The Negro in South Carolina During Reconstruction* . . . (Chapel Hill, 1965)

Okon Edet Uya, *From Slavery to Public Service: Robert Smalls* . . . (New York, 1971)

Edward F. Sweat, "Francis L. Cardozo: . . . Integrity in Reconstruction Politics," *Journal of Negro History*, XLVI (October, 1961)

E. Merton Coulter, *Negro Legislators in Georgia During the Reconstruction Period* (Athens, Ga., 1968)

Joe M. Richardson, *The Negro in the Reconstruction of Florida* . . . (Tallahassee, 1965)

Vernon L. Wharton, *The Negro in Mississippi, 1865–1877* (Chapel Hill, 1947)

Melvin I. Urofsky, "Blanche K. Bruce: United States Senator, 1875–1881," *Journal of Mississippi History*, XXIX (May, 1967)

John Hope Franklin (ed.), . . . *The Autobiography of John Roy Lynch* (Chicago, 1970)

Charles Vincent, "Negro Leadership and Programs in the Louisiana Constitutional Convention of 1868," *Louisiana History*, X (Fall, 1969)

Agnes S. Grosz, "The Political Career of P. B. S. Pinchback," *Louisiana Historical Quarterly*, (April, 1944)

Alrutheus A. Taylor, *The Negro in Tennessee, 1865–1880* (Washington, 1944)

William B. Hesseltine, "Economic Factors in the Abandonment of Reconstruction," *Mississippi Valley Historical Review*, XXII (September, 1935)

Patrick W. Riddleberger, "The Radicals' Abandonment of the Negro during Reconstruction," *Journal of Negro History*, XLV (April, 1960)

Alfred B. Williams, *Hampton and His Red Shirts: South Carolina's Deliverance in 1876* (Charleston, 1935)

Garnie W. McGinty, *Louisiana Redeemed: The Overthrow of Carpetbag Rule, 1876–1880* (New Orleans, 1941)

C. Vann Woodward, *Reunion and Reaction: The Compromise of 1877* . . . (2d edition, Garden City, N.Y., 1956)

Vincent P. DeSantis, *Republicans Face the Southern Question* . . . (Baltimore, 1959)

Stanley P. Hirshon, *Farewell to the Bloody Shirt: Northern Republicans and the Southern Negro* . . . (Bloomington, Ind., 1962)

II *The Gilded Age, 1877–1892*

John A. Garraty, *The New Commonwealth, 1877–1890* (New York, 1968)

Robert H. Wiebe, *The Search for Order: 1877–1920* (New York, 1967)

Fred A. Shannon, *The Centennial Years* . . . (Garden City, N.Y., 1967)

Leonard D. White, *The Republican Era: 1869–1901* (New York, 1958)

H. Wayne Morgan, *From Hayes to McKinley* . . . (Syracuse, N.Y., 1969)

Matthew Josephson, *The Politicos: 1865–1896* (New York, 1938)

Albert V. House, "Republicans and Democrats Search for New Identities, 1870–1890," *Review of Politics*, XXXI (October 1969)

David J. Rothman, *Politics and Power: The United States Senate, 1869–1901* (Cambridge, Mass., 1966)

Irwin Unger, *The Greenback Era: A Social and Political History of American Finance, 1865–1879* (Princeton, 1964)

Allen Weinstein, *Prelude to Populism: Origins of the Silver Issue, 1867–1878* (New Haven, 1970)

Walter T. K. Nugent, *Money and American Society, 1865–1900* (New York, 1968)

F. W. Taussig, *The Tariff History of the United States* (8th edition, New York, 1931)

Mary R. Dearing, *Veterans in Politics: The Story of the G. A. R.* (Baton Rouge, 1952)

H. Wayne Morgan (ed.), *The Gilded Age* . . . (2nd edition, Syracuse, N.Y., 1968)

Paul Kleppner, *The Cross of Culture: A Social Analysis of Midwestern Politics, 1850–1900* (New York, 1970)

Richard Jensen, "The Religious and Occupational Roots of Party Identification: Illinois and Indiana in the 1870's," *Civil War History*, XVI (December 1970)

C. Vann Woodward, *Origins of the New South, 1877–1913* (Baton Rouge, 1951)

William I. Hair, *Bourbonism and Agrarian Protest: Louisiana Politics, 1877–1900* (Baton Rouge, 1969)

Joy J. Jackson, *New Orleans . . . Politics and Urban Progress, 1880–1896* (Baton Rouge, 1969)

Robert D. Marcus, *Grand Old Party: Political Structure in the Gilded Age* (New York, 1971)

Harry Barnard, *Rutherford B. Hayes and His America* (Indianapolis, 1964)

R. G. Caldwell, *James A. Garfield: Party Chieftain* (New York, 1931)

George F. Howe, *Chester A. Arthur* (New York, 1934)

Harry J. Sievers, *Benjamin Harrison* . . . (3 vols., Chicago and New York, 1952–68)

William G. Eidson, "Who Were the Stalwarts?" *Mid-America*, LII (October 1970)

L. L. Sage, *William Boyd Allison: A Leader in Practical Politics* (Iowa City, 1956)

David S. Muzzey, *James G. Blaine* . . . (New York, 1934)

Leon B. Richardson, *William E. Chandler, Republican* (New York, 1940)

David M. Jordan, *Roscoe Conkling of New York* . . . (Ithaca, N.Y., 1971)

J. W. Neilson, *Shelby M. Cullom: Prairie State Republican* (Urbana, Ill., 1962)

Richard E. Welch, Jr., *George Frisbie Hoar and the Half-Breed Republicans* (Cambridge, Mass., 1971)

Mark D. Hirsch, *William C. Whitney: Modern Warwick* (New York, 1948)

Allan Nevins, *Grover Cleveland: A Study in Courage* (New York, 1932)

Horace Samuel Merrill, *Bourbon Leader: Grover Cleveland* . . . (Boston, 1957)

Alexander C. Flick, *Samuel Jones Tilden* . . . (New York, 1939)

David Lindsey, *"Sunset" Cox: Irrepressible Democrat* (Detroit, 1959)

John R. Lambert, *Arthur Pue Gorman* (Baton Rouge, 1953)

Festus P. Summers, *William L. Wilson and Tariff Reform* (New Brunswick, N.J., 1953)

Geoffrey Blodgett, *The Gentle Reformers: Massachusetts Democracy in the Cleveland Era* (Cambridge, Mass., 1966)

Gerald W. McFarland, "The Breakdown of Deadlock: The Cleveland Democracy in Connecticut . . . ," *The Historian*, XXXI (May 1969)

Alexander B. Callow, Jr., *The Tweed Ring* (New York, 1966)

Horace Samuel Merrill, *Bourbon Democracy of the Middle West, 1865–1896* (Baton Rouge, 1953)

Joseph F. Wall, *Henry Watterson, Reconstructed Rebel* (New York, 1956)

Leslie E. Decker, *Railroads, Lands, and Politics* . . . (Providence, 1964)

Lee Benson, *Merchants, Farmers, and Railroads: Railroad Regulation and New York Politics, 1850–1887* (Cambridge, Mass., 1955)

Stanley P. Hirshon, *Grenville M. Dodge: Soldier, Politician, Railroad Pioneer* (Bloomington, Ind., 1967)

Joseph F. Wall, *Andrew Carnegie* (New York, 1970)

Robert G. McCloskey, *American Conservatism in the Age of Enterprise* (Cambridge, Mass., 1951)

Sidney Fine, *Laissez-Faire and the General Welfare State* . . . 1865–1901 (Ann Arbor, 1956)

Richard Hofstadter, *Social Darwinism in American Thought* (rev. edition, Boston, 1955)

John G. Sproat, *"The Best Men": Liberal Reformers in the Gilded Age* (New York, 1968)

Ari Hoogenboom, *Outlawing the Spoils: . . . the Civil Service Reform Movement, 1865–1883* (Urbana, Ill., 1961)

F. W. Patton, *The Battle for Municipal Reform . . . 1875–1900* (Washington, D.C., 1940)

Arthur Mann, *Yankee Reformers in the Urban Age* (Cambridge, Mass., 1954)

Kermit Vanderbilt, *Charles Eliot Norton* (Cambridge, Mass., 1959)

Claude M. Fuess, *Carl Schurz, Reformer* (New York, 1932)

Charles A. Barker, *Henry George* (New York, 1955)

III   *Ferment in the 'Nineties, 1892–1900*

Harold U. Faulkner, *Politics, Reform and Expansion: 1890–1900* (New York, 1959)

Ray Ginger, *Age of Excess . . . 1877–1914* (New York, 1965)

George H. Knoles, *The Presidential Campaign of 1892* (Stanford, Calif., 1942)

Earl W. Hayter, *The Troubled Farmer, 1850–1900* (DeKalb, Ill., 1970)

Fred A. Shannon, *The Farmer's Last Frontier . . .* (New York, 1945)

Paul W. Gates, "The Homestead Act in an Incongruous Land System," *American Historical Review*, XLI (July 1936)

Allan G. Bogue, *Money at Interest . . .* (Ithaca, N.Y., 1955)

Theodore Saloutos, "The Agricultural Problem and Nineteenth-Century Industrialism," *Agricultural History*, XXII (July 1948)

Gerald Prescott, "Wisconsin Farm Leaders . . . 1873–1900," *Agricultural History*, XLIV (April 1970)

Solon J. Buck, *The Granger Movement* (Cambridge, Mass., 1913)

John D. Hicks, *The Populist Revolt* (Minneapolis, 1931)

Norman Pollack, *The Populist Response to Industrial America . . .* (Cambridge, Mass., 1962)

C. Vann Woodward, "The Populist Heritage and the Intellectual," in *The Burden of Southern History* (Baton Rouge, 1960)

Oscar Handlin, "Reconsidering the Populists," *Agricultural History*, XXXIX (April 1965)

Theodore Saloutos, "The Professors and the Populists," *Agricultural History*, XL (October 1966)

Walter T. K. Nugent, "Some Parameters of Populism," *Agricultural History*, XL (October 1966)

Karel D. Bicha, "A Further Reconsideration of American Populism," *Mid-America, LII* (January 1970)

George H. Knoles, "Populism and Socialism . . . 1892," *Pacific Historical Review,* XII (September 1943)

Jack Abramowitz, "The Negro in the Populist Movement," *Journal of Negro History,* XXXVIII (July 1953)

R. V. Scott, *The Agrarian Movement in Illinois* . . . (Urbana, Ill., 1962)

Martin Ridge, *Ignatius Donnelly* . . . (Chicago, 1962)

Frederick E. Haynes, *James Baird Weaver* (Iowa City, 1919)

Walter T. K. Nugent, *The Tolerant Populists: Kansas Populism and Nativism* (Chicago, 1963)

O. Gene Clanton, *Kansas Populism: Ideas and Men* (Lawrence, Kans., 1969)

David B. Griffiths, "Far Western Populism: The Case of Utah . . . ," *Utah Historical Quarterly,* XXXVII (Fall 1969)

Marion Harrington, *The Populist Movement in Oregon* (Eugene, Ore., 1940)

W. DuBose Sheldon, *Populism in the Old Dominion* (Princeton, 1935)

Stuart Noblin, *Leonidas F. Polk* . . . (Chapel Hill, 1949)

C. Vann Woodward, *Tom Watson: Agrarian Rebel* (New York, 1938)

William Warren Rogers, *The One-Gallused Rebellion: Agrarianism in Alabama, 1865–1896* (Baton Rouge, 1970)

Albert D. Kirwin, *Revolt of the Rednecks* (Lexington, Ky., 1951)

Roscoe C. Martin, *The People's Party in Texas* . . . (Austin, 1933)

Daniel M. Robison, *Bob Taylor and the Agrarian Revolt in Tennessee* (Chapel Hill, 1935)

Charlotte Erickson, *American Industry and European Immigration: 1860–1885* (Cambridge, Mass., 1957)

Thomas N. Brown, *Irish-American Nationalism, 1870–1890* (Philadelphia, 1966)

Frederick G. Leubke, *Immigrants and Politics: The Germans of Nebraska, 1880–1900* (Lincoln, Nebr., 1971)

John Higham, *Strangers in the Land: Patterns of American Nativism, 1860–1925* (rev. edition, New Brunswick, N.J., 1963)

Barbara M. Solomon, *Ancestors and Immigrants: A Changing New England Tradition* (Cambridge, Mass., 1956)

Norman J. Ware, *The Labor Movement . . . 1860–1895* (New York, 1929)

Gerald N. Grob, *Workers and Utopia: . . . Ideological Conflict . . . 1865–1900* (Evanston, Ill., 1961)

Donald L. McMurry, *The Great Burlington Strike of 1888* (Cambridge, Mass., 1956)

Leon Wolff, *Lockout: . . . the Homestead Strike of 1892* (New York, 1965)

Almont Lindsey, *The Pullman Strike* (Chicago, 1942)

Gerald G. Eggert, *Railroad Labor Disputes: The Beginnings of Federal Strike Policy* (Ann Arbor, 1967)

Philip Taft, *The A.F. of L. in the Time of Gompers* (New York, 1957)

Chester M. Destler, *American Radicalism, 1865–1901* (Menasha, Wisc., 1946)

Charles Hoffman, "The Depression of the Nineties," *Journal of Economic History*, XVI (June 1956)

Samuel Rezneck, "Unemployment, Unrest, and Relief . . . During the Depression of 1893–1897," *Journal of Political Economy*, LXI (August 1953)

Harry Bernard, *"Eagle Forgotten," The Life of John Peter Altgeld* (Indianapolis, 1938)

Benjamin R. Twiss, *Lawyers and the Constitution: How Laissez-Faire Came to the Supreme Court* (Princeton, 1942)

Arnold M. Paul, *Conservative Crisis and the Rule of Law . . .* (New York, 1960)

Alan F. Westin, "The Supreme Court, The Populist Movement, and the Election of 1896," *Journal of Politics*, XV (February 1953)

J. Rogers Hollingsworth, *The Whirligig of Politics: The Democracy of Cleveland and Bryan* (Chicago, 1963)

Paolo Coletta, "Bryan Cleveland the Disrupted Democracy . . . ," *Nebraska History*, XLI (March 1960)

Robert F. Durden, *The Climax of Populism* (Lexington, Ky., 1965)

Paul W. Glad, *McKinley, Bryan and the People* (Philadelphia, 1964)

Stanley L. Jones, *The Presidential Election of 1896* (Madison, Wisc., 1964)

Gilbert C. Fite, "Republican Strategy in . . . 1896," *American Historical Review*, LXV (July 1960)

Herbert Croly, *Marcus Alonzo Hanna* (New York, 1912)

H. Wayne Morgan, *William McKinley and His America* (Syracuse, N.Y., 1963)

Paolo E. Coletta, *William Jennings Bryan* . . . Lincoln, Nebr., 1964)

James A. Barnes, "Myths of the Bryan Campaign," *Mississippi Valley Historical Review*, XXXIV (December 1947)

William Diamond, "Urban and Rural Voting in 1896," *American Historical Review*, XLVI (January 1941)

Walter LaFeber, *The New Empire* . . . *American Expansion, 1860–1898* (Ithaca, N.Y., 1963)

William A. Williams, *The Roots of the Modern American Empire* (New York, 1969)

Julius W. Pratt, *Expansionists of 1898* (Baltimore, 1936)

Margaret Leech, *In the Days of McKinley* (New York, 1959)

William A. Swanberg, *Citizen Hearst* (New York, 1961)

Robert L. Beisner, *Twelve Against Empire: The Anti-Imperialists* (New York, 1968)

David F. Healy, *The United States in Cuba, 1898–1902* (Madison Wisc., 1963)

Howard K. Beale, *Theodore Roosevelt and the Rise of America to World Power* (Baltimore, 1956)

IV   *Reforms and Repressions, 1900–1920*

Richard Hofstadter, *The Age of Reform* . . . (New York, 1955)

Samuel P. Hays, *The Response to Industrialism, 1885–1914* (Chicago, 1957)

Gabriel Kolko, *The Triumph of Conservatism* . . . *1900–1916* (Glencoe, Ill., 1963)

Dewey W. Grantham, Jr., "Theodore Roosevelt in American Historical Writing . . . ," *Mid-America*, XLIII (January 1961)

George E. Mowry, *The Era of Theodore Roosevelt, 1900–1912* (New York, 1958)

Henry F. Pringle, *Theodore Roosevelt* (New York, 1931)

John M. Blum, *The Republican Roosevelt* (Cambridge, Mass., 1954)

Willard B. Gatewood, Jr., *Theodore Roosevelt and the Art of Controversy* (Baton Rouge, 1970)

Oscar Kraines, "The President versus Congress . . . 1905–1909," *Western Political Quarterly*, XXIII (March 1970)

Peter G. Filene, "An Obituary for 'The Progressive Movement,'"
    American Quarterly, XXII (Spring 1970)
Jack Tager, "Progressives, Conservatives and the Theory of the Status
    Revolution," *Mid-America*, XLVIII (July 1966)
David W. Noble, *The Paradox of Progressive Thought* (Minneapolis,
    1958)
J. Joseph Huthmacher, "Urban Liberalism and the Age of Reform,"
    Mississippi Valley Historical Review, XLIX (September 1962)
Samuel P. Hays, "The Social Analysis of American Political History,
    1880–1920," *Political Science Quarterly*, LXXX (September
    1965)

John D. Buenker, "Urban Liberalism and the Federal Income Tax
    Amendment," *Pennsylvania History*, XXXVI (April 1969)
Joseph F. Mahoney, "Women Suffrage and the Urban Masses," *New
    Jersey History*, LXXXVII (Autumn 1969)
Paul E. Isaac, *Prohibition and Politics: Turbulent Decades in Tennes-
    see, 1885–1920* (Knoxville, Tenn., 1966)
Samuel P. Hays, *Conservation and the Gospel of Efficiency . . .
    1890–1920* (Cambridge, Mass., 1959)
James Penick, Jr., *Progressive Politics and Conservation: The Ballin-
    ger–Pinchot Affair* (Chicago, 1968)
Oscar E. Anderson, *The Health of a Nation: Harvey W. Wiley and
    the Fight for Pure Food* (Chicago, 1958)
Gabriel Kolko, *Railroads and Regulation, 1877–1916* (Princeton,
    1965)
Stanley P. Caine, *The Myth of a Progressive Reform: Railroad Regu-
    lation in Wisconsin, 1903–1910* (Madison, Wisc., 1970)
Robert H. Wiebe, *Businessmen and Reform: A Study of the Progres-
    sive Movement* (Cambridge, Mass., 1962)
C. C. Regier, *The Era of the Muckraker* (Chapel Hill, 1932)
David M. Chalmers, *Social and Political Ideas of the Muckrakers*
    (New York, 1964)
Harold S. Wilson, *McClure's Magazine and the Muckrakers* (Prince-
    ton, 1970)
Samuel P. Hays, "The Politics of Reform in Municipal Government
    in the Progressive Era," *Pacific Northwest Quarterly*, LV (Oc-
    tober 1964)
Marguerite Green, *The National Civic Federation and the American
    Labor Movement, 1900–1925* (Washington, D.C., 1956)

Stephen B. Wood, *Constitutional Politics in the Progressive Era: Child Labor and the Law* (Chicago, 1968)

Walter I. Trattner, *Crusade for the Children: . . . the National Child Labor Committee* . . . (Chicago, 1970)

Jeremy P. Felt, *Hostages of Fortune: Child Labor Reform in New York State* (Syracuse, N.Y., 1965)

Robert H. Bremner, *From the Depths: The Discovery of Poverty* . . . (New York, 1956)

Roy Lubove, *The Progressives and the Slums . . . in New York City* (Pittsburgh, 1962)

Richard M. Abrams, *Conservatism in a Progressive Era: Massachusetts* . . . (Cambridge, Mass., 1964)

Richard B. Sherman, "The Status Revolution and Massachusetts Progressive Leadership," *Political Science Quarterly*, LXXVIII (March 1963)

Robert F. Wesser, *Charles Evans Hughes: Politics and Reform in New York, 1905–1910* (Ithaca, N.Y., 1967)

Arnold S. Rosenberg, "The New York Reformers of 1914: A Profile," *New York History*, L (April 1969)

Irwin Yellowitz, *Labor and the Progressive Movement in New York State* (New York, 1965)

Ransom E. Noble, Jr., *New Jersey Progressivism Before Wilson* (Princeton, 1946)

John D. Buenker, "Urban, New-Stock Liberalism and Progressive Reform in New Jersey," *New Jersey History*, LXXXVII (Summer 1969)

Russel B. Nye, *Midwestern Progressive Politics* . . . (East Lansing, 1951)

Hoyt L. Warner, *Progressivism in Ohio* . . . (Columbia, Ohio, 1964)

Zane L. Miller, *Boss Cox's Cincinnati: Urban Politics in the Progressive Era* (New York, 1968)

Robert M. Crunden, *A Hero in Spite of Himself: Brand Whitlock* . . . (New York, 1969)

Robert S. Maxwell, *La Follette and the Rise of the Progressives in Wisconsin* (Madison, Wisc., 1956)

David P. Thelen, "Social Tensions and the Origins of Progressivism," *Journal of American History*, LVI (September 1969)

E. Daniel Potts, "The Progressive Profile in Iowa," *Mid-America*, XLVII (October 1965)

Arthur S. Link, "The Progressive Movement in the South," *North Carolina Historical Review*, XXIII (April 1946)

Hugh C. Bailey, *Liberalism in the New South: Southern Social Reformers and the Progressive Movement* (Coral Gables, Fla., 1969)

James B. Crooks, *Politics and Progress: The Rise of Urban Progressivism in Baltimore* . . . (Baton Rouge, 1968)

William D. Miller, *Memphis During the Progressive Era* . . . (Memphis, 1957)

Sheldon Hackney, *Populism to Progressivism in Alabama* (Princeton, 1969)

William F. Holmes, *The White Chief: James Kimble Vardaman* (Baton Rouge, 1970)

George E. Mowry, *The California Progressives* (Berkeley, 1951)

John L. Shover, "The Progressives and the Working Class Vote in California," *Labor History*, X (Fall 1969)

Walton Bean, *Boss Reuf's San Francisco* . . . (Berkeley, 1952)

D. H. Leon, "Whatever Happened to an American Socialist Party? . . . the Spectrum of Interpretations," *American Quarterly*, XXIII (May 1971)

Donald Drew Egbert and Stow Persons (eds.), *Socialism and American Life* (2 vols., Princeton, 1952)

David A. Shannon, *The Socialist Party of America* (New York, 1955)

Howard H. Quint, *The Forging of American Socialism* . . . (Columbia, S.C., 1953)

Ira Kipnis, *The American Socialist Movement, 1897–1912* (New York, 1952)

Henry Bedford, *Socialism and the Workers in Massachusetts* . . . (Amherst, 1966)

Marvin Wachman, *History of the Social-Democratic Party of Milwaukee* . . . (Urbana, Ill., 1945)

Ray Ginger, *The Bending Cross: A Biography of Eugene V. Debs* (New Brunswick, N.J., 1949)

August C. Bolino, "American Socialism's Flood and Ebb . . . ," *American Journal of Economics*, XXII (April 1963)

R. Laurence Moore, *European Socialists and the American Promised Land* (New York, 1970)

Daniel Bell, *Marxian Socialism in the United States* (Princeton, 1967)

James Weinstein, *The Decline of Socialism in America, 1912–1925* (New York, 1967)

John Laslett, *Labor and the Left . . . Socialist and Radical Influences . . .* (New York, 1970)

Melvyn Dubofsky, *We Shall Be All: . . . the Industrial Workers of the World* (Chicago, 1969)

Murray Seidler, *Norman Thomas, Respectable Rebel* (Syracuse, N.Y., 1961)

Horace Samuel Merrill and Marion Galbraith Merrill, *The Republican Command, 1897–1913* (Lexington, Ky., 1971)

Jerome M. Clubb and Howard W. Allen, "Party Loyalty in the Progressive Years: The Senate, 1909–1915," *Journal of Politics*, XXIX (August 1967)

Blair Bolles, *Tyrant from Illinois: Uncle Joe Cannon's Experiment with Personal Power* (New York, 1951)

William R. Gwinn, *Uncle Joe Cannon, Archfoe of Insurgency* (New York, 1957)

Kenneth W. Hechler, *Insurgency: Personalities and Policies of the Taft Era* (New York, 1940)

Laurence J. Holt, *Congressional Insurgency and the Party System, 1909–1916* (Cambridge, Mass., 1967)

Stanley D. Solvick, "William Howard Taft and the Payne-Aldrich Tariff," *Mississippi Valley Historical Review*, L (December 1963)

Claude E. Barfield, ". . . The Democratic Party, Cannonism, and the Payne-Aldrich Tariff," *Journal of American History*, LVII (September 1970)

Richard Lowitt, *George W. Norris: The Making of a Progressive* (Lexington, Ky., 1963)

George E. Mowry, *Theodore Roosevelt and the Progressive Movement* (Madison, Wisc., 1947)

Norman M. Wilensky, *Conservatives in the Progressive Era: The Taft Republicans of 1912* (Gainesville, Fla., 1965)

Evans C. Johnson, "The Underwood Forces and the Democratic Nomination of 1912," *Historian*, XXXI (February 1969)

Charles Forcey, *The Crossroads of Liberalism . . .* (New York, 1961)

Arthur S. Link, *Woodrow Wilson and the Progressive Era, 1912–1917* (New York, 1954)

Richard L. Watson, Jr., "Woodrow Wilson and his Interpreters
. . . ," *Mississippi Valley Historical Review*, XLIV (September 1957)

Arthur S. Link, *Wilson: The New Freedom* (Princeton, 1956)

John M. Blum, *Joe Tumulty and the Wilson Era* (Boston, 1951)

Richard M. Abrams, "Woodrow Wilson and the Southern Congressmen," *Journal of Southern History*, XXII (November 1956)

Burton I. Kaufman, "Virginia Politics and the Wilson Movement
. . . ," *Virginia Magazine of History*, LXXVII (January 1969)

C. Vann Woodward, *The Strange Career of Jim Crow* (rev. edition, New York, 1964)

William A. Mabry, *Studies in the Disfranchisement of the Negro in the South* (Durham, N.C., 1933)

Margaret Law Callcott, *The Negro in Maryland Politics, 1870–1912* (Baltimore, 1969)

Charles E. Wynes, *Race Relations in Virginia, 1870–1902* (Charlottesville, 1961)

Dewey W. Grantham, "The Progressive Movement and the Negro," *South Atlantic Quarterly*, LIV (October 1955)

Seth Scheiner, "President Theodore Roosevelt and the Negro," *Journal of Negro History*, XLVII (July 1962)

Howard W. Allen *et al.*, "Political Reform and Negro Rights in the Senate, 1909–1915," *Journal of Southern History*, XXXVII (May 1971)

John B. Wiseman, "Racism in Democratic Politics, 1904–1912," *Mid-America*, LI (January 1969)

Willard H. Smith, "William Jennings Bryan and Racism," *Journal of Negro History*, LIV (April 1969)

Henry Blumenthal, "Woodrow Wilson and the Race Question," *Journal of Negro History*, XLVIII (January 1963)

Nancy J. Weiss, "The Negro and the New Freedom: Fighting Wilsonian Segregation," *Political Science Quarterly*, LXXXIV (March 1968)

Charles Flint Kellogg, *NAACP: A History of the National Association for the Advancement of Colored People*, Vol. I: 1909–1920 (Baltimore, 1967)

William E. Leuchtenberg, "Progressivism and Imperialism . . . ," *Mississippi Valley Historical Review*, XXXIX (December 1952)

Ernest R. May, *The World War and American Isolation* . . . (Cambridge, Mass., 1959)

John M. Cooper, Jr., *The Vanity of Power: American Isolationism* . . . *1914–1917* (Westport, Conn., 1969)

Howard W. Allen, "Republican Reformers and Foreign Policy, 1913–1917," *Mid-America*, XLIV (October 1962)

J. A. Thompson, "American Progressive Publicists and the First World War, 1914–1917," *Journal of American History*, LVIII (September 1971)

N. Gordon Levin, Jr., *Woodrow Wilson and World Politics* . . . (New York, 1968)

Seward W. Livermore, *Politics Is Adjourned: Woodrow Wilson and the War Congress, 1916–18* (Middletown, Conn., 1966)

Robert D. Cuff, "Woodrow Wilson and Business–Government Relations During World War I," *Review of Politics*, XXXI (July 1969)

H. C. Peterson and Gilbert Fite, *Opponents of War, 1917–18* (Seattle, 1957)

Harry N. Scheiber, *The Wilson Administration and Civil Liberties* (Ithaca, N.Y., 1960)

Donald D. Johnson, *The Challenge to American Freedoms: World War I and the* . . . *American Civil Liberties Union* (Lexington, Ky., 1963)

Carl Wittke, *German-Americans and the World War* (Columbus, 1936)

Arno J. Mayer, *Politics and Diplomacy of Peacemaking* . . . (New York, 1967)

Wolfgang J. Helbich, "American Liberals in the League of Nations Controversy," *Public Opinion Quarterly*, XXXI (Winter 1968)

Joseph P. O'Grady (ed.), *The Immigrants' Influence on Wilson's Peace Policies* (Lexington, Ky., 1967)

Thomas A. Bailey, *Woodrow Wilson and the Great Betrayal* (New York, 1945)

Ralph Stone, *The Irreconcilables: The Fight Against the League of Nations* (Lexington, Ky., 1970)

John A. Garraty, *Henry Cabot Lodge* . . . (New York, 1953)

Robert K. Murray, *Red Scare* . . . (Minneapolis, 1955)

Stanley Coben, "A Study in Nativism: The American Red Scare of
    1919–1920," *Political Science Quarterly*, LXXIX (March
    1964)
David Brody, *Labor in Crisis, The Steel Strike of 1919* (Philadelphia,
    1965)
Robert L. Friedheim, *The Seattle General Strike* (Seattle, 1964)
Stanley Coben, *A Mitchell Palmer, Politician* (New York, 1963)
Fred D. Ragan, "Justice . . . Holmes . . . and the Clear and Pres-
    ent Danger Test . . . 1919," *Journal of American History*,
    LVIII (June 1971)
Zechariah Chafee, Jr., *Free Speech in the United States* (Cambridge,
    Mass., 1941)
Samuel J. Konefsky, *The Legacy of Holmes and Brandeis . . .*
    (New York, 1956)

V *The Abnormal 'Twenties, 1920–1932*

Burl Noeggle, "The Twenties: A New Historigraphical Frontier,"
    Journal of American History, LIII (September, 1966)
Henry May, "Shifting Perspectives on the 1920's," *Mississippi Valley
    Historical Review*, XLIII (December 1956)
Don S. Kirschner, "Conflicts and Politics in the 1920's: Historiogra-
    phy and Prospects," *Mid-America*, XLVIII (October 1966)
William E. Leuchtenberg, *The Perils of Prosperity . . .* (Chicago,
    1958)
Karl Schriftgiesser, *This Was Normalcy: . . . 1920–1932* (Boston,
    1948)
John D. Hicks, *Republican Ascendancy . . .* (New York, 1960)

Wesley M. Bagby, *The Road to Normalcy* (Baltimore, 1962)
Gary W. Reichard, "The Aberration of 1920: An Analysis of Hard-
    ing's Victory in Tennessee," *Journal of Southern History*,
    XXXVI (February 1970)
Donald C. Swain, *Federal Conservation Policy, 1921–1933* (Berkeley,
    1963)
Burl Noggle, *Teapot Dome: Oil and Politics in the 1920's* (Baton
    Rouge, 1962)
J. Leonard Bates, "The Teapot Dome Scandal and the Election of
    1924," *American Historical Review*, LX (January 1955)
Kenneth C. MacKay, *The Progressive Movement in 1924* (New York,
    1947)

James H. Shideler, "The La Follette Progressive Party Campaign of 1924," *Wisconsin Magazine of History*, XXXIII (June 1950)

Arthur S. Link, "What Happened to the Progressive Movement in the 1920's?" *American Historical Review*, XLIV (July 1959)

Edmund A. Moore, A *Catholic Runs for President . . . 1928* (New York, 1956)

Ruth C. Silva, *Rum, Religion, and Votes: 1928 Re-examined* (University Park, Pa., 1962)

Paul A. Carter, "The Campaign of 1928 Re-examined . . . ," *Wisconsin Magazine of History*, XLVI (Summer 1963)

Jerome M. Clubb and Howard W. Allen, "The Cities and the Election of 1928: Partisan Realignment?" *American Historical Review*, LXXIV (April 1969)

Andrew Sinclair, *The Available Man: The Life Behind the Masks of Warren G. Harding* (New York, 1965)

Robert K. Murray, *The Harding Era: Warren G. Harding and His Administration* (Minneapolis, 1969)

William A. White, A *Puritan in Babylon: The Story of Calvin Coolidge* (New York, 1939)

Donald R. McCoy, *Calvin Coolidge* (New York, 1967)

David Burner, *The Politics of Provincialism: The Democratic Party in Transition, 1918–1932* (New York, 1968)

Lawrence W. Levine, *Defender of the Faith, William Jennings Bryan . . . 1915–1925* (New York, 1965)

Lee N. Allen, "The McAdoo Campaign . . . in 1924," *Journal of Southern History*, XXIX (May 1963)

Oscar Handlin, *Al Smith and His America* (Boston, 1958)

Howard Zinn, *La Guardia in Congress* (Ithaca, N.Y., 1959)

Bernard Bellush, *Franklin D. Roosevelt as Governor of New York* (New York, 1955)

Alex Gottfried, *Boss Cermak of Chicago* (Seattle, 1962)

Elmer L. Puryear, *Democratic Party Dissension in North Carolina, 1928–1936* (Chapel Hill, 1962)

Franklin D. Mitchell, *Embattled Democracy: Missouri Democratic Politics, 1919–1932* (Columbia, Mo., 1968)

John W. Prothro, *Dollar Decade: Business Ideas in the 1920's* (Baton Rouge, 1954)

Otis Pease, *The Responsibilities of American Advertising* . . . *1920–1940* (New Haven, 1958)

Keith Sward, *The Legend of Henry Ford* (New York, 1948)

Allan Nevins and Frank E. Hill, *Ford, The Times, The Man, The Company* (3 vols., New York, 1954–1963)

Joseph Brandes, *Herbert Hoover and Economic Diplomacy: Department of Commerce Policy, 1921–1928* (Pittsburgh, 1962)

Paul W. Glad, "Progressive and the Business Culture of the 1920's," *Journal of American History*, LIII (June 1966)

George B. Tindall, "Business Progressivism: Southern Politics in the Twenties," *South Atlantic Quarterly*, LXII (Winter 1963)

Theodore Saloutos and John D. Hicks, *Agricultural Discontent in the Middle West, 1900–1939* (Madison, Wisc., 1951)

James H. Shideler, *Farm Crisis, 1919–1923* (Berkeley, 1957)

Robert L. Morlan, *Political Prairie Fire: The Nonpartisan League, 1915–1922* (Minneapolis, 1955)

Donald L. Winters, *Henry Cantwell Wallace as Secretary of Agriculture, 1921–1924* (Urbana, Ill., 1970)

Gilbert C. Fite, *George N. Peek and the Fight for Farm Parity* (Norman, Okla., 1954)

William D. Rowley, *M. L. Wilson and the Campaign for Domestic Allotment* (Lincoln, Nebr., 1970)

Gilbert C. Fite, "The Agricultural Issue in . . . 1928," *Mississippi Valley Historical Review*, XXXVII (March 1951)

Don S. Kirschner, *City and County: Rural Responses to Urbanization in the 1920's* (Westport, Conn., 1970)

J. Joseph Huthmacher, *Massachusetts People and Politics, 1919–1933* (Cambridge, Mass., 1959)

John M. Allswang, *A House for All Peoples: Ethnic Politics in Chicago, 1890–1936* (Lexington, Ky., 1971)

Irving Bernstein, *The Lean Years: . . . the American Worker, 1920–1933* (Boston, 1960)

David Brody, *Steelworkers in America: The Nonunion Era* (Cambridge, Mass., 1960)

Robert H. Zieger, *Republicans and Labor, 1919–1929* (Lexington, Ky., 1969)

Paul A. Carter, *The Twenties in America* (New York, 1968)

Norman F. Furniss, *The Fundamentalist Controversy, 1918–1931* (New Haven, 1954)

Paul A. Carter, *The Decline and Revival of the Social Gospel* . . . *1920–1940* (Ithaca, N.Y., 1956)

Ray Ginger, *Six Days or Forever? Tennessee v. John Thomas Scopes* (Boston, 1958)

Charles Merz, *The Dry Decade* (Garden City, N.Y., 1931)

Andrew Sinclair, *Prohibition: The Era of Excess* (New York, 1962)

Anne Firor Scott, "After Suffrage: Southern Women in the Twenties," *Journal of Southern History*, XXX (August 1964)

Paul L. Murphy, "Sources and Nature of Intolerance in the 1920's," *Journal of American History*, LI (June 1964)

William Preston, Jr., *Aliens and Dissenters: Federal Suppression of Radicals, 1903–1933* (Cambridge, Mass., 1963)

Francis Russell, *Tragedy in Dedham:* . . . *the Sacco-Vanzetti Case* (New York, 1962)

David M. Chalmers, *Hooded Americanism:* . . . *the Ku Klux Klan* (rev. edition, Chicago, 1968)

Kenneth T. Jackson, *The Ku Klux Klan in the City, 1915–1930* (New York, 1967)

Emerson Loucks, *The Ku Klux Klan in Pennsylvania* (Harrisburg, Pa., 1936)

Charles C. Alexander, *The Ku Klux Klan in the Southwest* (Lexington, Ky., 1965)

E. David Cronon, *Black Moses: The Story of Marcus Garvey* . . . (Madison, Wisc., 1955)

Richard B. Sherman, "The Harding Administration and the Negro . . . ," *Journal of Negro History*, XLIX (July 1964)

John L. Blair, ". . . The Negro During the Coolidge Years," *Journal of American Studies*, III (December 1969)

Dewey W. Granthtam, Jr., "Recent American History and the Great Depression," *Texas Quarterly*, VI (Winter 1963)

Harris Gaylord Warren, *Herbert Hoover and the Great Depression* (New York, 1959)

Albert U. Romasco, *The Poverty of Abundance: Hoover the Nation, the Depression* (New York, 1965)

Carl N. Degler, "The Ordeal of Herbert Hoover," *Yale Review*, LII (Summer 1963)

Jordan A. Schwartz, *The Interregnum of Despair: Hoover, Congress, and the Depression* (Urbana, Ill., 1970)

VI *The New Deal, 1932–1945*

Otis L. Graham, Jr., "Historians and the New Deals . . . ," *Social Studies*, LIV (April 1963)

Richard S. Kirkendall, "The New Deal as Watershed: The Recent Literature," *Journal of American History*, LIV (March 1968)

Jerold S. Auerbach, "New Deal, Old Deal, or Raw Deal: Some Thoughts on New Left Historiography," *Journal of Southern History*, XXXV (February 1969)

Basil Rauch, *History of the New Deal* (New York, 1944)

Denis W. Brogan, *The Era of Franklin D. Roosevelt* . . . (New Haven, 1950)

Edgar E. Robinson, *The Roosevelt Leadership* . . . (Philadelphia, 1955)

Dexter Perkins, *The New Age of Franklin Roosevelt* . . . (Chicago, 1957)

Arthur M. Schlesinger, Jr., *The Age of Roosevelt* . . . (3 vols. to date, Boston, 1957–)

William E. Leuchtenberg, *Franklin D. Roosevelt and the New Deal* . . . (New York, 1963)

Paul Conkin, *The New Deal* (New York, 1967)

William E. Leuchtenberg, "The New Deal and the Analogue of War," in John Braeman (ed.), *Change and Continuity in 20th Century America* (Columbus, 1964)

Arthur A. Ekirch, Jr., *Ideologies and Utopias: The Impact of the New Deal on American Thought* (Chicago, 1969)

Clarke A. Chambers, "FDR, Pragmatist-Idealist: An Essay in Historiography," *Pacific Northwest Quarterly*, LII (April 1961)

Frank Freidel, *Franklin D. Roosevelt* . . . (3 vols. to date, Boston, 1952–)

James McGregor Burns, *Roosevelt: The Lion and the Fox* (New York, 1956)

Rexford G. Tugwell, *The Democratic Roosevelt* . . . (Garden City, N.Y., 1957)

Harold F. Gosnell, *Champion Campaigner: Franklin D. Roosevelt* (New York, 1952)

Alfred B. Rollins, Jr., *Roosevelt and Howe* (New York, 1962)

James A. Farley, *Jim Farley's Story* . . . (New York, 1948)

Rexford G. Tugwell, *The Brains Trust* (New York, 1968)

Raymond Moley, *The First New Deal* (New York, 1966)

Bernard Sternsher, *Rexford Tugwell and the New Deal* (New Brunswick, N.J., 1964)

Hugh S. Johnson, *The Blue Eagle—from Egg to Earth* [NRA] (Garden City, N.Y., 1935)

Sidney Fine, *The Automobile Under the Blue Eagle: Labor, Management and the Automobile Manufacturing Code* (Ann Arbor, 1963)

Thomas E. Vadney, *The Wayward Liberal: A Political Biography of Donald Richberg* (Lexington, Ky., 1970)

Cedric B. Cowing, *Populists, Plungers, and Progressives: . . . Stock and Commodity Speculation, 1890–1936* (Princeton, 1965)

Michael E. Parrish, *Securities Regulation and the New Deal* (New Haven, 1970)

Ralph F. DeBedts, *The New Deal's SEC . . .* (New York, 1964)

Ellis W. Hawley, *The New Deal and the Problem of Monopoly . . .* (Princeton, 1966)

C. Herman Pritchett, *The Tennessee Valley Authority . . .* (Chapel Hill, 1943)

Thomas K. McCraw, *TVA and the Power Fight, 1933–1939* (Chicago, 1971)

Charles O. Jackson, *Food and Drug Legislation in the New Deal* (Princeton, 1970)

Barry D. Karl, *Executive Reorganization and Reform in the New Deal* (Cambridge, Mass., 1963)

Josephine C. Brown, *Public Relief, 1929–1939* (New York, 1940)

Searle F. Charles, *Minister of Relief: Harry Hopkins and the Depression* (Syracuse, N.Y., 1963)

Roy Lubove, *The Struggle for Social Security, 1900–1935* (Cambridge, Mass., 1968)

Edwin E. Witte, *The Development of the Social Security Act* (Madison, Wisc., 1962)

Arthur J. Altmeyer, *The Formative Years of Social Security* (Madison, Wisc., 1966)

Paul K. Conkin, *Tomorrow a New World: The New Deal Community Program* (Ithaca, N.Y., 1959)

Jane DeHart Mathews, *The Federal Theatre, 1935–1939: Plays, Relief, and Politics* (Princeton, 1967)

Raymond Wolters, *Negroes and the Great Depression . . .* (Westport, Conn., 1970)

Leslie H. Fishel, Jr., "The Negro in the New Deal," *Wisconsin Magazine of History*, XLVIII (Winter 1964–65)

Rita Werner Gordon, "The Change in the Political Alignment of Chicago's Negroes During the New Deal," *Journal of American History*, LVI (December 1969)

Van L. Perkins, *Crisis in Agriculture: The AAA and the New Deal* (Berkeley, 1969)

Richard S. Kirkendall, *Social Scientists and Farm Politics in the Age of Roosevelt* (Columbia, Mo., 1966)

John A. Crampton, *The National Farmers Union: Ideology of a Pressure Group* (Lincoln, Nebr., 1965)

John L. Shover, *Cornbelt Rebellion: The Farmers' Holiday Association* (Urbana, Ill., 1965)

David E. Conrad, *Forgotten Farmers: . . . Sharecroppers and the New Deal* (Urbana, Ill., 1965)

Louis Cantor, *A Prologue to the Protest Movement: The Missouri Sharecropper Roadside Demonstration of 1939* (Durham, N.C., 1969)

Donald McCoy, *Angry Voices: Left-of-Center Politics in the New Deal Era* (Lawrence, Kans., 1958)

David H. Bennett, *Demagogues in the Depression* (New Brunswick, N.J., 1969)

Charles J. Tull, *Father Coughlin and the New Deal* (Syracuse, N.Y., 1965)

Abraham Holtzman, *The Townsend Movement: A Political Study* (New York, 1963)

T. Harry Williams, *Huey Long* (New York, 1970)

Frederick Rudolph, "The American Liberty League, 1934–1940," *American Historical Review*, LVI (October 1950)

George Wolfskill, *The Revolt of the Conservatives: . . . The American Liberty League . . .* (Boston, 1962)

Richard Polenberg, "The National Committee To Uphold Constitutional Government," *Journal of American History*, LII (December 1965)

Otis L. Graham, Jr., *An Encore for Reform: The Old Progressives and the New Deal* (New York, 1967)

James T. Patterson, *Congressional Conservatism and the New Deal . . .* (Lexington, Ky., 1967)

Robert H. Jackson, *The Struggle for Judicial Supremacy* . . . (New York, 1941)

Leonard Baker, *Back to Back: The Duel Between FDR and the Supreme Court* (New York, 1967)

William E. Leuchtenberg, "Roosevelt's Supreme Court 'Packing' Plan," in H. M. Hollingsworth (ed.) *Essays on the New Deal* (Austin, 1969)

Richard C. Cortner, *The Wagner Act Cases* (Knoxville, Tenn., 1964)

Richard C. Cortner, *The Jones and Laughlin Case* (New York, 1970)

Charles A. Leonard, *A Search for Judicial Philosophy: Mr. Justice Roberts and the Constitutional Revolution of 1937* (Port Washington, N.Y., 1971)

Samuel Hendel, *Charles Evans Hughes and the Supreme Court* (New York, 1951)

Alpheus T. Mason, *Harlan Fiske Stone* . . . (New York, 1956)

C. Herman Pritchett, *The Roosevelt Court* . . . 1937–1947 (New York, 1948)

Irving Bernstein, *Turbulent Years: the American Worker, 1933–1941* (Boston, 1970)

J. O. Morris, *Conflict Within the AFL* . . . 1901–1936 (Ithaca, N.Y., 1958)

Walter Galenson, *The CIO Challenge to the AFL* . . . 1935–1941 (Cambridge, Mass., 1960)

Saul Alinsky, *John L. Lewis* (New York, 1949)

Matthew Josephson, *Sidney Hillman* . . . (Garden City, N.Y., 1952)

Milton Derber and Edwin Young (eds.), *Labor and the New Deal* (Madison, Wisc., 1957)

Irving Bernstein, *The New Deal Collective Bargaining Policy* (Berkeley, 1950)

Jerold S. Auerbach, *Labor and Liberty: The La Follette Committee and the New Deal* (Indianapolis, 1966)

Sidney Fine, *Sit-down: The General Motors Strike of 1936–37* (Ann Arbor, 1969)

Donald H. Grubbs, *Cry from the Cotton: The Southern Tenant Farmers' Union and the New Deal* (Chapel Hill, 1970)

James T. Patterson, *The New Deal and the States* . . . (Princeton, 1969)

J. Joseph Huthmacher, *Senator Robert F. Wagner* . . . (New York, 1968)

Allan Nevins, *Herbert H. Lehman* . . . (New York, 1963)

Frank Freidel, *F. D. R. and the South* (Baton Rouge, 1965)

Joseph L. Morrison, *Governor O. Max Gardner: A Power in North Carolina and New Deal Washington* (Chapel Hill, 1970)

Allan P. Sindler, *Huey Long's Louisiana: State Politics, 1920–1952* (Baltimore, 1956)

Richard B. Henderson, *Maury Maverick: A Political Biography* (Austin, 1970)

Leonard Arrington, "The New Deal in the West," *Pacific Historical Review*, XXXVIII (August 1969)

Michael P. Malone, *C. Ben Ross and the New Deal in Idaho* (Seattle, 1970)

T. A. Larson, "The New Deal in Wyoming," *Pacific Historical Review*, XXXVIII (August 1969)

Robert E. Burke, *Olson's New Deal for California* (Berkeley, 1953)

Thomas Mathews, *Puerto Rican Politics and the New Deal* (Gainesville, Fla., 1960)

Arthur Mann, *La Guardia Comes to Power: 1933* (Philadelphia, 1965)

William J. McKenna, "The Negro Vote in Philadelphia Elections," *Pennsylvania History*, XXXII (October 1965)

Bruce M. Stave, *The New Deal and the Last Hurrah: Pittsburgh Machine Politics* (Pittsburgh, 1970)

Lloyd Wendt and Herman Kogan, *Big Bill of Chicago* (Indianapolis, 1953)

Lyle W. Dorsett, *The Pendergast Machine* (New York, 1968)

A. Theodore Brown, *The Politics of Reform: Kansas City's Municipal Government, 1925–1950* (Kansas City, 1958)

Donald R. McCoy, *Landon of Kansas* (Lincoln, Nebr., 1966)

Milton Plesur, "The Republican Congressional Comeback of 1938," *Review of Politics*, XXIV (October 1962)

Donald B. Johnson, *The Republican Party and Wendell Willkie* (Urbana, Ill., 1960)

Harry Barnard, *Independent Man:* . . . *Senator James Couzens* (New York, 1958)

Selig Adler, *The Isolationist Impulse* (New York, 1957)

Manfred Jonas, *Isolationism in America, 1935–1941* (Ithaca, N.Y., 1966)

John E. Wiltz, *In Search of Peace: The Senate Munitions Inquiry* . . . (Baton Rouge, 1963)

Wayne S. Cole, *America First: The Battle Against Intervention* . . . (Madison, Wisc., 1953)

Richard W. Steele, "Preparing the Public for War: Efforts To Establish a National Propaganda Agency, 1940–41," *American Historical Review*, LXXV (October 1970)

Mark Chadwin, *Hawks of World War II* (Chapel Hill, 1968)

James M. Burns, *Roosevelt: The Soldier of Freedom* (New York, 1970)

Robert E. Sherwood, *Roosevelt and Hopkins* . . . (New York, 1948)

H. Bradford Westerfield, *Foreign Policy and Party Politics: Pearl Harbor to Korea* (New Haven, 1955)

Edward S. Corwin, *Total War and the Constitution* (New York, 1947)

Eugene V. Rostow, "The Japanese American Cases—A Disaster," *Yale Law Journal*, LIV (June 1945)

Morton Grodzins, *Americans Betrayed: Politics and the Japanese Evacuation* (Chicago, 1949)

Jacobus tenBroek *et al.*, *Prejudice, War, and the Constitution* . . . (Berkeley, 1954)

Joel Seidman, *American Labor from Defense to Reconversion* (Chicago, 1953)

Alonzo L. Hambly, "Sixty Million Jobs . . . : The Liberals, The New Deal, and World War II," *Historian*, XXX (August 1968)

Davis R. B. Ross, *Preparing for Ulysses: Politics and Veterans During World War II* (New York, 1969)

Elias Huzar, *The Purse and the Sword: Control of the Army by Congress* . . . 1933–1950 (Ithaca, N.Y., 1950)

Donald H. Riddle, *The Truman Committee* . . . (New Brunswick, N.J., 1964)

Roland Young, *Congressional Politics in the Second World War* (New York, 1956)

John R. Moore, "The Conservative Coalition in the United States Senate, 1942–1945," *Journal of Southern History*, XXXIII (August 1967)

Donald R. McCoy, "Republican Opposition During Wartime . . . ," *Mid-America*, XLIX (July 1967)

VII   *The Search for Equilibrium, 1945–1960*

Cabell Phillips, *The Truman Presidency* . . . (New York, 1966)

Barton J. Bernstein (ed.), *Politics and Policies of the Truman Administration* (Chicago, 1970)

Alfred Steinberg, *The Man from Missouri* (New York, 1962)

Allen J. Matusow, *Farm Policies and Politics in the Truman Years* (Cambridge, Mass., 1967)

Richard O. Davies, *Housing Reform During the Truman Administration* (Columbia, Mo., 1966)

Richard E. Neustadt, "Congress and the Fair Deal . . . ," *Public Policy*, V (1954)

Susan M. Hartmann, *Truman and the 80th Congress* (Columbia, Mo., 1971)

Clifton Brock, *Americans for Democratic Action: Its Role in National Politics* (Washington, D.C., 1962)

William C. Berman, *The Politics of Civil Rights in the Truman Administration* (Columbus, 1970)

Richard M. Dalfiume, *Desegregation of the U.S. Armed Forces* . . . (Columbia, Mo., 1969)

Louis Ruchames, *Race, Jobs, and Politics: The Story of FEPC* (New York, 1953)

Robert A. Garson, "The Alienation of the South: A Crisis for Harry S Truman . . . ," *Missouri Historical Review*, LXIV (July 1970)

John M. Redding, *Inside the Democratic Party* (Indianapolis, 1958)

Irwin Ross, *The Lonliest Campaign* . . . (New York, 1968)

Karl Schmidt, *Henry A. Wallace, Quixotic Crusade, 1948* (Syracuse, N.Y., 1960)

Athan G. Theoharis, *The Yalta Myths: An Issue in U.S. Politics, 1945–1955* (Columbia, Mo., 1969)

Harold L. Hitchens, "Influences on the Congressional Decision To Pass the Marshall Plan," *Western Political Quarterly*, XXI (March 1968)

Annette B. Fox, "NATO and Congress," *Political Science Quarterly*, LXXX (September 1965)

Earl Latham, *The Communist Controversy in Washington* (Cambridge, Mass., 1966)

Walter Goodman, *The Committee: . . . the House Committee on Un-American Activities* (New York, 1964)

Eleanor Bontecou, *The Federal Loyalty-Security Program* (Ithaca, N.Y., 1953)

Alan D. Harper, *The Politics of Loyalty: The White House and the Communist Issue, 1946–1952* (Westport, Conn., 1969)

C. Herman Pritchett, *Civil Liberties and the Vinson Court* (Chicago, 1954)

Alan Schaffer, *Vito Marcantonio, Radical in Congress* (Syracuse, N.Y., 1966)

Ronald J. Caridi, *The Korean War and American Politics* (Philadelphia, 1968)

Richard H. Rovere, *Senator Joe McCarthy* (New York, 1959)

Robert Griffith, *The Politics of Fear: Joseph R. McCarthy and the Senate* (Lexington, Ky., 1970)

Michael Paul Rogin, *The Intellectuals and McCarthy . . .* (Cambridge, Mass., 1967)

Richard H. Rovere, *Affairs of State: The Eisenhower Years* (New York, 1956)

Emmet John Hughes, *The Ordeal of Power: A Political Memoir of the Eisenhower Years* (New York, 1963)

Arthur Larson, *Eisenhower: The President Nobody Knows* (New York, 1968)

David A. Frier, *Conflict of Interest in the Eisenhower Administration* (Ames, Iowa, 1969)

Seymour E. Harris, *The Economics of Political Parties, with Special Reference to Presidents Eisenhower and Kennedy* (New York, 1962)

Louis Harris, *Is There a Republican Majority?* (New York, 1954)

Samuel Lubell, *Revolt of the Moderates* (New York, 1956)

Heinz Eulau, *Class and Party in the Eisenhower Years* (Stanford, Calif., 1962)

Stuart Gerry Brown, *Conscience in Politics: Adlai E. Stevenson in the 1950's* (Syracuse, N.Y., 1961)

Herbert J. Muller, *Adlai Stevenson* (New York, 1967)

James Q. Wilson, *The Amateur Democrat: Club Politics in Three Cities* (Chicago, 1962)

Jay S. Goodman, *The Democrats and Labor in Rhode Island, 1952–1962* (Providence, 1967)

Robert W. Anderson, *Party Politics in Puerto Rico* (Stanford, Calif., 1965)

Henry Lee Moon, *Balance of Power: The Negro Vote* (Garden City, N.Y., 1948)

Oscar Glantz, "The Negro Voter in Northern Industrial Cities," *Western Political Quarterly*, XIII (December 1960)

Hanes Walton, Jr., *Black Political Parties* . . . (New York, 1969)

James Q. Wilson, *Negro Politics: The Search for Leadership* (Glencoe, Ill., 1960)

Everett Carl Ladd, Jr., *Negro Political Leadership in the South* (Ithaca, N.Y., 1966)

Donald R. Matthews and James W. Prothro, *Negroes and the New Southern Politics* (New York, 1966)

Albert P. Blaustein and Clarence C. Ferguson, Jr., *Desegregation and the Law* . . . (2nd edition, New Brunswick, N.J., 1962)

Loren Miller, *The Petitioners:* . . . *the Supreme Court* . . . *and the Negro* (New York, 1966)

Numan V. Bartley, *The Rise of Massive Resistance: Race and Politics in the South During the 1950's* (Baton Rouge, 1969)

Anthony Lewis, *Portrait of a Decade: The Second American Revolution* (New York, 1964)

Alpheus T. Mason, "Understanding the Warren Court . . . ," *Political Science Quarterly*, LXXXI (December 1966)

Archibald Cox, *The Warren Court* . . . (Cambridge. Mass., 1968)

Lee Katcher, *Earl Warren: A Political Biography* (New York, 1967)

Richard C. Cortner, *The Apportionment Cases* (Knoxville, Tenn., 1971)

James A. Gazell, "One Man, One Vote: Its Long Germination," *Review of Politics*, XXIII (September 1970)

Clifford M. Lytle, *The Warren Court and Its Critics* (Tucson, 1968)

Walter F. Murphy, *Congress and the Court* [1954–59] (Chicago, 1962)

Adam C. Breckenridge, *Congress Against the Court* [1958–68] (Lincoln, Nebr., 1970)

VIII   *The Modern Distemper, 1960*

James M. Burns, *John Kennedy* (New York, 1960)

Theodore H. White, *The Making of the President, 1960* (New York, 1961)

Philip E. Converse *et al.*, "Stability and Change in 1960 . . . ," *American Political Science Review*, LV (June 1961)

Lucy S. Dawidowicz and Leon J. Goldstein, *Politics in a Pluralist Democracy: A Study of Voting in the 1960 Election* (New York, 1963)

V. O. Key, Jr., *The Responsible Electorate: Rationality in Presidential Voting, 1936–1960* (Cambridge, Mass., 1966)

Hugh Sidey, *John F. Kennedy, President* (New York, 1964)

Richard E. Neustadt, "Kennedy in the Presidency . . . ," *Political Science Quarterly*, LXXIX (September 1964)

Amitai Etzioni, "The Kennedy Experiment," *Western Political Quarterly*, XX (June 1967)

Theodore C. Sorensen, *Kennedy* (New York, 1965)

Arthur M. Schlesinger, Jr., *A Thousand Days* (Boston, 1965)

Pierre Salinger, *With Kennedy* (New York, 1966)

Edward Jay Epstein, *Inquest: The Warren Commission* . . . (New York, 1966)

Theodore H. White, *The Making of the President, 1964* (New York, 1965)

Robert D. Novak, *The Agony of the G.O.P. 1964* (New York, 1965)

George F. Gilder and Bruce K. Chapman, *The Party That Lost Its Head* (New York, 1966)

John H. Kessel, *The Goldwater Coalition* . . . (Indianapolis, 1968)

Stephen Hess, *The Republican Establishment* (New York, 1967)

William S. White, *The Professional: Lyndon B. Johnson* (New York, 1964)

Alfred Steinberg, *Sam Johnson's Boy* . . . (New York, 1968)

Eric F. Goldman, *The Tragedy of Lyndon Johnson* (New York, 1969)

Edward C. Banfield, *The Unheavenly City* . . . *Our Urban Crisis* (Boston, 1970)

Gilbert Y. Steiner, *Social Insecurity: The Politics of Welfare* (Chicago, 1966)

Nathan Wright, *Black Power and Urban Unrest* (New York, 1967)

Benjamin Muse, *The American Negro Revolt* . . . *1963–1967* (Bloomington, Ind., 1968)

Jerome H. Skolnick, *The Politics of Protest* (New York, 1969)

Philip L. Geyelin, *Lyndon B. Johnson and the World* (New York, 1966)

George M. Kahin and John W. Lewis, *The United States in Vietnam* (New York, 1967)

Theodore H. White, *The Making of the President, 1968* (New York, 1969)

H. G. Nicholas, "The 1968 Presidential Elections," *Journal of American Studies*, III (July 1969)

George Christian, *The President Steps Down* . . . (New York, 1970)

Jack Newfield, *Robert Kennedy* . . . (New York, 1969)

Norman Mailer, *Miami and the Siege of Chicago* (New York, 1968)

Joe McGinnis, *The Selling of the President, 1968* (New York, 1969)

Gottfried Dietze, *America's Political Dilemma* (Baltimore, 1968)

Walter Dean Burnham, "The End of American Party Politics," *Trans-Action*, VII (December 1969)

Samuel Lubell, *The Hidden Crisis in American Politics* (New York, 1970)

Andrew Hacker, *The End of the American Era* (New York, 1970)